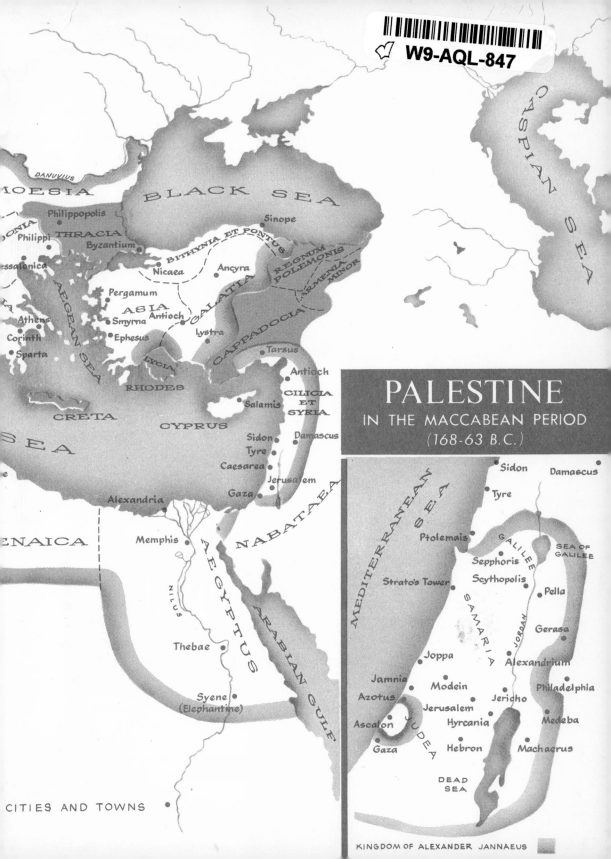

CASPIAN SEA

BLACK SEA

DANUVIUS

MOESIA

Philippopolis

THRACIA

Philippi

Sinope

BITHYNIA ET PONTUS

REGNUM POLEMONIS

ARMENIA MINOR

essalonica

Byzantium

Nicaea

Ancyra

Pergamum

ASIA

Antioch

GALATIA

CAPPADOCIA

Athens

Smyrna

Corinth

Ephesus

Lystra

Sparta

AEGEAN SEA

LYCIA

Tarsus

Antioch

RHODES

CILICIA ET SYRIA

CRETA

Salamis

CYPRUS

Sidon

Damascus

SEA

Tyre

Caesarea

Jerusalem

Gaza

Alexandria

NABATAEA

ENAICA

Memphis

AEGYPTUS

NILUS

Thebae

ARABIAN GULF

Syene
(Elephantine)

PALESTINE
IN THE MACCABEAN PERIOD
(168-63 B.C.)

Sidon

Damascus

Tyre

Ptolemais

GALILEE

SEA OF GALILEE

MEDITERRANEAN SEA

Sepphoris

Scythopolis

Pella

Strato's Tower

SAMARIA

Gerasa

JORDAN

Joppa

Alexandrium

Jamnia

Modein

Philadelphia

Azotus

Jericho

Jerusalem

Hyrcania

Medeba

Ascalon

JUDEA

Hebron

Machaerus

Gaza

DEAD SEA

CITIES AND TOWNS

KINGDOM OF ALEXANDER JANNAEUS

W9-AQL-847

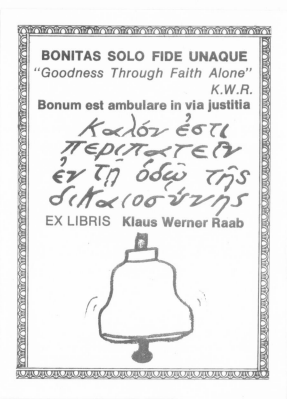

BONITAS SOLO FIDE UNAQUE
"Goodness Through Faith Alone"
K.W.R.
Bonum est ambulare in via justitia

Καλόν ἐστι
περιπατεῖν
ἐν τῇ ὁδῷ τῆς
δικαιοσύνης

EX LIBRIS   Klaus Werner Raab

UNDERSTANDING THE NEW TESTAMENT

UNDERSTANDING

Prentice-Hall, Inc., Englewood Cliffs, N. J.

Second Edition

THE NEW TESTAMENT

HOWARD CLARK KEE

*Professor of the History of Religion, Department of Religion,
Bryn Mawr College, Bryn Mawr, Pennsylvania*

FRANKLIN W. YOUNG

Princeton University, Princeton, New Jersey

KARLFRIED FROEHLICH

The Theological School, Drew University, Madison, New Jersey

PRENTICE-HALL INTERNATIONAL, INC., *London*
PRENTICE-HALL OF AUSTRALIA, PTY., LTD., *Sydney*
PRENTICE-HALL OF CANADA, LTD., *Toronto*
PRENTICE-HALL OF INDIA PVT. LTD., *New Delhi*
PRENTICE-HALL OF JAPAN, INC., *Tokyo*

Current printing (last digit):
12   11   10   9   8

Understanding the New Testament

Second Edition

Howard Clark Kee, Franklin W. Young, and Karlfried Froehlich

Except in a few instances where the authors have provided their own translations of certain key words or phrases, the translation used throughout this book is the Revised Standard Version of the Bible, copyright 1946 and 1952 by the Division of Christian Education, National Council of Churches, and is used by permission. Quotations from *Gospel Parallels* by permission of Thomas Nelson and Sons and the Division of Christian Education, National Council of Churches.

Design by John J. Dunleavy

93602—C

PREFACE

More than a decade ago, when the authors were asked by the Society for Religion in Higher Education to prepare the original edition of this book (concurrently with the companion volume, *Understanding the Old Testament*, by Bernhard W. Anderson), it was acknowledged that the approach adopted by the authors toward the New Testament did not fit the usual categories of introductory Biblical studies. The book was not an historical introduction, although it was written out of the conviction that only by historical reconstruction of the life and thought of the first-century Christian community and its cultural environment could the writings of the New Testament be understood. Neither was the book a treatise in theology, although it was recognized that theological convictions were the major content of the New Testament. Further, the book was not intended to be primarily an introduction to the literature of the New Testament, although the literary form and content of the books had to be taken into account if the intention of the writers was to be grasped by the modern reader of the New Testament. Accordingly, it was decided to combine historical, theological, and literary perspectives in a unifying approach to the New Testament. The response that the book received has given the authors the impression that many found this method helpful in seeking to better understand the New Testament. In the new edition, therefore, the basic method remains unchanged.

In the intervening years, however, the intellectual and religious climate has changed. New discoveries and more detailed studies of the New Testament writings have altered the situation in the field of Biblical scholarship. The prevailing attitudes of the 1960's are more skeptical and critical than those of the 1950's. The mood of uncertainty, which characterized the opening years of the Christian Era, is even more characteristic of our present era than it was of the decade following the Second World War. It seems appropriate, therefore, that the study of the New Testament should reflect something of these changes in atmosphere, as well as the effects of more recent research. Readers familiar with the earlier edition of this work will note that we have devoted less space to the presentation of a synthesis and more to the setting out of critical problems or divergent viewpoints. The footnotes are more abundant, and the list of suggested readings at the back of the book is considerably fuller. Expanded discussions of Gnosticism and of the Dead Sea Scrolls are found in the opening chapters; details of the results of these discoveries are noted throughout the book.

One of the new features of this edition is the inclusion of separate chapters dealing with the theological viewpoints of each of the gospels. This, combined with a greatly extended treatment of the oral tradition and the literary questions concerning the origins of the synoptic gospels, results in a wholly different approach to the gospels and the question of the historical Jesus. The reader especially interested in these themes will find in the notes throughout these chapters suggestions for wider exploration of the issues briefly discussed in this section of the book.

In the last third of the book, we discuss more fully than in the first edition matters relating to the organizational development of the early Church. These issues seem to be of particular importance today, when the spirit of ecumenicity requires every thoughtful person to reexamine the roots of his own religious heritage, not only with regard to beliefs but with regard to institutional development as well. The works referred to in this part of the book likewise are intended to provide the basis for more detailed investigation of this time of the Church's transition from a community living in expectation of an imminent End to an ongoing institution with the necessity to in some way come to terms with the surrounding world.

The present edition of this work shares with its predecessor, however, the conviction that the visible form of the unity which underlies the diverse writings that we call the New Testament is the community, the Christian Church. The inner unity lies in the message—in the variety of its forms—which was proclaimed in and by the Church, and in which the community believed that it was being addressed by God. The reader may share this belief or he may not, but the recognition of these two factors—message and community—seem to us to be necessary presuppositions for understanding this collection of writings. It is our hope that this work will serve to further the reader's understanding by laying stress on these factors.

We acknowledge our indebtedness to those whose works we have drawn upon explicitly, as well as those who have helped to shape our thinking by their insights.

In as comprehensive a work as this, the authors cannot mention all those whose scholarly contributions have been drawn on. We are grateful to the Division of Christian Education of the National Council of Churches for its grant of permission to quote extensively from the Revised Standard Version of the Bible. And finally, our thanks to the staff of the Project Planning Department of Prentice-Hall, Inc., for their skilled assistance in the preparation of this book, and especially to Mr. George A. Rowland for his able editorial aid.

Howard Clark Kee

Franklin W. Young

Karlfried Froehlich

CONTENTS

PART ONE

ILLUSTRATIONS

MAPS

End-paper maps and all maps listed above, except *Plan of the Temple Area* and *Ancient Rome*, are based on maps in *The Westminster Historical Atlas to the Bible* (Revised Edition), edited by George Ernest Wright and Floyd Vivian Filson, copyright 1956 by W. L. Jenkins, published by the Westminster Press, and are used by permission.

Plan of the Temple Area is based on the plan in *Sacred Sites and Ways*, by Gustav Dalman, copyright 1935 by The Macmillan Company, and is used by permission.

PART ONE

THE COMMUNITY

EMERGES

THE SEARCH
FOR COMMUNITY
IN THE
GRAECO-ROMAN WORLD

CHAPTER ONE Every age is an age of transition, for the

world never stands still. But in some ages the rate of change

seems to speed up. Ideas move swiftly from place to place,

the population shifts about restlessly, social classes become

more mobile, loyalties are made and unmade overnight, and

political and economic institutions are dramatically reshaped.

Rapid changes of this sort always dislocate groups and in-

dividuals, creating an atmosphere of uneasiness or even of

anxiety. Life seems to be open at both ends; the past seems to be crumbling and the shape of the future has not yet become clear. Fascination with new developments breeds insecurity, and men and women tend to cling uncertainly to the discredited beliefs of the past or else grasp frantically at any new proposal that offers a solution to the perennial problems of life. It is as though some sinister hand had written across the face of the present: "Subject to change without notice."

Unsettled by the insecurity of such an age, men search for certainty. Some seek for a more profound understanding of the nature of the universe and the ultimate meaning of life. Others may shun the search, preferring rather to put their confidence in the fantastic promises of would-be saviors, or in the secret formulas of those who purvey quick and easy answers. An age of transition is a flourishing time for religions and philosophies that promise security and for governments that promise stability. When the old patterns of society break up and men are set adrift in a hostile, unpredictable world, they seek for security in some group that is bound together by common concerns and common aspirations. They search for true community—that is, for community of interest, for a common destiny, and for a sense of belonging.

It was in such an age of transition and search that the New Testament was written. To understand these writings, we must try to imagine ourselves possessed of the anxieties and aspirations of the age; we must see how the writers of the New Testament spoke to men's needs. These writers spoke, not as isolated individuals proposing solutions of their own, but as the spokesmen for a group, a tiny minority struggling for existence in the vast Roman Empire at the opening of the Christian era. Although the events that gave rise to the convictions recorded in the New Testament took place among the Jews of Palestine, the community that arose around these convictions soon spread across Asia Minor and into Europe, where it welcomed Jew and Gentile alike into its membership, and where it grew with astonishing speed.

The community that produced the New Testament began, not in a vacuum, but in an age of conflicting social, political, philosophical, and religious forces. So we must look closely at the state of the world in New Testament times if we are to understand how the Christian community came into being. Our effort to understand the New Testament begins, then, with a sketch of the Roman world at the opening of the Christian Era. Then we shall focus somewhat more sharply on the Jewish world out of which the Christian community emerged.

WAR AND PEACE: FROM ALEXANDER TO AUGUSTUS

One of the most familiar stories in the New Testament—the birth of Jesus according to the Gospel of Luke (Lk. 2:1 ff.)—reminds us that Christianity began during the reign of Octavian (27 B.C.-A.D. 14), better known by his title of

AUGUSTUS *the first emperor. It was during his reign that Jesus was born.*

Caesar Augustus, the first and in many ways the greatest of the Roman emperors. "In those days a decree went out from Caesar Augustus that all the world should be enrolled." Augustus was acclaimed by many throughout the empire as a deliverer and savior. And it is true that he had brought to an end the power struggle among the Roman leaders that had led to the murder of Julius Caesar in 44 B.C. He had driven the pirates from the seas, making them safe once more for travel and commerce. He had quelled Rome's enemies, some of whom had harassed her borders for decades. Above all, he had managed to create an atmosphere of peace and unity throughout the far reaches of the empire. On landing at ports, sailors gave thanks to Augustus that they had been able to sail unmolested by pirates. The Italian peasants, with their strong sense of morality, were profoundly grateful to Augustus for combating the immorality that had become rampant among the upper classes of Rome in the years before his rise.

Caesar as Savior and Divine King

The people of the empire acclaimed Augustus not merely as a human deliverer from conflict and struggle, but as a divine savior-king. Temples were erected in his honor; sacrifices were made and incense was burned on the altars. In Palestine, for example, the fawning puppet king, Herod, built an imposing seaport in honor of Augustus. From it one could see glistening on the distant

ALEXANDER THE GREAT *on a silver coin (tetradrachm) minted during his reign.*

Samaritan hills white limestone columns of the Temple of Augustus, which stood at the west gate of the city that Herod had built on the site of ancient Samaria and had named Sebaste (the Greek equivalent of Augustus). Although the Jews themselves did not pay divine honors to Augustus, most of the other eastern peoples accepted him as divine, in keeping with their ancient tradition of regarding the king as a god. Augustus carefully avoided accepting the title of king, and even tried to preserve the fiction that he was no more than the leading citizen (*princeps*) among equals in the empire.

The world-wide acclaim given Augustus was not without precedent: in the fourth century before Christ a young Macedonian prince named Alexander had been hailed as a divine king in Egypt, in Asia Minor, and throughout much of western Asia. The military conquests of Alexander the Great, as he came to be called, were aided by the popular belief that he was a divine ruler before whom resistance would be useless and impious.

Although Augustus did not publicly seek divine honors as had Alexander the Great (356-323 B.C.), he benefited from Alexander's success in establishing himself in the minds of men from the Mediterranean basin to the borders of India as a divine king destined to unify the civilized world. Even the three centuries that intervened between the time of Alexander and that of Augustus had not tarnished the popular image of the divine ruler; so Augustus took on a familiar role when he set about extending the empire from the Nile to the Seine and from Gibraltar to Jerusalem.

Caesar Re-creates Alexander's One World

But Augustus inherited from Alexander more than the tradition of divine kingship; the atmosphere of outward peace and inner unrest that characterized the age of Augustus was a direct development of forces that had been set in motion in the time of Alexander.

Alexander's conquests had begun in Greece at a time when the city-states were in decline (336 B.C.). The weakening of the Greek social and political structure resulted in both military weakness and a breakdown in the sense of group loyalty that had reached its height in the golden age of the city-states. Although Alexander managed to build up an administrative unity among the Greek cities, he failed to create a common allegiance to himself to take the place of the old devotion to the city-states. In the eastern territories, however, where the tradition of divine kingship reached back for centuries, Alexander did succeed in winning great personal devotion from the conquered peoples.

A story arose that the tide along the coast of Asia Minor had retreated at his coming to enable him to pass along a narrow beach between sea and cliff. Since there was an ancient legend that the sea would recede at this point to herald the coming of a world ruler, word of the event sped before him and prepared the way for his acceptance in the East as a divine king. Had Alexander lived, there is little doubt that he could have developed tremendous support and affection—even veneration—from the peoples he had conquered, for legends of his divinity had begun to flourish even during his brief lifetime. But his efforts to create a politically unified world were cut short by his death in 323 B.C.

Alexander's vision of one world stretched far beyond the political sphere, however; he took with him a small army of scholars to record descriptions of the peoples, customs, animals, plant life, and terrain that he and his armies encountered. He had caught from his old teacher, Aristotle, a love of knowledge and an insatiable curiosity about the world around him. And he shared Aristotle's conviction that Greek learning was superior to all other, and that it was his responsibility as a leader of men to spread Greek culture wherever he went. This process of "Greek-izing" the world became known as *Hellenizing,* since the Greeks called their own land *Hellas* and themselves *Hellenes.* In their intensive efforts to disseminate Greek culture, Alexander and his followers established Greek-style cities as far east as the Indus Valley and as far north as the territory now included in the Central Asia states of the Soviet Union. Reports have come down to us of petty monarchs in Central Asia who staged Greek tragedies as entertainments for their courtiers.

Yet Hellenization never succeeded in laying more than a thin veneer of Greek culture over the oriental parts of Alexander's realm, either during his reign or after his death. The mass of the people in the subject lands remained faithful to their native customs and ways of life. Among the aristocracy, however, there was a strong desire to ape the ways of the Greeks. The aristocrats changed the names of their temples to honor local gods under new Greek titles. They built gymnasia and hippodromes and theaters to provide a setting for Greek-style entertainment. The upper classes even adopted Greek dress. But most of the people in these conquered lands continued to live and amuse themselves much as they had before Alexander began his Hellenizing conquests.

In one area of life, however, Hellenization had a profound and lasting effect, for Greek was widely accepted as the common language of commerce and international correspondence. Although men continued to speak their native language among themselves, Greek became the *lingua franca* of the Hellenistic world. So readily did it gain acceptance that some colonies of expatriates—such as the Jews living in Alexandria—stopped using their native tongues altogether and spoke only Greek. The Alexandrian Jews finally had to translate their Hebrew Bible into Greek so that their own people could understand it. This translation, known as the Septuagint (*i.e.*, seventy, since a Jewish legend claimed that seventy men had prepared independent translations that miraculously turned out to be identical), was widely used by Jews and was known to educated Gentiles throughout the world.

With Alexander's death in 323 B.C., all appearances of political unity vanished. His generals vied with one another to gain power over their dead leader's domain, and conflict among them and their successors raged on until the rise of Rome in the middle of the first century B.C. Only two relatively stable centers of power remained in the Hellenistic empires: one was Syria, where the Seleucids (successors of Seleucus, one of Alexander's generals) ruled, and the other was Egypt, where Ptolemy (another general) established the Ptolemaic dynasty. But in Asia Minor and Greece there was an unending series of wars and dynastic disputes.

In spite of the widespread disruption created by the continuing struggles, important centers of learning managed to grow up during the period between Alexander and Augustus. Athens had already begun to decline as the center of philosophical thought, although the Academy founded by Plato (427-347 B.C.) continued to exist until A.D. 529, eight centuries after his death. Tarsus, on the southern coast of Asia Minor, however, became an important university city. But most significant of all was Alexandria, the city that Alexander had founded at the western edge of the Nile Delta as a center for commercial and cultural interchange between East and West. There Alexander had founded the Museum, by definition a shrine to the Muses, but in actuality a great library with more than half a million volumes, and a center of learning and research unparalleled in the ancient world. It was there that Euclid developed his principles of plane geometry, that Archimedes performed his famous experiments with water, and that Eratosthenes discovered the formula by which he was able to calculate the size of the earth.

At the eastern end of the Mediterranean Sea there was continual conflict between the Seleucids and the Ptolemies. As we shall see later, one victim of this conflict was the Jewish nation, situated as it was in the buffer zone between the two great centers of power. The Ptolemaic kingdom enjoyed a high degree of stability because of the great desert that protected it on three sides and because of the immense wealth that it acquired, both through the agricultural produce of its own lush valley and through the luxuries that were shipped across it on the way from India to the Mediterranean cities. The Seleucids, on the other hand, had vast territories to the east over which they exercised only feeble control and beyond which lived powerful hostile tribes who constantly threatened to engulf them. Except for a century of relative independence, Palestine, from the time of Alexander until the coming of the Romans in 63 B.C., was subject to either Egypt or Syria, the one rich and indolent, and the other aggressive but insecure.

The Failure to Create Unity

In spite of the efforts of Alexander's successors to bring unity to their realms, they succeeded only in creating profound unrest. The simpler units of society, like the Greek city-states and the petty oriental kingdoms, had been ruined by the military and cultural conquests of Alexander and his successors. And nothing had risen to fill the void. Merchants could no longer look ahead in the certainty that their business would continue as usual. Villagers never knew when a pillaging army might sweep through and leave them impoverished. The old worship of local gods had been disrupted by attempts to make all men worship universal deities, or at least to give new and unfamiliar names to the old ones. Politically, a man's allegiance to his city or to his petty prince was irreparably shaken; religiously, the world revealed by these widening horizons was too vast to be controlled by local gods.

In Rome itself the ancient gods of the Latin people were still worshiped after a fashion, but the daily round of sacrifices and incantations had become increasingly pointless. Moreover, the Romans had been subjected to powerful influences from Greece and the Orient which on the one hand increased skepticism about the traditional gods and on the other introduced an emotional kind of religion that was far more colorful and satisfying than the formal worship of the state gods.

Rome's contact with the religious philosophy of Greece and the gods of the East was an outcome of her commercial and military operations in the eastern Mediterranean. For centuries, Romans had modestly busied themselves developing and safeguarding agriculture and commerce within the limits of the Italian peninsula. But in the process of extending their power over all of Italy, they fell into conflict with the Phoenicians, who dominated the sea from their capital, Carthage, across the Mediterranean in North Africa. In the course of her long struggle with Carthage (264-146 B.C.), Rome gained control of the southern coast of France and Spain, and became mistress of the western Mediterranean. Only then was she ready to extend her power to the east.

Rome's sympathy with the democratic ideals of the Greek city-states moved her to aid Greece in her struggles during the early second century B.C. against the Macedonians and other Hellenistic kingdoms that were competing for the opportunity to absorb her. But Rome's motives in turning to the aid of Greece were not altogether unselfish, for her commercial success in the West had led her to cast ambitious eyes toward the East. When a Seleucid ruler (Antiochus the Great) intervened to support Macedonia in an invasion of Greece, he was defeated by the Roman army and driven back into Syria (192-190 B.C.). Now Rome was in control of Greece, Illyria (modern Yugoslavia), and Asia Minor as far east as the Taurus Mountains. By treaty and military conquest, her expansion continued steadily for more than a century (200-63 B.C.), until at last Syria herself, including Palestine, became a Roman province. Egypt continued her independence under the Ptolemies, although Rome had to intervene in 168 B.C. to keep the Seleucids from taking over. The final round in Rome's battle for the East came in 30 B.C., when, following the defeat of Anthony by Octavian (Augustus) and the suicide of Cleopatra, Egypt too became a part of the Roman Empire. Augustus' victory was the crowning one; the Mediterranean had become a Roman lake; what began as a defense of democracy had ended in the establishment of the most powerful empire the world had ever seen.

The calm that fell after Augustus' destruction of his enemies brought peace to the empire but not peace of mind to its peoples. In the long struggle for power, the Roman ideals of democracy had been crushed. Public and private morality had declined appallingly in the presence of new wealth and power. The local Roman gods had been offered up on the altar of political expediency, for over and over again the Roman leaders had honored foreign gods in order to win the favor of subject peoples. The strict moral philosophy that the Roman ruling classes had borrowed from the Greeks had withered away. And, in spite of efforts to create a kind of universal religion by identifying the Greek and Roman gods with those, for example, of Egypt, men everywhere were left with no sense of religious certainty. Instead of worshiping the gods who were meant to keep things as they were, men searched for a religion that would deliver them from the evils of this world and would provide a promise of new life in the next.

THE DECLINE OF PHILOSOPHY

Although the Greeks tried hard to spread their culture throughout the civilized world, the rich tradition of Greek philosophy degenerated on foreign soil. And even at home, the lofty heights of philosophy reached by Plato were never attained by any of his successors in the Academy.

THE AGORA AT ATHENS *with the reconstructed Stoa of Attalos in the center. The Theseum, a temple of the god of fire and the best-preserved ancient temple in Greece, is visible at left center.*

The Decline of Platonism

In the golden age of Greek philosophy, Plato had taught that reality does not consist of specific, tangible objects or observable activities like houses, men, and good or evil deeds. Rather, reality consists of *the idea or universal pattern of any particular class of object.* For example, the *idea* of "house" exists independently of whether or not a particular house exists; the *idea* of "goodness" exists independently of whether or not men do in fact perform good deeds. These "ideas," Plato suggested, exist eternally; they are not concepts that exist only in men's minds; they are the true and perfect realities of which the objects and actions we know in this world are only imperfect copies. Even though by the beginning of the Christian era philosophers who claimed to subscribe to Plato's thought had debased his system, his understanding of reality had an important influence on Christian thinking almost from the start.

The Appeal of Stoicism

The name Stoic was originally given to the philosophical school founded by Zeno (336-264 B.C.), who instead of giving his lectures in a hall, as did other teachers of the day, gathered his pupils around him in one of the colonnades or *stoas* adjoining the public market place of Athens. During Zeno's lifetime, and for centuries after his death, the Stoic way of life continued to attract a large following among both aristocrats and the common people. Perhaps the chief appeal of the great Stoic figures was their personal character and quality of mind, for they were earnest men of great moral integrity. Their outlook on life was one of quiet joy and serenity, and they accepted suffering and tragedy with calmness. Although their ascetic ways discouraged pleasure-seekers from following them, their ability to discipline themselves appealed to many in an age when the moral standards of public officials and private individuals were notoriously low.

The Stoics rejected the Platonic belief that ideas exist independently of man and of the physical universe, and affirmed instead that the real world is the world of material bodies acting and reacting upon one another. They believed that the universe is a single organism energized by a world-soul, just as man is a body energized by a human soul. Soul itself is an extremely fine bodily substance that penetrates everything and is to be found in greater degree in man, in lesser degree in animals and inanimate objects. This world-soul is Reason, an impersonal force that operates throughout the universe, shaping its destiny, and bringing it to its predetermined goal. Then evil will be overcome, and great happiness unknown since the legendary past will again prevail. The true unity of man will be realized in the establishment of a great brotherhood of mankind. The world will be absorbed by God, who is all in all; a great conflagration will purge the universe, and a new cycle of the ages will begin.

Critics of the Stoics scoffed at the notion that the history of the world is the unfolding of a divine purpose, claiming instead that man is free to make his own decisions on the basis of what serves his natural desires, and that there are, after all, no certainties in this world, only degrees of probability.

In spite of critical attacks, Stoicism continued to exert a powerful influence down into the Christian era. The two greatest figures in the later period of Stoic thought were Epictetus, a contemporary of Paul the Apostle, and Marcus Aurelius, the philosophizing Roman emperor of the second century A.D.

Epicurus' Vision of the Pleasant Life

A more sophisticated philosophy than Stoicism was that of Epicurus (341-270 B.C.), whose views were adopted by such outstanding Roman thinkers of the first century B.C. as Lucretius and the Latin poet, Horace. Epicureanism never exercised a wide popular appeal, however, largely because it pictured the gods as far removed from the world and utterly indifferent to human affairs. Contrary to popular misconception, Epicureanism did not teach self-indulgence; rather, it taught peace of mind based on the conviction that the universe operates according to fixed laws over which man has no control, and in which the gods have no interest. Its chief concern was to free man from anxieties over the terrors of hell, and from fear of the acts of capricious gods. Although the scientific treatises of the Epicureans (like Lucretius' *On the Nature of Things*) are filled with quaint and fascinating speculations on the natural world, their ethical and religious statements sound like commonplaces from the pen of some contemporary writer telling his readers how to stop worrying, how to find inner peace, how to live bravely in the face of adversity, and so on.

The Hybrid Philosophies

None of these philosophies continued for long in a pure form. As the years passed, elements from all of them were merged into a kind of generalized religious philosophy, which became immensely popular among self-styled intellectuals during the last century B.C. and the first Christian century. To this philosophical mixture each of the philosophical schools contributed some facet of its thought. Stoicism provided its stress on reason, thereby permitting the hybrid philosophers to claim that they were essentially rational in their approach to truth. From Platonism came the yearning for a vision of the eternal world. But Platonism itself provided no mediators to bridge the gap between the finite world, known to human senses, and the eternal world. Accordingly, the popular philosophies developed hypotheses about ways of mediation through which men might attain direct knowledge of the eternal. From Stoicism and Epicureanism came curiosity about the physical world; so the composite philosophy had its quasi-scientific interests as well.

One of the best-known of the eclectics (*i.e.*, a thinker who chooses what suits his fancy from a variety of philosophical systems) was Seneca (4 B.C.-A.D. 65), a chief adviser at the court of the emperor Nero. Even though his basic viewpoint was a modified Stoicism, Seneca drew heavily on Plato and Epicurus and on anyone else whose moral teachings happened to appeal to him at the moment.

Perhaps the most prolific of the eclectic philosophers of the first Christian century was a Jew named Philo. Born into a prominent family among the nearly third of a million Jews of Alexandria, Philo distinguished himself in public affairs as leader of an embassy to the court of the emperor Gaius Caligula (A.D. 37-41), and in intellectual circles as the first thinker to join together in thoroughgoing fashion rational philosophy and the revealed religion of the Jews.

Philo's voluminous writings consist chiefly of long treatises on the spiritual (*i.e.*, philosophical) meaning of the narratives and laws included in the Hebrew Bible. For example, Abraham's journey from Ur in Mesopotamia to Hebron in Palestine is really not a narrative of ancient Semitic nomads, but a description of the spiritual journey of the seeker after truth, who moves from the world of the senses (Ur) to the place where he has a direct vision of God (the promised land of Palestine). By fanciful explanations of Old Testament stories, names, and numbers, Philo tried to show that the sacred books of the Old Testament were really saying the same things as the religious philosophers of his own day. Although we have no evidence that Philo's writings attracted a wide following among Gentiles, they do show how eager the Jews of the first century A.D. were to find in the Bible some knowledge of God that would be rationally defensible and that would at the same time provide an experience of God's living presence. In his interpretations of the Old Testament, Philo uses many of the commonplaces of Stoic and Platonic philosophy as they had come to be understood in his time.

Growing rapidly alongside these movements in philosophy, and at times overlapping them, were three other closely related approaches to the universe: astrology, magic, and gnosticism.

EFFORTS TO CONTROL A HOSTILE UNIVERSE

Astrology developed in Mesopotamia, where for centuries men had observed and recorded the orderly movements of the stars and planets. At last they had come to the conclusion that the stars possessed power over human affairs, and that the particular configuration of the stars at the time of a man's birth shaped his destiny. To gain happiness in life, therefore, man must try to understand and, if necessary, to placate the star spirits. Plato's belief that the stars were gods (*Timaeus*, Section 40) had provided a link between those astrological speculations and the Greek philosophical tradition. Other Hellenistic philosophers, by combining astrology with Greek mathematics, heightened the sense of order and precision with which the stars moved. As a result, men of the late Hellenic and early Roman periods grew apprehensive about the power of the stars, and more eager than ever to learn their secrets in order to gain the favor of the star spirits. Only in this way could men guarantee that the fate ordained for them by the stars would be a happy one.

The intense desire to curry the favor of the star spirits, and of other seemingly hostile forces of nature, gave rise to formulas by which one could ward off evil, drive away pain, avert accidents. Societies sprang up that claimed to possess such secrets as astral knowledge, or the trick of staying on the right side of Asclepius, the god of healing. The magic formulas invoked the name of as many deities as possible in order to assure a happy outcome. One crudely written manuscript has been discovered in which the name of Jehovah (or Yahweh), the God of the Hebrews, is linked with Zeus, the chief god of the Greeks, and with the Egyptian god, Serapis. Presumably the man who knew the most magical words and how to invoke the greatest number of deities stood the best chance of gaining happiness in this world and the next.

As kingdoms fell and as life grew more uncertain, people of every class became more interested in life beyond the grave and more anxious to escape the catastrophes of life on this side of it. Even the magic formulas fell into disrepute, and many people turned elsewhere in their search for the secrets of life and death. Some believed that they possessed superior knowledge of history and secrets of the universe that had been revealed to them through visions of divine oracles. They claimed that they could help a man to learn his own fate, or, better still, to secure a happier one; they offered to teach the topography of the underworld to aid men on their journey back from death to the next life.

THE RISE OF GNOSTICISM

During the first century of the Christian Era, the Church carried on a running battle with groups within and outside the Church organization who claimed that they possessed superior knowledge of God and his purposes. In the second century A.D. these groups came to be known as *Gnostics,* a name taken from the Greek word *gnosis,* meaning "knowledge." They were the ones who were "in the know." We have no certain information about the origins of these groups, nor even whether the beginnings of this movement were among Jews or pagans. That Gnosticism was strongly influenced by pagan religious and philosophical developments cannot be doubted. The sharp dualism of the Gnostics, according to which light and darkness, good and evil, matter and spirit are set in sharpest contrast, seems to have arisen under the impact of Persian thought, within whose bounds precisely these pairs of realities were central. But whether there was a pre-Christian Gnosticism, as is often assumed,[1] we cannot determine. Indeed, it is even difficult to decide on a definition of Gnosticism.

Until recently, the oldest evidence available to us concerning Gnosticism was in the form of polemical attacks on Gnostics contained in the writings of second-century Fathers of the Church. Chief among these was Irenaeus, who left his native Asia Minor in the middle of the second century A.D. to become Bishop of Lyons in France. His best-known work was titled *Refutation and Overthrow of Gnosis Falsely So-Called* (usually known as *Against Heresies*). In this writing he quoted at length from Gnostic writings and refuted their claims by appeal to scripture and Church tradition.[2] Gnosticism, as depicted in its various forms by Irenaeus, was elaborately mythological, with multiple

---

[1] This is the assumption of Rudolf Bultmann, as is evident in his *Theology of the New Testament,* I (New York: Scribner's, 1951), 164-183. This point of view, which has been taken by many New Testament scholars as self-evident, has been discredited by the work of Carsten Colpe, *Die Religionsgeschichtliche Schule,* I (Göttingen: Vandenhoeck & Ruprecht, 1961), who has shown that all the documentation we have for the Gnostic redeemer myth—the existence of which in pre-Christian times has been so widely assumed—is from the Christian Era.

[2] The full text (in translation) of Irenaeus' *Against Heresies* is found in *Ante-Nicene Fathers,* I (Grand Rapids, Mich.: Eerdmans, n.d.), 315-358. Excerpts from Irenaeus, together with translations of most of the available material relating to Gnostic origins, are given in *Gnosticism: a Sourcebook,* R. M. Grant, ed. (New York: Harper & Row, 1961).

heavens and complex patterns of deities and celestial powers. In the teachings of one group called Sethians (for Seth, one of the sons of Adam and Eve, through whom these Gnostics traced their origin) or Ophites (since the serpent —in Greek, *ophis*—was worshiped by them) there is an elaborate account of the origins of the Trinity and of seven lesser deities generated by the Son. After giving their names, which are Greekized versions of Hebrew names of God, the account continues:

> These heavens and excellences and powers and angels have places in heaven according to the order of their generation, and they invisibly reign over things celestial and terrestrial. When they had been made, his sons turned to a struggle for the primacy. Therefore in grief and despair Ialdaboth (the first of the lesser divinities) looked down on the dregs of matter and solidified his desire into it and generated a son. This son is Mind, twisted in the form of a serpent and is also Spirit and Soul and everything worldly. From him were generated all forgetfulness and wickedness and jealousy and envy and death.[3]

From even this brief excerpt, which differs in detail from the other Gnostic systems, it is evident that the basic problem with which the Gnostics were struggling was the involvement of man in the material world, subject as it is to decay, death, and defeat. As a part of the Creation, man is to some extent composed of matter, and the world of matter is subject to catastrophe and destruction. How can one believe in a just God and see the evil and disintegration that pervades the created world? Stated more personally, how can man become free from this involvement?

The divine process as seen by the Gnostics was one in which the lesser deities made unwitting errors, or in which their offspring became filled with pride and sought to usurp the powers of their betters. Man was considered to be a divided being: on the one hand he was imprisoned in the world of matter; on the other hand, the ultimate source of his being was the supreme deity, who was free of involvement in the Creation, dwelling in eternal light. The promise of the Gnostics was that by heeding secret knowledge and by the appropriate worship of the deities, man could ascend to the realms of light. In most of the Gnostic systems there was a redemptive figure who had come from the heavenly regions and had become ensnared and suffered in the material world, but who, having triumphed over these adversities, could lead the faithful back to the realm of pure spirit.

Until 1945, all that was available for the study of Gnosticism consisted of quotations from Irenaeus and other Church Fathers, in addition to some rather late (fifth century) manuscripts, which unfortunately were not published until 1955 and subsequently. But in 1945 there was found in upper Egypt a large clay jar containing a number of manuscripts. Although it was nearly a decade

---

[3] Quoted from *Gnosticism: a Sourcebook*, R. M. Grant, ed. (New York: Harper & Row, 1961), p. 54.

before they began to become available for scholarly study, it was soon learned that the manuscripts were part of a library of works, written in Coptic,[4] which had once belonged to a church or monastery, the ruins of which were near the site of the discovery. It was obvious from the first information that was released concerning these finds that they were preserved by a Gnostic group, and that several of the documents were first-hand Gnostic writings. Others showed Gnostic tendencies. There are about 50 different treatises in the collection, some of them known previously only by title, some by quotations in the Church Fathers or from translations in other languages, and some not known at all. One writing, called the Gospel of Truth, is a thoroughly Gnostic document, and may have been written by Valentinus, one of the leading Gnostics whose ideas were attacked by Irenaeus. The Gospel of Thomas, which was known from a few quotations, and a few fragments of which had been found among other Egyptian papyri, was discovered apparently complete. Although it is not a gospel in the sense that it describes the ministry of Jesus, culminating in his crucifixion—no activities of Jesus are depicted at all, only his sayings—it does parallel many of the sayings in our New Testament gospels, and at some points it may preserve an older form of the sayings of Jesus than those found in the gospels as we know them.[5]

We may ask what light these discoveries shed on the origins of Gnosticism. The answer cannot be categorical, but the fact that all these documents employ Jewish-Christian vocabulary in spite of their heterodox views would suggest that Gnosticism as an organized movement arose on Christian soil. It is an aberration from, or rose concurrently with, Christian teaching. A major ingredient in the development of Gnostic thought, however, seems to have been the Jewish apocalyptic writings,[6] since the names of the demons and angels and the elaborate descriptions of the celestial regions in the Gnostic writings closely resemble or are in some cases identical with those found in the apocalyptic writings. We have already noted that the dualistic view of the world that is expressed in apocalypticism came into Judaism under pagan (Persian)

---

[4] Coptic is a language descended from ancient Egyptian, written in the Greek alphabet, with the necessary addition of extra letters to cover sounds not provided for in Greek.

[5] Already an extensive literature has appeared dealing with these Gnostic documents. A brief, reliable account of the discovery and contents is by W. Van Unnik, in *Newly Discovered Gnostic Writings* (London: SCM Press, 1960). A fuller description of the discovery, together with a translation of the Gospel of Thomas, was written by J. Doresse, *The Secret Books of the Egyptian Gnostics* (New York: Viking, 1960). *The Gospel of Truth* was edited and translated by K. Grobel (New York: Abingdon, 1960). *The Gospel of Thomas* was published with text and translation by Harper & Row in 1959.

[6] Apocalyptic, from the Greek *apocalyptō*, meaning "reveal, disclose," is used with reference to a body of literature that arose in the last centuries before the birth of Christ and in the first century A.D. These writings purport to predict how God will act in the future in behalf of his Chosen People. The picture of the future is given in elaborate imagery and symbols, often recounted in the form of dreams. It is a primitive way of viewing history, the consummation of which is expected in the near future. A discussion of the historical situation in Judaism out of which this literature arose is given in the next chapter.

influence, but the Gnostic movement itself seems to have developed from Jewish and Christian sources. Although our sources are late and fragmentary, there is evidence that the Jewish sects in the east Jordan and southern Syria regions were or became Gnostic by the second century A.D. One such group, the Mandaeans—whose name means "knowers" (Gnostics)—originated in this area, and then moved to Iraq, where they still exist as a small practicing Gnostic group.[7] But the only Gnostic writings we have that go back to the early stages of the movement are based on Christian and Old Testament ideas and language, even though the whole complex of ideas has been set in a new framework.

One explanation which has been offered for the emergence of the new framework in which Gnosticism placed old material is the failure of the expectation held by Jews and early Christians that God was very soon going to establish a New Age.[8] Instead of locating the fulfillment of redemptive hope in the Future Age, as Jewish prophetism and apocalyptic did, it was now envisioned as occurring in another sphere of existence in a timeless present. Instead of taking place on the plane of world history, this redemption was seen as happening in cosmic history—or perhaps in the realm of man's own personal history as an inner experience. Indeed, the fruitfulness of Gnostic perspectives for providing man with an understanding of himself is evident even today in the interest of existentialist philosophers [9] and theologians,[10] as well as depth psychologists,[11] in Gnostic literature.

Although we cannot regard developed Gnosticism as an antecedent of Christianity, we can see that the use of Gnostic modes of interpretation in the early centuries of the Church's life was of profound importance in enabling Christian

---

[7] For a sympathetic account of this group, see E. S. Drower, *The Mandaeans of Iraq and Iran* (Leiden: E. J. Brill, 1962). The Mandaean literature has been pointed to as preserving pre-Christian Gnostic material, but in its present form we cannot with any confidence go behind the fifth- or sixth-century stage of development of the Mandaeans. It sheds little light on Gnostic origins.

[8] The theory that Gnosticism arose through the transformation of apocalyptic eschatology in the speculative climate of the Hellenistic world is developed by R. M. Grant, *Gnosticism and Early Christianity* (New York: Columbia University Press, 1959), especially pp. 150-185.

[9] A comprehensive survey of the rise of Gnosticism by a sympathetic philosopher is presented in Hans Jonas, *The Gnostic Religion* (Boston: Beacon Press, 1958). Unfortunately, this penetrating survey relies too heavily on the late Mandaean materials for its reconstruction of what is presented as pre-Christian Gnosis.

[10] Especially R. Bultmann, whose two-volume *Theology of the New Testament* (New York: Scribner's, 1951), shows how attractive the Gnostic attempt at providing man with an understanding of his existence can be for modern man. It is significant that Bultmann's *Commentary on John*, soon to be published in an English translation, interprets the central Christian message along lines that are wholly sympathetic with the Gnostic motifs that Bultmann sees at work in John's gospel.

[11] Psychologists of the Jungian school have long been attracted to Gnostic writings in their search for the "master images" in terms of which C. C. Jung set forth his analysis of man's collective history, his self-consciousness, and his place in the universe. It is not surprising that one of the most important of the Egyptian Coptic manuscripts, the Gospel of Truth, was purchased for the Jung Institute and named the Jung Codex.

propagandists to appeal to sophisticated pagans. Unfortunately, the Gnostic modes very soon crowded out the essence of Christian faith, so that Gnosticism in its fully developed forms had to be repudiated by the Church. Yet, even over the span of centuries, we can sense what an enormous appeal it must have exerted for men foundering in an uncertain or even meaningless world.

THE RISE OF THE MYSTERY RELIGIONS

Among those who claimed access to the secrets of life were the groups of worshipers who made up the so-called mystery cults. Through participation in religious dramas and other ceremonies, the initiates of these cults believed that they could share in the life of the gods. The myths on which the mysteries were based varied from country to country, but the basic intent and the general pattern of the myths were common to all. In most cases there is a wife (or mother) who grieves for her lost husband (or child). After a period of suffering, the son or daughter is restored to the mother—usually from the dead —and begins a new life.

The Mystery of Osiris

· In the Egyptian cults, the myth tells of Isis and her consort, Osiris, a divine king of ancient Egypt. Osiris was seized by his enemies, killed, and dismembered, and Isis wandered over the earth searching for his body, burying each part as she found it. Part of Osiris' corpse was eaten by the fish in the Nile, which the Egyptians believed to flow into the underworld; as a result, Osiris became god of the underworld, where he ruled over the dead. In a series of elaborate ceremonies, described in detail in the *Metamorphoses* of Apuleius, a Latin writer of the second century A.D., an initiate re-enacts the suffering and journey to death that Osiris experienced. As a result of the initiate's union

BACCHUS, *the god of wine, shown among a procession of his worshipers in this well-preserved Greek vase painting.*

with Osiris, the king of the dead, death has no more fears for him and he is assured of life beyond death. The dignity of the cultic ritual, the splendor of the robes worn by the priests, and the awesomeness of the drama combined to give the worship of Isis and Osiris a tremendous appeal, not only in Egypt but in Rome and throughout the empire as well.

Greek Mystic Saviors

In Greece, the mystery cults developed around the myth of Dionysus, the god of wine, and Demeter, the goddess of grain. Dionysus was the son of Zeus, the father of the gods, and was destroyed and devoured by the Titans. His heart, however, was snatched from them and given to Semele, one of the wives of Zeus, who bore another Dionysus to the father of the gods. Since the race of man sprang from the Titans, the divine spark that the Titans took in by eating Dionysus was also present in man. Through mystical union with Dionysus, man could purge away the earthly aspect of his existence and, by rekindling the divine spark, could enter more closely into the life of the gods. From the classical era of Greece down into the Roman period, union with Dionysus was sought by groups of people—especially women—who through night-long ceremonies and the drinking of wine entered into a state of frenzy in which the god allegedly appeared to them. A gruesome account of one such ecstasy is preserved in *The Bacchae*, by Euripides (*ca.* 485-406 B.C.), one of classical Greece's greatest dramatists.

In the cluster of myths that have survived, Demeter is pictured as the goddess of earth, whose daughter, Persephone, was stolen from her by the god of the underworld. In her grief, she neglects the earth, and all vegetation withers and dies. Through the intervention of other gods, Persephone is restored to her, but since Persephone has eaten food in the lower world she

THE TELESTERION *was the great assembly hall at Eleusis, where the mystery rites of Demeter, the goddess of grain, were annually enacted by the faithful.*

must return there for a part of each year. During the months of the year when mother and daughter are united, the earth rejoices and vegetation flourishes; but during the winter months Demeter mourns her lost child. While Demeter was searching for her daughter, she disguised herself as a child's nurse and stayed at Eleusis, a town about 12 miles from Athens. From early Greek times, a series of ceremonies was conducted here every year, beginning with a procession from Athens, and including the re-enactment of the mourning of Demeter, the journey of Persephone into the underworld, and her joyous return.

Only the general outline of the Eleusinian and other mysteries is known, but we know they were attended by thousands every year from all over the civilized world. From the time of Caligula (A.D. 37-41), who granted permission for the worship of Isis to be carried on in Rome, to the initiation of Julian (A.D. 331-363) into the cult of Attis, the mysteries found support in high places in the empire.

Scholars have offered various theories to account for the origin of the mysteries. The fact that one of the most important of the sacred objects displayed to the initiates at Eleusis was a stalk of grain suggests that the rites originated as a magical means of guaranteeing good grain crops. This conjecture is confirmed by the way in which the sacred mystery dramas follow the pattern of recurrent death (sowing), mourning (the winter period when seeds are dormant), and life from the dead (growth and harvest). In one of the cultic liturgies, the priest shouted at the sky, "Hu-eh" (meaning "rain"), and at the earth, "Ku-eh" (meaning "bring forth"). The myth of Isis was clearly associated with the annual flooding by the Nile, which was the sole source of fertility for the land of Egypt.

But it is obvious that by Hellenistic times the ceremonies had become far more than rituals performed to insure good crops. The crops' cycle of life and death had become a symbol of man's cycle of life and death, and the intent of the mystery drama was to assure new life, not for the crops, but for the worshiper. In an age when the future held so little promise, and when the old order had broken down, men turned with enthusiasm to these cults with their secrets of life beyond death and their guarantees of immortality.

The mystery religions had another strong appeal: the initiates of each cult were united in a brotherhood from which the barriers of race and social standing were erased. All presented themselves to the deity on the same level, and through participation in the sacramental rites all were united into a fellowship that was to endure forever. That the mysteries were ridden with superstition, that the myths on which they were based were jumbled and contradictory, and that they provided no basis for social or individual morality seem to have mattered only to cynics and critical satirists. Slaves and freedmen, middle-class merchants and artisans, men and women of the upper classes—all flocked to the mystery cults in their search for security and a sense of community in an age of uncertainty.

THE SEARCH
FOR COMMUNITY
IN ISRAEL

CHAPTER TWO   There was one community in the Graeco-
Roman world which, more than any other, shared a common
life and thought. This was the community of Israel—the
Jews—who looked to Palestine as their homeland and to
Jerusalem as their capital city. And yet Jerusalem was not a
political capital for the Jews, for they had been without political power for the better part of five centuries. Rather, it
was a religious capital for a people who were indissolubly

bound together by a religious faith and a history that reached back into the distant past. After their political community was wiped out, the Jews succeeded in developing a remarkably homogeneous religious community which, though it looked to Palestine as its homeland, was scattered throughout the Graeco-Roman world. At the beginning of the first century A.D., there were more Jews living outside Palestine than in it; large Jewish settlements were thriving in the major cities, such as Rome and Alexandria, and in many smaller cities as well. Jews had continued to live in Mesopotamia since the sixth century B.C., when they were carried there as captives by the Babylonians. In spite of their being scattered over the civilized world, the Jews were forced by historical circumstances and by religious convictions into a tightly knit community.

THE JEWS UNDER FOREIGN DOMINATION: THE PERSIANS AND THE GREEKS

In the late sixth century, Persia overthrew the Babylonians who had led the Jews into slavery, and granted the exiles permission to return to their homeland (538 B.C.). Many of them were content to remain where they were, but others began a slow migration homeward that continued for a century. By 516 B.C., the Temple in Jerusalem (destroyed by the Babylonians in 586 B.C.) had been reconstructed and work had been started on rebuilding the city and its walls. Because of opposition from hostile neighbors, however, the walls were not completed until shortly after 450 B.C.

By the end of the fifth century B.C., then, Jerusalem had once again become the center of Jewish national and religious life, even though the Jews were the political subjects of Persia. Though stripped of political power, the Jews were free to develop their religious life and thought with little interference from the Persian authorities. Under the leadership of their High Priest they developed into a small theocracy set within the confines of the Persian Empire.

When the Greeks under Alexander made their conquest of Persia and her territories, the Jews, like most of the oriental subjects of Persia, welcomed him as a liberator. During the period following Alexander's death, when the Jews were subjected first to the Ptolemies and then to the Seleucids, they enjoyed the same religious toleration they had experienced under Persia. So long as they paid their tribute and offered no resistance to their rulers this condition continued—until the reign of the Seleucid king, Antiochus IV Epiphanes (175-164 B.C). It was at this time that the Jewish people experienced the most serious threat to their existence that had arisen since the Babylonian Captivity.

The Maccabean Revolt

Ancient and modern historians have offered many reasons for Antiochus IV's attack on the Jews. Among them was a very practical economic reason. For some time, the Seleucids had been hard pressed for funds not only to carry on their feud with the Ptolemies but also to maintain control over their vast holdings in the East. One of their sources of revenue was the Jewish nation. In addition to increasing the taxes levied on the Jews, Antiochus decided to offer the Jewish office of High Priest to the highest bidder. He deposed the rightful High Priest, Onias, and in his place appointed a man named Jason, who offered large sums of money for the office and agreed to support Antiochus in the Hellenization of the Jewish nation. Antiochus, who fancied himself a true representative of Hellenistic culture, was eager to force this culture upon all

ANTIOCHUS IV (Epiphanes) on a Greek coin. The reverse side carries the Greek words: Basileos Antiochou, Theou Epiphanous, Nikephorou—"(coinage) of King Antiochus, God Manifest, Bearer of Victory." The king represents himself as Zeus, seated on a throne, holding in his left hand a royal staff and in his right the figure of the goddess of victory, Nike, who holds in her hand the laurel wreath, symbol of victory.

his subjects. It was this effort, in which Jason joined, that led to conflict between Antiochus and the Jews.

Jason built a gymnasium in the heart of Jerusalem in which young Jews, some of them from priestly families, exercised in the nude, according to Greek custom. Some Jews even submitted to surgery to remove the distinctive marks of circumcision. These Greek practices horrified many of the Jews, who regarded them as contrary to their Law and in violation of their covenant with God. Consequently, a strong opposition party called the Hasidim (pious ones) arose in opposition to Jason and to the Jews who were sympathetic to Hellenization. The Hasidim fought against all efforts to adopt Greek ways, for to them these customs were inseparably bound up with the idolatry and immorality that they associated with the Greek religion and way of life.

Antiochus finally realized that he could not bend the Jews to his will until he had first destroyed their religion. So in 168 B.C. he issued an edict of proscription. Under penalty of death all Jews were forbidden to circumcise, to celebrate religious festivals, or to observe the Sabbath. He ordered all copies of the Law to be destroyed, and anyone found in possession of it to be punished.

Antiochus' men set up a Greek altar to Zeus in the Temple in Jerusalem, and sacrificed swine upon it. Heathen altars were erected throughout the land, and the Jews were compelled to worship heathen gods. To enforce his edict, Antiochus stationed troops throughout Israel.

Although the Jews who had favored Hellenization in the first place acceded to Antiochus' demands, the stubborn Hasidim refused to comply with the edict even though they were faced with martyrdom. Finally, the Jews revolted under the leadership of a priest named Mattathias (from the Hasmon family —Hasmoneans), who came from the village of Modin. After killing a Jew who was in the act of sacrificing on a pagan altar, Mattathias fled with his five sons to the rugged hill country outside Jerusalem. There they gathered around them followers who were ready to fight the Syrian oppressors in the name of God and in defense of their right to live according to their Law.

This action marked the beginning of the Maccabean Revolt, named for Judas Maccabeus, Mattathias' son who assumed command of the forces when his father died. The Syrians were little disturbed by the uprising, for the Jews had no trained militia, no arms, and almost no financial backing. But Antiochus underestimated their religious zeal, their bravery, and their ingenuity. Since the Jews were greatly outnumbered and had only crude weapons, they turned to guerrilla tactics against the Syrians in the rugged hill country of Judea. After suffering a number of discouraging defeats, Judas and his men made a heroic effort and finally managed to win a peace treaty from Antiochus' general, Lysias. In December, 165 B.C., Judas entered the Temple in Jerusalem, cleansed it, and re-established the traditional Jewish worship. To the present day, Jews commemorate this triumphant event in the festival of Hanukkah (Rededication), the Feast of Lights.

Now that religious liberty had been restored, many of the Hasidim were apparently ready to withdraw from the revolt. But Judas and his followers carried on raids against the Ammonites and Idumeans, traditional enemies of the Jews, and led expeditions to Galilee and Gilead to rescue Jews who were suffering retaliation at the hands of Gentiles. The fact that the Syrians still were in control of strong fortifications in Judaea and in Jerusalem itself (the Acra) also must have increased Judas' reluctance to disband his forces. Furthermore, there was still an active Hellenizing party among the Jews that continued to seek the high priestly office and was quite ready to call upon the Seleucid king for assistance.

What had begun as a revolt for religious liberty now became a struggle for political freedom, a struggle that was carried on by the brothers of Judas after his death. Under the leadership of Simon (142-135 B.C.), the Jews took several strategic Syrian fortresses, including the Acra in Jerusalem, and thereby gained virtual independence. The people acknowledged Simon's success by naming him the legitimate High Priest, even though he was not a member of a high priestly family. As the years passed, efforts were made to enlarge the boundaries of the kingdom, and the Hasmonean rule became more obviously political. John Hyrcanus (135-104 B.C.), Simon's son, made notable strides toward his goal of restoring the boundaries of the former kingdom of David. This ambition was more nearly realized by Simon's son, Alexander Jannaeus (103-76 B.C.), who was more ambitious than his father and more ruthless in his tactics. Using mercenary troops, he even attacked fellow Jews who opposed his insatiable desire for expansion, and put to death many of the Jewish leaders. Under Alexander Jannaeus, the religious aims of the original Maccabean revolt were all but obliterated, and most Jews looked upon him as disloyal to the cause of the original Maccabean heroes.

After Alexander Jannaeus' death, his widow Alexandra (76-67 B.C.) restored some degree of stability to the Jewish nation. But when she died, a dispute sprang up between her two sons over the succession. Each had his following among the Jews, and each sent an embassy to Pompey, in Syria, to seek Roman support. A third embassy, representing the Jewish people, requested that Pompey reject the monarchy altogether and restore the Jewish nation to its pre-Maccabean nonpolitical status.

UNDER ROMAN RULE: THE HERODIANS

In 63 B.C., with Pompey's arrival in Jerusalem, the political independence of the Jews was cut off once again. The territory now passed under Roman rule, and was made subject to Rome's representative in the territory of Syria. Hyrcanus II, a son of Alexandra who was appointed High Priest by Pompey, faithfully carried out Rome's policy with the help of his minister, Antipater, an Idumean who was clearly motivated by personal ambition. During the long period of disturbances in Rome at the close of the Republican period, Antipater and his son Herod, through political astuteness and cunning, managed to stay in favor with a succession of Roman leaders. In 40 B.C., Rome named Herod ruler of both Judea and Samaria, with the title of king, although disturbances in Jerusalem made it impossible for him to ascend the throne until 37 B.C. Herod's rule (37-4 B.C.) was confirmed by Augustus Caesar in 30 B.C. Before Herod died, his kingdom had come to include not only Idumea, Judea, and Samaria, but also Perea in Transjordan, Galilee, and a territory north and east of the Sea of Galilee. It was this Herod who was ruler at the time of Jesus' birth.

Herod proved one of the most successful of Rome's puppet rulers, and he was given the title of Herod the Great. He restored some degree of law and order to troubled Palestine and set it up as a buffer state between Rome's territories and the marauding Arab peoples who constantly threatened the peace and Rome's lines of communication. Furthermore, in the fashion of a true Hellenistic monarch, he tried to foster in his kingdom Augustus' hopes for a common Graeco-Roman culture throughout the Roman Empire. Herod, as

THE ROMAN FORUM *and part of a temple at Sebaste, the Greek-style city of Samaria built by Herod the Great and named in honor of Augustus ("Sebaste" in Greek).*

we noted above, gave support to the imperial cult and built temples honoring Augustus in cities of Palestine and Asia Minor. He rebuilt many old cities according to the Hellenistic pattern, and throughout the land he constructed gymnasia, theaters, and stadia to encourage the Hellenistic way of life.

But most of the Jews despised Herod for his Idumean ancestry and for his tireless efforts to Hellenize the kingdom. Furthermore, his ambitious building programs cost money that had to be raised by excessive taxation. Desperately jealous of his power and fearful lest he lose it, Herod filled the land with secret police and severely punished any Jew who aroused the least suspicion of disloyalty. He went so far as to have his mother-in-law, two of his sons, and his favorite wife (he had nine others) murdered because he suspected their loyalty. Herod did try, though in vain, to conciliate the Jews, for in hard times he eased their taxes and during famine he provided food. And he began the construction of a beautiful new Temple in Jerusalem (20 B.C.), though it was not completed until after his death. But all these efforts were to no avail. The land was seething with parties of dissatisfaction, and there is evidence that Herod shrewdly played one off against the other to heighten the internal unrest.

It is not surprising, then, that when Herod died in 4 B.C. the Jews sent an embassy to Augustus imploring that Rome refuse to execute Herod's will, in which he had appointed his sons as successors. When riots broke out in Judea, Varus, the Roman governor of Syria, was sent to quell them, and Augustus shortly approved Herod's will dividing the kingdom among his three sons. Archelaus was appointed ethnarch in Judea (4 B.C.-A.D. 6), Herod Antipas tetrarch of Galilee, Perea (4 B.C.-A.D. 39), and Philip tetrarch of Iturea, Trachonitis, Batanea, Auranitis, Gaulinitis, and Panias. Philip, most of whose subjects were Gentile, enjoyed a very successful rule. Herod Antipas was relatively successful in the eyes of Rome but distasteful to the Jews; it was under his rule that John the Baptist and Jesus carried on their ministries (see Chapters

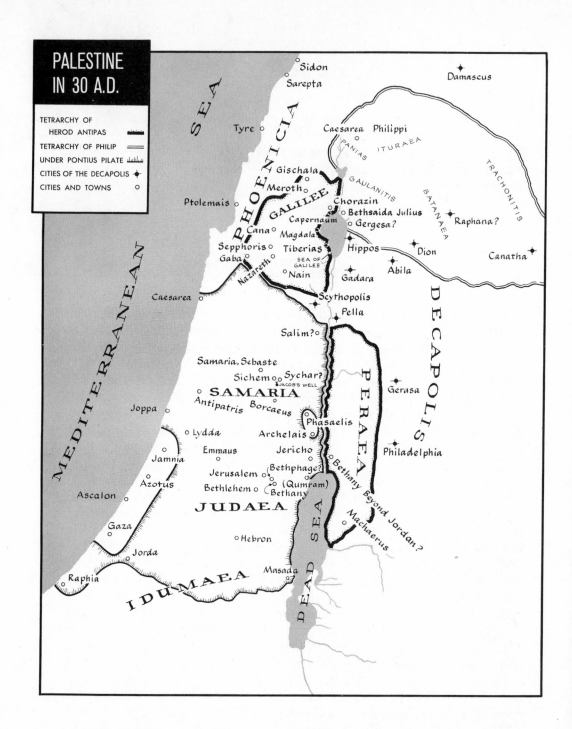

5 and 6). Archelaus, who proved totally incompetent, was deposed after offending both Jews and Romans. Following Archelaus' deposition, Jerusalem and Judea passed under direct Roman rule administered by a succession of procurators. There was just one short break in the administration (from A.D. 41 to 44), when Herod Agrippa I, Herod the Great's grandson, was granted the rule of his grandfather's entire territory. Since the welfare of the Jewish nation during the years of Roman rule depended directly on the relations between the people and the procurators, we must consider more carefully the events of this period.

The Procurators (A.D. 6-66)

No less than 14 procurators were sent to Judea during the 60-year period from A.D. 6 to 66. As the years passed, tension between Rome and the Jewish people increased steadily, partly because of the character of the procurators themselves. With few exceptions, these men failed to measure up to the highest standards of Roman administrative personnel, and their caliber seemed to decline with each successive appointment. Repeatedly, they made foolish judgments in administration, and often they were guilty of inordinate cruelty in carrying out official policies.

But the lot of the procurators was not easy, for they were appointed to govern one of the most troublesome territories under Roman rule—a territory that had grown increasingly resentful under years of alien control. Furthermore, they could not understand the Jews' stubborn resistance to Hellenistic religion and customs, and their persistent loyalty to their own religious faith—a faith that procurators looked upon as superstitious and barbarous. In the name of that faith, minor figures arose time and time again promising release from Roman rule. To the Romans, such promises carried with them the threat of political treason. A good example of the procurators' failure to understand the Jews occurred under Pontius Pilate (A.D. 26-36), before whom Jesus stood trial. On one occasion, in order to build a new aqueduct, Pilate appropriated funds from the Temple treasury in Jerusalem that were specifically designated for maintaining sacrifices. Then, when the people protested this outrage against their religion, he turned them away by force of arms. On another occasion, he offended the religious sensitivity of the Jews by bringing military insignia bearing the emperor's image into the city of Jerusalem. Pilate finally had to be removed from office when he commanded his soldiers to attack a crowd of defenseless Samaritans who had gathered to watch a self-styled prophet perform a miracle on Mt. Gerizim.

As time went by, an increasing number of Jews were drawn into groups (Zealots) that openly or secretly favored armed rebellion. Open hostility often flared up. Under Felix (A.D. 51-60), before whom the Apostle Paul was brought for a hearing, the Jewish reactionary groups became even more fanatical, and assassinations on both sides were common. Felix's ruthless reaction to his opponents drove still more Jews to adopt radical ways of showing their hatred. Albinus (A.D. 62-64), who was recalled by Rome because of his graft and his maltreatment of innocent people, emptied the jails of prisoners before he left Judea, flooding the country with brigands who added to the confusion of the times. By the time of Florus (A.D. 64-66), the last of the procurators, open fighting had become common. To add to the fury, Florus plundered the Temple treasury, and when the people demonstrated against his action he ordered many of them crucified. By A.D. 66, the situation had become so critical and the promise of improvement so remote that organized revolt against Rome finally broke out.

But the rebellion of the Jews against the Romans was lost before it began, for the trained and powerful forces of Rome could not be overcome. Under the Roman generals Vespasian and Titus, the war was successfully concluded by Rome in A.D. 70, though the last remnants of resistance were not wiped out until A.D. 73. The city of Jerusalem suffered heavy damage during the fighting, and the Temple itself was destroyed. For the third time in their history, the Jews had suffered what appeared to be annihilating defeat; yet once again they managed to survive.

Although political, social, and economic factors contributed to the outbreak of the Jewish War, the desperate venture sprang primarily from religious motives. Most of the leaders of the revolt saw themselves as the true successors of the Maccabean heroes, and they fought the enemy for the sake of their faith. Like the revolt itself, the Jews' survival as a community can be understood only in terms of faith. And, since it was the religious development within the community that determined to a large degree the community's development, we must turn now to the faith of the Jewish community that sustained its life through these decisive periods in its history.

THE FAITH OF THE JEWISH COMMUNITY

After the calamity wrought by the Babylonians in 587 B.C., it was a resurgence of religious faith that had brought about the reconstitution of the Jewish community. The Jewish prophets and leaders during the Exile boldly declared that the victory of the Babylonians was not a sign of the weakness of their God Jehovah, but rather the means whereby he had revealed his judgment on his people for their sins. Looking back to the words of the great prophets Amos, Hosea, Isaiah, and Jeremiah, the Jews saw that through them God had repeatedly warned his people that continual refusal to obey his commands would lead to destruction. In the Exile, destruction had indeed come as testimony to the truth of all that the prophets had said.

The prophet whose words are found in the last chapters of the book of Isaiah (40-66) saw in Cyrus' permission to the Jews to return to their homeland a sign of God's continuing concern for his people. By granting them an opportunity to renew their loyalty to him, God had provided the Jews with further evidence that he was not only their God but the only true God in all the universe. It was the mission of his people to bear witness to him to all the nations through their loyalty and obedience.

When the leaders of the returning Jews tried to understand just how the people had sinned and had brought down the judgment of God, they emphasized three major failures: First, the Jews had succumbed to idolatry and had turned to foreign gods rather than to Jehovah alone. Second, they had not worshiped Jehovah in purity but had permitted their worship to become corrupted by all manner of foreign practices. Third, they had not obeyed the commandments that he had given them. With these failures in mind, the post-exilic Jews determined to guard against any intrusion into their religious belief and life that might turn them from worshiping God as he ought to be worshiped. They realized that all through their history God had been seeking to lead them to what they fully came to understand only through the Babylonian Captivity. They had been chosen by the one true God to know him, to worship him, and to live according to his commandments.

These convictions led to what has been called Jewish "particularism" or "exclusivism." It was not merely their belief that they were God's Chosen People that set the Jews apart from all other people. Given their firm conviction that belief, conduct, and worship were all of one piece, it was inevitable that they would seek to separate themselves from any mode of life that threatened the purity of any of the three. The book of Ezra shows the lengths to which this particularism was carried, for in it the Jews returning to Judaea after the captivity are forbidden to marry foreigners, and those who have married non-Jews are asked to put them aside. Such exclusivism can be understood only in the light of the religious zeal that prompted it—the earnest desire to avoid at all costs the disloyalty of their fathers. And since loyalty to Jehovah involved every aspect of life, it was dangerous to enter into close relations with those who lived in accordance with other ways. This exclusivism at its worst could become a cloak for the derision and hatred of other peoples. But at its best it was the Jews' testimony to the reality of the God they worshiped and the way of life into which faithfulness to him inescapably led them.

In the Hellenistic Age, when polytheism and idolatry were commonplace, and when religion and morality were not so clearly related as they were in Judaism, the exclusivism of the Jews stood out sharply against the pagan world. Concerted efforts to Hellenize the Jews, by such rulers as Antiochus Epiphanes, drove loyal Jews to defiance, since they felt that their way of life had been given by God himself, in the form of the Jewish Law. More than anything else, it was the Law that provided the bond between Jews and that distinguished them as a community from all other people.

THE CENTRALITY OF THE LAW

The Jews were convinced that to avoid the recurrence of such a tragedy as the Babylonian exile, they must know God's will as revealed in the Law of Moses and live in accordance with it. The Jews fervently believed that his Law had been given by divine revelation through Moses and was contained in the Pentateuch (the first five books of the Old Testament). It is now common knowledge that these books contain materials that were gradually brought together over many centuries and that it was not until the end of the fifth century B.C. that they reached their present state.

By the end of the third century B.C., the prophetic books (Amos, Hosea, Isaiah, and so forth) had also assumed the form in which they now appear and had been accepted as part of God's divine revelation to his people. In the New Testament, the phrase "the Law and the Prophets" is a reference to God's revelation to his people as it was contained in these holy scriptures. By the end of the first century B.C., all the books in the Old Testament, except for a very few, were regarded as divine revelation.

The English term *law* is not a precise equivalent of the Hebrew word *Torah*, a fact that is obvious to anyone who reads the Pentateuch carefully. For the Pentateuch contains a great deal of legend, history, and myth, as well as specific rules or regulations. To the Jews, Torah was a very inclusive term that referred to all that God had revealed about himself, their history, and the conduct that was required of them. In time, the entire written revelation came to be referred to as Torah, though in the more narrow sense Torah always meant the Pentateuch, and often specifically God's commandments.

It is this centrality of the Torah in Judaism that accounts for the rise of a body of Jewish scholars known as the Scribes (*Sopherim*). Since knowledge of the Torah was so essential, there had to be authorities who were competent to interpret the meaning of Torah to the people. In the early post-exilic period, the priests had been the learned men who were looked to as authorities. By the end of the third century B.C., some laymen had become Scribes charged with the responsibility of preserving the writings and giving the official interpretation of them. The conviction had arisen by that time that God was no longer revealing his will through the prophets but that the authority for understanding and interpreting God's will now resided largely with the Scribes, who accordingly thought of themselves as the successors to the prophets.

The Torah, then, provided the basis for the common belief and conduct that characterized Jewish life and bound Jews together wherever they might be. But no institution in Judaism was more important in transmitting knowledge of the Torah and in nurturing deep reverence for it than the synagogue (transliterated from a Greek word meaning *assembly*). It is impossible to speak with certainty of the precise origins of the synagogue. It may have had its inception during the exile in Babylonia, when the Temple no longer stood and the Jews, far from their home, came together for worship, deliberation, and mutual support. Long before the end of the first century B.C., the synagogue had become a well-established institution, though its significance had evolved gradually. Not only in Palestine, but wherever Jews lived throughout the Graeco-Roman world, the synagogue served as the center of Jewish life and thought. Indeed, the term *synagogue* referred not so much to a place of meeting as to the coming together of Jews in any locality. It was an assembly for worship for Jews who had no temple, an occasion to read and interpret the Torah in the presence of the community. And it was in the synagogue that the "elders," the respected counselors of the local Jewish community, sought ways in which the Jews could adjust to an alien environment without being unfaithful to the Torah. When the Romans destroyed the Temple in A.D. 70, the synagogue continued as the vital center of Jewish faith and life.

THE TEMPLE AND THE PRIESTHOOD

When the Jews returned to Jerusalem from the exile after 538 B.C., one of the first things they did was to rebuild the Temple. This step was in keeping with their strong desire to re-institute the proper worship of God. The priests who did the final editing of the Law of Moses (Torah) were careful to include specific instructions on the temple structure and the form of temple worship. The Temple itself consisted of a series of courts; the innermost court was the Holy of Holies, which only the High Priest was permitted to enter. This secret chamber was the place where God dwelled, and it symbolized his presence with his people. Naturally enough, the Holy of Holies provoked endless curiosity among non-Jews, who circulated scandalous rumors about the contents of the room and what went on inside.

The heart of the temple worship consisted of sacrificial offerings, including daily sacrifices morning and evening, and special sacrifices and more elaborate rituals on festival occasions. Then there were daily private offerings by individuals to cover the multitude of sacrifices required by Torah. Consequently, the temple area was constantly crowded with priests and Jews making offerings, and with the sacrificial animals and the men who sold them. In addition, money-changers were always on hand, since Torah required that financial transactions in the Temple could be carried on only with a particular kind of coin.

It is hard to tell just what meaning the sacrifices had for the average Jew at the end of the first century B.C. But there is no doubt about one point: the whole sacrificial system was essential to Jewish worship, for it was required by Torah itself.

To officiate at the numerous sacrificial rites there were multitudes of priests from a long line of priestly families whose genealogies were recorded in the Torah. Admission to the priesthood was carefully controlled, since the Jews were determined that worship be conducted only by properly qualified men. Only descendants from the sons of Aaron could be priests, although descendants from the line of Levi could perform restricted functions alongside the priests. The Torah's regulations to insure the purity of the priests were meticulously observed, as was the Torah's requirement that the priests and the Levites be supported from offerings made by the people.

At the head of the priesthood was the High Priest, an office that seems to have emerged during the Persian period. As the titular head of the Jewish people, the High Priest carried on negotiations with the various governments to which the Jews were subject. From the beginning, this meant that the High Priest, together with the other priests whom he represented, exercised unusual authority in the community. By the second century B.C., and perhaps earlier, he served as head of the Sanhedrin, a court that handled cases involving infraction of the Torah. Since the Jews made no distinction between civil and religious law, the Sanhedrin could control every aspect of the daily life of the Jewish people. In practice, however, the Sanhedrin concerned itself with only the most obvious infractions of Torah. Since the Romans recognized the Sanhedrin as the ruling body over the Jews, except in matters of treason, the Sanhedrin with the High Priest at its head wielded a great deal of authority.

In the Temple itself, the High Priest's importance was most dramatically symbolized on the Day of Atonement (Yom Kippur), when he entered into the Holy of Holies, into the very presence of God, as the representative of all the Jews. There he offered sacrifices for all the unwitting sins committed by the people during the year, and in response God assured the Jews of his continuing presence and love.

Although the High Priest and the priesthood continued to occupy a place of great importance up to the time of the destruction of the Temple in A.D. 70, their influence had begun to wane. Since the families from which the High Priests came were typically wealthy and aristocratic, they were separated in sympathy and understanding from the masses of the people. Probably the most important factor in the decline of the priesthood was the rising influence of the Pharisees, who were in dispute with the priests on many points of interpreting the Torah and who usually represented a position more sympathetic toward the people.

Nevertheless, as long as the Temple stood it provided a unifying bond. Whether in Palestine or the Diaspora, the Jew looked to the Temple as a symbol of his status as one of God's people. Every year, Jews throughout the world sent their contribution to the Temple, and most Jews longed to make a pilgrimage to the Temple in Jerusalem at least once in their lives. When the Temple was destroyed, it was only a remarkable resurgence of religious faith and the centrality of the Torah that enabled the community to survive.

THE HOPE OF THE JEWISH COMMUNITY

Underlying the growth and development of a strong Jewish community lay a hopefulness that came to play an increasingly important role in its life. Paradoxically, the greater the hardships and calamities the Jewish people suffered, the more fervent became their hope for the future.

Although the expectations of the Jews were expressed in many ways, two concepts were basic to all others in popular thought. The first expectation, which had its roots in pre-exilic times, was for the coming of an ideal ruler who would establish a reign of righteousness and peace throughout the world. As time passed, the Jews came to believe that this ruler would be a descendant of David and that he would restore the kingdom of David, which the Jews increasingly tended to idealize. This expectation obviously implied that the Jewish nation would regain the political prestige it had once enjoyed, but its ultimate meaning was that the nation's resurgence would vindicate the faith of the Jews and the righteousness of God.

The second expectation was that God himself would establish his heavenly rule throughout all the world, a hope that gradually found expression in the concept of the kingdom of God, God's perfectly righteous rule that one day would supplant the imperfect rule of man. During the last two centuries B.C., this concept received particular emphasis, for two principal reasons. First, as the result of repeated defeats by the Seleucids and the subjection of the Jewish nation to Rome, the Jews came to believe that only through some act of God himself could they ever be vindicated and their oppressors brought under judgment. Second, there was a growing belief that the world lay in the power of evil spirits who could not be defeated by human agencies alone. Under the influence of Persian religious thought, the Jews had developed dualistic tendencies in their thinking. They conceived of the world as the battleground of two opposing realms, the realm of God and the realm of Satan, with all men divided between those who fought in faithfulness for God and those who served Satan. Although the powers of evil seemed to have the upper hand for the time being, the Jews were confident that God was still in control. The day was coming when he would once and for all destroy the realm of Satan and bring in a new age in which his people would be vindicated.

During the last two centuries B.C. there emerged a whole body of literature [1] dealing with the conflict between the kingdom of God and the kingdom of Satan, and with the great victory that God would eventually bring about. In

---

[1] Such writings have been brought together in modern times into two great collections, called *The Apocrypha* and *The Pseudepigrapha*. See R. H. Charles, *The Apocrypha and Pseudepigrapha of the Old Testament*, 2 vols. (Oxford: Clarendon Press, 1963). The literature has been expanded with the discovery of the Dead Sea Scrolls.

general, the struggle was portrayed as growing increasingly worse until a violent conflict broke out among mankind, accompanied by violent disruptions in the whole natural order. Finally, in a totally renewed order of existence, God's kingdom would prevail, God's faithful servants who had died would be raised up to live in joy and peace, and God's purposes in creating the world would be brought to fulfillment.

Although the Jews felt that it was God himself who would bring about this final renewal, there was a growing tendency to think that it would be accomplished by the Messiah, one anointed by God as his agent in carrying out his purposes. Not all the Jews thought of the Messiah in the same way. Some expected him to be a human being who would emerge from the Jewish people, perhaps the long-expected ruler from the Davidic line. Others believed the origin of the Messiah was cloaked in mystery. Some texts suggest the expectation of a divine being who would descend from heaven and lead the righteous to a transformed life in the kingdom of heaven. The messianic figure of the Son of Man in the Book of Enoch might be such a Messiah. But most Jews agreed that the Messiah's coming would mark the beginning of God's victory over the powers of evil.

This type of thinking about the events related to God's final judgment on evil is referred to technically as *eschatological,* a term that comes from the Greek word meaning "final" or "end." Another term used to describe such speculative thought is *apocalyptic,* derived from a Greek term meaning "revelation." Writers who dealt with eschatology presented revelations regarding the end that purportedly had been given to ancient worthies such as Enoch, Noah, and Abraham. Although the various apocalyptic and eschatological writers made use of a wide range of mythological images, they were all interested in making one point: that God would triumph over evil and bring to completion his purposes.

Throughout the period from the Maccabean Revolt to the end of the war with Rome, the eschatological hopes of the Jews fanned the flames of their religious zeal and held them firm in their resistance to any violation of the Torah. Soon after the Maccabean War broke out, the apocalyptic book of Daniel was written, urging the Jews to stand firm in their faith since God's kingdom was at hand and the kingdom of evil was about to be destroyed. Appropriately, evil was personified in the Seleucid kingdom. Later, under Roman domination, other apocalyptic writings appeared in which Rome was identified with the reign of evil. The sharper the crisis, the more brightly the Jewish hopes flamed.

When the final battle with Rome took place in A.D. 66, these hopes undoubtedly played a major role in rallying the Jews to action. Those who thought of God's victory in political terms stood side by side with those who looked for some cataclysmic transformation of the world and a renewed order of existence. For Rome was both the political enemy of the Jewish nation and a personification of the evil that thwarted the rule of God himself. But it was primarily the religious hope that led the Jews to throw themselves into conflict with Rome. This was a hope common to all Jews, for all had been nourished on the conviction that God would vindicate their faithfulness to him before the eyes of the whole world.

JEWISH SECTARIAN GROUPS

Although the world-wide Jewish community was bound together by Torah and Temple, certain differences did spring up in the interpretation of that faith. The most obvious disagreements arose between the Jews of Palestine and those of the Diaspora, such as Philo of Alexandria (see pp. 13-14). Under the influence of Hellenistic thinking, the non-Palestinian Jews began to make various modifications and accommodations in their religious thought. But even within the confines of Palestine, certain differences developed. These differences are clearly illustrated by three sectarian groups that originated in Palestine: the Sadducees, the Pharisees, and the Essenes.

The Sadducees

Concerning the origin of the term *Sadducee*, and of the sect itself, there is considerable uncertainty. The first mention of the sect is given by the Jewish historian, Josephus, discussing events in the time of John Hyrcanus (135-104 B.C.). According to one hypothesis which has received considerable support, the term *Sadducee* was derived from *Zadok* (*Zadokite*). In the Old Testament the legitimate priestly office of Aaron is said to have been given to Zadok and his descendants. According to this hypothesis, since the principal claim and concern of the Sadducees was the legitimate succession of the priestly office, this derivation of the name and the movement seems justified.

Since no literature of the Sadducees is extant, and our knowledge about them is derived from the writings of rival movements, it is difficult to reconstruct a full and accurate account of their beliefs and practices. In comparison with the *Pharisees* and the *Essenes* their religious outlook was conservative. Their central guide in religious matters was the Law of Moses, the first five books of the Old Testament. In these books are contained the basic rules and regulations governing the Temple, the priesthood, and the sacrificial rites. How the Scribes of the Sadducees interpreted the meaning of the sacrifices cannot be known. This much seems clear: they believed that faithful and literal fulfillment of God's provision for sacrificial worship in the Temple was the crucial requirement in maintaining Israel's covenant relationship with God. Here was their focus of religious piety.

The influence and prerogatives of the Sadducees reached beyond the confines and activities of the Temple and its priesthood. They enjoyed a dominant position in the Sanhedrin, whose presiding officer was the High Priest. Considering the authority of the Sanhedrin, the potential for wielding influence over the life of the Jews is quite obvious. Only the Pharisees, who gradually increased in strength, were powerful enough to challenge both their influence and their interpretation of the Torah. The sphere of Sadducean involvement and influence was even broader. Through their dominant role in the Temple and the Sanhedrin, the Sadducean priesthood and its supporters were the official spokesmen for the Jews in their dealings with Rome. Drawn largely from the wealthy, aristocratic, priestly families, they were concerned and in close touch with both the economic and political problems of the harassed nation. When possible they followed the road of peaceful co-existence with the civil authorities. Nevertheless, on occasion they were capable of resistance when a political authority ventured to control and manipulate the office of High Priest, or plundered the treasury of the Temple.

Placing supreme value upon the Law of Moses, the Sadducees relegated the prophetic and other writings of the Old Testament to a place of secondary importance. They were particularly opposed to apocalyptic and eschatological thought, on the grounds that such speculation was not compatible with the Torah. For the same reason, they disavowed the popular belief in angels, demons, evil spirits, and the resurrection of the dead. Firmly ensconced in their theocratic conservatism, which saw the life blood of Judaism pulsing in the Temple cult, they looked with particular fear and horror on eschatological speculation and apocalyptic hopes, especially when these fanned the flames of anti-Roman nationalism. While the Sadducees' political sagacity undoubtedly was an important factor in keeping a potentially hot war cold, the succeeding years were to show that the Sadducees had cut themselves off from those vital movements in Jewish religious life and thought that were to play such a decisive role in the resurgence of Judaism after the tragedy of 70 A.D. From that date, when the Romans sacked Jerusalem and destroyed the Temple, the Sadducees quickly disappeared from the Jewish scene. Their understanding of the Torah was so literalistically and unimaginatively limited, and their religious piety was so narrowly centered in the Temple, that once the Temple was destroyed their reason for existence ceased. The disappearance of the Sadducees marked the triumph of their chief rivals, the Pharisees.

The Pharisees

The origin of the Pharisees was closely related to the revolt of the Hasidim in the Maccabean period, and, like them, they were rigorous supporters of the Torah. According to their own traditions they looked back to the time of Ezra as the formative period. But even if they could legitimately claim such early antecedents for their movement, it was not until after the Maccabean Revolt that the patterns of thinking emerged that were to be determinative for the later development of the movement. It was also in this period that they became a coherent force in Jewish life. Concerning the derivation of the name, Pharisee, there is even less agreement among scholars than in the case of the Sadducees. One plausible hypothesis derives the name from a Hebrew word meaning "separatists." Whether this was a self-designation or a derogatory label of their opponents is uncertain. The problem of determining specifically what it was from which they were separated is likewise difficult to decide. One possibility would be the group's withdrawal of support from the Hasmonaean monarchy when in the second century B.C. it pursued a more decidedly political course and tended to veer from a distinctly religious orientation.

Pharisaism was a nonpriestly lay movement in Judaism. Whatever its background in pre-Maccabean times, during the second century B.C. there appeared a succession of prominent teachers and scholars whose teachings, along with those of their successors, were the beginning of that vast body of religious literature known as the *Mishnah* and the *Palestinian* and *Babylonian Talmuds*. Though this literature took written form only after the second century A.D., it contains much earlier tradition which had been orally preserved, and from which the expert can learn much about the origins and development of the movement.

Like the Sadducees, the Pharisees looked upon the Torah of Moses as a definitive revelation of God's will. Unlike the Sadducees, they paid great respect to the prophetic writings, and to another group called "holy writings" (*hagiographa*) that were eventually to be accepted as authoritative. Indeed, it was the Pharisees who finally (about 90 A.D.) determined the contents of the Hebrew Bible. But the Pharisees went a step further, for they also acknowledged the existence and validity of an Oral Torah (Oral Tradition). According to rabbinic tradition it had its inception with Moses himself. In this point they were in radical conflict with the Sadducees, who rejected the Oral Torah and all doctrines not found in the Written Law.

In their insistence on the validity of the Oral Torah, the Pharisees exercised a liberalizing influence on Judaism; through the Oral Torah it was possible for Judaism to keep the Written Torah relevant to changing conditions. The Pharisees believed that God had fully revealed his will in the Written Torah, but that new rules of conduct had to be worked out if the Written Torah were to be understood and obeyed in the face of ever-changing external circumstances. It was their firm conviction that every decision in life must be governed by Torah (the revelation of God's will) that led them to develop elaborate principles of interpretation whereby they could derive specific rules to govern conduct in every conceivable situation. A rule or instruction so derived to set forth the relevant meaning of the Written Torah was called a *halakah*. In the development of these *halakoth* (plural) the Pharisees employed an important principle called the "hedge." According to their tradition an important early Pharisaic teacher had said, among other things, "Build a hedge around the Torah." In practice this meant the formulation of additional *halakoth* to assist in faithfully obeying the requirement of some injunction of Written Torah or previously formulated *halakah*. But the Oral Torah consisted of more than these succinct instructions. It also contained *haggadah*. *Haggadah* could take a variety of forms, such as a parable, simile, legend, myth, historical reminiscence. Its purpose might be to illustrate and elicit response to the moral injunctions of Written or Oral Torah. But its range of concern was much broader. In it such subjects as the relation of God to Israel and the world, the meaning of Israel's past, present, and future, the problems of life, death, sin, temptation, etc., were dealt with in an imaginative way. If the *halakah* served as an arrow pointing to God and his will, the *haggadah* was intended not only to emphasize the urgency of following the arrow, but to evoke the faith, understanding, and motivation that brought active response.

Through the Oral Tradition the Pharisees found an outlet for their religious imagination, always of necessity oriented toward the Written Torah. Among other things, it enabled the Pharisees to incorporate into their thinking the apocalyptic and eschatological insights which became increasingly important during the second century B.C. and later. Such expectations as the victorious coming of God's kingdom, the coming of the Messiah, and the resurrection of the dead, assumed an important place in Pharisaic thought. They were accustomed to thinking of the history of Israel and all men in terms of the "two Ages": "this Age," and the "Age to Come." By "this Age" they referred to the then present world situation, wherein evil powers and lawless men sought to frustrate God's purposes and God's will. Within "this Age" the one certain path was that of obedience to the Torah through which the powers of temptation and sin could be overthrown and overcome. In God's own time he would bring the "Age to Come," in which his final victory over sin and evil would be disclosed to mankind, and a new order of existence would characterize human life. But compared with such a sect as the Essenes, most Pharisees were restrained in their attitude toward eschatological speculation.

If the piety of the Sadducees was centered in the Temple, that of the Pharisees was centered in the Torah. Even their hopes for the "Age to Come" were understood basically from the standpoint of obedience to the Law. There were some Pharisees who could say that if Israel should obey the Torah for one day then the kingdom of God would come. And so, their zeal for the Torah was conditioned not only by their desire for Israel not to be faithless as in the past, but also by their belief that obedience was determinative for the future. It is in this context that their rigorous emphasis on obedience to the Law must be understood.

To the Pharisees, the Torah was God's great gift to Israel, and through Israel, to all men. They emphatically taught that it was sin that stood between man and God. Residing in each man's heart is an evil and a good desire, the former leading to sin, the latter to obedience and good deeds. God gave the Torah in order that his good desire might overcome the evil. When the

Pharisee spoke of the "joy of the Law" he meant not only its ability to show man what God requires, but also its power to lead man to overcome his evil desire. And if he failed, God in his mercy had also offered man the gift of repentance. The power of the Law and the power of repentance were two of the great themes of Pharisaic teaching.

The Pharisees set a rigid standard of adherence to Torah that few could follow. But there is no doubt that many respected them. Their influence was dominant in the synagogue, whose existence and worship was validated by Oral Tradition, and in the home, where they encouraged study and obedience to the Torah. On the other hand, it was inevitable that their rigorous attitude would tend to cut them off from many of their fellow Jews, and bring with it the danger of self-righteousness, a problem they recognized and combated in their teachings.

It was the Pharisees who led the Jewish community to recovery after the fall of Jerusalem and the destruction of the Temple. The Pharisees had lost no love on Rome or her puppet rulers in Palestine, but the majority of leaders seem to have cautioned against open revolt as demanded by the more radical elements of the population. They were not motivated by political or economic ambitions, but by their understanding of Torah and their belief that the destiny of the Jews was religious rather than political. Pharisees rallied to the support of the nation once Rome attacked. But even as the terrible siege of Jerusalem was on, they managed to smuggle out of Jerusalem Johannan ben Zacchai, the famous teacher who was later to play a major role in recovery. Strengthened by a religious faith and piety so deeply grounded in the Torah, by applying the Oral Torah to the new situation they confronted after the destruction of the Temple, they were able to withstand the shock and proceed to create an even greater unity of life in the Jewish community—a unity that has persisted to the present day.

The Essenes

The Essenes were the third important sectarian group to develop in the Jewish community during the last two centuries B.C. Although they are not mentioned in the New Testament, they have long been known from the writings of both Philo and Flavius Josephus, the Jewish historian of the first century A.D. Until recently, many questions regarding the Essenes and their origins had never been answered. However, a new flood of light has been thrown on the Essene movement with the discovery (beginning in 1947) of the now famous Dead Sea Scrolls, more recently called the Qumran Scrolls after the name of the site (Khirbet Qumran) of the community's dwelling adjacent to the caves where the scrolls were stored. From the beginning, scholars recognized certain differences and omissions in the accounts of Philo and Josephus, as compared with the Scrolls themselves. There is now general agreement that these discrepancies can be explained, and there is little doubt that the community

THE MONASTERY AT QUMRAN: *the excavated ruins, with the Dead Sea in the background. The cave in the cliff in the right center foreground contained manuscript fragments of the Dead Sea Scrolls.*

which composed and treasured these scrolls belonged to the Essene movement. Since the day when a shepherd accidentally stumbled upon the first cave in the rugged hills on the western shore of the Dead Sea, numerous caves (11 are of major importance for the sect) have been found and their valuable manuscripts and fragments of manuscripts recovered. The task of publication and research is far from complete. Nevertheless, study of the literature has proceeded sufficiently to provide a tentative reconstruction of the beliefs, practices, and history of the sect. The information derived from the documents has been enhanced by the knowledge gained from archeological excavation and study of the ruins at Khirbet Qumran.[2]

---

[2] There is an immense bibliography for Qumran studies. Among the many excellent works, the following are notable for their conciseness as well as their dependability: Frank M. Cross, *The Ancient Library at Qumran and Modern Biblical Studies* (Garden City, N.Y.: Doubleday, 1958); J. T. Milik, *Ten Years of Discovery in the Wilderness of Judaea* (Allenson, Inc., 1959); and Helmer Ringgren, *The Faith of Qumran* (Philadelphia: Fortress Press, 1963). For a translation of the documents that were accessible at the time of its publication, see: Theodor H. Gaster, *The Dead Sea Scriptures* (Garden City, N.Y.: Doubleday, 1964). Many of the important documents are included.

The Essenes, just as the Pharisees, were spiritual descendants of the movement of religious protest generated by the Hasidim. In the case of the Essenes this protest, culminating in the establishment of the community at Qumran, entailed a radical withdrawal from normal social and religious associations. Scholars continue to debate the date of the sect's origins; suggestions range widely from the beginning of the Maccabean Revolt (167-165 B.C.) to the reign of Alexander Jannaeus (103-76 B.C.). If its beginnings were contemporaneous with the settlement at Qumran, we arrive at a date either during, or shortly before or after, the reign of John Hyrcanus (135-104 B.C.). Archeological evidence points decisively to settlement within this period. On the basis of the primary literary evidence, mainly Josephus' works and the historical allusions in the Scrolls, events which motivated the sect's withdrawal to Qumran can be satisfactorily harmonized, through several alternative interpretations, with what is known of Jewish history at that time. There are good grounds, however, for believing that the Essene movement antedated the withdrawal to Qumran. According to one interpretation of an important Essene writing, the *Damascus Document*, the sect existed for "twenty years" before the crisis that sparked the withdrawal to Qumran. It is quite possible, however, that "twenty" has symbolical meaning. On one fact there is general agreement: the establishment of the community at Qumran, and the circumstances accompanying that

TABLES *on which scribes of the Qumran sect copied manuscripts. The tables' inkwells contain traces of dried ink. At the far end is a ceremonial basin in which the scribes washed their hands before copying the sacred writings.*

event, were decisive in the formation of Essene religious life and thought as they are described in the Qumran Scrolls.

The withdrawal of the sect to Qumran represented a drastic reaction to the increased Hellenizing and secularizing tendencies of the Hasmonean rulers, and a repudiation of their illegitimate claims to the high priesthood. The specific event which provoked the departure was the persecution of the Righteous Teacher, whom the sect venerated as its founder, by a "wicked priest." Efforts to identify these persons with known historical figures has produced a flood of hypotheses. This much seems certain: the wicked priest was one of the Hasmonean rulers. Concerning the Righteous Teacher, there has been less success in overcoming his anonymity. His significance for the development of the Essene movement is acknowledged by all, but most interpreters are inclined to limit our knowledge about him to the information contained in the sectarian writings. Specific references are scarce, and in certain cases, downright controversial. Fortunately, the writings are clear on two essential facts about the Teacher. In the first place, his followers believed that he was the true representative of the legitimate line of priesthood, the Zadokite. This, in part, accounts for the priestly character of the sect and its violent opposition to the established priesthood in Jerusalem. In the second place, they believed that God had revealed to the Teacher a new interpretation which was the true interpretation of the Law and the Prophets. According to their *Habakkuk Commentary*, God had revealed to the Righteous Teacher "all the secrets of the words of his servants the prophets." Through their inspired Teacher the Essenes were constituted as the community who alone possessed and exercised the legitimate priestly offices, and alone had received the authoritative interpretation of the Torah.

INTERPRETATION OF AND OBEDIENCE TO SCRIPTURE. Like the Hasidim, who rallied in Maccabean times to the defense of the Torah, the Essenes ardently sought to understand and obey the holy scriptures. However, it was their peculiar mode of interpretation which made for the distinctive features of their life and thought. Fortunately, among the Scrolls are several commentaries on Biblical books, the earliest extant literature of this type, and from these, in particular, their peculiar way of interpreting the sacred writings can be discerned. While it is questionable if any of these writings can be attributed to the Teacher, the method of interpretation, which the sect called the *pesher*, undoubtedly derives from him. Simply stated, the sect read the sacred writings, especially the prophetic books, in the belief that the words and events contained in them were written with specific reference to the events occurring in their own time. For example, their understanding of a passage from Isaiah (40:3) was of crucial importance: "Prepare in the wilderness a way . . . make straight in the desert a highway for our God." It is clear that they read these words as if they were spoken to them, and their retreat to Qumran was seen as the obedient response to prepare in the wilderness for the coming of God's kingdom. It was not only their belief that the prophets were to be understood in terms of the sect's contemporary history that was important. Equally significant was the conviction that the prophets' words referred to the last days before the final victory of God's kingdom. The Essenes believed they were living in those last days. Their religious outlook was eschatological, and this way of viewing history exercised a decisive influence over all they thought and did. The Essenes were an eschatological community; more than any other Jewish sect they were nourished on the eschatological hopes that touched the lives of so many Jews during the troubled times of Hasmonean, Herodian, and Roman domination. The strength of these hopes was manifested in their rigorously disciplined life, which they believed was God's true way for his people during the short interval before his long-expected deliverance.

The sect was organized on the pattern of the early days of Israel's history when the people paused on the edge of the wilderness, preparing to enter into the inheritance of the Promised Land as a sequel to God's covenant with them. The Essenes clearly thought that the end of Israel's earthly pilgrimage would be a recapitulation of her beginnings under Moses and Aaron and Joshua. But they were forced to recognize the actual situation in their day— as they saw it. The Promised Land was in the hands of the wicked, who were unfaithful to the covenant and ignorant of the truth of the Law and the Prophets. But now God was about to bring to fulfillment the establishment

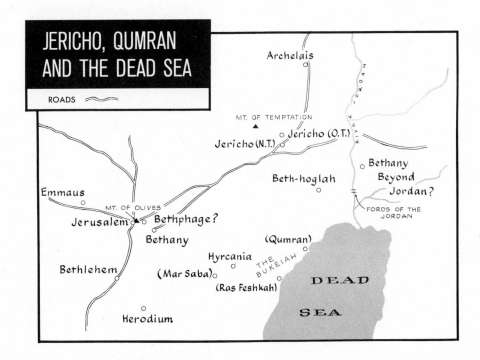

of a new covenant which he had promised through his prophets. It was an eternal covenant. If its fulfillment involved the defeat of the enemies both within and without Israel, its culmination was eternal life. The Essenes believed God had called them into the wilderness in order to lead them out by way of the new covenant; indeed, they called themselves the *Community of the New Covenant.* They alone were the true Israel, the faithful remnant, who in their way of life already celebrated the anticipated fulfillment of God's promises.

THE DISCIPLINE AND ROUTINE OF THE COMMUNITY.   The Essenes residing at Qumran lived, as we have said, a life of strict discipline. The character of this discipline is reflected throughout their writings, but particularly in the *Rule of the Community* (or, *Manual of Discipline*), a document which sets forth the sect's principal doctrines, rites, and governing rules and regulations, with precise penalties for infractions. The community was tightly organized into groups of Priests, Levites, and Laymen, each enjoying a special status determined by specific privileges and responsibilities. A central council consisting of twelve Laymen and three Priests served as a judiciary body to deal with certain well-defined problem areas. The superior status of the Priests clearly indicates the priestly character of the community's organization. This division into orders was set within the context of a strong sense of unity. Indeed, the characteristic Hebrew word used by the Qumran sect to designate themselves can be translated *unity* as well as *community.*

The daily life of the sect included work, assemblies for prayer and worship, study of the Law, and meals of a distinctly religious significance. Members engaged in those trades necessary to furnish a modest subsistence for the group, each in return drawing on the communal goods for his needs. In the ruins of Qumran were found the remains of a smith shop, pottery kilns and shop, bakery, grain mills, and storage silos. The sect also appears to have occupied an additional site at 'Ain Feshka, about two miles south of Qumran, where they engaged in small-scale irrigation farming, and maintained their herds. Those who entered the community pooled their possessions voluntarily. A vow of poverty was a feature of their discipline—they called themselves the *Congregation of the Poor.* As the sect's commentary on Psalm 37 shows, they were the "meek [who] shall inherit the earth"—of course, in the eschatological sense in which they understood "inheritance."

Early in the morning, before going about their work, and again in the evening, the sect assembled for prayers, probably in the large assembly hall which was located in the central building at Qumran. The many original psalms found in the Scrolls, especially the *Thanksgiving Scroll,* and remains of liturgical texts, suggest the liturgical form of their worship. Considering their zeal for the Torah and its interpretation, it is probable that reading and exposition of the Torah was an important part of their worship. Study of the Torah absorbed much more of their time. The discovery of a large *scriptorium* at the Qumran site, as well as the many remains of Biblical texts, bear witness to the energy they devoted daily to studying, copying, preserving, and commenting upon the scriptures. According to the *Rule of the Community*, the Torah was to be read throughout the night for one-third of the nights of the year, in the wakeful presence of the whole community.

The two daily meals of the sect, at noontime and evening, were central to their life of religious devotion. The *Rule of the Community* designates participation as one of the culminating privileges of full membership; it was one of their principal religious rites. The *Rule* stipulates that these meals were to take place in the presence of an officiating priest, whose prayer of blessing was of primary importance. It is generally maintained that these meals should be understood within the eschatological framework of their thinking. They were eaten in anticipation of the great Messianic Feast in which the Essenes expected to participate when God's final victory had been achieved. In the present, their meals were an anticipation and celebration of the certain joys of the impending future, which were symbolized by that banquet.

Throughout the year the Essenes celebrated the great religious festivals of the Jews, such as sabbath, Passover, Pentecost, and the Day of Atonement. However, they followed a religious calendar at variance with the authoritative calendar of the Jerusalem Temple—undoubtedly an important source of contention in their continuing conflict with the established priesthood. To understand the significance of this feud it is necessary to recognize the Essenes' strong conviction that the times for the great religious festivals were ordained by God for the world, and fixed according to the movements of the heavenly bodies. Since a solar calendar was employed at Qumran, and a lunar calendar in Jerusalem, serious discrepancies were inevitable. To the Essenes, irregularities at Jerusalem were a defiance of God's will.

BAPTISMAL POOLS *at the Qumran monastery.*

In view of the freedom and ingenuity which marked their scriptural interpretation, and their absence from the Temple, the Essenes' rites probably varied
from those of the Jerusalem Temple. One important problem concerns their
attitude toward sacrifices. There is no clear evidence that they performed
sacrifices at Qumran, and good reason to believe that they tended to "spiritual-
ize" the concept of sacrifice. How far they went in this direction remains a
highly controversial question. Did they abstain from sacrifices at Jerusalem
merely because of their opposition to the priesthood? Or did their abstention
reflect a radical reinterpretation of sacrifice, consequently reflected in their
theology and rites?

TRAINING, RITES, AND DOCTRINE.   Entrance into the community was preceded by a two-year-long novitiate of instruction and of testing the candidate's
"knowledge," culminating in full membership. The *Rule of the Community*
describes the ceremonial rite of initiation, in which each of the orders—Priests,
Levites, and Laymen—had its special part to play. The new members were
placed under a solemn oath of secrecy, and confronted with an impressive
recitation of curses and blessings, a testimony to the alternate consequences
of disobedience or obedience to their vows. Apparently the admission of new
members was an annual event, at which time the old members submitted to an
examination of their obedience, and renewed their entrance into the new
covenant. Such a ceremony surely augmented the solemnity of the occasion.
The initiation was climaxed by a purificatory rite of baptism, in which the
baptized was purified by the Holy Spirit. The Essene writings, as well as the
discovery of cisterns and water channels fed by aqueduct from Wadi Qumran,
testify to the importance of ritual ablutions and baptisms. From the time of
his initial baptism the Essene was admitted to the privilege of, and obligation
for, such ritual ablutions.

The zeal with which the Essenes embraced their rigoristic discipline is to
be understood in the context of their dualistic interpretation of the world and
their eschatologically determined hopes. Beyond the visible world there existed
a host of wicked angels or spirits under the dominion of their ruler, Belial, also
called the Spirit of Wickedness and the Prince of Darkness. Arrayed against
them were the heavenly hosts of God, led by the Spirit of Truth, also named
the Prince of Lights and the Angel of Truth. God, they believed, had permitted Belial and his forces to pursue their wicked course, but only for an
allotted time. Why God had permitted this was one of the deep mysteries
known only to God. But there is no suggestion that Belial existed outside God's
ultimate sovereignty. There is no hint of an absolute or metaphysical dualism.
This has led scholars to coin the phrase "eschatological dualism" to describe it.
The wicked course of Belial was manifested principally through men of Belial's
lot, Sons of Darkness, who rejected God and his will. These men of Belial's
lot were identified not only with the enemies of the Jews, such as the Roman

oppressors, but also with Jews who were not a part of the true remnant. Against these angelic and human forces were arrayed the angels of God's lot, and the men of God's lot, the Sons of Light, the *Community of the New Covenant*.

According to the Essenes, God had predestined each man's lot. Entrance into the community was evidence of being in God's lot, and assured a man of the support of the Spirit of Truth in fulfilling his destiny. That destiny for the Essene would be fulfilled when Belial's allotted time came to an end, and he and those of his lot were destroyed. For the Essene, life was already a battle against the Spirit of Wickedness which sought to overcome him; the struggle served as a discipline and preparation for the final conflict. For the end of Belial's lot was to come in a mighty battle. In one of their writings, the *War of the Children of Light Against the Children of Darkness*, the details of the progressive stages in that Holy War, and the military organization of the community, are meticulously described. The Essenes with the hosts of God would prevail in the battle which marked the end of the hosts of wickedness, both angelic and human.

THE ESCHATOLOGICAL HOPE OF THE COMMUNITY.   Messianic speculation played an important role in the sect's eschatological expectations. Their preoccupation with messianism is especially evident in their *Testimonia Document*, a collection of scriptural verses which they interpreted as messianic prophecies. Like many other Jews, the Essenes looked forward to the coming of a prophet as the forerunner of the Messianic Age. They were distinctive in their expectation of *two* Messiahs, the Messiah of Aaron and the Messiah of Israel, the former from the priestly line, the latter from the royal line. The Messiah of Israel was to be instrumental in leading the community in its victorious war; the Messiah of Aaron was to be instrumental in the establishment of the New Jerusalem and the New Temple. It is significant that the Messiah of Aaron takes precedence over the Messiah of Israel. This precedence undoubtedly harks back to the centrality of the priesthood in the theocratic pattern of Israel's early history. No doubt it was further strengthened as a result of the disillusion over the secularistic tendencies of the Hasmoneans, and the later despair of the this-worldly victory over the Romans. The priestly ascendancy is clearly seen in the sect's expectation of the great Messianic Feast, participation in which was the privilege of those who entered into the New Age. Among the writings, the *Rule of the Congregation* contains a description of this feast, in which the priestly Messiah plays the primary, and the royal Messiah a secondary, role. This Messianic speculation regarding Israel in the New Age was consistent with the Essenes' belief concerning God's purpose for Israel throughout her history. She was to be a priestly people whose only king was God, and a holy people whose only Law was Torah. On the basis of this conviction the sect withdrew to achieve the life which such a purpose demanded.

A very important question concerns the extent to which the Righteous Teacher was the subject of the Essenes' messianic speculation. Since the discovery of the Scrolls many theories regarding the Teacher have been promulgated—such as the theory that he had been crucified and had risen from the dead. Further study has decisively shown that this particular theory was founded on a mistaken reading of the texts. On somewhat firmer grounds other scholars have assigned a messianic role to the Teacher, identifying him with the expected prophet or even one of the messiahs. But such identifications are not generally maintained any longer. Most interpreters do acknowledge that his role as the herald of the Last Days, of the Messianic Age and its messianic figures, must be described as eschatological, if not messianic.

Nurtured on their eschatological hopes, the Essenes viewed the present world order pessimistically. We have already noted that, staunch in their Biblical doctrine of God the Creator and sovereign over his Creation, they avoided anything approaching a metaphysical dualism. But in their writings, especially their psalms, there is an emphasis on the lowliness of man which goes beyond the Biblical writings in intensity. At points it seems to exude the pessimism expressed in the body-spirit dualism found in the religious thought of the Hellenistic world. However, it is not so much the problem of the weakness of the body or flesh as such that troubles them; it is the perverseness of the heart, mind, and will—the inadequacy of all human righteousness, the hopelessness of man apart from the righteousness of God—without God's justification of man. Such thinking stands in an unresolved tension with their predestinarian tendencies; but it also mitigates clear-cut legalistic tendencies. It is also in harmony with their confession that only through the guidance of the Holy Spirit do they achieve purity, obedience, and salvation. However much their pessimism must have been accentuated by the repeated political and religious frustrations of the Jewish people during 200 troubled years, it was basically rooted in their conviction of man's moral weakness and the necessity of God's action to displace the grounds of pessimism.

The monastic life of the Essenes at Qumran must have had a peculiar appeal for many Jews who were world-weary, and looked to God for a new understanding of his ways with his people, Israel. The fact that there were Essene communities in places other than Qumran has long been known from Josephus' account. One of their writings, the *Damascus Document*, describes the organization of these camps, which were founded on a nucleus of 10 persons, provided one was a priest. Obviously, accommodations in religious practices were necessary for the dispersed communities that did not enjoy the seclusion of Qumran. But the monastic life and thought at Qumran surely exercised a continuous influence upon them. Numerically the movement was small (Josephus says 4,000). However, the Essenes must have played an important role in spreading and nurturing the eschatological hopes and apocalyptic visions that pervaded the atmosphere of Jewish religious thought. This is one of the most important aspects of the discovery of the Dead Sea Scrolls. Now, in a way that was not possible before, we can better understand this atmosphere. It is significant that the sect's library included a number of writings [3] which are either identical with, or bear a literary relationship to, writings of the *Apocrypha* and *Pseudepigrapha*. Essenes, undoubtedly, were the authors of many such writings. It is particularly important for the student of the New Testament to have some understanding of the eschatological mode of thought represented by the Essenes. For it was just this mode that was one major characteristic of the thought of Jesus and the New Testament writers.

THE END OF THE COMMUNITY. The conclusions of the archeologists point to the grim fact that sometime during the siege of Jerusalem (probably in 68 A.D.) Roman legionaires attacked and devastated the settlement at Qumran. The disappearance of the sect after 70 A.D. affords persuasive evidence that the community pinned its hopes on the expectation that this was the Holy War for which they had waited. It appears that those who did not suffer death in the tragic war with Rome came to the shocking and disillusioning conclusion that their way of understanding Torah had been wrong. Their precious library, which they managed to conceal in their caves before the Roman onslaught, bears testimony to their incredible zeal for God and his Torah, and their consuming desire to be the faithful community established by his covenant.

The existence of the sectarian movements we have discussed shows a degree of flexibility in Judaism that is often overlooked. Although each movement in its own way claimed the Torah as the basis of its life, common loyalty to Torah helped provide the Jewish community with its sense of unity. This unity of life and thought must have attracted non-Jews by its religious and ethical fervor, and repelled them by its exclusiveness.

Earlier we saw that men and women in the Hellenistic age sought eagerly for membership in a religious community, but the Jews seemed to have been *born into* such a community. The Jews had made efforts to share their religious life with Gentiles, but with little success. Now, however, there arose out of Judaism a new movement—one that succeeded where the parent had failed. We turn next to a consideration of this new community: the Christian Church.

---

[3] These include from the *Apocrypha*: Tobit; Ecclesiasticus; Epistle of Jeremy; and from the *Pseudepigrapha*: Testaments of Levi and Naphtali (portions of Testament of the Twelve Patriarchs); Jubilees; Enoch.

THE
NEW COMMUNITY
AND ITS
CONVICTIONS

CHAPTER THREE   About the year A.D. 30 there appeared

in Palestine a Jewish community that shared with much of

Judaism the hopes for the New Age that God had promised

through the prophets and seers. But it differed from the rest

of Judaism radically on one crucial point: it was convinced

that the New Age had already begun to dawn. More spe-

cifically, it believed that God had acted in Jesus of Nazareth

to inaugurate the New Age, and that the community itself

was the nucleus of the People of the New Age. The basis for this conviction was the belief that God had raised Jesus from the dead. The resurrection of Jesus was understood to be more than merely the resuscitation of his physical body; it meant that one whom the civil and religious leaders had rejected and executed as a common criminal had been exalted by God as his chosen instrument for establishing the New Age. In the words of one New Testament writer:

> This Jesus whom you crucified, God has made both Lord and Christ.
> —ACTS 2:36

Both these terms "Lord" and "Christ" come, of course, directly out of the Jewish tradition. The Christian community was not inventing terms and categories in which to express its claims concerning Jesus and the coming of the New Age; rather, it affirmed that the promises set forth in the Old Testament and uttered by the seers whose predictions found such an eager audience in the decades preceding and following the opening of the Christian Era were now being fulfilled. Such titles as "Messiah" (in Greek, *Christos*, meaning "anointed"), "Son of Man," "Servant," "King," "Savior," all came out of this Jewish tradition with its roots in Old Testament prophecy and its flowering in the sayings of the apocalyptic seers. The terms took on other connotations when they were translated into their Greek equivalents, as we shall see (Chapter 9), but the basic background against which they are to be understood is that of Jewish eschatological expectation. The Christian community was now claiming that *it*, rather than the historic people of Israel, was the group in and through whom the promises made to Israel were being fulfilled.

The basis on which this claim rested—the Resurrection—was even more astounding than the claim itself. There were stories in the Old Testament about men who had been brought back to life after they had died. Both Elijah and Elisha, for example, are reported as having restored to life the young sons of grief-stricken mothers (I Kings 17:22; II Kings 4:22 ff.). In the gospels, Jesus is depicted as reviving the dead (for example, the raising of Jairus' daughter in Mt. 9:18 ff., and the restoration of the widow's son in Lk. 7:11 ff.), as are the apostles in the book of Acts (20:9, 10). But the resurrection of Jesus is without precedent or parallel in the Jewish tradition. It was understood to be a permanent triumph over death by which Jesus entered into a new kind of life, not merely a resumption of life as it was before death or a postponement for a few years of life's inevitable end. Because his followers had encountered him risen from the dead they were assured that the long-awaited era of deliverance from death and the powers of evil had begun to break in upon them.

For the Christian community to have made this claim in behalf of a heavenly being who had come incognito in their midst as a kind of divine masquerade would have been easier to understand. At least there would have been an abundance of comparable claims made for various savior-gods who were so widely venerated in the Hellenistic and Roman periods. Jewish apocalyptic itself depicted figures like Enoch who, though hidden with God from past ages, were now to be revealed for the redemption of the Chosen People. The Christians, however, claimed that this man who was now exalted by God as Lord was the very same one whose home in Nazareth, whose ministry in Galilee, whose audacious actions in Jerusalem, and whose condemnation to death were matters of public knowledge. What then is the historical evidence on which these claims rest?

THE HISTORICAL EVIDENCE CONCERNING JESUS

Our contemporary common-sense view of historicity leads us to search for objective evidence, preserved and reported if possible by impartial observers of the events which we are seeking to investigate. When we approach the events connected with the life of Jesus and the beginnings of Christianity with these procedures in mind, however, the results are disappointing. Nearly all the evidence that we have to go on has been preserved by partisan observers and is to be found within the New Testament itself.

There is evidence from non-Christian sources sufficient to demonstrate that Jesus lived, that he was put to death during the governorship of Pontius Pilate, and that the movement which sprang up in his name had spread to Rome within a dozen years of his death. Jewish sources of the period refer to Jesus as a sorcerer who was executed.[1] Josephus, the Jewish historian, refers to Jesus twice in his *Antiquities* (XVIII. 3.3 and XX. 9.1), although Christians have certainly expanded Josephus' original statements in the first of these passages, in order to make Josephus bear a Christian witness to Jesus. Suetonius, the Roman biographer of the early emperors, in his *Life of Claudius* (A.D. 41-54) mentions the expulsion of Jews from Rome as a result of trouble stirred up by someone named Chrestus. This is usually interpreted as a confusion by Suetonius of the familiar name of Chrestus for the unfamiliar and, on first hearing, meaningless name, Christus. The assumption is that when Christian preachers came to the Jewish community in Rome talking about Jesus Christ (Christus, in Latin), the results were so disruptive that the imperial government had to intervene in order to quell the disturbance. Another Roman historian, Tacitus, in his *Annals*, describes the persecution of the Christians in the reign of Nero, and refers back to the crucifixion of Jesus by order of Pontius Pilate in order to explain to his readers the unsavory origins of this trouble-making movement.[2]

When we turn from non-Christian to Christian sources, however, our his-

---

[1] The material relating to Jesus is conveniently presented and assessed in Joseph Klausner's *Jesus of Nazareth* (New York: Macmillan, 1926), pp. 18-60.

[2] The relevant quotations from the historical sources are available in translation in *New Testament Background: Selected Documents*, ed. C. K. Barrett (New York: Harper & Row, 1959), pp. 14-16.

torical difficulties are further complicated rather than resolved. Quite apart from the fact that none of the Christian sources can qualify as objective evidence (a matter which we shall consider later in this chapter) is the difficulty that none of the accounts on which our knowledge of Jesus and his immediate followers rests was written down until about 40 years after the events of which they tell. It is highly questionable that any of them was written by an eyewitness. Not only did Jesus himself write nothing, but the attribution of the gospels to his disciples did not occur until the late first century at the earliest. The one gospel for which the strongest case can be made that it was written by the man whose name it bears, Luke, acknowledges that its author was not himself an eyewitness of the events he portrays (Lk. 1:1, 2). The date of composition of the gospels and the special interests that they represent will be considered in detail in Chapters 11-14. That they were produced by the second generation of Christians seems clear, so that they cannot be used as they stand for direct, first-hand reports of events they describe.

That the gospels are from a later time than the generation of eyewitnesses of Jesus' ministry would not in itself disqualify them from serving as objective historical evidence. But it must be acknowledged further that they cannot be considered nonpartisan reports about Jesus. They are in the truest sense of the term propaganda literature. If one had to provide a single statement of purpose that would suit all four of the gospels he could probably not find a better one than the explanation given by the author of the Gospel of John:

> These are written that you may believe that Jesus is the Christ, the Son of God, and that believing you may have life in his name.
> —JOHN 20:31

Both the claim that is made in behalf of Jesus as the Christ and the appeal to respond in faith to that claim are present in the intention of the Gospel writers. The gospels are, above all, documents for the propagation of the faith.

The oldest writings in the New Testament, the letters of Paul, are to be dated between the years A.D. 50 and 65. If these contained information about the life of Jesus, we should be able to move closer in time to these crucial events by 20 to 40 years than the gospels in their present form take us. Unfortunately, Paul has almost nothing to say about the earthly career of Jesus, although he does refer repeatedly to both Jesus' death and resurrection. He presupposes the origin of the Church and the emergence of the apostolic circle—that is, the group of Jewish leaders in Jerusalem, many or most of whom had been followers of Jesus from the beginning. Although he claims to possess authority in the community equal to that which they possess, he acknowledges certain basic differences between his understanding of the intention of Jesus and theirs. His letters are written to strengthen established Christian communities, not to found them. Accordingly, the story of Christian beginnings and the basic events concerning Jesus are assumed to be matters of common knowledge which Paul in his letters need not recount. Therefore, his letters do not give us direct information about the founding of the communities in the area of his evangelistic work, much less about the events concerning Jesus and the very beginning of the Christian community. The question remains, then: How do we reach back historically behind the relatively late documents of the New Testament to gain understanding of the events which gave rise to the Christian community?

THE NATURE AND VALUE OF ORAL TRADITION

The question is put in a different light when we realize that among Jews of the first century the orally transmitted word was at least as highly valued as the written word. Even though the Jewish Law was believed to have been written down by direct inspiration of God, the living interpretation of the will of God contained in the Law was carried on by orally transmitted interpretation of the scriptures; passed on by word of hearing from teacher to pupil, as was noted in the preceding chapter. Paul refers to this transmission of the tradition within the Christian community, and does so in such a way as to suggest how very important a factor it was as a guarantee of the unity and continuity of the community's preaching and teaching. Paul could be fiercely independent, as he portrays himself in telling the Galatians that his revelation from God was communicated to him directly, rather than being mediated through the apostolic group in Jerusalem (Gal. 1:15, 16). He needed no human ("flesh and blood") corroboration of his divinely given call and commissioning. Yet in writing to the church at Corinth (I Cor. 15:1-8) he acknowledges that the message of the Gospel that he proclaimed to them was basically the same that he had received from those who preceded him in the community of faith. In describing the message and the process of transmission, Paul uses a verb, *paradidomi*, which has come to have a technical meaning: to pass on what one has received. The verb is almost the exact equivalent of the Latin verb *traditio*, from which of course comes the English word *tradition*. Similarly, there is a correlative verb in Greek, *paralambano*, which meant for the early Church "receiving the tradition from those who have passed it on." Paul is acknowledging, then, that he is no innovator when it comes to the basic conviction about the significance of Jesus; he is rather the transmitter of the tradition which he received from those who before him had joined themselves to the People of the New Age. Paul uses similar language when he is reminding the Corinthian Christians of the origins of the central act of Christian worship, the Lord's Supper (I Cor. 11:23 ff.). What was the content of the tradition about Jesus that Paul is transmitting?

The tradition as reproduced by Paul in I Cor. 15 is little more than a framework, consisting of two main themes and a subsidiary one. The main themes are: Christ died "for our sins"; he was raised on the third day and appeared to a succession of witnesses, beginning with Peter and ending with Paul. The minor observation is that he was buried—possibly an apologetic note introduced to attest that Jesus had really died, rather than having merely swooned or disappeared, as enemies of the Christian faith sometimes claimed. Overarching the whole of this affirmation is the declaration that what happened to Jesus had occurred "according to the scriptures"—that is, in fulfillment of the purpose and promise of Israel's God. The death of Jesus had been more than a tragic end to a good man, and the Resurrection was more than an astonishing sequel to a seeming tragedy: his death is declared to have atoning significance for man's sins, and his resurrection has constitutive results, in that those whom he encounters after he has risen from the dead are commissoned by him to proclaim the good news of what God has done for man in Jesus Christ.

The proclamation that Paul and the other apostles have been charged with disseminating is referred to by him (I Cor. 15:14) as the *kerygma*. This is a verbal noun, from a verb which means "to herald, announce, proclaim." In recent theological and Biblical study, the word *kerygma* has been taken over as a technical term to refer to the content of the early Christian message. According to some scholars,[3] the message in the earliest days of the Church's life was, in spite of deep differences and even dissension, essentially one. As evidence of this, one may point to the sermons attributed by the author of Acts to Peter and Paul (Acts 2, 3, 10, 13), which in spite of the differing circumstances under which they were supposed to have been spoken are strikingly similar in tone and content. This unity is the more striking when one observes that Peter and Paul were at least sometimes sharply at odds with each other, as Paul attests in writing to the Galatians (Gal. 1 and 2).

In the gospels brief statements are attributed to Jesus concerning his death and resurrection (Mk. 8:31; 9:31; 10:33, 34 and parallel passages in Luke and Matthew). Although these are written in the form of predictions of his Passion, they are similar in form and content to the summary statements of the Christian message which can be found elsewhere in the New Testament. The assumption has been made on the basis of the apparent uniformity that there was basically one *kerygma*, which was proclaimed by all the first generation of Christians, with only relatively minor local and theological variations.

For several reasons, however, the assumption of such a high degree of kerygmatic unity seems unwarranted. In the first place, the sermon reports and kerygmatic summaries are, on closer examination, not so unified as has been assumed. Although Paul sets forth as his cardinal point in the *kerygma* (I Cor. 15:3) that there is redemptive significance in the death of Jesus, the sermons of Acts attach no such value to it. Peter is reported in Acts 10:36 ff. as including a brief account of the public ministry of Jesus in his kerygmatic summary. Paul, on the other hand, never alludes to it, concentrating instead on the final events

---

[3] The classic statement of this position was given by C. H. Dodd, in *The Apostolic Preaching and Its Development* (New York: Harper & Row, 1951), especially pp. 7-35.

of the Cross and Resurrection. Only in a brief passage which many commentators think was taken over by Paul from some traditional formulation (Rom. 1:4) does he draw attention to the earthly origins of Jesus; elsewhere Paul is content to stress the fact *that* Jesus was truly man (Gal. 4:4) even though he was sent from God (II Cor. 8:9; Rom. 8:3; Phil. 2:6, 7).

It is not possible to identify even a short list of specific themes or beliefs that are expressed in all forms of the *kerygma* preserved in the New Testament. As we shall see, the kerygmatic form is present in materials related not only to preaching, but to worship (I Tim. 3:16) or to prayer (Acts 4:24-30). The content of the kerygmatic statements varies with each writer and often with the occasion. What is uniform in relation to the *kerygma* is twofold: (1) Each kerygmatic statement presupposes that in Jesus Christ God has acted decisively for the redemption of man, so that the New Age has begun to break into the present situation; (2) the form of each kerygmatic passage includes some reference to the humiliation of Jesus Christ during his earthly life, culminating in his death, and the exaltation by which God has vindicated him.[4] The *kerygma* in all its variations is concerned, therefore, not with the teachings of Jesus alone, nor with the redemptive results accomplished by or through him alone, but with Jesus Christ as a person who lived in humiliation and who now lives in exaltation.

The question that the Church is asking itself in the New Testament is not merely "What did he say and do?" but "Who was this man who said and did these things?" As a result of this concern, the community was not content merely to prepare a collection of his ethical teachings or even a series of illustrative anecdotes about their revered but now departed teacher. What is recalled and recounted about Jesus is transmitted in the interest of the *kerygma;* that is, to illumine the significance of this one who, though humiliated and rejected on earth, has been raised by God and exalted as Lord. In the interests of the *kerygma,* then, the Church transmitted sayings of Jesus and stories about him.

THE HISTORICITY
OF THE TRADITION ABOUT JESUS

Before proceeding with a brief examination of the process and forms by which the tradition was transmitted, we must face the question as to the value of such kerygmatically oriented tradition as historical evidence for our knowledge of Jesus and the beginnings of the Christian Church. To acknowledge that the gospel tradition is all that we have does not necessarily heighten our estimate

---

[4] This pattern and the variety of ways in which it appears in the New Testament is presented concisely by Eduard Schweizer in *Lordship and Discipleship* (London: SCM Press, 1960), especially pp. 98-103.

of its historical value. For someone who considers historical research to be an objective science, the acknowledgment of the prejudiced nature of the evidence contained in the tradition would disqualify it from consideration as useful for historical research.

In response to such a challenge, several observations about the possibility of historical reconstruction of the life and teaching of Jesus may be made. First, it must be acknowledged that neither the gospels nor any other source provides us with the kind or quantity of information about Jesus that would make possible the preparation of a biography. A serious modern biography tries to understand a man not only against the background of the times in which he lived, but in the light of the specific personal and psychological forces which helped to shape his decisions and to affect his response to the challenges and opportunities that confronted him. No such materials are available to us for preparing a psychological study of Jesus. We cannot determine with any certainty the order of events that are reported by the tradition, apart from the obvious fact that his baptism by John the Baptist came toward the beginning of his public career and the Crucifixion came at the end. It is impossible, therefore, to trace with any confidence a pattern of development or change in the life or thought of Jesus—another factor which would be indispensable in writing a biography.

The Uncertain Order of Events in Jesus' Life

A careful study of the four gospels in comparison with each other will show that there is little agreement among the gospel writers as to the order in which Jesus said and did what is reported of him. John depicts him cleansing the Temple at the outset of his public ministry; in the other three gospels, the incident occurs at the end of his career. Sayings placed at the opening of his teaching ministry by Luke are located toward the end of it by Matthew. The nearest we can come to an outline of Jesus' public life is the one offered by Mark and followed with some modifications by Matthew and Luke. John goes his own way in complete independence of the other three gospels (see Chapter 14). But Mark's outline is not really much help, since a close analysis of Mark shows that the framework is contributed by Mark himself, and was not a part of the tradition which he received. Almost all the chronological and geographical references in Mark are vague or even artificial in nature. The tradition reached Mark in the form of independent story or sayings units; Mark arranged them on his own narrative line. As someone has expressed it, Mark began his gospel writing with only a heap of unstrung pearls. How these units of the tradition took shape and how they are to be classified and evaluated will be touched on briefly in this chapter and dealt with more fully in the next. Here, however, it is enough to recognize that the Gospel tradition does not furnish the material for reconstructing the course of the life of Jesus. Of his childhood we learn next to nothing; of his training we hear nothing at all; of his adult life prior to his public ministry we are left without a clue. Everything in the tradition is concentrated on the kerygmatic significance of the words and acts that came out of the brief period of his public career.

THE GOSPELS AS HISTORICAL EVIDENCE

Although it must be acknowledged that the tradition does not make possible the writing of a biography of Jesus, the nonobjective quality of the traditional material should not lead us to despair concerning the possibility of historical knowledge about Jesus. Indeed it would be a mistake to conceive of history-writing as an "objective" science. History does not deal with mere facts, but with the interpretation of events. To string out a list of occurrences in random fashion and without interpreting their inner connections would not be to write history; it is the historian's task to discern within the events a pattern of significance. Although there would be no events without something having happened, a happening becomes an event only when it carries meaning for a person or community. There is no such thing as an uninterpreted event. The fact that it is an "event" shows that it was an event *for* someone, and that therefore the subjective factor of meaning is already a part of the event itself. This does not imply that one can speak of an event where nothing occurred outside the mind of the reporter. That would be hallucination rather than history. It means rather that an occurrence becomes an event when the reporter is no longer describing in a detached manner something that happened, but is setting forth the meaning that he discerns in what happened—a meaning in which he is no longer observer but has become a participant. His stance may be that of critic or champion, of debunker or devotee. But he feels himself to be involved for good or ill.[5]

In this sense, the gospel materials are wholly appropriate as historical evidence. They are reports of events prepared and preserved by those who have found in the central actor of these events Jesus of Nazareth, the key to the ultimate meaning of life. The traditions are reported in order not only to inform but to persuade. This does not mean, however, that their value as historical evidence is worthless. We must begin by recognizing the tradition for what it is, and we must avoid expecting it to become what it is not: detached, objective information. Reports of these same events written by Pharisaic or Roman observers would not be more objective; they would only represent a different set of presuppositions and interests, and a different interpretation based thereon.

As thinking persons, reared in the thought patterns of Western rational

---

[5] A creative and widely influential treatment of historiography by an outstanding historian is to be found in *The Idea of History*, by R. G. Collingwood (New York: Oxford, 1957).

learning, and the historical consciousness that emerged in late eighteenth-century Europe, however, we cannot avoid raising questions about the tradition that earlier generations and other cultures might not have raised. How much of the reports transmitted by the tradition go back to the events themselves and how much comes from later interpretations read back into the events by the community? This is an entirely legitimate question, even though it is difficult to answer. Indeed, there is no single answer to be given; rather, the question must be raised in relation to each item present in the tradition.

Changes in the Tradition: Textual Variants

It cannot be denied that modifications did in fact occur in the process of transmitting the tradition. These changes can be classified under two categories, the second of which is more important for our investigation. The first category is *textual variants*—that is, the changes which occurred in the records of the tradition *after* they had been put in writing and were handed down in manuscript form through succeeding generations. There are thousands of such variants among the several thousand manuscript copies of the New Testament that have been preserved down to the present. No two of the manuscripts are alike in every detail. The task of analyzing and classifying these manuscripts is a highly technical and never-ending one.[6] Although there are hundreds of interesting interpretive points which turn on the choice that is made among the possibilities offered by the various manuscripts, there is no essential historical or theological point that is determined one way or another by textual variants. (At certain places throughout this book, the bearing of textual variants on interpretation will be noted.)

Changes in the Tradition: Oral and Written

The other type of change in the tradition occurred much earlier in the process of transmission and is far more significant for an understanding of the New Testament. The more important change is the modification which the tradition received during the period of *oral* transmission and at the hand of the gospel writer when he placed it in the framework of his own interests. The changes can be most readily detected where the gospel writers differ among themselves as to the details of Jesus' sayings or activities. For example, Matthew reports Jesus as proclaiming the nearness of the kingdom of heaven; Mark and Luke say that he spoke of the nearness of the kingdom of God. Mark describes

---

[6] A recent, concise, and reliable summary of the results and problems of textual studies of the New Testament has been prepared by Vincent Taylor, in *The Text of the New Testament* (New York: St. Martin's Press, 1961).

Jesus passing through Jericho and then, as he was leaving the town, healing a blind man seated by the road. Luke reports that the incident occurred as Jesus was entering Jericho. Matthew agrees that it happened on the way out, but claims there were two blind men! (Mk. 10:46; Lk. 18:35; Mt. 20:29). The point of these incidents is not greatly affected by the difference in details, but the fact that modification has taken place is obvious. The method of critical study by which these units of the tradition are recognized, classified, and analyzed is known as *form criticism*.[7] This is not a wholly satisfactory term, since the analytical process carried on by form critics is as much concerned with content as with literary form. *Tradition history* might be a more satisfactory designation.

In the next chapter we shall examine in detail how the tradition in the process of transmission acquired certain recognizable forms or patterns. In part, these patterns are traceable to the teaching methods of the time, used by both Jesus and the Jewish teachers who were his contemporaries. Such a common pattern is discernible in the short proverbial or poetic sayings attributed to Jesus. The parables, which are also a teaching form used by Jewish teachers and interpreters of the Law of Moses, were developed by Jesus in a distinctively powerful and penetrating way. Other forms of the tradition resemble the patters into which the folk literature and oral tradition of any people are shaped by the transmission process itself. A stylized opening ("And it happened that as Jesus was passing by . . .") and an equally stylized concluding comment ("the crowds were amazed. . . .") enable the hearer—or reader—to concentrate attention on the main point of the incident, free of extraneous reference to the accompanying circumstances of the event. Some of the patterns seem to have been more or less consciously developed by the community in order to serve its own special interests, as when in Matthew 5 the ethics of Jesus are set in explicit contrast to the ethics of the Mosaic Law, thus reflecting the situation in the early church when Christians and Jews were engaged in controversy as to which group had the proper understanding of God's will for his people.

The analytical methods of form criticism enable us, therefore, to fulfill two objectives: to distinguish older from later forms of the tradition, and to tell us a great deal about the primitive Church, whose concerns and controversies are to be detected in the modifications it made in the tradition in the process of transmitting and finally of recording it. The gospels, then, are the end product of the process that began with the proclamation of the Gospel. Those

---

[7] The basic works in which this method was developed are Martin Dibelius' *From Tradition to Gospel* (New York: Scribner's, 1935), and R. Bultmann, *History of the Synoptic Tradition* (New York: Harper & Row, 1963). Both works appeared in the original German editions in the post-war World War I period (1919 and 1921, respectively); both have passed through several editions and have subsequently been translated into English.

who claimed to have encountered Jesus risen from the dead were in a position to understand the meaning of his life of humiliation and rejection. Their proclamation of the good news ("Gospel" is an old English equivalent for the Greek word roughly pronounced *evangelion,* meaning "good news") dated from this confrontation by Jesus, whom God had exalted as Lord and Christ by raising him from the dead. This Resurrection encounter now put the whole of Jesus' earthly life and public ministry in a new light. The recounting of Jesus' words, deeds, and death in the light of the Resurrection took the form of a gospel.

For reasons which will be set forth in the next chapter, it would appear that Mark's is the oldest of the four gospels included in the New Testament, although there may have been written collections of sayings by, and stories about, Jesus before Mark wrote his gospel. The production of gospels continued for centuries, as we know from references to other gospels in the writings of the leaders of the Church during the next three centuries, and as we have learned from manuscript copies of other gospels that have been discovered over the years. We shall shortly have more to say about the criteria by which the Church decided which writings should be considered authoritative, and which were not to be so regarded.

THE PURPOSES OF THE WRITERS

It was not only the gospels which were called into existence by the Gospel. Nor was the preaching of the Gospel the only objective which the New Testament writers had in view. Throughout the New Testament the writers seek to serve not only the interests of preaching and evangelism, but of worship, of catchetical instruction of new converts, of moral instruction of members of the community, of a counterattack against enemies of the faith and its detractors. In most of the New Testament books, the authors have not limited themselves to any single one of these objectives. In few of the books are all these interests respresented. In some books the purpose is obvious and explicit; in others, it can only be inferred or conjectured. We shall briefly sketch some of the ways in which these objectives are served and the tradition reinterpreted.

The oldest writings in the New Testament, the letters of Paul, show concretely how the early Church dealt with the problem of translating the Christian message for non-Jewish hearers. Although the Gospel had originated on Jewish soil and was couched in Jewish terms, its implicit claim was that it was the good news for all the human race. As such it could and should be addressed to the Gentiles, or as Paul phrased it, "to the Greeks and the barbarians" (Rom. 1:14), meaning both the civilized Gentiles who spoke Greek and those who did not. In his letter to the Galatians, Paul's vivid words enable the reader to participate in the painful struggle that ensued when it became clear to him that certain changes had to be made in what the Jerusalem church considered to be basic Christianity if non-Jews were to be admitted to the fellowship.

There were difficulties in deciding what were the appropriate moral standards for the life of the community when new members who joined the circle of believers had not had the preparatory training in morals that Judaism provided. Paul's Letter to the Corinthians gives us vivid evidence of the problems of behavior in a Gentile church. Both the Gospel and its ethical implications had to be reinterpreted for the Gentiles who were entering the Christian Church. Inevitably both the Gospel itself and the Jesus tradition underwent modification in the process. In I Corinthians we can see Paul wrestling with the question of legislating for someone who had recently become a Christian but whose spouse had not been converted. He appeals to the Jesus tradition where it is applicable, and expresses hope that the Spirit is guiding him where there is no word of Jesus to which he can appeal for precedent (I Cor. 7). In I Thessalonians Paul explicitly identifies his readers as those who have turned to God from idols—that is, who have entered the Christian community straight out of paganism, rather than having first accepted Jewish faith and then being converted to the Christian faith (I Thess. 1:9). It was persons of this sort who stood in need of a translation of the tradition; it was this need that Paul set himself to supply, as we see evidenced in his letters.

At the same time, since it was the claim of the *kerygma* that God had fulfilled for the Church the promises made to Israel, the Christian community could not avoid an interpretation of itself over against Judaism. Paul deals with this question in one form in his letter to the Romans (Chapters 9-11). It is a major concern of the writer of the Gospel of Matthew, who alone among the gospel writers portrays Jesus as a kind of second Moses, giving the New Law on a mountain in Galilee as Moses had given the Old Law at Sinai. Matthew alone makes Jesus set his interpretation of the will of God against and above that found in the Mosaic code (Mt. 5). More than the other gospels, Matthew is at pains to show that at every important point, what Jesus did was "in order that the scriptures [that is, the Old Testament] might be fulfilled." Although the Letter to the Hebrews adopts a very different approach to the problem, it agrees with the Gospel of Matthew in claiming that Jesus Christ is superior to the best that the Old Testament has to offer. When in the second century a brilliant theologian named Marcion declared that Christians should repudiate the Old Testament and purge the Christian tradition of all dependence upon it, he was condemned by the rest of the Church as a heretic. The theme in the *kerygma* that saw in Jesus Christ the fulfillment of the promises made in the Jewish scriptures was too strong and too important to be set aside, although the defense of this proposition in detail and in answer to Jewish opposition exercised the ingenuity of the New Testament writers.

THE GOSPEL AND EARLY CHURCH CONFLICTS

The conflicts which confronted the Church were not only with Judaism, however: as the first century drew to a close, the Church began to experience mounting suspicion, and finally active hostility from the authorities of the Roman Empire. The issue of the relationship of the Christian to the state is set forth in Paul's Letter to the Romans (Chapter 13), but does not seem to have become a serious issue until the period from A.D. 90 to 110. From this period come the First Epistle of Peter and the Book of Revelation. The response of the writers of these books is quite different: I Peter urges quiet obedience and acceptance of persecution; Revelation is more revolutionary and in veiled and symbolic language counsels active resistance to the state as the instrument of the Devil. But both writings appeal to the faithful endurance of Jesus in the midst of his trials at the hand of Rome as the basis of encouragement to his people in the trials that they are to undergo in his name and for his sake.

Not all the difficulties that the community had to face were from without. One recurring problem was that of moral laxity among the members of the community. The Letter of James, which is more sermon or diatribe than letter, lashes out against moral indifference, placing much of the blame on Paul's doctrine of justification by faith, which he feels has led people to suppose that once they have faith they may do as they please. The Letter to the Hebrews warns its readers that the same God who has acted in grace in sending Jesus as the pioneer and perfecter of faith will also one day act in judgment on the wicked and the apostate. Paul must also deal with moral problems, as we noted above, and does so where possible by an appeal to the words or example of Jesus.

Another kind of internal problem in the light of which the tradition must be reinterpreted was that of false teaching. Although there was from the beginning great freedom allowed within the Church as to the content of faith and the interpretation of the *kerygma*, the Church had by the beginning of the second century to draw the line between what might and what might not be allowed as true Christian teaching. It would be anachronistic to suppose that a fully developed credal orthodoxy had emerged by this time, but false teaching had to be differentiated from the truth. If Paul is the author of Colossians (see discussion in Chapter 8), then already in his time there were those of a speculative turn of mind who were laying claim to esoteric knowledge of a kind that demoted Jesus Christ to a minor rank among the celestial beings and placed Christians under obligation to fulfill ascetic obligations. An interpretation of the *kerygma* was called for, one that moved far beyond the material preserved in the synoptic tradition to interpret the role of Jesus as redeemer of man in cosmic terms. Denials of the reality of the humanity of Jesus called forth emphatic declarations of the reality of his having come "in the flesh"—that is, as a true human being (I Jn. 4:3). Even when a current intellectual category such as the *logos* (a Greek term meaning "word," "reason," rationale") was applied to Jesus, as it was by the Gospel of John it was balanced by the insistence that in him the Word had "become flesh" (Jn. 1:14).

The most serious problem of all confronting the Church in the first century of its existence was that its expectation that Christ would be revealed as Lord and Judge was not realized. Since the exaltation of the risen Christ was one of the fundamental claims of the *kerygma*, and since the purpose which lay behind his ministry of humiliation and his promise of redemption was the establishment of the kingdom of God, the next great event that would be awaited was his disclosure as Lord and the bringing into complete and visible reality the reign of God over the world which he created. But the apostolic generation passed away, and the consummation of the kingdom did not occur. What then was one to think of the *kerygma* or of the hope of redemption that it held out?

One way of dealing with this problem was to lay stress on the results of the death and resurrection of Jesus Christ as they affected the inner life of the individual. The man who had entered the new life of faith need not be concerned about a resurrection or a coming of Christ as an event in the future, since for him the life of the Age to Come was already a present reality. It was this way of coming at the question that was taken with great effectiveness by the Gospel of John. Another way of facing the difficulty was to say that there had been a mistake in calculation by those who awaited the return of Christ in the immediate future. It could be argued, as it is in II Peter, that God's time is different from man's time, so that by His computation a thousand years' delay would be no more than a brief interval; or one could suppose that the fulfillment would not take place in the temporal sphere, but in a heavenly, eternal sphere, where chronological time had no meaning or existence. This approach to the problem is represented by the Letter to the Hebrews.

Closely bound up with the chronological problem of the expectation of the end of the Age was the question of how the continuing existence of the Church was to be understood. It had begun as an eschatological community announcing and awaiting the New Age. But what if the New Age did not arrive? If the Church continued to function in spite of the delay, it would be necessary to work out regulations to govern the inner life of the community, as Paul was required to do in the churches under his charge even while awaiting the imminent End. The Letters to Timothy and to Titus (usually referred to collectively as *the Pastorals*) develop the specific requirements for and obligations of leadership roles in the community. But there was still a need for some positive understanding of the Church as an on-going reality in the midst of the world, not simply as a group waiting for the next world. Luke and Acts, which were written as companion volumes by the same author, provide the most complete solution to this issue by attaching positive significance to the Church as God's instrument of redemption in the present age, yet without denying the hope of a future Day of Fulfillment. This thesis of Luke will be developed in Chapter 13, where it will be shown that, in spite of the novel elements in Luke's perspective on the purpose of God through the Church, he remains faithful to and dependent upon the older tradition of the life and ministry of Jesus. As in the *kerygma* itself, the crucial event around which all of Luke's story turns is the resurrection and exaltation of Jesus as the Christ.

The twin forces at work in the writing of the books of the New Testament during the hundred years or so that they were being produced were (1) the *kerygma*, in all the diversity of emphasis and modes of expression that it received by the various writers; and (2) the consciousness of standing in a tradition, which had come down from Jesus and the apostles, but which was to be interpreted in the changing situations in which the Church found itself. Luke could be said to speak for all the New Testament writers when he set forth his own statement of purpose in writing his gospel and Acts:

> Inasmuch as many have undertaken to compile a narrative of the things which have been accomplished among us, just as they were delivered to us by those who from the beginning were eyewitnesses and ministers of the word, it seemed good to me also, having followed all things closely for some time past, to write an orderly account for you, most excellent Theophilus. . . .
>
> —LUKE 1:1-3

The New Testament writers are concerned to hand on a tradition, not to develop a new religion. Their task is one of interpretation, of unfolding the implications of the Christian message for the worship and moral life of the members of the community, of defending the community and its message in the face of opposition from whatever source. The New Testament, therefore, cannot be understood apart from the historical development of the community that produced it, and it is in this perspective that we must study it today.

DECIDING WHICH CHRISTIAN WRITINGS
ARE AUTHORITATIVE

There is one other general question concerning the New Testament as a whole with which we must deal before turning to more detailed analyses of its individual books: How do we explain the fact that out of all the writings produced by the Christian Church in the century and a half after the birth of Jesus, only the 27 books that the New Testament contains were selected for inclusion? Many have survived from this period—some that are more than a half-century older than books that were included. From the lists of books considered authoritative by various leaders of the Church during the second and third centuries, we can infer that there was no complete consensus, but that the final decisions emerged only gradually. But how were decisions made at all?

At the outset, we can observe that when Paul, for example, speaks of "the scriptures," he is referring in a general way to what we call the Old Testament. There was, however, no fixed definition accepted by all Jews as to what constituted their scriptures. All of them accepted Torah (the five books of Moses) as the Word of God, but the Pharisees accepted and the Sadducees rejected the Prophets and the later poetical and historical works as constituting part of scripture. The *canon*, as we call it (from a Greek word meaning "rule," "standard") was probably not drawn up by Jews until A.D. 90. It is likely that the formation of the Jewish canon was a reaction against Christians who were claiming authority for their writings equal to that of the Jewish scriptures, so that Jewish officialdom felt obligated to draw up its authoritative list. Furthermore, a number of additions to the collection of Old Testament writings had attracted a wide reading audience among Jews and perhaps among others as well. Some of these works had already found their way into the Septuagint, and very nearly became part of the Jewish scriptures, even though they were of recent origin and incorporated speculative ideas that were simply incompatible with the traditional books of Hebrew scriptures. The Greek work known as the Wisdom of Solomon, which uses ideas and terms nearly identical with the opening of the New Testament book of Hebrews, is an example of this speculative type of religious literature against which the orthodox rabbinic group in Palestine felt it must take a firm stand. Accordingly, only works that existed in Hebrew (or Aramaic) were included, and only those that were adjudged to be in accord with the legal and prophetic tradition of ancient Israel. The criteria that were employed led to the inclusion of a speculative apocalyptic writing, the Book of Daniel, on the supposition—certainly erroneous—that it had been written during the time of Israel's exile in Babylon. Actually it was written in the second century B.C. at the time of the Maccabean Revolt described in Chapter 2. The intention and the effect of this drawing-up of a Jewish canon was the establishment in the seat of religious authority of the pharisaic segment of Judaism, for whom the Law was central and whose tradition of legal interpretation provided the link with the ancient past.

Within the New Testament itself, there is only one passage which refers definitely to Christian writings as scripture. This is II Pet. 3:15-16, where the letters of Paul are mentioned along with "the other scriptures." The evidence available is scanty for determining what books were at any given stage considered authoritative, or by what procedure they were pronounced to be canonical, and when.

In addition to this general reference to Paul's letter as scripture, we have definite evidence that about the year A.D. 150, Marcion, a brilliant, though unorthodox, leader in the Church, published his own list of Christian books that he considered worthy of the true faith. He was violently anti-Judaistic, and would admit as genuinely Christian only the letters of Paul and an expurgated edition of Luke-Acts. It may have been by way of answer to Marcion that the main body of the Church drew up its own list of books that it regarded as authoritative. Although we do not have available the criteria by which such a hypothetical anti-Marcionite list might have been made, we do have some hints in three short prologues to the gospels of Mark, Luke, and John, probably written between A.D. 160 and 180. These lay stress on the continuity between the testimony included in the gospels and the witness of the apostles who saw these events for themselves. The fullest statement concerning the four gospels that has been preserved from this period comes from Irenaeus, who was originally from Asia Minor but who became Bishop of Lyons in France about A.D. 180. Irenaeus in his book, *Against Heresies*, explains why there are only four gospels: Matthew, Mark, Luke, and John. Although a modern reader might not find his arguments persuasive ("there are four zones of the world and four principal winds . . . it is fitting that the Church should have four pillars breathing out immortality"; *i.e.*, the gospels. From *Against Heresies*, III.11.8), it is evident that by the end of the second century there were only four serious contenders for inclusion in the Christian canon among all the purported Gospel writings. Irenaeus rests his claim for the canonicity of these four gospels not only on the analogies with the natural world, quoted above, but on the grounds of the tradition that associated these four with the apostles.

A fuller statement concerning the canon, though without using the term itself, is to be found in an eighth-century Latin manuscript which is generally recognized to be a translation from a second-century Greek list of books which are to be accepted for public reading in the churches, *i.e.*, as scripture. The manuscript was published in 1740 by a Milanese scholar named Muratori; hence the canon list is known as the Muratorian Canon.[8] In both these lists, the criterion for acceptability of any book is its dependence directly, or by way of an intimate associate, on an apostle. At the oral stage of the transmission of the tradition had been fidelity to the *kerygma* and correspondence to the Old Testament promises. Now to these was added a third factor: apostolicity.

It is impossible to discover how apostolicity was defined, although it was clearly not sufficient to declare that a certain work had been written by or rested upon the witness of an apostle. The Gospel of Peter, a spurious work of the mid-second century that builds on the canonical gospels but dissolves into myth the historical reality of the incarnation, death, and resurrection of Jesus, was first approved by the bishop of Antioch for public reading as scripture and then denounced as heretical. On every count it failed to meet the test: it betrayed the *kerygma*, it misused the Old Testament prophecies, and therefore

---

[8] An English translation of the text of this manuscript is included in Hennecke-Schneemelcher, *New Testament Apocrypha*, I, tr. R. McL. Wilson (Philadelphia: Westminster, 1963), 43-44.

it could not be considered the work of an apostle. There does not seem to have been any formal agreement by the various churches, nor any official decree by its leaders. Rather, the decisions emerged on the basis of growing consensus. Some books, such as the Revelation to John, were under dispute down to the tenth century at least. The distinguished American translator and Biblical scholar, E. J. Goodspeed, proposed the theory that the original nucleus around which the canon began to form was the letters of Paul, with the Letters to the Ephesians prepared by the collector on the basis of Pauline themes and intended to serve as a covering letter for the whole group. Whether there was a stage of the canon before Marcion's time we cannot be certain, but the letters of Paul were surely the main element in the oldest list known to us.

The Complex Problem of the Gospels

The situation in relation to the gospels is even more complex, since in the opening decades of the second century there seems to have been no common agreement as to which of the gospels were to be considered canonical. As we have noted, by about the year 180 all four of our present gospels were accepted as canonical. Eusebius, the fourth-century historian whose *Ecclesiastical History* was commissioned by the Emperor Constantine, records some rather vague reports about the origins of the gospels which he attributes to Papias, bishop of Hierapolis in Asia Minor in the early second century. Our confidence in the accuracy of these reports (which will be discussed in Chapters 11, 12, 13, and 14, where we deal with the individual gospels) is not increased by the comment of Irenaeus, who said that Papias was a man of limited capacities. Papias makes no mention of the Gospel of John, although

A PAPYRUS FRAGMENT *of the Gospel of John, written in Egypt around* A.D. *125 and found on an island in the Upper Nile. The writing style enabled scholars to date it.*

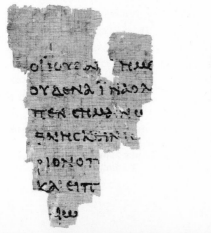

later second-century tradition reports that Ephesus; one of the chief cities of Asia Minor, was its place of origin.

Paradoxically, the oldest manuscript of any part of the New Testament that has yet been found is a fragment of the Gospel of John, unearthed in the present century on an island in the upper Nile in Egypt. Its style of hand-writing enabled specialists to date the papyrus scrap to about the year A.D. 125. In the early second century, Papias, then, attests to the existence and use of three gospels; we have manuscript evidence for the existence of the fourth. In the Christian writings which originated in the period from about A.D. 85 to A.D. 150, but which were not included in the Christian canon and are given the general designation of the *Apostolic Fathers*, there are quotations from all the gospels, though no one author quotes from all four. In short, in the early second century all four gospels are used, but they are not generally or officially recognized as authoritative. Indeed, there is evidence that the Apostolic Fathers did not always quote from the written gospels, but sometimes quoted merely variant forms of the Gospel tradition still circulating orally among the churches.[9]

By the late second century, the four gospels now included in the Christian canon had been woven together to form a continuous narrative by Tatian, a Syrian leader whose orthodoxy was challenged by many and whose harmony of the gospels (which he called the *Diatessaron*) was later condemned by the main body of the Church. By the latter part of the fourth century, the situation was clearer. As we can infer from the Festal Letter sent out in A.D. 367 by Athanasius, bishop of Alexandria, there was operative in the politically and intellectually influential church there a canonical list that corresponds exactly to our own except for the order of the books.

Beginning in the early second century and during several succeeding centuries, other gospels, purportedly of Jewish origin, circulated and were highly regarded. The names, or mere fragments in quotation, are all that have survived of many of these. The Gospel of the Hebrews and the Gospel of the Egyptians, for example, are known only from quotations in the writings of orthodox teachers who were seeking to refute the heresies contained in these documents. The Gospel of Thomas, which was until recently known only by name and a few scattered quotations, was discovered in a collection of ancient books unearthed in the village of Nag Hammadi in upper Egypt in 1945. The text and translation into English are now available.[10] It now appears that sayings drawn from the Gospel of Thomas or incorporated by its author from other sources into his gospel are included in collections of sayings attributed to Jesus that were found over a period of years in Egypt, beginning in the last

---

[9] Research into this question has been carried on by H. Köster, in *Synoptische Uberlieferung bei den apostolischen Vätern* (Berlin: Akademie Verlag, 1957).

[10] *The Gospel of Thomas*, Guillaumont, Puech, *et al.* (New York: Harper & Row, 1959). This edition is often referred to as the "Brill text," since the Dutch firm of Brill first published it.

decade of the nineteenth century.[11] The Gospel of Thomas has affinities with Gnosticism, a speculative, esoteric type of thought that flourished in many forms in the early centuries of the Christian Era, and which denied that the Creation was good and that the Incarnation was real.

There is no evidence that the main body of the Church was ever inclined to include any of these writings within its canon of scripture. That was done by certain heretical groups, but the books were quoted by orthodox Church leaders only for purposes of refutation or to warn the faithful against using them. As such they stand in contrast not only to the canonical books but to the Apostolic Fathers, which were books considered to be edifying and worthwhile reading for Christians, but which failed to meet the tests of canonicity. Although the term "apocrypha"[12] is often applied to these writings, it is misleading to do so. Among the noncanonical works that were highly regarded in the early Church were the Apostolic Fathers. These writings are of three main types: works written to a specific church, but with implications for the whole Church; works of moral exhortation, with no particular address; general works intended for the edification of the Church at large. An example of each type will indicate something of their contents, and will show how, by the turn of the second century, subtle changes were taking place in the life of the Church as an institution.

The Apostolic Fathers

The First Epistle of Clement, prompted by a dispute within the church in Corinth about A.D. 95, is a lengthy exhortation from the bishop of Rome to the brethren at Corinth, appealing to them to submit to ecclesiastical authority. In discussing the issues, the author of I Clement lays down clearly the lines along which the doctrine of apostolic succession (i.e., the transmission of spiritual authority within the Church from generation to generation of its leaders) was to develop.

A second type of writing is the *Didache*, or *Teaching of the Twelve Apostles*, which consists of moral instruction and regulations for the administering of baptism and communion. This document, which is thought to have been written in the first decades of the second century, is the earliest treatise on ecclesiastical regulations that has survived, and may in fact be the first that was ever produced by Christians.

The third type of writing is the general exhortation to the Church at large or a group of churches, as exemplified by the seven letters ascribed to Ignatius, bishop of Antioch in Syria. Although these letters purport to have been written by him as he was on his way to martyrdom in Rome, they are little more than

---

[11] Hennecke-Schneemelcher, pp. 278 ff.
[12] From a Greek word meaning "concealed." It refers to secret works originating in esoteric groups, but it came to be used of writings which were deemed heretical or spurious, or both.

a series of appeals to churches everywhere to submit to the authority of their bishops, and to allow moral exhortation to take the place of the exciting predictions about the future that were so popular in the Church in times of actual or impending persecution.

Although the Church as a whole never accepted these writings as of equal authority with those in the canon—a few, like the Shepherd of Hermas, were at times included with the canonical group—they were considered as valuable for the edification of the churches, and they are surely of great worth to the historian in filling in the details of the life of the Christian community at the close of the first century and the opening of the second. No serious effort has been made in the nearly two thousand years that have elapsed to reopen the question of the canon. There have been occasional objections raised over individual books. Luther, for instance, objected strongly to James, because it seemed to be opposed to Paul's doctrine of justification by faith, which Luther considered to be central for the New Testament. Some books entered the canon belatedly; Hebrews was included only because it was attributed (wrongly) to Paul, and could therefore be considered of apostolic origin. But the validity of the threefold criteria—fidelity to the *kerygma*, fulfillment of the Old Testament, aspostolicity—once accepted by the Church, determined its selection, and it is with this group that we are primarily concerned in this book. The canon is in a sense the end-product; to understand how it came into being we must look back behind and through the tradition embodied in the gospels to the events which the tradition reports and interprets: the life, ministry, death, and resurrection of Jesus of Nazareth.

JESUS
IN THE GOSPELS

In the previous chapter attention was directed to some of the problems which complicate the task of reconstructing the life and teachings of the historical Jesus. It was pointed out that the four gospels, the principal sources for such information, were not composed for the express purpose of providing the kind of information which a modern biographer would hope to have at his disposal. The gospels are not biographies in any modern sense of the word.

74

To say this is not to make a snap judgment regarding the character of these writings; this view has been reached on the basis of the accumulative evidence of years of intensive study of the gospels. To test the validity of this judgment about the gospels, as well as other statements made about them in the previous chapter of this book, it is necessary to examine the kind of evidence which underlies these conclusions.

THE SYNOPTIC PROBLEM

When a close comparison is made between the general outline and content of the four gospels, two major problems emerge. First, there are striking differences between John and the other three gospels. Very few of the events in Jesus' life recorded in the latter are to be found in John. Those missing include such important events as the Temptation of Jesus, the Transfiguration at Caesarea Philippi, Jesus' words at the Last Supper, the Gethsemane scene, to mention only a few. The place and chronology of Jesus' ministry are different in John, and the style and language of Jesus' message contrasts markedly with that of the other three. The problem of accounting for these differences has challenged scholars for years. Later (Chapter 14) when the Gospel of John is considered in detail, attention will be given to this enigmatic problem of differences. For the present it is sufficient to note that for purposes of reconstructing the life and teachings of Jesus, Matthew, Mark, and Luke have been given priority in the work of critical scholarship.

Another problem is posed by a comparative examination of the Gospels of Matthew, Mark, and Luke.[1] Attention has already been called to certain similarities between them in contrast to John. Each of these gospels is constructed on a common arrangement which underlies any variations. For example, the beginning of Jesus' ministry is associated with John the Baptist, for the most part its scene is Galilee, and it concludes with a final trip to Jerusalem where, after a brief period, Jesus dies. In addition to this agreement in general content and plan it is apparent that in long individual passages not only is subject matter similar, but phrase after phrase of the Greek texts are identical.[2] When it is remembered that the original oral tradition was in the Aramaic language, it is incredible that the agreements between the synoptic gospels could have resulted from independent translations of this original tradition. The conclusion is inescapable that there must be some other explanation for the close literary relationship between the three gospels. Because of the broad agreement

---

[1] Serious comparative study of the Gospels of Matthew, Mark, and Luke requires the constant use of a text which presents the three in parallel columns. The following discussion will be enhanced by reference to such a text. The text based on the Revised Standard Version (1952) is *Gospel Parallels: A Synopsis of the First Three Gospels* (New York: Nelson, 1957).

[2] Usually reflected in English translations.

in content and outline, these gospels have come to be called the *synoptic gospels*, or *the Synoptics*. And the problem of accounting for their literary relationship is an important aspect of what is known as the *Synoptic problem*.

The Priority of the Gospel of Mark

One of the most widely accepted conclusions of gospel studies is the hypothesis that Mark was the earliest written gospel and that Matthew and Luke used Mark as the basis for writing their gospels.[3] This provides the clue for understanding the literary relationship between the three synoptic gospels. More than a century of intensive research has amassed such overwhelming evidence in support of this hypothesis that alternative explanations have been given up. While we cannot survey all the arguments which have been given to support this hypothesis, a few of the most important ones will be considered to illustrate the nature and weight of the evidence.

The first and most obvious argument is based on the recurrence of Mark's subject matter in Matthew and Luke. Most of Mark, with the exception of eight brief passages, is found in Matthew, and all but 12 Markan passages are found in Luke. Dependence on Mark seems necessary since it is usually the case that when a Markan passage is missing in either Matthew or Luke it is found in the other gospel. This is one of the major arguments against the older view that Mark was an abridgment of Matthew. Further evidence against such a possibility is the fact that on actual word count in many passages Mark is the longer. In the analysis of such passages there is convincing evidence that Matthew and Luke have abridged, and the reason is not obscure. Stylistic changes and the elimination of redundancies are everywhere evident, and the presence of a good deal of non-Markan material in both Matthew and Luke suggests that these authors intentionally abridged Mark in order to include these non-Markan traditions.

The arrangement and sequence of material also supports the theory of dependence on Mark. It is not just the fact that the Markan sequence regularly recurs. In most instances when one of the two gospels varies from Mark in sequence, the other follows Mark. Sometimes such variations from Mark do not make good sense. For example, Mark gives an account of a visit of Jesus to Nazareth some time after the beginning of his ministry (Mk. 6:1-6). Luke places this episode at the very outset of the ministry (Lk. 4:16-30). In Luke's account Jesus says: "Doubtless you will quote to me this proverb, 'Physician, heal yourself; what we have heard you did at Capernaum, do here also in your

---

[3] This is true of both Protestant and Roman Catholic scholarship. For a Roman Catholic interpretation see Alfred Wikenhauser, *New Testament Introduction* (New York: Herder & Herder, 1963), pp. 239-252. An elaborate attempt to demonstrate that Mark was dependent on Matthew is in W. R. Farmer, *The Synoptic Problem* (New York: Macmillan, 1964).

own country.' " But according to Luke's sequence Jesus has not carried on a ministry in Capernaum before this time; the saying seems out of place. In Mark, however, the same words occur and make sense. According to the Gospel of Mark, Jesus has already been active in Capernaum (Mk. 1:21 ff.; 2:1 ff.). Luke's passage must presuppose Mark's sequence to make sense out of the content of the passage. That Luke has actually relocated a Markan passage is further substantiated by the fact that Matthew follows Mark in his order.

Another argument supporting dependence on Mark is based on the numerous parallel passages where the Greek of Matthew or Luke, or both, exhibits a refinement of style in contrast with Mark. In some instances Aramaisms of Mark are missing; in other passages the phraseology of Mark contrasts with the more "literary" style or language of Matthew or Luke. This strongly suggests that the latter authors have consciously improved upon the Markan original. There are occasions when the differences represent substantive modifications. For example, phrases in Mark which describe emotional states of Jesus frequently are either modified or omitted in Matthew and Luke. It is a good guess that the religious sensitivity of the latter has prompted such revisions. In certain cases more radical differences are to be found. In the story of the Rich Young Man (Mk. 10:17-22), according to Mark's account Jesus is addressed by the young man as "Good Teacher," and Jesus responds, "Why do you call me good?" In Matthew's version of this story, Jesus' question is missing in a complete recasting of the dialogue (Mt. 19:16-22). That Matthew has purposely reworked the Markan passage is further substantiated by the fact that Luke follows the Markan story (Lk. 18:18-23).

No one of these several arguments is sufficient in itself to support the theory of dependence on Mark. It is the accumulative weight of the evidence and the inadequacy of alternative explanations which demand explanation.

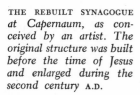

THE REBUILT SYNAGOGUE *at Capernaum, as conceived by an artist. The original structure was built before the time of Jesus and enlarged during the second century* A.D.

Fig. 1. A Selection from the Synoptic Gospels in Parallel

THE RICH YOUNG MAN

MATTHEW 19:16-22	MARK 10:17-22	LUKE 18:18-23
16 And behold, one came up to him, saying, "Teacher, what good deed must I do, to have eternal life?" 17 And he said to him, "Why do you ask me about what is good? One there is who is good. If you would enter life, keep the commandments." 18 He said to him, "Which?" And Jesus said, "You shall not kill, You shall not commit adultery, You shall not steal, You shall not bear false witness, 19 Honor your father and mother, and, You shall love your neighbor as yourself." 20 The young man said to him, "All these I have observed; what do I still lack?" 21 Jesus said to him, "If you would be perfect, go, sell what you possess and give to the poor, and you will have treasure in heaven; and come, follow me." 22 When the young man heard this he went away sorrowful; for he had great possessions.	17 And as he was setting out on his journey, a man ran up and knelt before him, and asked him, "Good Teacher, what must I do to inherit eternal life?" 18 And Jesus said to him, "Why do you call me good? No one is good but God alone. 19 You know the commandments: 'Do not kill, Do not commit adultery, Do not steal, Do not bear false witness, Do not defraud, Honor your father and mother.'" 20 And he said to him, "Teacher, all these I have observed from my youth." 21 And Jesus looking upon him loved him, and said to him, "You lack one thing; go, sell what you have, and give to the poor, and you will have treasure in heaven; and come, follow me." 22 At that saying his countenance fell, and he went away sorrowful, for he had great possessions.	18 And a ruler asked him, "Good Teacher, what shall I do to inherit eternal life?" 19 And Jesus said to him, "Why do you call me good? No one is good but God alone. 20 You know the commandments: 'Do not commit adultery, Do not kill, Do not steal, Do not bear false witness, Honor your father and mother.'" 21 And he said, "All these I have observed from my youth." 22 And when Jesus heard it, he said to him, "One thing you still lack. Sell all that you have and distribute to the poor, and you will have treasure in heaven; and come, follow me." 23 But when he heard this he became sad, for he was very rich.

The Two-Source Hypothesis

There is another side to the Synoptic problem. Examination of these three gospels not only shows a large body of material common to all three; a little more than one-third of Matthew and one-fourth of Luke consists of material common to these two but missing in Mark. The question immediately arises: How can we account for the absence of this material in Mark and its presence in the other two? It is not impossible that Luke borrowed the material from Matthew, or vice versa. But there are such serious arguments against this solution that it is commonly rejected. For example, the different arrangement of the material in each gospel weighs heavily against it. In Luke this common material is incorporated in two insertions in the Markan narrative; these are called the "Little Insertion" (Lk. 6:20-8:3) and the "Great Insertion" (Lk. 9:51-18:14). Matthew, on the other hand, includes most of the material in five major discourses by Jesus in Chapters 5-7, 10, 13, 18, and 23-25, working his material into either the narrative or the specific sayings as presented in Mark. Such treatment of the material points more forcefully to an independent source rather than mutual dependence.

A more telling argument against the possibility that one author borrowed from the other is the fact that in various passages where there are variations of a minor sort, in some cases Matthew seems the more original, in others, Luke. It may be asked on what grounds one version can be determined the more original, since the only versions we have are those found in Matthew and Luke. Of course, there can be no absolute determination. However, a number of helpful principles have been developed in an effort to deal with the problem. For example, on the basis of the analysis of the linguistic style and religious interests of both gospels, constructions and religious motifs characteristic of one author may be identified in his version of the common material. This suggests that the version in which such obvious evidences of the author's hand are absent *may be* the more original. Since the more original version of the common material is not confined to either one of the gospels, it would appear more reasonable to assume that both authors have made use of an independent source rather than that either borrowed from the other.

On the basis of such analyses it is commonly acknowledged today that Matthew and Luke did have access to a separate source which each employed in his own way, in addition to Mark, in the composition of his gospel. In gospel studies this source is designated "Q," a symbol introduced by nineteenth-century German scholars as an abbreviation of the German *Quelle*, meaning source. The Two-Source Hypothesis maintains that both Matthew and Luke used two sources, Mark and Q, in composing their gospels. While the hypothesis continues to be tested, even challenged, it is normally accepted as a basic working hypothesis in the study of the synoptic gospels.

When it comes to the matter of reconstructing the hypothetical Q source, there is anything but unanimous agreement. The problem is obvious. While Matthew and Luke verbally agree at many points, in many instances they differ (see Fig. 2, p. 80). The problem of determining which is the more original is great. Furthermore, there is always the possibility that Q consisted of more than has been preserved by Matthew and Luke. But on the basis of what they have incorporated in their gospels the contents of Q are fairly clear. While it consisted largely of sayings of Jesus, it also included traditions about John

Fig. 2. A Selection from Q

THE WATCHFUL HOUSEHOLDER

MATTHEW 24:43-44	LUKE 12:39-40
43 But know this, that if the householder had known in what part of the night the thief was coming, he would have watched and would not have let his house be broken into. 44 Therefore you also must be ready; for the Son of man is coming at an hour you do not expect.	39 But know this, that if the householder had known at what hour the thief was coming, he would have been awake and would not have left his house to be broken into. 40 You also must be ready; for the Son of man is coming at an hour you do not expect.

the Baptist, several parables, an account of the Temptation of Jesus, several controversy stories and miracles. Some scholars would include in Q materials found only in Matthew or Luke, but such decisions are highly subjective. It is commonly agreed that Q was not a gospel in form. It is quite certain that it contained little, if any, connective narrative. Matthew and Luke apparently knew it and used it in Greek translation; but it is almost certain that it first circulated in Aramaic.

One of the continuing debates centers on the question of whether Matthew and Luke had access to a written document or knew Q as an oral tradition. The strongest argument for its existence as a written source is the frequency of verbal agreements between the two gospels. Whether Matthew and Luke used two versions of Q, whether oral or written, is also a much debated question. The collection of traditions known as Q undoubtedly existed prior to the composition of Mark, perhaps as early as A.D. 50. Indeed, there are some scholars who believe that Mark used Q, and explain certain peculiarities in passages common to Matthew, Mark, and Luke as evidences of the text of Q.

There has been a good deal of speculation regarding the explanation of why the Q collection was first created. One very attractive hypothesis maintains that it was brought together for the purpose of instruction of newly baptized Christians. However its origin may be explained, its function was not primarily biographical. A typical reconstruction of Q can be seen in the appendix.

The Problem of Additional Sources

When all the Markan material, as well as the Q material, has been isolated from Matthew and Luke, we find that there remains a considerable amount of material in each gospel. On examination it will be found that this material is peculiar to each gospel. For example, while both gospels have birth stories, they are quite different in content. Such familiar parables as the Prodigal Son (Lk. 15:11-32), the Good Samaritan (Lk. 10:29-37), and the Pharisee and the Publican (Lk. 18:9-14), and the story of the Rich Man and Lazarus (Lk. 16:19-31) are found only in Luke. Such parables as the Weeds (Mt. 13:24-30), the Hidden Treasure (Mt. 13:44), the Pearl (Mt. 13:45-46), and the Last Judgment (Mt. 25:31-46) are found only in Matthew. Luke alone has the story of John the Baptist's birth (Lk. 1:5-25; 57-80), the raising of the widow's son at Nain (Lk. 17:11-17), and Mary and Martha (Lk. 10:38-42). Matthew alone has such sayings of Jesus as that concerning alms (Mt. 6:1-4) and fasting (Mt. 6:16-18), and the description of Judas' death (Mt. 27:3-10; cf. Acts 1:15-20).

No one disputes that Matthew and Luke had access to independent sources; there is, however, no unanimity as to the character of these sources. In the first place, it is possible that some of the material peculiar to either gospel came from the Q source. But after allowance is made for such possibilities, a large body of material remains to be accounted for. Perhaps some of these materials are the outright composition of the author of the gospel. The genealogy of Jesus in Matthew may be an example of such a composition (Mt. 1:1-17). However, after allowance is made for such creativity on the part of the author, there is still a considerable bulk of material remaining. The dispute does not revolve around whether there were sources; the question is whether there were two written documents that were roughly equivalent to the special material in each gospel. A number of years ago this thesis was strongly maintained as integral to what has been called the Four-Document Hypothesis.[4] Simply stated, this theory presupposed four written documents behind the Gospels of Matthew and Luke: Mark, Q, a written source peculiar to Matthew, and a written source peculiar to Luke. Matthew's special source was designated "M," and Luke's "L." In recent years there has been increasing scepticism regarding the existence of such written documents.

In recognition of the divergence of scholarly opinion regarding sources, it is preferable to presuppose that each author had access to *several* sources, perhaps written and oral, from which he incorporated material into his gospel. This does not eliminate the possibility that among the sources, in the case of each author, there might have been one collection of traditions from which he drew heavily in writing his gospel. The symbols M and L have become convenient terms to designate the special material of Matthew and Luke rather than any specific theory about the character of the sources. The reader can consult the appendix for the contents of M and L.

Up to this point in our consideration of the synoptic gospels we have dealt with the major conclusions reached during a century and a half in the effort

---

[4] The classic statement of this position is found in B. H. Streeter's *The Four Gospels*, rev. ed. (London: Macmillan, 1930).

to explain the similarities and differences among these gospels. The conclusions of this particular discipline of study, technically known as *source criticism,* can be summarized diagrammatically as follows:

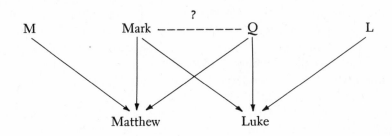

BEHIND THE WRITTEN SOURCES

The intensive examination of the synoptic gospels eventually led to a question opening the door to a new epoch in gospel studies. It was actually certain startling conclusions with respect to the character of the Gospel of Mark which prompted the new departure. On the basis of a close scrutiny of the connective narrative in Mark's gospel, attention was called to the generally vague notices of time (*e.g.,* "after John was arrested," 1:14; "one Sabbath" 2:23; "again," 3:1; "in those days," 8:1, etc.) and place (*e.g.,* "Galilee," 1:14; "by the Sea of Galilee," 1:16; "a lonely place," 1:35; "beside the sea," 2:13; "the grainfields," 2:23; "the sea," 3:7; "his own country," 6:1; "among the villages," 6:6, etc.). These investigations led to a conclusion that was to find general acceptance among critical scholars: generally speaking, the chronological and topographical narrative framework of Mark's gospel was the creation of the author. This literary analysis was supported by the further argument that the selection and arrangement of materials bore the marks of the author's religious insights and purposes. Concerning this important aspect of the argument more must be said. When the Gospel of Mark is considered in detail (Chapter 11), the reader's own conclusions must be drawn in view of that discussion. For the present, attention must be given to the implications of the conclusion. If the author of Mark himself supplied the general chronological and topographical framework, then obviously the traditions which he incorporated into his Gospel, with few exceptions, came to him devoid of any framework. This conclusion shattered a long accepted tradition that Mark had preserved in his gospel a reliable and accurate account of the life of Jesus, dependable in its general chronological sequence and place setting for the events in Jesus' life. Now it was acknowledged that Mark had been the first to bring the early traditions about Jesus into a sequential pattern, endeavoring to provide the setting of time and place. Before Mark the traditions circulated independent of such a framework.

With this development a new epoch in Gospel studies was launched. Attention now moved on from a preoccupation with the literary relations between the synoptic gospels—that is, from *source criticism*—to *form criticism*, the new discipline (briefly discussed in the previous chapter) which continues to play an important role. Basically, form criticism has been concerned with the study of the period of oral transmission before the gospel traditions reached their written stage in the synoptic gospels. It is a basic thesis of form criticism that the traditions contained in the written gospels are analyzable in terms of definite forms in which they circulated orally. Form criticism also maintains that in the course of transmission there were changes and developments in these forms, and it is part of its task to identify and account for these changes. In so far as the discipline is concerned with this latter investigation, it is more appropriately called *form history*.

From the beginning there have been, and still are, important differences of interpretation among those who acknowledge the importance of form criticism.[5] But there are broad agreements which must be seriously considered in any effort to understand the history and transmission of the traditions now contained in the gospels. In the first place, it is agreed that, generally speaking, at the beginning the traditions about Jesus circulated orally as independent units. That is, in most cases they were not specifically set within a chronological or sequential or topographical framework of his ministry. The major exception is the Passion narrative in its basic outline of Last Supper, arrest, trial of Jesus before the High Priest and Pilate, crucifixion, and resurrection appearances. In the second place, it is acknowledged that the situation in life (*Sitz im Leben*) or the needs of the first Christians to transmit the traditions, played an important role in the selection, formation, and transmission. What these needs were presupposes some understanding of the beliefs and activities of the earliest Christians. Such understanding depends not only on careful interpretation of the gospels but interpretation of the rest of the New Testament writings as well. In the reconstruction there are differences in emphasis, but consideration would have to be given to the following: (1) Christian preaching; (2) teaching or instruction; (3) community worship; (4) debate with the Jews (and Gentiles when the mission to the Gentiles began); (5) community organization and discipline. The traditions about Jesus were remembered and transmitted not primarily to perpetuate the memory of past happenings, but to guide the community in its daily life in the world. Earlier (Chapter 3) we saw that central to the *kerygma* of the earliest Church were the death and resurrection of Jesus whom they believed to be God's Messiah. Therefore, form criticism's conclusion that the Passion narrative was the one episode in the life of Jesus which from the beginning consisted of a minimal sequence of events is not

---

[5] These differences are evident in the two major studies by M. Dibelius and R. Bultmann mentioned previously (Chapter 3, fn. 7). For another important evaluation of form criticism, see Vincent Taylor, *The Formation of the Gospel Tradition* (London: Macmillan, 1953).

surprising. Not only would the occurrences surrounding Jesus' death have left an indelible mark upon the memories of the first disciples; just these events were at the heart of the message which they proclaimed as the Gospel.

The Forms of the Oral Tradition

Form critics have generally agreed in their classification of the units in which the tradition circulated during the period of oral transmission. They have differed in their choice of the technical terms by which they designate the forms, and to a certain extent there has been disagreement in their identification of the forms where, for various reasons, certain passages seem to fit the definition of more than one form. While these divergencies cannot be overlooked, the areas of agreement are impressive and provide the consensus which commends the form-critical method as an essential tool for understanding the period of oral transmission. In the present discussion of the various forms the nomenclature of Vincent Taylor [6] will be employed; the comparable terminology of two other form critics, Rudolf Bultmann and Martin Dibelius, will be given in footnotes.

PRONOUNCEMENT STORIES. *Pronouncement stories* (See Fig. 3, below) [7] are brief narratives purporting to describe an encounter between Jesus and one or more persons. The setting, which is regularly general and often vague, contains details sufficient only to provide the setting for the distinctive feature of the story: a culminating statement or pronouncement of Jesus which occurs at the end. While the pronouncement of Jesus can be understood in the immediate context of the story (often a conflict between Jesus and other persons), it is of such a nature as to lend itself to more general application. These stories were remembered and transmitted basically because of the pro-

---

[6] Taylor, *The Formation of the Gospel Tradition.*
[7] Dibelius uses the term *Paradigm,* and Bultmann *Apophthegmata.*

Fig. 3. A Pronouncement Story

MARK 12:13-17

And they sent to him some of the Pharisees and some of the Herodians, to entrap him in his talk. And they came and said to him, "Teacher, we know you are true, and care for no man; for you do not regard the position of men, but truly teach the way of God. Is it lawful to pay taxes to Caesar, or not? Should we pay them, or should we not?" But knowing their hypocrisy, he said to them, "Why put me to the test? Bring me a coin, and let me look at it." And they brought one. And he said to them, "Whose likeness and inscription is this?" They said to him, "Caesar's." Jesus said to them, "Render to Caesar the things that are Caesar's and to God the things that are God's."

nouncements which the Christian community valued as an authoritative guide for their own lives.

MIRACLE STORIES. *Miracle stories* [8] (Fig. 4, below) have as their principal point the narration of a miraculous act of Jesus. With rare exceptions the narrative contains a threefold pattern of development: (1) a description of the situation which prompts the miracle (*e.g.*, in the case of a healing this would involve the description of the condition of the person to be healed); (2) a description of the miraculous act; (3) a description of the consequences of the miracle (*e.g.*, the reaction of those who witnessed the miracle). The focus of the miracle story is the miracle itself, and when the narrative follows the above outline it is a *proper* miracle story. There are, however, certain narratives which appear to be a mixture of a pronouncement story and a miracle story (*e.g.*, Mk. 2:3-12). And in at least one instance we find two miracle stories combined in one narrative (Mk. 5:21-43). Like the pronouncement stories, the miracle stories circulated independently at first though it is possible that in the period of oral transmission they already circulated in collections.

Fig. 4. A Miracle Story

MARK 1:40-45

And a leper came to him beseeching him, and kneeling said to him, "If you will, you can make me clean." And being moved with pity, he stretched out his hand and touched him, and said to him, "I will; be clean." And immediately the leprosy left him, and he sternly charged him, and sent him away at once, and said to him, "See that you say nothing to anyone; but go, show yourself to the priest, and offer for your cleansing what Moses commanded, for a proof to the people." But he went out and began to talk freely about it, and to spread the news, so that Jesus could no longer openly enter a town, but was out in the country; and the people came to him from every quarter.

SAYINGS. The oral tradition included a large number of sayings [9] of Jesus which originally circulated independently, without a narrative framework relating them to the specific occasion in Jesus' ministry when they were uttered. During the oral period there already was a tendency for these sayings to be grouped in small collections as illustrative of a common theme (Fig. 5, p. 86). In some instances, certain important sayings continued to be transmitted independently, as can be seen from the different contexts in which such sayings are found in the written gospels (see Mt. 23:12; Lk. 14:11; 18:14). It

---

[8] Dibelius designates these *Novellen* and Bultmann *Wundergeschichten.*

[9] Dibelius prefers the term *Parenesis.* Bultmann classifies "saying" in five categories. His most comprehensive term is *Logia.*

is likely that in certain instances the gospels retain a sequence of sayings which were originally uttered in that form by Jesus and were transmitted as a cluster throughout the oral period.[10] Luke's shorter version of the Beatitudes may reflect such an original cluster (Lk. 6:20-22; cf. Mt. 5:3-11). Such instances are the exception to the rule that in general the collections were made by the community in the course of oral transmission.

Fig. 5. A Cluster of Sayings

MARK 8:34-9:1

[And he called to him the multitude with his disciples, and said to them,] "If any man would come after me, let him deny himself and take up his cross and follow me. For whoever would save his life will lose it; and whoever loses his life for my sake and the gospel's will save it. For what does it profit a man, to gain the whole world and forfeit his life? For what can a man give in return for his life? For whoever is ashamed of me and of my words in this adulterous and sinful generation, of him will the Son of man also be ashamed when he comes in the glory of his Father with the holy angels." [And he said to them,] "Truly, I say to you, there are some standing here who will not taste death before they see the kingdom of God come with power."

PARABLES. One of the most characteristic forms of Jesus' words preserved by the oral tradition was the parable.[11] A parable is a narrative which vividly describes a commonplace incident or experience (see Fig. 6, p. 87). A lifelike quality is essential to the parable. It was important that the hearer recognize the incident described as something he had already seen occur, or at least, could imagine the incident as within the realm of possibility. The parables were originally intended to call attention to some truth by comparing the principal impression left by the parable with that truth. For example, many of the parables were told to suggest some truth about the kingdom of God. The parable is a story employed to illustrate a truth which is independent of the parable itself. In oral transmission, parables tended to be allegorized. In some instances the parable itself maintained its internal structure and was accompanied by an allegorical interpretation; an example of this is the Parable of the Sower (Mk. 4:1-9), with its accompanying interpretation (Mk. 4:13-20). But in numerous instances the allegorizing has already affected the internal structure of the parable (e.g., Mt. 22:1-14).

In another case we have a parable which already bears the marks of al-

---

[10] See C. F. Burney, *The Poetry of Our Lord* (Oxford, England: Oxford University Press, 1925). The author endeavors to recover the original sayings of Jesus by a retranslation of the Greek into original Aramaic.

[11] Both Dibelius and Bultmann use the term *Gleichnis*.

legorizing, but is nevertheless accompanied by an allegorical interpretation (Mt. 13:24-30; 36-43). There were two primary reasons for this tendency toward allegorization. First, a proper understanding of the parable depended upon the concrete situation to which it was addressed. Since most of the parables soon circulated in isolation from the specific situation to which they were addressed by Jesus, one way to read them meaningfully was to allegorize them, for example, through understanding them as symbolic stories describing the early Church's situation. Second, allegorizing apparently resulted from a tendency to look for esoteric meaning in the words of Jesus.

While parables circulated as independent units it is likely that at the oral stage of transmission some were already transmitted in groups of two or more. For example, it is likely that Mark found in oral tradition the group of three parables he presents in 4:26-32.

Before leaving the parables attention must be given to one literary form which stands in close relation to them. I refer to the *simile*, a term regularly used to designate a brief saying which, like the parable, implies a comparison, but unlike it does not have the extended narrative form. Since the similes, like the parables, were first uttered to provide clarification of some specific point Jesus was endeavoring to make by comparison, when they were detached from their original setting in oral transmission they posed problems for understanding. Like other sayings, they were often preserved in groups (see Fig. 7, below). The group of two similes found in Mk. 2:21-22 may have been found by the author in the oral tradition.

Fig. 6. A Parable

MARK 4:3-8

[Listen!] A sower went out to sow. And as he sowed, some seed fell along the path, and the birds came and devoured it. Other seed fell on rocky ground, where it had not much soil, and immediately it sprang up, since it had no depth of soil; and when the sun rose it was scorched, and since it had no root it withered away. Other seed fell among thorns and the thorns grew up and choked it, and it yielded no grain. And other seeds fell into good soil and brought forth grain, growing up and increasing and yielding thirtyfold and sixtyfold and a hundredfold.

Fig. 7. A Cluster of Similes

MARK 2:21-22

No one sews a piece of unshrunk cloth on an old garment; if he does, the patch tears away from it, the new from the old, and a worse tear is made. And no one puts new wine into old wineskins; if he does, the wine will burst the skins, and the wine is lost, and so are the skins; but new wine is for fresh skins.

STORIES ABOUT JESUS. These stories,[12] unlike the pronouncement story, have no special features which constitute a definable literary form. The category is intended to designate a sizable number of stories of wide-ranging subject matter which fail to fall clearly under other classifications (see Fig. 8, below). They include such stories as the birth stories of Jesus in Matthew and Luke (Mt. 1:18-25; Lk. 2:1-20), the Temptation of Jesus (Mt. 4:1-11; Lk. 4:1-13), the call of the disciples (Mk. 1:16-20), the Transfiguration (Mk. 9:2-8), the guard at Jesus' tomb (Mt. 27:62-66), and many others. To be exact, numbered among these are stories about persons other than Jesus: for example, the story of the birth of John the Baptist (Lk. 1:57-80). These stories generally circulated as independent units of the oral tradition; there are possible exceptions, such as each of the two independent cycles of stories concerning the birth of Jesus and John the Baptist which probably were transmitted together.

Fig. 8. A Story About Jesus

MARK 11:15-18

[And they came to Jerusalem.] And he entered the temple and began to drive out those who sold and those who bought in the temple, and he overturned the tables of the money-changers and the seats of those who sold pigeons; and he would not allow any one to carry anything through the temple. And he taught, and said to them, "Is it not written, 'My house shall be called a house of prayer for all the nations'? But you have made it a den of robbers."

THE GOSPEL WRITERS AS AUTHORS

We have been considering the contribution of form criticism to our understanding of the traditions about Jesus during the oral period of transmission. One of the indirect consequences of form-critical studies has been a re-examination of the gospels with an eye to discovering the extent to which their authors have left the marks of their interpretation upon the traditions that provided the basic content for their writings. An acute awareness of the important role of the authors of the gospels followed from the realization that in the oral period the traditions circulated as independent units. The question was asked: Did the first author, Mark, and his successors, merely take the oral traditions, and such written traditions as were available, and with a minimum of organizing principles lay them side by side? Study of the gospels has made it increasingly clear that this was not the case. Methodologically speaking, by examination of

---

[12] Dibelius uses the terms *Mythen* and *Legende* and Bultmann *Geschichtserzählung* and *Legende*.

his arrangement of material, his narrative additions, and the intrusion of explanatory words and phrases, it is possible to discover not only the governing purposes of each author, but his theological interests and interpretations. In the case of Matthew and Luke the possibilities of success are further enhanced by the possibility of studying their treatment of Mark, and with less certainty, their revisions and employment of Q.

The role of the gospel authors in interpreting their traditions is so important that we must later devote a chapter to each (Chapters 11-14). Here it is important to make two observations: first, that they mark the final stage in the interpretation of the original traditions about Jesus; and second, as form criticism has made abundantly clear, the traditions at their disposal did not provide that kind of information which would make it possible for them to compose biographies of Jesus even if they had desired to do this. But they did not. Their intentions in preserving and transmitting the traditions of the historical Jesus were more nearly in harmony with the community which passed on the oral tradition from the beginning than with those of modern biographers.

THE GOSPELS AND THE JESUS OF HISTORY

By now the reader is undoubtedly aware of the problems which confront the task of reconstructing the life and teachings of the historical Jesus. It is difficult to assess fully the change which has come about since the nineteenth century, when scholars labored in a confidence inspired by the recent achievements of source criticism. Accompanying the conclusion that Mark was the earliest gospel was the conviction (now known to have been unjustified) that in Mark they possessed an account of the life and ministry of Jesus which reliably reported the sequence and progress of Jesus' ministry. In Q they believed they possessed an early source containing sayings of Jesus which were close to the very words (*ipsissima verba*) of Jesus. Many believed it was possible through Mark and Q not only to reconstruct the progress of Jesus' ministry, but to explore the consciousness of his mission, even to trace a development in that consciousness from the beginning to the end of his ministry.

The story of the quest of nineteenth-century scholars to write the life of the historical Jesus, and the many "Lives" that were produced, has been thoroughly told by Albert Schweitzer in a book that is now one of the great landmarks of New Testament studies, *The Quest of the Historical Jesus*.[13] Schweitzer leveled a severe criticism on much of their efforts. His criticism was based mainly on his contention that the efforts were misguided because of the neglect of the

---

[13] Albert Schweitzer, *The Quest of the Historical Jesus*, tr. W. Montgomery (New York: Macmillan, 1948). The original German title was *Von Reimarus zu Wrede: Eine Geschichte der Leben Jesu Forschung* (Tübingen, Germany: J. C. B. Mohr, 1906).

eschatological character of Jesus' message and mission.[14] It had receded into insignificance, he claimed, as scholars uncritically interpreted Jesus' life and teachings on the basis of their own ideas, which were derived mainly from nineteenth-century theology and philosophy. They had wrenched Jesus from his historical environment and clothed him in the garb of their own age.

The substance of Schweitzer's criticism of the nineteenth-century scholars continues to be a decisive factor in the differences between studies of Jesus in the nineteenth and twentieth centuries.[15] The truly decisive factor was yet to come. Schweitzer himself in one important respect continued the tradition of nineteenth-century scholarship. At the conclusion of his book, with a confidence as great as that of any of his predecessors, he sought on the basis of the content and sequence of events in the gospels to penetrate and explain the intentions, purposes, and decisions of Jesus' inner life. And on the basis of this he presented his own detailed "historical" analysis of the development of Jesus' life and message from its beginning to its earthly end. Schweitzer's critique of the nineteenth-century studies, and his stress on the importance of eschatology in Jesus' message, were supremely significant in determining the future direction of interpretations of the historical Jesus. But it was the conclusions of the form critics which drove the final wedge between the hopes and aims of the nineteenth- and mid-twentieth-century study of Jesus. Not only was the possibility of writing a full biography or life of Jesus called into question, but all pretensions to be able to penetrate recorded traditions to his life and thought were shown to be beyond the realm of historical research.

THE NEW QUEST FOR THE HISTORICAL JESUS

One of the firstfruits of form-critical studies was a profound scepticism. Not only was the possibility of writing a life of Jesus discarded; it was seriously believed that only a minimal content of Jesus' message could be recovered with any certainty. In the words of one form critic, only a "whisper" remained.[16] The crucial issue was the extent to which the Christian community not only interpreted the traditions about Jesus, but created them. Two of the most influential form critics, Dibelius and Bultmann, tended to assign a major creative role to the early Church. For example, Dibelius believed that the pronouncement stories were largely the creation of the non-Palestinian Christian community and served mainly as illustrative stories in the preaching mission

---

[14] Schweitzer was not the first or only scholar to make this criticism. Equally important in the scholarly world was the earlier work of Johannes Weiss, *Die Predigt Jesu vom Reiche Gottes* (Göttingen, Germany: Vandenhoeck and Ruprecht, 1900). Schweitzer's work was so important because of his review of the nineteenth century and because of the wider reading his book received.

[15] An account of the study of the historical Jesus in the twentieth century is presented in C. C. McCown, *The Search for the Real Jesus* (New York: Scribner's, 1940).

[16] R. H. Lightfoot, *History and Interpretation in the Gospels* (London: Hodder & Stoughton, 1935).

to the Gentiles. Bultmann, on the other hand, was inclined to trace the origin of the stories to Palestinian Christian communities. But he believed the settings which provided the context for the pronouncements were the creation of the community and reflected the conflicts in which the community found itself engaged. Both scholars believed that the miracle stories were largely the product of the religious imagination of the Gentile churches. And both likewise considered that most of the stories about Jesus, which they chose to describe as myths, legends, or tales, were the creation of the community, many for the purpose of transferring the origin of later beliefs and practices to the ministry of the historical Jesus. Many of the sayings, and even the parables, were similarly viewed through sceptical eyes.

The reaction to the form critics was varied. Some scholars, shocked by their sceptical conclusions, refused to take them seriously. There were from the beginning, however, many thoughtful scholars who after serious examination recognized the validity of certain basic claims of form criticism. But there were serious objections made against certain historical judgments, principally the creative role assigned to the early Christian community.[17] Among the many criticisms of form criticism which have been made from the beginning, two have particular importance in the eyes of many. First, it has been charged that the more extreme form critics have neglected the impact of the words and deeds of Jesus on those followers who after his death and resurrection formed the nucleus of the earliest Christian community. Second, they have neglected the importance of the presence of these eyewitnesses in the early Christian community during the formative period when the traditions about Jesus were remembered, interpreted, and transmitted. Recently, reaction to this neglect has been expressed in the form of theories which suggest that the character of Jesus' teaching and the religious awe in which his words were held were such as to guarantee their almost inviolable transmission.[18] Such conclusions have not found a widely favorable response; nevertheless, a more moderate yet persistent insistence on the relative historical reliability of the Gospel tradition is increasingly evident among many scholars,[19] who at the same time acknowledge the indispensability of the contribution and method of form criticism in research into the mission and message of Jesus.

The contemporary trend of research into the words and deeds of Jesus is

---

[17] One of the early responsible reactions to the form critics which is both appreciative and critical is found in B. S. Easton, *The Gospel Before the Gospels* (New York: Scribner's, 1928).

[18] See Harald Riesenfeld, *The Gospel Tradition and Its Beginnings* (London: A. R. Mowbray & Co., 1957), and B. Gerhardsson, *Memory and Manuscript: Oral Tradition and Written Transmission in Rabbinic Judaism and Early Christianity* (Uppsala, Sweden: C. W. K. Gleerup, 1961).

[19] See Amos Wilder, "Form-History and the Oldest Tradition," in *Neotestamentica et Patristica*, supplements to *Novum Testamentum*, VI (Leiden, Netherlands: E. J. Brill, 1962), 3-13; W. D. Davies, "Reflections on a Scandinavian Approach to 'The Gospel Tradition' " in *Neotestamentica et Patristica*, supplements to *Novum Testamentum*, VI (Leiden, Netherlands: E. J. Brill, 1962), 14-46. The latter article is a critique of Gerhardsson (see previous footnote).

characterized by a positive attitude toward the possibilities for new understanding afforded by the advances in the field of source- and form-critical studies. If form criticism has established the fact that the Gospel traditions continually bear witness to the interpretation of the early Church, its intensive study of the theological and practical interests of the emerging Church has enhanced the possibility of arriving at a more proximate, if not an absolute, understanding of the bedrock traditions of the historical Jesus. This increasing knowledge of the early Church's beliefs and practices has been supplemented by an ever-expanding knowledge of the Jewish background of Jesus' ministry. The sudden discovery of such unexpected evidence as the Qumran Scrolls, as well as a more adequate knowledge of various sects and the general historical situation in Palestine, provide a context most favorable to historical research.

It is common today to speak of a "new quest" for the historical Jesus.[20] It differs from the old nineteenth-century quest in its disavowal of any hopes to write a biography of Jesus.[21] It is generally agreed that methodological problems are far from solved. What is striking is the areas in which agreement is to be found.[22] A pioneering work in the new quest has been written,[23] and an increasing number of specialized studies, utilizing the critical insights of form criticism, but turning them to the positive task of understanding the words and deeds of Jesus, have appeared. One of the most important developments has been a critical but positive reaffirmation of the authenticity of the parables of Jesus in the synoptic tradition; important progress in their interpretation has shed new light on both the content of Jesus' message and the meaning of his mission.[24] There is a fresh new critical-but-appreciative understanding of the miracle tradition [25] in the gospels, and significant strides have been taken toward further illumination of the content and meaning of the ethical teaching of Jesus in the historical setting of his ministry.[26] It is within the limitations as well as the possibilities provided by the new situation in gospel studies that we now turn to a consideration of what can be said regarding the mission and message of Jesus of Nazareth.

---

[20] See J. M. Robinson, A New Quest of the Historical Jesus (Naperville, Ill.: Alec R. Allenson, Inc., 1959). The major impetus for this quest came from an address by Ernst Kaesemann now in English translation, in Essays on New Testament Themes (Naperville: Allenson, 1964).

[21] There are also major differences created by the new theological context in which the quest is pursued. We have not dealt with these. For a discussion see J. M. Robinson, op. cit.

[22] See the stimulating essay by J. M. Robinson, "The Formal Structure of Jesus' Message," in Current Issues in New Testament Interpretation, William Klassen and Graydon F. Snyder, eds. (New York: Harper & Row, 1962), pp. 91-110.

[23] Günther Bornkamm, Jesus of Nazareth (New York: Harper & Row, 1956).

[24] Consult the monumental work of J. Jeremias, The Parables of Jesus, 6th ed., tr. S. H. Hooke (New York: Scribner's, 1962).

[25] E.g., Reginald H. Fuller, Interpreting the Miracles (Philadelphia: Westminster, 1963).

[26] Representative of these new studies in the English-speaking world are Harvey K. McArthur, Understanding the Sermon on the Mount (New York: Harper & Row, 1960); T. W. Manson, Ethics and the Gospel (New York: Scribner's, 1960); W. D. Davies, The Setting of the Sermon on the Mount (Cambridge, England: Cambridge University Press, 1964).

THE CLAIMS
OF JESUS

For anyone in search of "what Jesus was

really like," it may be disconcerting to discover—as we have

in the last two chapters—that nearly all the material in the

gospels is kerygmatic in nature and that it does not provide

us with the basis for writing an objective biographical ac-

count of Jesus. The lack of reliable sequence in what is

available to us means that about all we can be sure of, as

far as the order of events in Jesus' life is concerned, is that the baptism came at the beginning of his public life and the Crucifixion came at the end. About the nature of his ministry and the content of his message, however, we are quite well informed, even when we take fully into account the modification and accretions that the tradition underwent before it reached the state that we now find in the gospels.[1]

Many New Testament scholars, especially in the Anglo-Saxon world,[2] think that there is one additional fixed point in the sequence of Jesus' career in the experience at Caesarea-Philippi (Mk. 8:27-33), when Peter confesses Jesus to be the Christ. As Wilhelm Wrede noted at the opening of this century, however, the confession of Peter does not mark a transition in the life of Jesus, since the "secret" of Jesus' messiahship had been disclosed prior to Caesarea-Philippi (according to Mark) and the secrecy about the messiahship continues after Peter's confession.[3] We have already noted in the previous chapter how freely Matthew and Luke and John relocate the incidents reported in the life of Jesus, and that they do so to serve their own literary and theological purposes, with no sense that there is an historical sequence to preserve.

THE ANCESTRY AND BIRTH OF JESUS

Although Mark begins his account of the ministry of Jesus at the time of Jesus' baptism (Mk. 1:1-6), both Matthew and Luke start their respective gospels with stories of the birth of Jesus. Matthew goes still farther back, and confronts his reader with the genealogy of Jesus. Mark is content to mention at a few points that Jesus had a family, and in one instance to give the names of his brothers (Mk. 6:3) while merely referring to his sisters. Matthew implies that Jesus is the son of a carpenter (Mt. 13:55), and John assumes that Jesus is the son of Joseph (Jn. 6:42).

A comparison of the genealogy given by Matthew (Mt. 1:1-17) with that given by Luke (Lk. 3:23-38) [4] shows that, beginning with David, the genealogies go their separate ways, Luke tracing his through Nathan, and Matthew following the royal line through Solomon. The lists meet at one point (Shealtiel and Zerubbabel), but continue to diverge down even to identifying two different persons as Joseph's father. In Matthew, Joseph is the son of Jacob (Mt. 1:16);

---

[1] An attempt to write a "factual" account of Jesus' life has been made by Ethelbert Stauffer, *Jesus and His Story* (New York: Macmillan, 1960). For a telling criticism of this effort, see Hugh Anderson, *Jesus and Christian Origins* (New York: Oxford, 1964), pp. 57-61.

[2] Vincent Taylor's *The Life and Ministry of Jesus* (New York: Abingdon, 1955) is a prime example of this approach. See especially pp. 140-144.

[3] The classic treatment of the messianic secret is Wilhelm Wrede, *Das Messiasgeheimnis in den Evangelien* (Göttingen: Vandenhoeck & Ruprecht), pp. 115-116. Originally published in 1901, it was re-issued unchanged in 1963.

[4] Luke's genealogy is conveniently set out in parallel to Matthew's on p. 1 of *Gospel Parallels* (New York: Nelson, 1957). Since Luke begins with Jesus and works backwards—to Adam!—it is helpful to have Luke's version printed in the same order as that of Matthew.

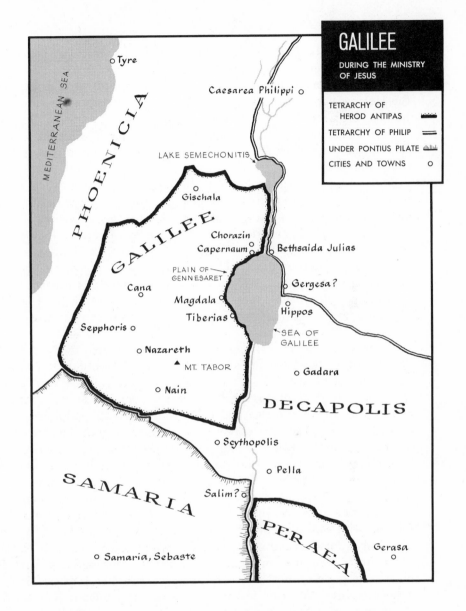

GALILEE

DURING THE MINISTRY OF JESUS

TETRARCHY OF HEROD ANTIPAS	▬▬▬
TETRARCHY OF PHILIP	═══
UNDER PONTIUS PILATE	⺤⺤⺤
CITIES AND TOWNS	o

MEDITERRANEAN SEA

o Tyre

Caesarea Philippi o

PHOENICIA

LAKE SEMECHONITIS

GALILEE

o Gischala

Chorazin o
Capernaum o ○ Bethsaida Julias

PLAIN OF GENNESARET

Cana o

Magdala o ○ Gergesa?

Tiberias o ○ Hippos

Sepphoris o

SEA OF GALILEE

o Nazareth

▲ MT. TABOR

o Gadara

o Nain

DECAPOLIS

o Scythopolis

o Pella

SAMARIA

Salim? o

PERAEA

o Samaria, Sebaste

Gerasa o

in Luke, Joseph is the son of Heli (Lk. 3:23). Valiant efforts have been made to reconcile the two conflicting genealogies,[5] but the results are not convincing. Neither Mark nor John nor Paul seems to know anything of this direct lineage, although Paul does refer—perhaps quoting an old tradition [6]—to Jesus as de-

---

[5] An elaborate attempt to harmonize the genealogies was presented by J. G. Machen, *The Virgin Birth of Christ* (New York: Harper & Row, 1930), who based his argument on the appeal to the distinction between actual and legal parentage (pp. 188-209). Luke, Machen proposes, gives the actual descent; Matthew traces the royal line from David.

[6] The possibility that Paul is here using a formula developed by others is discussed by C. K. Barrett, *The Epistle to the Romans* (New York: Harper & Row, 1957), pp. 18-21.

scended from David according to the flesh (Rom. 1:3). The probable explanation for the origin of these genealogies is that they were created by the early Church to demonstrate concretely the lineal connection of Jesus with David and the Hebrew patriarchs. The artificiality of the Matthean genealogy, by which he sets forth Jesus' ancestors in groups of 14 (Mt. 1:17) has long been recognized.[7] Names well known from Old Testament records are omitted from the list, and centuries are compressed in order to make each set of names come out to 14.

Since both genealogies come down to Joseph, rather than Mary, it is puzzling to know why the evangelists have included them along with accounts of the virgin birth of Jesus to Mary, since they establish the ancestry of Joseph, who—according to the virgin birth stories—was not the father of Jesus at all. It has sometimes been suggested that, since Joseph accepted Jesus into his family, the genealogies present Jesus' official ancestry, even though biologically he had none. But the fact that *two* ancestral lines are traced weakens the force of this argument. It would appear that the dogmatic belief in the Davidic descent of Jesus gave rise to these two independent attempts to construct a genealogy for Jesus.

A more extensive set of divergencies is evident between the Matthean account of the birth of Jesus and the one found in Luke. According to Matthew, Jesus was born in the house of Joseph (Mt. 2:11) in Bethlehem. When Herod learned from the Wise Men of this significant birth (2:1), which had apparently taken place up to two years earlier (hence the need for killing children of two years or less, Mt. 2:16), he sought to destroy the "king of the Jews." Joseph is warned in a dream to flee to Egypt, and then after Herod's death, is advised in a dream to move his place of residence to Nazareth, where he will be out from under the control of Herod's son, Archelaus. In addition to the repeated mention of dreams, by which God's will is communicated to Joseph and Mary and the Wise Men, Matthew's account points at each stage of the story to the fulfillment of scripture, by which God's will is achieved.[8]

In Luke's birth narrative, however, Mary and Joseph reside in Nazareth, but are in Bethlehem in connection with a Roman census (Lk. 2:1-4). They can find no accommodations, so that the new-born child is placed in a manger. The only visitors reported to have come are the shepherds from nearby fields. Eight days after Jesus' birth, the parents present their child to the Lord in the Temple at Jerusalem, following which they return to their home in Nazareth (Lk. 2:21-40).

These two accounts have been harmonized by popular Christian piety, rein-

---

[7] Cf. Vincent Taylor, *The Historical Evidence for the Virgin Birth* (Oxford: Clarendon Press, 1920), pp. 89, 90.

[8] The importance of the fulfillment of scripture in Matthew is discussed exhaustively by K. Stendahl, *The School of St. Matthew* (Uppsala, Sweden: C. W. K. Gleerup, 1954), pp. 143-217.

forced by countless Christmas cantatas and nativity pageants. But the details are not really compatible. Indeed, they do not really meet, except on the location of the birth in Bethlehem, and the names of Joseph, Mary, and Jesus. Once again, as in the case of the genealogies, we seem to have quite independent traditions about the birth of Jesus. Similarly, neither Mark nor Paul nor John knows anything of the virgin birth; at least there is no evidence of it in any other New Testament writings than the Gospels of Luke and Matthew. As we have already seen, Mark and John assume that Joseph is the father of Jesus. The explanation for this wide divergence of view about the origins of Jesus—that is, whether or not he was virgin-born—reflects the differing ways in which Jesus' relation to God was understood by the writers of the New Testament. Since the Church spoke of Jesus as "Son of God," there were those (represented by Luke and Matthew) who supposed that this must have involved a miraculous birth. Others, like Mark and Paul and John, could conceive of Jesus as Son of God in the sense that he was the man designated by God to fulfill a unique redemptive function in the Creation. He was, as C. K. Barrett has translated the credal formula quoted by Paul in Rom. 1:4:

> . . . in the sphere of the flesh, born of the family of David;
> in the sphere of the Holy Spirit, appointed Son of God.[9]

The birth stories, therefore, lie in the realm of the theology of the Church (probably toward the end of the first century); they tell us nothing of historical value about the family origins of Jesus. Beginning in the later second century, pious imagination tried to fill in the gaps in our knowledge creating legends about the miracles performed by Jesus as a child, but the Church has always regarded these accounts as apocryphal.[10] The history of Jesus begins only with the account of his baptism.

JESUS' BAPTISM BY JOHN

In all three of the synoptic gospels, Jesus' designation by God as his Son is directly connected with the story of his baptism at the hand of John the Baptist. But who was John that he should have played so important a role in the launching of the public ministry of Jesus?

Our information about John the Baptist is not limited to the references to him in the New Testament: Josephus mentions him appreciatively in connec-

---

[9] *The Epistle to the Romans* (New York: Harper & Row, 1957), p. 18.

[10] See the translation of these Infancy Gospels in Hennecke-Schneemelcher, *New Testament Apocrypha*, I (London: Lutterworth, 1959), 363-408; see especially the Protevangelium of James, the (Infancy) Gospel of Thomas. The stories include such fantastic accounts as Jesus' stretching a piece of wood that his father had cut too short, his transformation of some peevish playmates into goats, and his changing some clay pigeons into real birds.

tion with his account of the destruction of the army of Herod Antipas, son of Herod the Great (*ca.* A.D. 37). Antipas, Josephus tells us, was suspicious of John because of the persuasive powers that he exercised over the populace. Fearing that John might use his popularity with the masses to launch a revolt, Antipas had him imprisoned and finally executed. Although Josephus replaces the eschatological message preached by John according to the gospels with an innocuous moral appeal, he at least confirms the New Testament account of the widespread effects of John's preaching and the official disfavor which led to his death at the hands of Herod Antipas.[11]

According to the gospels, John was a preacher of repentance, calling men to turn from their evil ways and to prepare for the eschatological judgment which God was about to visit on the earth. The brief account in Mk. 1:1-6 is supplemented from Q by a résumé of his message (Mt. 3:7-10; Lk. 3:7-9), in which he denounces his contemporaries as unworthy to bear the name of children of Abraham, and warns of the fires of divine judgment that are about to fall. But further, Mark and the other gospels report John's proclaiming that "one mightier than I" is to follow him, who will carry out the judgment which he has only announced. These familiar details raise important and difficult historical and interpretive questions, however: What is John's background? What did baptism mean for him? Was the role of the Coming One expected by John the same as the role fulfilled by Jesus? Did John know Jesus beforehand, and did he subsequently acclaim Jesus as the Messiah?

These questions cannot be explored fully here,[12] but some summary observations may be offered. According to Luke 1, John was born of a priestly family in such a way that he was clearly set aside from before birth for a special place in the purpose of God. From Josephus [13] as well as from the Dead Sea Scrolls,[14] we learn of sects in the Jordan Valley that practiced daily lustrations. Whether they should be called baptisms or not is a matter of dispute,[15] but among Jewish sects in the first half of the first century the conviction seems to have been widespread that cleansing with water was a necessary step in preparation for the New Age. Notable among these movements was that associated with John the Baptist. Under his influence there came on the scene Jesus of Nazareth; through this influence, Jesus was launched on his public ministry.

For John, baptism was a way by which one might be cleansed now in order

---

[11] For a translation of the relevant section of Josephus' *Antiquities* (XVIII, 116-119), see C. K. Barrett's *New Testament Background* (London: SPCK, 1957), pp. 197, 198.

[12] A full examination of the historical questions relating to John is presented by C. H. Kraeling, *John the Baptist* (New York: Scribner's, 1951).

[13] Josephus, *Life of Josephus*, I. 2. 11, tr. W. Whiston, in *Harper Torchbook No. 74* (New York: Harper & Row, 1960), p. 277; also *Jewish War*, II. 8.5, p. 77.

[14] E.g., *Rule of the Community*, 5:13; 3:4-9.

[15] See W. H. Brownlee, "John the Baptist in the New Light of Ancient Scrolls," in K. Stendahl, ed., *The Scrolls and the New Testament* (New York: Harper & Row, 1956), pp. 33-53; H. H. Rowley, "The Qumran Sect and Christian Origins," in *From Moses to Qumran* (New York: Association Press, 1963), pp. 263-264, especially Note 4.

THE WILDERNESS OF JUDEA *through which passes the modern road from Jericho to Jerusalem. In the background are the Dead Sea and the delta of the Jordan River.*

to be pure when the fires of judgment swept over the earth in the Last Day. Among Jews, there was a practice known as *proselyte baptism,* by which one born a Gentile could become a member of the community of Israel through accepting circumcision and baptism.[16] It has been suggested that John thought that all Israel had disqualified itself to be the People of God, so that all now needed to come like proselytes and be baptized. But what seems to have been in John's mind was the creation of an eschatological community that was prepared and waiting for the New Age that would follow upon the divine judgment that was about to fall. John—or the tradition that informs us about him—saw in his work the fulfillment of the prophecy of II Isaiah:

> The voice of one crying in the wilderness,
> "Prepare the way of the Lord."

When Christians considered John as preparing the way of the Lord, it was not the way of Yahweh, but of the Lord Jesus Christ of which they thought. Accordingly, John came to be considered the forerunner of Jesus.

The evidence in the gospels suggests that John may not have understood Jesus to be the One through whom the kingdom of God would be established; indeed, he may not have recognized him at first in any special way. According to a Q tradition (Mt. 11:2-6; Lk. 7:18-23), John at the end of his life sent to Jesus to ask him if he were in fact the Coming One. Neither Mark nor Luke indicates that at the time of the baptism of Jesus, John took any special notice of Jesus, much less that he recognized him then as Messiah. Matthew

---

[16] A concise discussion of proselyte baptism is presented by G. R. Beasley-Murray, *Baptism in the New Testament* (New York: St. Martin's Press, 1962), pp. 18-31.

THE JORDAN VALLEY *at its lower end, near the traditional site of Jesus' baptism, looking toward the hills of Judea.*

and John have added this detail, but it is probably the result of later conflicts between the followers of John and those of Jesus rather than an authentic historical recollection (cf. Mk. 1:9-11 with Mt. 3:13-17 and Jn. 1:29-31). The hint of conflict between the two groups is present in the report of hostile relations between Jesus and John in Jn. 3:25-4:3.[17]

Although there is probably an historical basis for the tension between Jesus and John implied in the Gospel tradition, Jesus seemed to have respected John to the point of delaying the beginning of his public ministry until John was off the scene, in prison (Mk. 1:14; Mt. 4:12; Lk. 3:20; Jn. 3:24). Further, Jesus had words of highest praise for John, even though he deemed John's work to be only the last phase of the old era, before the kingdom of God began to break into the present (Mt. 11:11, 12).

The Gospel tradition reports that it was at the time of Jesus' baptism that God designated him as his Son (Mk. 1:11; Mt. 3:17; Lk. 3:22), as we have noted. It is likely that (1) Jesus' experience at the time of baptism was regarded by him as the moment of his divine call to the work of announcing the coming of God's kingdom; and (2) the story of this call was told by the early Church in the light of their acclamation of him as Son of God in whom the scriptures were fulfilled (with Mk. 1:11 cf. Isa. 42:1; 44:2). In view of the difficulties raised for the early Church by Jesus' having accepted baptism at the hand of John, it is scarcely conceivable that the Church would have invented the baptismal story. Baptism by John is one of the best-attested events of Jesus' career.

"THOU ART MY SON"

Among the messianic titles assigned to Jesus in the Gospel tradition, the first that the reader encounters (apart from the infancy stories) is "Son of God." This title is often thought of as affirming that Jesus possesses a divine nature

---

[17] This conflict is reconstructed by M. Goguel, *Life of Jesus* (New York: Macmillan, 1946), pp. 270-279.

which is in some way derived from God. The Greeks seem to have conceived of a god-man in this way, although the evidence for this belief is rather slim.[18] There was, however, a widespread belief in the Hellenistic world that kings were begotten by the gods. The term "Son of God" in the gospels was developed from the Christian interpretation of Ps. 2.7, as some ancient manuscript copies and early versions of Luke make clear. They read at this point:

> Thou art my Son; this day have I begotten thee.
> —LUKE 3:22

Together with other psalms of similar type and viewpoint, this psalm assumes that the king of Israel was God's vicegerent. Some scholars think there was a ceremony in ancient Israel held on the first day of the New Year at which the king was acclaimed as God's son—that is, as the one chosen and empowered by God to rule in his behalf over his People.[19] Sonship on these terms is a matter of function, rather than of supernatural birth or conception. The instances in the gospels where Jesus refers to himself as "Son" are few, and even in the one such verse which has the strongest claim of authenticity (Mk. 13:32), it is precisely the use of the term "Son" which is most suspect of being an addition of the later Church.[20] While Jesus surely spoke of God as Father— and did so in such an intimate way as to offend his contemporary Jews [21]—he seems not to have referred to himself in a special way as "Son."

"YOU ARE THE CHRIST"

Other titles which are given to Jesus in the Gospel tradition include Messiah (*Christos*, in Greek) and Lord (*kurios*, in Greek). Much has been written on the "messianic consciousness of Jesus"; actually, we have no access to the consciousness of Jesus, except through the testimony to him preserved in the gospels, and these as we have seen are all written from the post-Resurrection perspective in the light of which Jesus is acclaimed by faith as Lord and Christ. We should not be surprised, therefore, if the perspectives of faith affect the form and content of the tradition. To put it another way, it is to be expected that the early Church read back its views into the story of the pre-Cross, pre-Resurrection Jesus.

Even in the Gospel tradition, however, Jesus never uses the term "Christ"

---

[18] The evidence for Hellenistic use of "son of God" has been assembled by O. Cullmann, *Christology of the New Testament* (London: SCM Press, 1959), p. 272. The parallels with Philostratus' *Apollonius of Tyana* probably show dependence of the latter on the gospels, rather than that the evangelists copied the style and content of secular Hellenistic writers.

[19] See S. Mowinckel, *He that Cometh* (New York: Abingdon, 1956), especially pp. 56-95.

[20] See the discussion of the term "Son" in W. G. Kümmel, *Promise and Fulfillment* (London: SCM Press, 1957), pp. 39-43.

[21] Cf. G. Kittel, article on *abba* in *Theological Dictionary of the New Testament*, I (Grand Rapids, Mich.: Eerdmans, 1963), 6.

of himself. It appears only on the lips of his followers, as in Mk. 8:29; Mt. 16:16; Lk. 9:20. It is easy for the modern reader to blur over distinctions, so that wherever he sees any of the titles of Jesus—for example, Son of Man, Lord, Holy One of God, the Coming One—he automatically assumes that they are interchangeable terms for Messiah. But in fact, each of these comes out of a separate tradition, each has its own history and its own special connotations. "Messiah" is most often a specific term for the anointed king of Israel, as in Psalm 2, although it is also used of the anointed prophet (I Kings 19:16) or priest (Zech. 4:14) which refers to the king and the priest as anointed ones.[22] The primary meaning of "Messiah" in Jesus' time seems to have been the kingly ruler who would establish God's kingdom on earth, or who would prepare for God's own coming to rule over his Creation.

The political implications of this belief among the Jews were apparent to Rome, so that stern measures were taken to suppress messianic movements, as Josephus' writings repeatedly attest (*e.g., Jewish War,* Book II, Chapters 4 and 5). It is going beyond the evidence to say that Jesus repudiated political messiahship; indeed, he never commented on messiahship at all. Some interpreters, however, have seen in the Temptation stories (Mt. 4:1-11; Lk. 4:1-13)

---

[22] The theme of the two messiahs is now well documented in the Dead Sea Scrolls. See K. G. Kuhn, "The Two Messiahs of Aaron and Israel," in K. Stendahl, ed., *The Scrolls and the New Testament* (New York: Harper & Row, 1956), pp. 54-64.

an insight into the inner struggle through which Jesus passed in defining his role before God. As they stand in the tradition, the stories are stylized, allegorical representations of the determination of Jesus to fulfill God's purpose in God's way.[23] The role of Messiah was not a sharply defined one to which Jesus must conform, but a redemptive function in the purpose of God, the full implications and details of which would become apparent only after the Resurrection.

The title *kurios* ("lord" or "sir") is somewhat ambiguous, since it can be simply a form of polite address (Mk. 7:28) as well as a form of Christian confession (Jn. 20:28, "My Lord and my God!"). The lordship of Christ was affirmed by the Church only in the light of the Resurrection. His earthly life was viewed as the time of humiliation; the Resurrection was his exaltation as Lord. This is the point of the pre-Pauline hymn quoted in Phil. 2:8-10:

> And being found in human form he humbled himself
> and became obedient unto death, even death on a cross;
> Therefore God has highly exalted him and bestowed on him
> the name which is above every name,
> that at the name of Jesus every knee should bow . . .
> and every tongue confess that *Jesus Christ is Lord*,
> to the glory of God the Father.

Those places in the Gospel tradition where the term *kurios* is used to refer to Jesus, therefore, are probably all written in view of the early Church's confession of Jesus as Lord.

THE SON OF MAN

We have left for consideration until last the most common of all designations in the synoptic tradition: Son of Man. (The reader should notice that the RSV Bible does not capitalize "man." We prefer to use the capitalized version of the word when not citing scripture.) In popular understanding, the term points to the humanity of Jesus. While it is true that the Old Testament uses this phrase to stress man's humanity (most notably in Ezekiel), the phrase had taken on certain superhuman connotations in Judaism which must be presupposed for an understanding of the gospels' use of the phrase.

The first step in the process can be discerned in Dan. 7, where the kingdom of God is given to "one like a son of man" (Dan. 7:13). There the stress falls on the humanity of this figure (representing the faithful remnant of God's People: "the saints of the Most High") in contrast to the fantastic beasts which represent the wicked earthly kingdoms and which are destroyed by the coming of God's kingdom. In one section of the Book of Enoch [24] (Chapters

---

[23] See F. W. Beare, *Earliest Records of Jesus* (New York: Abingdon, 1962), pp. 42, 43.

[24] Although several fragments of the Book of Enoch have been found among the Dead Sea Scrolls, thereby guaranteeing that the Enoch writings are pre-Christian, none of the fragments includes parts of Chapters 37-71. Some scholars think the absence of this section is accidental, while others conclude that this section must be later and therefore post-Christian. See J. T. Milik, *Ten Years of Discovery in the Wilderness of Judaea* (SCM, 1959), p. 33.

37-71 in the Ethiopic versions), there is a figure, the Son of Man, whose coming brings about the establishment of God's kingdom. Although this writing may be post-Christian in its present form, it may nevertheless embody an idea that was abroad in pre-Christian Judaism. In the late (first century) Jewish apocalypse of IV Ezra, a figure called "the Man" appears, who is the agent of God's judgment in the last days, thus fulfilling a role identical with that of the Son of Man in the Book of Daniel. "The Man" is a common figure in oriental religions in the period of Hellenistic syncretism; [25] it was almost inevitable that this redemptive title and its functions should be recognized as appropriately applicable to Jesus Christ, who was viewed as God's final Chosen One to bring about the transformation of the whole Creation. The theme of the New (or Second) Man appears in Paul's Letter to the Romans (Rom. 5:12 ff.).

More important than the historical development of the "Son of Man" term, however, is the diversity of connotations that the term carries within the Gospel tradition itself. The Son-of-Man sayings in the synoptic gospels may be conveniently classified into three groups: (1) those that speak of the Son of Man as presently at work on earth; (2) those that predict his suffering and death; (3) those that announce his Coming in triumph and/or judgment.[26]

Typical of the first group are two stories from Mk. 2, one telling of Jesus' healing the paralytic (Mk. 2:1-12), and the other in which Jesus announces that the Son of Man is Lord of the sabbath (2:23-28). Since in Aramaic, the phrase "son of man" can mean simply "man," it has been proposed that Jesus is simply saying that man has power to forgive sins, that man is lord of the sabbath. In this view, the tradition has misunderstood the force of the Aramaic *bar-nasha* ("son of man") and has treated it as a title. Since Mk. 2:27 is speaking about "man," it is suggested that "Son of man" in verse 28 means only "man." A similar argument can be made for "Son of man" in Mt. 8:20, where the fate of man is contrasted with that of the beasts of the field: birds and foxes have resting places; "man" has none. If these sayings are authentic, then Jesus seems to have used the term "Son of man" in designating himself as the humiliated, suffering, Righteous One.[27] Although the term "Son of man" is not used, the motif of the Righteous One is a common one in certain of the psalms (*e.g.*, Psalms 25, 27, 38) and in the Wisdom of Solomon, 4-5, and could have provided the background for Jesus' designation of himself as Son of man in this sense. Another view which considers these sayings as not authentic,

---

[25] A thorough study of the complex beliefs about "the Man" are found in C. H. Kraeling, *Anthropos Son of Man* (New York: Columbia University Press, 1929). A brief summary of the material is presented by O. Cullmann, in *Christology of the New Testament* (London: SCM Press, 1959), pp. 137-152.

[26] This classification is developed by R. Bultmann, in *Theology of the New Testament*, I, (New York: Scribner's, 1951), 30-31.

[27] Thus E. Schweizer argues in "The Son of Man," in *Journal of Biblical Literature*, LXXXIX, Part II, June, 1960, 119-129.

but as based on actual words and claims of Jesus, is set forth in the section dealing with Jesus' authority (pp. 109-113).

Some of the sayings in which Jesus refers to himself as the Son of Man who is to suffer and die—that is, the second category named above—seem surely to come from the early Church rather than from Jesus himself. The three stylized predictions of the Passion, that follow upon Peter's confession in Mk. 8, sound like summaries of the Church's *kerygma* rather than authentic predictions by Jesus, especially since they detail at whose hands he will suffer and under what circumstances he will die and when he will be raised from the dead. Unless Jesus' suffering and death was a kind of charade in which he merely acted out a prescribed part, it is not likely that he knew in advance all the details of what he must undergo (cf. Mk. 8:31; 9:31; 10:33, 34; and parallel sayings in Luke and Matthew).

There are other Son of Man words, however, in which Jesus' Passion is predicted or anticipated in a more indirect way, and of these the authenticity cannot so quickly be affirmed or denied. Most difficult to account for as having been supplied by the early Church are the following passages:

> But first he [the Son of man] must suffer many things and be rejected by this generation.
>
> —LUKE 17:25

> ... and how is it written of the Son of man, that he should suffer many things and be treated with contempt?
>
> —MARK 9:12

Neither of these sayings gives details of the circumstances of Jesus' death; indeed, they do not even speak directly of death. Some scholars have insisted that in Jewish thinking of the time, the Son of Man was never associated with a sacrificial death for the redemption of others, while other scholars have pointed to the great importance attached by Judaism in the first century to the death of the martyrs as having redemptive value for the Jewish nation.[28] While recognizing that the detailed predictions of the Passion probably come from the early Church, it is possible to make a case for a saying like Lk. 17:25 as originating with Jesus, even though its present setting gives it a somewhat different force from its original intention.[29] There are other sayings, however, in which the Son of Man is not found, but in which Jesus seems clearly to have anticipated his death as a part of the purpose of God. The best such example is the dialogue between Jesus and the sons of Zebedee—James and John—who have asked for places of special favor in the coming kingdom of

---

[28] This view is summarized by E. Schweizer, *Lordship and Discipleship* (London: SCM Press, 1960), pp. 22-41.

[29] See W. G. Kümmel, *Promise and Fulfillment* (London: SCM Press, 1957), p. 71.

God and who are warned of the "baptism" of suffering and death that must precede the coming of glory in the kingdom (Mk. 10:35-40).[30] If these words— along with a similar declaration in Lk. 12:50—are taken as authentic, then Jesus foresaw both his death and the participation in the kingdom that God was soon to establish, though without connecting himself thereby with the Son of Man title. (In the next chapter we shall consider Jesus' attitude toward his death.)

It is with the third category of Son of Man words that we reach the group of sayings that seems to have the strongest claim to authenticity. In this group, Jesus seems to differentiate between himself and the coming Son of Man. Since the Son of Man in the Jewish tradition was an eschatological figure primarily, it is wholly appropriate that he should appear in these sayings as one who was to come. His Coming is connected with judgment and the vindication of God's faithful people; in Jesus' words, those who have been ashamed of him will be denounced by the Son of Man when he comes (Mk. 8:38). The saying appears in all three of the synoptic gospels, and in several different forms (Lk. 12:9, for example, reads: ". . . he who denies me before men will be denied before the angels of God"). A casual reading of these passages might lead one to think that Jesus is simply referring to himself in the third person under the title, "Son of man"; many readers of the New Testament draw this conclusion. Taking the words at face value, however, forces one to infer that Jesus is distinguishing between himself and the coming Son of Man. Similarly, he speaks in the third person of the coming Son of Man in Lk. 17:24, although in this case it is not primarily man's fate, but the suddenness of the Coming of the Son of Man that is in view. It seems more plausible to suppose that the early Church modified the words of Jesus so as to have him directly identify himself with the Son of Man than that the Church changed Jesus' statement about the Son of Man from the first to the third person. In the light of the Resurrection encounter, the early Church acclaimed Jesus as Son of man (cf. Mt. 16:13 with 16:15; in verse 13 the Son of man is mentioned, but it obviously means Jesus; in verse 15, the pronoun "I" is used by Jesus. Comparison with Mk. 8:27 and 29 shows that in the older form of the tradition, "I" was used in both instances). But Jesus himself during his ministry must have referred to the Son of Man as one who was yet to be revealed.

To affirm this, however, is not to deny that Jesus made any claims for himself in relation to the coming of the kingdom. When one examines Mk. 8:38 closely, he sees that the criterion by which one will stand or fall in the Day of Judgment by the Son of Man is the way in which one has responded in this life to Jesus. The Son of Man will at that time confirm one's response to Jesus

---

[30] Kümmel, op. cit., pp. 69-70. The authenticity of this passage is denied by R. Bultmann, in History of the Synoptic Tradition (New York: Harper & Row, 1963), p. 24, and challenged by F. W. Beare, in Earliest Records of Jesus (New York: Abingdon, 1962), pp. 197-200.

and his claims *now*. The requisite for entrance into the kingdom of God is faithful, obedient acceptance of Jesus' claims.

A MAN OF AUTHORITY

Alongside the tendency in the gospels to assign to Jesus messianic or christological titles, there runs the phenomenon which has been called "implicit christology." [31] That is, the authority with which he speaks and acts, and the interpretation of his words and deeds as the in-breaking of God's kingdom into the present, imply that he sees himself as one uniquely commissioned by God to prepare for the kingdom's coming. Jesus fulfills a kind of messianic office quite apart from the question as to whether or not he used messianic titles with reference to himself. Even if we attribute to the early Church all the titles, the function of God's agent in preparing for the coming of the New Age remains fixed in the oldest layers of the synoptic tradition, and presumably goes back to Jesus himself.

Overcoming Disease and the Demonic

Mark brings out these factors with great emphasis, but they are present in the Q material as well. The first of the claims made by Jesus or implied by his actions is that God has given him power over demons (Mk. 1:21-28). Closely related to this power of Jesus over the demons is his ability to heal, as in the case of Peter's mother-in-law (Mk. 1:29-31) and the paralytic who was brought to Jesus' house by friends (Mk. 2:1-12).

In some instances the healings are reported to have occurred at a distance from where Jesus was, or without his being aware that healing had taken place (Mk. 5:21-43). In the case of the two stories just mentioned, and in all of the miracle stories reported in Mk. 5 (and the parallel accounts in Matthew and Luke), there is a great deal of narrative detail, depicting the circumstances surrounding the afflicted person and the stages by which the healing took place. It is likely that these stories were embellished in the process of transmission in the early Church; some scholars think they were created by the Church as illustrations of the powers of Jesus. But even in the simplest accounts of demonic exorcisms and healing, the authority of Jesus is evident.

Sometimes an attempt has been made to provide a rationalistic explanation for these stories of exorcisms and healing by appeal to modern psychological techniques and particularly to psychosomatic medicine.[32] But such explanations are not really helpful. In the first place, they require us to read contemporary insights into first-century situations. And secondly, they do not account for the

---

[31] See R. Bultmann, *Theology of the New Testament*, I (New York: Scribner's, 1951), 43.
[32] For example, S. V. McCasland, *By the Finger of God* (New York: Macmillan, 1951).

meaning which the gospel writers and the Christian community as a whole saw in these events.

Fortunately, the Q source included traditions which do embody the primitive community's understanding of Jesus' actions in these exorcisms. In their present form, these traditions appear at a point where it is difficult to draw the line between Mark and Q: Mk. 3:23-27 overlaps with or is interwoven with a somewhat enlarged version of the same sayings in Mt. 12:25-29 and Lk. 11:17-22. Two themes stand out. First is the affirmation that the conflict with the demonic is really a battle between the kingdom (or rule) of God and the rule of Satan (meaning *adversary*). The same point is made with a changed figure in Mk. 3:27 and parallels: the "strong man" (= Satan) must be bound (*i.e.*, by Jesus) before what he now possesses can be taken away from him; that is, the world and its inhabitants, now under his sway, are to be freed from his domination by the power of the kingdom at work through Jesus.

The implication of these parabolic words is made explicit in the second theme: Jesus performs exorcisms "by the finger of God" (Lk. 11:20), and thereby is demonstrated that the kingdom of God has come into the present situation. Others may and do perform exorcisms, as Jesus acknowledges (Lk. 11:19), but Jesus is able to do his work of overcoming the demons because God's power [or spirit (Mt. 12:28)] is upon him. The house or kingdom of Satan, then, is the tradition's—and Jesus'—way of portraying the powers at work in the world that thwart God's purpose for man, that hold him enslaved, that warp and destroy man's existence. God's power is at work through Jesus to overcome these demonic forces and to set man free. In Mark's account of the ministry of Jesus, the demons recognize that their doom is assured by the coming of Jesus ("What have you to do with us, Jesus of Nazareth? Have you come to destroy us?"—Mk. 1:24), but Jesus orders them to be silent. The theme that Jesus demanded that all who recognized his authority be silent about it pervades much of Mark, although there is some contrary evidence that he told some on occasion to tell others what he had done (*e.g.*, Mk. 5:19).

On the basis of this evidence, a theory was proposed [33] that Mark (or the community for which he was spokesman) tried to account for the failure of Jesus' fellow Jews to recognize him as Messiah by asserting that he had insisted on keeping his messiahship a secret. While some of Jesus' injunctions to silence do seem to have come from the later tradition, for example Mk. 1:34, the claims to divine authority remain even when the use of the messianic titles is assigned to the later Church.

It is not appropriate, however, to make a complete break between what God was doing through Jesus and who he was or is. This comes out clearly in the question addressed to Jesus by John the Baptist, and in Jesus' answer. During John's imprisonment, he sent to Jesus to inquire, "Are you the one who is to

---

[33] By Wilhelm Wrede. See the brief discussion at the beginning of this chapter, and especially footnote 3.

come, or should we look for someone else?" (Mt. 11:3). Jesus replied: "Go and tell John what you hear and see; the blind receive their sight, and the lame walk, lepers are cleansed and the deaf hear, and the dead are raised up, and the poor have good news preached to them. And blessed is he who takes no offense at me." [34] We have had occasion to refer to this incident in another connection and will consider it again when we come to the question of Jesus' ministry to the outcasts ("poor"); but here it is important to note two aspects of his response: (1) Jesus does not answer the question directly, but throws the responsibility back on the questioner to assess the importance and source of authority in his acts of healing. The hearer must decide; Jesus will not decide the question for him. (2) The decision about the source of power at work through Jesus comes down finally, however, on the estimate of Jesus himself. Hence the force of the declaration about the blessedness of the one who does not take offense at Jesus. To combine the force of these two, Jesus rests his case on his words and acts; he makes no explicit claims for himself. Yet his response to the questioners clearly implies by its content and by its appeal to Isaiah (his answer is a mosaic of quotations from Isa. 29:18; 35:5; 61:1) that his work is God's working toward the establishment of his kingdom.

Authority in Dealing with Sinners

The authority of Jesus in forgiving sins is set forth explicitly in the familiar story of the paralytic who was lowered through the roof of the house where Jesus was. His persistent friends, unable to reach Jesus by the usual means because of the throng in and around the house, broke open the packed-earth roof and let their friend down into the room below where Jesus was. Jesus, seeing their faith, healed the man, the story runs (Mk. 2:1-12). But inserted in the middle of the story (from verse 5 to 10) is a report that Jesus pronounced the forgiveness of the man's sins, and then, in reply to the charge of blasphemy leveled by his scribal opponents, he declared that it was as Son of Man that he had authority to forgive sins.

The section of the story from verse 5 to 10 reflects the old Jewish idea that sickness is the result of sin; in this narrative, Jesus cures both cause and effect. It is likely, however, that this part of the story is told in the light of the early Church's belief that man (= Son of Man) has been authorized by God to forgive sins. The same viewpoint is given in a unique passage in Mt. 18:18, which is surely not an authentic saying, but the Church's justification of its exercise of authority by appeal to an alleged saying of Jesus.[35]

---

[34] This passage is considered a product of the early Church by R. Bultmann, in *History of the Synoptic Tradition* (New York: Harper & Row, 1963), p. 23. The authenticity of the words is defended by W. G. Kümmel (*Promise and Fulfillment*. London: SCM Press, 1956), pp. 109-111, following M. Dibelius.

[35] See p. 286. For an analysis of the Mk. 2 passage, see F. W. Beare, *Earliest Records of Jesus* (New York: Abingdon, 1962), pp. 76, 77.

There is an important strand of authentic material in the gospels which depicts Jesus as offering two basic challenges to the view widely held in his time that God was chiefly concerned with "good people." On the one hand, Jesus by word and act befriends the religious outcasts; on the other hand, he announces that God's joy over the repentant sinner exceeds his concern for the "righteous."

In a passage which can scarcely have been invented by the early Church (Mt. 11:16-19), since it places Jesus in a somewhat unfavorable light, he contrasts the reaction of his fickle contemporaries to the ascetic John ("he has a demon") with their response to him in his friendship for tax collectors (hated collaborators with Rome) and sinners ("a glutton and a drunkard"). Jesus' action in accepting invitations (Mk. 2:13-17) or inviting himself to the home of the religiously disapproved (Lk. 19:1-10) furnishes the evidence that he believed God through him was calling the outcasts to repentance in preparation for the coming of God's kingdom. He knows that many, like John the Baptist, will find his befriending sinners and outsiders to be scandalous (Mt. 11:6).

In his parables he portrays God as one who takes the initiative in calling the outsiders into the fellowship of his People. For example, the Parable of the Great Supper (Lk. 14:15-24) seems intended to picture the People of God gathered in the New Age; the religiously respectable have declined the invitation to participate, while the outcasts and outsiders have responded to the offer and are in the kingdom. The Parable of the Lost Son (Lk. 15:11-32) is really the portrait of the Joyous Father, who rejoices at the return of his dissolute son, even while the prosaic, stay-at-home brother sulks and refuses to share in the festivities. It is the despised Samaritan who is honored as the one who obeyed the command to love one's neighbor, rather than the pious and scrupulous religious leaders (Lk. 10:29-37). An even more direct and forceful word is attributed to Jesus (in the Q source), which warns that those who pride themselves on being children of Abraham, Isaac, and Jacob may well be excluded from the kingdom, while men "from east and west" will "sit at table in the kingdom of God" (Mt. 8:11, 12; Lk. 13:28, 29). In this way, Jesus redefined the requirements for being part of the People of God and therefore for sharing in the life of the New Age. What is required, Jesus announced, was willingness to accept God's favor as a gift to be received, rather than as a merit to be earned.

Nowhere is this view of God more forcefully set forth than in the difficult Parable of the Laborers in the Vineyard, according to which all, regardless of the length of time they labored in the fields, receive the same. No justification for this seeming inequity is offered; the lord of the vineyard simply asks his disgruntled critics, "Do you begrudge me my generosity?" (Mt. 20:1-15). It expresses the same understanding of what God is like as is declared in the familiar words of Jesus:

[God] makes his sun rise on the evil and on the good, and sends rain on the just and on the unjust.

—MATTHEW 5:45

But it is not only the general providence of God that is described by Jesus; it is rather the joy of God at the restoration of what had been lost. The Parables of the Joyous Housewife, glad for the recovery of her lost coin, and the Rejoicing Shepherd, happy over the return of his lost sheep, depict the nature of God as One who rejoices that his estranged creatures are restored and reconciled. In this way, Jesus not only transforms the picture of God prevalent among his Jewish contemporaries, but he by implication redefines the way by which one may participate in the common life of the People of God.

Authority to Redefine the Law

In first-century Judaism, there was virtually unanimous agreement that the seat of authority was Torah, the Law given by God through Moses. As we have seen (Chapter 2), some groups thought the Law should be supplemented by other authoritative writings (Pharisees); others thought the scriptures needed a special kind of interpretation (the Qumran Essenes). Some clung exclusively to the Law itself (Sadducees), while others felt the need for an on-going process of interpretation (Pharisees). But each of these positions was essentially a variation on the theme of the eternal, binding authority of the Law. Although there is considerable doubt that Jesus spoke these words, Matthew quotes Jesus as affirming this conservative position with respect to the Law:

For truly, I say to you, till heaven and earth pass away, not an iota, not a dot, will pass from the law until all is fulfilled.

—MATTHEW 5:18

Almost certainly, the present form of the section of the Sermon on the Mount (Mt. 5-7) which runs from Mt. 5:21 to 48 has been given to it by the evangelist. This is apparent in the repeated phrases, "you have heard it has been said . . . but I say to you" which recur in Matthew (5:21, 27, 31, 33, 38, 43), but which are not found at all in the Lukan form of the same passages. But in spite of this Matthean modification of the tradition (see Chapter 12), there has been faithfully preserved the fact that Jesus did challenge the Law in detail and in different ways: the Law permitting divorce and remarriage was rejected in favor of the insistence of the permanency of the relationship intended by God in creating male and female (cf. Mt. 5:31 f. with Mk. 10:11, 12). He insisted that the commandments were basically ineffective, since a lustful look was in reality tantamount to adultery and a hateful attitude was the equivalent of murder.

Beyond this set of antitheses between Jesus' teaching and the Law, he challenged the validity of the ceremonial cleansing laws and commended the setting aside under certain circumstances of the sabbath law, which prohibited all work on the seventh day (Mk. 7:15; 2:23-28). Though not without precedent or parallel in Judaism of the period, these were revolutionary proposals, especially if we regard Mk. 2:27 as authentic: "The sabbath was made for man, not man for the sabbath." Many commentators, however, think that the story as it stands has been reworked in the light of the early Church's conflict with Judaism over sabbath observance, so that the original form of the words of Jesus is no longer recoverable. Nevertheless, his action on the sabbath in the healing of the man with the withered hand is one that shows that the inbreaking of the kingdom as evident in Jesus' power to heal is undermining even the venerable law of the sabbath. From the standpoint of official Judaism, it is no wonder that Jesus was regarded as a subversive who threatened its very foundations by his setting aside the Law on no other authority than that which he claimed to have from God. Without training in rabbinic interpretation, without credentials or sanction from known authorities, he exercised authority on his own, and claimed God was with him.

ENTERING THE KINGDOM

Jesus declared that man's fate in the day of the Coming of the Son of Man turned upon his response to Jesus now (Mk. 8:38). This astounding claim is found in other forms in the synoptic tradition (cf. Lk. 12:9; Mt. 10:33) but the point is in each case the same: the decision for or against Jesus is an eschatological decision, by which one's destiny before God is determined. Those who acknowledge him as master are expected to do what he says (Lk. 6:46). But what did he say about entering the kingdom?

First, it is to be received as a gift; it is not bestowed as a reward for faithful service. It is not the noble, or the honored, or the esteemed of this world who receive the kingdom, but the poor in spirit (Mt. 5:3), the hungering, the persecuted (Mt. 5:6, 10). In all probability, the Lukan form of these Beatitudes ("Blessed are you poor. . . ."—Lk. 6:20) is the original; Matthew has shaped them into general statements, whereas Luke has retained their form as eschatological promises ("you are poor now; you shall possess the Kingdom"). Although the following words are likely to have originated in the early Church rather than with Jesus, they accurately display the expectation that Jesus' followers received from him concerning the coming of the kingdom:

> Fear not, little flock, for it is your Father's good pleasure to give you the kingdom.
>
> —LUKE 12:32

The early Church did, however, soon set about establishing structures of authority for controlling admission to the kingdom of God. This is evident especially in Matthew, where twice there is repeated the theme that the authority over admission to the kingdom has been given to the apostles (Mt. 16:19; 18:18). These passages are found only in Matthew, and have no counterpart in the other synoptic gospels. They come almost certainly from a time when the Church had begun to struggle with the question of authority within the life of the community, as we see to have been the case in Paul's dealings with the church at Corinth (I Cor. 5:3 ff.). The community, recalling the authoritative way in which Jesus spoke of entering the kingdom, sought to transfer this authority to itself. Elsewhere, however, we see the later Gospel tradition [36] retaining the belief that admission to the kingdom was the consequence of God's gracious action:

> Come, O blessed of my Father, inherit the kingdom prepared for you from the foundation of the world.
>
> —MATTHEW 25:34

The fact that admission to the kingdom is not a reward does not exclude the possibility that rewards may be received by those who enter the kingdom. And here again the promise is bound up with the response which must be given to Jesus:

> Truly, I say to you, there is no one who has left house or brothers or sisters or mother or father or children or lands . . . who will not receive a hundredfold now in this time . . . and in the age to come eternal life.
>
> —MARK 10:29, 30

This is a strange saying, since it alone in the tradition speaks of the reward that is to be received "now"; however, its difficulty speaks *for* rather than *against* its authenticity. In any case, it points to the claim of Jesus that response to him—or if Luke's version is correct, to the kingdom which he proclaimed as coming (Lk. 18:29)—determines man's standing in the Age to Come.

THE COMING OF THE KINGDOM

The first thing that we learn about Jesus' public ministry in Mark's account is that he appeared in Galilee announcing:

> The time is fulfilled, and the kingdom of God is at hand; repent, and believe in the gospel.
>
> —MARK 1:15

We have already seen earlier in this chapter that the conflict of Jesus with the demons was understood by him to betoken the overthrow of the kingdom of

---

[36] The special viewpoint of Matthew's gospel is examined more fully in Chapter 12.

Satan and the inbreaking of the kingdom of God. Thus far, however, we have not considered what the phrase "kingdom of God" means, and what Jesus asserted to have been the time and circumstances of its "coming."

When we use the term "kingdom" it usually conveys the meaning of realm or territory over which kingly power is exercised. The Greek word *basileia*, which is translated in English as "kingdom," is itself to be understood as a translation of the Hebrew word *malkuth*, which means "kingly power." In Psalm 145, for example, we have set in parallel with each other "thy kingdom," "thy power." "thy mighty deeds," "thy dominion," and again in conclusion, "thy kingdom" (vv. 10-13). Set as this is in the context of extolling God as King, it is evident that *malkuth* is a verbal noun of action, describing the effective exercise by God of his kingly authority and power. But the word took on more precise connotations in the intertestamental period; under the impact of Jewish apocalypticism, "kingdom" came to mean the final state of the Creation when everyone and everything are subjected to the will of God. Usually, this was conceived as occurring indirectly through the Messiah, or else the Messiah brought about a transitional situation which then gave way to the final state where God himself was king.

To speak of the kingdom of God as "at hand" (or more precisely, as having drawn near) is not to affirm merely that God is always ready to take control when men submit to his will, but that a new situation is about to occur in which the apocalyptic promise of God's kingdom will be fulfilled. The word used by Jesus for time (in Mk. 1:15) is a term in Greek which focuses on the strategic or decisive moment of time (*kairos*), rather than on the notion that qualitatively a sufficient amount of time has passed for such an event to occur (*chronos*). (The distinction between these two Greek words has often been overdrawn.)

How near in time the coming of the kingdom was for Jesus is shown in his declaration to his followers:

> Truly, I say to you, there are some standing here who will not taste death before they see the kingdom of God come with power.
>
> —MARK 9:1

Attempts have been made to blunt the force of this statement, since it appears not to have been fulfilled.[37] The first generation of the Church died and the kingdom did not come in any visible way. It has been proposed that the kingdom came at the Resurrection, or at Pentecost when the Spirit was poured out, but there is no evidence whatsoever that the New Testament writers so understood the promise as having been fulfilled. Others have proposed that the kingdom comes when the Church meets in worship, especially in the celebration

---

[37] For a concise history of these interpretational developments see N. Perrin, *The Kingdom of God in the Teaching of Jesus* (Philadelphia: Westminster, 1963), especially pp. 13-57.

of the Lord's Supper,[38] or in identifying the present moment of decision as the time when the kingdom "comes." [39] The nonfulfillment of the expectation must not prevent us from seeing the original force of the promise, however: although Jesus refused to engage in date-setting or other common forms of apocalyptic speculation (cf. Mk. 13:32), he predicted that the rule of God would be consummated within the lifetime of his followers. It is inconceivable that the early Church would have introduced such a saying, since it was and is a problem for the Church in its estimate of the words of Jesus.

Jesus' message of the coming of the kingdom was not limited to predictions about the future: he pointed to his own actions as signs that the powers of the kingdom, which would be fully disclosed in the Day of Consummation, were already manifesting themselves in the present. The classic word on this is Lk. 11:20, which we have already looked at in connection with our discussion of Jesus' authority over the demons (p. 107).

> If it is by the finger of God that I cast out [demons], then the kingdom of God has come upon you.

In offering this assessment of the significance of his own work, Jesus attracted the hostility of the religious leaders, who sought from him some unambiguous, outward indication that God was behind what he was doing. To them he replied:

> The kingdom of God is not coming with signs to be observed; nor will they say, "Lo, here it is!" or "There!" for behold, the kingdom of God is in the midst of you.
>
> —LUKE 17:20-21

Some interpreters have rendered the Greek for "in the midst of you" as "within you," thereby claiming that the kingdom is a spiritual reality within man, rather than a future, apocalyptic reign. This interpretation, which received its classic formulation in Adolf von Harnack's What Is Christianity?,[40] has enjoyed wide popularity, but it cannot be supported by an examination of Jesus' teaching on this subject as a whole. Rather, there is strong evidence that the meaning is: the signs of the kingdom are not external, confirmatory proofs given by God to establish publicly that Jesus' work is God's activity in establishing his kingdom; they are acts of mercy and works of liberation in which faith can discern

---

[38] Thus C. H. Dodd, in Apostolic Preaching in the New Testament (New York: Harper & Row, 1951), pp. 93, 94.

[39] Thus R. Bultmann, in Jesus and the Word (New York: Scribner's, 1958), p. 131. This interpretation calls for the transformation of eschatology from a term depicting the consummation of the creation history to one describing the discovery of meaning in the life of the individual. See R. Bultmann, The Presence of Eternity (New York: Harper & Row, 1957), especially pp. 150-155.

[40] Originally published in German in 1900; translated into English and republished (New York: Harper & Row, 1957) in the Harper Torchbook series. This view is wholly compatible with philosophical idealism, especially that of Kant with his "moral law within."

and from which it can infer that God is at work through Jesus preparing for the coming of his kingdom.

This interpretation finds support in another reply of Jesus to the request for a confirmatory sign. His response appears in the Synoptic tradition in two different forms. In Mk. 8:11-12, the Pharisees are reported to have asked for a sign from heaven (*i.e.*, for God's direct attestation of Jesus). Jesus replied in words which carry the force of a Semitic oath, "No sign shall be given." The point of his statement is that "signs" are not available on request. His actions carry the force of signs for those who can see within them the work of God, but he will not perform a "sign" as a form of self-vindication.

The other form of this saying preserved in the tradition appears in Q: Lk. 11:29-32 and Mt. 12:38-42. The saying has been added to, as is most evident from the Matthean addition (Mt. 12:40) which makes the sign of Jonah refer to the death and resurrection of Jesus, even though the timing ("three days and three nights") scarcely fits. Possibly Lk. 11:31 and 32 have also been added to the original saying, in the light of the early Church's identification of Jesus as the Son of Man. But since the judgmental role of the Son of Man is described as taking place for "this generation" (Lk. 11:30), the saying must have arisen before the passing of the first generation of Christians raised the acute problem of the delay of the Coming of Christ. Standing alone, apart from its present context, the sign of Jonah is the impact of the message and messenger of repentance, calling men to prepare themselves for the judgment that will precede the coming of God's kingdom. Jesus' words and works are the criterion by which men will stand or fall in the judgment, in the Day of the Son of Man. No external aids in the form of miracles-on-demand will be offered; they must decide for themselves what they see in him.

FOLLOWING JESUS

In addition to the claims made for Jesus and by him, the synoptic tradition includes material in which Jesus addresses his hearers with an appeal to follow him. What sort of claim does Jesus make upon his followers? [41]

The account of Jesus' call to his disciples (Mk. 1:16-20) may well summarize what was in fact a process. If there is historical validity to the report in the Gospel of John about the earlier relationship between Jesus and those disciples who were formerly followers of John the Baptist (Jn. 1:35-51), then the "call" described in Mk. 1 (and parallels) would be a summons to resume an association that had been broken off after Jesus' return from the Jordan to Galilee. To be a follower of Jesus demands a loyalty to him and his work; it is not merely a matter of adopting his point of view or subscribing to his ideas. It involves

[41] See on the matter of discipleship Eduard Schweizer, *Lordship and Discipleship* (London: SCM Press, 1960), especially Chapter 1, pp. 11-21.

close association with him in his itinerant preaching and teaching, and participation in the kind of work in which he engaged.

It is difficult to determine the extent to which the disciples were specifically commissioned and empowered to carry further Jesus' work during his lifetime, since the gospels in their present forms read back into the pre-Cross period formal accounts of Jesus' sending the disciples—sometimes anachronistically called by the early Christian term, apostles!—which can only have developed after the Resurrection and in subsequent decades. In Matthew 10, for example, the account of the sending of the 12 disciples must have been written much later than the time of Jesus, since it envisions situations which came about only later in the first century, and since it draws on a late source in Mark (*ca.* A.D. 70). Luke's own version of the sending of the apostles (in addition to the one he reproduces from Mark; cf. Mk. 6:6 ff. with Lk. 9:1 ff.) is told in the light of Luke's convictions about the mission of the Church to the Gentiles, here represented symbolically in the form of the Seventy. (There was a belief in the first century that the number of the nations was 70 or 72 in all. See pp. 305-306.)

In spite of the modification of the tradition in the light of the changed situation in which the Church found itself, there is no reason to doubt that behind the stories of the sending of the Twelve (or Seventy) is an authentic strand, according to which Jesus commissioned his followers to share in and further the work of preparing men for the coming of the kingdom of God. Although the question of the disciples in Mk. 9:28 and the answer in v. 29 are placed in an artificial setting (the remarks about the inability of the disciples to deal with the demon seem to be added to the story), it is nevertheless presupposed that the disciples do perform exorcisms and that on some occasions they failed. Their success in exorcisms and healings in the post-Resurrection time is described in Acts (*e.g.*, 3:1 ff.; 5:12 ff.; 14:8 ff.). In John's gospel, Jesus' followers are told that after the Spirit has come, they will be able to do even greater works than those performed by Jesus (Jn. 14:12). The historical beginnings of this later development seem to lie in the participation of the disciples in the activities of Jesus' ministry.

Jesus' encouragement to his followers in the proclamation of the Gospel of the kingdom is the point of several of his best-known parables: the Sower, the Drag-Net, the Weeds and the Wheat (Mk. 4:3-8; Mt. 13:24-30; 13:47-48). In each case, the later Church has appended interpretations to these parables (Mk. 4:13-20; Mt. 13:36-43; 13:49-50), which have had the effect of shifting the point of the parable [42] from the proclaimer of the Gospel to the hearer, so that the appeal of the parables is now, "Be the right kind of hearer." Originally, the import of the parables was that the preacher of the Good News

---

[42] For a discussion of the change of audience in the interpretation of the parables see J. Jeremias, *The Parables of Jesus*, rev. ed. (New York: Scribner's, 1963), especially pp. 33-48.

should be prepared for mixed results from his work ("thirty-fold . . . sixty-fold," "good and bad fish," "wheat and weeds"), but that in spite of this, God would achieve a significant outcome. Jesus called his hearers to proclaim the Gospel; the results were to be left up to God and his purposes.

Leaving Everything

Mark represents Peter as the spokesman for the disciples in reminding Jesus that in following him, they have left everything behind—business, family, means of livelihood, security (Mk. 10:28). Their decision to leave all was considered by Jesus to be a necessary part of their discipleship, since he declared to be unfit for the kingdom those who looked back longingly to what they had left behind (Lk. 9:62) or who refused to respond to the invitation to prepare for its coming because of preoccupation with affairs of this world, commendable and constructive though they might be (Lk. 14:15-21).

Among other sacrifices that the disciples were called upon to make was the willingness to relinquish religious respectability. Jesus had befriended religious outcasts; he had chosen a tax-collector for membership in the inner circle of his followers (Mk. 2:13-14). There is no trait of Jesus that comes through the tradition more clearly than that he violated the rules of social and religious separatism that were prevalent in Judaism of his day, and that he did so, not in the name of irreligion, but as a part of his claim that God was working through him to prepare for the New Age. His critics asked:

> "Why does he eat with tax collectors and sinners?" And when Jesus heard it, he said to them, "Those who are well have no need of a physician, but those who are sick; I came not to call the righteous, but sinners."
>
> —MARK 2:16, 17

To become a follower of Jesus meant to align oneself with, among others, this collection of outcasts and religious outsiders.

Discipleship also involved a break with one's family. Jesus himself was mis-understood by his own family, and seems to have been suspected of being mad. The tradition utilized by Mark beginning at 3:21 appears to have had quite another meaning than the one given it by Mark, who charges the Pharisees with having accused Jesus of madness. The text reads smoothly, however, from Mk. 3:21 to 31, omitting verses 22 to 30. In this case, the meaning is restored when we see that the Greek (literally, "those of him") referred originally to his family, as verse 31 confirms. The actual situation was that his family came to take him away on the assumption that his claims and his extraordinary powers were indications that he was "beside himself." He refused, however, to heed their appeal to leave quietly, and declared instead that in the light of the inbreaking kingdom, the whole notion of family and family obligations must be reconceived: what is primary is to do the will of God (Mk. 3:35).

The Impending Crisis

The prospect for the disciple was a sobering one, not only because of the general expectation of hostility and misunderstanding, but because there was to be an eschatological crisis which would bring the present Age to a close and bring in the New Age. The crisis is directly described in such passages as the Synoptic Apocalypse (Mk. 13; Mt. 24-25; Lk. 21), where the original words of Jesus have been added to considerably in the light of the destruction of Jerusalem (see especially Lk. 21:20; cf. Mk. 13:14), as a consequence of the growing hostility of official Judaism toward the Church in the later first century, and as a result of the problem created by the delay of the Consummation (Mk. 13:31-37).[43]

But the eschatological crisis is also pointed to less directly in the parables of Jesus.[44] The blindness of his hearers and their preoccupation with their own pursuits is as grave as that of the rich farmer who foolishly supposed he could guarantee his own future even up to the very night that he died (Lk. 12:16-20). God's visitation of judgment will not be endlessly delayed: like the farmer who allows a fruit tree a few more chances to produce before he cuts it down (Lk. 13:6-9), or like the members of the wedding party who were unprepared for the bridegroom when he came at a late hour (Mt. 25:1-13), so his hearers will not be ready for the judgment that will fall unless they now repent. More shocking is the Parable of the Unjust Steward, which seems on the surface to violate all our principles of justice. But it is used by Jesus as an argument from the lesser to the greater: that is, if a crafty, unscrupulous steward has the shrewdness to make ready for the crisis that will come when his master finds him out and dismisses him, how much more should Jesus' hearers prepare themselves now for the coming of the New Age by responding in faith to the Good News (Lk. 16:1-8)? Jesus exhorts his hearer to make ready like the wise man who built his house on a secure foundation (Mt. 7:24-27) for the eschatological crisis that is impending.

We have already considered the question of the time of the eschatological crisis, and have concluded that although Jesus did predict the coming of the kingdom in power before the passing of the then present generation, he did not engage in specific statements as to the exact time and circumstances of its coming. Rather, he urged his listeners to make their decisions now, before it was too late. Only thus could they be certain that, when they sought to enter the kingdom, they would not confront a closed door (Lk. 13:25).

---

[43] See the discussion of the Synoptic Apocalypse in Chapter 11.

[44] See J. Jeremias, op. cit., pp. 160-198.

On Being Perfect

To be a follower of Jesus was far more demanding than the superficial reading of the Sermon on the Mount might lead one to suppose. The so-called "Golden Rule" ("As you wish that men would do to you, do so to them."— Lk. 6:31) is neither the heart nor the high point of the teachings of Jesus. Similar utterances are to be found in one form or another in the writings of most of the world's great religions. What is far more radical is the command, "You must be perfect" (Mt. 5:48), together with the implications that are spelled out in the same context. Judaism knew love of neighbor as a part of its ethical heritage (Lev. 19:18), although because of the exclusiveness of the nation this tended in practice to mean love of one's Jewish neighbor. According to Mt. 5:43, Judaism also taught hatred of one's enemies. This attitude cannot be documented from the Old Testament, but it was taught at Qumran.[45] Jesus, however, enjoins his hearers to go far beyond the commandment: even one's enemies are to be the objects of love.

Equally radical is the basis for Jesus' ethical appeal. He does not suggest that such action as love of enemies will be beneficial in the long run or that it will evoke similar attitudes from one's opponents. Rather, he appeals directly to the nature of God: man should act in love toward his enemies because God acts in mercy with compassion on all men, sending sun and rain on evil and good alike. Since man is a creature of God, nothing less than the love and mercy of God is the standard which man is called upon to achieve:

> You, therefore, must be perfect, as your heavenly Father is perfect.
> —MATTHEW 5:48

Losing One's Life

In both Mark and the Q source there is preserved for us in several different forms and in different contexts the word of Jesus:

> Whoever would save his life will lose it, and whoever loses his life for my sake will find it.
> —MATTHEW 10:39; 16:25; MARK 8:35; LUKE 9:24; 17:33

When a man decides to become a follower of Jesus, he must realize that his obedience may be extremely costly, even to the point of his losing his life. There can be no compromise with other attachments and obligations; the call to follow Jesus must take precedence over all the rest:

---

[45] Discussed by W. D. Davies in *The Setting of the Sermon on the Mount* (Cambridge: Cambridge University Press, 1964), pp. 245-248.

> If any one comes to me and does not hate his own father and mother
> and wife and children and brothers and sisters, yes, and even his own
> life, he cannot be my disciple.
>
> —LUKE 14:26

Before one even sets out to follow, he should weigh carefully what is involved
in order to carry through on his intentions. Like a farmer who prepares to build
a watchtower in his field or like a king making preparations for war, one must
be ready to pay the price, to provide sufficient strength to fulfill one's commit-
ments (Lk. 14:28-32).

We have no way of telling when the full import of this teaching came through
to the disciples. If we consider as authentic the word of Jesus about taking up
one's cross as a part of following him (Mk. 8:34; Mt. 16:24; Lk. 9:23), then
the disciples should have been well aware of what the cost of discipleship
would be. (Luke has spiritualized the force of this word of Jesus by adding the
term "daily"; originally, it seems to have referred to the willingness to accept
martyrdom, which would have had special relevance if Mark was written in
Rome not long after the martyrdom of Peter.) [46] If we were to accept the
genuineness of the predictions of the Passion, then it would be difficult to explain why the disciples did not realize the consequences of their associations
with Jesus. It is likely, however, that the seriousness of discipleship became real
to them only in the light of the Crucifixion. In Mark's account (10:38-39),
shortly before the Crucifixion the two disciples, James and John, asked for
places of special favor in the Age to Come. Jesus replied:

> Are you able to drink the cup that I drink, or to be baptized with the
> baptism with which I am baptized? And they said to him, "We are
> able."

Subsequent events were to show that they were not.

---

[46] See F. W. Beare, *Earliest Records of Jesus* (New York: Abingdon, 1962), pp. 140-141.

THE CROSS
OF JESUS

The gospels help to prepare the reader for

Jesus' death by presenting in dramatic fashion his decision

to leave Galilee and go to Jerusalem. Jesus' public ministry

was concentrated in Galilee and the regions immediately

adjoining, according to the synoptic gospels. The Gospel of

John describes an extended ministry of Jesus in the Jordan

Valley (Jn. 3:22-4:2), and much of the action in this gospel

takes place in Jerusalem (Jn. 5, 7, 8, 9, 10-20). Since John's

THE MOUNT OF OLIVES *stands out in the background above the eastern hill of Jerusalem. The domed structure is the Dome of the Rock—a Muslim shrine erected in the seventh century A.D.—which stands on the site of the altar of sacrifice of the Jewish Temple.*

gospel concentrates on discourse material, rather than on narrative, it seems unwarranted to assume that Jesus spent most of his time in Jerusalem rather than in the Galilean setting where the Synoptics present him. This does not exclude the possibility of a period of activity by Jesus in Judea, which Mark has omitted in the interests of telescoping the time of Jesus' work into as short a period as possible. John's locating the Cleansing of the Temple at the beginning (Jn. 2:13-22), rather than at the end as it seems properly to come in Mk. 11:15-17, shows that John is presenting a stylized view of Jesus' ministry seen as a whole, rather than an attempt to offer an historical sequence of events.

THE JOURNEY TO JERUSALEM

For Mark (followed by Matthew and Luke), there is only one journey to Jerusalem. It occurs in the final weeks of Jesus' ministry and has as its intention Jesus' confronting the authorities in Jerusalem with his claims. That Jesus did go to Jerusalem in the last period of his life is undeniable; the extent to which the gospels record accurately his motives and the actual course of events is debatable.

According to Luke, Jesus rather early in his career (Lk. 9:51) determined to go to Jerusalem. The rationale for this decision was disclosed by him in response to some seemingly well-meaning Pharisees who reported to him that Herod Antipas was seeking to kill him, as earlier he had had John the Baptist put to death (Lk. 13:31-33). Some scholars think this tradition is misplaced, since Jesus had already left Galilee by this point in Luke's narrative.[1] Others think the incident is wholly unhistorical. Most likely, however, it is a somewhat expanded version of an authentic saying of Jesus,[2] in which he pictures himself as a prophet whose destiny is to die in Jerusalem. There is here no hint of redemptive significance to his death, nor are any specific details of his death predicted. The probability is the greater, therefore, that here we have an insight into the intention of Jesus in going up to Jerusalem.

Mark and Matthew tell us (Mk. 10:1; Mt. 19:1) that the journey to Jerusalem was made by way of Perea, the territory east of the Jordan Valley which was also under the control of Herod Antipas. We learn from the gospels nothing of Jesus' activity there, except that Jn. 10:40 f. reports that Jesus returned to the place east of the Jordan where John the Baptist had carried on his baptizing activities. The geographical allusions are somewhat confused ("Judea beyond the Jordan"—Mt. 19:1), but the Synoptics unite to depict Jesus passing through Jericho in the Jordan Valley on his way up to Jerusalem for the last time (Mk. 10:46; Mt. 20:29; Lk. 18:35).

THE CLIMAX OF THE CONTROVERSIES

It is not only in geographical movement, however, that the Synoptics prepare the reader for the climactic event of the Cross. Following Jesus' entry into the city (which we shall examine below), Mark has presented a series of somewhat stylized incidents in which the issues are drawn between Jesus and his opponents. As they now stand, the stories seem to be told in the light of the controversies that the early Church was carrying on with its detractors, but the issues may well go back to Jesus himself. The issues and situations are varied. Jesus' refusal to answer the question about the source of his authority (Mk. 11-27-33 and par. [parallel passages]) is in keeping with his refusal to give a sign in order to confirm the divine origin of his powers. The controversy over paying tribute to the Roman authorities comes out of a real situation in the life of Jesus, but his pronouncement ("Render to Caesar the things that are Caesar's, and to God the things that are God's."—Mk. 12:17) was of great importance for the early Church in its struggle to live under the increasingly hostile influence of the empire.

The question about the Resurrection (Mk. 12:8-27) reflects the controversy that went on within Judaism between the Pharisees, who believed in resurrec-

---

[1] J. M. Creed, *The Gospel According to St. Luke* (London: Macmillan, 1930), p. 186.
[2] See Rudolf Bultmann, *History of the Synoptic Tradition* (New York: Harper & Row, 1963), p. 35.

tion even though it could not be documented in Torah, and the Sadducees, who rejected it because it lacked scriptural support. The argument from scripture does not sound convincing to modern ears as unassailable proof for the Resurrection.

> " '. . . I am the God of Abraham, and the God of Isaac, and the God of Jacob. . . .' He is not God of the dead, but of the living; you are quite wrong."
>
> —MARK 12:26, 27

The mode of argumentation is rabbinic, which could imply that it comes out of the life situation of Jesus or out of the experience of the early Church in debate with Judaism. In either case, the issue at stake is not the resurrection of Jesus Christ, but the possibility of a resurrection at all. What was basic in the Christian belief in the Resurrection was the encounter with the risen Christ, not the theoretical possibility of *a* resurrection.

The question as to which is the primary commandment (Mk. 12:28-34) and Jesus' reply (. . . "you shall love the Lord your God with all your heart . . . and . . . your neighbor as yourself.") have a parallel in the lawyer's question told in Lk. 10:25-28 and Mt. 22:34-40. Luke's version seems to be independent of Mark's, and may even be more original, since it credits the lawyer with giving the perceptive answer to his own question. In this incident can be seen the fact that neither Jesus nor the early Church created a new ethic; rather, both built upon Jewish ethics, presenting the demand of God with a new radicalness and urgency in the light of the nearness of God's kingdom.

The question about David's son (Mk. 12:35-37) seems to have arisen in a situation of conflict with Jewish scribal interpreters as to whether or not the Christian's claim that Jesus is the Messiah can be justified from the scriptures. Since we have assumed that Jesus did not use the messianic titles with reference to himself, it seems inappropriate to have him speak of himself as "son of David," "Christ," and "David's Lord." It sounds rather like a stock dilemma that Christians presented to Jewish opponents: How can David's descendant also be his Lord? A Jew would have to answer that this could not be so; the Christian, who affirmed Jesus' Davidic descent, also claimed Jesus' superiority to David and the whole royal line of Judaism. Mark ends the section of his gospel (Mk. 12:37-40) with a series of sayings in which the Pharisees are condemned; Matthew has greatly expanded this passage to point up the hypocrisy of the scribes and Pharisees (see fuller treatment in Chapter 12).

THE WITNESS IN JERUSALEM

These controversy encounters are depicted by Mark as occurring in Jerusalem. Thus far we have only implied that Jesus entered the city; now we must examine the gospel account of the so-called Triumphal Entry. The details of the ar-

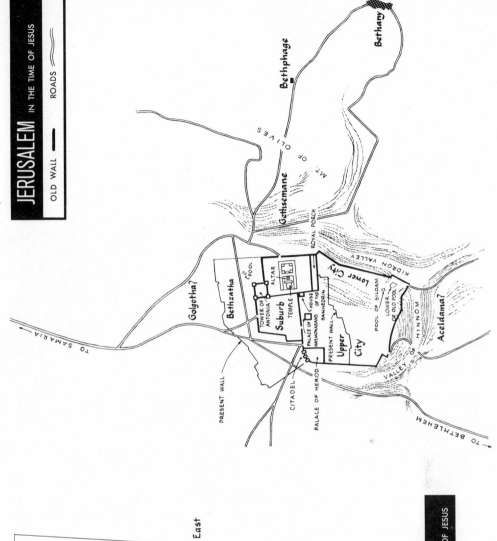

JERUSALEM IN THE TIME OF JESUS

OLD WALL ▬▬▬ ROADS ~~~

TO SAMARIA

PRESENT WALL

Golgotha?

Bethzatha

Suburb

TOWER OF ANTONIA

TEMPLE

PALACE OF HASMONAEAND

HOUSE OF THE SANHEDRIN

CITADEL

PALACE OF HEROD

PRESENT WALL

Upper City

Lower City

POOL OF SILOAM

LOWER OR OLD POOL

VALLEY OF HINNOM

Aceldama?

TO BETHLEHEM

KIDRON VALLEY

ROYAL PORCH

Gethsemane

MT. OF OLIVES

Bethphage

Bethany

POOL

ALTAR

North

Cross-Section West–East

West

East

PLAN OF THE TEMPLE AREA IN THE TIME OF JESUS

RAMPS

South

A. "THE HOUSE"
B. PORCH
C. ALTAR
D. LAVER
E. COURT OF THE PRIESTS
F. COURT OF ISRAEL
G. COURT OF WOMEN
H. ROYAL PORCH
I. SURROUNDING WALL
J. MOUNTAIN OF THE HOUSE

rangements for Jesus to use a colt have led some to suppose that there had been organized a kind of secret society in the Jerusalem vicinity, whose members now cooperate in helping Jesus to enter their city in enactment of the prophecy of Zech. 9:9—"Lo, your King comes to you . . . humble and riding on an ass." By comparing Mark with Matthew and Luke, we can see the tradition in the process of growth. Matthew has made explicit (Mt. 21:4, 5) the Markan allusion to the prophecy of Zechariah. A group of disciples of indeterminate number in Mark (Mk. 11:8) has become a crowd in Matthew, and a whole multitude in Luke. Furthermore, the purely eschatological shout of the followers ("Blessed be the kingdom of our father David that is coming."—Mk. 11:10) has been changed into a direct acclaim of Jesus as Son of David (Mt. 21:9), and King (Lk. 19:38). It is likely that the messianic significance of Jesus' entry was apparent, if at all, to only a small group of his followers and that it may not have been intended consciously by Jesus. Only in the light of his exaltation as Lord and Christ in the Resurrection would the significance of his action and the fulfillment of prophecy have become apparent. It was not the entry into the city, however, but his actions in the Temple, including his prediction of the destruction of the Temple, which attracted the attention and anxiety of the authorities.

The Temple in Jerusalem was not only the seat of the Jewish cultus, but it was the focus of unity of the scattered nation and its chief source of pride. Here was one of the great structures of the ancient world, as even pagan geographers of the era acknowledge. The operation of the Temple was a big and highly remunerative business; any threat to it could only be regarded as having the gravest economic, social, and religious consequences. Control of the Temple rested in the hands of the High Priest, whose appointment was theoretically hereditary, but in fact at the sufferance of Rome. Any disturbance of the *status quo* in the administration of the Temple, therefore, had important political implications as well.

When Jesus appeared in Jerusalem announcing the destruction of the Temple and the judgment of God on the nation, the authorities could not ignore his words. When he entered the Temple and arrogated to himself authority to purify it, and did so in the name of God, his action could not be overlooked. To Rome, here was one who threatened the order it sought to maintain. To official Judaism, here was a man without authorization or credentials who claimed to act in God's behalf. His challenge to the established authority could not go unmet.

Mark reports (11:11) an inconclusive visit of Jesus in the Temple, with the action of purification coming later (11:15-19). Matthew and Luke have combined his account into one incident. But the point in all three gospels is the same: the traffic through and commercialism in the midst of the Temple courts must be halted. It was intended as a place of prayer. Mark records that it was to be a house at prayer "for all nations" (Mk. 11:17), perhaps with reference to the Court of the Gentiles, where even a non-Jew could approach God. Now, however, its purpose had been lost, Jesus was saying; it had become a "den of thieves."

The story as a whole was worked over in the light of the growing hostility of Judaism and the Church, especially in connection with the fall of Jerusalem (see Chapter 10) and the flight of the Jerusalem church from the city. But there is no reason to doubt that Jesus did act in such a way as to render judgment in God's name against the Temple, and that he predicted its destruction.

The prophecy that the Temple will be destroyed (see Mk. 13:1-4 and par.) serves as an introduction to the Synoptic Apocalypse (Mk. 13:5-37, which has been expanded in Matthew and Luke). The prediction and the Apocalypse in their present form give evidences of modification in the light of the actual course of events at the time of the Roman siege and the ensuing destruction of the city in A.D. 70, as is unmistakably clear from Lk. 21:20. Mark has spoken of the desecration of the sanctuary, with apparent reference to the pollution of the Temple in the time of Antiochus Epiphanes (see pages 23-26). Luke, however, at the same point in the Apocalypse gives as the sign of the disaster, not the desecration of the Temple, but the siege of the city by armies.

Not only by direct prediction, but by parable, the downfall of the nation is foretold in the synoptic tradition. One such "parable" is the Cursing of the Fig Tree (Mk. 11:12-14); the original form of this tradition is probably the genuine parable of Lk. 13:6-9, where the point is the forebearance of God, who delays a little longer the bringing down of judgment on the unrepentant. In Mk. 11, the parable has become a parabolic act: Jesus' curse on the fig tree points to God's judgment on the people who will not hear the message of the inbreaking kingdom.

Even more pointed is the Parable of the Wicked Tenants (Mk. 12:1-12 and par.). Building on an allegory from Is. 5, in which the vineyard is Israel and the owner is God, who awaits in vain the fruits of obedience from the nation, this parable introduces the figure of the son of the owner, who has come to collect the income from the produce of the vineyard. Servants who had come before had been treated shamefully; some were killed. The owner's son, however, is also seized by the tenants and killed, in the hope that they can then claim the property of the absentee owner.[3] The conclusion of this parable is a prediction of divine judgment on the nation and an appeal to the fulfillment of Ps. 118:22-23, one of the early Church's favorite scriptural texts:

> The very stone which the builders rejected has become the head of the corner; this was the Lord's doing, and it is marvelous in our eyes.
>
> —MARK 12:10-11

---

[3] A full, concise analysis of this parable, including the modification of it in other strands of the tradition, is given by J. Jeremias, in *The Parables of Jesus*, rev. ed. (New York: Scribner's, 1963), especially pp. 70-77.

What we see at work here is the tendency to transform parables, in which the story as a whole conveys symbolically one or two main points, into allegories, in which every detail of the story has a symbolic significance. If there is an original nucleus behind the present allegorical form of this parable, its point was probably that God will judge the nation for its failure to respond in faith to the Good News. Now, however, it has become a prediction of the course of sacred history, culminating in the rejection and crucifixion of God's Son. The point of the allegory is further sharpened by Matthew's addition of the prophecy that the kingdom will be taken from Israel and given to "a nation producing the fruits," i.e., the Church (Mt. 21:43). Surely this "parable" has been either created, or at least reworked, in the light of the Fall of Jerusalem, which was interpreted in the early Church as God's judgment upon and rejection of the nation Israel.

THE LAST SUPPER

Since the Last Supper of Jesus and the traditions that came to surround it became the prototype for the Church's celebration of the Lord's Supper throughout history, it is legitimate to raise the question as to what occurred that night which gave rise to the varied liturgical forms and practices by which the rite is celebrated in the Church. While it is not possible to raise, much less to answer, all the related questions about the origins of the Lord's Supper, some important corollary issues may be considered: Is it an anachronism to think of a churchly rite as originating during the lifetime of Jesus? How can one account for the widely diverse forms by which the Eucharist is celebrated, even though all forms claim to trace their origins back to the Last Supper?

As for the origins of the Church during Jesus' lifetime, it must be acknowledged at the outset that the term "Church" occurs only twice in all four of the gospels (Mt. 16:18 and 18:17). It should be kept in mind that the English word "Church" carries certain organizational and ecclesiastical overtones which the Greek word ekklesia does not. Ekklesia is in turn the translation of the Hebrew word kahal, which is the term for the People of Israel gathered in the wilderness. It has been argued that Jesus could have used the term in this sense inasmuch as his messianic role presupposed the existence of a messianic People or a new community of the People of God.[4]

Other phrases and figures in the Gospel tradition report Jesus as speaking in advance of the new People of God, as for example, the "little flock" (Lk. 12:32). While it is true that Jesus' work was in effect summoning a people who

---

[4] Authenticity of the words of Jesus in Mt. 16:16ff. and 18:17 is defended by K. L. Schmidt in *Bible Key Words: The Church*, J. R. Coates, ed. (New York: Harper & Row, 1951), pp. 35-50. See also the discussion of these passages by O. Cullmann, in *Peter*, rev. ed. (Philadelphia: Westminster, 1962), pp. 192-217.

would be prepared for the coming of God's kingdom, the present form of these words comes from the later situation of the Church, following the Cross and Resurrection. There is a self-consciousness about the Church in Mt. 18, with its own judicial processes, which is scarcely appropriate in the midst of the eschatological urgency created by Jesus' message of the inbreaking kingdom.

But what of the words reported as spoken by Jesus at the Last Supper? Are these, too, the product of a worshipping Church? It is widely recognized that the present form of the words of institution betrays the effects of liturgical and theological development within the early Church. Furthermore, the evidence available to us shows widespread diversity of viewpoint and seems to manifest different conceptions of the nature of the meal underlying the synoptic material.

In the traditions included in the gospels and Acts, there are at least two different ways of understanding the significance of Jesus' last meal with his followers: (1) as a solemn act, patterned after the Jewish Passover celebration, and instituted as a memorial celebration of Jesus' impending death, and (2) as a joyous celebration of fellowship, with the focus on the eschatological fulfillment that will come when God's People are united in the kingdom of God.[5]

Although it is not possible to harmonize these two strands, it is probable that a single historical action underlies the two eucharistic patterns which have developed, not only in the New Testament tradition but subsequently in the Church.[6] The primary reference was almost certainly the eschatological expectation: Jesus promised that the fellowship with the disciples—now about to be ruptured by his death—would be renewed in the future by God's design. As an intimate, though informal fellowship of teacher and disciples, Jesus and his disciples would have eaten common meals together often; the final meal in this series would have left deep impressions on their minds. The main point of his ministry had been to prepare for the coming of the kingdom. One of the declarations that it is most certain that he made at the Last Supper was:

> I shall not drink again of the fruit of the vine until that day when
> I drink it new in the kingdom of God.
> —MARK 14:25; LUKE 22:18; MATTHEW 26:29

The fellowship which had begun in their common commitment to the ministry of the Gospel of the coming kingdom would be restored when the kingdom came in its fullness. The bread and wine—in keeping with the Jewish tradition

---

[5] The classic statement of this distinction is by Hans Lietzmann, *Mass and Lord's Supper*, tr. D. H. G. Reeve (Leiden: E. J. Brill, 1953-58). The view that the Supper was a Passover with special messianic meaning is held by J. Jeremias, *Eucharistic Words of Jesus* (Oxford: Blackwell, 1955).

[6] See the analysis by R. D. Richardson in the supplementary essay to Lietzmann's work as translated by D. H. G. Reeve, described in Note 5 above. See especially pp. 272-274.

of table fellowship—were the visible symbols of their fellowship. But further, the meal was a tangible evidence that God would include among his people those who were religious outcasts when adjudged by official standards. Their corporate actions in sharing the meal bore witness to the sense of incompleteness that they felt: the kingdom of God was yet to be consummated. It was in this hope that they gathered. Although Lk. 22:28-30 should probably be considered a word that arose in the post-Resurrection time, it fittingly summarizes what the early Church understood the meaning of the Last Supper to be:

> You are those who have continued with me in my trials; as my Father appointed a kingdom for me, so do I appoint for you that you may eat and drink at my table in my kingdom, and sit on thrones judging the twelve tribes of Israel.

It is easy to see how the theme of the New Covenant could develop from this understanding of the Supper, as is reflected in the familiar words, "This is my blood of the [new] covenant which is poured out for many" (Mk. 14:24). The sacrificial nature of Jesus' death would become meaningful in retrospect, and the wine poured out would become the symbol of the life (blood) given for their benefit. Later, Paul—or the tradition on which he drew—would lay stress on the memorial aspect of the Supper: "Do this in remembrance of me" (I Cor. 11:25). But the original significance was a meal of fellowship eaten in the spirit of eschatological expectation. Perhaps the closest analogy we have to this ceremony is the messianic meal that was eaten at Qumran, where the community expected that at the End Time there would be present the priestly Messiah of Aaron and the lay Messiah of Israel:

> And when they gather for the community table, or to drink wine, and arrange the community table and the wine to drink, let no man stretch out his hand over the first-fruits of the bread and wine before the Priest; for it is he who shall bless the first-fruits of bread and wine and shall first stretch out his hand over the bread. And afterwards, the Messiah of Israel shall stretch out his hands over the bread. And afterwards, all the congregation of the Community shall bless, each according to his rank.[7]
> —RULE OF THE FUTURE COMMUNITY: II: 17-21

The Last Supper could not but be remembered and re-enacted in the light of the Cross; but its original intent looked beyond the Cross to the Consummation.

---

[7] Quoted from *The Essene Writings from Qumran*, by A. Dupont-Sommer, tr. G. Vermes (New York: Meridian, 1962), pp. 112, 113. A full discussion of the communal meal at Qumran in relation to the Christian Eucharist is given by K. G. Kuhn in "The Lord's Supper and the Communal Meal at Qumran," from *The Scrolls and the New Testament*, ed. K. Stendahl (New York: Harper & Row, 1956), pp. 65-93.

THE CHRONOLOGY OF HOLY WEEK

In addition to the question about the original meaning of the Last Supper, and in some ways closely related to that question, is the matter of the chronology of Holy Week. According to the synoptic gospels, the Last Supper took place on Thursday evening during the Jewish celebration of the Passover. Since the Passover was a movable feast tied in with the phases of the moon, it could fall on any day of the week; the sabbath, of course, came at the same point in each week, beginning at sundown on Friday and continuing to sundown on Saturday.

By the synoptic report, the Passover would have begun 24 hours before the sabbath. In the Gospel of John, however, it is carefully pointed out that the trial of Jesus took place on the Day of Preparation—that is, the day before the Passover began (Jn. 13:1; 18:28; 19:31, 42). Moreover, none of the essential elements of the Passover celebration is present in the synoptic account of the meal: unleavened bread, bitter herbs, and the recital of the Passover story from the Old Testament.[8] The cups of wine before and after the breaking of bread required in the Passover celebration are likewise missing in the synoptic accounts, unless a rather poorly attested text of Luke is followed.[9] In the Lukan account (Lk. 22:15, 16), if we follow those manuscripts that omit "again," there is the suggestion that Jesus had wanted to eat the Passover with his disciples, but knew by Thursday evening that he would not be able to do so. Some of the early Christians observed the Jewish Passover by fasting while the Jews celebrated, as though to dramatize the discontinuity between the Jewish covenant community and the New Covenant People.[10] This suggests only that the Last Supper and the Passover were linked in the memory of the early Church; it does not prove that the Supper was a Passover celebration.

Even though some early Christians sought to differentiate the Lord's Supper from the Passover, it is clear that the imagery of the Passover (sacrificial lamb, deliverance from bondage, constitution as a Covenant People) affected the understanding of the Eucharist as well as its liturgy. The suggestion does not carry conviction that John and the Synoptics were using different calendars and that therefore both Thursday and Friday were Passovers in the same week.

---

[8] The relevant passages from the rabbinic tradition dealing with the Passover regulations are quoted by C. K. Barrett, in *New Testament Background: Selected Documents* (London: SPCK, 1957), pp. 155, 156.

[9] Some of the so-called "Western" ancient versions of Luke add a verse and a half, following verse 19 in the Revised Standard Version, which simply reproduce I Cor. 11:25. The added passage seems to have resulted from harmonizing Luke with Paul.

[10] See K. G. Kuhn, in *The Scrolls and the New Testament* (ed. K. Stendahl), pp. 90-92.

THE GARDEN OF GETHSEMANE *is where Jesus was arrested the night before his death. Beyond the garden is the Jewish cemetery on the Mount of Olives. Here the pious were buried to be near the Lord, who, according to Zechariah, will stand on the mountain on the Day of Judgment.*

Historically, it seems that a non-Passover meal came to be understood in the light of Passover practice.

The hypothesis that the events between the entry of Jesus and the Crucifixion must have extended over a longer period of time than a week is plausible, and has been defended with vigor and learning.[11] There is simply not enough evidence on which to construct a chronology. Although it is reasonable to suppose that a period of time somewhat longer than three or four days may have ensued between Jesus' action in the Temple and his seizure by the authorities, the fact that we cannot work out such a chronology bears further witness to the nature of the synoptic tradition as originally consisting of disconnected units— even in much of the Passion narrative.

The Arrest and Trial

For the sake of convenience, we shall follow the approximate order of Mark's account of the arrest and trial of Jesus, although this does not carry with it the confidence that Mark is presenting a straightforward historical account of what actually occurred. Here too we see the effects of theological interests and apologetic concerns, particularly in relation to the later conflicts between the Church and official Judaism.

THE BETRAYAL. That Judas Iscariot betrayed Jesus to the authorities is uniformly attested to in the tradition. What Judas' motives and background

---

[11] As for example by M. Goguel, *Life of Jesus* (New York: Macmillan, 1946), where it is proposed that Jesus entered the city of Jerusalem in early Fall, remained until December, and withdrew until his final return at Passover season in the Spring (p. 44).

were, we have no way of knowing. The attempt to picture him as a frustrated revolutionary whose disappointment in Jesus' quietism led him to betray his Teacher is nothing more than a conjecture. That he was a member of the Sicarii, a group sworn to assassinate the enemies of Israel, rests on a guess about the meaning of "Iscariot" (= Sicarii!) and an historical error, since the group did not appear on the stage of history until about A.D. 50, long after Jesus' death.[12] The details of Judas' action have been filled in from Old Testament prophecies, such as Ps. 41:9 ("Even my bosom friend in whom I trusted, who ate of my bread, has lifted his heel against me.") and Zech. 11:12-13 (which has been combined with Jer. 32:6-15 to form a prediction of Judas' acceptance of 30 pieces of silver as his reward for perfidy). Even the circumstances of his death and his replacement within the circle of disciples (Acts 1:20) are seen as the fulfillment of scripture. This motif pervades the whole of the Passion narrative, not just the details connected with Judas.

But *what* did Judas betray? Not the secret of Jesus' messiahship,[13] since it appears that he never made such a claim either in public or to his disciples, and the actions which could be interpreted as messianic signs were not done in secret. There was nothing clandestine about his cleansing the Temple courts. Since the priests were eager to avoid arresting Jesus in a public situation and yet to seize him before the Passover feast began (Mk. 14:1, 2), all that they needed to know was where he spent the night. The tradition reports that this was in a place called Gethsemane on the side of the Mount of Olives, across the Kidron Valley to the east of Jerusalem. In order to make certain of Jesus' identity in the darkness, it was agreed that Judas would kiss his master. The plot went according to plan, and Jesus was taken into custody by the authorities.

The synoptic tradition implies that the guards who seized Jesus were from the Temple (Lk. 22:52) and under the jurisdiction of the High Priest. John 18:3 and 12, however, indicate that the guards were Roman, who were not under orders from the High Priest, but who took Jesus to him for a hearing. Since John elsewhere (Jn. 1:1-16) is at pains to show that it was the Jews, not Pilate, who insisted on Jesus' death, it is not likely that John would have invented the detail of Jesus' seizure by Roman guards unless he had found it in the traditional sources on which he was drawing.[14]

THE TRIALS OF JESUS.   The synoptic gospels report three trials of Jesus: before the High Priest and the Sanhedrin; before Herod Antipas (in Lk. 23:6-16

---

[12] See Foakes-Jackson, F. J. and K. Lake, *Beginnings of Christianity*, I, Part 1 (London: Macmillan, 1920), 422-423.

[13] As supposed by A. Schweitzer, *The Quest of the Historical Jesus* (London: A. & C. Black, 1954), p. 394.

[14] For a discussion of this question, and for details of the trial and crucifixion of Jesus, see Paul Winter, *On the Trial of Jesus* (Berlin: Walter de Gruyter, 1961), especially pp. 44 ff. The reconstruction which follows is dependent at many points on Winter's analysis.

only); before Pilate. Only the last of the three was a trial in the proper sense of the term, and only in that situation was sentence passed upon Jesus.

There is no evidence that the Sanhedrin could conduct a legal hearing during the night or that its official meetings could be held in the residence of the High Priest.[15] The probable course of events is that the Roman guards, out of courtesy and respect for the right of the High Priest and the Sanhedrin to adjudicate purely local affairs, brought Jesus to the residence of the High Priest during the night. At that time certain charges were brought against him, although the basic complaint was not religious but political: that he was a disturber of the peace and a threat to administrative stability. The Sanhedrin convened in the morning—presumably in its own council chamber (Lk. 22:66) —and then agreed to turn him over to the Roman authorities for official trial and sentencing.

The story in Lk. 23:6 ff. of the hearing before Herod Antipas appears to be part of the apologetic concern of Luke to show that Jesus and the apostles were often haled before royal and local courts, always with the outcome that no charge could be made to stand against them. The implication intended by Luke was that Christians were neither subversives nor enemies of the state.

The desire to exonerate Jesus is carried further in the hearing before Pilate, where he is portrayed as unable to find in Jesus any crime deserving the death penalty (Lk. 23:22). Matthew heightens the picture of Jesus as guiltless by recounting the dream of his innocence that came to Pilate's wife (Mt. 27:19). A corollary of the innocence of Jesus is the effort of the tradition to assign to the Jews the responsibility for his death. This motif reaches its height—or depth! —in Mt. 27:25: "His blood be on us and on our children." Actually, neither the sentencing nor the mode of execution was Jewish. Although it was to the best interests of the Jewish ruling class to have Jesus out of the way, they did not condemn him on the basis of their own laws. For him to call himself "King of the Jews" would have invited from Jews scoffing, not execution. But the charge that he sought to be a king was a serious matter for the Roman authorities, who placed kings on thrones and allowed them to reign only so long as it served the best interests of the empire. Although the charge of blasphemy is mentioned in the tradition (Mk. 14:64), had Jesus been convicted and executed on that charge, his death would have been stoning. It is possible that the acted symbol of the broken loaf at the Last Supper was Jesus' way of anticipating his death by stoning. Though the fact has been questioned, there is every evidence that the Sanhedrin had the right to condemn and execute when the person was found guilty of infraction of a Jewish religious law [16] in the

---

[15] P. Winter, op. cit., pp. 20-30. The attempt to prove that the trial could have occurred under these circumstances is not convincing: J. Jeremias, The Eucharistic Words of Jesus (Oxford: Blackwell, 1955), pp. 52-53.

[16] P. Winter, op. cit., pp. 67-74.

period preceding A.D. 70. That Jesus was executed by crucifixion, a Roman practice, shows that he was condemned as a violator of the civil code of the empire. This conclusion is confirmed by the inscription that was placed on the Cross: "The King of the Jews." [17] The title as it stands in Mk. 15:26 has no special Christian connotations; the incident reported in Jn. 19:19-22 shows that Christians were seeking to transform Pilate's placement of the inscription into a witness to the true kingship of Christ. The historical evidence is that Jesus was put to death by the Romans as a threat to the political stability of Judea. The inscription was the public announcement of the charge.

The incident of the release of Barabbas (Mk. 15:6-15 and par.) is told by the evangelists to heighten the guilt of the Jews who, it is claimed, preferred to have a real insurrectionist released from prison rather than to save the innocent Jesus from dying under a false accusation of being a revolutionary. There is no evidence that there was a special custom of granting amnesty to political prisoners at festival times during the Roman administration of Palestine. According to some old versions and manuscript traditions of the Gospel of Matthew (27:16), the full name of the rebel prisoner was Jesus Barabbas. It is easy to see that Christian scribes would want to omit the name "Jesus" because of its place in the earliest Christian confessions (for example, "Jesus Christ is Lord"). What may have happened is that there were two prisoners brought before Pilate on the same day, both of whom were accused of being insurrectionists. One, Jesus Barabbas, was known to be a rebel, but even so the crowd called for his release. In the case of the nonrevolutionary Jesus of Nazareth, they shouted for his death. Although the story has been characterized as a legend,[18] it may have some basis in historical occurrence.

The Crucifixion and Burial

Luke has expanded the rather spare Markan account of the crucifixion of Jesus by introducing prophecies and a prayer attributed to Jesus (Lk. 23:28-31, 34). The derision of the crowd in mocking Jesus as King of the Jews and calling him to save himself is a kind of unwitting testimony to him as both king and savior. The final cry of despair consists of words from Psalm 22, an Old Testament passage which seems to have had extensive influence on the development of the Passion narrative tradition (cf. Mt. 27:43 with Ps. 22:8, Jn. 19:24 with Ps. 22:18). Some scholars think that the word of Jesus, "My God,

---

[17] O. Cullmann goes so far as to say that Jesus was condemned as a Zealot. See *The State in the New Testament* (Philadelphia: Westminster, 1956), p. 48. M. Goguel says: "Jesus was condemned as an aspirant to royal power," in *Life of Jesus* (New York: Macmillan, 1946), p. 521. The original form of the inscription is discussed by P. Winter, *op. cit.*, 105-109.

[18] So R. Bultmann, *History of the Synoptic Tradition* (New York: Harper & Row, 1963), p. 272.

my God, why hast thou forsaken me?" is itself the product of the interpretation of Jesus' death in the light of the Psalms (especially Psalms 22 and 69). It is assumed that the inarticulate cry mentioned in Mk. 15:37, rather than the prayerful allusion to scripture, was the last sound uttered by Jesus. On the other hand, the cry of despair has been such a source of theological embarrassment to the Church that it is thought to be unlikely that the Church would have invented the saying. Standing as it is, the prayer is a paradox—half despair and yet an appeal to God in the midst of seeming abandonment. It bears witness to the genuine humanity of Jesus, and stands in sharpest contrast to the depiction of Jesus in the gnosticizing gospels, according to which Jesus disappeared from the Cross and then reappeared on it, following his successful conquest of Hades.[19] The Synoptic account has stressed rather than suppressed the reality of the suffering of Jesus on the Cross.

[19] See, for example, the Gospel of Bartholomew, in *New Testament Apocrypha*, I, W. Schneemelcher, ed.; tr. R. McL. Wilson (London: Lutterworth, 1963), pp. 488-490.

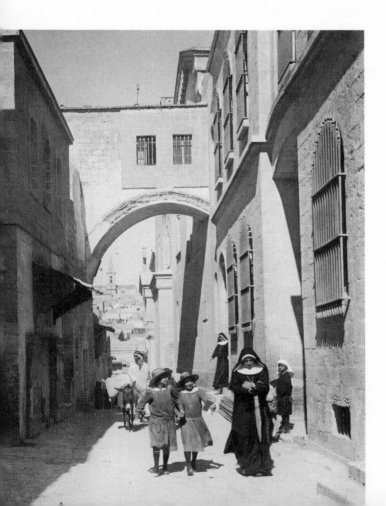

THE VIA DOLOROSA *is the traditional route through which Jesus carried his cross to Golgotha. In the basement of the building on the right are enormous paving stones that are believed to have formed the courtyard of the Roman fortress that adjoined the Temple area. The arch over the street was probably part of a building erected by Hadrian in the second century* A.D.

THE GARDEN TOMB *outside the wall of the Old City of Jerusalem. Though it probably dates from the late first or early second century* A.D., *it is thought by some to have been the tomb in which Jesus was laid.*

The place of Jesus' crucifixion and burial has from the fourth century to the present—and perhaps as early as the second century—been identified as the rocky area now covered by the Church of the Holy Sepulchre. In the course of reconstruction work, there have recently come to light elements of the shrine built there by order of the Empress Helena, mother of Constantine, in the fourth century on the site of an earlier public structure, probably the pagan temple built by Hadrian on the site about the time (*ca.* A.D. 135) of the destruction of Jewish Jerusalem and the rebuilding of the city in Hellenistic-Roman fashion. The Christians have claimed that Hadrian intentionally desecrated the spot venerated by Christians as the place of Jesus' death and burial by erecting a pagan temple there. It is of course possible that the Christians wanted to consecrate a site already hallowed as a religious shrine by pagan practice, as was the case in the choice of a cave, originally sacred to the memory of Venus and Adonis, as the spot to be honored in Bethlehem as the birthplace of Jesus. The traditional site of the Crucifixion and tomb, although they are now in the center of the Old City of Jerusalem, then lay outside the city walls on the northwest side. Under Jewish laws, which forbade contact with the dead except when unavoidable, it would have been necessary to have a place of execution and burial outside the city. The Citadel, where Pilate probably had his place of residence when in Jerusalem, was not far away, just within the city walls. The traditional Via Dolorosa would not then be authentic, since it leads from the site of another fortress that overlooked the Temple area, but which is thought not to have been the location of Pilate's garrison.

The body was laid in a tomb, apparently close at hand, carved out of the soft limestone of the Judean hills. The burial was done in haste, because of the approach of the sabbath, and was performed in charity by Joseph of Arimathea, who was willing to undergo ceremonial pollution and to risk opprobrium in order to prevent the corruption of the sabbath by allowing the body to be exposed. Christian tradition claimed both Joseph and Nicodemus (Jn. 19:38, 39) as secret believers. The body was placed in the tomb hastily; Jesus' followers returned within the city in order to rest on the sabbath, which began at sundown on Friday. Only the faithful women remained to witness the death and burial; the disciples appear to have fled, perhaps back to Galilee.

THE CROSS
IN THE LIGHT OF THE RESURRECTION

There is little uniformity in the gospel accounts of the empty tomb, and wide divergence on the matter of the post-Resurrection appearances. Matthew and Luke follow Mark's account up to the point of the discovery of the empty tomb, although Matthew has added considerable dramatic detail, such as the earthquake, the descending angel, the terror of the guards, the broken seal. Luke, on the other hand, has abridged Mark's account and replaced the note of fear (Mk. 16:8) with an attitude of faith on the part of the women, and incredulity on the part of the disciples (Lk. 24:8-11).

How are we to account for the report of the empty tomb? It has been observed [20] that some ancient copies of Mark imply that the women in their excitement and sorrow went to the wrong tomb! Some interpreters think that the empty tomb stories arose as an inference from the encounters with the risen Christ experienced by the apostles, and that the Resurrection was then made more concrete by the development of narrative detail concerning the observers of the empty tomb. Whatever the origin of the stories—and the other gospels are obviously dependent on Mark—the disappearance of the body of Jesus proved nothing. Indeed, it appears to have been in some circumstances something of an embarrassment to the Church, since Matthew has developed the rather elaborate apologetic story of the guard at the tomb and the false explanations circulated by the Jewish authorities (Mt. 27:62-66). It is significant that Paul makes no mention of the empty tomb (see p. 152). The diversity of the gospel accounts seems to preclude the possibility that there was one set of historical circumstances which came to be interpreted in different ways by the evangelists. One must conclude, rather, that each of the gospel writers brought his account to a close in a way which seemed to him most appropriate, with no firm tradition to guide him.

Mark's ending is especially puzzling, since in terms of syntax and content it ends quite awkwardly: the Greek text ends with the word *gar* (=“for”).

---

[20] By K. Lake, in *The Historical Evidence for the Resurrection of Jesus Christ* (London: Williams & Norgate, 1907), pp. 250-253.

It has been conjectured that the original version of Mark ended with an account of the appearance of Jesus to his disciples in Galilee.[21] This is most plausible, since such an appearance is twice anticipated by Mark, when he speaks of Jesus going before his disciples into Galilee (Mk. 14:28; 16:7). We do not know whether "go before" means here "precede you" or "lead you." But an appearance in Galilee is surely what is expected (see p. 257).

Matthew's version of the Resurrection story ends with (1) the account of bribing the soldiers to spread the story that the disciples had stolen the body of Jesus (Mt. 28:11-20), and with (2) the appearance of Jesus to his disciples in Galilee, at which time they are commissioned to launch the world mission of the Church. Luke's account (which is treated at some length in Chapter 13) reflects in detail such practices of the early Church as the Eucharist ("made known in the breaking of bread") and the Christian interpretation of the Old Testament ("He interpreted to them in all the scriptures the things concerning himself"), as well as the missionary outreach of the Church "to all nations." The Resurrection appearances in the Gospel of John occur both in the vicinity of Jerusalem (Jn. 20) and in Galilee (Jn. 21). In both locales, the purpose of the appearances is to commission and instruct the followers of Jesus in the work that they are to carry on. A distinctive element is present in the story of Thomas, who doubts the corporeal resurrection of Jesus. The story is apparently an effort by the early Church to answer the heretical claim that the Resurrection was no more than a vision of Christ.

There is little by way of detail that is shared among these "appearance stories." The persons involved, the location, the words attributed to Jesus—all differ with each evangelist. Two factors are present in all of them, however: that the appearances were not expected, and that they resulted in commissioning by the risen Christ to carry forward the work that he had begun.

In addition to the direct effect of the appearances on those who were encountered by Christ, there was one result which was of basic importance for the faith of the Church. Without it, there would have been no *kerygma*. The Resurrection made it possible to understand the Cross.[22] The encounter with the living Christ enabled the apostles to declare that the Cross was not the end. Otherwise, his death would have been the tragic, untimely fate of an innocent man. In the light of the Resurrection, however, the Cross took on prime importance. Let us examine some of the ways in which the Cross came to be understood, since these modes of understanding directly affected the modification of the synoptic tradition.

---

[21] M. Dibelius, in *From Tradition to Gospel* (New York: Scribner's, 1935), pp. 189-190.

[22] R. Bultmann, in *Kerygma and Myth*, I, H. W. Bartsch, ed. (London: SPCK, 1953), 41, 42, seriously overstates the case when he says that the Resurrection is nothing more than a way of understanding the Cross.

The Cross: Divine Necessity

First of all, the death of Jesus was understood as a matter of divine necessity, rather than an historical accident. This insight is placed on the lips of the risen Christ (Lk. 24:26):

> Was it not *necessary* that the Christ should suffer these things and enter into his glory?

But this point of view has been written into the accounts of the whole of Jesus' ministry, not simply in the post-Resurrection appearances. Mark reports Jesus as saying (Mk. 9:12):

> How is it written of the Son of man, that he should suffer many things and be treated with contempt?

The predictions of the Passion (Mk. 8:31; 9:31; 10:33, 34) are all written in the light of the Resurrection. Even though they purport to have been spoken during Jesus' earthly ministry, the evangelists acknowledge that the disciples did not understand the predictions. Only after the Resurrection, so the tradition reports (Lk. 24:44 ff.), could the disciples discern the significance of Jesus' death. This was as God intended it to be.

The Cross: Fulfillment of Scripture

In the second place, the death of Jesus was in accordance with the scriptures. This point is made in Mk. 9:12, quoted above, even though it is difficult to tell what specific scripture the tradition had in mind. Often the reference to the Old Testament is direct, as in Lk. 22:37:

> For I tell you that this scripture must be fulfilled in me, "And he was reckoned with transgressors"; for what is written about me has its fulfillment.

Several times repeated in Jn. 19 is the phrase, "This was to fulfill scripture," or its equivalent. The pattern of Jesus' suffering, therefore, was divinely ordained and its course disclosed in the Old Testament scriptures, although the Church recognizes that only in light of the Resurrection can this meaning in scripture be discerned.

The Cross: Prelude to Glorification

The third aspect of the death of Jesus is that it was a prelude to his glorification. The divine pattern is: suffering, followed by glory. The ancient Christian hymn quoted by Paul in Phil. 2:8, 9 asserts this:

. . . he humbled himself and became obedient unto death, even death
on a cross. Therefore God has highly exalted him and bestowed on him
the name which is above every name.

The theme is evident in the development of the synoptic tradition as well as
in the Book of Acts.[23] The suffering/vindication motif is implicit in Jesus' word
about losing one's life in order to find it (Mk. 8:35 and par.). It is explicitly
mentioned in Lk. 24:26, which declares that it was necessary for Christ first
to suffer and then enter into his glory. It is the same viewpoint expressed in
the sermons of Acts 2, 10, and 13. Even though these sermons be adjudged to
represent the theology of Luke rather than that of the first apostles,[24] they
give evidence of one theological tendency that was at work at the time that the
gospels were being written—that is, one way in which the Resurrection provided the meaning of the Cross.

The Cross in the Plan of Redemption

Finally, the death of Jesus on the Cross was understood as having
redemptive effects. The clearest statement of this is in Mk. 10:45:

For the Son of man also came not to be served but to serve, and to
give his life as a ransom for many.

Although the authenticity of this verse has been stoutly defended,[25] it would
appear that verse 45 has been attached by Mark or by the tradition on which
he is dependent as a theological comment on the appeal of Jesus to his followers to adopt the role of a servant. In the words reported to have been
spoken by Jesus at the Last Supper, his life is seen as the sacrifice by which
the New Covenant is ratified (Mk. 14:24); the passage, as we have observed,
then leads on immediately to speak of the fulfillment that is to come in the
kingdom of God.

While it is an overstatement to speak of the gospels as Resurrection stories
with long introductions,[26] the influence of the Resurrection faith is pervasive.
Without the Resurrection, there would be no need even to recall the Cross,
except perhaps out of pity for an innocent man's death. But without the life
and ministry characterized by authority and eschatological promise, the death of
Jesus would have been as obscure as that of any common criminal executed by

---

[23] This motif is developed at length by E. Schweizer in *Lordship and Discipleship* (London:
SCM Press, 1960), especially pp. 32-41.

[24] For a discussion of the authenticity of the sermons in Acts see pp. 317-319.

[25] For example, Vincent Taylor, *The Gospel According to St. Mark* (London: Macmillan,
1953), pp. 445-446.

[26] Ernst Fuchs, *Studies of the Historical Jesus* (Naperville, Ill.: Alec R. Allenson, 1964),
p. 26).

Rome. It was the Resurrection that made the Cross meaningful and the ministry memorable. We shall consider in Chapters 11, 12, 13, and 14 how the tradition about Jesus came to be modified by the four evangelists and the communities for which they were spokesmen. But we must turn now to the work of the one man who, transformed by the Resurrection encounter, took his place among the followers of Jesus, and became the chief agent of the spread of Christianity beyond the borders of Palestine and the boundaries of Judaism.

PART TWO

THE COMMUNITY EXPANDS
THROUGH THE
MINISTRY OF PAUL

PAUL

AMONG THE APOSTLES

The oldest documents we possess that report the death of Jesus are the letters of Paul, a Jew of the Dispersion to whom are attributed nearly half the writings in the New Testament. The earliest of these letters probably goes back to about a decade after the Crucifixion. Their author in the years immediately following the death of Jesus was, by his own acknowledgment, a vigorous enemy of the Church (Gal. 1:13). Indeed, his goal was to destroy both

the Church and its faith (Gal. 1:23). There are two obvious historical infer-
ences which can be drawn from Paul's testimony about his past role as persecutor of the Church: (1) that the Church and its faith were going concerns when
Paul became a Christian, and (2) that some radical change took place that
brought Paul to faith and into the Church. Let us examine the evidence that
Paul provides on both these points.

PAUL'S PREDECESSORS IN THE FAITH

The Letter to the Galatians has as its immediate occasion a challenge to the
authority of Paul as an apostle. Ordinarily, when writing to the churches, Paul
observed the literary conventions of his day as to salutations and formal introductory remarks.[1] So great is his concern over the situation among the Galatians,
however, that he hurries quickly to the main point (Gal. 1:12); namely, that
as an apostle he is not in any way dependent upon other human beings—not
even the other apostles—for the Gospel which he preaches or for the revelation
of Jesus Christ which God had been pleased to grant him (Gal. 1:12, 16). His
missionary work had been begun independently; only "after three years" had
he had a brief conference in Jerusalem with two of the leaders of the Church
there, Peter and James (1:18, 19). Apart from a second consultation with an
inner group of the Jerusalem leaders of the Church 14 years later, Paul claims
to have had no further contact with the apostolic group prior to his writing
his Letter to the Galatians (Gal. 2:1 ff.). As far as authorization for carrying
on his work was concerned, Paul saw himself as completely independent of
the other apostles.

THE COMMON APOSTOLIC MESSAGE

There is one point, however, on which Paul acknowledged his dependence on
his predecessors in the faith: the Christian message itself. In writing to the
Corinthian church (I Cor. 15:3-8), he declares that the message which he had
preached among them had been transmitted to him by others and that he had
simply passed it on to his hearers in Corinth (and presumably elsewhere).
The Greek words that are used in 15:3 are technical terms for the transmitting
or handing down of a tradition. Paul had taken his place in the line of those
passing on a tradition; he had not been an innovator. When we compare this
statement about the Gospel tradition with Paul's word to the Galatians in Gal.
1:12, however, we see that Paul is not assuming that the Gospel consists merely

---

[1] The form of Paul's letters is discussed in Chapter 8.

of a set of informative statements about the death and resurrection of Jesus Christ. It is an appeal to the hearer that his destiny is involved in the destiny of Jesus. He is not merely reporting that Jesus died and rose again, although these events are central to his message (or *kerygma*, as it has come to be called, on the basis of Paul's term in I Cor. 1:21, "the foolishness of *what we preach*" —*kerygma* [2]).

We have already discussed attempts made by scholars [3] to show that the *kergyma* was primarily a series of declarations concerning Jesus Christ: his origin, his ministry, his death, his resurrection, his Coming as judge and king. Our criticisms of this procedure were, however: (1) There is no clearly uniform pattern of affirmations associated with the New Testament formulations of the *kerygma*, and (2) The *kerygma* is not simply a recital of facts, but a declaration of the significance of Jesus Christ and of events in which he is the central figure. Attention has been drawn to the brief, hymn-like statements incorporated in the writings of the New Testament. These credal-type statements are sometimes referred to as kerygmatic summaries of primitive Christian confessions.[4] We have already had occasion to note that there is usually discernible in these kerygmatic passages a pattern which proclaims the humiliation of Christ and his final exaltation.[5] But the details of the kerygmatic formulations vary widely.

The summary of the Christian message just referred to (from I Cor. 15:3 ff.) speaks first of the humiliation of Jesus (". . . Christ died for our sins . . . he was buried . . .") and then of his exaltation (". . . he was raised on the third day . . ."). But Paul goes beyond stereotyped formulation, to enumerate those to whom Jesus Christ had appeared risen from the dead: ". . . To Cephas, then to the twelve . . . to James, then to all the apostles. . . ." At the end of the list (". . . last of all, as to one untimely born . . .") comes Paul himself. Here Paul points to the central reality which effected Paul's conversion and which placed him in his role among the apostles. To state it another way, the encounter of Paul with the risen Christ may be viewed from three perspectives: (1) it transformed Paul from persecutor of the Church to proclaimer of the Gospel; (2) it confirmed the Gospel for Paul, so that he now preached the faith he once tried to destroy (Gal. 1:23); (3) it placed Paul among the witnesses of the risen Christ, and therefore among the apostles. Each of these affirmations requires some elaboration.

---

[2] This term, *kerygma*, though widely used by modern Biblical scholars, occurs only eight times in the entire New Testament. More common terms are *Gospel*, and *logos* (a Greek word meaning message, word, account).

[3] Notably by C. H. Dodd in *The Apostolic Preaching* (New York: Harper & Row, 1951).

[4] A convenient summary treatment of these materials is given by O. Cullmann in his *Earliest Christian Confessions* (London: Lutterworth, 1949).

[5] See p. 57, and the fuller presentation of the evidence in E. Schweizer, *Lordship* and *Discipleship* (London: SCM Press, 1960).

THE GOSPEL BECOMES GOOD NEWS FOR PAUL

What was Paul like before his conversion? In Rom. 7:7-23 he describes a man ("I") in a hopeless struggle with sin; only in Christ does he find deliverance. Some interpreters have assumed that, prior to his conversion, Paul was a particularly wicked man, who is here depicting his own moral conflict. This passage probably is only indirectly autobiographical, in the sense that all of us inevitably tend to generalize on the basis of our own experience, however much we may consciously seek to avoid doing so. What Paul is pointing to here is the sense of moral impotence that any man feels when, knowing full well what he *ought* to do, he cannot bring himself to do it. Actually, in terms of the Law, under whose precepts Paul had been reared and by whose demands his religious life and convictions were shaped, he was an effective and obedient man:

> . . . circumcised on the eighth day, of the people of Israel, of the tribe
> of Benjamin, a Hebrew born of Hebrews; as to the law a Pharisee, as
> to zeal a persecutor of the church, as to righteousness under the law
> blameless.
>
> —PHILIPPIANS 3:5, 6

This self-description does not sound like one written by a moral weakling. It is rather the frank statement of one who knows that he has achieved what he has within the strict standards of Jewish legalism. Elsewhere, Paul shows himself to have become aware of the inadequacies of the whole legalistic approach to God. What made Paul discontented was the sense that all he had done was to achieve status in the eyes of the Law alone; what he longed for was a sense of acceptance in the eyes of God. Paul's transformation from one who honored God to one who honored God in Christ (II Cor. 5:19) was not a conversion in a radical psychological sense, but was rather a change from striving to be justified before God as a reward for good works to a willingness to rely in faith on what God had provided man in Jesus Christ. What God had done was to provide the grounds of the forgiveness of man's sins in the death of Jesus Christ and the grounds of his hope of deliverance from sin and death in Christ's resurrection.[6] (The meaning of the Cross and the Resurrection in the thought of Paul is developed more fully in Chapter 9.)

Paul was convinced that he had met Jesus Christ risen from the dead ("Have I not seen the Lord?"—I Cor. 9:1). The fact that this man Jesus, who had been despised and rejected as a traitor to his nation, had been raised from the

---

[6] From W. G. Kümmel, *Römer 7 und die Bekehrung des Paulus* (Leipzig: J. C. Hinrich'sche Buchhandlung, 1929), p. 158. This view is developed in relation to man's common experience of inner struggle by R. Bultmann, in "Romans 7 and the Anthropology of Paul," from *Existence and Faith*, S. Ogden, ed. (New York: Meridian, 1960), pp. 145-157.

dead, was interpreted by Paul—together with others of the first generation of Christians—to mean that God had vindicated Jesus. At one point, Paul puts it in even stronger terms:

> Jesus Christ . . . was . . . designated Son of God in power . . . by his resurrection from the dead. . . .
>
> —ROMANS 1:1-4

For Paul, as for the Jewish prophetic tradition, to be the "Son of God" meant to be the Messiah (Ps. 2:7), the one anointed and therefore commissioned of God to establish his kingdom, to rule in his stead. If the Church, which Paul had persecuted, honored this one now vindicated by God, how could Paul dare to oppose him or his Church? The claim of the Church that God had exalted Jesus as Lord (Phil. 2:11) was not a lie to be combatted, but good news to be proclaimed to all mankind. The turning point had come when Paul was confronted by Christ, or as he phrased it:

> . . . he who had set me apart before I was born, and had called me through his grace, was pleased to reveal his Son to me. . . .
>
> —GALATIANS 1:15, 16

PAUL'S CLAIM TO HAVE BEEN COMMISSIONED BY THE RISEN CHRIST

Apart from the effect on Paul's own faith, the confrontation by the risen Christ had its most significant effect in providing Paul with the grounds for his claim to be numbered among the apostles. The other apostles [7] were those who had been associated with Jesus during the period of his ministry. According to Acts 1:22, the period of association with Jesus must have extended from the time of the baptism of Jesus until his ascension. Obviously, Paul could not qualify by this criterion. It may be that his description of himself as "one untimely born" (I Cor. 15:8) is an acknowledgment of his failure to qualify on this particular point. But he is insistent that his authority as an apostle is equal to that of any others, even though they may not acknowledge him as an apostle (I Cor. 9:1-2). At the beginning of a majority of his letters, Paul identifies himself as an apostle of Jesus Christ. On one occasion, when Paul's authority was called into question by some traveling preachers who visited the churches founded by Paul—almost certainly these were not the Jerusalem leaders, and were likely not even emissaries from Jerusalem—Paul responded sarcastically: "I think that I am not in

---

[7] The English word *apostle* is a transliteration of the Greek noun *apostolos*, which is related to the verb, *apostello*, meaning "send" or "commission." The term *apostolos* takes on the technical meaning of "one commissioned by God for the work of the Gospel." For a full discussion of the background of the term, see the article on "Apostleship" in *Bible Key Words*, ed. J. R. Coates (New York: Harper & Row, 1958).

the least inferior to these superlative apostles."—(II Cor. 11:5). Later (II Cor. 11:13) he denounced them as "false apostles." Clearly, then, Paul was in no doubt as to his apostolic authority, even though he had not been a companion of the earthly Jesus.

Thus far we have said nothing about the nature of the encounter of Paul with the risen Christ. Was it only a vision that took place in Paul's imagination? Or was the physical body of Jesus objectively present before Paul? Was the experience of Paul any different from that of men of faith in any age who claim to have "met" Christ?

To answer the questions in reverse order: Paul apparently wanted to stress the fact that the appearances of the risen Christ which he was enumerating (I Cor. 15:4-8) were unique and unrepeatable, and that they terminated with the appearance ("last of all") to Paul himself. Although he provides us no information as to the nature of the resurrection appearance of Jesus Christ, Paul assumes the direct connection between the resurrection of Jesus and the resurrection of all men of faith:

> (But) each in his own order: Christ the first fruits, then at his coming
> [Greek: *parousia*] those who belong to Christ.
>
> —I CORINTHIANS 15:23

Accordingly, what Paul has to say about the resurrection of the faithful is applicable presumably to the resurrection of Christ. On the subject of the resurrection body, Paul is somewhat more explicit. His argument in I Cor. 15 runs like this:

(1) The ground of Christians' belief that God has forgiven their sins is that Christ died for their sins and was raised from the dead. If he is not raised, then their hope of forgiveness is futile (15:12-17).

(2) In fact, Christ *has* been raised from the dead. His resurrection is the ground of hope that those who belong to Christ by faith will share in the resurrection in the day when God's kingdom is established in its fullness (15:20-28).

(3) There are various forms of bodies. Some are terrestrial; some are celestial. Among the celestial bodies there are differences: the sun, the moon, the stars. It should not be surprising, therefore, that the human body may take different forms. Just as a seed when sown reappears in a new form (or "body"), so the human form of man when "sown" (*i.e.*, buried) will re-emerge in a new form, or "body" (15:35-41).

(4) The new body will not be perishable or physical, but imperishable and "spiritual." The body of the resurrection, with which man will enter the kingdom of God, will not be characterized by "flesh and blood," but will "bear the image of the man from heaven"—that is, of the risen Christ (15:42-50).

We might wish that Paul had told us more fully what he understood by the term "spiritual body." At least he rejects many of the popular notions of what is involved in resurrection: it does not consist in the resuscitation of a corpse. While the "body" is thought of by Paul as preserving personal identity with one who was known under earthly conditions, the new body does not share the limitations of human existence as it is now known to us on earth. As he puts it succinctly, "We shall be changed" (15:52)..

It is worth noting that Paul does not engage in the discussion of the empty tomb, nor does he try to demonstrate that the body of the risen Christ could be touched and handled, or that he could eat and build a fire, as the writers of the Gospel report (see especially Mt. 28:1-10; Jn. 20:19-28, 21:9-14). The absence of these details from Paul's discussion of the subject does not diminish in the slightest his confidence that God had raised Jesus from the dead or that at "the last day" all would be transformed and thus enter the kingdom (see I Thess. 4:13-18).

Apart from Paul's hope of sharing in the resurrection (Phil. 3:11), the encounter with the risen Lord was of primary importance, in that through this experience Paul was commissioned as the apostle *to the Gentiles* (Gal. 1:16). Although the account of Paul's conversion in Acts 9 (repeated with differing details in Acts 22:4-16 and 26:9-18) includes dramatic elements not even hinted at by Paul, the Acts accounts and Paul join in asserting that he was God's "chosen instrument" to carry the message "before the Gentiles" (Acts 9:15). It was on the basis of this call and commission that Paul the persecutor of the Church became Paul the apostle to the Gentiles. It was his understanding that the summoning of the Gentiles to faith was in a special way his task, and that he must go into unevangelized territory, step by step around the Mediterranean basin, in order to fulfill his God-given assignment:

> (For) I will not venture to speak of anything except what Christ has wrought through me to win obedience from the Gentiles, by word and deed, by the power of signs and wonders, by the power of the Holy Spirit, so that from Jerusalem and as far round as Illyricum [8] I have fully preached the gospel of Jesus Christ, thus making it my ambition to preach the gospel, not where Christ has already been named, lest I build on another man's foundation. . . .
>
> —ROMANS 15:18-20

Paul's claim to apostolic authority did not and could not rest on historically demonstrable continuity between his work and the ministry of Jesus. From a purely human viewpoint, he had had no contact with Jesus. Paul insisted, how-

---

[8] Illyricum was the name of a Roman province, located east of the Adriatic Sea in what is now Yugoslavia. It cannot be determined whether Paul means that he has carried on evangelistic work in Illyricum or only that he has gone as far as the border of Illyricum. The first possibility is the more likely.

ever, that his call by the risen Christ was as real and as effective as that experienced by the original disciples. ⸙

THE QUEST FOR THE HISTORICAL PAUL

Is it possible to trace the antecedents of this startling transformation in the life of Paul? What in the way of biographical sources is available for tracing the development of his personality and career? The answer is: very little, apart from the information we can extract from his own letters.

If we were to accept Acts as providing on the whole reliable historical information about Paul, our supply of biographical sources would be greatly increased. But we are discouraged from doing so by the disagreements between the accounts of certain events in Paul's letters and what appear to be reports of the same events in Acts. The most notable example of this conflict is the story of the meeting of Paul with the leaders of the Jerusalem church to settle

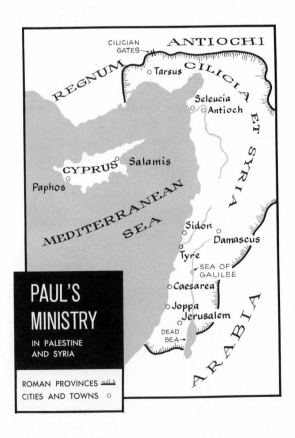

DAMASCUS *is believed by some historians to be the oldest continuously inhabited city in the world. A few traces of Roman times remain in the old covered markets, but most of the city presents the modern appearance pictured here.*

their differences on the question of requirements for admission of Gentiles to the Church.

Acts vs. the Letters of Paul

The question of the time and circumstances of Paul's consultation with Church leaders in Jerusalem is important, not only as a problem in itself, but because of its implications for the chronology of Paul, and beyond that, for the reliability of Acts as an historical source. Before examining the specific question of the Jerusalem Council, however, we should raise the broader issue of the value of Acts as a source for the life of Paul, and the relation of the evidence from Acts to the evidence from Paul's own writings.

On the basis of Paul's letters alone, we can learn a good deal about Paul's life before his conversion, and even more about the progress of his ministry as the apostle to the Gentiles. Let us sketch briefly what the main outline of material tells us about Paul, and then compare it with what we are told by Acts.

THE EVIDENCE FROM PAUL'S LETTERS. In Phil. 3:4-6 Paul outlines the Jewish background in which he had been reared. From birth he had been brought up in accord with Jewish Law: "circumcised on the eighth day. . . ." He believed that he could identify not only the nation (Israel) into which he had been born, but the tribe (Benjamin) as well, although we have no clear evidence that such genealogical precision was possible in his day. He was a

Hebrew of Hebrew stock. On the issues of the interpretation of the Law, he took his stand with the Pharisees,[9] which meant that he accepted both the Law and the Prophets as scripture, and that he believed in the resurrection and other forms of eschatological hope that were rejected by the Sadducees, the Pharisees' chief opponents. On the basis of the Pharisaic interpretation of the Law, Paul could boast that he was "blameless" with regard to the righteousness that it was claimed that the Law could provide.

His legal achievements were recognized by his contemporaries, Paul tells us in another autobiographical passage, Gal. 1:13-2:10, so that his zeal for the traditions of the fathers had brought him an outstanding reputation among Jews. Then, as we have seen, he was converted by the appearance to him of the risen Christ. Although he does not include any of the detail surrounding this experience that the Acts account offers, he does indicate that it occurred near Damascus. At least, he implies that the place where he was living at the time of his conversion and to which he returned following it was Damascus (Gal. 1:17). Then he withdrew to "Arabia," although he does not tell us whether he means by that the border of the Arabian desert south or east of Damascus— territory controlled by the Nabatean Arab king, Aretas (II Cor. 11:32)—or whether he traveled farther south in the Arabian peninsula.

Three years after his conversion (Gal. 1:18), Paul went up to Jerusalem for a private conversation with Peter, and James, the brother of Jesus. After that, he went into the area known as Syria and Cilicia, a Roman province in the vicinity of Antioch at the northeastern corner of the Mediterranean Sea. Fourteen years afterward—whether 14 years after his conversion or after the first visit is not clear—he returned to Jerusalem, again for a small conference with the inner circle of apostles there. On this occasion the issue under discussion was whether or not Gentiles should be circumcised in accordance with the Law of Moses before their being admitted to the Church. The decision reached was that no such requirement should be made of Gentile converts to Christianity. The Jerusalem apostles recognized the distinctive mission of Paul to the Gentiles, and asked of him only that the Gentile churches "remember the poor," which seems to mean that the Gentile churches were to make a contribution to the Jerusalem church. (Gal. 2:1-10). We cannot tell whether the term "poor" is meant literally or is a religious self-designation on the part of the Jerusalem Christian community. It is attested in Acts that the Jerusalem Christians were impoverished as a result of a famine (Acts 11:27-30), in which case the term would be meant literally. On the other hand, there is some evidence that the early Palestinian Christians called themselves "the poor," just as the later Jewish Christian sect, the Ebionites, did.[10] There may be further

---

[9] For a characterization of the Pharisees, see p. 38.

[10] For a discussion of the Ebionites, see pp. 246-247. The attempt to identify the Ebionites with the Dead Sea community at Qumran has been effectively refuted by J. Fitzmyer in "The Qumran Scrolls, the Ebionites and their Literature," from *The Scrolls and the New Testament*, K. Stendahl, ed. (New York: Harper & Row, 1957), pp. 208-231.

evidence of this usage in Luke's version of the Beatitude, "Blessed are you poor!" (Lk. 6:20). To the end of his public ministry, Paul was concerned to discharge his obligation to collect funds for the poor among the saints in Jerusalem (Rom. 15:25-27).

Most of what other information we can gather from Paul's letters about his travels and plans is connected with the collection for the Jerusalem church. In I Cor. 16:1-4 he tells that the churches of Asia Minor, Macedonia, and Achaia have been asked to share in the contribution, and that he plans to revisit them in order to gather up the money offered. The importance of this visit is underscored by the several references to it that Paul makes in the course of his correspondence with the Corinthian church (I Cor. 16:5; II Cor. 8, 9). From this report of the collection plans (I Cor. 16:3, 4) we learn that Paul expects to go with the approved representatives of the churches that participate in the contribution when they take the gift to Jerusalem. When this offering is completed, and since the evangelization of the area from Jerusalem to the western limits of Greece is now accomplished (Rom. 15:23-32), Paul expects to visit the church in Rome on his way to begin evangelistic work in Spain, as yet unreached by the Gospel.

Another group of Paul's letters—Philippians, Colossians, and Philemon— appear to have been written from prison (Phil. 1:12 ff.; Col. 4:3, 10, 18; Phm. 1:1). But the question is: "When were they written, and from where?" It has been vigorously denied that Paul was in prison at all when he wrote these letters, the references to "bonds" being interpreted in a purely metaphorical way as the hindrances and entanglements in which Paul found himself and which hampered his work.[11] An elaborate hypothesis was worked out by G. S. Duncan to prove that Paul had been imprisoned in Ephesus and that he wrote the letters of Philippians, Colossians, and Ephesians from there.[12] Al-

---

[11] The theory that Philippians was written from Ephesus but that Paul was not in prison at the time was developed by T. W. Manson in an essay, "The Date of the Epistle to the Philippians," in *Studies in the Gospels and the Epistles*, ed. M. Black (Philadelphia: Westminster, 1962), pp. 149-167.

CLAUDIUS *as pictured on a coin of his reign* (A.D. 41-54). *He was the emperor who drove the Jews from Rome about the year 50. Some of the exiles found their way to Corinth and became Paul's aides.*

though it is conceivable that Paul spent time in prison in Ephesus, there is no direct evidence for it either from Acts or from his letters. The claim that Paul could not have written from Rome about a hoped-for visit to Philippi because the two cities were so far apart does not carry much weight, since there was a direct route from Rome to Philippi, and travel between the two was safe and common. The proposal of E. Lohmeyer that the letters were written during the imprisonment of Paul in Caesarea, reported in Acts 23-26, has even less to commend it than the Ephesian theory, since Caesarea is half again as far from Philippi as Rome is.[13] The most convincing theory as to the place of origin of the Letter to the Philippians is the traditional one: it was written from Rome by Paul during his imprisonment there. It may in its present form include fragments of other letters—Chapter 3, for example, may be part of a separate writing—but it represents the thought of Paul toward the end of his life when he must face the likelihood of execution.[14] Colossians is a letter which we shall consider in connection with the pattern and themes of Paul's message for Gentiles (Chapter 9).

THE EVIDENCE FROM ACTS. Here, then, is a summary of what we can infer from Paul's letters as to the course of his life. It is obvious that there is no fixed chronology, and only a general pattern as to the place and sequence of his work. In Acts, on the other hand, we have a series of events described that can be dated with reasonable certainty.[15] These are:

---

[12] The theory is set forth fully by G. S. Duncan in *St. Paul's Ephesian Ministry* (New York: Scribner's, 1930), pp. 59-161. The thesis was proposed earlier by such scholars as Adolf Deissmann, in *Paul* (New York: Harper & Row, 1957, first published in 1912), p. 17, where full bibliography up to 1927 is given.

[13] E. Lohmeyer, *Der Brief an die Philipper*, in *Kritisch-exegetischer Kommentar über das Neue Testament* (Göttingen: Vandenhoeck & Ruprecht, 1928), p. 3.

[14] For a discussion of the details of questions relating to the origins of the Letter to the Philippians and the possibility that Chapter 3, is an interpolation, see F. W. Beare, *The Epistle to the Philippians* (New York: Harper & Row, 1959), pp. 1-46.

[15] For a discussion of these dates and a presentation of the basis for arriving at them, see G. B. Caird, "Chronology of the New Testament," in *Interpreter's Dictionary of the Bible*, I (Nashville: Abingdon, 1962), 603. The date of Agrippa's death can be inferred from the account of his reign in Josephus' *Antiquities*, Books 18 and 19, although the circumstances of his death are differently described by Acts and Josephus. The date of the famine is difficult to fix precisely, since Josephus (Book 20) does not specify who was procurator at the time. Probably he intends his reader to conclude that Tiberius Alexander was procurator, in which case the year would be A.D. 46. Claudius' decree of expulsion of the Jews is reported by the Roman historians Suetonius (*Life of Claudius*) and Dio Cassius (*History of Rome*), but only Orosius, a Christian historian of the fifth century (*Historia contra Paganos*) specifies that it was in the ninth year of Claudius' reign, i.e., A.D. 49 or 50. An inscription found at Delphi, across the gulf from Corinth, fixes the date of Gallio's coming as governor of Achaia at A.D. 52-53, although it might have been a year earlier or later. On the basis of the accounts of the political fortunes of his predecessors as procurators of Judea (reported by Josephus, Tacitus, and Suetonius), it may be inferred that Festus became governor in A.D. 56, although if we follow the report in Eusebius' *Ecclesiastical History*, it may have been as late as A.D. 59. For a full presentation of the evidence for arriving at these dates, see F. J. Foakes-Jackson and K. Lake, *The Beginnings of Christianity*, V, eds. K. Lake and H. J. Cadbury (London: Macmillan, 1933), pp. 445-474.

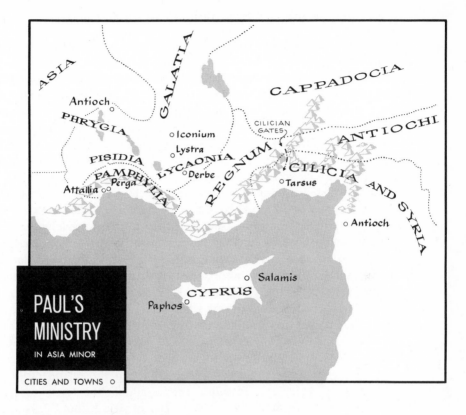

PAUL'S
MINISTRY
IN ASIA MINOR

CITIES AND TOWNS o

The death of Herod Agrippa I (described in Acts 12:23); A.D. 44

The famine in Palestine in the time of Claudius (Acts 11:28): A.D. 46

The decree of Claudius banning the Jews from Rome (Acts 18:2):
  A.D. 49 or 50

The arrival of the Roman governor, Gallio, in Corinth (Acts 18:12):
  A.D. 51

The arrival of the Roman governor, Festus, in Caesarea (Acts 24:27):
  A.D. 56 or 59

Of all these dates, the only ones that help us in fixing a date that ties in with Paul's autobiographical notes are those of the time of the decree of Claudius and the arrival of Gallio in Corinth. Both of these point to the likelihood that Paul began his ministry in Corinth about the year 50. We have no way of checking this date or the other dates as they relate to later events in Paul's career. Using this date as a base, however, we could conjecture that Paul left Corinth in 52, that he remained in Ephesus, visiting the churches of Greece and Asia Minor, until about 56 (I Cor. 16:8; II Cor. 12:14; I Cor. 16:5), after which he went to Jerusalem. That would have been about A.D. 57; allowing for the years of imprisonment in Caesarea, we come to the year 59 or 60 for his arrival in Rome. According to a tradition which we shall consider in Chapter

10, Paul was executed in Rome toward the close of the reign of Nero—that is, about A.D. 64.

In addition to providing us with a chronology of the life of Paul, Acts presents a picture of Paul significantly different from the one we have just inferred from his letters. According to Acts, Paul's home was not Damascus, but Tarsus in Cilicia. From there he traveled to Jerusalem to study under the famous rabbinic interpreter of the Law, Gamaliel (Acts 22:3), who has already been mentioned to the readers of Acts as cautioning Jewish officialdom against hasty opposition to Christianity (Acts 5:34-37). Paul is pictured as the leader of the opposition to Christianity in Jerusalem itself (Acts 9:1-2), even though he reports that he was not known by appearance to the Jerusalem Christians (Gal. 1:22). The Jerusalem church, however, is reported by Acts (11:19-26) to have chosen Paul to carry on a program of instruction of the new Gentile converts in Antioch. Paul was assisted in his work there by Barnabas (Acts 11:26; 12:25). These two were commissioned by the church in Antioch to carry an offering to the Jerusalem church during the famine period when the Judean church was in such great want (Acts 11:27-30). After their return to Antioch, Barnabas and Paul were again appointed to a special task: to begin the evangelization of the nearby island of Cyprus (Acts 13:1-12). The sphere of activity was soon extended to the mainland of Asia Minor, when Paul and Barnabas began preaching Jesus as the Christ in the inland cities of Pisidian Antioch (Acts 13:13-43), Iconium, Lystra, and Derbe (Acts 14:1-23), returning to Antioch in Syria via the coastal cities of Asia Minor (Acts 14:24-28). At first the preaching was done in the synagogues, but in the face of heightening opposition, the itinerant evangelists announced that they were turning from the Jews to the Gentiles (Acts 13:44-51); accordingly, they brought back to the church in Antioch the report of God's favor on their evangelism among the Gentiles (Acts 14:26-27). (See the map on p. 159 for the location of the cities Paul and Barnabas visited.)

THE PROBLEM OF THE JERUSALEM COUNCIL

Thus far in our examination of the evidence about the course of Paul's career, taken from Acts on the one hand and from his letters on the other, there is little by way of conflict or direct contact between these two sources.

Superficially, it would appear that the "council" described in Acts 15 is the one that Paul mentions in Gal. 1 and 2, since the issue in both cases is the grounds of admission of Gentile converts to Christian fellowship. The question is raised as to whether Gentile Christians should be obligated to observe the Law of Moses, and the answer in each case is that they should not be so required. Beneath this surface appearance, however, the genuine differences begin to appear.

According to Paul, the meeting with the leaders of the Jerusalem church was a private affair (Gal. 2:3) including presumably only Peter, James (the brother of Jesus) and John (Gal. 2:9). In Acts, however, it would appear that the entire body of "apostles and elders" was gathered together for a kind of public disputation on the issue (Acts 15:6 ff.). In Gal. 1:18, Paul's defense of his independence of the Jerusalem leaders rests in large measure on the rarity of his contacts with them. It is important for him, therefore, to represent the facts with strict accuracy when he says that the conference visit was only the second time he had been in Jerusalem since his conversion. But in Acts, it is clear that he had been there at least twice before: once following his conversion, and once on the visit with the relief for the famine-stricken Judean church (Acts 11:27-30). Some manuscripts of Acts report in 12:25 that Paul returned once more to Jerusalem, though the original reading is probably the one followed in most translations, which tells that he returned to Antioch following the relief visit.

The accounts of the Jerusalem Conference vary even more widely on the reports of the outcome of discussion. In Acts there are four rules which are agreed to by the opposing parties: (1) abstinence from idolatry; (2) abstinence from unchastity; (3) abstinence from eating flesh of animals that have been strangled (it was forbidden by Jewish Law for anyone to eat the flesh of an animal that died of itself or was torn by a wild beast—cf. Ex. 22:31, Lev. 17:15); and (4) abstinence from eating meat that still contained the animal's blood. The latter was strictly prohibited in many Old Testament passages, of which Gen. 9:4, Lev. 7:26, 27, and Deut. 12:16, 23 are representative. On this evidence it would seem that Paul agreed to four basic legal requirements for the admission of Gentiles to the Christian community, two of them of a moral-religious type and two of them of a ritual type.

In Galatians, however, Paul's main point is that he did not yield to the Jerusalem church leaders on a single point of legal obligation ("not even for a moment"—Gal. 2:5), in order that the truth of the Gospel free of legal obligations might be preserved for the Galatian Christians, and by extension for the whole Church. The only obligation to which Paul agreed was to take up the collection for the Jerusalem community, and this was an obligation of charity and sharing, not a legal requirement. It would seem that for Paul to have agreed to place these ritual and religious regulations as binding on the Gentile churches would have destroyed his entire understanding of the Gospel (see fuller discussion in Chapter 9). Paul did deal with the moral problems that arose among the Gentile Christians, but he did not do so by imposing on them a new or revised version of the Jewish Law (the problems of morality in the Gentile churches are considered in Chapter 8). How then are we to understand the conflicting evidence of the nature and outcome of Paul's conference with the Jerusalem church?

Several explanations are possible. First, there is the supposition that Acts

15 and Gal. 2 are discussing the same event, but are doing so from different points of view, with the Acts account dependent on Jerusalem sources. The difficulties with this thesis are many and great. If Paul had agreed to the regulations reported in Acts, his whole argument in Galatians could have been undermined by producing the document to which he had subscribed, in which the decrees were set forth. There is no evidence that such decrees were ever circulated among the Gentiles, as was reportedly agreed upon (Acts 15:21-30). Not only does this reconstruction lead us to conclude that Paul went back on his word, but that the church in Antioch professed to rejoice in obligations (Acts 15:31) that it had no intention of meeting.

A second possibility is that Paul in Galatians is speaking of a conference that took place on the occasion of the famine relief visit (Acts 11:27 ff.), but which is not described by Acts. The reason that Paul did not mention the formal council described in Acts 15 would be that it had not taken place at the time he wrote his letter to the Galatians.[16] The author of Acts has con-

---

[16] This theory is advanced by G. H. C. MacGregor in the "Exegesis of Acts," in *The Interpreter's Bible*, IX (Nashville: Abingdon, 1954), 198-201. It was also proposed in the first edition of the present work.

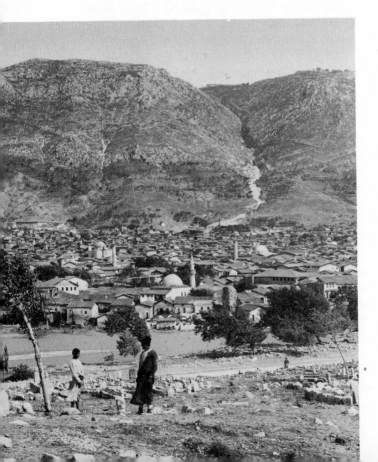

ANTIOCH *on the Orontes, with Mt. Silpius in the background. Located near the Mediterranean Sea, it was the seat of Paul's operations and one of the most important centers of Christianity in the first three centuries* A.D.

fused the record by failing to report the earlier consultation between Paul and "the pillars" of the Jerusalem church (Gal. 2:9). It may be argued against this thesis that it places Galatians as the earliest of the surviving Pauline letters, even though it is closely akin to Romans, which is demonstrably a late product, written toward the end of Paul's ministry.

A third possible explanation for the disagreement of the records is that the author of Acts has transformed the account of the Council in order to make it serve more effectively his own special interests. (On the theological and apologetic interests of Luke-Acts, see Chapter 13.) Luke was presumably writing at a time when both Jews and Christians had been driven from Jerusalem, following the fall of the city in A.D. 70. The consequences of this catastrophic event, which will be examined in some detail in Chapter 10, were that Jewish Christianity of the Torah-abiding type became isolated from the mainstream of the developing Church, so that the issue of Gentile obedience to the Jewish Law became a thing of the past. The decline of influence of the James-type leadership, following his death in A.D. 64, removed any reason for keeping alive the older hostilities which shine through Paul's letters so clearly. Accordingly, Luke smooths over the earlier difficulties and plays up the emerging consensus of the whole Church in his account of Christian origins in Acts. His report of the Jerusalem Council, therefore, far from requiring him to narrate the conflict between the church in Antioch and the leaders of the mother church in Jerusalem, provides him with an opportunity to show how differences were resolved and unity achieved. Out of this period of struggle there emerged a sense of the universality of the Church—called "catholic," from the Greek word meaning "concerning the whole." [17] Part Three of this book will discuss the developments within the Church in the post-Apostolic period, but it should be noted here that Acts does seem to have been written at a time when the conflict over keeping the Jewish Law was only a somewhat dim memory of a past generation. This would mean that Acts 15 ought to be used only with extreme caution as a source for historical reconstruction. Although there is no objective basis for doubting the reliability of the historical information included by Luke in the later parts of Acts, where we have no parallel material from Paul by which to check Luke's accuracy, we must accept the fact that Luke's major aim in writing Acts was not factuality but a theological understanding of the progress of the Gospel from Jerusalem to Rome.

---

[17] F. C. Baur (1792-1860), whose critical hypotheses were the basis for the so-called Tübingen school of Biblical criticism, proposed that in this development can be seen the classic pattern of historical movement described by the philosopher Hegel (1770-1831): every idea evokes its opposite; the opposites unite to form a new synthesis. The thesis, Baur said, was the Jewish, legalistic version of Christianity espoused by Peter and the Jerusalem leaders; the antithesis was the Law-free Gospel of Paul; the synthesis was catholic Christianity, which came into being at the end of the Apostolic Age. This theory has been sharply attacked, most recently and fully by J. Munck in *Paul and the Salvation of Mankind* (Richmond: John Knox Press, 1959), especially Chapter 3.

HOW MANY LETTERS DID PAUL WRITE?

A careful reading of the letters of Paul preserved in the New Testament will show that he wrote more letters than those that have survived. In Col. 4:16, for example, he refers to "the letter from Laodicea," by which he presumably means the letter he had written to the church at Laodicea. In I Cor. 5:9 Paul mentions a letter that he had previously sent to the Corinthian church, which in turn had written letters to him (I Cor. 7:1), so that we must suppose that an extended correspondence passed between them, of which only a small portion remains. Similarly, in II Cor. 2:4 there is a reference to an earlier letter of Paul to the church at Corinth, so that we can by no means assume that the entire output of Paul's letters has survived in the New Testament. Furthermore, there is some evidence that some of the letters of Paul that we now treat as units actually include parts of what were originally *several* letters. This seems to be most certainly the case in II Cor., where the train of thought is several times broken off abruptly: *e.g.*, at 6:13, 10:1, and possibly 9:1. Similar proposals for dividing up the Letter to the Philippians have been advanced,[18] based chiefly on the abrupt break in thought and mood that occurs between Phil. 3:1 and 3:2.

> Finally, my brethren, rejoice in the Lord. To write the same things to you is not irksome to me, and is safe for you.
>
> —PHILIPPIANS 3:1

> Look out for the dogs, look out for the evil-workers, look out for those who mutilate the flesh.
>
> —PHILIPPIANS 3:2

It appears that the passage extending from Phil. 3:2 to 4:1 is an interpolation from some other writing of Paul, inserted by an editor of his letters at this point in the original Letter to the Philippians.

Similar partition or rearrangement theories have been proposed for both the Letter to the Romans and the First Letter to the Corinthians, though none of them has been widely accepted. The uncertainty with regard to Romans, for example, centers around the questions: To whom was it originally addressed (was it a kind of encyclical, or a specific epistle to the church at Rome)? And how did it originally end? Some manuscripts of Romans include the long doxology usually found at 16:25-27, but locate it at the end of Chapter 14. One of the oldest and best manuscripts of Paul's letters includes the doxology at

---

[18] A concise statement of the theories and possibilities concerning Philippians as a composite document is set forth in *The Epistle to the Philippians*, by F. W. Beare (New York: Harper & Row, 1959), pp. 1-5.

the end of Chapter 15.[19] Many scholars have concluded from this evidence that Romans existed in the early Church in several editions, some of which ended at one point, others at another point. A few ancient copies of Romans omit the mention of Rome at 1:7, which has led to the suggestion that the book was originally an encyclical that was circulated among many churches.

The differences in copies of Romans serve only to demonstrate that there was considerable freedom in the form and manner in which the writings of Paul were used and circulated in the ancient Church. They are differences so great that we cannot determine with exactitude what the original form was, and yet so slight in content that we have no doubts about what was the essence of Paul's message contained in this letter.[20]

The more important question as to the extent of Paul's letters is: How many of those attributed to him actually were written by Paul? In the King James (or Authorized) version of the New Testament, the following letters are designated in the title as having been written by Paul:

Romans	I and II Thessalonians
I and II Corinthians	I and II Timothy
Galatians	Titus
Ephesians	Philemon
Philippians	Hebrews
Colossians	

Of this list, Hebrews makes no claim to have been written by Paul, and was already believed by the end of the second century to have achieved its present form by the work of someone other than Paul. Modern scholarship is virtually unanimous in seeing in the Letter to the Hebrews the creative product of an unknown writer whose views and orientation were quite different from those of Paul and his immediate followers (see Chapter 17 for a fuller discussion of Hebrews). In Chapter 3 we noted that Ephesians was likely written by a disciple of Paul, rather than by Paul himself. Differences in literary style, in vocabulary, and in theological detail make a convincing case against the Pauline authorship of the book.[21] Some scholars have questioned the authenticity of Colossians, but its genuineness is here assumed, as will be evident from the treatment of its contents in Chapter 9, where we shall be considering the main themes of Paul's message for Gentile hearers.

---

[19] This is the so-called Chester Beatty Papyrus, which was discovered in Egypt in 1931, and which was written in the third century. It contains both the gospels (called by textual scholars, p^{45}) and the letters of Paul (p^{46}).

[20] A concise, comprehensive presentation of the evidence concerning the ending of Romans is given by C. K. Barrett in *The Epistle to the Romans* (New York: Harper & Row, 1957), pp. 9-13.

[21] A thorough, technical examination of this question of the authorship of Ephesians is given by C. L. Mitton in *The Epistle of the Ephesians* (Oxford: Clarendon Press, 1951). A brief discussion of the authorship of Ephesians is presented in Chapter 10 of this book.

The question with regard to the authorship of the two Letters to Timothy and the Letter to Titus is more complex. The letters clearly claim to have been written by Paul, although the probability that the author has used Paul's name as a pseudonym should not trouble us. Far from such a practice being considered deceitful or dishonest, it was regarded in ancient times as a way of honoring a great figure of the past to write a work in his name. The best-known instance of this is in the *Dialogues* of Plato, who put his thought and words in the mouth of Socrates. There may be Socratic thoughts in this work, but the words as we have them are those of Plato. In the case of these three disputed Pauline letters, however (which are usually referred to in a group as the *Pastorals* [22]), it seems that Pauline words are used with meanings quite different from those given them in Paul's own works. In Paul's undisputed writings, for example, "faith" means trust in God, especially with reference to what God has promised or performed through Jesus Christ. In the Pastorals, on the other hand, "faith" is a body of knowledge which is to be guarded and preserved intact (see I Tim. 3:9; II Tim. 1:11-13; Tit. 1:1). The life of faith, according to the Pastorals, is not the struggle of flesh against spirit, of grace against sin, as we find it in Paul's letters, but a reasonable life in accord with religious virtues: sobriety, good conscience, piety. Similarly, the rather vague lines of responsibility that gave Paul so much difficulty in the administration of the churches during his lifetime have given way to quite carefully delineated classifications of ecclesiastical responsibility in the Pastorals. Clearly, then, these letters come from a later period—perhaps from the middle of the second century. The significance of these letters for the life and thought of the Church is presented in Chapter 16. The Pastorals, therefore, are of no assistance in our reconstruction of the life and work of Paul, with the possible exception of authentic fragments of a letter or letters of Paul which may be included in the Pastorals. This possibility is considered in Chapter 10.

We have now surveyed the sources for our knowledge of Paul, as well as the problems and the possibilities for recovering the history of his work. The limitations for one interested in biography are very considerable, though not so great as for one who might attempt a biography of Jesus. But the possibilities are very great for gaining an understanding of how Paul presented the Christian faith to pagans, and how he nurtured the struggling Christian communities that he founded in his travels throughout the Roman Empire. We turn now to a sketch of the range of his travels, and to a reconstruction of his methods and problems in dealing with Gentile churches.

---

[22] For a full discussion of the questions of authorship and distinctive qualities, see J. C. Beker, in *Interpreter's Dictionary of the Bible*, III (Nashville: Abingdon, 1962), 668-675.

PAUL,
THE PIONEER

CHAPTER EIGHT   There were no precedents by which

Paul could be guided as he set about his work of preaching

the Christian message to Gentiles and establishing churches

among the converts to the new faith. The account in Acts

reports that Paul's strategy was to preach at the synagogue

in any given city as long as he was permitted to do so, after

which he would withdraw to a convenient home or meet-

ing place where the gatherings of the Christian community

would take place. According to Acts 16, for example, Paul's first evangelistic activity in the mainland of Europe was launched by the side of a river near Philippi, at a spot where a group of Jews were accustomed to gather on the sabbath for prayer (Acts 16:11-15). In Corinth, Acts tells us, Paul preached in the synagogue until he was forced to leave, whereupon he moved into the adjoining house and continued his preaching there (Acts 18:5-8).

On the basis of his own letters, it is more difficult to trace any such details of strategy or of shift in procedure when the Jewish community in any given place had rejected Paul and his message. Paul does, of course, at all times presuppose the authority of the Old Testament scriptures in the Gentile churches. Even in writing to what seem to have been strictly Gentile churches, such as the one at Thessalonica (I Thess. 1:9), the scriptures are referred to often but by way of allusion rather than extensive quotation, as in the Letter to the Romans. That the church at Thessalonica had been brought straight out of paganism into Christianity is suggested by Paul's phrase "you turned to God from idols" (I Thess. 1:9).

At Rome, on the other hand, the nucleus of the church seems to have been a group of Jews who came to believe in Jesus as the Christ. This is surely implied in Acts 18, where Priscilla and Aquila, who have been driven out of Rome because of a disturbance among the Jews, are already Christians when Paul meets them, and join immediately in assisting him in his work. That Priscilla and Aquila did, in fact, assist Paul in Corinth and elsewhere is confirmed by Paul's own writings (e.g., Rom. 16:3; I Cor. 16:19).

STRATEGY AND STRUCTURE IN THE GENTILE CHURCHES

A major concern of Paul as he began work in a city was a thoroughly practical matter: to establish himself as financially independent of the community in which he was to carry on his evangelistic work. From II Corinthians it can be inferred that one of the charges against which he had to defend himself was that he was engaged in his work for the sake of the money he could get out of it (II Cor. 12:14-18). Accordingly, Paul was extremely careful to have thoroughly reliable persons, including representatives of the participating churches, as members of the delegation charged with carrying out one of his major projects: transporting the gift of the Gentile churches to the church in Jerusalem (II Cor. 8:16-23).

There is some evidence that Paul managed to live by supporting himself. He mentions in writing to the Corinthians that he worked with his own hands (I Cor. 4:12; 9:6). Acts reports that his means of livelihood was tentmaking (Acts 18:3), which probably means that he worked with leather rather than cloth. There is likewise some evidence that rabbis were encouraged to develop skill in a trade such as leather-working, but no claim is made by Paul or for him in the New Testament that he was a rabbi. Whatever his means of livelihood, he chose to work in order to guarantee his financial independence of the churches he founded. This is the whole force of the argument in I Cor. 9.

Under certain circumstances, however, Paul did accept money from a church in which he had previously worked. That churches were not often so generous is evident from the thank-you note appended to the Letter to the Philippians (Phil. 4:14-19). There Paul declares that they were the only ones at the beginning of his work in Macedonia who helped to support him, and that they had done so on several occasions. Whether the generosity of the Philippians toward Paul was matched by other churches, or whether the sensitivity of the Corinthian church on financial matters was matched by any other, we have no way of knowing. One thing is clear: no matter how spiritually motivated the ministry of Paul may have been, he could not ignore such material problems as finances.

The Foolishness of Preaching

The ultimate concern of Paul in beginning his work, however, was not finances but evangelization. His was the unprecedented commission to preach the Good News of Jesus Christ to those who had never heard—including those who had heard scarcely if at all of the God of Israel, the Father of Jesus Christ (Col. 1:3). We have already noted that the prime consideration in Paul's ministry was the *kerygma*, in which it was declared "as of first importance":

> ...that Christ died for our sins in accordance with the scriptures, that he was buried, that he was raised on the third day in accordance with the scriptures, that he appeared to Cephas, then to the twelve.
> —I CORINTHIANS 15:3, 4

The difficulty involved in choosing the Cross as a starting point in the propagation of a strange new religious message can scarcely be exaggerated. Jesus was an unknown figure, without training or position, from an obscure part of a remote province. Under some peculiar circumstances, which involved brash aspirations of the tiny Jewish nation to gain political independence, he had been executed by order of the provincial governor, with the consent of the local political and religious authorities. Now the Christians were not only appealing to men to pay heed to the teachings of this man who had been convicted as an enemy of the state, but to claim that he had overcome death and had reappeared alive to his former followers. We shall examine this message in greater detail in the next chapter, but here it is important to recognize the enormous difficulties that Paul and his fellow workers faced in trying to put across this claim.

Paul neatly summarizes for us the kind of reception he had come to expect from the majority of his hearers:

> . . . we preach Christ crucified, a stumbling-block to Jews and folly to Gentiles. . . .
>
> —I CORINTHIANS 1:23

Jesus did not fit any of the patterns of Jewish expectation about the Deliverer whom God would send at the End Time. He was not a king in any ordinary sense of the word, nor did he appear to be a divine being, disguised in human form. His birthplace and parentage were known, and they did not fit the details of messianic expectation. Furthermore, in the exercise of his extraordinary authority in the course of his ministry, he had achieved the result of undermining Jewish institutions, such as the laws of separation and sabbath. He had predicted the destruction of the Jews' greatest pride, the Temple in Jerusalem. One would have expected the authority of the Messiah to be used in liberating the people from Gentile domination; instead, he seemed to acquiesce in Caesar's sovereignty and even told his followers to love their enemies. Those of the Jewish nation's leaders who had had an opportunity to hear him at first hand had largely rejected him; how could Jews as a whole be expected to respond to him otherwise?

To compound the objectionable quality of this Christian message, from the standpoint of the Jews, the preachers of the Gospel claimed that Judaism did not really understand the import of its own scriptures, but that the Christians did. What the God of Israel intended and what he had promised were now actually fulfilled in the coming of Jesus as Messiah and in its consequent effects on the Christian community.

The Greek hearers of the Gospel had just as great difficulty with it, though on different grounds. They were familiar with claims of various religions that a certain divine man or a certain god masquerading as a man—whether Osiris or Adonis or Dionysius—had died and then been restored to life, thereby becoming savior of those who worshiped him. (See discussion of the mystery religions in pp. 19-21.) But the claim that an historical figure who had been recently executed as a criminal had now been exalted by God and was the savior of the world—such a claim was utterly foolish. In full recognition of "the folly of what we preach" (*i.e., kerygma;* I Cor. 1:21), Paul continued to proclaim to Greeks the "foolish" message of Jesus Christ crucified and risen from the dead.

Joy in Affliction

Inevitably, Paul encountered hostility and hardship. We gain an insight into the frame of mind that was his as he went about his itinerant evangelism,

in the autobiographical note—one of those brief but very revealing passages—
included in one of his letters to the Corinthians:

> ...even when we came into Macedonia, our bodies had no rest,
> but we were afflicted at every turn—fighting without and fear within.
> —II CORINTHIANS 7:5

Paul would have been less than human if he had not been disheartened by
the difficulties he encountered and by the opposition that his work engendered
from both Jewish and Gentile sources. Added to these problems, however, was
some sort of personal handicap, of a nature that is never specified by Paul.
He refers to it metaphorically as "a thorn in the flesh" (II Cor. 12:7). Some
modern writers have guessed that he was subject to epilepsy. Others have conjectured that he had an eye ailment, on the basis of his reference to writing
"with large letters" (Gal. 6:11) and the willingness of the Galatians to "pluck
out their eyes" and give them to him (Gal. 4:15). He quotes his detractors at
one point as commenting contemptuously on his unimpressive bodily appearance
and his despicable speech (II Cor. 10:10). He commends the Galatians, however, because they were not put off by his bodily condition and did not scorn
or despise him on account of it (Gal. 4:14). But what precisely the condition
was, we do not know. All that we can conclude is that it was for Paul an
abiding annoyance and for the Christians a source of embarrassment.

There were two forms of compensation for these difficulties that Paul reports
in his letters: the gratification that came from those who did respond to the
Gospel, and the support from his fellow workers. In one of the passages where
he is commenting on the embarrassment that his appearance created, he declares that the Galatians, unlike others who had scorned him, had received
him as a messenger (or angel) of God (Gal. 4:14). In spite of all the difficulties that he encountered, the Gentiles did respond in faith. They did turn
to God (I Thess. 2:13). They did believe (I Cor. 15:11). In the midst of
persecution and harassment, Paul was filled with joy:

> For what is our hope or joy or crown of boasting before our Lord
> Jesus at his coming? Is it not you? For you are our glory and joy.
> —I THESSALONIANS 2:19

"Partners and Fellow Workers in Your Service"—II Corinthians 8:23

To establish churches in Gentile lands would not have been possible
without the assistance that Paul received from his co-workers, and especially
from those who traveled with him. The tradition by which the messengers of
the Gospel went out in pairs is at least as old as the Church itself, and may

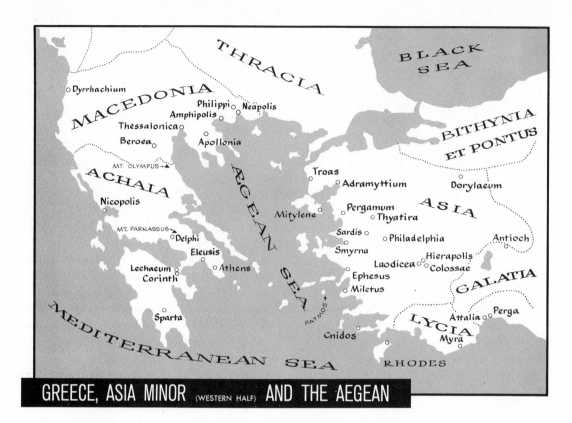

GREECE, ASIA MINOR (WESTERN HALF) **AND THE AEGEAN**

go back to the period of the ministry of Jesus (Mk. 6:7). Paul regularly associates himself with a fellow worker at the beginning of his letters. Sometimes the mention of the other worker may be purely formal, or it may refer merely to the amanuensis who actually did the writing for Paul. This would seem to be the case in the mention of Sosthenes in I Cor. 1:1. But at other times Paul refers to those who are known to have shared with him in the ministry of preaching in the very churches with which he carried on correspondence (cf. II Cor. 1:19 with I Thess. 1:1). The pattern of two-by-two is more precisely observed in Acts, where Paul travels first with Barnabas (Acts 13:2), then with Silas, or Silvanus (Acts 15:40). Later we might infer from the sudden shifts from "they" to "we" in the course of the Acts narrative (*e.g.*, at Acts 16:10; 21:1), that Paul was frequently accompanied on his journeys by an anonymous companion who has preserved the accounts now embodied in Acts. In addition, Acts reports that Paul sent out other workers in pairs; for example, Timothy and Erastus in Acts 19:22.

Even clearer than the pattern of traveling pairs of evangelists is the picture of Paul relying heavily on his associates to complete the work he had begun or to move into a situation where problems had arisen. At Corinth, for example, Paul had done the pioneer work ("I planted"), and Apollos had nurtured the faith of the new-born church ("Apollos watered"). But Paul is unwilling to take credit to himself for what he had done, or to give special honor to Apollos for his contribution, since in his judgment all that occurs in Christian growth is the work of God (I Cor. 3:6). Other important tasks are reported as having been performed by Timothy and Titus (II Cor. 7:5-16; I Cor. 16:10-11),[1] including assistance with the collection for the Jerusalem church, the project by which Paul sought to demonstrate tangibly the unity of the whole Church.

In his chosen role of pioneer missionary, Paul could not and would not remain for long periods of time in one place. According to Acts he resided and worked in Ephesus for about two years (Acts 19:10), but this is the longest such period of which we have any record. The eagerness to press on to new, unevangelized territory is apparent at many points in his letters, and explicitly set forth in Rom. 15, where he speaks of his "ambition to preach the gospel, not where Christ has already been named" (Rom. 15:20). In the light of this aim, he is already seen as laying plans to go on beyond Rome to Spain, where Christian preachers had not yet penetrated (Rom. 15:24). But what is to happen to the churches that have been established by Paul and by those who have been working directly with them?

As in founding the churches, so in maintaining them, Paul was heavily dependent on his fellow workers. Among them he singled out for special honor Priscilla and Aquila, who had aided him first in Corinth, according to Acts (Rom. 16:3; cf. Acts 18:2). But following the mention of Priscilla and Aquila there is in Rom. 16 a long list of those to whom Paul sends greetings, many of whom are designated as "fellow workers." Of one woman in the list, it is said simply that "she worked hard among you" (Rom. 16:6). In Ephesians and in the Pastorals, the transfer of authority from Paul to his successors is at times implied, at times directly affirmed. Mention of the gift of God which was received by the laying on of the apostles' hands and of the consciousness of having been entrusted with the Gospel (I Tim. 1:11, 13), implies that the transmission of authority and function in the Church was conceived in a quite formalized way. The apostles pass on to their successors both the content of the Christian message and the power to minister effectively. Even though we do not recognize the Pastorals and other deutero-Pauline literature as authentic, we can assume that something like the process they describe actually did occur from the beginning—namely, that those who took over from the apostles exercised authority in their names and believed that they were authorized to build on the foundation that the apostles had established (Eph. 2:20).

---

[1] For a fuller statement of the roles of Timothy and Titus see the articles by H. C. Kee on these two figures in *Interpreter's Dictionary of the Bible*, IV (New York and Nashville: Abingdon, 1962), 650-651, 656-657.

THE IMPORTANCE OF APOSTOLIC AUTHORITY
TO THE STABILITY OF THE CHURCHES

Reference has just been made to the authority of Paul as an apostle. We have
already considered the problem which Paul experienced in finding and maintaining his place among the Apostolic Circle.[2] Especially in the Corinthian
letters, we can see that Paul had a constant battle to maintain his position as
one who bore the authority of an apostle. The danger was always present that
he would be treated as a second-class apostle, since he had not been one of
Jesus' original followers, and since he had at the outset been a persecutor of
the Church (I Cor. 15:9). Against such charges Paul had to speak out—at
times with some bitter sarcasm—in protest that he was as worthy and as authoritative as any of the rest of the apostles (II Cor. 11, 12). All the signs
that might be expected of an apostle had been evident through Paul: signs,
wonders, and mighty works (II Cor. 12:12). The one thing he acknowledged
that differentiated him from the rest of the apostles was that he refused to
accept money from the Corinthians in order that he might keep his freedom:

> For in what were you less favored than the rest of the churches,
> except that I myself did not burden you? Forgive me this wrong!
> —II CORINTHIANS 12:13

But positively, Paul was certain of his possessing apostolic authority by reason
of the transformed lives of those who became members of these fledgling
Christian communities:

> Do we need, as some do, letters of recommendation to you, or from
> you? You yourselves are our letters of recommendation, written on
> your hearts, to be known and read by all men.
> —II CORINTHIANS 3:2

Paul's authority was exercised in many ways in his relationships to the
churches. Most striking of all its manifestations, perhaps, was the command
issued to the church at Corinth to execute judgment on an unrepentant member. Although he could not be present for the occasion, his spirit would be
there, together with the power of the Holy Spirit; by this authority the man was
to be delivered to Satan for the destruction of the flesh, in order that his spirit
might be saved at the last day (I Cor. 5:3-5). Since this is the only such
instance of which we have knowledge from the New Testament, we cannot
tell how widespread the practice was of pronouncing corporate judgment on
an incorrigible brother. But what this passage does show is that Paul saw his

---

[2] See in the previous chapter, pp. 151-152.

authority ("spirit") as appropriately bracketed with the Holy Spirit in the exercise of authority in God's name in the churches.

Another facet of the apostolic authority of Paul is evident in his handing down decisions on moral questions that arose among the churches. In doing so, he placed his own commandments alongside those of Jesus. Thus, on the question of divorce, he simply transmitted (in his own paraphrase) the commandment of Jesus forbidding divorce and remarriage, which is preserved in the synoptic tradition (Mk. 10:1-9; cf. I Cor. 7:10). Paul indicated clearly that this rule was not his own, but was from "the Lord," meaning from Jesus Christ. But in the next sentence Paul presented his own decision about the problem of the believer who is married to an unbelieving spouse (I Cor. 7:12). Here the command was issued with an authority equal to that of the word of Jesus, but now it is as the word of *Paul:* "To the rest I say, not the Lord. . . ." In the passage that follows this decree, Paul continues to offer to the Corinthian church guidelines or even specific commands, and to do so by virtue of the authority that he possesses—or rather that possesses him.

The chief means by which Paul expressed and transmitted this authority was—at least so far as we can now observe it—his letters. He quoted his detractors at one point as acknowledging that, in spite of his weak bodily presence, "his letters are weighty and strong" (II Cor. 10:10). In form, Paul's letters do not differ greatly from other letters which have been preserved from this period.[3] The similarities and differences have been sharply detailed by Martin Dibelius:

> A Greek private letter begins with a prescript: "(The sender) gives (his) greetings to (the recipient)." Paul employs this formula, but instead of the Greek greeting *chairein* (salutation) he employs the similar sounding but far deeper *charis* (grace) and adds the Semitic greeting "peace," *e.g.,* "Grace and peace from God our Father and the Lord Jesus Christ." This combination of words of greeting had possibly already become customary in Greek-speaking Judaism, but it may originate with Paul. Sometimes two or three writers are named, a feature which springs from the apostle's desire to let his fellow workers express themselves, but it is no indication that they took part in composing the letter. . . . Frequently in a Greek private letter, an assurance of prayer for the recipients follows on the prescript. Characteristically in Paul an expression of thanks grew out of this feature; when he mentions his readers his prayer is one of thanksgiving. That is the form in which Paul gives praise to his churches. When he departs from this form, as in Galatians: "I marvel that you are so soon removed" as we read in this case, we can see that he consciously departed from custom and thereby sharply censured them.[4]

---

[3] Several representative letters from the Graeco-Roman era are reproduced, translated, and analyzed in A. Deissmann, *Light from the Ancient East* (New York: Harper & Row, n.d.), especially pp. 146-251.

[4] From M. Dibelius, *A Fresh Approach to the New Testament and Early Christian Literature* (New York: Scribner's, 1936), pp. 142-143.

THE ACROPOLIS *at Athens, with the hill of Areopagus in the foreground. According to Acts 17, Paul preached before the court that traditionally met on the Areopagus.*

The string of exhortations that come at the end of most of Paul's letters are likewise his own variant on the conventional manner of closing a letter. Even the content of these exhortations is not wholly original with Paul, who seems to have taken over more or less conventionalized moral exhortations of the day—perhaps of Stoic origins—and Christianized them by inserting here and there the phrase "in the Lord" (*e.g.*, Col. 3:18-22).[5] With regard to their outward form and their location within the over-all framework of the letter, they correspond precisely to standard usage in the Graeco-Roman period. As to both form and content, therefore, Paul has adapted the conventions of his time to serve his own purposes in the upbuilding of the churches. Thereby the letters of Paul became one of his most effective instruments in implementing his apostolic authority.

THE PROBLEMS OF GENTILE CHURCHES

The correspondence with the Corinthian church provides us with our best insight into the social and moral difficulties that the Church faced as it sought to establish itself in Gentile, pagan cities. We do possess a dramatic, rather

[5] *Ibid.*, p. 220.

full account of Paul's evangelistic efforts in the great city of Athens, reported in Acts 17. Even though we regard the Acts account as the author's attempt to describe the way he thought Paul should have undertaken such a task, rather than a straightforward historical record, there is a certain appropriateness in the description and even a sensitivity to the kind of difficulty that Paul would have faced under the circumstances.[6] It may therefore be illuminating to examine this report in some detail.

The Setting of Paul's Evangelism of the Gentiles

According to the Acts narrative, Paul had encountered both success in winning converts and hostility from local Jewish authorities in the cities of Thessalonica and Beroea. In order to avoid arousing greater antagonism, Paul is reportedly asked to leave, moving on southward to Athens, where his companions Silas and Timothy are to meet him (Acts 17:1-15). Whether Paul traveled from Beroea to Athens by land or sea, he would have seen two of Greece's glories: the majestic peak of Olympus, legendary home of the gods, towering over the Gulf of Thessalonica, and the spectacular Acropolis at Athens, crowned with the glistening marble of the Parthenon. A second-century traveler tells us that the light of the sun, reflected from the huge bronze statue of Athena located within the precincts of the Parthenon, was visible to sailors miles away as they entered the harbor of Athens at Piraeus. Among the cluster of buildings that topped the hill were the temple known as the Erectheum, with its famous Porch of the Maidens, and the complex of graceful colonnades and shrines that formed the portal to the temple precincts, the Propylaea.

It was, however, not the splendor of Athens' marble shrine that caught Paul's attention; it was the activity in the city center, several hundred feet below at the foot of the Acropolis. The six acres of open market place (or *agora*, as it was called) had long since become so cluttered with monuments and altars to assorted deities that the Roman rulers had felt obliged to construct annexes in the area to the east. Around the original square were the colonnades and public structures in which were carried on the commercial, political, social, and, to an extent, the intellectual life of this great center of Hellenic culture. Athens' leadership in the cultural world was declining, to be replaced by that of Alexandria and later the cities of the West. But even in Paul's day the successors of Zeno were to be found teaching in the very public porches (*stoa*)

---

[6] M. Dibelius has shown that Luke has seen in the journey of Paul to Greece "an event affecting the entire world." Paul's appearance in Athens, of which Luke would have had knowledge from I Thess. 3:1, represented a confrontation of the Gospel with the highest level of pagan culture, as symbolized by and embodied in the city of Athens. His visit to Athens becomes, therefore, "the focal point in this great event in the history of evangelism and religion." M. Dibelius, *Studies in the Acts of the Apostles* (London: SCM Press, 1956), p. 76.

that had given the name Stoic to their philosophical school. To the west of the agora were the imposing council chambers and shrines that had served as public gathering places since before the days of Socrates. Intruding into what was originally the open court of the market place were the Temple of Ares, god of war, and an enormous music hall, which seem in retrospect to have symbolized the devotion to power and pleasure that brought Greece to ruin. The great days of Greek literature and political thought were centuries past, but the pride of culture and the fondness for matching wits remained.

Converting the Intellectuals

According to the account in Acts 17, Paul divided his time between the synagogue, where the most fertile field for conversion was normally to be sought, and the agora, where the prospects were dim but the need great. His remarks about Jesus and the Resurrection were greeted in the market place with amused interest by some and with open scorn by others. It has been suggested that the Athenians mistook the term "resurrection" for a female deity (the word is feminine in Greek) and thought that Jesus was her consort,

THE STOA OF ATTALOS *has been reconstructed at the foot of the Acropolis. The original was built as a public portico by Attalos II, King of Pergamum, and the marble for the reconstruction was taken from the same quarry that he used in the middle of the second century* B.C.

after the fashion of such pairs of deities as Isis and Osiris, and Venus and Adonis. In any case, the excitement that Paul's disputing stirred up led to his being summoned before the council of city officials who were charged with maintaining order in the agora. Originally, this court had convened only in the open-air space carved out of the rock on top of the Hill of Ares (Areopagus in Greek), but in later years it often met in one of the council chambers adjoining the agora. The staircase leading to the summit and the benches carved from the living rock of Areopagus are still to be seen in Athens today. Whether on this occasion the session of the Areopagite council was held on the hilltop or in the Stoa is impossible to determine.

If it was from the vantage point of the Hill of Ares itself that Paul spoke to the council, he could have indicated with a single sweeping gesture scores of the idols and altars to which he referred in his opening remarks. Far from condemning the Athenians as irreligious, Paul sought to guide them to the goal of their religious quest, which was epitomized for him in their dedication of an altar to an unknown god. In other Greek cities inscriptions have been found on altars that were dedicated to unknown *gods*, but none to a *single* undesignated deity. Two famous travelers of antiquity, Pausanias (around A.D. 150) and Apollonius of Tyana (first century A.D.), are reported to have seen altars to unknown gods in Athens, and an Athenian legend tells how an ancient hero averted a plague by offering a sacrifice to an unknown god. It is not impossible, therefore, that such an altar may have existed in the agora of Athens, even though none has been discovered. In any case, the reference provided an effective opening wedge for the address that Paul is reported to have given.

Scholars have pointed out that neither the style nor the approach of this sermon is quite like what we find in Paul's letters.[7] The famous phrase, "In him we live and move and have our being," sounds pantheistic, as though God were a world-soul that permeated all the universe. What Paul is reported as doing, however, is quoting a familiar passage from Epimenides, a popular semi-legendary figure of ancient Greece. He uses the words to establish a common point of reference with his audience, not as proof for a major point in his sermon. Paul's attack is against idolatry, with its notion that God can be represented in tangible form. He insists on the spiritual nature of God, who is active throughout all his creation, and who is the true goal of those who have erected an altar to the god that they admit they do not know. The god whom they worship without knowing is the one who orders events and fulfills his purpose in his creation. That purpose is a moral one, and in order to prepare themselves for the time when God will fulfill it men must repent.

---

[7] See the essay by M. Dibelius, "Paul on the Areopagus," in *Studies in the Acts of the Apostles* (London: SCM Press, 1956), pp. 26-77. An attempt to demonstrate that the Areopagus speech belongs to a tradition going back to Paul is made by Bertil Gärtner in *The Areopagus Speech and Natural Revelation* (Uppsala, Sweden: C. W. K. Gleerup, 1955), especially pp. 248-252.

Only through repentance can they be made ready for the end of the present age and the judgment that will usher in the Age to Come. Paul is not seeking to compete with the philosophers on their own ground by means of an erudite discourse; rather, by using commonplaces of religious verse and sentiment, he is trying to gain a sympathetic hearing from the council before proceeding to controversial matters.

Results in Athens

So long as Paul confined himself to the denunciation of idolatry and the affirmation of the spiritual nature of God, few of his examiners could have felt much antagonism. But when he introduced the notion of a man through whom the world is to be judged, and when he talked about the Resurrection, it was too much for most of his listeners. Had Paul spoken of immortality, he would have given no offense; even if he had affirmed only that some dead hero had been revived or deified, the audience would have understood, although they might not have been convinced. But the distinctively oriental (Iranian and later Jewish) idea of the resurrection of the dead seemed an absurdity to the educated Athenians. The results of Paul's approach were meager, and he seems never to have used it again.

The narrator has given a tantalizing twist to the account by mentioning that among the converts was a man named Dionysius the Areopagite. This would imply that Paul converted one of his judges in much the same way that the martyr Stephen's courage had contributed to Paul's own conversion (Acts 6:8; 8:3; 9:1-30). Actually, nothing further is known of this Dionysius, although his name was a favorite nom-de-plume for quasi-philosophers in the fifth century and later. As enigmatic as Dionysius is the subsequent history of the community of Christians in Athens; we know nothing more about the Athenian church in the Apostolic Age.

There is one city—Corinth—where we know on the evidence of his own letters that important work was carried on by Paul. If we combine the account of his journey to Corinth as reported by Acts with what is known of the city from sources contemporary with Paul as well as from extensive archaeological work done on the ancient site, a vivid picture emerges. According to Acts 18:1 ff., Paul traveled westward from Athens along the shore of the Saronic Gulf, past the Island of Salamis, which is forever associated with the Greeks' spectacular defeat of the Persian navy in 480 B.C. As he approached the narrow isthmus that separates the Peloponnesus from the rest of Greece, he could see Cenchreae, the eastern port of Corinth and the seat of the famous Isthmian Games. Here goods were transported across the narrow neck of land to Lechaeum, just west of Corinth, where ships carried them on to the ports of Rome. Corinth itself sits on a series of ledges facing out over the gulf that bears its name. To the northwest are the jagged snow-patched slopes of Mount Parnassus, with the famous Delphic Oracle nestling at its foot.

Looming up behind the city nearly 1,900 feet above the sea is the massive rock known as Acrocorinth. From its summit can be seen the Gulf of Corinth stretching to the west, the rugged hills of the Peloponnesus to the south, and the eastern gulf through which ships sailed to the ports of Asia Minor and the Levant. This impressive vista symbolized the strategic position that Corinth occupied at an important commercial and cultural crossroad.

Morality and Religion in Corinth

Located atop Acrocorinth was a small structure that dramatized in grosser fashion the cultural mingling at Corinth. It was a temple, ostensibly in honor of Aphrodite, the Hellenic goddess of love and beauty, but actually a center for the worship of Astarte, the sensual Phoenician deity whose orgiastic cults had shocked the sensibilities of the ancient Israelites. Strabo, the indefatigable geographer and chronicler of the early first century A.D., reports that at one time more than a thousand temple prostitutes were maintained in connection with the worship at this shrine.

In the city itself were temples to Isis, the Great Mother, and to other oriental deities. So low was the level of morality in Corinth that the very name of the city had become synonymous with profligacy and degradation. "To corinthianize" meant "to debase."

In addition to all the other eastern cults, there was a colony of Jews in Corinth. The size of the colony had been sharply increased just before Paul's arrival as the result of an imperial decree that banned all Jews from Rome. Suetonius, the Roman biographer, referring to this incident in his *Life of Claudius*, explains that there had been a disturbance among the Jews, instigated by a man named Chrestos, which Claudius had sought to settle by dispersing

THE TEMPLE OF APOLLO *at Corinth, with the Gulf of Corinth beyond.*

THE BEMA *at Corinth (the public rostrum), with the Acrocorinth in the background. Paul was accorded a hearing on this platform before Gallio, the Roman governor.*

the Jewish community. What Suetonius took for an internal conflict may actually have been caused by the arrival in Rome of preachers of the Christian Gospel, which would certainly have stirred up discord among the Jews. Among those who fled to Corinth were Aquila and Priscilla, with whom Paul struck up a lasting friendship (Acts 18:1-3). It may be that this couple had already heard the Gospel, or had even accepted it, before leaving Rome, and were thus favorably disposed to cooperate with Paul in his missionary work in bustling, corrupt Corinth. Perhaps the reason Paul does not list Aquila and Priscilla as his first converts in Achaia [8] (I Cor. 16:15) is that they had been converted long before he arrived.

The synagogue in Corinth seems to have been located on the main road that led from the agora down to the port at Lechaeum. More than 50 years ago a heavy stone lintel was discovered with an inscription that almost certainly reads, "Synagogue of the Hebrews." The crudeness and unpretentiousness of this lintel suggest that the synagogue itself was a modest affair. If so, it would have contrasted sharply with the structures that surrounded the gate a short distance away where the Lechaeum Road ended. The gate itself was an imposing, white marble arch surmounted by a bronze statue of the sun-god in his fiery chariot. Surrounding the archway were glistening colonnaded shops and spacious public markets. Passing through the gate, one entered the agora itself, flanked on the left by the legendary fountain of Peirene, which still supplies water to the little village of Old Corinth. The ruins along the road immediately adjoining the site of the synagogue indicate that the houses and shops that once stood there were of a humble sort; it was in such a house that Titius Justus, Paul's host, must have lived. At this strategic spot, Paul could continue his proselytizing work among the Jews (even though he had made a show of public withdrawal from such work) and could also carry on a program of open-air preaching in the nearby agora (Acts 18:5-11).

---

[8] The name Achaia was given by the Romans to the province that included the southern half of the Greek peninsula.

Paul's Strategy

Judging from the amount of time and attention Paul gave to the Corinthian church both on this visit and on his return, the results of his efforts in such an unpromising city must have been very encouraging. Even criminal charges and a hearing before the civil ruler did not deter him (Acts 18:12-17). The remains of the public rostrum, or tribunal, at which Paul was tried and upon which the proconsul Gallio sat, are still standing among the ruins of the Corinthian market place. Gallio is less well known than his brother, Seneca, who achieved fame as philosopher-royal and court adviser until he fell into disfavor with the irresponsible emperor Nero. The date of Gallio's consulship, as we noted in Chapter 7, provides one of the few relatively fixed points for the chronology of Paul's life.

Apart from a mention of Paul's converting one of the leaders of the synagogue and gaining an acquittal before the Roman authority, the account in Acts tells us little about Paul's problems and tactics in founding a church in this predominantly Gentile community. We have to infer his methods from the letters that he later wrote to the Christians there. More than any of Paul's other letters, I Corinthians gives us a clear picture of the problems that beset the struggling churches whose members were recruited from heathendom.

THE PROBLEM OF HERO WORSHIP.   The first of these problems (touched on in I Cor. 1, 4, and 12-14) was their reluctance to be a community at all! Pride, hero worship, and rivalry were stronger forces than the desire for unity. The Corinthian Christians felt a greater sense of loyalty to particular favorites among the men who had founded the church ("I belong to Paul . . . I belong to Cephas . . .") than they did to their common Lord. Each man was so inflated with pride over his special spiritual gift ("the utterance of wisdom . . . the interpretation of tongues . . .") that he forgot that one Spirit was the source of strength for all these ministries in the life of the Church. The ability to serve in any capacity was a "gift"; each gift was necessary to the functioning of the whole Body of Christ, as Paul sometimes called the Church. To make matters worse, the Corinthian Christians, among whom the manifestations of the Spirit's power were still novel, chose to parade their newly acquired talents before the unbelieving citizenry, who—far from appreciating the spiritual nature of the gifts—thought the Church was an aggregation of madmen. The community in Corinth needed to be reminded that a spirit of order was essential to its corporate life and worship. Divisiveness, disorder, and display must all give way before love, the greatest gift of all.

THE WISDOM OF THIS WORLD.   Some interpreters of Paul have concluded from the discussion of "wisdom" in I Cor. 1:18-25 that Paul was struggling with those at Corinth who held a Gnostic point of view. One scholar has gone so far as to say that the Corinthian "heresy," as it can be reconstructed from the Corinthian letters, is the best example we have of Gnostic self-consciousness.[9] As we have already observed in Chapter 1, it is—at the present stage of research into the origins of Gnosticism—an anachronism to speak of pre-Christian Gnosticism. There are, in both the New Testament and Jewish literature contemporary with it, certain tendencies and terms which later came to be incorporated into what can then be identified as Gnosticism. In spite of learned efforts to do so, the Dead Sea Scrolls cannot be appealed to convincingly as giving evidence of Gnosis in the pre-Christian period. All that the evidence from the scrolls (as well as from the apocalyptic writings) enables us to say is that there were certain forms of religious speculation of a dualistic nature which provided Paul with a vocabulary by which he portrayed the cosmic dimension of God's redemption of the world through Christ, and which later became incorporated into the highly speculative, thoroughly dualistic systems that we know from the second century A.D. onward as Gnosticism. Paul's picture of the demonic struggle that will be brought to victory by God's power in the New Age (I Cor. 15) develops straight out of Jewish apocalypticism. But the wisdom/foolishness conflict with which he is dealing in I Cor. 1 and 2 does not appear to be of the esoteric, Gnostic variety. As Paul clearly declares (I Cor. 1:22), his difficulty in preaching and teaching the Gospel is that the Jews seek some sort of public, divine confirmation for the claims expressed in the Gospel ("signs"), while the Gentiles (Greeks) want to have its rationality demonstrated ("wisdom"). Paul, in meeting these challenges to the Gospel, utilizes the wisdom speculation of late Judaism, of the type found in the Wisdom of Solomon. In this writing, which probably originated in Alexandria, Wisdom—virtually personified—is pictured as the agent through whom God worked to create the world, and through whom knowledge of himself is given:

> Therefore I prayed, and understanding was given me;
> I called upon God, and the spirit of wisdom came to me. . . .
> I learned both what is secret and what is manifest,
> for wisdom, the fashioner of all things, taught me.
> —WISDOM OF SOLOMON 7:7, 21-22

Until unambiguous evidence for the existence of pre-Christian Gnosticism is available, it seems wiser to assume that Paul is trying to combat the charge of irrationality in the Gospel by an appeal to the revealed nature of its "wisdom,"

---

[9] This is the claim of W. Schmithals in *Die Gnosis in Korinth* (Göttingen: Vandenhoeck & Ruprecht, 1956), p. 239. R. Bultmann also points to I Corinthians as evidence that Paul utilized Gnostic terminology in interpreting the gospel for Gentile hearers. See R. Bultmann, *Theology of the New Testament* (New York: Scribner's, 1951), p. 181.

foolish though it may appear to Gentiles trained in philosophy. It is as yet unwarranted to suppose that he is setting forth his own version of esoteric "knowledge" to compete with the Gnostic claim to inside information about the nature of reality. In Chapter 16 of this book we shall consider how in some later New Testament writings the problem of false teaching is more explicitly dealt with. To label Paul's difficulty here as opposition to Gnosticism is anachronistic, since it requires us to read a second-century heresy back into the middle of the first century.

THE PROBLEM OF IMMORALITY. Quite in keeping with the proverbial Corinthian character, the first of the questions raised by the church there concerned immorality (I Cor. 5). The Christians had come to tolerate among their number a man who had taken his stepmother as his wife. Such flagrant immorality was not condoned even among the pagans. Could the Christians be less severe in condemning it? If the action of such men brought disrepute on the whole community, they were to be rejected by group action. Contacts with them could not be avoided, but fellowship with them was unthinkable! Some Corinthians had exploited their freedom from law to the extent of having sexual intercourse with prostitutes (I Cor. 6). To enter such a union was to ignore the fact that what man does with his body is inseparable from his spiritual condition. The corrupting influence of such an association is completely incongruous with the presence within him of the Holy Spirit, Paul maintained.

Another reason for the ridicule that the city of Corinth heaped on the church was the group's habit of settling internal disputes by airing them in public courts (I Cor. 6). The authority to settle such disputes resided in the community itself, and, it appeared to the people of the city, as it did to Paul, there was no excuse for stirring up such adverse publicity.

ATTITUDE TOWARD MARRIAGE. Questions regarding sex had been raised in the Corinthian church on grounds that were more matters of personal piety than of morality (I Cor. 7). Some overly pious members insisted that a Christian was more holy if he did not marry. The issue at stake was not the morality of sex relations, but the piousness of asceticism as demonstrated by sexual self-control. Paul's conviction was that the believer was neither more nor less holy if he married than if he remained single, but that the unmarried Christian had fewer obligations, and thus was freer to devote himself to "the affairs of the Lord." Those in whom the sex urge was so strong that they wasted time thinking of marriage would do well to marry, since their bachelorhood did not actually provide them more time to serve the Church. Although Paul felt that freedom from time-consuming marital responsibilities was a great aid to his work, he recognized that everyone could not follow his example. He reminded his readers, however, that the end of the Age was soon to come, and that in light of the shortness of time the Corinthian Christians should avoid doing anything or entering into any relationship that might interfere with their missionary activities. No one was to change his marital status or seek to alter his social position. Rather, each was to serve God in the condition in which he found himself. Paul's belief that the present state of the world would soon undergo a radical transformation made the development of any detailed social ethic unnecessary.

Paul's critics have often maligned him for his alleged woman-hating. Although he shared with his fellow Jews the belief that the woman's place in society was subordinate to that of man, he was happy to welcome women into full membership in the Christian community, and even to give them places of responsibility in the missionary work of the Church. It was at Corinth that Paul came to rely so heavily on Priscilla and her husband, Aquila, and in his letters to Corinth he indicates that this couple had major roles in the work at Ephesus as well (I Cor. 16:19). But Priscilla was not the only woman to whom Paul assigned a place of prominence in the churches he established, as we can infer from the numerous greetings and admonishments to women included in his other letters. Although he did believe that the woman's role was a secondary one, his attitude cannot with justice be termed "anti-feminine."

SOCIAL CONTACTS WITH UNBELIEVERS. In Corinth, as in any pagan city, the sacrifices offered in the temples were later sold by the priests in the public markets. This practice provided a cheap source of food for anyone who was not squeamish about eating slightly used meat. The Christians in Corinth, reveling in their newly acquired knowledge that idols were not gods but nonentities, had adopted the practice of buying and eating meat from this source. The well-instructed Christians knew that there could be no harm in this practice, but some of the folk who were still at the inquiring stage thought that the Christians were in some way participating in the pagan sacrifices when they ate the sacrificial meat. To the unenlightened, this behavior seemed a gross inconsistency, and potential converts were turning away from the Church because of an otherwise harmless practice. Paul reminded his readers that the enlightened have a responsibility toward the weak and uninstructed. Even though he agreed that there was no harm in eating sacrificial meat, he advised against it because the action was being misunderstood by the less well informed. By way of example, Paul pointed out (I Cor. 9) that he had certain privileges that were his by right of his apostleship (for example, the right to claim material support from those among whom he worked), but that he had purposely refrained from using his prerogative lest people misunderstand his motives and suppose that his ministry was motivated by greed. The work of the Christian minister, he reported, is not an individual matter, nor does it follow a single pattern: the minister must learn to adapt and adjust and exercise restraint in order to be most effective.

The temptation to slip back into idolatry and other pagan modes of living was a constant problem among the Gentile Christians. In this connection, Paul had a word of warning that he stated in the form of an allegory based on a narrative from the Old Testament. This method of discovering moral significance in Biblical stories by means of allegorical interpretation was a traditional practice among the rabbis of Paul's day. The experiences of the Children of Israel in the wilderness were the source of many ethical lessons for both the Jewish and Christian communities (I Cor. 10). On the basis of several of these stories, Paul developed a solemn reminder of the risk of divine judgment upon those participating in idolatry. Some of the Corinthians had supposed that there was no harm in taking part in the sacred meals connected with pagan worship. But Paul pointed out that participation in the rites of idolators involved the participant in a real way with the evil forces that were represented by the idols. A Christian can eat the sacrificial meat with impunity, but when he partakes of the ceremonial meal itself he is actually sharing in the worship of the idols, and this is inadmissible for a Christian.

EUCHARISTIC MEAL OR COMMUNITY PICNIC?   Paul took this occasion to rebuke the Corinthians who, forgetting the true significance of the Church's common meal, had allowed it to become a kind of riotous picnic. Some of the members went at the food and drink with such gusto that they were soon drunk, while the timid souls and the poor had little or nothing to eat. There was a desperate need for the Corinthians to be reminded of the solemn origin and deep meaning of this meal. In recalling the words of Jesus at the Last Supper, Paul uses phrases that are very close to those of the gospels—something that rarely occurs in his letters. Scholars have suggested that the gospels must have copied Paul at this point, but an equally plausible explanation is that both were relying on common ancient tradition. This explanation is substantiated by Paul's use of the words "received" and "delivered," which (as we saw in Chapter 2) are technical terms to indicate what has come down from the primitive traditions of the Church. Paul did not invent these words concerning the Last Supper; he merely passed on to the Corinthians what was transmitted to him from the apostolic tradition (I Cor. 10, 11). In the Jerusalem community, as we can infer from Acts 2:46, the common meal of the Church was thought of more in terms of fellowship than of commemoration. Just as Luke records that the Risen Christ was made known to the disciples "in the breaking of bread" (Lk. 24:35), so the Christians in Jerusalem looked upon their meal together as a continuation of the fellowship they had known when Jesus was visibly in their midst, and they looked forward joyfully to the day when they would share the cup with him again "in the kingdom of God" (Mk. 14:25).

For Paul, however, the meaning of the meal was primarily a memorial of Jesus' death, suggested both by the broken bread (symbolizing the broken body of Jesus) and the blood (symbolizing the life offered up to God). In Jewish thinking, blood was regularly identified with life (Gen. 9:4), so that drinking the cup was not considered to be drinking the blood of God in order to share his life; rather, it was a sign that the whole life of the victim had been offered up. The reference (I Cor. 11:25) to the covenant is a further reminder of the Jewishness of Paul's thinking, since throughout Old Testament history a covenant with God was always ratified by the offering of a sacrifice. Thus, Jesus gave his life as the sacrifice to inaugurate the "New" Covenant, which brought into being the New People of God spoken of by the prophet Jeremiah (Jer. 31:31 ff.). Although the words of Jesus in the Gospels (Mk. 14:22-25) do not refer to the "New" Covenant, it seems safe to assume that Jesus was consciously referring to the Old Covenant established through Moses (Ex. 24:8), which he now looks upon as being supplanted by the new community of the faithful that he established. Paul is warranted, therefore, in referring to the newness of this Covenant, even though Jesus may or may not have had in mind the specific words from Jeremiah.

Although Paul sought to correct the exclusive emphasis on fellowship in the common meal, with its sensual excesses, he shared with the Jerusalem community its belief that the communion looked forward to the Great Supper that the People of God would share in the Age to Come. Until that time arrived, however, he was insistent that the loaf and the cup should be considered as a memorial of Jesus' death. This solemn note is understood when Paul points out that the judgment of God has already fallen on those who partook unworthily of this sacred feast.

THE RAISING OF THE DEAD. Judging by the amount of space devoted to it in Paul's First Letter to the Corinthians, the resurrection of the dead was one of the most perplexing problems for the Gentile Christians. It would appear from Paul's full statement on the subject (I Cor. 15) that some members of the church at Corinth were minimizing the importance of the resurrection, or even denying it altogether. Similar doubts about this cardinal element of Christian faith were expressed by the Thessalonians, as we can infer from Paul's reply to them in I Thess. 4. There were all manner of related questions about the resurrection: Is it essential to the faith? How can anyone be sure it will take place? What form will man have in the resurrection? When will the resurrection come? Paul tried to deal with each of these questions in careful, logical fashion.

He recalled to the minds of his Corinthian readers that the resurrection was the foundation stone of the whole Christian faith, and that the authentication of the *kerygma* depended upon the appearance to chosen witnesses of Jesus *risen from the dead*. Because Christ had risen, the dead will indeed rise. Just as the devout Israelite farmer brought the first of his harvest to present before the Lord, so Jesus has now presented himself before God as the first fruits of the great harvest: the new People of God. God's purpose in the resurrection was not to bring the dead back to life, but to bring into being a new order of humanity, which would be characterized by obedience to God, as the old order had been characterized by the disobedience of Adam. The outcome of this renewal of creation is to be the subjection of all the universe to the reign of God. Faith in this divine program has consequences for the individual Christian's present and future as well. In the present he is to be diligent in service, fearless even in the face of the threat of death, knowing that in Christ death has been conquered. But should death come, he is to have confidence that the same power that brought Jesus from the dead is able to transform his perishable body into one of incorruption. This is not merely resuscitation: rather, it involves the exchanging of mortality for an immortal body. Death itself will be utterly defeated. In the light of this confidence, Christians are to be zealous in service, and undeterred by fear of failure or even fear of death. Such faith is the one sure ground of stability and perseverance in the life and work of the community.

THE UNITY OF THE PEOPLE OF GOD.   Paul brought his First Letter to the Corinthians to a close with specific instructions and exhortations concerning the collection which was to be made among all the Gentile churches for the "saints" in Jerusalem (I Cor. 16:1, 3). We shall be considering this collection and its importance for Paul in Chapter 10, but here it is sufficient to observe that this collection was a symbol of the unity of the Church. Gentile converts shared tangibly in the life and work of the mother church in Jerusalem. Paul had agreed in the Jerusalem Council to gather this offering, when the question of the relation of Gentile Christians to Jewish Christians was discussed and at least ostensibly settled (Gal. 2:7-10). But the question of the unity of the Church was Paul's overarching concern throughout I Corinthians.

Paul began, as we have noted, with the problem of the divisions that had fragmented the Church and all but destroyed its fellowship. The theme of I Cor. 12, 13, and 14 is the unity of God's People. Here the theme is developed in an extended metaphor of the Body of Christ, with its many members, each of which has its own appropriate function, and each of which is necessary for the proper functioning of the whole.[10]

Viewed from the side of God's gift, the power which binds the Body of Christ into one is the Spirit. It is given in baptism, quite apart from man's action, and welds diverse mankind into the unity of the true humanity which is the People of God. Viewed from the perspective of man's experience and

---

[10] The image of the Church as the Body is treated more extensively in Chapter 9, where it is set in the context of the message of Paul to the Gentiles.

consciousness, the bond of unity is love. It is love which enables the Body to function free from discord (I Cor. 12:24-26), and which preserves man from pride concerning the spiritual gifts which he has been granted (I Cor. 13:1-3; 14:1 ff.). Neither superior knowledge, nor outstanding gifts, nor abundance of faith is of ultimate value, or will indeed even endure. Not only is love the greatest of all these qualities, but it alone can transform the others so that they too become of infinite worth. Thus, in the hymn-like words and cadences of his lines extolling love, Paul declares that love is the ultimate ground of the experiential unity of God's People (I Cor. 13).

In the midst of strife and struggle, Paul carries on his work with joy and confidence. Love, which is the motivating force behind all that he does, is not a personal quality that he has produced within himself, but a power that has been given to him by God through Jesus Christ:

> Therefore, since we are justified by faith, we have peace with God through our Lord Jesus Christ. Through him we have obtained access to this grace in which we stand, and we rejoice in our hope of sharing the glory of God. More than that, we rejoice in our sufferings, knowing that suffering produces endurance, and endurance produces character, and character produces hope, and hope does not disappoint us, because God's love has been poured into our hearts through the Holy Spirit which has been given to us.
>
> —ROMANS 5:1-5

THE MESSAGE
FOR GENTILES

CHAPTER NINE

Even though a sizable collection of

Paul's letters is preserved in the New Testament, it is no

simple task to determine the precise nature of his message.

Since Paul wrote his letters for specific occasions, they are

not in the form of orderly theological treatises. For the most

part, the main outlines of his thought have to be recon-

structed by inference, and the details arranged into a system

only with caution. Fortunately, however, Paul's Letter to the

Romans is a fairly systematic presentation of the major aspects of his thought. Written from Corinth to affirm to the church at Rome his intention of visiting them as soon as possible, the Letter to the Romans has no other objective than to introduce Paul and his version of the Gospel before he arrives. There are no burning issues to be settled and no questions from the Romans to be answered. As a result, Paul writes in a deeply thoughtful mood, choosing his words with care, and developing his lines of argument as precisely as he can. Adopting this letter as a framework, supplemented by references to his other letters, we shall try to summarize Paul's message to the Gentiles. Using phrases selected from his letters, we shall trace seven major strands that Paul weaves into his discussion and that together provide the structure for his message.

"ALL HAVE SINNED AND FALL SHORT"
[ROMANS 3:23]

In the Jewish world-view, which was a part of Paul's heritage and by which the early Church was guided, morality was not a matter of living up to ideals, but of obedience to a living, personal God. It is true that in Torah there were many specific precepts by which Israel was expected to live, but these were thought of as concrete expressions of the will of God, rather than as abstract

THE ROMAN FORUM *and the Arch of Septimius Severus from the Palatine Hill. The plain, squarish building across the Forum is the Curia, where the Senate convened. At the lower right are the steps and column bases of the Basilica Julia, one of the colonnaded porticos used for transacting business in ancient Rome. Behind the arch appears the flat roof of a small church that was built over the ruins of the Mamertine Prison, where, according to tradition, Peter and Paul were imprisoned.*

ethical principles. Immoral action, therefore, could be traced to two major causes: (1) rebellion against God's will, and (2) subjection to a power that was opposed to God rather than subjection to God himself. This might be a voluntary subjection to the forces of evil, or it might result from a divine judgment by which God permitted the evil power to possess a person, or it might be a wholly involuntary seizure by an unusually potent demonic power. The one general term to describe a man's condition when he is outside an obedient relationship to God is *sin*. The acts that a man performs as a result of this broken relationship to God and the consequent lack of proper direction in his life are *sins*. Paul devotes the opening section of his Letter to the Romans to a development of the theme of the sinfulness of man.

Since the time of the Protestant Reformation, many within and without the Christian Church have thought of sin and redemption in purely or largely individualistic terms. A sin is a wrong committed by a person. If he seeks forgiveness, it is as a private matter between himself and God. This attitude has been sharpened in America where so much is said and written about the rights of the individual. Every man is expected to be able to determine his own destiny by making up his own mind. Even though sociologists and social psychologists have shown how powerful the group is in shaping decisions and influencing behavior, the notion of individual autonomy persists. For those who share this view of human existence as a solitary matter, it is difficult to sense the import of the picture of man that is assumed by the New Testament writers, who in turn draw on the image of man found in the Old Testament.

For Paul, together with the other writers in the early Church, man is inevitably part of a human *community*. The Biblical writers conceive of man as bound by birth to his nation, his tribe, his family. But above all, man is bound to the human race as a whole in its seeking to be independent of God. The story of Adam, with its report of Adam's longing to be like God (Gen. 3:5), is the story of every man. It is not something that happened "way back then"; it is an insight into an attitude of self-seeking autonomy that characterizes the whole human race in every age. Is there a remedy for such a predicament?

Paul shares with the Old Testament writers the belief that there is a remedy. Out of the race of disobedient mankind, God called into being a new people—a People of God—who would obey and serve him. This was the nation Israel, which was designed by God to be his own People in a special way, as we can infer from the words addressed to Israel at Sinai:

> Now therefore, if you will obey my voice and keep my covenant, you shall be my own possession among all peoples; for all the earth is mine, and you shall be a kingdom of priests and a holy nation.
>
> —EXODUS 19:5, 6

In words apparently addressed to the nation, depicted by the prophet as the Lords' servant, II Isaiah wrote:

> I am the Lord, I have called you in righteousness,
>   I have taken you by the hand and kept you;
> I have given you as a covenant to the people,
>   a light to the nations,
> To open the eyes that are blind,
> To bring out the prisoners from the dungeon,
> From the prison those who sit in darkness.
>   —ISAIAH 42:6, 7

The mission of the People of God, therefore, was to be a holy nation and thereby to serve as a light to bring the knowledge of God to the Gentiles, who sit imprisoned and in darkness. In the judgment of Paul—and his view is shared by the other New Testament writers—this mission had not been fulfilled. God was accordingly bringing into being through Jesus Christ a New People of God, in whom these unfulfilled objectives would be achieved. The concept of the New Covenant had been set forth by Jeremiah:

> Behold the days are coming, says the Lord, when I will make a new covenant with the house of Israel and the house of Judah, not like the covenant which I made with their fathers . . . which they broke. . . .
> I will put my law within them, and I will write it upon their hearts; and I will be their God and they shall be my people.
>   —JEREMIAH 31:31-33

This New Covenant, Paul is convinced (I Cor. 11:25), had been brought into being by the sacrificial death of Jesus Christ. Other New Testament writers shared his view (Lk. 22:20;[1] Heb. 9:15 ff.; 10:16 ff.) that the New Covenant People consist not of those obedient persons descended biologically from Israel and Judah, but of those persons of whatever race or national origin who respond in faith and obedience to the God of Israel who has addressed all mankind in Jesus Christ.

The question, therefore, is not, "How will individuals believe and be saved?" but, "How in the midst of disobedient humanity is God calling into being his New People?" The familiar Pauline theme—justification by faith—is therefore not the major theme of the Letter to the Romans, nor is the defense of his Gentile mission Paul's main concern. Both these themes are part of the larger objective: to show how God is establishing his People.

After a brief introduction, in which Paul outlines the Gospel and explains his delay in visiting the community in Rome (Rom. 1:1-15), he plunges into the argument that occupies most of the remainder of the letter. It is clear from the outset that, although he thinks of himself as commissioned to preach primarily to the Gentiles, he is gravely concerned for the Jews and for their status—now apparently forfeited—as the People of God. He believes that both Jew

---

[1] A number of important Greek manuscripts of Matthew add "new" before "covenant" at Mt. 26:28; a somewhat less impressive group add "new" at Mk. 14:24.

and Greek (*i.e.*, Gentile) are to share in God's salvation—that is, the deliverance of man and the universe from the power of evil, and the fulfillment of God's purpose for man and all creation. The direction that the argument will take is set in the key phrase: "The righteousness of God revealed through faith" (1:17). But before Paul can state what righteousness involves, he must show how it has been revealed and why it can be known only through faith.

The knowledge that God exists, and that he is the power behind the universe, is not the property of any favorite group of men to whom alone it has been revealed; rather, it is an inescapable inference from the majestic order of the natural world. Man, when he ignores the Creator and chooses to worship instead some created thing, is guilty of willful defiance of God. Paul paints a fearful picture of the moral degradation that results from man's alienation from his Creator (1:18-32). Even though the Jews were given a more direct revelation through Torah, or perhaps *because* they had this unique opportunity of knowing God's will, they are the more reprehensible for failing to fulfill his demands. Their moral shortcomings are symptoms of the fact that they, like the unenlightened Gentiles, are alienated from God, and hence "under the power of sin" (2:1-3:9). The condemnation under which the human race stands is sweeping, and man cannot possibly escape from it by striving to be better. Torah itself serves only to remind man of his failure, and thus to increase his sense of guilt.

Into this apparently hopeless situation, God himself has come in the person of Jesus Christ. (The relationship between God and Jesus will be considered below.) Through Christ, the enmity of man toward God is overcome, the alienated are reconciled, man's sense of guilt is removed, and he stands delivered from the powers of evil that have kept him enslaved. Once he has been liberated from his condition "under the power of *sin*," man can then turn his attention to the matter of *sins* and ethical demands. Until he is liberated, it is useless to talk to him about ridding himself of any particular sins, since these are only symptoms of his real problem.

Man's failure to gain divine approval is not the result of occasional or even perennial moral lapses: he is simply manifesting his oneness with the entire human race, which has lost the splendor of the image of God in which man was created (3:23). The reference here is to the account of Creation in Gen. 1, where man and woman are said to have been created in God's image. That Paul accepts this as the true account of the origin of man and the character God intended him to possess is evident from the description of man as the "image and Glory of God" in I Cor. 11:7. We have seen that Paul believed that all mankind shared in the responsibility for Adam's sin of disobedience to God (Gen. 3) and that all men justly suffer under the judgment resulting from that sin. The conviction was a part of the traditional Hebrew belief in the solidarity and inner unity of the nation. In ancient times, all Israel suffered when David, their king, sinned by taking a census. Presumably, the number of

God's People was supposed to be a divine secret into which no man could inquire; hence, the judgment fell on David—and on all Israel—for his wicked act.

Since all men stand under condemnation because of their share in Adam's sin, the hope of redemption must involve the creation of a new race. The old race is characterized by Adam's disobedience; the new race will be characterized by the complete obedience of Jesus to the will of God. Simply to tell men they ought to be better is useless; unaided by divine grace, men cannot be good. Conversely, merely to trim off a man's imperfections is not to solve his basic moral problem. A complete reorientation to God and an inner transformation are the prerequisites of goodness.

"A MAN IS JUSTIFIED BY FAITH"
[ROMANS 3:28]

Justification by Good Works

Paul had respect for the terminology and even the precepts of the moral philosophies of his Greek contemporaries. But he was convinced that to talk ethics to a man bound to a morally impotent race was not only a waste of time, but grossly misleading. Such an approach to righteousness suggested that if man only tried hard enough, he could arrive at the state in which God would be obligated to accept him. Paul, as we have seen, was convinced that the finest moral injunctions that he knew (those embodied in Torah) only frustrated man by reminding him of his shortcomings. The real hindrances to obedience—a sense of estrangement from God, and the lack of inner motivation to do what was right—were aspects of the problem that remained untouched by mere moral appeal. Laws do not make men good; they only remind men of what is wrong (Rom. 3:20).

Justification by Faith

Now, however, God has begun to work on an entirely new basis: justification by faith. This possibility for man has been declared with fresh clarity and with finality through Jesus Christ, but it was the basis for the relationship that had existed between God and men of faith as far back as the time of Abraham (Rom. 4), as we have already seen in Paul's Letter to the Galatians (p. 161). The goods news of salvation that has come by Jesus Christ is not, therefore, a radical break with the past. It is not as though God had dealt in a legalistic way with Israel, and then had set up faith as a basis for dealing with the Church. Throughout Torah it is clear that what God desired was the devotion of his People, not the performance of empty ceremonies or the scrupulous observance of regulations out of a sense of obligation. The burden of the prophets of Israel was to protest against formalism and to issue a summons to loving, obedient trust in God. The essence of Paul's Gospel, as stated succinctly in Rom. 3:21-26, is that God has acted decisively through Jesus Christ to free men from bondage to sin and the evil forces that held them captive (redemption), to remove the barrier of guilt that kept men from God's presence (expiation), and to restore men to a right relationship with God in spite of their sins (justification). Since this statement is so compact, and since the way of thinking that it represents is so strange, let us examine in some detail the meaning of these words.

The word "righteousness" in English usage usually means a moral quality of uprightness and justice; as such, it could be ascribed either to God or to man. "To justify," which is the cognate verb, would signify "to make right" or "to declare right." To justify God would be to demonstrate his righteousness; and to justify man would be either to declare him to be morally right or to make him right. In any case, righteousness would be regarded as a moral attribute.

In the thought of the Hebrews, however, the concept is quite different. The word that we usually translate as "righteousness" is not primarily a quality, but an activity. When a judge in ancient Israel "justified" a man who had been wronged, he did not instill a quality of uprightness, nor did he publish a decree that the man was innocent of wrong; rather, he rectified the situation, and thus restored the wronged man to his rightful place. In a psalm included in one of the Dead Sea Scrolls, dating from the beginning of the Christian Era, there is a passage in which both "justification" and "righteousness" are used in the sense of what God does for those who trust in him:

> For as for me, my justification belongs to God;
> And in His hand is the perfection of my way,
> Together with the uprightness of my heart.
> Through His righteousness my transgression shall be blotted out. . . .[2]

The emphasis here clearly falls on God's work, by which the oppressed are vindicated; the uprightness of the heart is regarded as a by-product of God's justifying, or vindicating, act. Similarly, when Paul speaks of "the righteousness of God" (Rom. 3:25), he is not merely describing the character of God, nor is he suggesting that God infuses his own qualities into certain persons. He is declaring that God has taken the initiative in restoring man to his proper relation to God and man.

The earlier part of the letter has shown the degradation that man suffers when he is apart from God, and the hopelessness of man's attempts to deliver himself from alienation from God and from enslavement to sin. Now, we see that being set right in relation to God is not a condition that man is called on to strive for, but that right relationship results from an action that God has

---

[2] Quoted from *The Manual of Discipline*, or *Rule of the Community*, the translation by W. H. Brownlee in *Bulletin of the American Schools of Oriental Research*, Supplementary Studies, Nos. 10-12, "The Dead Sea Manual of Discipline," pp. 42, 43. New Haven, 1951.

performed in Jesus Christ, the benefits of which are offered as a gift, to be received by faith (Rom. 3:24). God's work of vindication is not dependent upon man's fulfillment of Law, although Torah and the writings of the prophets bear witness that God's nature is such that he does vindicate the oppressed (Rom. 3:21).

The Ground of Justification by Faith

God's justifying activity is focused in the death of Jesus on the Cross. That death is looked upon by Paul, as it was reported to be by Jesus himself (Mk. 10:45), as a ransom. The ransom was thought of as a means of release for one in bondage, not as a price to buy off the captor. The conviction that the death of Jesus was the means for freeing men from subjection to the evil powers is elaborated in the Letter to the Colossians (2:13-15). There, in words that are reminiscent of Jesus' allusion to pillaging Satan's household, Paul declares that in the Cross man's bondage to law was broken and the powers that oppress man in this age were decisively defeated. If these powers had realized that the seeming tragedy of the Cross would be the means of God's triumph over them, they would not have instigated his crucifixion. (The early Church was convinced that behind every temporal authority was an unseen spiritual power, and that it was these invisible powers that plotted against the purposes of God. See Chapter 17.) Later in the Letter to the Romans (6:20), Paul describes the former condition of the Roman Christians as "slaves of sin"; here in a single phrase he proclaims that God has acted to free men from such bondage.

The agent through whom God's justifying act was achieved is Jesus, whom God ordained for this role. When Paul speaks of Jesus as "an expiation by his blood" (Rom. 3:25), it sounds as though God were a vengeful deity whose wrath could be appeased only by the slaughter of a bloody victim. The term "propitiation," which is used in the King James Version to translate the Greek word that is here rendered "expiation," heightens the picture of a God of wrath. Actually, the term in question is used in the Septuagint to describe the removal of the guilt that stands as a barrier between man and God. If guilt is removed by man's action, the proper rendering is "expiation"; if it is simply a matter of God's gracious removal of the barrier, "forgiveness" is the appropriate translation.[3] As we saw earlier, in Hebrew usage blood means life. The point of Paul's phrase, then, is this: Through Jesus' offering up his life to God, obedient unto death, the barrier of guilt that separated man from God has been removed.

The idea that the obedience of Jesus removes the guilt is explicitly stated in Rom. 5:19 and is reaffirmed in Phil. 2:8. But the logic of the idea is not clear

---

[3] For a full discussion of the key words in this passage, see C. H. Dodd, *The Epistle to the Romans* (New York: Harper & Row, 1932), pp. 48-61.

to a modern mind unaccustomed to thinking of religion in terms of sacrifice. From the gospel records it is clear that the major reason for the determination of Jesus' enemies to have him executed was their belief that he was undermining the moral standards and the institutional structures of their religion. He refused to abide by the regulations that required him to keep separate from defiled people; he persisted in befriending religious outcasts; he would not condemn sinful people; he enjoyed deflating those who, according to accepted standards, excelled in piety. His parables told of a God of grace and forgiveness. So it is not surprising that he was regarded as a religious subversive. It was in large measure because he was the friend of "tax collectors and sinners" (Lk. 7:34) that he was put to death. In spite of the growing opposition to his ministry, Jesus continued to challenge the religious institutions and to proclaim the grace of God, because he believed it was God's will for him to live and teach in this way. Paul was not drawing on his imagination when he said that Jesus was "obedient unto death," or when he connected Jesus' death with the forgiveness of sin; it was part of the tradition he had received.

The initiative of God in bringing men into the right relationship with himself has been fully and finally made known in Jesus Christ (Rom. 3:25, 26). Up until the time of Jesus' coming, God has been forgiving toward man, and forbearing towards man's sins, but man's sense of guilt and spiritual blindness kept him from understanding the true nature of God. Weighed down by guilt, man fled from God's presence and sought peace and safety in the worship of false gods. But now Jesus has come, completely dedicated to God, even to the extremity of death. Thus he has demonstrated once and for all that God is One who vindicates the oppressed, removes the barriers that separate man from him, and brings man into relationship with himself. In response to what God has done, man is expected to trust God and to rely for his salvation on God's justifying act in Christ.

Jew and Gentile

There is no place in such a scheme for human pride, since a man is accepted before God not on the basis of what he does, but on the strength of what God has done for him in Christ (Rom. 3:27, 28). So there is no place for any distinction between Jew and Gentile, since both must come to God on the same basis: faith. Even circumcision, which the Judaizers had been insisting on as a requisite for admission to the Christian community, was not required of Abraham until after he had trusted God, and had been accepted by him. There is, therefore, neither reason nor precedent for demanding that the Gentiles be circumcised in order to enjoy salvation. The fulfillment of the promise to Abraham rested solely on faith (Rom. 4:13 ff.).

We might conclude from this line of argument that a man who has faith can live as he pleases. Paul puts the issue in an exaggerated form: If our sins cause God to display his gracious forgiveness, we should sin more so that more grace might be available (Rom. 6:1 ff.). But the answer to such a suggestion is an emphatic no. The believer who is convinced that God has revealed himself in Jesus Christ, and that God has taken the initiative in removing the barrier that separates man from God, comes under the control of an influence which is strong, yet unlike the burdensome necessity of keeping the Law. The new influence is the love of God, as the believer has experienced it in Christ (II Cor. 5:14, 15). Man is free either to respond to God's love or to ignore it. But when he does respond in faith, he feels himself overmastered by Christ's love, which was demonstrated by his willingness to die in order that all men might be reconciled to God. The force, then, which compels the believer to do the will of God is not a sense of obligation, but an overwhelming feeling of gratitude for what God has done for man in Christ.

"GOD WAS IN CHRIST"
[II CORINTHIANS 5:19]

So far in what we have said about Paul's formulation of the Gospel, we have referred only in passing to the relationship between Jesus and God. Actually, Paul never defines this relationship, although he gives considerable attention in his letters to what God has done through Jesus. It is important to remind ourselves that the Hebrew mind does not express itself in abstract concepts, but in terms of action and concrete events. Ancient Israel did not construct a set of ideas or theories about God; she gloried in what God had done for Israel and how he had made himself known in her historic experiences. Similarly, when Jesus was asked to define "neighbor," he did not launch into a lengthy discourse on neighborliness, or on the ideal qualifications of being a neighbor; rather, he told the unforgettable story of the Good Samaritan, who demonstrated what a neighbor was by what he did (Lk. 10:29-37). It is this action type of thinking, rather than the conceptual or theoretical type, that must be foremost in our minds if we are to understand Paul's belief about the nature of Jesus' relation to God. Before attempting to trace out what it was that Paul believed God to have done in Christ, let us look briefly at the titles that Paul gives to Jesus in his redemptive role.

Jesus As Lord

Paul never says that Jesus is God. He does, however, so closely identify Jesus and God that it is sometimes difficult to tell to which one he is referring—as in his many references to "the Lord," for example. This title for God, which is *kurios* in Greek, was the one used by the translators of the Septuagint when they found in the Hebrew text "YHWH," the unpronounceable name of

God. It was Jewish practice to read this "YHWH" as though it were the Hebrew word, *adonai*, which means "Lord." The Greek translators translated the substitute word, *adonai*, rather than the original Hebrew, YHWH, the meaning of which was no longer known. Therefore to any reader of the Septuagint—and of course every Dispersion Jew was familiar with it—*kurios* was the most common name for God.

As it happened, the term *kurios* was also widely used by the pagans, particularly by the devotees of the mystery cults. In the worship of Osiris or Dionysus, for example, *kurios* was the common designation for the savior-god. Paul acknowledged in writing to the Corinthians (I Cor. 8:5) that in the Roman world there were many competing "lords" or *kurioi*. The earliest Christian preachers had affirmed that God had made Jesus "Lord" (Acts 2:36); Paul echoes this conviction in his words to the Philippians (Phil. 2:9-11). The affirmation "Jesus is Lord" is the earliest form of Christian confession (cf. Rom. 10:9, 10).

Because this term *kurios* is first widely used in the New Testament by Paul, we must not infer that Paul invented the idea of calling Jesus *kurios* in order to put him into competition with other Hellenistic saviors. Paul's quotation (in I Cor. 16:22) of the Aramaic phrase, *Maranatha*, which means, "Our Lord, come!", shows that Jesus was called "Lord" by the earliest Christian community in Palestine; Paul simply adopted the practice from them, translating it into Greek, the language that was meaningful to those among whom he was working. Later theological elaborations of the nature of Jesus were aided by the connotations of the word *kurios* among both Jews and Greeks of the day. But the term was a part of the earliest Christian tradition and was not introduced as part of a process of deifying the man Jesus. Paul goes so far as to apply to Jesus passages from the Old Testament that referred in their original context to the God of Israel. A prime instance of this occurs in the Letter to the Romans, where Paul quotes the promise of the prophet Joel that "everyone that calls upon the name of the Lord will be saved." Here the title "Lord" is clearly taken to mean Jesus (Rom. 10:9-13).

Jesus As Son of God

Another of Paul's favorite designations for Christ is "Son of God." In the usage of ancient Israel, this phrase was applied to the ideal king, who, because he had been designated by God to reign over God's People, was called the "Son of God" (Ps. 2:7). The term continued to be used throughout Israel's history, although later it was not applied to a historical personage, but rather to the king who would one day come and establish the reign of God over creation. The belief in Jesus as the one anointed to bring in God's reign was clearly in the back of Paul's mind when he applied the title to Jesus. But Paul added to this traditional meaning for "Son of God" the conviction that there was an intimate relationship between Jesus and God which gave Jesus a unique claim to the title (Col. 1:13), even though the term was commonly applied to the saviors of the Hellenistic religions. Furthermore, the character of Jesus was such that his concerns for mankind and his selfless attitudes were identified by Paul as divine qualities. He described the death of Jesus in behalf of sinners as "God showing his love" (Rom. 5:8). The fluid way in which Paul shifted from speaking of Jesus to speaking of God is puzzling grammatically, but it is thoroughly compatible with Paul's conviction that Jesus' relation to God was unique.

Paul rarely referred to Jesus as simply "Jesus." He preferred such expressions as "Jesus Christ," or "Christ Jesus," or "the Lord Jesus Christ." The title "Christ," as we have seen, is simply the Greek form of the Hebrew word "Messiah," meaning "anointed." It was often used in referring to the king, as one anointed to rule for God, but it could be used of any man who had a special role to play in the purpose of God. It was used of Cyrus, the Persian ruler who gave orders for the nation Judah to return to Palestine from captivity in Babylon (Is. 45:1). It is applied to the Servant of God through whom the coming of the day of Israel's redemption is announced (Is. 61). When Paul called Jesus "Christ," he meant that Jesus was the one through whom God was working to defeat the forces of evil and to restore man to a right relationship with God.

Jesus As Redeemer

In later centuries, after Christianity had become the official religion of the Roman Empire, theologians devoted a great deal of discussion to questions about the relation of the human to the divine elements in the person of Jesus. They tried to decide whether Jesus had a divine will *and* a human will, or simply one *composite* will; whether he had a divine *and* a human nature, or just *one*. They struggled with the problem of what happened to the divine characteristics (for example, omniscience, omnipresence) during the time that Jesus was on earth and was subject to the human limitations of localization, hunger, thirst, and incomplete knowledge (Mk. 13:32). Paul, however, had no such interest in theorizing; for him the important fact was that God had acted decisively in Christ for the redemption of his Creation. Paul had himself experienced this deliverance, and had taken his stand within the community that had similarly come to a new understanding of God's nature and purpose and that felt a new sense of kinship with him. Paul's task in his letters, therefore, was to inform the members of the community about what God has done through Christ, and what the implications of this work of redemption were for the life and faith of the community.

Paul's classic statement of what God did through Christ is found in the Second Letter to the Corinthians (5:19): "God was in Christ, reconciling the world to himself. . . ." The meaning of these words is developed more fully in the fifth chapter of Romans, where Paul describes the whole human race as alienated from God, and actually at enmity with him. Man, conscious of his disobedience and burdened with a sense of guilt, had fled from God's presence as Adam had in the Genesis story. In his estranged state, man's resentment against God had mounted to the point where man became an enemy of his Creator. It was in this spiritually helpless condition that man had languished prior to the coming of Christ. In the obedient life of Jesus, man could see in concrete form what complete dedication to the will of God meant. Even though Jesus' life had ended in seeming defeat, God had vindicated him by raising him from the dead and exalting him at his right hand. There could be no doubt that God in Christ was victor over both sin and death. But in the extremity to which God went to achieve his redemptive purpose, the depth of God's love was made known. There was no limit to the grace of God, since he was willing to "put forward" (Rom. 3:25) his Son to die in order that men might understand his love and be reconciled to him.

When men responded in faith to God's redeeming act in Jesus Christ, they realized that Jesus, by his "obedience unto death" (Phil. 2:8), had removed the barrier of guilt that separated man from God, and had defeated the powers of evil who had sought to destroy him. The new relationship with God that results from his work of reconciliation in Christ is contrasted in detail with the results of Adam's disobedience (Rom. 5:12-21). Adam, the man who typified the Old Creation, had violated the will of God, and had brought condemnation and death on all humanity as a result. Christ's justifying act will result in the transformation of men from sinners into righteous, obedient People of God.

As the rest of the Letter to the Romans shows, this transformation is not merely a matter of juggling the records, as though God arbitrarily listed as righteous those who believed what he said. Paul makes clear that what God did in Christ was to remove the barriers that stood between man and himself, but that until man responds in faith to God's offer of reconciliation the work of redemption will have no effect on him. When man comes to a realization of what God has done, and responds in grateful trust, God's Spirit will begin to work in his heart, transforming and shaping his desires and aspirations in order to conform them to God's will. (This aspect of Paul's teaching about redemption will be treated more fully below.)

Christ As Pre-Existent

Paul did not feel that the importance of Jesus began with Jesus' birth, nor that it was confined to the promise of salvation to all mankind. Paul believed that Jesus had existed before his birth, and that he was God's agent in creating the world. Furthermore, the program of redemption would not be complete until all Creation was restored to the condition that God had intended for it when he brought it into being. The idea of pre-existence was a common one in the Judaism of Paul's day. In the Book of Psalms (139:13-16), the belief is expressed that a man's form and the whole pattern of his life are in existence in the plan of God before man is born. The claim to pre-existence would not, therefore, in itself be unique. The uniqueness of Jesus lies in the creative role that he is described as having fulfilled before his incarnation—that is, before he assumed human form.

In the Wisdom Literature of Judaism, of which the Book of Proverbs is the most important representative in the Hebrew canon, there is the conviction that God is too sublime and exalted to have been involved in the business of creating the universe, and that this work was done through an intermediary. Usually, the intermediary is Wisdom, personified; at other times, Torah is described in personal terms as the creative agent. Paul adopted this concept of the intermediary through whom the Creation was accomplished, and modified it for his own purposes. Jesus Christ was the one in whom "all things were created, in heaven and earth . . . all things were created through him and for him" (Col. 1:16, 17). When the New Age has fully come, the whole of Creation will share in the benefits of redemption. The powers of evil that have held the created world in subjection will be overcome, and Creation will enter a new era of freedom comparable to the freedom that men of faith experience in the new life into which they enter through Jesus Christ (Rom. 8:18-23). Just as believers are called on to suffer in this life so that they may partake of glory in the Age to Come, so Creation itself groans like a woman in childbirth until the day of its deliverance from the powers of evil.

In barest outline, these are the chief meanings behind Paul's phrase, "God was in Christ." Although Paul refrains from saying that Jesus was God, he comes within a hair's breadth of doing so. He speaks of Jesus as "in the form of God" and as refusing to grasp at equality with God (Phil. 2:6). He ascribes to him the qualities and functions of God, as we have seen. He turns with ease from speaking of the grace of God to mention "the grace of our Lord Jesus Christ." Later New Testament writers define the relationship between Jesus and God in terms of virgin birth (Matthew and Luke), or develop the idea that Jesus was the pre-existent Logos of God (Jn. I). Paul introduces his convictions about the nature of Jesus Christ only incidentally, when they help to drive home a practical point that has arisen in connection with the life of one of his churches. For example, the magnificent passage on Jesus' taking human form appears in Phil. 2[4] as an encouragement to the Christians to be humble. The description in Col. 1:15-20 is built up to pave the way for Paul's

---

[4] R. Bultmann has declared that Paul is here drawing on a pre-Christian Gnostic's redeemer myth, which he has adopted and christianized. E. Kaesemann has elaborated on this theory in *Exegetische Versuche und Besinnungen* (Tübingen: J. C. B. Mohr, 1962), pp. 51-95. Although it is generally agreed that Paul is using a pre-Pauline hymn at this point in Phil. 2, and although it might be conjectured that oriental syncretism of some sort may have affected the viewpoint and terminology of the hymn, there is as yet no evidence for the existence of Gnosticism in pre-Christian times. (See pp. 184-185.)

attack on a serious error that has developed in the Colossian church. Paul's chief concern in all that he wrote about the significance of Christ was to inform his readers of what God had done for them, and to relate to them his own liberating, transforming experience of the Christ who had appeared to him risen from the dead.

"IF ANY MAN BE IN CHRIST"
[II CORINTHIANS 5:17]

The man who by faith in Jesus Christ had experienced reconciliation to God, Paul believed, was part of a whole new order of being. He was not just a reformed sinner; he was part of the "New Creation" to which everyone belonged who trusted Christ to bring him into right relationship with God. The new sphere of existence that was constituted by Christ's renewal of the Creation Paul identified by the simple phrase "in Christ" (Rom. 6).

All believers who have been baptized have, by participation in that rite, attested to their identification with Christ in his death, burial, and resurrection, which the rite symbolizes. Since they share with him by faith in his obedience unto death, they also now share with him in the new life that is brought into being by the Resurrection. Here is a form of human existence that is not subject to death, and that is triumphant over sin and the powers of evil which held the old life in subjection. Paul states the concept of the New Creation succinctly in writing to the Corinthians (I Cor. 15:22): "As in Adam all die, even so in Christ shall all be made alive." Again, we see the Hebrew conviction of the solidarity of God's People expressing itself in the inclusion of all humanity under two heads: Adam and Christ.

The fact that a man is "in Christ" does not free him from responsibility for his actions. His life should correspond to his spiritual status in the New Creation. Even though from the divine perspective the final outcome of the whole scheme of redemption is foreseen, it is man's responsibility to guide his actions and order his life in a manner befitting a Christian. So long as man is in his physical body, temptations to sin will always be present and the possibility of his yielding to the pull of the old life will continue to be very real. Nothing in his new status before God makes it impossible for him to allow sin to control his body. But Paul appeals to those who have discovered the potential for new life in Christ to avail themselves of their spiritual resources, and to allow God to use them for his purposes. We shall see later on that the service of God was a corporate rather than an individual matter, but each member was to see to it that the controlling influence of his life was obedience to God and not a yielding to sinful impulses. To sharpen the issue, Paul speaks as though there were no halfway house between the life of obedience and the life of sin. Either a man devoted himself to the service of God or he became the servant of sin, in spite of his having been set free from the power of sin. If he chose voluntarily to return to his former enslaved condition, God would permit him to exercise his own will in the matter.

But we must not infer from this passage in the Letter to the Romans that Paul thought a man must be either sinlessly perfect or hopelessly sinful. He makes this clear in writing to the Philippians (Phil. 3), when he tells them that he is himself bending every effort to increase in righteousness and to become more like Christ in his unconditional obedience to God's will. But he also warns them that he has not achieved perfection. Although failures have plagued him, he tries to leave them behind, pressing on to the prize that awaits the obedient. Yet the compelling force behind Paul's earnest striving was not "the prize," but an eagerness to express gratitude and devotion for the redemption that he and the whole community had experienced "in Christ."

"WE WERE ALL BAPTIZED INTO ONE BODY"
[I CORINTHIANS 12:13]

Paul's favorite metaphor to describe the community is "the body." This is a highly useful figure, since it is obviously familiar to everyone, and since it is capable of being developed in several ways to illustrate various aspects of the corporate life of the community.

The Unity of the Body

The first of these aspects—the unity of the body—we have already considered in Paul's dealing with the problem of the schisms that marred the unity of the Church at Corinth. But for Paul, the unity of the Church was not merely a feeling of togetherness but a belief in a mystical oneness "in Christ," with whom the Church was identified in death and resurrection. Developing the figure of "the body" in connection with another illustration, Paul demonstrates that the Christian, because he is a member of the Body of Christ, is free from obligation to the Law, just as a widow has no legal obligation to her husband after he has died (Rom. 7:1-6). And just as she is free to remarry, so the believer is now free to be joined in mystical union with Christ. The marital relationship as an illustration of religious experience is common in the Old Testament (cf. Hosea, Isaiah), but it was also widely used among devotees of the popular religions and mystery cults. Gentiles, then, would find this analogy familiar, even though they were not familiar with Torah.

Diversity Within the Body

In Rom. 12, Paul speaks of the need for the Church to recognize the diversity that must exist within the unity of the body. The one Spirit that came upon all believers in baptism is now at work in their midst to perform through them the various functions that are needed to carry on the work of God. The "gifts"—that is, the duties bestowed or the qualities granted by the Spirit to believers—include both participation in the active ministry of the Church (prophecy, exhortation, teaching) and simple good works (contributions, acts of mercy). The body cannot function when every member wants to do the same job, or when any member thinks the others are negligent or unspiritual because their share in the work of the Church does not correspond to his. The Spirit is the one who operates within the members to show them their appointed tasks; the diversity of ways in which the Spirit manifests itself must never obscure the fact that there is just one Spirit behind all these differing functions.

The life of the community, like the life of the human body, is dependent on certain central organs. No member of a human body can live independently, although the body can continue to function even after some members have been removed. For Paul the central organ in a human body was the head, which he regarded as the seat of life. Analogously, the life of "members" in the Body of Christ was dependent upon the "Head" (Col. 2:18, 19)—that is, Christ. The head is not only the source of life for the entire body; it also determines the form of the body's growth and integrates the life of the whole body. The theme of the oneness of the body and its dependence on the head is developed much more elaborately in the Letter to the Ephesians, which, though it parallels Paul's thought, was probably not written by him (see pp. 236 ff.).

The community, therefore, cannot consider itself as autonomous. It depends for its existence and for its continuance on Jesus Christ, who called the community into being, who died to seal the Covenant on which the community is founded, and who has sent the Spirit to guide and empower its corporate life.

"WALK ACCORDING TO THE SPIRIT"
[ROMANS 8:4]

The Spirit As Power

In the thinking of the Gentiles to whom Paul sought to interpret the Christian message, the existence of spirits and their power over human life were among the accepted facts of life. The phenomenon of demonic possession was a commonplace: the spirit that took control of a man might be beneficent, as in the case of the inspired prophetess of Apollo at the Delphic Oracle, or it might have a ruinous effect on a man's life and personality. The Greek word *pneuma*, like the Hebrew word *ruach*, meant "breath" or "wind" as well as "spirit"; so the evanescent, intangible quality of spirit was emphasized in the word itself. When Paul spoke of "the Spirit," however, he did not mean a generalized, immaterial force. In the thinking of the Stoic philosophers of

Paul's day, even *pneuma* was a material substance, though a highly refined one. For Paul, "the Spirit" was the pervasive power of God through which his purposes were fulfilled. It is not surprising, therefore, that in Paul's letters the person of Jesus and the Holy Spirit are very closely related. Occasionally, Paul will shift from one to the other without warning, as for example in Romans 8:10, 11, where he speaks of "Christ . . . in you" and, in the next breath, of "the Spirit . . . in you." It is as though the character and personality of God's continuing work of redemption were demonstrated in the person of Jesus, but as though the unseen yet efficacious power behind the work were defined as the Holy Spirit. In keeping with this relation between Christ and the Spirit, Paul describes the life "in Christ" as a life lived "according to the Spirit."

The Flesh Against the Spirit

It has sometimes been supposed that it was frustration over his own inability to keep the Law that drove Paul into the Christian faith. If one were to read Rom. 7:7-25 as a straightforward autobiographical account, then perhaps this understanding of Paul's alleged moral impotence would be justified. Probably, however, Paul is describing in this passage what he believed to be the struggle of every man in his own moral consciousness, as he was confronted on the one hand by what he acknowledged to be just moral requirements and on the other hand by his inner compulsion to ignore or defy those moral demands. Paul tells us in Phil. 3:4-6 that, so far as righteousness could be gauged by the Law, he was "blameless." What troubled him was not his inability to be law-abiding, but the unsatisfactory nature of his relationship to God in spite of his outward conformity to the demands of the Law.

The injunctions of Torah had proved to be a stimulus to disobedience rather than a means of moral achievement (Rom. 7:5-25). Now that he found himself liberated from the Law, and free to serve God through the new power that the Spirit had brought into his life, he characterized the life of defeat that he had previously experienced as life "in the flesh." By "flesh" Paul does not mean simply "the material body." Rather, "flesh" is the quality of being human, with such inevitable limitations as transitoriness, apprehension, and weakness. The flesh relies on insecure foundations in its misguided effort to stabilize life. It judges by appearances and fails to understand the nature of reality. It mistakes the worldly standards of wealth, force, and social approval for the real values in life. It was through these susceptibilities in man that the tempter in Eden was able to lead man to disobey God, by arousing his pride and by promising power that was supposed to come through increased knowledge. It is these ethical and religious considerations that Paul has in mind when he contrasts the life "in the flesh" with the life "in the Spirit." He is not identifying "flesh" with matter and then simply echoing the dualistic belief that matter is inherently evil and that only spirit is good.

All humanity, or, to translate literally, "all flesh" (Rom. 3:20), stood under condemnation and moral helplessness because of the inability of man to do the will of God even with the aid of Torah, the classic statement of God's purpose for his people. Undeterred by the ineffectiveness of Torah to bring man into right relationship with God, God sent his son, who was identified with humanity in every way, except that he was wholly obedient. Thus the hold which sin maintained upon humanity, through the weakness of the flesh, was broken; or, as Paul phrases it "[Christ] condemned sin *in the flesh*" (Rom. 8:3). Now, those who are in Christ measure up to the requirements of the Law; but they do so, not by moral striving, but through the power of the Spirit at work within their lives. Men of faith, therefore, "walk, not according to the flesh, but according to the Spirit" (Rom. 8:1-11).

In the life according to the Spirit, Paul testifies that he found peace and a sense of kinship with God that striving to obey the Law had never brought. That feeling of intimacy with God is epitomized in the term of address that Paul uses in prayer: "Abba" (Rom. 8:15), a word that is commonly used by Aramaic-speaking people when talking to their fathers. For Paul, therefore, the working of the Spirit was not some vague, impersonal force, but an intimate experience of closeness to God that his former life in Judaism had never made possible.

Life "in the Spirit" was not, however, free from difficulty or conflict. Paul was able to endure the difficulties that overtook him because he was convinced that they were the prelude to a New Age of Righteousness that was to come. Here, too, the role of the Spirit was an important one: the presence of the Spirit was an anticipation of the new situation that would obtain throughout Creation when the will of God triumphed over all opposition (Rom. 8:23). As he phrased it in writing to the Corinthians (II Cor. 1:22), the Spirit that dwelt within him was a guarantee or a kind of "down payment" on the time of consummation that lay in the future. Until that time came, however, the Spirit was at hand to give guidance to the man of faith in praying to God (Rom. 8:26-27). In the midst of trials, men of faith could look forward to the day when God's purpose for Creation would be fulfilled, confident that God was even now at work shaping events to his ends (Rom. 8:28 ff.). But until the time of total victory came, the man of faith might live his life free from guilt and fear, conscious that nothing could separate him from God's love (Rom. 8:31-39).

The Commands of the Spirit

Paul recognized, as Jesus had earlier, that it was not enough to tell a man that he should obey God; some specific indications of attitude and actions were needed. As real as Paul felt the power of the Spirit to be, he was careful in his letters to include a set of detailed, practical instructions by which the communities could regulate their corporate and personal lives. "What is good and acceptable and perfect" (Rom. 12:2) had to be spelled out in unmistakable terms. In the concrete ethical injunctions that are given in Rom. 12, 13, and 15, there are a few instances in which Paul's language parallels that of the Greek ethical systems of his day, but the whole orientation of Paul's ethics is much more Hebraic than Greek. His appeal rests on love and gratitude to God, rather than on the essential logic of his ethic. He does not discuss the abstract principle of the "good," nor does he even ask what the duty of man is. Rather, the life of service and dedication to which man is called is simply a response to "the mercies of God" that believers have experienced in Jesus Christ.

The nearest that Paul comes to a formal set of ethical precepts is the list of instructions in the Letter to the Colossians. There (Col. 3:5-4:6), Paul gives advice to the various members of the Christian families to guide them in their mutual relations. A similar, though longer, list is found in the post-Pauline Letter to the Ephesians (4:25-6:20). Yet even in didactic passages such as these, Paul is not merely telling men that they should be better. The whole appeal is set in the context of the forgiveness of God in Christ, the operation of the Spirit in the lives of the faithful, the love of Christ for the Church, the need of the Church for maintaining the respect of those who are not members. For Paul, the ideal was not conformity to a standard of virtue, but the dedication of oneself to God—that is, sanctification. It was the holy character of God with whom man had, through Christ, been brought into a relationship that required purity of life on the part of man; it was not merely that goodness was reasonable, or "according to nature," as the Stoics phrased it. Man's nature led him away from the will of God, but the Spirit of God at work within him both aroused the urge to do right and gave man the moral strength to achieve the right. To experience this inner transformation was to "walk according to the Spirit."

"WE SHALL ALL BE CHANGED"
[I CORINTHIANS 15:51]

As we have observed (p. 193), Christianity cannot be appropriately described as the religion of individualism, even though Protestant Christianity has, in fact, stressed individual freedom throughout its history. From the beginning, the Christian faith affirmed that God's purpose was to create a *community* of the obedient, not merely to snatch isolated individuals from destruction. We have seen that Paul was concerned with the establishment of the New People of God, a group that he believed to be already in the process of formation but that would come to its fullness at some time in the future.

Has God Turned from the Jews?

This conviction raised for Paul an acute problem, which he dealt with at length in the Letter to the Romans (Rom. 9-11)—namely, the relation of the former People, Israel, to the New People, the Church. In this extended passage he acknowledges the place of peculiar favor that Israel enjoyed because the earlier covenant was established with her, the prophets spoke through her, and the promises of future blessings for creation were given to her. But just as God acted in sovereign choice among various descendants of Abraham, choosing some for honor and passing others by, so God has now chosen to pass Israel by temporarily in order to have his message of redemption proclaimed to the Gentiles. Since God is the sovereign Creator of his universe, man is in no position to dispute the wisdom or justice of his actions (Rom. 9:14-24). Israel will share ultimately in the blessings that are now being enjoyed by faith among those who, whether Jew or Gentile, respond in faith to the Gospel. The tragic mistake of Israel has been her effort to gain standing before God by her own efforts in obedience to Torah (Rom. 9:24-10:4). At this point (Rom. 10:5 ff.), Paul uses a method of interpreting the Old Testament that seems strange to modern readers, but that was an accepted practice among the rabbis of his day. He takes a few phrases from the Book of Deuteronomy (30:12-14) which declare in a vivid way how the word of God has been made readily accessible to man in Torah; he then interprets these phrases as referring to the word of the Gospel, which has now been proclaimed to all men, whether Jew or Gentile. The one response demanded of man is that he confess "Jesus is Lord." His lips and his heart are to give outward expression to his inner trust.

If men are to be brought into the fellowship of the People of God by response to the *kerygma*, someone will have to serve as a proclaimer of the Good News. Faith can arise only when men have heard (Rom. 10:14 ff.). Israel has heard and has not responded in faith, however, because God's purpose is that the Gentiles should be saved as a result of Israel's failure. Israel's rejection of the Messiah made redemption possible; her rejection of the message about the Messiah had led the Christian preachers to turn to the Gentiles with it (Rom. 10:18-11:12). But Paul is convinced that Israel will not persist in her unbelief indefinitely; she will return to God. And when she does, the blessings that will follow for all the world will be immeasurably greater than before she turned away in disobedience.

Paul develops an extended allegory of the grafting of branches onto an olive tree. The allegory is difficult from the standpoint of logic as well as of horticulture (Rom. 11:13-24). But the point is clear: God still will have a purpose for Israel when his work of summoning the Gentiles to obedient trust has been completed. A divinely determined number of Gentiles must come into the fellowship of God's People, and the New Age will not come in its fullness until that number has been reached (Rom. 11:25 ff.). The argument in verses 28 to 32 is not clear, and it involves Paul in a series of contrasts that are perhaps overdrawn. But the passage ends in a majestic hymn of praise to God, whose wisdom transcends man's capacity to comprehend. Man may rest assured that God's purpose is effectively at work throughout his creation. From his poetic outburst of praise to God, Paul turns to practical considerations (Rom. 11:33-36).

In contrast to the inconclusiveness of the discussion about the place of the Jews in God's plan, Paul was certain of two things: that he had reason to be proud of his heritage of Jewish faith and piety, and that God had called him to turn from the Jew to the Gentile as the major target of his evangelizing. The passage from Romans 9, 10, and 11 summarized in the preceding pages gives evidence of the importance Paul attached to the whole question of the relation between the community of the Old Covenant in which Paul had been reared, and the community of the New Covenant in which he was now at work in the service of God. He was convinced that "in Christ" there was no place for racial distinction (I Cor. 12:13), and yet he believed that the promises made by God to Israel were not simply abrogated by Israel's unbelief. The Jewish hope of the coming kingdom of God was a strong element in Paul's thinking (I Cor. 15:24 ff.), and, as a result, he made no attempt to legislate for a Christian society or to give instructions for the establishment of a new social order. At "the end," God would restore Israel to favor and to faith, and would defeat his enemies, thereby establishing his rule over Creation. Paul longed for the day of peace and deliverance, and labored for its coming. It was not his task to bring in the kingdom; he was charged with the mission of preaching the Good News, and thus preparing men for the kingdom that God was about to establish.

What Will Eternal Life Be Like?

Although Paul's major concern was for the future of the community, he did have words of comfort and admonition about the future for individuals as well. It is impossible to reconstruct a neat system out of Paul's thoughts on the theme of the future life. At times, he writes as though he expected to be transported immediately to the presence of Christ when he died (Phil. 1:23). At other times, he speaks of those who have died as being asleep, awaiting the trumpet call at the Day of Resurrection (I Cor. 15:51; I Thess. 4:13). In one famous passage, he describes a "body" in which the believer is "clothed" at death, when he is transported into the presence of the Lord (II Cor. 5:1-4). In I Cor. 15, however, Paul speaks of the "spiritual body" as though it were bestowed at the time of the resurrection, rather than immediately upon death. Efforts have been made to reconcile these two aspects of Paul's thought by assuming that in II Cor. 5 Paul was describing an intermediate state. A similar diversity of detail can be seen in a comparison of I Thess. 4 and II Thess. 2. In the first passage, the return of Christ is expected with little delay, since Paul expected to live to see that event; in the second passage, Paul explains what must happen in the interim before Christ's return. (This question will be dealt with in detail in Chapter 17.) But notice that Paul was not interested in developing a systematic theology; he was living in a time of crisis, during which his job was to preach, to exhort, to instruct, to prepare men for the coming of the New Age.

Paul's consistent conviction, which overarches the divergent details, was that Jesus would again appear but this time in triumph, that the resurrection would take place, and that the Day of Consummation would thus arrive. Man's hope, then, was that God would change his People, so that their present bodies of humiliation (Phil. 3:21) would become glorious bodies. Corresponding to the hoped-for transformation of individuals would be the transmutation of the weak and imperfect "Body of Christ" into the fullness of the community of the New Covenant. Since the coming of this time of "salvation" was near at hand (Rom. 13:11-14), there was no place in the lives of Christians for frivolity or dissipation. Believers belong to the Lord, and are to conduct themselves worthily until the time of fulfillment comes (Rom. 14; 15).

In the concluding chapters of Paul's Letter to the Romans, he told the Roman Christians that he intended to visit them after he had gone from Corinth to Jerusalem to take the contribution from the churches of Greece and Asia Minor to the "saints" in the Holy City (Rom. 15:25 ff.). Rome was to be just a stopping-off place for him on his way to Spain, where he intended to go in order to preach the Gospel in territory untouched by Christian evangelists. The fact that Paul here greets by name so many of the members of a community that he never visited has raised a question about whether this chapter is an authentic part of the Letter to the Romans. But Paul's indication that some of the contacts had been made in the Corinth area (16:3), in addition to the ease and frequency of travel between Corinth and Rome, suggests that there may already have been considerable visiting back and forth by Christians between the two cities, although Paul himself had not made the journey to Rome. If this explanation is correct, it would account for his feeling close enough to them to solicit their prayers that he might not be deterred from his projected travels by any opposition in Judea. The seriousness of the opposition that Paul did encounter in Jerusalem, the subsequent history of the Jerusalem community, and the circumstances of Paul's going to Rome, are matters that we shall discuss in the next chapter.

THE DEATH OF PAUL
AND THE END
OF THE
APOSTOLIC AGE

In Paul's later letters he indicates that he intends to go to Jerusalem in order to take to the mother church there the collection for the "poor" (I Cor. 16:1-4; cf. Rom. 15:25-29). He expects to be accompanied by accredited representatives of the churches that have shared in the gift. And further, he anticipates that he will experience some difficulties at the hands of "unbelievers in Judea" (Rom. 15:30-32). From his own hand, we have no hint of what these difficulties may have been, or what the outcome of the journey to Jerusalem was. These gaps in our information are supplied by Acts, which details the journey to Jerusalem, the seizure by the authorities there, and the voyage to Rome. We might wish that we could turn to Acts as an unqualifiedly reliable historical source for this phase of Paul's life. But as we have seen in recounting those events concerning Paul where we have a basis of comparison between Acts and Paul's own writings, Acts must be used with caution. It is scarcely sound methodological procedure to discount Acts where we can test it by Paul's letters, but then rely on it where we have no way to check.[1] What follows in the description of Paul's final travels is offered with reservations: we cannot automatically doubt its accuracy, but neither can we treat it as unquestionably historical.

PAUL'S RETURN TO JERUSALEM

The decision to return to Jerusalem is announced in Acts 19:21; the account of the journey begins at Acts 20:3. When the narrative reaches the point of Paul's return to Philippi, the story shifts from "they" to "we," presumably marking the reappearance of the anonymous traveling companion (traditionally identified as Luke). The most unusual incident connected with the journey to Judea occurs in Troas, where Paul's preaching until midnight reportedly puts a

---

[1] See the discussion of the historical reliability of Acts on pp. 154-163.

EPHESUS *today: the ruins. In Paul's day, Ephesus was one of the great cities of the eastern Mediterranean, but the silting up of its harbor rendered it useless as a port and caused it to be abandoned.*

TOWER OF CITY-WALL

THE PRESENT SEA COAST

THE HARBOR OF ROMAN TIMES

ROAD TO THE HARBOR

GYMNASIUM AND BATHS

THE THEATRE

young man to sleep; he topples from the window ledge where he has been perched and is taken up for dead. Paul restores him to life, Acts 20:10 reports; by this the reader is led to see that the same power over life and death that was evident through Jesus is at work through the apostles.

Stopping at various spots along the western coast of Asia Minor, Paul is met at Miletus by the elders from the church at Ephesus, in whose midst he had worked for so long, according to Acts 19:10. In a touching address (Acts 20:18-35), Paul looks back with mingled humility and confidence over the course of his career and, in particular, at his three years' work in Ephesus. Since he had earned his own way during his stay in that city, no one could accuse him of having profited in any material way from his preaching the Gospel of the kingdom among the Ephesians. But Paul had two premonitions: he felt that he would probably never return to Ephesus, and he feared that discord and false teaching would arise after his departure. After joining with the Ephesians in prayer, he bids them farewell (Acts 20:36-38) and returns to the ship.

As Paul and his companions travel toward Jerusalem, they stop off for brief visits with various Christian communities, notably in Tyre, Ptolemais, and Caesarea. In Caesarea lived Philip, the evangelist whom we have already met in connection with the launching of the Christian message in the territory outside Jerusalem. The fact that Philip's daughters are described as "virgins" (Acts 21:9) suggests that certain wings of the Church were already commending celibacy, although we have seen that Paul himself thought that abstinence from marriage was a practical rather than a moral question. Philip's daugthers later moved to Ephesus and were counted among the luminaries of the Church in Asia Minor, as we discover from the account of Philip's work given by Eusebius of Caesarea (who died in A.D. 339) in his *Ecclesiastical History* (Book III, xxxi).

At Tyre, and again at Caesarea, men who claim to be inspired by the Spirit try to dissuade Paul from going up to Jerusalem. They seem to have a sense of foreboding about the treatment Paul will receive there. (Their anxiety may have been based on information about the plotting against him that was going on in Jerusalem, or it may have been a premonition of some sort.) In reading Acts, we cannot be sure whether Paul doubts their claim to be speaking "in the Spirit" when they try to discourage him from going to Jerusalem, or whether he is convinced that the Spirit is simply trying to test his faith by these words of discouragement. In either case, he will not be deterred. In spite of the tearful protests of his loyal friends (Acts 21:10-14), he goes up to the Holy City, accompanied by disciples from Caesarea and Cyprus.

The Jewish Legalists

According to the account in Acts (21:17 ff.), Paul was in a conciliatory mood from the moment of his arrival in Jerusalem. The old question about the necessity for Christians to keep the Law of Moses was still the major issue in

THE "WAILING WALL" *was a part of the massive masonry built by Herod to enclose the area around the Jewish Temple. Sections of masonry like this are all that remain of the network of structures connected with the Temple in the time of Jesus.*

the minds of the leaders of the Jerusalem church in spite of the agreements they had made in the past. Paul's reputation for laxity on this matter of keeping the Law was so notorious that James and the other leaders were embarrassed by their association with him. They suggested that he might ease the Jewish opposition against him if he would make some public demonstration of his willingness to conform to Jewish ritual requirements. As it happened, Paul had already taken a step in the direction of conformity to ritual requirements by cutting his hair in preparation for his pilgrimage to the Temple (Acts 18:18). The practice of cutting the hair or shaving the head as a part of an act of consecration had its roots in the rites of ancient Israel (Num. 6), and a man consecrated in this way was called a Nazirite. The most famous Nazirite was Samson, although in his case the vow of dedication made by his parents demanded that his hair should never be cut. Why Paul performed the rite at this time is impossible to determine. Now, when the leaders of the church suggested that Paul should pay the expenses for a group of four other Christians who had shaved their heads as a part of their vow of consecration, Paul agreed. It was considered an act of piety for a man of means to pay the expenses of a poor man who wished to take a vow but could not afford to do so.

The logic of Paul's position on the question of Torah should have led him to refuse to cooperate in this scheme, since his action gave the impression that he was a strict observer of the Law when in fact he was not. Critics have raised the question of whether this incident may not have been invented by the author of Acts to document his thesis that peace prevailed in the relations between Paul and the Jerusalem church. Even if we were to assume that the account as we have it is substantially accurate, we should still be unable to decide whether Paul's motivation was a desire for peace-making, or a surge of sentiment for the traditional practices of Judaism, or a strategic compromise with his own convictions. But whatever his objectives may have been, they were not fulfilled. Instead of gaining the favor of the Jews by this attempt at conciliation, Paul brought the wrath of the mob down upon his head.

Mob Violence in Jerusalem

One day toward the close of the seven-day period of ritual obligation, Paul was in the Temple preparing to complete the offerings for himself and the others who were consecrating themselves. Some of his enemies—perhaps including men who had been active in the opposition to him in Asia Minor (Acts 21:27)—spread the word that he had brought a Gentile, Trophimus, into the inner courts (see Temple plan, p. 127).

The Temple area was divided into a series of courts and terraces, mounting upward to the innermost sanctuary, and Gentiles were permitted to enter only the outermost of these courts. Separating the Court of the Gentiles from the more sacred sections was a carved stone screen on which were placed at intervals stone tablets bearing the following warning: "No stranger [is permitted] to enter within the screen and enclosure around the sanctuary. Whoever is seized will be answerable to himself for his death which will follow therefrom." Two of the blocks of stone bearing this inscription have been discovered in Jerusalem. The punishment that followed a violation of the sacredness of the Jewish Temple was carried out by the crowd of the faithful gathered in the precincts; no formal trial was held.

Word of the alleged desecration spread instantly through the throngs gathered for worship. Paul's notoriously liberal attitude toward Gentiles made the charge seem plausible, and the crowds rushed to the scene of the riot, eager to witness, if not to share in, the death of this enemy of the traditional religion.

The mob had already begun to beat Paul when word of the melee reached Claudius Lysias, the tribune in command of the Roman garrision stationed in the massive Tower of Antonia, which overlooked the Temple area from the north. The tribune rushed down the stairway leading from the tower into the Temple's outer court and attempted to quell the riot. His first thought was that Paul was an Egyptian trouble-maker who was wanted by the Roman authorities for an earlier insurrection. But, since the noise of the mob was so great that the tribune could not hear Paul's defense against the charges, he decided to take the prisoner up into the fortress, away from the excitement and shouting (Acts 21:27-36).

As they were mounting the stairs, Paul spoke in Greek to the tribune, who concluded immediately that he had been wrong about Paul's identity. Thereupon, Paul identified himself as a citizen of the Roman colony of Tarsus, and asked permission to speak to the people. Standing high on the stairs, he spoke to the crowd in Aramaic—a choice that helped him command the crowd's attention. Hebrew was no longer spoken by the Jews, although both Jews and Christians continued to refer to Aramaic, the Semitic dialect that had replaced Hebrew by the beginning of the Christian era, as "Hebrew" (Acts 21:40).

In diplomatic fashion, Paul began his address by telling the crowd of his Jewish background and training, and of his former violent opposition to Christianity (Acts 22:1-6). The story of his conversion seems to have entranced the people, but when he began to identify himself with Stephen and the mission to the Gentiles that developed as a result of Stephen's death, the fickle mob again demanded his death (Acts 22:6-22). So violent was the hatred of the crowd toward Paul that the tribune concluded there must be some more serious charge against him, and that Paul might be forced to confess if he were scourged. Before the ordeal began, Paul reminded the centurion, a minor officer who was supervising the scourging, that extorting a confession by such means from a Roman citizen was illegal. When Paul's remark was relayed to the tribune, he stopped the proceedings immediately, fearful of the punishment that he might suffer for such a careless violation of Roman law (Acts 22:22-29).

Because of all the confusion, the real nature of the Jewish accusation against Paul had never come through clearly. Now, determined to get all the evidence he could, the tribune permitted the Jewish council to examine Paul. But there was no opportunity for a fair hearing, for the leaders had already decided before they heard his case that Paul must be destroyed. Paul's strategy, therefore, is understandable even if it is not commendable. Sensing that he would receive no justice at the hands of the council, he seized the opportunity to set the two major factions within the group against each other. By taking his stand with the Pharisees on the questions of resurrection and the messianic hope, he stirred up an internal conflict that diverted attention from the real reason for the trial: his alleged violation of the sanctity of the Temple precincts. Finally, through the intervention of the tribune and his troops, Paul escaped (Acts 23:1-10).

The Plot on Paul's Life

But the Jewish religious leaders' determination to kill Paul continued to mount. At last, upwards of 40 men plotted to ambush him. Paul learned of the plot and had it reported to the tribune, who decided to take Paul secretly to Caesarea, where it would be easier to protect him from his enemies. Since

Caesarea was the capital of the province, the governors spent most of their time there on the coast, traveling inland to Jerusalem at festival times when peace was threatened by the throngs of excitable pilgrims. With an escort of guards and cavalrymen, and with an explanatory letter for Felix, the governor, Paul was sent off by the tribune to Caesarea (Acts 23:16-32).

Once Felix had ascertained that Paul was from Cilicia, and that the case was therefore within his jurisdiction, nothing more could be done until the accusers had arrived from Jerusalem. Meanwhile, Paul was imprisoned in "Herod's Praetorium" (Acts 23:35), which was evidently the palace built by Herod that the Romans had taken over as the seat of imperial authority in the province. There has been a good deal of speculation over what Paul did with his time during his two years (Acts 24:27) of imprisonment. The mention of the "praetorium" here, combined with Paul's statement about the "praetorium" found in Phil. 1:13, might suggest that it was while Paul was in prison that he wrote his letter to the Philippians. If this were so, we might infer that the other prison letters—Colossians, Philemon, and possibly Ephesians—were also written at this time. "Praetorium" was a general term, however, that was applied to the imperial headquarters anywhere in the empire. If any of Paul's correspondence from this period has survived, it is probably limited to the few personal notes addressed to young Timothy and incorporated by a disciple of Paul into the post-Pauline writing we know as the Second Letter to Timothy (4:16 ff.), in which Paul tells that all his associates deserted him at the time of his trial.[2]

When the priests and elders arrived from Jerusalem, they made their charges through an official spokesman or advocate, who gave evidence of his training in rhetoric by the flowery and flattering words he used to address the governor (Acts 24:1-8). The accusation was that Paul was a trouble-maker, and a leader of the Nazarene sect. The very fact that Jesus had come from the obscure Galilean village of Nazareth was enough to discredit his followers, since Galileans were considered to be lacking in culture and in religious and racial purity. Paul did not deny his connection with the Nazarenes, but he pointed out that he had come to Jerusalem solely as a bringer of alms and as a pious worshiper in the Temple. Charges that he had disturbed the peace were simply not true. The real issue—Paul's success in preaching a Law-free Gospel in Asia Minor— was not raised by the Asiatic Jews (Acts 24:18, 19) who had roused the mob against Paul in Jerusalem. Such an accusation, resting on a point of mere theological disagreement, would not be weighty enough for Rome to take punitive action. So Felix postponed taking any action at all until he could talk again with Lysias, the tribune in Jerusalem. Meanwhile, Paul was permitted to visit with and receive assistance from his companions.

---

[2] Another theory, which claims that Ephesus is the place of origin of Colossians, Philippians, and Philemon, has been considered in pp. 157-158. For a full statement on the theory that the verses from II Tim. originated during the Caesarean imprisonment, see P. N. Harrison, *The Problem of the Pastoral Epistles* (Oxford: Oxford University Press, 1921), pp. 121, 122.

The Inconclusive Trials

Felix already had become interested enough in the new Christian sect to learn for himself what they taught and what their practices were (Acts 24:22). But he arranged for his young wife, Drusilla, to hear Paul, perhaps supposing that her own Jewish background would give her a basis for estimating the worth of Paul's claims more accurately than his own Gentile training. His liberal attitude toward Paul during his imprisonment (24:23) and the haste with which he dismissed Paul after Paul had preached to him about the judgment (24:25) suggest that he was attracted by the Gospel, even though he could not bring himself to accept its claims. It may be that the reports of the large sum Paul had brought from Greece and Asia to Jerusalem had reached Felix's ears, leading him to believe that Paul was personally wealthy and that he might bribe Felix to release him. The acceptance of bribes from prisoners, though forbidden by Roman law, was not uncommon. In any event, at the end of two years, Felix was still unconverted, Paul was still in jail, and no bribe had been paid (Acts 24:24-26).

Felix's successor, Porcius Festus, sought to ingratiate himself with the leaders of the Jewish people in Jerusalem by keeping Paul imprisoned. The leading Jews requested that Paul be brought back from Caesarea to Jerusalem for another hearing, intending to ambush and kill him en route (Acts 25:1-3). But Festus refused to comply with the request, announcing instead that the hearing would take place in Caesarea and that Paul's accusers might come and bring charges against him there. At the hearing, the same charges that had been made at the earlier trials were repeated before Festus. And Paul's defense took the same line as it had before; only on this occasion he decided to extricate himself and his case from the web of petty, provincial politics by appealing to Caesar, as was the privilege of any Roman citizen. Festus agreed to have the case brought before the emperor—pleased, no doubt, to have the matter off his hands.

Before arrangements were made to take Paul to Rome, however, Festus was visited at Caesarea by Agrippa II, the puppet king of Batanea, Gaulanitis, and Trachonitis, arid regions north and east of the Sea of Galilee. Agrippa was accompanied on this official welcoming visit by his sister, Bernice, who completely dominated her fawning, pomp-loving brother. Agrippa had secured from the emperor Claudius authority to appoint the High Priests and to oversee the Temple in Jerusalem, and because of his royal blood and his connection with the Hasmonean dynasty [3] through his great-grandmother, Mariamne, he had deemed it his right to occupy the Hasmonean palace when he was in Jerusalem. In order to get a good view of the activity within the Temple courts nearby, he had erected a tower on top of the palace, which provided an unsurpassed

---

[3] The Hasmoneans were the royal line of the Jewish nation from 162 B.C. until the Roman invasion in 63 B.C. See pp. 25-26.

vantage point. But the priests, who detested him for his pagan ways and for his connivance with Rome, had built a high wall that completely obstructed his view. Agrippa's complaints to the Roman authorities were unavailing, and he had to find other pastimes during his Jerusalem visits.

During the course of Agrippa's extended stay in Caesarea, Festus mentioned to Agrippa that he had inherited from his predecessor a curious case of a prisoner against whom no civil charges, but only religious accusations, had been brought by the leaders of the Jews. Since Agrippa had a Jewish heritage, Festus thought he might be able to clarify some the religious issues involved. Agrippa was pleased to have been asked, and agreed to hear Paul's case. Agrippa's reputed concern about Jewish religious practices and the sectarian differences among Jews seems to have been more a matter of curiosity than piety, however. And his own participation in Jewish religious life seems to have been motivated more by politics than by conviction. It is reported that Bernice also tried to keep up an appearance of piety by performing a Nazirite vow, but her moral standards were so low that they raised even Roman eyebrows. The show of fidelity to Judaism that this pair made was more than counterbalanced by the thoroughly profligate lives they lived.

In Agrippa's presence, Paul recounted his conversion and the conflict that had developed around him at the instigation of the Jewish leaders (Acts 25:23-26:23). He took care to include a brief statement of the Gospel, in which he emphasized the Resurrection and the mission to the Gentiles. Festus' reaction was one of astonishment, since Paul's words sounded to him like those of a madman. Turning to Agrippa, Paul tried to press him for a decision regarding the validity of the Christian belief in Christ as the fulfillment of the prophets,

PUTEOLI *may be the harbor on the Campanian coast represented in this mural. Puteoli is where Paul landed in Italy. The painting was on the wall of a house that was destroyed by the eruption of Vesuvius in* A.D. *79.*

but Agrippa quickly terminated the hearing (Acts 26:24-30), disturbed and perhaps moved by Paul's eloquence.

In private, Agrippa told Festus that his earlier decision had been correct: there was nothing in what Paul had done that would justify executing him. There was not even any reason to keep him in prison, except that he had appealed to Caesar, and the law required that he be kept in custody until the hearing before the emperor could be arranged (Acts 26:31, 32). This was a safe conclusion. It gave Agrippa the appearance of a man of insight and mercy, but it saved him from possible trouble with Rome or Jerusalem, since Paul could not be freed under the circumstances. The craft and political acumen of the Herodians [4] surely flowed in Agrippa's veins. No further delay was possible: Paul must go to Rome. Along with several other prisoners, he was assigned to a centurion named Julius, whose task it was to escort his charges to Caesar.

THE JOURNEY TO ROME

The account of the journey to Rome and the shipwreck en route is the most vivid and detailed section of Acts (27:1-28:16). There is a ring of authenticity in the allusions to such navigational problems as the prevailing winds in the various parts of the Mediterranean. Shipping was a dependable means of travel in those days, but only during the summer months. Paul and his party were late in starting, and their early progress was so slow that it was late September or early October [5] by the time the ship reached Crete. Paul's advice against going any farther was ignored. What was at first a helpful breeze from the south became a raging northeaster that threatened to drive them across the Mediterranean to the shoals off North Africa. Actually, they drifted westward, across the opening of the Adriatic, and finally ran aground on the island of Malta. In a vision, Paul had received a promise that he would in fact stand trial before Caesar. Not all the factors that contributed to Paul's deliverance from disaster were of the miraculous kind, however, for the centurion was instrumental in saving Paul's life when the soldiers, fearful of the consequences if any prisoners escaped, were about to put Paul and the other prisoners to death.

While Paul was on the island of Malta, his life was miraculously preserved, according to Acts, after he had been bitten by a poisonous reptile. The Maltese natives had concluded that the goddess of justice, Dike, had sent the viper to strike him down even though he had survived the storm and the shipwreck. But when he came through unharmed, they concluded that he was under the special protection of the gods, or perhaps he was a divine person in human form. The admiration of the natives increased when Paul was able to heal the sick, especially when he cured the father of the "chief," as the man designated by Rome

---

[4] See pp. 26-29 for details about Herod the Great and his family.

[5] This dating is based on the assumption that "the fast" in Acts 27:9 is a reference to the Day of Atonement, which came after the fall equinox.

to rule the island was known. When the weather began to clear—early the following spring—the centurion, the prisoners, and the friends of Paul who had accompanied him all the way from Caesarea set out for the Italian mainland, reaching the harbor of Puteoli near Naples, after stops at Syracuse and Rhegium. At Puteoli there was already a community of Christians, founded, we may assume, by the missionary activity of the thriving church in Rome. A delegation from the community in Rome traveled southward along the famous Appian Way to meet Paul and to escort him into the Imperial City (Acts 28:1-15).

PAUL IN ROME

Having arrived in Rome, Paul extended the usual courtesies to the Jewish community. First, he invited them to hear his version of the conflict with the Jews in Jerusalem, and then he arranged a time for them to hear a statement of the Christian message. Since there had as yet been no adverse reports on Paul from Jerusalem, the Roman Jews came in large numbers to hear what he had to say. As on similar occasions in the past, the response to Paul's preaching of the Gospel was mixed. But to those who rejected it, Paul had a word of warning: The prophet Isaiah had predicted that the people Israel would not receive his message to them. It was in accord with the word of the prophet, therefore, that Paul had turned his attention to the Gentiles, confident that they would continue to respond in faith to the *kerygma*.

During Paul's imprisonment in Rome, he was permitted considerable freedom, both in personal activities and in the preaching of the Gospel. According to the account in Acts (28:30, 31) he lived at his own expense, although he was attended constantly by a Roman guard (28:16). The record in Acts ends incon-

THE APPIAN WAY *just south of Rome, with the arches of the Claudian aqueduct in the background. Paul traveled this road on his way to Rome.*

clusively, without telling us whether or not Paul came to trial, much less whether he was acquitted or sentenced at the trial.[6] Since the words in 28:31 sound like the formal statements with which the author closes the other sections of his book (5:42; 15:35; 19:20), it does not appear that the text has been artificially broken off at this point. It has been conjectured that the author intended to write a third book (in addition to Luke and Acts), but it seems odd that he should have left unresolved such an important issue as the outcome of the trial while he shifted from one volume to another. A more plausible explanation is that the book was to serve as an apology for Paul and the Christian movement, by presenting evidence (1) that the Jewish rejection of Paul and his message was arbitrary and contrary to their own scriptures, and (2) that the Roman authorities had dealt fairly with Paul, and had never found him guilty of violating Roman law. If this was the author's purpose, he closed his account at a dramatic moment. The "two years" (Acts 28:30) of waiting may refer to a statute of limitation, during which period either the accusers of a prisoner were obliged to appear in court or else the prisoner could be set free. We may infer from the absence of any mention of Paul's accusers appearing in Rome that the Jewish leaders from Palestine who originally brought the charges against Paul must not have appeared in the two-year period. But what happened to Paul afterward, we do not know.

Correspondence with the Asian Churches

The matters that occupied Paul's mind can be inferred from the letters he is believed to have written during this time of imprisonment: the Letters to the Philippians, to the Colossians, and to Philemon (and possibly the Letter to the Ephesians). These letters contain clear references to the fact that Paul is in prison (Phil. 1:12; 1:17; Col. 4:10; 4:18; Phm. 23; Eph. 4:1). The fact that Paul mentions several times his hopes of visiting friends in Philippi and Colossae (Phil. 2:24; Phm. 22) has given rise to the theory that it was from an Ephesian rather than a Roman prison that Paul was writing. Would he have told his friends in Colossae to prepare the guest chamber for him when he was 1200 miles away? On the other hand, if he were only 100 miles away (that is, in Ephesus) the possibility of a visit would seem more likely. There is no direct evidence of Paul's having been imprisoned in Ephesus,[7] and, conversely, the personal references in the imprisonment letters fit well into the probable

---

[6] For full discussions of the trial of Paul and the end of Acts, see Foakes-Jackson and Lake, *The Beginnings of Christianity*, Part 1, Vol. V, Additional Note XXVI; and G. H. C. Macgregor in *The Interpreter's Bible*, IX (New York: Abingdon, 1954), 349-352.

[7] The fullest statement of the hypothesis of an imprisonment in Ephesus is in G. S. Duncan, *St. Paul's Ephesian Ministry* (New York: Scribner's, 1930). A summary of the whole question is given by M. S. Enslin, *Christian Beginnings* (New York: Harper, 1938), pp. 273-275. The arguments based on the difficulty of traveling from Rome to Philippi or Colossae are weakened by the evidence of the relative speed and dependability of sea travel in imperial Rome. See *Cambridge Ancient History*, X (Cambridge: Cambridge University Press, 1927), 387.

course of events at the close of Paul's life. In the following paragraphs, we shall attempt to reconstruct the situation.

While Paul was waiting in Rome for his accusers to appear, information came to him from Asia Minor about the church in Colossae and the sister church in Laodicea. These were both vigorous communities, the report ran, but certain unnamed adversaries were trying to convince the Christians there that Paul's Gospel was incomplete. As all the ancient evidence suggests, Asia Minor was fertile territory for religious speculation. Under the influence of the Iranian belief in intermediaries, false teachers had been telling the Colossians that they must purify themselves by means of certain ritual observances (Col. 2:16, 20-23) in order to prepare themselves for the presence of God, and that they must aspire to more complete knowledge of the other intermediary beings—in addition to Christ—if they were to travel the path that leads from the earthly world of darkness to the heavenly realm of light. It was in answer to these false teachings and practices that Paul wrote the Letter to the Colossians.

After expressions of commendation and gratitude (Col. 1:1-12), Paul tells the Colossians that they have already been transferred through Christ to the realm of light, and have already been purified. There are no angelic agents of

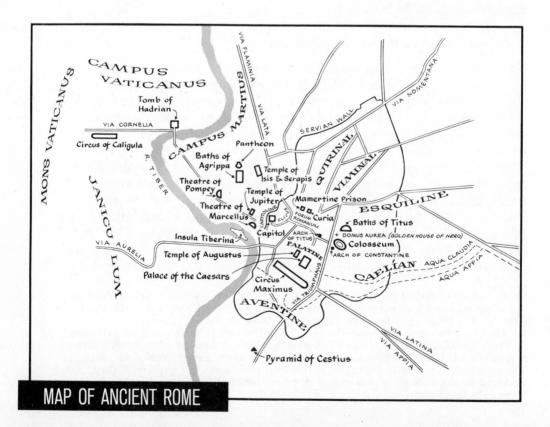

MAP OF ANCIENT ROME

creation of whom they must gain knowledge: Christ is the one through whom God made the universe, and Christ is superior to all other beings. The whole *pleroma* (that is, the totality of God's means of disclosing himself to man) dwells bodily in Jesus Christ (1:13-19). He has already, by his death on the cross, brought man into relationship with God (1:20-23). To Paul, and through him to the Colossian Christians, has been committed the task of declaring the message of what God has done in Christ. There is no need to seek further wisdom about God; it has all been made known in Christ. The effort to delve into religious mysteries is futile; the "mystery" has been revealed, and its meaning is now to be proclaimed (1:24-2:4). The Colossian community is to use its own spiritual resources; it is to shun involvement in ascetic ritual, which subjects the participant to the hostile spiritual powers from which Christ has set men free (2:8-23). The legitimate task of the Colossians is to develop the corporate life of the community, in the power of the Spirit and under its guidance, so that their unity in Christ will appear in their Church life as well as in their personal relationships (3:1-4:5).

The concluding paragraphs of the letter tell us the means by which Paul was carrying on correspondence with distant churches. He was sending Tychicus and Onesimus to carry to the Colossians a first-hand report on his condition and on his prospects for the future. Presumably Paul was reluctant to put in writing his opinions of Rome and its judicial system, lest his comments fall into the hands of the authorities. (We shall see in Chapter 17 how a Christian from Asia Minor veiled his denunciation of Rome in elaborate symbolic imagery.) The names of Paul's companions who aided him during his imprisonment are of interest to us: Mark has already appeared in association with Paul's early work (Acts 12); Aristarchus was one of the delegates who carried the offering from the Greek churches to Jerusalem (Acts 19:29; 20:4); and Luke has been identified traditionally as the author of Acts and the gospel that bears his name (4:7-10, 14).

In addition to the Letter to the Colossians, Paul sent two other letters with Tychicus. One of these was a letter to the Laodiceans, which Paul mentions (Col. 4:16), but which has not survived. Marcion, a learned heretic of the second century, believed our "Letter to the Ephesians" was the letter to the Laodiceans mentioned by Paul. Curiously, several of the oldest and best manuscripts of the New Testament omit the phrase "at Ephesus" in Ephesians 1:1. It has been inferred that the Letter to the Ephesians was originally an encyclical, intended for general circulation among all the churches founded by Paul.[8] The other letter that Tychicus took with him was a personal note to Philemon, in whose house the Colossian church convened (Phm. 2). The purpose of the

---

[8] This theory is defended by Edgar J. Goodspeed in *The Meaning of Ephesians* (Chicago: University of Chicago Press, 1933). In the same author's *Introduction to the New Testament* ([University of Chicago Press, 1937], pp. 238, 239), it is further suggested that Onesimus is the compiler of Ephesians and the one who first brought together all of Paul's letters into a single collection.

letter was to plead with Philemon to accept with gracious forgiveness Onesimus, a slave of Philemon's who had run away. Onesimus had found his way to Rome, where he had come in contact with Paul and had become a Christian (Phm. 16). Paul had found him valuable as a helper in his work, but felt that justice demanded he be returned to his rightful owner. If Onesimus has taken anything from his master, Paul offers to repay it. It is tempting to conjecture that Onesimus, the bishop of Ephesus mentioned by Ignatius (a writer of the early second century) may have been this same runaway slave!

In writing to Philemon, Paul speaks as though he hoped soon to visit his friends in Colossae, which would imply that he expected to be released from prison. But apparently Paul's earlier hopes for release had begun to weaken. He may even have been set free for a time, at the expiration of the waiting period prescribed by Roman law, and again imprisoned—perhaps in connection with Nero's persecution of Christians in A.D. 64—and finally executed. Since both the language and the point of view of the Pastoral Letters (see pp. 393-406) show that they were not written by Paul, but in about the turn of the second century, we have no evidence at all that Paul undertook any further journeys. The wish that Paul expresses in Rom. 15:24, that he might preach the Gospel in Spain, probably went unfulfilled. It seems likely that the charges brought against the Christians in Rome during the reign of Claudius (see p. 159) were revived during the early years of Nero's reign, and that Paul was executed as a disturber of the peace. This must remain, however, a mere conjecture. The whole series of questions about Paul's death should serve as a reminder that the Christian movement, which was later to play such an important role in the history of the empire, was at this time nothing more than a minor nuisance.

Paul's Final Word

It was probably during the closing months of Paul's life that he wrote his most personal message to one of the churches: the Letter to the Philippians. His hope for freedom is not extinguished (Phil. 1:19, 26), but at the same time he has faced up to the fact that death awaits him (1:20; 2:17). He reminds the Philippians (2:8) that it was Jesus' obedience unto death that led to his exaltation by God, and he prays that he may be made like Christ, even in his death (3:10). For Paul, death has no terrors; it will be "gain" (1:21) for him, although his removal by death will be a loss for the Philippians and for all other communities among whom Paul has worked.

The letter begins with words of profound gratitude for the participation of the Philippian Christians in Paul's work through the gift they have sent (1:3-5), and to his thanks he adds a heartfelt prayer for their continued growth in understanding and spirituality (1:6-11). He urges them not to be alarmed by the fact that he has been imprisoned as a result of the schemes of his enemies:

his presence in prison has brought the message of Christ into the imperial household itself; the work he has carried on in prison has helped to strengthen the Roman Christians. Even Paul's opponents are "preaching Christ" by their acts of opposition, since they are drawing attention to the movement and its claims, and are providing Paul with an opportunity to bear witness to Christ in such unexpected places as the imperial establishment itself.

It is at this point in the letter that Paul expresses the hope that the prayers of the Philippian Christians for his deliverance from prison will be answered, even though his personal preference would be to die and so enter the presence of the Lord (1:19-23). He feels, however, that it is more important for the work of the Gospel that he live, and in the light of this conviction he hopes to visit Philippi again (1:24-26). Meanwhile, it is his prayer that they continue steadfast in the face of opposition and even suffering, free from selfishness and factionalism. The supreme illustration of humility and dedication to the welfare of others is Christ, who did not grasp at equality with God even though he possessed the divine qualities characteristic of God. Instead, he humbled himself in obedience to God, to the extreme of dying on a cross. God had publicly acclaimed this complete obedience by exalting Christ as Lord, and by bringing all creation in subjection to him, so that all the universe confesses that "Jesus is Lord."

In the light of Christ's obedience, the Philippians are to be earnest in service to God, pure in mode of life, faithful as witnesses to the truth. Paul hopes to see them again, and is sending messengers to tell them of his own fate (2:23). He warns them against men who take pride in Jewish legalism, and reminds the community at Philippi that he has as enviable a heritage in Judaism as any of the Judaizers. Unlike those who are trying to impose Jewish ritual on the Gentile Christians, Paul is not relying on his religious credentials, but is earnestly striving to live and serve acceptably before God. He is conscious that his new life was given him by God, and that he cannot pride himself on his spiritual achievement; rather, he presses on, longing for the day when the transformation that God has begun in him through Christ will be complete (3:3-21).

The letter closes with a series of warm, personal exhortations and an expression of profound gratitude for the contribution that the church at Philippi has made to his work. There is something unexpected and poignantly powerful about a man who is facing possible death and who can still write: "Rejoice . . . always. Have no anxiety about anything. . . ." (4:4, 6). If the closing lines of II Timothy are authentic notes from Paul's last days, we can see that his confidence never wavered: "For I am already on the point of being sacrificed; the time of my departure has come. . . . Demas has deserted me. . . . Only Luke is with me. . . . But the Lord stood by me and gave me strength. . . . To him be the glory for ever and ever. Amen." (II Tim. 4:6, 10, 11, 17, 18).

AFTER THE APOSTLE'S DEATH

The importance of the work of Paul for the expansion of the Christian movement can hardly be overestimated. Luke's account of Christian beginnings
gives an impression of the high esteem in which the apostle was already held
by early generations. He not only parallels Paul's role with that of Peter, the
leader of the Twelve, but implies that it was through Paul alone that God
carried his purpose beyond the limited beginnings to the "ends of the earth."
Soon numerous legends about the person of the apostle were in circulation,
celebrating him as a unique hero of the cause of God. As in the case of other
apostles, we have fragments of so-called "Acts" of Paul which in a popular
fashion tell of the adventures of the apostle on his journey from Asia Minor
to Rome, using the itinerary of the canonical Acts as a basis but filling in with
fabulous details and legendary stories.[9] The book ends with a fictitious "Martyrdom of Paul," according to which Paul was beheaded, but after his death
appeared to the frightened emperor (Nero), prophesying to him God's punishment for his wickedness.

On the other hand, the figure of the great apostle was also subject to much
controversy. The opposition of a strict Jewish-Christian wing against Paul's
Gospel of freedom from the Law kept growing, and has even found literary
expression. Under the name of Clement of Rome, we have preserved for us a
rather sentimental Christian novel, perhaps the first one of its kind. It tells
the story of the reunification of Clement's family, which through various mis-
fortunes had been dispersed all over the world. Instrumental in the happy
reunion is the Apostle Peter, the true hero of the story. Presented as a traveling preacher and philosopher, Peter is involved in a fierce battle with the
"sorcerer" Simon (cf. Acts 8:9 ff.), following him through various cities along
the Syrian coast and refuting his teaching in lengthy sermons until he finally
convicts him publicly in a discussion at Laodicea. The writing, known as the
"pseudo-Clementine novel," has come to us in two different recensions, the
so-called "Homilies" and the "Recognitions," both of which seem to go back
to an earlier version, perhaps written in Syria early in the third century.[10]
Obviously, various sources have been used in the composition. Many scholars
assume that the oldest one of them, the "Preachings of Peter," is a Jewish-
Christian document from the beginning of the second century A.D. In this

---

[9] The texts are conveniently collected by M. R. James, *The Apocryphal New Testament*,
corrected edition (Oxford: Clarendon Press, 1953), pp. 270 ff. and 570 ff.

[10] A full translation of both recensions is found in Volume VIII of *The Ante-Nicene Fathers*
(Grand Rapids, Mich.: Eerdmans, n.d.), pp. 73 ff. The latest comprehensive study of the novel
has been undertaken by G. Strecker in his book *Das Judenchristentum der Pseudoklementinen*
(Berlin: Akademie Verlag, 1958—*Texte und Untersuchungen zur Geschichte der altchrist-
lichen Literatur*, Volume LXX).

document, Paul and his "lawless" teaching seem to have been the target of most violent attacks, and there can hardly be any doubt that this attitude was typical for many Jewish Christians. In the later orthodox recension of the novel, these attacks of course had to be eliminated; this was done simply by substituting the figure of the arch-heretic Simon, who now displayed the same features the original document had used to characterize Paul.

Paul seems also to have become the favorite authority of certain heretical movements. Ascetic as well as antinomian and even libertine tendencies were justified by an appeal to his position, and Marcion (see pp. 64, 69 f.) reveals his intention of merely drawing out the implications of Paul's theology by giving 10 epistles of Paul (Galatians, I and II Corinthians, Romans, I and II Thessalonians, Ephesians [here called Laodiceans], Colossians, Philippians, Philemon) the prominent place in his canon. This trend seems to have caused quite some embarrassment in the Church. The latest book of the New Testament, the so-called Second Epistle of Peter, contains a remark illustrating this uneasiness. The author, who is fighting libertine Gnostics and defending the Christian hope of the Second Coming against doubts arising from its long delay, connects his final appeal with a reference to the epistles of Paul.

> So also our beloved brother Paul wrote to you according to the wisdom given him, speaking of this as he does in all his letters. There are some things in them hard to understand, which the ignorant and unstable twist to their own destruction, as they do the other scriptures.
> —II PETER 3:15-16

The passage, in the first place, witnesses to the authority of the Apostle Paul in the Church of this time. The collection of his letters is already Christian literature of equal standing with "the other scriptures," *i.e.*, especially the Old Testament. They are regarded as common possession and therefore as being addressed to every Christian generation. But the text also issues a warning. In the new situation, the "wisdom" given to the great apostle may have its limitations and therefore needs supplementation and interpretation—just as the other scriptures (cf. II Pet. 1:20 f.). The polemic obviously is directed against false teaching that claims to stand in the Pauline tradition.

Paul's Influence on History through Letters

It probably was Paul's letter writing more than anything else that insured his influence upon the history of the following decades. Although these letters were genuine pieces of private correspondence, written only for a momentary purpose, they quickly gained exemplary importance. Not only did the churches exchange them among themselves for edifying reading in their assemblies, but they were soon collected, circulated, and imitated throughout the Church in East and West. In fact, Paul's letters set the pace for most of the literature of the post-Apostolic period, which consisted mainly of letters or "epistles" (literary documents styled as letters). In many cases the dependence upon the Pauline model is easily visible; the "Christianized" form of the initial greeting, the basic division of the letter into doctrinal and ethical parts, became standard convention among Christian writers.

PSEUDONYMOUS LETTERS AND PAULINE CORRESPONDENCE. We even know of writings composed under Paul's *name* by later authors. They partly try to fill in gaps of the authentic Pauline correspondence. An exchange of letters between the Corinthians and Paul, known as III Corinthians, capitalizes on allusions in the two genuine Corinthian epistles. The composition of an "Epistle to the Laodiceans," which is mainly drawing from Philippians, obviously was inspired by the reference to such a letter in Col. 4:16. There even exists a fictitious correspondence between Paul and the Roman philosopher Seneca, which tries to show how much the two men admired each other.[11]

We call such literature written under the name of another person "pseudonymous" (Greek for "under false name").[12] For us, this practice seems to be fraud, which seeks willfully to deceive the reader. It is shocking to hear that pseudonymous writing was widely practiced in antiquity. In our historical and psychological age, we connect every work of literature immediately with the personality of the author; and conversely, the author enjoys public protection for his intellectual production. We must remember that this situation did not exist in antiquity; *our* understanding of personality and intellectual property was not known. Thus, instead of looking at the problem of pseudonymity as a moral one, we should see it in its historical perspective.

Most of the Jewish apocalyptic writings, for example, are pseudonymous. Although none of them was written before the second century B.C., they claim the authority of such ancient heroes as Daniel, Baruch, Enoch, and even Adam. Since apocalyptic knowledge is presented as prophecy, it seemed appropriate to claim a venerable figure from ancient times—the older the better—as author of a book which aimed at disclosing the mysteries of the End Time. Knowing the true identity of the author would not have helped the reader to get the message. The author deliberately remained in the background—precisely for the sake of his message.

Another example: the legendary figure of King Solomon was regarded as *the* model of a wise man. Thus a whole wisdom literature developed under his name (cf. Proverbs, Ecclesiastes, Wisdom of Solomon, Psalms of Solomon, etc.). Here, another motif of pseudonymous writing enters in. The writer of a

---

[11] Translations of these writings again are found in M. R. James' *The Apocryphal New Testament*, pp. 288 ff. and 479 ff.

[12] See the instructive article by K. Aland, "The Problem of Anonymity and Pseudonymity in Christian Literature of the First Two Centuries," *The Journal of Theological Studies*, new series, XII, 1961, 39-49.

later epoch regarded the ancient figure as his master, whom he would like to match. His declared intention was to write exactly what and how the master would have written were he still alive. It was a claim of a certain self-achievement, and at the same time a humble tribute to the genius of the imitated master if an author chose to use the famous name for his own work. Letter writing was a favorite field for this kind of pseudonymity in Hellenistic and early imperial times. Many unknown writers took pride in composing letters purportedly written by Alexander, Cicero, or Brutus. In most cases it is perfectly clear that these are literary fiction and are intended to be enjoyed as such.

We may assume a similar background for most of the pseudonymous Pauline literature mentioned above. What Tertullian says concerning the "Acts of Paul" [13]—namely, that they were written by a presbyter in Asia Minor "out of love for the Apostle" in an attempt to "enhance Paul's reputation by adding to it something of his own"—is probably a good explanation for much of the later pseudonymous writing under the name of an apostle. But we must realize that beyond this "pious fraud" or the naïve ambition to attract a public of Christians under the cover of a prestigious name, the rise of pseudonymity in the post-Apostolic period had far more serious reasons, which have to do with the basic problems of that age. Thus, in the last instance, pseudonymity evidences a changing self-understanding of the Church. We have to take a look at this development before we can evaluate fully the problem of pseudonymity in the New Testament.

The Changing Self-Understanding of the Church

Much of the change in the Church's self-understanding was due to the simple fact of ongoing time. Christians originally had not reckoned with this possibility, since their hope was that within their lifetime the End would come. But by A.D. 70, the 12 apostles and Paul all were probably dead, and as more and more second- and third-generation Christians found their way into the community, the intense expectation of the imminent Coming of the Lord was beginning to diminish. In situations of stress and suffering, like the period during which the Book of Revelation was written, the coals of expectancy were fanned to white heat. But there was a growing feeling that things were probably going to continue pretty much as they were, at least for a time. The Church, which saw itself as God's People of the End Time, as the vanguard of the kingdom, proclaiming the Gospel to all the world in order to "hasten" the Coming of the Lord, now had to take seriously the realities and demands of an *extended*, perhaps *very* extended, intermediate period. In the conflicts in which it soon was involved, it realized that being chosen as God's People of the End Time

---

[13] Tertullian, *On Baptism*, 17.

meant being sent on a long and hard pilgrimage—a pilgrimage of people who are aliens and strangers in this world, yet who have to walk through it in order to reach their goal.

All the dominant themes of the post-Apostolic period reflect this basic change. They are not really new. But they appear in the context of new questions, and thus demand new answers.

There is, first, the theme of *unity*. From the very start, the Christian community had taken its unity for granted. Those who entered the Church believed that they were becoming members of a new community which God had called into being through the Messiah, Jesus, and together they awaited Christ's coming and the consummation of God's purpose. They felt that they had a sure sign that they were the People of God: the presence of the Holy Spirit or the spirit of Jesus Christ in their midst. They were living in the Last Days that had been proclaimed long ago by the prophets of Israel. By their missionary efforts, little communities of Christians had sprung up throughout the Roman world. As a result, there was a strong feeling of unity, which was largely unpremeditated and spontaneous.

However, as time went on, this feeling of unity became problematical. It was not that an originally existing unity was now being broken by human error and ill will. To be sure, this is the image of the beginnings which later generations, themselves suffering under schism and division, have projected. A golden time of such undisturbed unity probably never existed. We must remember that from earliest times on, unity in the Christian Church did not exclude variety, even tension, among those who worshiped Christ as Lord. The sources of Acts as well as the Pauline epistles constantly remind us of this fact. But variety and even tension were never felt to endanger the unity in Christ as long as the Spirit was at work and drove Christians to seek and find means of expressing their unity in acts of solidarity.

In the post-Apostolic period, this spirit seemed to be no longer a standard by which unity could be determined. In the growing Church herself, the gift of the Spirit no longer manifested itself as intensely as it used to; too many "Spirits" were claiming to speak in the name of Christ. The Church had to raise the question of the marks of her unity; moreover, this unity itself had now to be defined in terms of its ground, its practical possibilities, and its limits.

Another theme is that of *holiness*. Christians of the earlier days called themselves "the saints," a title which probably is derived from the self-designation of esoteric Jewish groups. It expressed the conviction of being elected by God, of being purified, made holy in order to fulfill the mission of the holy remnant in the world. It obviously included the expectation that with the God-given new life, sin would cease to dominate this group in which the kingdom of God had already broken in upon the world.

Again, this concept of holiness was rendered problematical as time went on.

Not that now sin was gradually inundating the Church of the "holy ones." In fact, there had never been a really sinless period. But the expectation of the imminent End had made it easier to deal with the problem of sin in a spontaneous way. Sinners were simply excluded from the community of the saints, and Paul could even explain death and sickness in Corinth as the means by which God himself guarded the holiness of his Church.

In the post-Apostolic period, this was no longer a sufficient answer to the problem. Sin proved to be a constant reality, not only outside the Church, but within as well. Facing its long pilgrimage through the world, the Church had to find ways of living with this reality. It had to redefine what it meant to speak of itself as "holy" and had to help Christians to distinguish between "holy" and "unholy" by the development of an ethical code.

A third theme is that of *apostolicity*. The earliest Church of course was "apostolic" inasmuch as its leadership was in the hands of the apostles, who represented the authentic continuation of Jesus' own authority. So long as they were living, they provided a ready court of appeal for all problems confronting the Church. Christians were confident that the apostles were in possession of the tradition that had been delivered to them by Jesus Christ. Paul, who claimed the direct commission by the Lord, also insisted that he was faithful to this tradition. In fact, the major debate between Paul and the "pillar" apostles of Jerusalem—Peter, James, and John—centered on whether or not Paul's teaching was true to the tradition.

With the passing of the apostles, the meaning of the Church's apostolicity necessarily became a problem. Where could the true Apostolic Tradition be found? The difficulty in answering this question became clear when Gnostic teachers claimed that they were in the possession of "secret teachings" of the apostles. How was the Church to show that this claim was false? It had to develop standards by which the true Apostolic Tradition could be distinguished from false teaching. This is the context in which the emergence of a new concept of tradition and of its guarantee—the regular, organized ministry—is to be seen. It also is the background for much of the pseudonymous writing in the early Church.

Modern scholarship recognizes that numerous writings in the New Testament are pseudonymous, particularly among the Epistles. In the Pauline corpus, the three Pastoral Epistles and Ephesians are generally reckoned in this category, and the Catholic Epistles are probably all pseudonymous. The authors who put these writings under the authority of an apostle certainly did not intend to deceive nor simply to entertain their readers; in some cases, it even is possible that the addressees knew the true identity of the writer. Their only intention was to preserve the *true* Apostolic Tradition as they saw it at a time of great confusion, and for this purpose they used a current literary device that enabled them to give their message the strongest backing possible. They were convinced that they wrote in the way the Apostle himself would have written, were he in their place. It was *his* message that they wanted to proclaim in their situation—a situation which needed a clearer word on the issues of right doctrine and conduct than they found in the existing letters of the Apostle.

It still remains true that our New Testament canon does contain books which are not written by the author under whose authority they have been accepted by the Church. We simply have to face this fact. To be sure, the Church did not consciously encourage such pseudonymous writing. But by accepting these specific books into its "apostolic" canon, the Church made clear that it regarded them as representative of the Apostolic Tradition and therefore as part of the standard in the fight against false doctrine. That this decision, arising out of a specific historical situation, was not a guarantee against historical error, and that it is the Spirit alone who can lead to a right understanding of the tradition, is a truth which the Church at all times has humbly to acknowledge.

A CALL TO UNITY: THE EPISTLE TO THE EPHESIANS

Among the pseudonymous epistles of the New Testament, it is the Epistle to the Ephesians, written during the latter half of the first century, which stands out most clearly as a witness for the developing new self-understanding of the Church, and its implications. The writing purports to be an epistle of Paul, and there is certainly a similarity in language and thought between Ephesians and Paul's epistles. But in spite of the similarities, careful study shows that words are often used in Ephesians with different shades of meaning from what they have in the epistles of Paul. Furthermore, there are several significant terms in Ephesians that do not occur in Paul's writings. This alone would not be reason enough to doubt Paul's authorship, but there are other significant differences. In Ephesians, the conflict with Judaism lies in the past, whereas in the Pauline epistles, it was still a burning issue. Ephesians also refers to the "holy apostles" (3:5), a phrase that would be almost inconceivable for Paul to use in referring to himself.[14]

According to one theory, the author of Ephesians put together the first collection of Paul's letters, and then appended his own writing as a general introduction.[15] Since Ephesians shows clear literary dependence on Paul's Epistle to the Colossians, it has been suggested that the author was very familiar with it and used it as his model. Ephesians is the most Pauline of all the later writings of the New Testament: its emphases on justification by faith, the in-dwelling of Christ, and the Spirit, are highly reminiscent of Paul. (The

---

[14] For a perceptive study of Ephesians on this line see C. L. Mitton, *The Epistle to the Ephesians, Its Authorship, Origin, and Purpose* (Oxford: Clarendon Press, 1951).

[15] *Ibid.*, pp. 45-54.

fact that from the earliest times Ephesians was associated with the Church in Asia Minor points to that region as the place where it was written.) Unlike the genuine Pauline epistles, which were written to specific churches to deal with specific problems, Ephesians appears to have been written for general reading by a number of churches. The phrase "in Ephesus" is missing from the address in several of the oldest manuscripts.

The First Theme: The Unity in Christ

Two great themes dominate the thought of Ephesians: *the unity of all things in Christ,* and *the Church as the visible symbol of that unity.* The author unfolds these two themes (1:3-23) in a long benediction and thanksgiving with many liturgical phrases. In Jesus Christ, God has revealed his purpose, which was present from the creation of the world; *through* Christ men were destined to be sons of God, and *in* him all things were destined to find their ultimate unity. Although the author speaks of unity in cosmological terms ("things in heaven and on earth"), it is perfectly clear that he does not regard the disunity of the world as some tragic flaw in Creation.

Rather, the cause of the disunity is man's sin (1:7), which prevents him from realizing the unity God has intended from the beginning. But those who have been laid hold upon by God through the Holy Spirit (1:13) have been enlightened; to them, the power of God has been revealed in the death and resurrection of Christ. God has given Christ dominion over all powers in heaven and on earth, evil or good, in order that now and forever all things may be subject to him. The evil powers that disunite the world have been overcome by Christ, who is the head of the Church, in which this unity is made known to the world.

This unity that the author speaks about is not just a theoretical concept, however (2:1-21). In the first place, he reminds his readers that before they were Christians they were enslaved to the evil powers of this world, and that through their sin they have contributed to the disunity of mankind. But through the mercy and love of God, Christ has released them from this dead past and has re-created them for good works (2:1-10). The sin that made them servants of the evil that disunites mankind has been marked out and declared dead through Christ. The grasp that evil powers had on their lives has been broken.

In the second place, the author points out that through Christ the greatest division among men has been healed (2:11-21). The Gentiles, who were not the chosen People of God, who did not worship the true God and who were separated in hostility from God's People (the Jews), have now been made God's People through Jesus Christ. A new household of God has been created through the preaching of the apostles and Christian prophets. Men from all nations have been knit together into a community in which God dwells through his Spirit and in which all men are united in one great family.

The Second Theme: The World Mission of the Church

Ephesians emphasizes that God has revealed through Christ the mystery of Creation; in Christ, mankind is to find power to overcome its divisions and to be united in a new community, the Church, which God has called into being. The Church's sole reason for existence is to bear witness in the world to this purpose of God (3:9-13). The author concludes his declaration of the unity of the Church with one of the most beautiful prayers in the New Testament (3:14-21). This is a petition to God who is the Father of all nations, that his spirit may so prepare Christians in mind and heart that Christ may dwell in them and that Christ's love may become the bond that unites them. In the doxology that concludes the prayer (3:20-21), the author acknowledges the power of God that is at work in Christ and in the Church. It is accomplishing his purposes in ways that surpass understanding. Above all, the author has in mind the unity of mankind that God is bringing about through Christ and the Church.

But again, the author emphasizes that there must be tangible evidence of this unity in the Church if the world is to believe its message (Chapters 4-6). The Church testifies to the truth that its unity is founded upon the belief in one God who has been revealed through one Lord (Jesus Christ) and one Spirit (4:1-6). But God has given the Church a ministry that is to lead it to an ever increasing unity of thought and action (4:7-16). Through knowledge of Christ, it is to move toward ever greater maturity: it must overcome the strange teachings that disunite it (4:14) and make it appear foolish to the world, for it cannot proclaim unity while a conflict rages within. The Church must grow strong in the bond of love—the true basis of its unity—as it fulfills its mission in the world (4:16).

A Final Theme: Ethical Conduct

In the final section, the author speaks of Christian unity in terms of specific ethical conduct (4:17-6:9). Since God, through Christ, has re-created Christians in newness of life (4:22-24), they are to put aside their former way of life, especially those vices that disrupt rather than unite the community (4:25-32). Since Christians are called to be "imitators of God," they must shun all immorality and walk in the light whereby God has revealed to them what is good and right (5:7-10). All their relationships—marriage, family, social —must bear single testimony to the new life in Christ (5:21-6:9) that they share in common.

THE GROWING CONFLICT
BETWEEN JUDAISM AND CHRISTIANITY

At the close of the Apostolic Age, leadership in the Church passed from Christians brought up in a Jewish religious setting and converted as adults to Christianity, to Christians brought into the faith from paganism or nurtured in it by non-Jewish Christian parents. One might suppose that the effect would have been to lessen the tension between Jew and Christian, but unfortunately this is not the case. In fact, the antagonism *mounted* as Palestinian-Jewish Christianity waned in numbers and importance; indeed, the Jerusalem church itself seems to have been subjected to an unprecedented persecution by Jewish authorities in the years immediately following the death of Paul. Since the conflict reached a crisis in connection with the fall of Jerusalem to the Roman army in A.D. 70, we shall consider both the antecedents and the consequences of that event, so important to the subsequent history of both Judaism and the Church.

Evidence from Literary Sources

Evidence of mounting hostility between Jew and Christian in the later first century is found in both Jewish and Christian sources. The rabbinic traditions that have been preserved from this period regularly refer to Christians as heretics, and heap scorn and slander on Jesus and his followers. For example, the story that Jesus was the illegitimate son of Mary by a Roman soldier appears to have originated with Jewish polemicists of this time.[16] Concurrently, the Christians were modifying the stories in the gospels to intensify the hatred against the Jewish leaders by portraying them as having assumed full blame for the death of Jesus. Matthew quotes the Jews as saying at Jesus' trial, "His blood be on us and our children" (Mt. 27:25). The fact that these words condemn the Jews in such strong terms, coupled with the fact that they are found in none of the other gospel accounts of Jesus' trial, suggests that they were added as a polemic against the Jews at or shortly before the time Matthew wrote his gospel.

Similarly, the harsh treatment that Jewish converts to Christianity received at the hands of the leaders of the synagogues throughout the empire during this period is reflected in the gospels in various ways: the Jewish-Christian tension appears in the heightening of the element of conflict in the accounts of Jesus' encounters with the Pharisees; it is included in the predictions of persecu-

---

[16] For a survey of the anti-Christian elements in the rabbinic tradition, see J. Klausner, *Jesus of Nazareth* (New York: Macmillan, 1926), pp. 18-54.

tion for faithful disciples in the apocalyptic section of Mark (13:5 ff.) and in the stories of Jesus' sending the disciples out to preach (Mt. 10:17-25). In three different passages the Gospel of John speaks of the practice of putting a man out of the synagogue if he confesses that Jesus is the Christ (9:22; 12:42; 16:2). These specific warnings of Jewish opposition were probably added by the early church to Jesus' predictions of the general resistance that preachers of the Gospel would meet, and the additions were probably made just when Jewish hostility to Christianity was mounting.

The high point of animosity between Christian and Jew in the New Testament is reached in the Gospel of John, especially in the story of the Passion. Although it is true that Matthew is the writer who has added to the Markan tradition the dreadful words, "His blood be on us and on our children" (Mt. 27:25), the whole movement of the trial scenes in John points up the belief that Pilate could find no cause for condemning Jesus, but that he yielded to the pressure of "the Jews." The very phrase "the Jews" demonstrates that the wide differences between the Jewish sects that prevailed in Jesus' day no longer existed in the time of the writing of the Gospel of John, but that all opposition from Jewish quarters could be lumped together as traceable to "the Jews." Even Jesus is quoted in John as putting the major blame on his own people: "He who has delivered me to you has the greater sin"—that is, the Jews are really responsible. Further evidence of conflict between Jew and Christian in the time in which John's gospel was written is probably to be found in the questions that appear throughout the book, always on the lips of Jewish antagonists: "Is not this Jesus, the son of Joseph, whose father and mother we know?" (6:42); "How can this man give us his flesh to eat?" (6:52); "Are you greater than our father, Abraham?" (8:53); "How can you say that the Son of man must be lifted up?" (12:34). From the words of the prologue (Jn. 1:11), "His own people received him not," throughout the book the theme recurs that "the Jews" were obstinate and blind in their failure to accept Jesus as the Christ.

Evidence from Historical Sources

The mutual ill will between Christian and Jew that developed at this time is apparent not only in the literature of the period, but also in direct reports of events from Christian and non-Christian sources. Herod Agrippa had gained favor with the Jews in Judea by executing James (and possibly his brother John), though it seems unlikely that the idea of persecuting the Christians originated with Herod. At any rate, he continued the persecution primarily to please the Jews (Acts 12:3), and quickly lost interest in the undertaking when one of his victims escaped (Acts 12:19). With Peter, James, and John removed as leaders of the Jerusalem community (about A.D. 44), the tension between Christians and Jews seems to have relaxed. When James, Jesus' brother, took over as head of the church in Jerusalem, he was eager to maintain good relations with the Jewish leaders, especially since his own convictions and practices were strongly legalistic. It was he who took the initiative in demanding that Gentile Christians respect certain aspects of Jewish regulations (see p. 161), and it was he who was most embarrassed by Paul's presence in Jerusalem, since Paul was notorious for his contacts with Gentiles and for his concessions to their way of life. The Jerusalem Christians were, until A.D. 62, zealous to demonstrate their loyalty to Judaism.

There is no evidence of any further conflict between Judaism and the Jerusalem church until A.D. 62, when James, the brother of Jesus, was put to death by order of the High Priest. Even the riot stirred up by Paul in A.D. 55 does not appear to have resulted in any unfavorable reaction against the Jerusalem Christians; in any case, they remained aloof from the incident, and made no effort to come to Paul's aid. There are two independent—and probably irreconcilable—accounts of the execution of James.[17] Josephus, the Jewish historian of the period, tells in his *Antiquities* that Annas, the High Priest, sentenced James to death on an alleged violation of Jewish Law. The sentence was passed and the execution performed during the interim between the death of Festus (A.D. 62) and the arrival of Albinus, his successor; so the absence of a Roman governor provided Annas with an opportunity to act independently. Probably Annas wanted to destroy James out of resentment for his popularity with the people, who seem to have admired James for his piety. Since James was famous for his fidelity to the Law, the charge brought against him by Annas was almost certainly false. There was a strong reaction to Annas' plot, both from the Jewish officials, who sought to have Annas deposed, and from the procurator himself, who did in fact remove Annas from the high priesthood.

The other account of the death of James comes to us in two forms from Eusebius, who quotes from two of the Church Fathers, Clement of Alexandria (around A.D. 200) and Hegesippus (around A.D. 180). According to these stories, James was first thrown down from a pinnacle of the Temple and then beaten on the head by a workman with a club until he died. The details of the story are what we would expect to find in a legend of the death of a martyr. Although Josephus' more sober version of James' death is to be preferred to the accounts in Eusebius, the stories agree that James was executed by official Jewish action in spite of, and in part because of, his popularity with the people of Jerusalem.

THE CLIMAX OF THE CONFLICT

In the years A.D. 66-70, the position of the Church in Jerusalem became increasingly difficult as a result of the Jewish revolt against Roman occupation. The cruelty and corruption of the Roman procurators had been increasing. Nero had made important concessions to the Gentiles in Palestine, and they had begun to interfere with Jewish worship in the synagogues. In the year 66, as

---

[17] These accounts are quoted and analyzed in detail by M. Goguel in *The Birth of Christianity* (New York: Macmillan, 1954), pp. 124-132.

a reaction against maltreatment at the hands of the Roman administrators, the Jews refused to permit the sacrifices to the emperor to continue, although these sacrifices were required by Roman law throughout the empire. Riots broke out in every city; Gentile towns were burned; the Roman garrisons were attacked in cities where they were weak; and Jews were slaughtered in reprisal in cities where the garrisons were strong. At first, the Jews succeeded in liberating

A SHEKEL OF ISRAEL *as minted by the Jews during the Jewish revolt of* A.D. *66-70. The reverse side is inscribed "Jerusalem the Holy."*

parts of the land from Roman control; the independence of the Jewish nation was declared, and Jewish coinage was issued. But the poorly armed bands of revolutionaries could not withstand the 60,000 seasoned troops that Rome sent in to quell the revolt. By the year 69 all of Palestine, except for Jerusalem and some outlying fortresses near the Dead Sea, was once again under Roman control.

Vespasian, who commanded the Roman troops, could have quickly destroyed all resistance, but his mind was occupied with other matters: the emperor, Nero, had died under mysterious circumstances in 68, and Vespasian's chances of succeeding him were excellent. Accordingly, Vespasian held back from the fighting for a time to see what the outcome of the contest for the imperial throne would be. When it became clear that the army in the East would declare for him, he returned to Rome. His rivals faded from the scene, and he became emperor in 69. His son, Titus, who had been left in charge of the troops in Palestine, pressed the siege of Jerusalem.

The Fall of Jerusalem

The city's resistance might have been greater if the people had not been torn by internal dissension. At the start of the revolt there had been two main parties: the peace party, whose members believed God would free the nation from Rome in his own time and by his own methods; and the resistance party, whose adherents were convinced that the time had come for them to take the initiative in driving the Romans out. With the advent of the Roman troops, the peace party was overwhelmed by the rebels, but any prospect of

VESPASIAN *invaded Palestine in* A.D. *67. He let his son Titus capture Jerusalem, and returned to Rome to be acclaimed emperor in 69.*

success for the revolt was ended when the rebels began to fight among themselves under rival leaders. The civil strife continued within the city even during the siege. Although the revolutionaries had killed Annas, who had caused James' death, the Christians appear to have been in sympathy with the peace party. They believed that the hope of the nation lay in the return of their Messiah to establish the reign of God, not in military victory. The siege, which began in April of the year 70, lasted five months, and during this time thousands died of starvation. Then, when the city fell, the Romans laid it waste and demolished the Temple. A generation later, during the reign of Hadrian, the Jews attempted a second revolt (A.D. 132-135), but at the order of Hadrian the city of Jerusalem was leveled and a pagan city called Aelia Capitolina was built on the site.

The Flight of the Christians

Presumably it was just before the siege began that the Christians decided to flee to a place of safety. At first glance, it seems clear that the reason they fled was to escape destruction at the hands of the Romans, but Eusebius tells us that they went to the Gentile city of Pella, east of the Jordan in the region of the Decapolis, in response to a divine oracle. Certain questions immediately arise: What was the nature of the oracle? Why did it tell them to go to a despised Gentile city like Pella, which had been among those attacked by the Jewish nationalists only a few years earlier? Why were the Jewish Christians—traditionally so fastidious about maintaining separateness from Gentiles —willing to seek refuge in a Gentile stronghold? Considering these questions in reverse order, the probability is that the Jerusalem Christians were willing to compromise their religious scruples for the sake of saving their own necks. The only place of safety in the whole area for Jews who had opposed the revolt would be a place like Pella, which was Gentile and hence free of Jewish nationalist feeling. There they would be safe from the Romans, who might have taken them for rebels in Jerusalem, and safe from the rebels, who might have killed them as traitors.

Eusebius gives another theory to explain the flight of the Christians from Jerusalem. He suggests that the Roman emperors, from Vespasian on, sought out all descendants of David in an effort to exterminate the Jewish hope of a revival of the Davidic dynasty. Since Jesus was from "the seed of David" (Rom. 1:3), he and his relatives would have been in the royal line, and his brothers

THE ARCH OF TITUS *in Rome contains this bas-relief. The structure was erected to celebrate Titus' triumph over the Jews. The victors are carrying off from the Temple of Jerusalem the seven-branched lampstand, the sacred trumpets, and the table where the sacred bread was kept.*

THE MAUSOLEUM OF HADRIAN *on the west bank of the Tiber River, with the dome of St. Peter's in the background. In Christian times, the top of the structure was rebuilt and served both as a fortress and as a chapel.*

and other surviving relatives would have been the victims of Vespasian if they had remained within his reach at Jerusalem. On this theory, the flight to Pella would have been a communal effort to protect Jesus' family, to whom had passed the leadership of the Jerusalem community. This story of Eusebius, like the ones about James mentioned above, bears the marks of legendary embroidering, and really conveys little more than the general impression that (1) the Romans did not understand the nature of Christian messianic beliefs, and mistakenly identified them with the nationalistic hopes of Judaism, and (2) the Jerusalem wing of Christianity had already lapsed into such complete obscurity by the end of the second century that there were no precise recollections of what had happened to it after the city of Jerusalem fell to the Romans.

As for the oracle that instructed the Christians to flee, there is a possibility that it may be imbedded in the apocalyptic section that precedes the Passion story in each of the synoptic gospels (Mt. 24; Mk. 13; Lk. 21). The phrase in Mk. 13:14, "let the reader understand," is often interpreted as referring to the reader of the oracle, which Eusebius tells us was circulated in Jerusalem at the time of the Roman invasion.[18]

Although we do not know what happened to the Christians after they fled from Jerusalem, we do know that the destruction of Jerusalem by the Romans was interpreted by Christians generally as a divine judgment on Judaism for its rejection of Jesus as the Christ. This conviction is plainly and repeatedly stated in Eusebius, and it is easy to read it between the lines of the gospels. The very

---

[18] The attempt by G. R. Beasley-Murray to demonstrate the authenticity of the Little Apocalypse of Mark cannot be called successful. See Beasley-Murray's *Commentary on Mark 13* (New York: St. Martin's Press, 1957).

245

fact that the apocalyptic section mentioned above was incorporated into the Synoptics shows that the fall of Jerusalem was considered a major event in the unfolding of the purpose that God had begun with the coming of Jesus. The destruction was understood to be the final proof that the Old Dispensation had come to an end; the New Age was already beginning to dawn.

THE HERITAGE OF JEWISH CHRISTIANITY

Although we have no direct knowledge of the fate of Jewish Christianity after A.D. 70, certain developments both inside and outside the main body of the Church are probably a heritage from this vanished wing of Christianity. Writers in the second, and again in the fourth, centuries tell of various groups living east of the Jordan who may have been the survivors of Jewish Christianity. One of these sects, known as the Ebionites (meaning "poor"), appears to have been directly related to the Jerusalem community, which also called itself "the poor" (Gal. 2:10; Rom. 15:26; cf. Lk. 6:20). The Ebionites are reported to have regarded Jewish Law and tradition as the basis for their outlook and practices. From all the Christian writings, they accepted as scripture only the Gospel of Matthew, although they denied the virgin birth of Jesus. The attempt to identify the Ebionites with the community that produced the Dead Sea Scrolls has proved fruitless.[19] Judged by the standards of Pauline Christianity or by the growing orthodoxy of the second-century Fathers of the Church, the Ebionites seem scarcely to be Christian at all.

Later writers speak of another group, called "Nazorenes" or "Nazarenes," who were also more Jewish than Christian in character, and who spoke a Semitic dialect rather than Greek. But these Jewish-Christian groups east of the Jordan did not retain unchanged the Jerusalem type of Christianity; under the influence of the unorthodox Jewish sects in the Jordan region, they engaged in the wildest kind of elaboration of the faith. Early in the second century there appeared a prophet named Elxai (Alexis in Greek), who insisted on the observance of the full Jewish ritual, but who recognized Christ as Son of God. Elxai had first-hand knowledge of Christ, since he had seen him in a vision in which Christ appeared as a mountain ninety-six miles high!

Fortunately for the subsequent history of Christianity, this type of bizarre speculation never became a dominant force in the Church. Like the rivers of Damascus, it flowed out to the edge of the desert and vanished. The church buildings that have survived in this territory east of the Jordan date from the time of Constantine (fourth century) or later, and demonstrate by their form

---

[19] See the article, "The Qumran Scrolls, the Ebionites and Their Literature," by J. Fitzmyer, in *The Scrolls and the New Testament*, K. Stendahl, ed. (New York: Harper & Row, 1957), pp. 208-231.

and decoration that the orthodox type of Christianity eventually prevailed here as elsewhere. Jewish Christianity simply died out.

The Fate of the Other Apostles

Only traces remain of the careers and fates of the other apostles. Acts reports the departure of Peter from Jerusalem at the time of the persecution of the Church under Herod Agrippa (A.D. 44), but gives us no information as to where he went. He reappears briefly in Acts 15 at the time of the so-called Jerusalem Council, though he is called "Symeon" on that occasion (Acts 15:14). Later Church tradition claims that Peter went to Rome and that he became the first bishop of the church there. There is considerable plausibility in the theory that he was martyred in Rome under Nero (A.D. 64) at the same time that Paul was executed. Since Peter was not a Roman citizen, he could have been crucified, as tradition reports he was. The site of his execution and burial is thought to have been in the gardens of Nero, which lay across the Tiber from the main part of Rome. It is in this area that archaeologists have uncovered a pagan cemetery, in the midst of which is a memorial thought to have been erected in honor of Peter. Over this spot was built the Church of St. Peter in the time of Constantine; over it now stands the Renaissance Basilica of St. Peter.[20]

The death of James, the brother of Jesus, has been discussed in connection with the fall of Jerusalem. Jude, in the epistle that bears his name, is depicted as calling himself "Jude, the brother of James." About Jude we know nothing, although there was a person of this name among the brothers of Jesus (Mk. 6:3; Mt. 13:55). He would have been dead at the time of the Emperor Domitian when his grandsons were tried before the emperor as being descendants of David—and therefore as possible pretenders to the Jewish throne—but were released upon showing their hardened hands as proof that they were merely hard-working farmers.

As to the fate of James and John, the sons of Zebedee (Mk. 1:29; 10:35), apart from Acts, we have only brief accounts in the Church Fathers of the second century to go on. Irenaeus is probably relying on Papias for his report of the residence in Ephesus of the venerable John, "a disciple of the Lord." Papias' own account seems to differentiate between John the Elder (to whom Irenaeus is evidently referring) and John the son of Zebedee. It is possible that John of Ephesus (sometimes referred to as John the Elder) was one who had become a follower of Jesus during his lifetime, and who had become the leader of the Church in the vicinity of Ephesus following his migration there from

---

[20] For a full discussion of the historical and archaeological questions concerning the fate of Peter, see O. Cullmann: *Peter: Disciple, Apostle, Martyr*, rev. ed. (Philadelphia: Westminster, 1963).

Palestine. The mention by Bishop Polycrates that John of Ephesus was a priest (cf. Jn. 18:15) would fit with this conjecture. It is significant that in these patristic references, John of Ephesus is described as a "disciple," not as an "apostle." Thus, the tradition that connects the Gospel and Epistles—and Apocalypse—of John with John of Ephesus does not make the claim that the works were written by the Apostle John, the son of Zebedee. Indeed, there is evidence that John, son of Zebedee, was martyred at the same time as was James, son of Zebedee—i.e., in A.D. 44, since a calendar of martyrs used in the Eastern Church celebrates the martyrdom of both James and John on the same day—which would scarcely be the case if John lived to an advanced age and died in Ephesus at the end of the first century. We are therefore left with the probability that *both* the sons of Zebedee died at the hand of Herod Agrippa about A.D. 44 (Acts 12:2).

We have only traces or pious legends about the fate of the other apostles. Thomas is said to have gone to India, where the Mar Thoma Church preserves his name. Mark was believed to have traveled to Alexandria, whence the Venetians stole his bones for their cathedral in the late Middle Ages. But the most significant monument of all that the apostles left was their witness to the risen Christ, and the power of the Spirit by which the Church believed God was guiding it in the changing situations that it confronted as the first Christian century ended and the new one began.

In the post-Apostolic age, as the Church sought to adjust to the pressures of change from within and without, its restatements of the *kerygma* regularly appeared under the authority of the apostles. At times the appeal to an apostle was explicit, as in the pseudo-Pauline writings; at times the apostolic claim is only implicit, as in the gospels. The assignment of apostolic authorship to these gospels seems to have developed a generation or so after they were written. While each of them reflects the peculiar circumstances of its own origin, each seeks faithfully to transmit the apostolic witness to Jesus as the Christ.

PART THREE

THE COMMUNITY SEEKS
NEW UNDERSTANDING
OF ITSELF AND ITS MESSAGE

THE COMMUNITY
CONFRONTS
MAJOR CRISES

CHAPTER ELEVEN   Of all the problems that confronted

the Christian community in the first century, there were

none more serious than (1) the passing of the Apostolic

Generation, with the profound question that it raised con-

cerning the hope of the establishment of God's kingdom

within their lifetime; (2) mounting hostility between the

Church and Judaism; and (3) the first signs of official Roman

opposition to the Church and its message about the coming

of God's kingdom. Closely associated with the passing of the apostles was the scattering of the Jerusalem church, which presumably occurred just prior to the destruction of Jerusalem by the Roman armies (see Chapter 10). With this sober reminder of Roman vindictiveness, the struggling Christian community could not but view with alarm the mounting signs that it would soon encounter imperial opposition.

Directly under the influence of these crisis situations were written several of the New Testament books: Revelation, I and II Peter, Mark, possibly Hebrews. At least indirectly, all the later New Testament writings give evidence of the crises that affected their authors. How the Church met these problems is a recurring theme in the remaining chapters of this book. We begin with Mark, which reflects the situation of the Church on the occasion of the fall of Jerusalem and includes a warning of hostility to be expected from civil and synagogal authorities. But Mark is even more directly concerned with the problem created by the death of the apostles upon whose first-hand witness the *kerygma* rested.

THE IDEA OF A GOSPEL

For the task of interpreting the will of God, first-century Jews and Christians considered the living word of oral communication preferable to the preparation of a written record. As long as there were first-hand witnesses of the events of Jesus' ministry, who could report personally on what he did and said, the living word was a preferred vehicle for communicating the Gospel. Until the late sixties, by which time all the apostles had died, there were apparently no written records except for letters, such as those of Paul. In addition, some scholars have conjectured that there were in existence collections of sayings of Jesus, often identified as the hypothetical document Q. Possibly John still was alive, if we give credence to the ancient tradition which describes him as living at an advanced age in Ephesus at the end of the first century. But there is perhaps stronger evidence that he died at the same time as did his brother, James. It is probable that in the year A.D. 44 both were martyred by Herod Antipas. This would mean that, so far as our records go, the martyrdom of Peter and Paul in A.D. 64 marks the end of the Apostolic Age. It may well have been that the passing of the last of the apostles and the termination thereby of the oral witness was the event that precipitated a crisis and led to the preparation of the first of the gospels.

It would be a mistake, however, to suppose that the crisis was met by the publication of a kind of official biography of Jesus. As we have learned, the gospels do not claim to be (and in fact ought not to be) classified as attempts at writing biographies. The intention of the Gospel is to flesh out the *kerygma*—to show that the power of God that brings to men of faith a foretaste of the life of the Age to Come was already at work in the ministry of Jesus and that the call to obedience which he proclaimed was embodied in his own obedience unto death. There was no interest in preserving archives of Christian origins for posterity, since it was still believed that the present age was very soon coming to an end. The writer was concerned rather to meet the needs of the Church—that is, to provide Christian preachers and teachers, as well as interested inquirers into the faith, with a document that would show forth in Jesus' words and works the redemptive meaning that faith discerned in him.

There was no precedent for this undertaking, although there might have been collections of sayings of Jesus distributed among the churches in written form before Mark wrote the first gospel. Since there were likely no prior documents, with the possible exception of these hypothetical sayings collections, it is most unlikely that there was any reliable information available as to the sequence of events. We have already noted that there is no real chronological order to be detected in Mark; the explanation for this omission is not that the author chose to ignore the sequence, but that there simply was none available for him to utilize. The material included in Mark is correlated, therefore, not with a known chronology of Jesus' life, but with the *kerygma*.

The *kerygma* which Mark chose to develop in his gospel is not precisely that presented in compressed form by Paul in I Cor. 15, or in such other Pauline kerygmatic statements as Rom. 1:4. The nearest we come to the major kerygmatic emphasis of Mark is the passage written or quoted by Paul in Phil. 2, where he speaks of Jesus as the one who chose not to grasp at equality with God but humbled himself, becoming obedient unto death. The hymn in Philippians implies that Christ was pre-existent before he assumed the humble role of the servant, but in Mark there is no mention of prior existence. Mark's implication is rather that he became the Son of God at the moment of his baptism (Mk. 1:11). The major stress in the form of the *kerygma* which lies behind and is worked out in the Gospel of Mark is the Passion. Indeed, Mark has been characterized as a Passion story with a long introduction.[1] Certain it is that the death of Jesus is anticipated almost from the outset by the writer of the Gospel of Mark.

The author is not content to show merely *that* Jesus died; he must show *how* he died, and how his death was in fulfillment of a divine plan of redemption. This served not only to show the faithful that God's purpose was working itself out in the ministry of Jesus from the outset, but to combat the scornful charge of the detractors of Christianity that the so-called savior of the Christians was no more than an executed criminal. The crucified Messiah could now be proclaimed as Lord because his lordship and his unique rôle in the fulfillment

---

[1] See M. Kähler, *Der sogennante historische Jesus und der geschichtliche biblische Christus* (Leipzig: A. Deichert'sche Verlagsbuchhandlung, 1892), p. 80. E. Fuchs has discussed the possibility of considering the gospels as resurrection stories from beginning to end, in *Studies of the Historical Jesus* (Naperville, Ill.: Alec R. Allenson, 1964), p. 26.

of God's purpose had been at least potentially discernible in his words and actions from the outset of his career. In addition to the more subtle hints of his death in the stories about Jesus, the author has described Jesus as three times—and in each case with mounting detail—having predicted his death and resurrection (Mk. 8:31; 9:31; 10:32-34). Later in this chapter we shall examine the force and details of these predictions; here we shall only observe that the Gospel as a whole serves to amplify the claim made in these kerygmatic summaries included by Mark in his gospel.

THE SITUATION IN WHICH MARK WAS WRITTEN

It is not enough to say, however, that Mark wrote his gospel at the end of the Apostolic Age in order to expand upon the *kerygma*. We still must inquire as to what the specific circumstances were which led Mark to the preparation of his gospel. Chief among these is the problem of the expected end of the Age.

In the Gospel of Mark, the disciples ask Jesus when the end of the Age will occur, and "what will be the sign that all these things [*i.e.*, the destruction of the temple and the accompanying catastrophes] are about to be consummated?" (Mk. 13:4). The answer Jesus gives, in addition to some stock apocalyptic pronouncements about wars, tribulations, and the like, makes specific reference to the desecration of an unspecified sacred place. Matthew, in the parallel passage, declares that this is the same "holy place" that was desecrated according to the prophecy of Daniel; that is, the Jerusalem Temple (Mt. 24:15). Luke states even more explicitly that the prophecy concerns the siege of Jerusalem (21:20). Probably Mark's oblique statement refers to the same incident: the attack on Jerusalem by the Roman army under Vespasian (and later under Titus) in the years A.D. 67-70. This despoiling of the Temple was seen as an analogy to the pollution of the altar more than two centuries earlier by the mad Syrian king, Antiochus Epiphanes, in 168 B.C. (see p. 25). That famous incident lies behind a passage in Daniel (Dan. 9:27; 12:11) which reads as a prediction but which almost certainly was written after the event. The fact that Mark's version of the prediction of desecration does not mention either the Temple or Jerusalem directly has led some scholars to conclude that it is a genuine prophecy, rather than having been written after the event, as other critics have assumed. But the predictions of apocalypticists are often vague and allusive, so that one cannot determine by its lack of precision whether this "prophecy" was written before or after the event that it purports to predict. Even if it were certain that the prophecy had been written before the fall of Jerusalem, it could still have been incorporated at a later time by the evangelist. The only thing that is clear is that the evangelist saw in the destruction of the Temple an event of paramount importance for the fulfillment of God's purpose. There is no reason to assume that the event was long past at the time of writing; the intensity of the writing suggests that the crisis was a living reality for the evangelist, perhaps only a few years or even months before he wrote.

In Chapter 3 we noted briefly the early second-century tradition which attributes the Gospel of Mark to an associate of Peter. Mark, the tradition reports, had been the interpreter of Peter while the apostle was in Rome, and after his death recorded the sayings of Jesus and the incidents of his life that Peter had repeated in his preaching and teaching on the basis of his own first-hand experience. When subjected to form-critical analysis, however, the indication is that the materials gathered together in Mark's gospel have a long history of oral transmission, rather than having been put down directly from memory by someone who had heard a single apostolic witness such as Peter. It may well be that there was a collection of sayings and stories prepared by an associate of Peter—perhaps even someone named Mark. But Mark in its present form shows that it rests on written sources, as when reporting on what is ostensibly a speech made by Jesus orally, the text says: "Let him who *reads* understand" (Mk. 13:14).[2] Even if one infers that this comment comes from the reporter of the discourse as a kind of parenthetic comment, the passage as a whole seems to have been inserted into a quite complex work that was fashioned from a string of small sayings and narrative units. Theories which claim to be able to identify specific written sources—for example, a twelve-source, coming from the 12 disciples—are something less than persuasive.[3] It has been proposed that among Mark's sources was the Q document, from which he allegedly drew such sayings material as his parables. Since we are using Q to refer to the non-Markan material common to Luke and Matthew, and since there is no light shed on Mark by attributing to Q some of the material that he used, we shall confine ourselves to the analysis of the tradition units on the assumption that they came to Mark directly from the oral tradition.

The tradition associating Mark with Peter in Rome may be nothing more than an inference from I Pet. 5:13, where Mark is spoken of as Peter's "son." The claim of a Roman origin which has been made for Mark from early times may or may not be accurate, since the alleged Latin words prove nothing one way or the other; the so-called Latinisms used by Mark no more prove a Roman provenance for the book than a modern author's use of *à la carte* and *bon voyage* would prove that he wrote in Paris. There may be traces of Semitic modes of expression lying behind the sometimes awkward Greek of Mark, but many of the idioms that an earlier generation labeled "Semiticisms" are now

---

[2] Even in a detailed analysis of this passage, which seeks to defend its "high claim to authenticity" [G. R. Beasley-Murray, in *A Commentary on Mark 13* (London: Macmillan, 1957), p. 11, n. 1], it must be acknowledged that there have been written sources and various redactions through which the discourse has passed.

[3] In W. L. Knox, *Sources of the Synoptic Gospels*, I (Cambridge: University Press, 1953), 17-31.

known to have been used by non-Semitic people speaking and writing the nonliterary Greek of the first century. In short, we must deal with Mark as we have it, and leave open questions as to its written sources, authorship, and place of writing.

THE PURPOSES OF THE GOSPEL OF MARK: THE END OF THE AGE

Although the fall of Jerusalem seems to have played such an important part in the thinking of the writer of Mark, its significance lay not in the catastrophe itself but in the greater event of which the destruction of the city was no more than the chief sign: the consummation of the Age. This Day of Fulfillment is pointed to by Mark both directly ("when shall all these things be consummated?" Mk. 13:4) and in symbolic language ("when the fruit is yielded up, then he puts in the sickle, because the harvest has come." Mk. 4:29). The climax of the apocalyptic discourse comes in 13:27, when, following the long list of difficulties and persecutions and upsetting of the natural order that serve as prelude to the end of the Age, there come the simple words:

> And then they shall see the Son of Man coming in the clouds with power and great glory, and then he shall send his angels and they will gather together his chosen ones from the four winds, from the corner of earth to the corner of heaven.

The explicit prediction is followed by two vivid metaphors: the harvest of the figs is ready; the messenger is already at the gates.

It is not only in the specifically apocalyptic section, however, that this theme recurs. Following Peter's confession that Jesus is the Messiah, when Jesus is outlining the conditions of discipleship, he is reported as declaring: "Truly, I say to you, there are some standing here who will not taste death before they see the kingdom of God come with power."—(Mk. 9:1). The coming in judgment of the divine messengers is made to be the main point of the great parable or allegory of the vineyard in Mk. 12:1-12, where the punishment meted out for Israel's rejection of God's Son is that the vineyard (i.e., the place of special favor as God's Chosen People) is taken away and given to others. It is this, and not the death, nor the Resurrection—which is not even mentioned in the parable—which serves as the climax to the last and greatest of Mark's parables. The coming of the kingdom is the time of fulfillment promised in the words of institution of the Lord's Supper, according to Mark (14:25). The establishment of the kingdom fellowship is pointed to in the twice-repeated promise that Jesus will go before his followers to Galilee (14:28 and 16:7). Although some scholars think that the abrupt ending of Mark in all the oldest manuscripts hides from us the fact that Mark originally ended with an account of the appearance of the risen Christ in Galilee,[4] it may well be that this gospel ended as it does now: with a note of expectancy of the coming in glory of the risen Lord—a coming to which the whole of the Gospel points.

The Messiah Is Jesus

This leads us to a second major objective of Mark: to express concretely the conviction that the Coming One is the same as the earthly Jesus. Some forms of the *kerygma* were content, as we have observed, to state the fact that the exalted Christ was once the humble Jesus; Mark demonstrates the humiliation of Christ in detail. This is apparent in the many incidents of hostility and rejection that he reports Jesus to have experienced from the outset of his ministry. To account for the fact that Jesus was rejected—in spite of his fulfillment of the messianic prophecies and in spite of his mighty works— was very difficult for the Church to explain, but it was understood positively as showing the genuineness of his days of humiliation on earth, culminating in his death.

Jesus' earthly activity is important for demonstrating not only his lowliness, but his authority as well. Although this theme of the authority possessed by Jesus is a pervasive one, it is perhaps set forth most vividly in the first five chapters of the gospel. Mark loses no time in making his point. Once the brief introduction to Jesus' ministry is presented, he describes the contest of Jesus with the demons—and the demons betray from the outset what the final outcome will surely be: their defeat (Mk. 1:21 ff.). Toward the end of the series of healing stories, Mark tells the most vivid of them all: the exorcising of the "Legion" of demons from the wretched tomb-dweller outside the pagan city of Gadara. The significance of the exorcisms and the explanation for the great anxiety of the demons in the presence of Jesus' power is presented in the controversy story of Mk. 3:22-27, where Jesus reveals that the real issue between himself and Satan is the struggle for mastery over the kingdom. The assumption here is that effective authority over the affairs of men in the present age has been wrested or is in danger of being seized by Satan and his hosts. This situation can be brought to an end only when someone comes along who can overcome Satan and strip him of his power. As the metaphorical word of Jesus phrases it:

> No one can enter a strong man's house and plunder his goods, unless
> he first binds the strong man; then indeed he may plunder his house.
> —MARK 3:27

---

[4] Cf. Dibelius, in *From Tradition to Gospel*, tr. B. L. Woolf (London: Ivor Nicholson & Watson, 1934), pp. 189 ff. E. J. Goodspeed can even tell how Mark probably ended! See *Introduction to the New Testament* (Chicago: University of Chicago Press, 1937), p. 156.

Jesus' victory over the demons, therefore, betokens the destruction of Satan's reign. This conclusion is reached, not merely on the basis of the triumph over death in the resurrection of Christ, but is depicted as having been a reality during his earthly ministry as well.

Other aspects of the authority of the earthly Jesus are set forth in these early chapters of Mark. He can overcome sickness, as he does in the case of a leper (1:40 ff.) and of Peter's mother-in-law (1:29 f.). He can not only heal diseases, but he can pronounce in God's name the forgiveness of sins, which were thought by Jews of the day to be the cause of sickness (2:1 ff.). Mark has reported this incident of healing the paralytic in such a way as to point up the paramount issue as he sees it. What is at stake is not simply the power of Jesus to heal; there were many professional healers abroad throughout the Hellenistic world in the first century, and at shrines of Aesclepius, the Greek god of healing, the lame and the ill gathered in great numbers in order to be healed. The issue that is of most importance both for Mark and for the opponents whom he here depicts is the authority which Jesus implicitly claims for himself in an-

GERASA *has been remarkably well preserved. The theaters, temples, and extensive baths of this city of the Decapolis are quite evident among the ruins. Some manuscripts of Mark report that it was outside the city of Gerasa that Jesus healed the demoniac.*

nouncing to this man that God has forgiven him. Jesus of course does not say, "I forgive you your sins." He uses instead the circumlocution, "Your sins are forgiven you" (*i.e.*, by God). But no one can miss what is implied: Jesus claims to be able to tell what God can and will do. There is an awkward turn midway in verse 10, where the direct address ("in order that you might know . . .") shifts abruptly to indirect address ("he says to the paralytic . . ."). This break in the flow of the story almost certainly indicates that Mark has here introduced a new element into the story as he received it in the tradition: the explicit claim that Jesus, as Son of Man, has authority on earth to forgive sins.

This is not the only passage where the term Son of Man is related to the authority which Jesus exercises during his public ministry. The phrase appears again when, on directly religious issues, Jesus speaks in an equally authoritative manner when he boldly sets aside venerable Jewish institutions—fasting, the sabbath, laws of separateness and ceremonial cleanliness. He modifies or even violates these laws in the name of the new fellowship that he claims to be establishing. In other acts described in these opening chapters of Mark, the authority of Jesus is displayed in similar manner, though without the use of the Son of Man title. When Levi, the tax-collector, is called by Jesus to be among his followers, Jesus flagrantly defies the Jewish regulations against eating with unclean persons by going to dinner with the most despised group of all, the hated tax-collectors, whose collaboration with Rome in collecting revenue rendered them in the eyes of their fellow Jews not only ceremonially impure but traitors to the hope of Israel. Jesus defends his action simply by saying, "I have not come to call the righteous but sinners." In what has been styled an "I-word," [5] Mark depicts the sovereign manner in which Jesus exercises authority in the act of calling into being the new People of God.

Jesus' sanctioning of the violation of the sabbath laws and his failure to require fasting of his disciples are presented by Mark in a similar way so as to underscore the authority of Jesus. In reply to a challenge from his interrogators as to why his disciples do not fast, Mark reports him (2:18-19) as uttering a parabolic word which depicts his presence in their midst as the presence of the bridegroom—that is, as the presence of the joyous New Age, for which the coming of the bridegroom was a favorite Jewish metaphor. Mark does go on (2:20) to speak of the fasting that will follow the taking away of the bridegroom, thereby presumably reflecting the practice in the early Church of fasting as a commemoration of the Passion of the Lord. When Jesus is called to account for allowing his disciples to violate the sabbath law, he replies: "The Son of man is Lord even of the sabbath" (2:28). And finally, when Jesus defends his healing of a man on the sabbath day—thereby bringing together both his

---

[5] See R. Bultmann, *Die Geschichte der synoptischen Tradition,* 3rd ed. (Göttingen: Vandenhoeck & Ruprecht, 1958), pp. 164-166. [English translation] *History of the Synoptic Tradition,* tr. J. Marsh (New York: Harper & Row, 1963), pp. 150-166.

NAZARETH *in Galilee. An insignificant village in Jesus' day, it was expanded by the Crusaders and given the appearance of a provincial town of northern Italy.*

authority over sickness and his sovereign setting-aside of the Law of Moses—Mark tells us that his religious and political enemies form their coalition to destroy him (3:6). Already, then, from the opening series of episodes in which Mark portrays the public ministry of Jesus, two things are made clear: the authority of Jesus and the certainty of his death.

When depicting the authority of Jesus, Mark does not restrict himself to matters relating to man, neither to man as an individual nor in his social relationships: the powers which Jesus displays in Mark's account extend to the cosmic powers which control what we would call "the world of nature." Since man's existence is involved not only with other humans but with the natural world, whose forces affect him directly and on which man is dependent for sustaining his life, the Lord of Life must be able to exercise authority in this sphere as well. Thus Mark tells us that Jesus exerted mastery over the forces of nature by calming the storm (4:35-41), by feeding the 5,000 (6:30-44), and by walking on the water (6:45-52). In these stories Mark wants us to understand that at certain points throughout the earthly ministry of Jesus, his divine powers as God's instrument for the redemption of the whole creation were briefly disclosed. Most clearly is this status revealed in the story of the transfiguration (9:2-8), whereby a chosen few of the disciples are enabled to behold —before the Crucifixion and Resurrection—the glory of the One who is to be exalted at God's right hand (see p. 264).

Beginning in the first five chapters, but more fully developed throughout the gospel, Mark sets forth the picture of the One whose authority on earth was veiled and misunderstood, but who is now about to be revealed to all the world as its Lord (13:10). As a kind of anticipation of the Resurrection event that betokens his exaltation, Mark describes Jesus' raising the daughter of Jairus from the dead (5:21-43). In language that reflects the early Christian vocabulary of death, Jesus assures the bereaved family that the child is not dead but sleeping (5:39). In response to the word of Jesus—"Arise!"—she returns to life. At precisely the point where human existence seems to reach its ultimate limit, and where man is about to be absorbed into the world of nature, the Lord of Life triumphs over death. Mark goes on to show, however, that even this demonstration of power is not convincing to those who are disposed not to believe in Jesus, so that the story of the raising of the dead is followed immediately by the account of Jesus' rejection in his home town of Nazareth. In Mark's words, "He could do nothing there because of their unbelief" (6:5). In spite of Jesus' authority, Mark is telling his reader, his tragic death was from the outset inevitable.

JESUS' DEATH AS PURPOSED BY GOD

Not only in the beginning, but throughout the gospel, Mark depicts the humiliation that Jesus had undergone. In this rejection at the hands of men, he had gone to the human extremity—death—and had done so not by accident, but by divine design. Death, then, was a necessary prelude to the glory to which God has now exalted him. In a passage unique to Mark (9:12), Jesus asks, "How is it written of the Son of man, that he should suffer many things and be treated with contempt?" Mark's answer is provided in the enigmatic words that point to the purpose behind Jesus' coming: ". . . the Son of man goes, as it is written of him. . . ."—(14:21). Interpreters have found in these and related passages, such as 10:45, possible allusions to the Suffering Servant poem of Isa. 53, where the redemptive significance of the death of the Servant of the Lord is set forth.[6] It was probably in these terms, drawn from the Jewish tradition, that Mark had come to understand the meaning of the death of Jesus. / Three times in the Gospel of Mark Jesus utters specific predictions of his own suffering and death: 8:31; 9:31; and 10:32-34. In addition, there are more veiled anticipations of his death: in 10:38-39, where death is spoken of as a baptism to be received; and in 14:24, where the symbolic act of the shared cup at the Last Supper is described as "my blood of the covenant, which is poured out for many."/Although it is likely that Jesus did anticipate that the path that he had chosen as being God's will for him would lead to his death, it is equally probable that the specifics of Mark's interpretation of his death are developed out of the Old Testament prophecies which he and the Christian community were convinced had been fulfilled by the death of Jesus. In the words of Paul's kerygmatic summary: "Christ died for our sins, according to the scriptures" (I Cor. 15:3). Mark shows in detail how Jesus' suffering and death corresponded to scripture. It is possible that Jesus himself so understood his own impending

---

[6] Rudolph Otto, *Kingdom of God and Son of Man* (London: Lutterworth, 1951), pp. 249-259.

death,[7] but it seems certain that the details of these predictions of the Passion have been provided by Mark or by the tradition on which he is directly dependent.

WHY JESUS' MESSIAHSHIP WAS NOT RECOGNIZED

If, however, the death of Jesus was, as Mark points out, so specifically in fulfillment of scripture, how is it to be explained that few, if any, recognized this during his ministry? As Mark acknowledges, even the disciples, to whom these predictions were uttered, did not comprehend them. Indeed, Jesus himself is reported as predicting that they would not comprehend the tragic events then impending, but would flee (14:27). Furthermore, in Mark the messianic mission of Jesus is regularly unrecognized or misunderstood, or both. Although there is a direct affirmation of Jesus' messiahship by Peter in 8:29, the subsequent course of events as described by Mark shows that the disciples did not understand what was involved in the acclaim: "You are the Christ." How are we to account for the fact that during Jesus' earthly life there apparently was no real recognition of him as Messiah, while after his death, affirmation that Jesus is Messiah and Lord became the central claim of faith?

Our concern at this point is not with how the messianic faith arose, but with how Mark accounts for the nonrecognition of Jesus as Messiah even though in Mark's view his was a fully messianic ministry. Nor is it enough to say that Mark has read messianic meaning back into the ministry of Jesus in the light of the Resurrection faith. The problem still remains that Mark depicts the messiahship of Jesus as at times to be kept a secret (8:30), at other times to be announced publicly by the beneficiaries of Jesus' power (5:19), and on at least one occasion as publicly acknowledged by Jesus himself (14:61, 62). A hypothesis which seeks to solve this problem solely by treating those passages in which the actual messianic titles are used will not be of much help in clarifying the whole picture of the mystery surrounding the authority and mission of the earthly Jesus in Mark's gospel, since the question of messiahship is often present in passages where the titles are not found.

At the turn of the present century, two epoch-making books were published which sought to explain this secrecy question in Mark. One book, by Wilhelm Wrede, attributed the element of secrecy concerning Jesus' messiahship to Mark, or rather to the community whose traditions he reproduced.[8] Wrede

---

[7] This is the judgment of William Manson, *Jesus the Messiah* (Philadelphia: Westminster, 1949); O. Cullmann, *The Christology of the New Testament* (London: SCM Press, 1957); J. Jeremias, *Servant of God* (with W. Zimmerli) (London: SCM Press, 1957), and many others.

[8] Wilhelm Wrede, *Das Messiasgeheimnis in den Evangelien* (Göttingen: Vandenhoeck & Ruprecht, 1901). For a critique, see A. Schweitzer, in *The Quest of the Historical Jesus* (London: A. & C. Black, 1954); for a discussion of this work and more recent related literature, see J. M. Robinson, *The Problem of History in Mark* (London: SCM Press, 1957), pp. 9-12.

accurately recognized that many of the injunctions to silence concerning messiahship appear in the generalizing or editorial material, rather than in the course of the narratives themselves (1:34; 3:12; 5:43; 7:36). But on the other hand, he observed that some of the orders forbidding the spread of knowledge about Jesus' power or identity occur in the body of the narratives: 1:25; 1:44; 4:39. Set over against both kinds of appeals for secrecy Wrede noted indications of widespread popular recognition of Jesus' extraordinary powers: 1:27, 28, 33, 45; 2:12; 3:7 ff.; 7:37. By analyzing the tensions among these strands of evidence Wrede thought he could distinguish three stages in the development of the messianic faith: (1) the earliest stage, in which Jesus did not regard himself as Messiah nor were his acts viewed as messianic in significance; (2) the stage in which the Confession of Peter and the triumphal entry portray Jesus' messiahship as a matter of knowledge during his lifetime, though in limited circles; and (3) the latest stage, in which Jesus' command to silence goes unheeded, inasmuch as his whole life is being viewed as messianic. According to Wrede, these developments were not apologetic in intent, but were simply stages whereby the life of Jesus became filled with messianic content.

Both the Markan theology and the development that lies behind it, however, are even more complex than Wrede recognized. For example, form-critical analysis of the narratives involved and philological studies of the terms used by Jesus in addressing the demons have shown that the "injunctions to silence" are part of the old tradition rather than editorial insertions. Furthermore, these stories employ the technical language of first- and second-century exorcists, as known from studies of literature roughly contemporary with the New Testament.[9] The words spoken by the demons, and Jesus' replies, cannot be accounted for as created by the Church's interest in providing messianic content for Jesus' life. They serve rather to lend the quality of realism—judged by first-century standards—to the demonic conflict in which Jesus engaged. The fact that Jesus performed exorcisms is attested to by Jewish authorities (see Chapter 3) and is at least as well established as that he spoke the parables. The manner of describing this activity understandably used the terms and thought-patterns of the day. Some of the injunctions to silence are to be accounted for on the basis of literary style and contemporary viewpoint, and cannot be considered as dogmatic formulations in the interests of a particular messianic theory. Nevertheless, it can scarcely be denied that Mark has heightened the sense of mystery that surrounds the messiahship of Jesus by incorporating the injunctions to silence concerning the person and powers of Jesus.

The second epochal work dealing with the same material was written by Albert Schweitzer. He treats the messianic secret as historical, on the assumption that Jesus kept to himself the belief that he was the eschatological Messiah until it was revealed to the inner group of his disciples (Schweitzer must trans-

---

[9] See especially O. Bauernfeind, *Die Worte der Dämonen im Markusevangelium* (Stuttgart: Kohlhammer, 1927).

pose the Transfiguration story, in order to make it precede the confession of Peter). Jesus' claim to be the Messiah was betrayed to the authorities by Judas, and finally acknowledged by Jesus openly to the High Priest on the night before his death.[10] But this way of handling the question fails utterly to deal with the artificiality of the commands to silence in the Markan editorial framework. /For Mark it was no accident that Jesus was not recognized as the Messiah; there was a divine necessity that he suffer and die if he was to enter the glory of the kingdom (9:11, 12). But it was also a part of the divine plan that men's eyes should be kept from seeing who Jesus was. For anyone accustomed to thinking of the meaning of the parables of Jesus apart from the setting in which Mark has placed them, it would be easy to think of these familiar analogies of Jesus as simple and direct means of communicating universal moral and religious truth./Mark characterizes the parables, however, as riddles, enigmas, mysterious sayings, intended to conceal, rather than reveal, the truth to "those on the outside." [11] (Mk. 4:11, 12). Jesus is here reported as saying that he teaches in parables *in order that men might not perceive* the mystery of the kingdom of God, and *in order that they might not repent*. Interpreters have endeavored to tone down the force of the words here, to try to make Jesus say that unless men repent they will not be forgiven. But such a meaning is not at all implicit in these words; rather, the force is that God has hardened men's minds so that they *cannot* grasp the truth. The secret of the kingdom is for the elect, for those to whom it has been given, *i.e.*, by God (4:11). Mark does not want his readers to infer that Jesus was not known widely as the Messiah because those who were in on the secret obeyed the command to silence; he is explicit in his declaration that all but the elect were divinely hindered from comprehending the mystery of the kingdom, and they fully understood only in the light of the Resurrection.

The present form of the belief in God's having prevented the outsiders from beholding the mystery of the kingdom seems to be late tradition, originating in a polemical situation—probably the late first-century mutual hostility between Judaism and the Church. But there is no reason to doubt that this theme builds on an authentic element of enigma in the teaching of Jesus himself.[12] By the same token, Mark and the other evangelists enlarge upon the dullness of the disciples, but their reported lack of insight may rest in part on their actual failure to penetrate the enigmatic words of Jesus. It seems unlikely that the gospel writers would have invented the stories which put the disciples—who were now venerated as apostles—in such a bad light by showing that they completely misunderstood the intention of Jesus. Not only did the predictions of the Passion fail to penetrate their understanding, but the message of the kingdom itself seems not to have been grasped. The human side of the divine

---

[10] A. Schweitzer, *The Mystery of the Kingdom of God* (London: A. & C. Black, 1956).

[11] A. Schweitzer, *op. cit.*, pp. 380-395.

[12] J. Jeremias, *The Parables of Jesus* (New York: Scribner's, 1963), pp. 13-18.

blinding, therefore, is the obtuseness of the disciples, of Jesus' family, and above all the self-will of his opponents.

The lack of understanding among the disciples is evident at some of the most important moments in the Gospel story. Peter, after confessing that Jesus is the Messiah, rebukes him for predicting that he must suffer in order to fulfill his mission (8:31-33). On the eve of the Passion, the disciples ask for places of special favor in the Age to Come (10:35-40). The flight of the disciples and the denial of Peter are familiar evidence of this same theme, in which Mark shows the inability of the disciples to comprehend God's purpose through Jesus.

If we treat the Beelzebub controversy of Mk. 3:22-30 as inserted into a story that originally dealt with Jesus' family relations, 3:21 ("those with him") would refer to his family, and it would be they who think he is beside himself. Verse 3:31 goes on to describe his mother and brothers waiting for him to come out of the house where he has been staying. In the words that follow (vv. 32-35), Jesus affirms that his real family is those who do the will of God, rather than his earthly family, who seem to have wanted to bring his public career to an end. We cannot be certain that Mark meant for his readers to understand the incident in this way,[13] but the force of the words about the true family are unambiguous. In his own hometown of Nazareth, Jesus encounters antipathy and is rejected (6:1-6).

The whole of Jesus' ministry is characterized by Mark from the outset as fostering suspicion and open hostility. His pronouncement of the forgiveness of sins is immediately considered as blasphemy (2:6 ff.), and his selection of a tax-collector as one of his intimate circle of followers scandalizes the Jewish separatists (2:16 ff.). The absence of a demand for his disciples to fast is viewed as a serious lapse of piety (2:18). His exorcisms are taken as a sign that he is in league with the demonic powers (3:22 ff.).

Mark takes care to show, however, that Satan is engaged in a death struggle to retain his hold on the world. He tests Jesus at the outset of the ministry (1:12-13); he snatches away the word of the Gospel lest it find root in the hearer (4:15). But the demons acknowledge that in him they have met their match (1:24; 5:7). Jesus declares that his mission is that of binding the strong man and plundering his goods (3:27); that is, he will overcome Satan, who is now in effective control of this Age, and thereby establish the rule or kingdom of God. Meanwhile, both the hostility of Satan and the antagonism of those who attribute Jesus' power to Satan stand in the way of Jesus' being recognized as Messiah during his earthly ministry.

It is sometimes assumed that Mark has reported the stories of Jesus' miracles in order to encourage his readers to have faith in him as Messiah. Actually, the

---

[13] See Maurice Goguel, *Life of Jesus* (tr. from the French by Olive Wyon), (New York: Macmillan, 1946), p. 334.

attitude toward miracles is more complex than this. Although faith may discern in the mighty works which Jesus performs the saving power of God, those who are disposed not to believe are simply confirmed in their unfaith. The story of the healing of the man with the withered hand does not convert Jesus' opponents; it simply stimulates them to conspire to destroy him (3:5, 6). When the demoniac from Gadara is cured, the townspeople do not welcome Jesus as a wonder worker, much less as a redeemer; they are filled with fear and urge him to go elsewhere (5:17 ff.). Most clear of all in this connection is his re-

A SILVER DENARIUS *from the time of the reign of Tiberius Caesar. Jesus held a coin like this one in his hand when he commanded the Pharisees to "Render to Caesar the things that are Caesar's."*

jection at Nazareth, previously referred to. The contrast between his humble origins and his mighty authority did not lead his fellow villagers to acclaim him as from God, but moved them to repudiate him. Mark has located this story at a strategic point in his narrative—namely, at the conclusion of a series of incidents in which the reader is presented powerful evidence that God has empowered Jesus to be man's deliverer from sickness and sin, and just before Jesus is described as sending out the 12 disciples on the missionary journey. The irony is impressive: at the very moment when others will have opportunity to hear and see the good news of God's grace at work in their midst, those closest to Jesus reject him.

Mark portrays scribes and/or Pharisees as witnesses of nearly every healing or act of deliverance that Jesus performs. And yet, a delegation of Pharisees comes toward the end of his Galilean ministry with a request that he give them a "sign from heaven"—that is, that he perform some act to prove to their satisfaction that God was really with him. In response to such a demand, Jesus refuses to act (8:11-13).

What lies behind this hostility toward Jesus, as Mark pictures it, is not simply human obstinacy, but the fact that his enemies rightly see in Jesus a threat to their institutions and authority. Chief among those who are depicted as threatened by Jesus are those loosely grouped together as "the scribes and the Pharisees." Precise definitions of these have been considered in the second chapter of this book, but Mark uses the double term (or one or the other member of the term) as a convenient designation for official Judaism in its conflict with Jesus. Jesus' teaching is described by Mark as "with authority" (1:27), presumably in contrast with the lack of a sense of authority communicated by their teaching. The Pharisees attack Jesus on the issue of the source of his authority, even accusing him of being in league with the demons (3:22). The persistence of their hostility toward Jesus in Mark's account and the vehemence of Jesus' counterattack suggests that Mark is writing under circumstances where the Jewish-Christian conflict has made these issues especially relevant for the Church. The questions of sabbath observance, fasting, and ceremonial cleanliness with which Mark deals are not merely dead issues recalled from the past, but living questions on which the Church wants the authority of Jesus in defending its own position (8:14 ff.; see especially 12:37b-40).

It is somewhat more difficult to understand on this basis the preservation by Mark of the stories about the conflict between Jesus and the Herodians (3:6), or indeed, about the opposition of Herod Antipas himself (6:14 ff.), since by the time Mark wrote, the Herodian family had vanished from the Palestine scene. Although we do not know who the Herodians were, it seems odd to have a group of those well-disposed toward Herod in league with the strict separatist Pharisees, unless the basis for their joint action was that they could meet on the common ground of interest in destroying a common enemy. There was a conflict between the early Church and another Herod, Agrippa I, but this took place more than a decade after the death of Jesus. The hostility of Agrippa I toward the Christians culminated in the murder of the disciple James in A.D. 44. It may be that the enmity toward Herod Agrippa is recalled by the Church in reporting the alleged conflict between Jesus and "the Herodians," of whom we otherwise know nothing.

In addition to Jesus' undermining the religious observances, such as keeping the sabbath, fasting, and avoidance of contact with unclean persons or things, Mark pictures Jesus as exercising authority in relation to two of the most important foundations of Judaism's existence: the Temple in Jerusalem, and the nation's place in the coming of God's kingdom. In both cases, Jesus' outlook is subversive: he predicts that the Temple will be destroyed (13:2), after having arrogantly cleansed its courts of those conducting business essential to the operation of the Temple cultus (11:15-19); and he twice predicts symbolically that the nation Israel will be set aside as an effective instrument of God (11:12-14 and 12:1-12). God will destroy the fig tree; he will give the vineyard to others. A new edifice with Christ as the cornerstone will replace the old Israel. Mark leaves us in no doubt as to the intended force of these parabolic sayings, since he tells us that the leaders of the nation "knew that he spoke the parable against them" (12:12). It is not surprising that "the chief priests and the scribes . . . kept seeking how they might destroy him" (11:18).

A FORETASTE OF FAITH IN JESUS

In spite of all the opposition which Mark pictures Jesus as evoking, in spite of the obtuseness and willful unbelief of followers and foes, the whole of the Gospel of Mark informs us that Jesus' words and works did in fact arouse a response of faith in some quarters. The wide following that Jesus attracted is described repeatedly by Mark—precisely in his editorial comments—in such passages as 1:45, 2:12, 5:20, 6:2, and 7:37. Mark wants his readers to know that what Jesus did and said was not unobserved, but that there was abundant opportunity to discern in him the saving power of God. Mark tells us that Jesus' divine sonship was known to him, at least from the time of his baptism on, although he indicates that only Jesus heard the voice acclaiming him as Son, in contrast to Matthew, who describes the voice as addressing the crowd (cf. Mk. 1:11 with Mt. 3:17).

As we have noted, Mark reports that the demons recognized not only the power of Jesus over them, but also his identity. In 1:24, the demon addresses Jesus as "the Holy One of God." In 3:11, he is called "the Son of God" and in 5:7, he is given the title "Son of the Most High God." Although Mark limits to the incident of Peter's Confession the use of the term, "Christ," the redemptive role of Jesus and his unique relationship to God are firmly attested to by the demons in the traditions which Mark has preserved and edited.

The followers of Jesus have abundant opportunity to see in him God's Messiah, even though in Mark's account Jesus was deserted by his disciples on the eve of the Crucifixion (14:50). The record in Mark could scarcely be more explicit in stating that the followers of Jesus are given special insight into the coming of the kingdom, and are permitted to witness extraordinary manifestations of Jesus' power, so that there is no human reason why they cannot recognize him for what he is: God's anointed. That they do not so recognize him, is in keeping with the *divine necessity* for him to be rejected and to suffer. In Mk. 4:11, Jesus tells the Twelve that they have been granted access to "the secret of the kingdom of God." They are given special insight into the meaning of the parables (4:10, 13 ff., 34). On the occasion of his stilling the storm, they are filled with awe and ask one another, "Who then is this, that even wind and sea obey him?" (4:41).

Even a non-Jew can—through persistent faith—gain access to the redemptive power that God is unleashing through Jesus (7:24-30). Although the theme of the access to faith for the Gentiles is not so clearly stated in Mark as in Luke, there are two points in the closing chapters of Mark at which the theme seems to be set forth: (1) In the story of the cleansing of the Temple, Mark alone reports Jesus as including in his quotation from Is. 56:7 that the Temple is to be a house of prayer *"for all the nations"* (11:17); and (2) Only Mark includes in his version of the Synoptic Apocalypse the declaration: "And the gospel must first be preached to *all nations*" (13:10).

In several ways Mark anticipates the new situation of comprehension and power that obtained after the resurrection of Jesus and his exaltation as Lord. The stories of the calling of the Twelve (3:13-19) and their commissioning to carry wider the messianic ministry begun by Jesus (6:6-13) are both told in language which seems to reflect the Apostolic Age rather than to be wholly appropriate to the period of Jesus' own minstry. Some ancient manuscripts actually add at 3:14 the words "whom also he named apostles." Even though we were to consider these to be later additions to Mark's original text, the apostolic quality of their activity is apparent. At 13:9 f. the hostility that the apostles will encounter is described in advance. Although Mark does not locate these "predictions" in direct connection with the sending of the Twelve, as Matthew does (10:17, 18), he clearly sees in the mission of the Twelve a foretaste of the mission of the Church. Not only are they thus commissioned: they actually carry out a ministry of preaching, exorcisms, healings, etc. Accordingly, Mark depicts the disciples as participating directly in the messianic activity, even though they do not fully comprehend the messianic meaning of Jesus until after the Resurrection.

The same can be said of Peter's Confession and the Transfiguration experience which follows it in Mark's account. Although Peter proclaims Jesus to be the Messiah, his protests against Jesus' predictions of suffering show that he does not understand what is involved in being Messiah. Even when the inner circle of disciples beholds the glory of Jesus as a preview of his exaltation that is yet to come, they are not prepared to stand by him in his time of difficulty, and lack utterly insight into what is meant by the coming of the kingdom of God (8:27 ff., esp. 33; 9:2-8). The import of Jesus' entry into Jerusalem in fulfillment of the messianic prophecy of Zech. 9 and of the sovereign authority that he exercises in cleansing the Temple, is completely lost on the disciples. Yet Mark seems to be telling his readers that the exaltation of Jesus as Messiah and Lord was not without advance notice, and that there were those who—however incompletely—grasped some clues as to the significance of Jesus even before the Cross and Resurrection. Ironically, it is a blind man, Bartimaeus, begging by the roadside in Jericho, who is able to "see" who Jesus is (10:46 ff.).

THE CALL TO SUFFERING

In Mark's scheme of things, it is significant that the call to men to become disciples moves from the initial formal stage of the commissioning of the Twelve to a series of solemn warnings as to what responsibilities and hardships discipleship involves. But this transition occurs only after Jesus has announced his impending Passion. Jesus has summoned the Twelve to share in his ministry of preaching and healing; now he calls a wider circle into what Paul has described as "the fellowship of his sufferings" (Phil. 3:10). The Confession of Peter and the first prediction of the Passion constitute a real watershed in Mark's gospel. From this point on, the Passion of Jesus which is clearly anticipated is set alongside the suffering of those who will be his followers. Faithfulness to him and his word will assure the disciple of a share in glory when the New Age fully comes (8:38).

The theme of following Christ is a pervasive one in the very chapters (8, 9, and 10) in which the predictions of the Passion occur. The necessity to adopt the role of the servant of the trusting child is described in several passages (9:33-37; 10:13-16; 10:43-45). Requirements of purity in the marriage relationship, of freedom from riches appear in this part of Mark (10:1 f.; 10:17 ff.). Both the joyous reality of sharing in Christ's ministry (9:38-41) and the solemn responsibilities that his followers must assume (9:42-50) are set forth here as well. The apocalyptic woes described in Mk. 13 are wholly in keeping with the suffering that Jesus expects to undergo in Mark's account. The twin themes of the Passion of the Lord and the passion of the disciples are effectively brought together in 10:43-45:

> Whoever would be great among you must be your servant, and whoever would be first among you must be slave of all. For the Son of man came not to be served but to serve, and to give his life as a ransom for many.

Any attempt to reconstruct what the situation was in the Church that produced the Gospel of Mark has less direct evidence to build on than is the case with any of the other gospels. There are no hints of organization, and few clues as to the kinds of internal needs that the Church felt. The stress laid on the controversy stories (Chapters 2, 3, 7, and 12 especially) in Mark would lead us to the conclusion that conflict with Jewish institutions and controversy over such regulations as sabbath observance and ceremonial and dietary purity were major issues for the Church. Its focus was not so much on the problems of the present as on the past and the future: on the past, since Jesus the Messiah had lived and taught and healed and died and been raised in their midst; on the future, because his Coming in glory was awaited imminently. In the light of that expectation such mundane questions as community organization or such transitory problems as conflicts and persecution faded into the background. What was paramount was the final deliverance when the New Age would be consummated.

THE NEW WAY
OF RIGHTEOUSNESS

Matthew

CHAPTER TWELVE   From the second century down to

the present, the Gospel of Matthew has been considered the

first gospel, not only in the list of the New Testament

books, but in importance as well. Its place at the beginning

of the canon means, of course, that it is probably the most

frequently read of all the New Testament writings. But more

significant than its location is the fact that the words of

Matthew's gospel are among the most familiar of all New

Testament themes. The coming of the Wise Men, the Sermon on the Mount, the familiar form of the Lord's Prayer, the Coin in the Fish's Mouth, the Parable of the Sheep and the Goats are found only in Matthew. Only in this gospel does Jesus address Peter as the Rock on which the Church will be built. There can be no question why Matthew has taken and held the prime place among the gospels in the esteem of the Church.

Mention has already been made (p. 70 f.) of Papias' report concerning the origins of the gospels. He stated that Matthew was the compiler of the sayings (in Greek, *logia*) of the Lord in Hebrew, and that every man interpreted or translated them as he was able. This testimony of Papias (written presumably about A.D. 140) has usually been understood to refer to the Gospel of Matthew, and therefore to affirm that that gospel was originally written in Hebrew.

There are many difficulties with Papias' testimony. First of all, we cannot be at all sure that he was talking about our Gospel of Matthew when he spoke of the "logia" of Jesus. If logia means "sayings," as it sometimes does, then we note immediately that Matthew's gospel contains far more than merely sayings; it is a careful blend of narrative and discourse material. In any case, Papias could not be referring to Matthew as we know it.

It has been suggested that *logia* was a term used in the early Church for collections of Old Testament texts, used by the Church to prove that Jesus was the fulfillment of the Hebrew prophecies. Among the manuscripts found at Qumran was a sheet of Old Testament passages which may have served to provide a ready list of messianic proof texts among the Essenes of the Dead Sea community. But Matthew, while attaching great importance to the fulfillment of the Old Testament, has far wider interests, and includes much more than scripture quotations in his gospel.

Papias has further been charged with error in his claim that the *logia* were in Hebrew, since the language in common use in Palestine in the first century was Aramaic, a Semitic dialect closely related to Hebrew. But the discovery of the Dead Sea Scrolls, most of which are in Hebrew rather than Aramaic, has weakened the force of this argument, since it is now evident that Jews in first-century Palestine were using Hebrew as the official tongue of their religious communities. But whether Papias meant Hebrew or Aramaic, he can scarcely have been referring to the original of the Gospel of Matthew, since it was clearly written first in Greek, and dependent on Greek sources.

At an early period in the Church's life, however, there were those who claimed to have found the Hebrew original of the first gospel. In the fifth century, Jerome (famous for his translation of the Bible into Latin, known as the Vulgate, the official Roman Catholic version) announced that he had discovered and translated the "original Hebrew" form of the Gospel of Matthew. What he actually found was a paraphrase in Aramaic of the Greek Gospel of

Matthew.[1] The paraphrase was known as the Gospel of the Nazarenes, a Jewish-Christian group that flourished in that part of Syria through which the Euphrates flows. Other fathers of the Church mistook other books—some of them heretical—to be the Hebrew original of Matthew's gospel. The fact is, however, that our Gospel of Matthew is based on the Greek Gospel of Mark, although of course the oral tradition drawn upon by Mark, as well as the tradition embodied in Matthew's other written sources, go back ultimately to the Semitic speech spoken by Jesus and his contemporaries in Palestine.[2]

There is no need to repeat here the evidence that Matthew had Mark before him, as well as a document (now known as Q) consisting mostly of sayings of Jesus (see pp. 79-82). What should be noted here, however, is the great skill with which Matthew has reworked and edited his material, supplementing it here, abridging it there.[3] Throughout, he has handled his materials in such a masterful way that both the over-all structure and the development of details contribute effectively to his major theological and polemical aims in writing his gospel. Before turning to an analysis of Matthew's aims, however, we direct our attention to the question of the probable time and place of writing of this influential document.

WHEN AND WHERE WAS MATTHEW WRITTEN?

Allusions to the Gospel of Matthew in the writings of Ignatius of Antioch (*ca.* 115) provide us the latest date to which the writing of this gospel can be assigned. That Ignatius quotes it as authoritative suggests that it had been in circulation for some time, perhaps since at least A.D. 100. On the other hand, Matthew's dependence on Mark as one of his sources proves that the gospel could not have appeared earlier than A.D. 70. This supposition of a post-70 date is confirmed by the direct mention in Mt. 22:7 of the fall of Jerusalem and the burning of the city which took place in the year 70. A likely date for the writing of Matthew would be, therefore, about 80 to 85.

To settle on so late a date as this virtually excludes the disciple Matthew from consideration as the author. We shall see that on other grounds it is not likely that this book was written by a disciple of Jesus, since a person so closely

---

[1] B. W. Bacon has denounced Jerome's claims of discovery as fraudulent; see his *Studies in Matthew* (New York: Holt, 1930), pp. 478-481. This gospel is also discussed in Hennecke-Schneemelcher, *New Testament Apocrypha*, I (Philadelphia: Westminster, 1963), 139-146.

[2] A comprehensive and judicious assessment of the Semitic element in the language of the gospels is presented by M. Black, *An Aramaic Approach to the Gospels and Acts* (Oxford: Clarendon Press, 1954).

[3] For a concise summary of the modification that Matthew has made in the Markan material, see R. Bultmann, *History of the Synoptic Tradition* (New York: Harper & Row, 1963), pp. 350-358.

connected with Jesus would not have had to depend as a literary source on Mark, who at best was reporting at second hand the recollections of an apostle. Indeed, the Gospel of Matthew itself makes no claim to have been written by an eyewitness, much less by one named Matthew. It is true that only in Matthew is the tax-collector who became a follower of Jesus (Mk. 2:13-14) called Matthew (Mt. 9:9; 10:3), but there is no hint of a connection between this man and the authorship of the gospel. The divergences among the lists of disciples found in the three synoptic gospels are such as to warn us against basing historical judgments on variations in the name. We must confess that, as with the other three gospels, we do not know who the author of Matthew was. For the sake of convenience, however, we shall continue to refer to him as "Matthew."

The author's use of a Greek source makes it obvious that the gospel was originally written in Greek, as we have noted. This conclusion is strengthened by the fact that a number of the quotations from the Old Testament are taken, not from the Hebrew text, but from the Septuagint, the widely used Greek translation of the Old Testament that had been prepared in the third and second centuries B.C. for the use of Jews scattered throughout the Hellenistic world who no longer readily understood Hebrew. We look, then, for a city or region where there were Greek-speaking Christians of Jewish origin as the likely place where Matthew was written. Alexandria has been proposed, but there is no evidence to connect Matthew with that city. Caesarea has been suggested, but largely on the basis that Peter, who is given a place of special importance in Matthew (especially 16:16-19), was the one through whom the Church was established in Caesarea, according to Acts 10. But as we shall see (pp. 313-314), the story of Peter at Caesarea serves the author of Acts as a stylized account of the transition from Jewish to Gentile evangelism rather than as a straightforward historical report. Antioch is the city where the first echoes of Matthew are heard in the form of quotations and allusions in the writings of Ignatius. The dominant view among Biblical scholars has been that Antioch is in fact that place where Matthew was written,[4] although it is more probable that the gospel originated in a community in the area to the east of Antioch near the Euphrates Valley. We know of the existence of strong Jewish communities in Aleppo, Edessa, and Apamea[5] in this period, and that Christian communities flourished there in the second century. The interest in the Magi and the miraculous star are fitting in such an environment, although astrological speculation had pervaded the whole of the empire by this time.

At best we can only conjecture, on the basis of hints from within the work

---

[4] The classic statement of this position is given by B. H. Streeter, in *The Four Gospels* (London: Macmillan, 1924). Streeter connects each of the gospels with one of the four great centers of Christianity.

[5] See the discussion of the possibility of this area as the place of origin of Matthew by B. W. Bacon, *Studies in Matthew* (New York: Holt, 1930) pp. 24-36.

itself, about the specific type of community in which the Gospel of Matthew might have arisen. It was, as we have seen, a Greek-speaking group, but one which was strongly influenced by Jewish perspectives and aspirations. As we shall see in our subsequent analysis of Matthean themes, there is on the part of the author of this gospel a paradoxical attitude toward Judaism. On the one hand he is deeply sympathetic with Judaism, especially its Law and the moral demands contained therein. But on the other hand, he is profoundly, at times bitterly, critical of Judaism, especially of its leaders, whom he regards as hypocrites (Mt. 23:1-36, especially vv. 13, 15, 16, 23, 25, 27, 29). The reader senses that Matthew has the mind and attitude of a convert from Judaism, who loves its institutions and shares many of its convictions, but who is profoundly troubled by what he considers to be its inability to grasp the fuller truth which God has now revealed in Jesus Christ. This truth is not antithetical to the faith of Judaism, but it is more than a mere supplement. Christianity is for Matthew the divinely disclosed fulfillment of the Law and of Jewish hopes; he cannot comprehend that those who stand in the tradition of the Law could fail to discern the truth as it is in Jesus. In presenting his gospel, therefore, Matthew meets his Jewish opponents on their own ground, arguing from scripture and employing typically Jewish methods of debate. Although the Gospel of Matthew contains polemics against Judaism, it is not written primarily as a polemical document; rather, it is a book of instruction for those living in a situation of tension with Jews. The author does not refute the claims of the Jewish scriptures; he claims instead that the Church is the true Israel,[6] while the people that calls itself "Israel" has actually forfeited that claim by its failure to recognize Jesus as God's Messiah.

The theory has been advanced that the primary aim of Matthew in writing his gospel was "to supply, from the treasure of the past, material for the homiletical and liturgical use of the Gospel in the future." [7] But apart from the traces of liturgical phraseology that have been introduced into the material included by Matthew in the Sermon on the Mount,[8] there seems to be no greater interest in worship here than in any of the other gospels. A more fitting characterization of the book is a manual of Church instruction and administration, perhaps comparable to the Dead Sea community's so-called Manual of Discipline.[9] In our examination of the themes and motifs that

---

[6] This understanding of the Church by Matthew has been convincingly developed by W. Trilling, Das Wahre Israel (Leipzig: St. Benno-Verlag, 1959).

[7] Thus G. D. Kilpatrick, The Origins of the Gospel According to St. Matthew (Oxford: Clarendon Press, 1946), p. 99.

[8] For example, the Beatitudes and the Lord's Prayer are both given by Luke in simpler form than by Matthew. Luke has Jesus pray simply, "Father"; Matthew has the more elaborate form suited for liturgical use: "Our Father who art in heaven." Luke presents the Beatitudes as direct address ("Blessed are you poor . . ."), while Matthew reproduces them as more general statements ("Blessed are the poor in spirit").

[9] This theory was developed by K. Stendahl, in his The School of St. Matthew (Uppsala, Sweden: C. W. K. Gleerup, 1954).

THE SEA OF GALILEE *looks much like a mountain mist in this photograph. Its surface is 685 feet below sea level. The gospels tell us that Jesus taught on the sides of low hills such as these.*

characterize the Gospel of Matthew, we shall see how devoted the author is to the matter of maintaining order in the Church.

STRUCTURE IN MATTHEW'S GOSPEL

Many interpreters of Matthew have drawn attention to the fondness for structure which is evident throughout the book. In the genealogy which opens the book, the author has arranged the generations in sets of 14, even though this process obviously requires the omission of several links in the genealogical sequence (Mt. 1:2-17). But the most striking instance of Matthew's having structured his material is in the main body of the gospel, which he has divided into five sections, each of which concludes with some such phrase as, "When Jesus had finished these sayings . . ." (cf. Mt. 7:28; 11:1; 13:53; 19:1; 26:1). Each of the sections begins with a series of narratives concerning the activities of Jesus, and each concludes with an extended discourse. Preceding the first such section is the story of the birth and infancy of Jesus; following the fifth discourse is the account of the Passion and Resurrection. The opening and closing parts of the gospel are, however, far more than mere prologue and epilogue; they are essential elements of the story as a whole. The structure of the Gospel of Matthew can be viewed schematically as shown on the next page.

I. The Coming of Jesus as God's Messiah—Chapters 1 and 2

II. The Ministry of the Messiah—Chapters 3 through 25

    (1) Preparation and Program of the Ministry—Chapters 3-7
        Narrative: Baptism, Temptation, and Call of Disciples—3:1-4:25
        Discourse: Sermon on the Mount—Chapters 5-7

    (2) The Authority of Jesus—Chapters 8 through 10
        Narrative: Healing and Forgiveness of Sins—8:1-9:38
        Discourse: Sending of the Twelve Disciples—10:1-42

    (3) The Kingdom and Its Coming—Chapters 11-13
        Narrative: Controversy Resulting from Men's Inability To Discern the Kingdom's In-breaking—11:1-12:50
        Discourse: The Parables of the Kingdom— 13:1-58

    (4) Life of the New Community—Chapters 14-18
        Narrative: Anticipations of Hostility toward and Common Life within the New Community—14:1-17:27
        Discourse: Regulations for the Common Life— 18:1-35

    (5) The Consummation of the Age—Chapters 19-25
        Narrative: Intensified Conflict between Jesus and Judaism—19:1-24:2
        Discourse: The End of the Age (Synoptic Apocalypse)—24:3-25:46

III. The Humiliation and Exaltation of the Messiah—Chapters 26-28
    The Passion and the Resurrection Stories; The Final Commissioning of the Disciples for the World Mission

A careful reading of the gospel following this outline will disclose that Matthew has not followed through his scheme with complete consistency. In Section II (4), for example, it is difficult to differentiate between narrative and discourse. In Sections II (1) and II (2), however, there is no mistaking the division, since the narrative portion in each case closes with a summarizing account of Jesus' public ministry. Thus Mt. 4:23 reads:

> And he went about all Galilee, teaching in their synagogues and preaching the gospel of the kingdom and healing every disease and every infirmity among the people.

And Mt. 9:35 reads similarly:

> And Jesus went about all the cities and villages, teaching in their synagogues and preaching the gospel of the kingdom, and healing every disease and every infirmity.

The other subsections of Section II are *not* thus marked off by summarizing statements.[10]

Some interpreters have suggested that the fivefold structure of Matthew's central section is a conscious imitation of the fivefold Torah. Thus Jesus would be giving the New Law on the mountain in Galilee as Moses had given the Original Law on the mountain in Sinai. But this proposal has several weaknesses. First, there is no real development in Matthew of the image of Jesus as a second Moses,[11] although Moses is depicted as appearing to him on the Mount of the Transfiguration (Mt. 17:3 f.), as is the case in the other synoptic accounts. More significantly, one of the main arguments of Matthew is that it is precisely the Law (*sc.*, of Moses) and the prophets that have their fulfillment in Jesus (Mt. 5:17). In addition to this explicit reference to the fulfillment of the Law, the book is marked from beginning to end by the claim that what God has done in Jesus Christ has been to effect the fulfillment of the scriptures. This leads us to an examination of the main themes developed by Matthew.

GOD'S MIGHTY WORKS

Although all the gospel writers present a picture of Jesus that is marked by marvelous powers on his part and by miraculous events that accompany his ministry, Matthew lays greater stress on this than do the other evangelists. The birth story consists almost entirely of divine disclosures through dreams and miraculous occurrences, chief among which is the supernatural conception of Jesus in the virgin's womb. Only slightly less wonderful is the guiding star that led the Magi to the birthplace. All these miracles are told in distinctive Matthean passages.

Matthew reproduced nearly all the miracle stories found in his sources, Mark and Q. At times he has abridged them; at other times he has expanded them. On occasion his modification has had the effect of heightening the miraculous element, such as when the ruler's daughter is not merely at the point of death, but dead (cf. Mk. 5:23 with Mt. 9:18), and when the blind man at Jericho in Mk. 10:46 becomes two men (Mt. 20:30). But for the most part, Matthew's changes in the miracle stories serve his theological objectives, by concentrating on the faith of the persons healed, or on the authority of Jesus, or on the demands of discipleship.[12]

---

[10] This and other inconsistencies in the structural arrangement of Matthew have been noted by F. V. Filson in his article, "Broken Patterns in the Gospel of Matthew," in *Journal of Biblical Literature*, LXXV, 1956, 17 ff.

[11] See the treatment of the theme, "New Exodus and New Moses," in W. D. Davies, *The Setting of the Sermon on the Mount* (Cambridge: Cambridge University Press, 1964), especially pp. 92, 93.

[12] The way in which Matthew has brought out these motifs in the miracle stories, partly by expansion of his sources and partly by condensing them, is set forth in detail by H. J. Held in his long essay, "Matthew as Interpreter of the Miracle Stories," in *Tradition and Interpretation in Matthew*, by G. Bornkamm, G. Barth, and H. J. Held (Philadelphia: Westminster, 1963), pp. 164-299.

The sheer joy in the miraculous, however, comes out most clearly in Matthew's account of the empty tomb. Mark soberly describes the stone as already rolled back, and a young man present who announces that Jesus has been raised from the dead. Matthew on the other hand reports a great earthquake, an angel descending from heaven, the terror that strikes down the guards. At the death of Jesus, according to Matthew alone, there had been an earthquake and the bodies of many saints were raised even before the resurrection of Jesus took place (27:52). The intention of all this is not simply to impress the reader with miraculous detail, but to demonstrate that God was at work throughout the whole of the earthly life of Jesus, and that his (God's) action had culminated in the greatest of all miracles, the Resurrection.

THE SCRIPTURES ARE FULFILLED

God's action in Jesus' behalf was not to be thought of as arbitrary or random; rather, it was the unfolding of a divine plan which the eye of faith could see as having been given beforehand in the Hebrew scriptures.

The Fulfillment of "Prophecy"

The foretelling of Jesus' ministry was not limited to the obviously prophetic sections of the Old Testament, but included passages which did not appear to be predictive at all, or which to an outsider might not even seem to apply. At least one scripture quoted by Matthew cannot be found in the text of the Hebrew Bible as we know it; there is nothing in the Old Testament that corresponds to the words that purport to be a quotation from the prophets: "He shall be called a Nazarene" (Mt. 2:23). Possibly the Old Testament reference that the writer had in mind was Judges 13:5, or Isa. 11:1, or a combination of the two. In the first of these passages, a person who in a special way is dedicated wholly to God is called a Nazirite; in the second, the coming Messiah of the Davidic line is called (in Hebrew) *nezer* (meaning "a shoot which springs from a cut-down stump"). The meaning is that, although the royal line that began with David is apparently dead, there will yet come one from that family who will be the ideal king. Since the Jews believed that the consonants (which alone were written in the original text of the Hebrew Bible) were sacred, and that they were capable of several meanings, depending on what vowels were supplied to fill out the words, perhaps Matthew recognized that a different set of vowels used with *nezer* would provide scriptural confirmation for Jesus' association with Nazareth.

A distinctive feature of Matthew's quotations from scripture is an introductory formula which he uses 11 times: 1:22; 2:5; 2:15; 2:17; 2:23; 4:14; 8:17; 12:17; 13:35; 21:4; 27:9-10. With variations, the formula runs: "This was done to fulfill what was spoken by the Lord through the prophet. . . ." It must

BETHPHAGE AND BETHANY *are villages east of Jerusalem through which Jesus passed on his final journey to the Holy City. This telephoto picture, taken from the eastern edge of the Mount of Olives, shows these villages, and also the Wilderness of Judea and the depression of the Dead Sea.*

be acknowledged that, by current standards of Biblical interpretation, none of these prophecies means in its original context what Matthew has made it mean in his setting. For example, "Out of Egypt have I called my son" is in Hosea a reference to the exodus of the nation Israel from its bondage in Egypt; here it is a prediction of God's calling Jesus back from his temporary residence in Egypt after the death of Herod, who had threatened his life. In at least one instance, Matthew seems to have created a story (Mt. 27:3-10) to fit his combination of two or three prophecies (Zech. 11:12-13; Jer. 32:6-15; 18:2-3). The actions of the prophets in neither of these passages has reference to the betrayal of the Messiah or to money received as a bribe. None of the other gospels reports this incident at all, so that it would appear to be a product of Matthew's concern to demonstrate how God's purpose revealed in scripture was fulfilled even in Jesus' betrayal by one of his own followers.

Although the prophecy of the king coming on an ass seems to lie behind the Markan version of Jesus' entry into Jerusalem, Matthew makes the allusion to Zech. 9 explicit. In doing so, however, he shows that he does not understand the nature of Hebrew poetic form in which the prophecy is set forth. Hebrew poetry is characterized by parallelism, in which the meaning of the first line is echoed or amplified in the second:

> The earth is the Lord's, and the fulness thereof,
> The world and those who dwell therein.
> —PSALM 24:1

When Zechariah wrote of Israel's king coming "on an ass, and on a colt the foal of an ass" (Zech. 9:9, as rendered literally from the Hebrew in the *King James Version*), he had in mind only one animal, as the other evangelists have recognized. Matthew, on the other hand, finding mention of two animals in the text, reports Jesus as giving orders to procure for his entry "an ass . . . and a colt."

Although it may not be warranted to speak of a school of interpretation standing behind these formula quotations,[13] there is a parallel between the method of applying the scriptures freely to the present situation, as was done at Qumran, and Matthew's procedure. In both instances, it was assumed that the group interpreting the scripture was an eschatological community awaiting the last days and the consummation of God's purpose. To them had been granted special insight into the future by means of the unlocking of scriptural mysteries. Therefore, even though—or perhaps more precisely *because*—the surface meaning of a passage of scripture did not seem to apply to the present, the inspired interpreter could see in these writings, out of an ancient setting, a clue to the divine purpose at work in the present historical circumstances.

The Fulfillment of the Law

The scriptures were also understood by Matthew to be fulfilled in another than the prophetic sense: that is, in fulfillment of the ethical demand contained in the Law and the Prophets. This claim is set forth in the opening section of the Sermon on the Mount (Mt. 5-7). Although Luke has also reproduced a "sermon" (Lk. 6:20-49) which shares some features in common with Matthew's better-known Sermon—both evangelists apparently drawing on Q— Matthew has given distinctive qualities to his version, and has included far more than has Luke. The Beatitudes which open the Sermon show that Matthew does not regard ethics as a matter of mere conformity to legal standards; membership in the People of God cannot be attained by meeting legalistic requirements. Rather, God's People are those who have received as a gift of his grace all that they have. By this world's standards they are the poor, the bereaved, the despised, the persecuted; but in the Age to Come, it will be evident that they are the special beneficaries of divine favor: theirs is the kingdom, they shall inherit the earth, they shall see God (Mt. 5:3-8). They are

---

[13] This is the view of K. Stendahl, *The School of St. Matthew* (Uppsala: C. W. K. Gleerup, 1954), especially pp. 20-35.

the salt of the earth, the light of the world: let them perform now their proper functions in doing good works, that men may glorify their heavenly Father (Mt. 5:13-16).

The heart of Matthew's attitude toward the Law, however, is disclosed in two passages: the general statements about the Law (Mt. 5:17-20) and the series of antitheses ("You have heard that it was said to the men of old . . . but I say to you. . . ."—(Mt. 5:21-48). Since these statements are found only in Matthew in this form, it is likely that they originated with him, or at least that they have been shaped by him to suit his purposes. Let us examine this passage in three parts:

> (1) Think not that I have come to abolish the law and the prophets;
> I have come not to abolish them but to fulfill them.
>
> —MATTHEW 5:17

The first part of the verse implies that the charge has been leveled against Jesus (or against the Church which honors him) that Christianity seeks the destruction of the Jewish Law. This accusation is denied, countered by the claim that Jesus intends to *fulfill* the Law and the Prophets. "Fulfill" cannot mean in this context what it meant in the formula quotations discussed above; instead, it means that Jesus has come to accomplish what the Law promised, to actualize in human existence the will of God which the Law summons man to obey. That the weight falls on the ethical demand is obvious from the third general statement in verses 19 and 20.

> (2) For truly, I say to you, till heaven and earth pass away, not an iota, not a dot, will pass from the law until all is accomplished.
>
> —MATTHEW 5:18

A parallel to this statement appears in Lk. 16:17, where it is apparently ironical; that is, Jesus mocks the Pharisees who would rather have the whole Creation pass away than for a single stroke or dot of the Written Law to be changed. As Matthew reproduces the saying, however, it is not ironical but affirms the unchangeability of the Law with an absoluteness that even some of the rabbinic interpreters did not enjoin. Matthew is convinced that what has been wrong with the nation that called itself Israel is that it has not in the proper and complete way expected the Law to be fulfilled; now the new community for which he is the spokesman looks forward to the true and total accomplishment of everything promised and commanded in the Law. Although this principle is not carried out with complete consistency in the interpretation of the Law that Matthew gives in the antitheses, the point of view expressed there is a full, radical affirmation of the Law. There is no hint of reducing the Law to a single principle, such as the law of love, nor is the Law presented as an instrument that will drive men to despair of their own moral abilities and thereby throw them back in repentance upon the grace of God. Interpreters of

Jesus have read these passages in this way, but without warrant from the texts themselves.

> (3) Whoever then relaxes one of the least of these commandments and teaches men so, shall be called least in the kingdom of heaven; but he who does them and teaches them shall be called great in the kingdom of heaven. For I tell you, unless your righteousness exceeds that of the scribes and Pharisees, you will never enter the kingdom of heaven.
>
> —MATTHEW 5:19-20

Several features of this astonishing passage must be noted. First, the role of the member of the community is twofold: doing and teaching. Unlike the Pharisees, whose teaching may conform to the Law but whose way of life does not (see Mt. 23:3), the true child of the kingdom teaches rightly and lives rightly. The person who aspires to leadership by assuming a teaching role in the community takes upon himself a serious and solemn responsibility.

The second part of this passage, rather than denouncing the Pharisees as immoral persons, calls for the member of the true Israel to go beyond them in obedience to the Law. The popular caricature of the Pharisee is that of a pedant, a prude, a prig—and a hypocrite. While denouncing the hypocrisy of the Pharisees (especially in verse 23), Matthew has no quarrel with the moral demands that they make; his complaint is that they do not live up to their own standards. The New People of God should not only live up to pharisaic standards, but should go beyond them in the stringency of their interpretation of and conformity to the Law. The Law, therefore, is understood to be binding in a most radical way.[14]

JESUS' ATTITUDE TOWARD THE LAW.   In the synoptic tradition as a whole, Jesus is represented as at times setting aside what is explicitly permitted or prohibited in the Law, and at other times as going beyond the statement of the Law to a more profound demand. Of the first type is the teaching about divorce, a practice which was explicitly permitted in Deut. 24:1. The rabbis of the first century disagreed as to the conditions implied in the specification of adequate grounds for divorce ("because he has found some indecency in her"), some interpreting the phrase strictly to apply only to adultery, others interpreting "indecency" more broadly. According to the version of Jesus' word on divorce in Mk. 10:11-12, there were to be no conditions under which divorce and re-marriage were to be permitted. In Matthew's versions of this saying (he re-produces the word twice: Mt. 5:31-32 and 19:9), there is provision for divorce in case of "unchastity." In this passage, Matthew therefore depicts Jesus as less

---

[14] A detailed analysis of the radical reinterpretation of the Law in the synoptic tradition and especially in Matthew is presented by H. Braun, *Spätjüdisch-häretischer und frühchrist-licher Radikalismus*, 2 Vols. (Tübingen: J. C. B. Mohr, 1957), especially II, 34-61.

See also in this connection the essay by G. Barth, "Matthew's Understanding of the Law," in G. Bornkamm, G. Barth, and H. J. Held, *Tradition and Interpretation in Matthew* (Philadelphia: Westminster, 1963), pp. 85-105.

radical than he actually seems to have been, according to the older form of the tradition preserved in Mark.

On the other hand, the radical nature of obedience is powerfully set forth in the words of Jesus on murder (Mt. 5:21-26), on adultery (5:27-30), on retaliation (5:38-42), and especially on love of enemies (5:43-48). In each instance the moral issue is moved clear out of the realm where one can calculate what is legally permissible and what is not. Not the overt act of murder, but hatred of one's brother is forbidden. Not extramarital intercourse, but lusting after a woman who is not one's wife is condemned. Not acquiescence in performing a burdensome duty, but willing cooperation in demands and obligations is enjoined. One is not to have love only for those who are friendly and close at hand, but for one's enemies.

These commandments are radical, not merely in the sense that they are stringent and demanding, but because they get at the root of man's relationships with his fellow man, rather than dealing with the externals of those relationships. It is too simple to say that Jesus is here pictured as concerned with the spirit rather than the letter; he is concerned about the letter of the Law as well, as we see from his appeal, in defense of his position on divorce, to the prior principle of God's intention in instituting marriage: "[So] God created man . . . male and female" . . . "and they become one flesh." "What therefore God has joined together, let not man put asunder."—(Mk. 10:6-9; Mt. 19:4-6—cf. Gen. 1:27; 2:24).

The basic appeal of the ethics of Jesus as shown in Matthew is to the nature and purpose of God himself:

> But I say to you, love your enemies and pray for those who persecute you, *so that you may be sons of your Father who is in heaven*; for he makes his sun rise on the evil and on the good, and sends rain on the just and on the unjust. . . . You, therefore, must be perfect, as your heavenly Father is perfect.
>
> —MATTHEW 5:44, 45, 48

The term "perfect" here does not mean simply absence of moral imperfection, but the wholeness and singlemindedness by which God goes about fulfilling his purposes and by which standard man is called to obey him.[15] Luke has toned down the force of this demand in his parallel form of this saying by substituting the word "merciful" (Lk. 6:36), but Matthew is closer to what was likely the original intent of Jesus' word.

Obedience to the Law, as Matthew describes it, was not confined to *ethical* performance, however: it included participation in such typical Jewish acts of piety as prayer (Mt. 6:5-8), giving of alms (6:1-4), fasting (6:16-18), and apparently offering the appropriate sacrifices as prescribed by the Temple regula-

---

[15] See the discussion of this term by G. Barth, *op. cit.*, pp. 97-103.

tions in the Law. These may have been empty requirements by Matthew's time, since the Temple was no longer standing,[16] but they show that in principle Matthew did not make our modern distinction between the ceremonial Law (as not binding on Christians) and the moral Law (as valid.)

THE WAY OF RIGHTEOUSNESS

A characteristic term of Matthew's is "righteousness." He has introduced incidents into his account where the term is used, and inserted it in accounts where he is paralleling Luke. (An example of the latter is Mt. 6:33: while Luke reads "seek first his kingdom," Matthew adds "and his righteousness.")

The theme of righteousness is laid down at the very beginning of Jesus' ministry in Matthew's account (3:15). At this point in the narrative of the baptism of Jesus, John protests that he is inferior to Jesus and needs to be baptized by him. Jesus, however, insists that "it is fitting for us to *fulfill all righteousness.*" Each of these italicized words is important. The demands of God's will are to be *fully* met. Even Jesus—nay, Jesus most of all—is under divine obligation to meet these demands. Righteousness is to be complied with in its *totality*; partial obedience will not suffice. Although the context in Mt. 3 does not tell us precisely what "righteousness" implies, we can see from the evangelist's use of the term throughout the gospel what it involves, and how Jesus is presented as the embodiment of righteousness. But that the term does not mean only ethical performance according to the will of God is made clear from Mt. 21:32, which speaks of John the Baptist as having come "in the way of righteousness."

There is an eschatological dimension to righteousness which is important for Matthew. This aspect is implied in Mt. 6:33, where "kingdom" and "righteousness" are linked. That is, the will of God is not fully achieved by the obedience of individuals; the whole sweep of human history is involved in the unfolding of God's purpose. Only when his goals are fulfilled in history—when his kingdom has come in its fullness—will the "way of righteousness" reach its divinely determined end. One aspect of that goal is set forth graphically by Matthew in the Parable of the Last Judgment. Strictly speaking, this is not a parable, but a highly stylized picture of the end of history, when all men—Jew and Gentile— are brought to account before God. In it we can sense Matthew's blending of eschatology and ethics: human behavior is the prime criterion in God's action to effect the consummation of history.

---

[16] K. W. Clark has sought to show that, even after the destruction of the Temple in A.D. 70, the sacrificial worship was continued, presumably in the ruins. This would account for mention of bringing sacrifices to the altar (*e.g.*, in Mt. 5:23), as well as the reference to the Temple cultus as continuing, in Heb. 8:4, 5. See "Worship in the Jerusalem Temple after A.D. 70," in *New Testament Studies*, VI, July 1960, 269 ff.

The specifics of the ethical demand are spelled out in the Sermon on the Mount as a whole, though especially in the antitheses, in which Jesus reportedly contrasts his interpretation of what the Law requires with the way it was understood by his Jewish contemporaries. Apart from one instance in which "righteousness" is used as a term for the alms given by the pious (Mt. 6:1), the word itself occurs in the Sermon in more general statements. That it has been introduced into the tradition by Matthew is evident from the comparison with the Lukan version of the same passages. Luke reads: "Blessed are you that hunger now" (Lk. 6:21); Matthew reads, "Blessed are those who hunger and thirst *for righteousness*" (Mt. 5:6). In contrast to Luke, who simply reports the blessedness of those whose names will be reviled on account of the Son of Man (Lk. 6:22), Matthew has a unique passage in which he declares blessed those who are persecuted "for righteousness' sake." It is not only for confession of the name of Christ ("on my account," Mt. 5:11), but for following the way of life called forth by Jesus' interpretation of the will of God. Matthew does not stop with the general appeal to do "good works" (Mt. 5:16); in the Parable of the Last Judgment he gives concrete examples: feeding the hungry, clothing the naked, visiting the imprisoned, welcoming strangers into one's home (Mt. 25:31-46). Conversely, to fail to perform these acts of mercy is to invite condemnation in the Day of Judgment. Yet the parable does not imply that works of kindness are to be done *in order to* achieve a reward. On the contrary, those who (according to the parable) performed them did so solely on the grounds that they had encountered another human being who was in need. They are represented as wholly astonished that they have done anything worthy of reward: "Lord, when did we see thee hungry . . . ?"

The way of righteousness, therefore, is not a path of legalism, by which the commandments are obeyed in order to "keep the rules." It is a way of life according to which the commandment to love is put into concrete action. It is not the one who says "Lord, Lord," but the one who does the Father's will who enters the kingdom (Mt. 7:21); it is not the one who *hears* Jesus' words, but the one who *does* them whose work endures (Mt. 7:26). It is to such, Matthew tells us (25:34), that the King will say at the Judgment: "Come, O blessed of my Father, inherit the kingdom prepared for you from the foundation of the world." It is they who are in truth "the righteous" (25:37).

Righteousness: a Community Responsibility

The way of righteousness is more than a matter of individual behavior; for Matthew it involves the life of the individual in the corporate experience of the community as well. In Matthew 18, the gospel writer has reworked synoptic material in such a way as to lay stress on community responsibility within the Church. Mark's account of the dispute of the disciples among themselves, as to which was greatest, is modified by Matthew (18:1-5) to a general statement that becoming humble like a little child is the way to greatness in the kingdom. Further, every true disciple is to be ever concerned for the welfare of the weaker members of the community. He is to exercise great care lest he offend one of the "little ones" (18:6-9). The Parable of the Lost Sheep, which in Luke (15:3-7) depicts the joy of God at the recovery of one of his lost creatures, has become in Matthew a warning to the Church to guard with care even the lowliest of its members from harm. In a uniquely Matthean verse (18:14), the point is made that God will hold the Church responsible for the loss of even "one of these little ones."

In 18:15-35, Matthew has brought together material from several sources to stress the obligation the Christian has for trying to restore an erring brother and to forgive one who has offended. Not seven times, but 70 times seven, the true follower of Jesus must be willing to forgive. A parable which must originally have carried the point that one dare not take advantage of God's forgiveness, lest it be withheld in the Judgment,[17] has been attached by Matthew to the appeal that the Christian be willing to forgive his brother repeatedly. While the parable does not intend to depict God as in every way like the king—complete with his own official torturers (18:34, where "jailers" should be translated "torturers"), he does want to impress his reader with the seriousness of the command of Jesus for Christian brothers to forgive one another.

GOOD AND BAD IN THE CHURCH

While Matthew, as we have seen, sets before the Church the goal of perfection, he is fully aware that the Church, like any other human institution, will have obedient members and disobedient ones, and that the leadership must be prepared to deal with disobedience. The mixed nature of the Christian community is clearly pictured in Matthew's versions of the Parables of the Kingdom, together with the interpretation of these parables which he offers. In addition to the general terms "kingdom" and "kingdom of heaven" (= kingdom of God), Matthew speaks of the "kingdom of the Son of Man" and the "kingdom of the Father." The former refers to the Church in the present Age in its mixed form, including good and bad. The kingdom of the Father is the Age beyond the Consummation, when only the faithful are present among the People of God.

In the Parable of the Weeds, which is found only in Matthew (13:24-30), and in the interpretation of it that is given (Mt. 13:36-40), we have two different points that are being made. In the original form of the parable, the point was that the messenger of the Gospel should go about his work without stopping to evaluate the outcome or to remedy unwanted results. The focus

---

[17] J. Jeremias, *Parables of Jesus*, rev. ed. (New York: Scribner's, 1963), pp. 210-214.

of the parable is on the eschatological judgment, portrayed under the figure of the harvest. God will evaluate in that day; man's task is to sow, leaving the results to God. Matthew, in the interpretation attributed to Jesus, has transformed this story into an allegory, warning members of the Church that some of them are worthy and some are not. The latter will be cast into the furnace of fire, where men weep and gnash their teeth (13:42). The task of sorting out in the Day of Judgment will be handled by the Son of Man, whose angels will gather "out of *his* kingdom" (= the kingdom of the Son of Man) the causes of sin and the evildoers. But the righteous "will shine like the sun in the *kingdom of the Father.*"

The Parable of the Net, which originally was addressed to the messengers of the Good News, encouraging them to leave to God the estimation of the results, is likewise made into an allegory warning men that they should not be "bad fish" whose destiny is to be thrown into the furnace. What we see at work in Matthew's modification of this parabolic tradition is concern about the mixed state of affairs in the Church. He is here warning the members to examine themselves, to see whether they will find their lot with the good or the bad in the Day of Judgment.[18]

Although there is no contrast between the kingdom of the Son of Man and the kingdom of the Father in Matthew's addition to the Parable of the Feast (Mt. 22:1-14; compare Lk. 14:16-24), the lesson is once more that the People of God are a mixed group. Luke's version of the parable stresses that the religious outcasts have responded to the Gospel invitation and are now certain of a place in the eschatological community. Matthew reshaped the parable so that those who have finally come to the feast are "both good and bad" (Mt. 22:10). Among them is one man who lacks the appropriate garb. He is cast out into outer darkness. Presumably the garment is the cloak of righteousness, which conforms to what we have already seen to be a dominant theme in Matthew.

The Church cannot wait, however, until the eschatological Judgment to settle matters of good and evil within its own group. There must be some system of adjudicating disputes and some structure of authority. Matthew alone among the gospels makes provision for this need. The story of Peter's confession of Jesus as the Christ is expanded by Matthew (16:17-19) to include the designation by Jesus of Peter as the rock on which the Church will be built. This passage cannot be original, since Mark, whose interest in Peter is great and obvious, would scarcely have omitted it from his account. Although "Church" would not here mean institution but eschatological community,[19] it is probably

---

[18] A detailed analysis of these parables is given by J. Jeremias in *The Parables of Jesus,* rev. ed. (New York: Scribner's, 1963), pp. 81-85, 224-227. Jeremias shows that on the grounds of vocabulary alone, the interpretations of these parables cannot be regarded as coming from the tradition; they originate with Matthew.

[19] For a defense of the authenticity of these words, see K. L. Schmidt, "The Church," in *Bible Key Words,* J. R. Coates, ed. (New York: Harper & Row, 1951), pp. 35-50.

anachronistic to attribute such a statement to Jesus.[20] For Matthew, however, Peter's central role is not that of broad ecclesiastical administration but the exercise of authority in regulating the inner life of the community. The binding and loosing mentioned here are repeated in Mt. 18:18, and echoed in Jn. 20:22-23. One of the functions of the rabbis, referred to in Jewish tradition as "binding and loosing," was the formulation of interpretations of the legal parts of the Old Testament in order to determine the situations in which a given law was or was not applicable. Matthew has obvious interest in and respect for rabbinic practices. In Mt. 13:52, Jesus is quoted as comparing a "scribe who has been trained for the kingdom of heaven" with "a householder who brings out of his treasure what is new and what is old." The leadership role in the Church, therefore, includes the task of interpreting the Law—whether old or new—in relation to the daily needs of the Church's life.

The strange and difficult Parable of the Laborers in the Vineyard, found only in Matthew (20:1-16) was originally a vindication of Jesus' Gospel against his critics.[21] God's nature is to be merciful toward all; he does not match his grace to man's performance. By adding the free-floating saying, "So the last will be first, and the first last," Matthew has shifted the meaning, so that the parable is in his setting a defense of the fact that the late-arriving Gentiles gain priority over God's People, the Jews, who were there from the beginning. As was the case with Paul in his struggle over the place of Israel in the purpose of God, Matthew here suggests that they have lost their place of special favor in God's sight. Whether this implication was intended by Matthew in 20:1-16 or not, it is clearly his meaning in his addition to the Parable of the Wicked Tenants in 21:33-46. Verse 43 reads:

> Therefore I tell you, the kingdom of God will be taken away from you and given to a nation producing the fruits of it.

Lest the reader be in any doubt as to the force of these words, he continues:

> When the chief priests and the Pharisees heard his parables, they perceived that he was speaking about them.

The most interesting feature of this prediction that the kingdom of God will be given to others is the use of the term "nation" to refer to the Church. The true nation, i.e., Israel, is no longer the Jewish people, Matthew declares: it is the Church.

What of the fate of Old Israel? In one of the bitterest passages in all the New Testament, Matthew describes the Jewish leaders as inviting upon them-

---

[20] O. Cullmann in the revised edition of his *Peter: Disciple, Apostle, Martyr* (Philadelphia: Westminster, 1962), argues that the words were spoken in a post-Resurrection appearance, rather than at Caesarea-Philippi (pp. 161-217).

[21] See J. Jeremias, *The Parables of Jesus*, pp. 33-40.

selves full responsibility for the death of Jesus: "His blood be on us and our children!"—(Mt. 27:25). Regrettably, this bit of Matthean polemic has been seized upon by anti-Semites ever since. But Matthew did not stop there: in 23:32-36 he went on to bring down on the heads of the Jewish leadership the guilt for the murder of all God's messengers, from the days of Cain and Abel to the present. Israel has, as Matthew sees it, forfeited its right to be called the People of God; that privilege has been granted the Church.

EXPECTATION OF THE END

The theme of the nearness of the kingdom of God (literally, of the heavens) is sounded by John the Baptist, according to Matthew alone. The other gospels speak only of his preaching of repentance. Drawing on Markan and Q material, Matthew builds up a vivid picture of John as announcing the coming of the kingdom, and as the instrument by which Jesus inaugurates the way of righteousness (Mt. 3:14). Only in Matthew, among the Synoptic writers, is John aware of Jesus' sonship at the moment of his baptism (Mt. 3:16). Jesus is represented as taking up John's message when, in Mt. 4:17, he begins his public ministry. The eschatological nature of the kingdom is emphatically stressed in Matthew's account of Jesus and John.

The summarizing statements in Mt. 4:23 and 9:35 concerning Jesus' ministry both use the peculiar phrase "the gospel of the kingdom," thereby pointing to the eschatological nature of his message. The signs which point to the in-breaking of the kingdom are evident in the works of healing and the exorcisms which Jesus performs. Similarly, the discourse on the sending of the Twelve (Mt. 10) instructs the messengers that they are to preach the nearness of the kingdom (10:7) and to manifest the signs of its coming. The eschatological dimension of their work is heightened by the inclusion in the mission discourse of Markan material that is found in the Synoptic Apocalypse (cf. Mt. 10:17-25 with Mk. 13:9-13), and which is obviously tied in with the judgment that Matthew believes fell when Jerusalem was destroyed; the Markan passage (Mk. 13:9-13), which Matthew has lifted out of its context and inserted in his mission discourse, leads directly into the prediction of the destruction of Jerusalem (Mk. 13:14 ff. = Mt. 24:15 ff.).

From various parts of Mark and Q, Matthew has brought together a series of sayings which he has modified in order to point up one of his major concerns, the Coming (Greek, *parousia*) of the Son of Man: Mt. 24:3 (where mention of the Consummation is also added to the Markan form of the word); 24:27, where a Q word mentioning the Son of Man "in his day" is converted into an explicit prediction of the *parousia*; 24:29-31, where the Markan prediction of the Coming of the Son of Man is expanded; 24:37, 39, where the Q expression "days of the Son of Man" becomes a direct reference to the *parousia*;

24:42, where Matthew introduces a distinctive word about watching, lest the Lord come on a day when he is not expected.

In three parables included by Matthew in his version of the apocalyptic discourse, the point is in each case the need for watchfulness in view of the delayed *parousia*. The Parable of the Faithful and Wise Servant furnishes both encouragement for those who remain faithful and ready in spite of the delay ("My Lord delays his coming"—Mt. 24:48), and a solemn warning of the judgment that will fall on those who are not watching at the time of his Coming. It reinforces the point we noted earlier, that the Church of Matthew is composed of worthy and unworthy, watchful and indifferent. In the Parable of the Ten Maidens the point is once more that when the *parousia* occurs, some will be ready and some will not. "No one knows the day nor the hour—watch, therefore." The Parable of the Talents, which like that of the Wise Servant comes from Q, calls for faithful stewardship of one's gifts during the interval before the Coming of the Master. That the interval is protracted in Matthew's view is evident from his adding the phrase (25:19): "after a long period of time" the Lord came again. Twice Matthew underscores the catastrophic consequences of failure to be ready, by appending his gloomy warning: there will be weeping and gnashing of teeth (24:51; 25:30).

There are hints in Matthew, however, that the interval between the First Coming of Christ and his *parousia* in glory is not to be viewed as an insignificant period of waiting. Rather, a new responsibility and a new reality have come into being as a consequence of the Resurrection. The new responsibility is the obligation of the followers of Jesus to preach the Gospel and to instruct in his teachings among all the people of the world. In contrast to the universal outreach commanded in the post-Resurrection words of Jesus in Mt. 28:19, 20, the mission discourse specifically instructs the disciples to limit their evangelism to the "lost sheep of the house of Israel" (Mt. 10:5, 6), by which is meant, not that all Israel is lost, but that the abandoned ones—the outcasts—from within Israel are to hear the Good News. We shall see in the next chapter that this theme is greatly developed by Luke. Nevertheless, the mission is to the Jews. The mission to the Gentiles has been anticipated, however, in the opening words of Matthew describing Jesus' public ministry (4:12 ff., especially v. 15), where Galilee is mentioned as "Galilee of the Gentiles [or nations]." The fact that there will—indeed must—be a mission to the whole world before the Consummation can occur is explicitly affirmed in Matthew's apocalyptic discourse, 24:14:

> This gospel . . . will be preached throughout the whole world [Greek, *oikoumene*], as a testimony to all nations, and then the end will come.

It is a fitting climax to this development, therefore, when the risen Christ commissions his followers to launch this world mission in 28:19, 20.

The new reality referred to above is the Church itself, composed not only of good and bad, but of Jew and Gentile. We have noted that the Church is represented by Matthew as a new nation, which will produce the fruits of righteousness that the People Israel have failed to do (Mt. 21:43). Upon Israel within the then-present generation will fall the doom appropriate to her guilt (Mt. 23:32 ff.):

> Fill up, then, the measure of your fathers. You serpents, you brood of vipers, how are you to escape being sentenced to hell? Therefore I send you prophets and wise men and scribes, some of whom you will kill and crucify, and some you will scourge in your synagogues and persecute from town to town, that upon you may come all the righteous blood shed on earth from the blood of innocent Abel to the blood of Zechariah the son of Barachiah,[22] whom you murdered between the sanctuary and the altar. Truly I say to you, all this will come upon this generation.

This fearful and vindictive indictment is surely written out of a situation of direct conflict between the growing church of Matthew and the Jewish community, torn as it was both with conflict with Rome and with the Church. Although the prediction of doom is addressed against the Pharisees (Mt. 23:13 ff.), it reads as a denunciation of the whole Jewish nation. These passages tell us a great deal about Matthew and his attitudes; they tell us nothing about Jesus. It is simply not possible to square this cruel invocation of wrath with the command of Jesus—ironically, also reproduced by Matthew (5:44)—to love one's enemies. The supreme irony in Matthew's viewpoint, however, is not that he denounces the Jews, but that he expects the Church to take over so much of Jewish institutions and practices: scribal interpretations, ceremonial requirements, alms, fasting, etc. He is able to view the Church in this way because, as we have already noted, the Church is for him the true Israel which takes the place of the nation which did not see in Jesus God's Messiah.

In the interval before the return of the triumphant Son of Man, the new community is to continue to confess him before men; if they fail to do so, they will not be vindicated by him at his *parousia* (Mt. 10:33). This Markan word (Mk. 8:38) has been placed by Matthew in the midst of instructions to the messengers of the Gospel. In fulfilling their work as witnesses, they function under the authority of the risen Christ: "All authority in heaven and on earth has been given to me."—(Mt. 28:18). It is by this power that they are to carry on their ministry, the specific tasks of which correspond precisely to the ministry that Jesus himself performed: healing, exorcisms, preaching the Gospel

---

[22] Abel is the first one murdered in the first book of the Bible; Zechariah is the last one to be murdered in the last historical book, II Chronicles. Matthew has, however, confused his Zechariahs, since the son of Barachiah was not a priest, but a prophet (Zech. 1:1) and was not murdered, so far as is known.

(Mt. 10:7, 8). But in addition, they are now to perform baptisms, and to do so in the trinitarian name of God. This is one of the few instances in the entire New Testament canon of an explicitly trinitarian formula; elsewhere, there are usually only implications of the Trinity (*e.g.*, II Cor. 13:14). Their lives are to be characterized by complete obedience to the commandments which he has given them during the period of his ministry among them; they are not only to teach these commandments, but to see that they are observed. They may rest assured that, though their Lord is not visibly present, he is nonetheless among them: "Lo, I am with you always, to the close of the age."—(Mt. 28:20). In this way, Matthew alleviates the problem created by the non-fulfillment of the *parousia* expectation. On the one hand, the passage of time must not permit the members of the community to grow lax or to lose their zeal, since the return of the Son of Man is certain; on the other hand, to consider him as absent is to misunderstand the facts, since he has promised his continuing presence in their midst until God's purpose through him is consummated and the Old Age has given way to the kingdom of the Father.

THE EPOCH
OF THE CHURCH
IN THE REDEMPTIVE
PLAN OF GOD

Luke-Acts

CHAPTER THIRTEEN Matthew was concerned to move beyond Mark's rather simple assumption that the End would come after a period of Gentile evangelism had been completed (Mk. 13:10). He felt it was important to provide for an understanding of the Church's existence, and did so by depicting it as the true Israel, in contrast to the historic Israel that had forfeited its right to that title. He had indicated the ground of the Church's authority in the apostolic designation of Peter (Mt. 16:18-20), and had sketched out the basis for the maintenance of discipline within the Christian community (Mt. 18:15-20). Nonetheless, he did not set forth a theory of the whole sweep of history by which the Church could understand itself and its reason for existence in the interim before the coming of the end of the Age. It was Luke who took on the task of developing an encompassing view in which the place of the Church in God's over-all purpose would be depicted. His story of Jesus and the Church in the perspective of God's historical purpose is set forth in the twofold work —unfortunately divided in our New Testament—known as Luke (Part I) and Acts (Part II).

WHY AND HOW
A CHRISTIAN HISTORY SHOULD BE WRITTEN

It is difficult for the man who looks back over the history of Christianity from the vantage-point of nearly 2,000 years to comprehend the seriousness of the question that must have confronted the Christians of the first century: Why should there be a Church? If the end of the Age was to be the next act in the redemptive drama of God, what meaning could be found for the Church as an ongoing institution? To provide a satisfactory answer to this kind of question, one would have to discover some positive significance in the situation before the End, rather than looking only to the End itself to provide meaning for human life.

There have, of course, been those in every century of the Church's existence who have looked on life in this age as merely transitional, and who claim to see no positive worth in anything that this age has to offer. Everything they want will become theirs in the sweet bye-and-bye. Luke [1] was not content with this viewpoint, and instead set about describing the redemptive purpose of God in such a way as to show the essential rôle of the Church in the achievement of that purpose. In his view, the establishment of the Church was as much a part of the fulfillment of the divine plan as the act of Consummation itself. Indeed, the act of the drama in which the Church has the center of the stage is an indispensable antecedent of the end of the Age. The Age of the Church is the midpoint in the whole drama, as Luke sees it. [2]

---

[1] Although we cannot be certain of the identity of the author of the two-volume work known today as Luke-Acts (see discussion of authorship, pp. 320-321), it is convenient to refer to him by the traditional name, Luke.

[2] The basic work on Luke-Acts in which the redemptive periods are traced out is *The Theology of St. Luke*, by Hans Conzelmann (New York: Harper & Row, 1960). This study is translated from the original German, which is titled appropriately, *Die Mitte der Zeit*: that is, *The Mid-Point of Time*. For details of this scheme, the reader is referred to Conzelmann's work, which is here presupposed.

Luke's Historical Method

Luke's scheme can be discerned not only from direct statements, but from the ways—at times subtle, at times more obvious—in which he modifies the tradition as he received it. The modifications are most clear, of course, where we have parallels from Mark and Matthew with which to compare Luke's handling of the material. But the special interests and even the distinctive vocabulary of Luke can be detected in material which he alone among the evangelists records. He was peculiarly well fitted for this task by his apparent knowledge of historical and literary methods of the cultured world of his own time, as well as by his thorough familiarity with the language of the Greek Old Testament. As a result of those two streams of literary influence, his work serves admirably as a bridge from the Jewish setting in which the Gospel arose to the Gentile world to which the message was to be interpreted. Luke is equally at home with the Semitic-sounding hymns of the infancy stories ("My soul magnifies the Lord"—Lk. 1:46) and the philosophical platitudes of the Hellenistic world ("In him we live and move and have our being"—Acts 17:28).

Luke's knowledge of his world extends beyond the literary to include precise political and historical information, as well. For example, in Acts 17:6 the city officials in Thessalonica are referred to as "politarchs." The term is used without explanation and occurs nowhere else in the New Testament. Inscriptions found in the region, however, confirm that the title was in use there and suggest that it was not used elsewhere. The accuracy of Luke's designation of the rulers of the city is thereby confirmed.

One of the few relatively fixed points of chronology in the whole of the New Testament is the stay of Paul in Corinth (Acts 18:12 ff.). Luke reports that the Roman governor in Corinth at the time of Paul's sojourn there was Gallio. From an inscription found across the Gulf of Corinth at Delphi it is possible to determine that Gallio began his term as governor in the first half of A.D. 51. This confirmation of Luke's account receives further support from the mention in Acts 18:1 ff. that two Jews who had recently arrived in Corinth and who later helped Paul in his work there had fled from Rome following a decree of the emperor Claudius against the Jews in the Imperial City. The date of that decree, as can be inferred from Suetonius' *Life of Claudius*, is approximately A.D. 49, which of course fits in precisely with Luke's account. In short, Luke has access to accurate information and uses it effectively in setting forth his story of the spread of the Gospel from Galilee to Jerusalem and on to Rome.

EVALUATING LUKE AS HISTORIAN. It would be unreasonable, however, to expect Luke to measure up to modern standards of historical reliability, much less objectivity. He compares favorably with his contemporary historians, and indeed uses many of their methods and literary conventions.[3] One sees this from the outset in the formal literary prefaces with which he has prefixed both volumes of his twofold work:

> Inasmuch as many have undertaken to compile a narrative of the things which have been accomplished among us, just as they were delivered to us by those who from the beginning were eyewitnesses and ministers of the word, it seemed good to us also, having followed all things closely for some time past, to write you an orderly account, most excellent Theophilus, that you may know the truth concerning the things of which you have been informed.
>
> —LUKE 1:1-4

And the second recalls the first:

> In the first book, O Theophilus, I have dealt with all that Jesus began to do and teach. . . .
>
> —ACTS 1:1

The complexity of the sentences, the acknowledgment of predecessors in the field, the expression of purpose by the writer, and the address to the patron are all part of the literary conventions of the time. Luke is making a bid to have his books regarded seriously by the literarily, perhaps even the intellectually, sophisticated of his day.

It is easier to assess Luke's place among the historians of his time than it is to evaluate his work as a historian for the modern man who seeks historical knowledge of the beginnings of Christianity. On the one hand, Luke uses his sources in much the same way as his contemporary historians, although the evangelistic purpose which lies behind his work gives his books a special quality that the other historical writings lack. On the other hand, he raises problems for the modern man in search of "historicity" by adopting the first-century custom of inventing speeches or modifying the accounts of events. This was done even when the historian was an eyewitness, since his aim was not verbatim reporting but portraying what was characteristic or what he thought was significant in the incidents which he was reporting. The late interpreter and historian of early Christianity, Martin Dibelius, has said:

> The ancient historian does not wish to present life with photographic accuracy, but rather to portray and illuminate what is typical, and his practice of aiming at what is typical and important allows the author of Acts partly to omit, change or generalize what really occurred. So it is that, where he sometimes appears to us today to be idealizing,

---

[3] For an appreciative study of Luke's literary and historical methods in comparison with those of other Hellenistic historians, see H. J. Cadbury, *The Making of Luke-Acts* (London: S.P.C.K., 1961), pp. 113-212.

and describing what was typical, he was really trying to discharge his obligations as an historian. Thus, through the literary methods of the historian, he was able to discharge his other obligation of being a preacher of faith in Christ.[4]

Basic for the work of an historian today is a chronological sequence of the events with which he is dealing; none such was available to Luke, however. In all probability, Luke had only an itinerary of Paul to follow for the sequence of events he depicts in Acts. Even there, his other objectives lead him to halt the course of his account of Paul to introduce other interests or to insert speeches attributed to Paul. This is especially evident in the famous sermon on the Areopagus in Acts 17. In preparing the Gospel of Luke, there was likely no

---

[4] M. Dibelius, in "The First Christian Historian," from *Studies in the Acts of the Apostles* (London: SCM Press, 1956), pp. 136, 137.

THE WILDERNESS OF JUDEA *is where John the Baptist carried on his ministry, in fulfillment of the prophecy: "In the wilderness prepare the way of the Lord." This treacherous wilderness road between Jerusalem and Jericho was the site of the attack by robbers upon the traveler mentioned in Jesus' Parable of the Good Samaritan.*

chronology or sequence of events available, except for Mark's. Luke follows Mark's sequence in a general way, but feels free to depart widely at the beginning and the end, and to make considerable modifications in the middle, since his avowed purpose of setting forth "an orderly account" seems to refer not so much to chronological order but to logical or even theological order. As we shall see, it is to his purpose to have the story of Jesus' rejection at Nazareth come right at the outset of his public ministry (Lk. 6), even though Mark locates it at the end of a period of successful activity in Galilee (Mk. 6). It is important, therefore, to try to discover what the pattern or "order" was which guided Luke in the arrangement of his material for the first Christian history.

A Christian Perspective
on the Whole Scope of History

Luke's undertaking is an ambitious one: he wants to place the ministry of Jesus and the work of the Church in the context of the universal purpose of God. Although the actual chronological scope of the events directly reported runs only from the birth of John the Baptist to the imprisonment of Paul in Rome, there are many pointers in both volumes which look backward to the story of ancient Israel and forward to the consummation of the Ages.

THE FIRST EPOCH: FROM ANCIENT ISRAEL TO JOHN THE BAPTIST. The best clue to the way that Luke regards history as divided into periods is Lk. 16:16. In Mt. 11:12-13, the more original version of the saying reads:

> From the days of John the Baptist until now, the kingdom of heaven has been suffering violence, and men of violence are seizing it. For all the prophets and the law prophesied until John; and if you are willing to receive it, he is Elijah who is going to come.

Luke has greatly reduced this saying (or this cluster of sayings) and has omitted the reference to John the Baptist as Elijah. But more important than these changes is the attitude implied toward John the Baptist: for Matthew, John marks the beginning of the new era of violence that presages the coming of the kingdom. For Luke, John marks the *end* of the epoch of the Law and the Prophets:

> The law and the prophets were until John; since then the good news of the kingdom of God is preached, and every one enters it violently.
> —LUKE 16:16

In Luke's view, John the Baptist brings to a close the old era of the Law and the Prophets, during which the promises of redemption were given, but in which the promised deliverance did not occur. It is the period of the ministry of Jesus that brings about the fulfillment of the promise. Luke tells us this in a unique passage, Lk. 4:16-30. He describes Jesus preaching in the synagogue at Nazareth. After reading the words of promised redemption ("good news to the poor, release to the captives, deliverance for the oppressed"), Jesus declares forthrightly:

> Today this scripture has been fulfilled in your hearing.
> —LUKE 4:21

Although he does not carry the theme of fulfillment to the extreme of Matthew, Luke is careful throughout his account of the ministry of Jesus to show how what Jesus did was the fulfillment of scripture. Before considering the subject of fulfillment in Luke in detail, we must identify the end of this period in Luke's scheme and the beginning of the next.

THE SECOND EPOCH: THE EARTHLY MINISTRY OF JESUS. The period of Jesus' ministry is the second great epoch, and is itself divided into three phases. The first opens with the launching of the ministry with the programmatic sermon already referred to above. By the time Luke reaches the point in his narrative that corresponds to Mk. 9:38-41 (*i.e.*, Lk. 9:50), we should expect the ministry to be nearing its close, as is the case with Mark's report. Instead, the ministry is now ready to go into its next phase: the preaching of the Gospel outside the land of Galilee, as 9:52 shows. The significance of the first phase is the gathering of the witnesses in Galilee, as is shown by the special attention and miraculous circumstances surrounding their call into his service (Lk. 5:1-11). The importance of these eyewitnesses has been anticipated in Luke's preface (1:2); it is confirmed by the special Lukan word to his followers on the eve of the Crucifixion, in which he addresses them as "you who have continued with me in my trials" (22:28), as well as by the choice of a replacement for the traitorous Judas from among those "who have accompanied us during all the time that the Lord Jesus went in and out among us, beginning from the baptism of John until the day that he was taken up from us. . . ." (Acts 1:21, 22.)

According to Luke 4, the rejection of Jesus by his fellow countrymen is expected from the outset. He must, therefore, turn to others in seeking a response of faith wherever it may be found. It is appropriate that Luke closes off the first phase of Jesus' ministry with the story of the strange exorcist, according to which Jesus rebukes the disciples for their exclusivism and encourages them to welcome support from whatever source (9:49-50): "Whoever is not against us is for us."

Although Jesus "must" now leave Galilee, he does not set out aimlessly: the clear goal that he has in view is Jerusalem, where his final rejection is to occur (9:51). Appropriately, this phase of his work is preceded by the sending of 70 evangelists to call men to repent and to announce the nearness of the kingdom

MODERN JERICHO *and the Jordan Valley. The road paralleling the dry creek bed is the old Roman road that leads up to Jerusalem. The mound in the left foreground contains the ruins of a Hellenistic fortress alongside which the Herodian kings built an elaborate villa.*

of God (10:1-16, especially v. 11). The number 70 seems to be here (as is often the case in Jewish tradition) symbolic of the 70 nations into which it was believed the human race was divided. Luke is here preparing for the mission to the Gentiles that is to be the theme of volume two of his work.

The event which signals the right time for the new phase is not simply the negative factor of the rejection in Galilee. Indeed, Luke reports widespread response to Jesus from Galilee, Judea, and Gentile regions beyond (*e.g.*, 6:17-19). The factor which brings about the change of locale and hence the change of procedure is the announcement by Jesus of his impending suffering and death (9:18-22). In Luke's version of the Transfiguration which follows the first prediction of the Passion, an incident occurs which he alone reports: the conversation of Jesus with Moses and Elijah ("the law and the prophets") concerning his "departure which he was about to fulfill in Jerusalem" (9:31). This theme is sounded again when Jesus' final departure from Galilee is recounted in 13:31-33. The immediate occasion for Jesus' statement is a report to him by Pharisees that Herod (Antipas, the tetrarch of Galilee) is seeking to destroy him:

> Go and tell that fox, "Behold, I cast out demons and perform cures today and tomorrow, and on the third day I finish my course. Nevertheless I must go on my way today and tomorrow and the day following; for it cannot be that a prophet should perish away from Jerusalem."

The first "journey" of Jesus and the Seventy begins after the fact of his suffering has been disclosed, but before its significance is understood.[5] The final journey begins (13:33) when the suffering is about to be undergone. Luke

---

[5] Cf. Conzelmann, *op. cit.*, p. 65.

moves up to this point his version of Jesus' lament over Jerusalem, in contrast to Mark (followed by Matthew), who assigns it to the last days of Jesus in Jerusalem. For Luke it serves as a symbolic indication that Jesus' rejection in Jerusalem and the subsequent judgment of God on the city are necessary elements in the outworking of the divine redemptive plan. The destruction of Jerusalem is mentioned unambiguously by Luke (21:20), whereas in Mark (13:14) and even in Matthew (24:15) the desecration of the Temple and the fall of the city are alluded to or described only in veiled language. It is also in Jerusalem that the triumphant Christ is to be revealed as judge at the consummation of the Age (Acts 1:8). Jerusalem, then, is central to the whole redemptive purpose of God in Luke's understanding, and it is to Jerusalem that Jesus *must* go.

The third phase of the activity of Jesus takes place in Jerusalem, beginning with the approach to the city by way of Jericho and reaching its climax in his rejection and crucifixion there. The nucleus of the new eschatological community is present at the Last Supper, according to a tradition found only in Luke (22:15-30).[6] The post-Resurrection appearances of Jesus occur in Jerusalem or in that vicinity, in Luke's account. On the other hand, Matthew reports them as taking place in Galilee, and Mark, who does not describe any appearances, nevertheless expects them to occur in Galilee. According to Luke, it is from Jerusalem that the world mission of the Church is to begin (Lk. 24:47), and it is there that the community will receive the gift of the Holy Spirit to empower it to fulfill its divinely appointed task (Acts 1:8).

THE THIRD EPOCH: FROM THE ASCENSION TO THE RETURN OF CHRIST. The ascension of Jesus Christ—reported only in Luke—marks the transition to the third major epoch in Luke's scheme of the Ages: the Age of the Church's mission to the world. During this period, Christ is seated at God's right hand (Acts 2:33; 3:20, 21). Having poured out the Spirit upon the Church, his next great work will be that of Judge of all men at the end of the Age (Acts 10:42; 17:31). God's work is, in the present epoch, being achieved by the power of the Spirit at work through the Church. It began with those who were eyewitnesses of Jesus' own activity (Acts 1:21-22) and is continued by those who succeeded them in the community of faith. It does not matter, therefore, how long the Last Day may be delayed: the ground of the redemptive activity has been laid in the work of Jesus Christ in fulfillment of the Law and the Prophets. The power of God is at work in the Church as it was in the ministry of Jesus. All is leading to the promised day, whose coming is now made certain by God's

---

[6] The account of the Supper is found, of course, in the other gospels, but the emphasis on the eschatological nature of the meal (22:16) and the words addressed to the disciples as the beginnings of a new community (22:28 ff.) are distinctively Lukan. If one assumes that the so-called Western text of the Greek New Testament is the original, and omits 22:19b-20, the eschatological nature of the Supper is all the more striking.

provision of the Messiah, by his triumph over death, by the power of the Spirit, and by the activity of the Church in fulfilling its mission.

ALL THINGS WRITTEN IN THE LAW
ARE NOW FULFILLED

Luke's conviction that the Law and the Prophets are fulfilled in Jesus Christ is far more pervasively present in both volumes of his work than the direct references to the fulfillment of scripture might indicate. We have already noted the explicit claim attributed to Jesus in his sermon at Nazareth that on that day the scripture was fulfilled in the hearing of those present (Lk. 4:16-30). Luke's gospel concludes on the same note; the doubting disciples are told:

> These are my words which I spoke to you while I was yet with you, that everything written about me in the law of Moses and the prophets and the psalms must be fulfilled.
>
> —LUKE 24:44

The sermons of Acts are full of allusions to the Old Testament and of the claim that the promises made to the Fathers (*i.e.*, the Fathers in Israel) have been fulfilled now in Jesus Christ (Acts 2:16, 30; 3:18; 4:11; 4:25; 7:52; 8:35; 10:43; 13:32). But to note the direct claims and specific promises which are believed to have been fulfilled is only part of the picture.

John the Baptist and the Old Testament

The stage is set for the development of this theme in the opening verses of Luke, following the formal preface (1:1-4). The birth of John the Baptist is described in its priestly environment and in an atmosphere of pious obedience to the Jewish Law. The miraculous circumstances surrounding John's conception and birth are reminiscent of the birth of Samuel (I Sam. 1, 2). He comes in the spirit of Elijah and his ministry will have its effect upon "the sons of Israel" (1:16, 17). The hymns of praise and gratitude uttered by the angels, by Mary, by Zechariah, and by the aged Simeon in the Temple (2:29-32) are written with the cadences, the vocabulary, the imagery of Old Testament poetry. So strong is the Semitic flavoring of the language in these passages, that some scholars think that the hymns have been translated from Hebrew or Aramaic originals. The same could be said, indeed, of the narrative context in which Luke has placed them. It is possible that there were Semitic originals, but it is perhaps even more likely that Luke, with his great literary skill, has written the narrative in the style of the Semitic-flavored Septuagint with which he was familiar and from which he regularly quotes. It would have sounded to him like Biblical language in much the same way that the language of the King James sounds "like the Bible" to us today.

The hymns may have originated in pre-Christian times and may have been adapted by Luke for his own purposes. It has been conjectured that they originally belonged to a sect that honored the Baptist as the eschatological prophet. Traces of such a sect may be discerned beneath the surface of John 3 and 4, as well as in Acts 18:24 ff. A sect that honors John the Baptist as redeemer survives to the present day in Iraq.[7] Some ancient Biblical manuscripts of Luke attribute the so-called Magnificat (1:46 ff.) to Elizabeth rather than to Mary, in which case the savior would be John and not Jesus. In any case, the continuity between the Covenant People of Israel and the new thing God is doing is vigorously set forth in the opening chapters of Luke. The venerable worshipers, Simeon and Anna, both of whom are looking "for the consolation of Israel" (2:25, 38), with true prophetic insight recognize in the infant Jesus the realization of their hopes.

Jesus' Ancestry as a Link to the Old Testament

The directness of the continuity between Jesus and Israel's hopes is affirmed in the genealogy of Jesus, which differs significantly from Matthew's (cf. Lk. 3:23-38 with Mt. 1:1-17). Matthew traces Jesus' ancestry back to Abraham; Luke traces it back to Adam. When linked with the expansion of John's quotation from Is. 40 to include the words "all flesh shall see the salvation of our God" (Lk. 3:6), it is obvious that Luke wants his readers to know that Jesus Christ is the *world's* redeemer, not merely the deliverer of Israel. Although we can recognize the artificiality of the genealogy, and although it is impossible to harmonize it with Matthew's, Luke's "historical" purpose still stands clear: God's guiding hand is to be seen throughout the whole range of history, culminating in the history of Jesus and the redemption of the world that is made possible through him.

Israel's Misunderstanding of the Prophecies

Even while affirming the hand of God at work in the history of his People, Luke asserts that the nation Israel has come under judgment because it has failed to comprehend the will of God through the prophets. The speech of Stephen in Acts 7 is the fullest and most vivid evidence of this, with its climactic accusation:

> You stiff-necked people, uncircumcised in heart and ears, you always resist the Holy Spirit. As your fathers did, so do you. Which of the prophets did not your fathers persecute? And they killed those who announced beforehand the coming of the Righteous One, whom you

---

[7] On this sect, called the Mandaeans, see E. L. Drower, *The Mandaeans of Iraq and Iran* (Leiden: Brill, 1962). For a discussion of the Baptist origin of the hymns, see C. H. Kraeling, *John the Baptist* (New York: Scribner's, 1951), pp. 166-171.

have now betrayed and murdered, you who received the law as delivered by angels and did not keep it.

—ACTS 7:51-53

The fault lies not with the Law or the promises contained in it, but with the people who have failed to hear in it God's Word for them. Yet even their rejection of his Word has been turned by God to good purpose. The Crucifixion itself, though accomplished "by the hands of lawless men," was nonetheless "according to the definite plan and foreknowledge of God" (Acts 2:23). Or in the words that Luke attributes to the risen Christ, "Was it not necessary that the Christ should suffer these things and enter into his glory?" And Luke goes on to say:

> And beginning with Moses and all the prophets he [Jesus] interpreted to them in all the scriptures the things concerning himself.
>
> —LUKE 24:26, 27

THE SPIRIT POURED OUT ON ALL FLESH

The effective agent in the accomplishment of God's purpose in the epoch of preparation through the prophets, the epoch of Jesus' ministry, and the epoch of the Church's mission, is the Holy Spirit. Thus David's prophecy about the Messiah and the demonic opposition he would encounter were uttered "by the Holy Spirit" (Acts 4:25). Israel's resistance to the Word of God proclaimed by the prophets was, according to Stephen's speech, "resisting the Holy Spirit" (Acts 7:51).

The Spirit Commissions Jesus

Similarly, the Spirit is operative in the preparations for the coming of Jesus Christ in the infancy stories of Luke 1 and 2: John the Baptist will be filled with the Holy Spirit; the Spirit will come upon Mary so that she may conceive and bear a son; Elizabeth is filled with the Spirit when she greets Mary; Zechariah prophesies by the Holy Spirit, as does Simeon. Luke alone depicts the coming of the Spirit upon Jesus at baptism as being "in *bodily* form, as a dove" (Lk. 3:22). The anointing by the Spirit characterizes Jesus' ministry from the outset, both in the initial return from the Jordan to the desert (4:1) and from the desert to Galilee (4:14), and in the sermon based on Isa. 61, which Jesus claims to be now fulfilled in him.

The Spirit Empowers the Church

The coming of the Spirit on the Day of Pentecost (Acts 2) is for Luke the sign that the promise made through Joel is being fulfilled: God's Spirit will be poured out on all flesh (*i.e.*, on all humanity) and whoever (*i.e.*, whether

Jew or Gentile) will call on the Lord's name will be saved. The day of universal salvation, or universal opportunity for salvation, is here. The miracle of simultaneous translation described by Luke (Acts 2:5-11) is told in a manner which parallels the Jewish tradition about the marvelous manifestations of divine power that accompanied the giving of the Law at Sinai. According to this Jewish legend, there were 70 tongues of fire on the mountain, representing the 70 languages of the 70 nations of the earth. The Law, however, remained largely the private possession of Israel, its light rarely reaching to the Gentiles. Now at the end of the Age, Luke is telling his reader, the goal is achieved: all men come under the power of the Spirit of God. And furthermore, the divine judgment at the Tower of Babel is reversed: mankind, who was then divided by language barriers into many hostile peoples, is now brought into one by the power of the Spirit in order to prepare all men to hear the one Gospel that can redeem the race.[8]

The Spirit is the effective power in enabling the ministry of the community to perform its work. The disciples, forbidden by the religious officials in Jerusalem to speak the message of God, are given courage through the Holy Spirit to defy the authorities and to speak the word (Acts 5:9). The criteria for selection of the "deacons" to assist in the ministry of the community include that they must be "full of the Spirit" (6:3). Stephen is given strength to go to a martyr's death faithful in his witness by the power of the Holy Spirit (7:55). The validity of the evangelistic work done among Samaritans (8:19) and Gentiles (10:44) is confirmed by the fact that those who hear the Gospel in faith receive the Holy Spirit. It is the gift of bestowal of the Spirit that the mercenary Simon Magus tries to purchase (8:18). The seal of Saul's conversion is the reception of the Spirit (9:17). The Spirit leads the community and its ministry in selecting persons for special tasks (13:2), in shaping the itinerary of the traveling evangelists (13:4; 16:7; 19:21), and in the supervisory rôles within the community itself (20:28). Angels at times lend assistance, according to Luke (e.g., Acts 8:26; 10:3; 12:7; 27:23), but it is the Spirit who is the chief agent of the achievement of God's purpose in this Age.

THE MISSION OF THE CHURCH
TO THE WHOLE WORLD

The first clear indication that Luke gives us of his concern for the universal benefits that are to come through Christ appears in the words of the aged holy man, Simeon, whose utterance now forms an important part in the liturgy of the Church:

---

[8] See the discussion of this difficult passage in E. Haenchen, *Die Apostelgeschichte* (Göttingen: Vandenhoeck & Ruprecht, 1959), pp. 130-139.

Lord, now lettest thy servant depart in peace,
    according to thy word;
for mine eyes have seen thy salvation
    which thou hast prepared in the presence of all peoples,
a light for revelation to the Gentiles,
    and for glory to thy people Israel.

                                        —LUKE 2:29, 30

The Light for the Gentiles

There is ample precedent in the Old Testament for the thesis that Israel's mission is to be a light to the Gentiles (Is. 42:6; 49:6), but Simeon as he beholds the infant Jesus affirms that it is through this child that the promise is to be fulfilled. We have already noted that Luke quotes a more extended passage from Is. 40 in connection with the ministry of John the Baptist, with the result that the savior for whose Coming John prepares the way is the savior of "all flesh" (Lk. 3:4-6). Even before Jesus launches his public ministry, Luke is letting his reader know that in the purpose of God the benefits which Jesus brings are to be extended to all humanity, and are not to be the exclusive privilege of the Jewish nation. In this way Judaism is not excluded from the grace of God, but the scope in which the grace of God is at work is extended beyond any ethnic bounds. In the words of the angels' song:

Glory to God in the highest, and on earth peace among men with whom he is pleased.

                                        —LUKE 2:14

Peace is for all who respond in faith, rather than the prerogative of a chosen few.

The occupations of the two groups of persons who are reported by Luke to have repented at John's preaching are such as to exclude them automatically from religious acceptability judged by Jewish standards. A tax-collector was considered a traitor to Judaism because of his collaboration with the hated Roman overlords and the dishonest dealings which seem to have been characteristic of his trade. Soldiers, who were always subject to duty on the sabbath or any other day, could not possibly keep the Jewish laws against work on the sabbath. Jews were excused from military service by Roman law; if a Jew chose a military career, he virtually forfeited his claim to participation in the life of the Covenant People. Luke tells us, however, that it was persons of this sort—that is, religious outcasts, when judged by Jewish standards—who heard John's message and repented. Even before Jesus appears, then, Luke is preparing us for the fuller story of the God who in Jesus Christ seeks the outcasts and accepts those who know their need and acknowledge it.

The Good News for the Outsiders

The converse of this concern for the outcasts is the constant attack on the rich. This theme is also sounded in the hymns of the infancy stories:

> He has scattered the proud in the imagination of their hearts,
> he has put down the mighty from their thrones,
> and exalted those of low degree;
>
> He has filled the hungry with good things,
> and the rich he has sent empty away.
>
> —LUKE 1:51, 52

The opening theme of the programmatic sermon at Nazareth is the claim that "The Spirit of the Lord . . . has anointed me to preach good news to the poor." The word "poor" resounds throughout the Gospel of Luke. Instead of the religious designation in the beatitude recorded by Matthew, "Blessed are the poor in Spirit," Luke has simply, "Blessed are you poor" (6:20). Only in Luke's version of the Parable of the Great Supper is it explicitly stated that those who are brought into the feast after the group originally invited has declined are the "poor and maimed and blind and lame" (Lk. 14:21). The invitation is symbolic of the Gospel invitation to share in the joys of the Age to Come. The Jews to whom the invitation was originally extended have refused to come; the offer now goes out to the outcasts. Only in Luke do we hear of the rich Fool whose wealth is his sole ground of security (12:13-21) and of the wretched Lazarus, who enters the realm of the blessed while the rich man lingers in torment (16:19-31).

Although Luke shares with Matthew the tradition about the questioners who come from John the Baptist, in which Jesus points to the works of healing and the proclamation of good news to the poor as evidence of his mission (Mt. 11:5; Lk. 7:22), Luke alone develops the theme widely. At times this motif appears in the form of a modification of material used by the other evangelists. For example, Matthew and Mark report at the end of Jesus' public ministry the story of the woman who anointed him for burial. In Mt. 16:8 and Mk. 14:4, the disciples complain about the waste of money, which might better have been given to the poor. Jesus' famous reply is that the poor are always on hand, but that he will not be on hand for long. In Luke's version, however, the story has become an account of the pronouncement of forgiveness to an outcast, a woman who is a "sinner." She comes to him in a spirit of devotion, seeking nothing. He offers her forgiveness and salvation (Lk. 7:36-50, see especially 48, 50). No mention is made of anointing for burial, and the whole point of the incident centers on the forgiveness of sin even to the one who most obviously violates the moral and ceremonial laws of Judaism. Luke underscores this by locating the incident immediately following the report of the contrast between Jesus and John the Baptist, in which Jesus quotes his critics as calling him, "A glutton and a drunkard, a friend of tax collectors and sinners" (7:34).

The same note is sounded in the story, reported only by Luke, concerning Zacchaeus, the tax collector (Lk. 19:1-10). Once more, Jesus violates the Jewish laws of ceremonial purity by not merely having contact with a tax collector, but actually inviting himself to his house for a meal. As in the case of the woman who anointed him, Jesus announces that "salvation has this day come to his house." The story is rounded off by a saying in which Jesus epitomizes his redemptive program: "The Son of man has come to seek and to save that which is lost."

God Takes the Initiative toward the Outcasts

In these narratives, Luke is telling us that not only is God willing to *accept* those who are estranged from him and to forgive those who are grievous sinners, but that he is actively *seeking out* those who are far from him, whether Jews who were excluded from the life of the Covenant People or Gentiles who never had a part in the Covenant. Luke underscores this conviction in both narrative and discourse material. Nowhere has he set this forth more powerfully than in the three parables which he presents in sequence: the Lost Sheep, the Lost Coin, and the Lost Son (Lk. 15:1-32). The last two of these are found only in Luke, and the first appears in an expanded version (cf. Mt. 18:12-14). In each case, the title of the parable might well be changed to lay the stress on the joy of the one who has recovered what has been lost, thereby making the point of the parable the nature of God rather than the condition of the one who is lost. Accordingly, the parables would become the Joyous Shepherd, the Joyous Housewife, and the Joyous Father. The story of the rejoicing father is actually in two parts, with the second focused on the disgruntled older brother who refuses to welcome back his wayward brother. He will not even acknowledge him as his brother, preferring rather to refer to him as "that son of yours." Luke (or Jesus?) is here striking out against the critics of his message of God's grace by comparing them with the self-centered, unforgiving, graceless brother, just as Jesus rebukes those who condemn him for his forgiving attitude toward the sinful woman. Luke views Jesus as the foe of prideful moralism and as the spokesman for God, whose grace flows out to all who will acknowledge their need and receive that grace by faith.

The Outcasts Are Ready To Respond

The readiness of the Gentiles to accept the grace of God is indicated by the two illustrations that bring to a close Jesus' sermon in the synagogue at Nazareth. The only person who was miraculously fed during the famine in the time of Elijah was a Sidonian woman—that is, a Gentile. Similarly, only the Gentile leper, Naaman, was healed in the time of Elisha. The implication is that others do not benefit from the divine redemption available to them because they are not ready to receive it. If God's grace can evoke no response of faith in Israel, it will turn to the Gentiles.

As we noted earlier in this chapter, Luke anticipates the Gentile mission when he depicts Jesus as sending out the Seventy. This mission of the Seventy is in addition to the sending of the Twelve that Luke has taken over from his Markan source (9:1; cf. Mk. 6:6 ff.), and which Matthew has greatly expanded in his account of the mission of the disciples (Mt. 9:35-10:16). Perhaps Luke intends the sending of the Twelve to symbolize the initial mission of the Gospel to Israel, and the sending of the Seventy to represent the subsequent turning of the messengers of the Gospel to the nations of the world. The shift of attention from the mission to Israel to the world mission is specifically pronounced in Acts. In Antioch of Pisidia, where Paul and Barnabas have been evangelizing, the success of their efforts has aroused violent hostility from the Jewish community. The apostles' reaction to their attack is a turning point in Luke's description of the apostolic mission.

> And Paul and Barnabas spoke boldly and said: "It was necessary that the word of God should be spoken first to you. Since you thrust it from you, and judge yourselves unworthy of eternal life, behold, we turn to the Gentiles. For so the Lord has commended us saying, 'I have set you to be a light to the Gentiles, that you may bring salvation to the uttermost parts of the earth.'"
>
> —ACTS 13:46, 47

The belief that the Gospel was to be heard first by the Jews and then by Gentiles is not peculiar to Luke (cf. Rom. 1:16), but it is declared by him with unique clarity and persistence.

Going into All the World

Just as Luke's gospel begins with a sermonic program outlining the ministry of Jesus, so the Book of Acts begins with a program laid down by the risen Christ to be effected by the power of the Holy Spirit through the Church. The disciples—now to be styled *apostles*, or *sent ones*—are to bear witness to the Gospel of Jesus Christ; first in Jerusalem, then in all Judea, then in Samaria, and then to the end of the earth (Acts 1:8). It is appropriate that the witness begins in Jerusalem, since, as we have seen, Jerusalem is for Luke the place of revelation *par excellence*. The proclamation of the Gospel in Judea brings the message to the Jews, in keeping with the divinely ordained order ("the Jew first"). The shift to Samaria brings the opportunity to hear the good news of Jesus Christ to those who are alienated from Israel but who share a common heritage. [The Samaritans were a Semitic people who shared with Judaism the belief that the Law of Moses was the Word of God, although their version of it differed slightly from the accepted Jewish version. But their chief point of disagreement was on the place of worship (Mount Gerizim rather than Jerusalem), where they had their own priesthood distinct from the Jerusalem priesthood. Samaria was a kind of enclave within predominantly Jewish territory.] Once the preaching of the Gospel moved beyond the borders of Palestine, it would know no bounds until it reached the ends of the earth.

Luke does not merely set out the program, however: he describes the progress of the Gospel as it moves on toward what is at least a symbolic achievement of its goal. The first seven chapters of Acts depict the efforts of the apostles to proclaim the Good News in Jerusalem. Their work met with considerable success ("... and there were added that day [of Pentecost] about three thousand souls."—2:42), as well as with violent opposition. As a result, the disciples were imprisoned, interrogated, warned (4:17-22), beaten, and forbidden to speak in the name of Jesus Christ (5:40). The threats and punishments were ineffective, however, and the work of evangelism in Jerusalem is described by Luke as continuing until, following the belligerent speech of Stephen, the Jewish leadership had little choice but to launch a counterattack. In that speech Stephen denounced the nation as having never been ready to hear God's messengers when they came (7:51-53), including Jesus, whom they have murdered. In response, the authorities turn on the infant community; as a result of the great persecution which follows, the friends and co-workers of Stephen flee (8:1b).

That this scattering is symbolic of the spread of the Gospel rather than an historical occurrence in which the Jerusalem community was wholly dispersed is evident from Luke's own account, since he reports continuing activities of the apostles in Jerusalem down to the time of the arrest of Paul there (21:17 ff.). Jerusalem continues to be the base of operations for the evangelists even in this same chapter of Acts (8:14, 25). The victims of the persecution and the subsequent scattering seem to have been, not the original circle of 12 disciples, but men whom Luke refers to as "Hellenists" (6:1), all of whom bear Greek names. Their assigned rôle in the Church is that of "deacon," which means "servant" or "assistant" (6:2, 3). Although their original assignment is reported by Luke as caring for "tables" (that is, taking care of the menial and more secular aspects of the community's life), they very soon are engaged in preaching the Word of God. This is most obvious in the case of Stephen (Chapters 6, 7) and Philip (Chapter 8).

It would appear that Luke has reworked some traditional material in such a way as to document several convictions: (1) that the division in the Church between Jewish Christians and Gentile Christians was by agreement and divine intention rather than a result of conflict; (2) that the proclamation of the Gospel to non-Jews carried the full sanction of the Jerusalem community; and (3) that the death of Stephen was the divinely planned occasion for drawing

Saul (Paul) under the influence of the Gospel, thus preparing him for the distinctive rôle he was to play in the spread of the Gospel to the Gentiles. There is a splendid irony in the fact that it is Paul who leads the very persecution that results in launching the Gentile mission of the Church (8:3). Apart from a general description of himself as a persecutor of the Church (Gal. 1:13), we have no word of this from Paul, so that we cannot determine whether or not it may rest on historical fact. But it is used here by Luke in a fitting way to show how the work of God's Spirit proceeds not only in spite of, but by means of, human opposition (8:4).

The Progress of the Gospel

The spread of the Gospel to the end of the earth has been anticipated by Luke in his description of the Day of Pentecost. This is the case, not only in the symbolic significance of the tongues of fire (p. 306), but in the enumeration of the widely scattered lands from which the dispersion Jews have come (2:9, 10). Luke goes so far as to say that they were present "from every nation under heaven" (2:5). Luke depicts them as including (1) Jews who had moved to these lands and were returning for the feast; (2) Gentiles who, by accepting baptism and circumcision, had become proselytes, members of the covenant community; and (3) devout Gentiles who had come to participate in the Jewish festival. But here for Luke they represent the whole of humanity. All mankind will soon have opportunity to hear the Gospel, Luke is telling his reader; from the outset these representatives had opportunity to witness the power with which the Gospel goes forth. The miracle of simultaneous translation was itself enough to fill them with awe and to foreshadow the coming of the Gospel to every nation:

> "We hear them telling in our own tongues the mighty works of God."
> And all were amazed and perplexed, saying to one another, "What does this mean?"
>
> ACTS 2:11, 12

Luke is not content, however, merely to anticipate the world mission of the Church: he depicts each stage of its development. The first is of course the preaching to the crowds in Jerusalem, and especially in the Temple itself, the religious center of Judaism (3:11-26), and before the Sanhedrin, Judaism's chief governing body (5:27-32). Following the first persecution (8:1 ff.), the next stage is launched when Philip preaches the Gospel in Samaria with impressive results, Luke reports (8:4-8). Soon thereafter the Gospel moves to a wider circle when Acts recounts the conversion of an Ethiopian eunuch (8:26-40). According to the Mosaic Law, a eunuch could not have participated in the covenant worship (Deut. 23:1), but the term "eunuch" is often used of a powerful court figure, without any of the usual connotations of the word. The story is filled with miraculous movements and coincidences. That the Ethiopian official was prepared in advance to hear the Gospel is evidenced by his reading from the Jewish scriptures the Suffering Servant text from Is. 53, which Philip immediately interprets for him as a prophecy of Jesus Christ (8:33-35). This story must have originated in Hellenistic circles, perhaps connected with Philip the evangelist, whose daughters joined him in his work (21:9), but it has been worked over by Luke to serve the over-all objectives of his work. Here it paves the way for the Gentile mission, which begins in full force with the conversion of Cornelius (10:1-48).

The importance of this story for Luke is emphasized by the fact that it is first told (Chapter 10) and then retold (Chapter 11). What is significant is not only that the Gospel was heard and received by a non-Jew, but that God had placed his stamp of approval on this by sending his Spirit on the new believers (10:44). The point is reaffirmed (10:45), and then put in question form by Luke (through Peter) to any potential critic of the practice of evangelizing Gentiles: "Can anyone forbid water for baptizing these people who have received the Holy Spirit just as we have?" (10:47). The apostolic circle in Jerusalem, Luke reports, approved the evangelism and gave its sanction to the results (11:18): "Then to the Gentiles also God has granted repentance unto life."

Opening the Door of Faith to the Gentiles

For a century and a half, critical study of the New Testament has debated the question as to why Acts depicts Peter as the one through whom the Gentile mission is launched, while the letters of Paul give one the impression that he was the pioneer in this field. An ingenious solution which still exerts wide influence originated with the so-called Tübingen School of interpretation, which was under the domination of Hegel's philosophy of history. According to Hegel's theory, all history moves by the emergence of an idea (*thesis*) which evokes its opposite (*antithesis*); the conflict between the two continues until there emerges a third possibility (*synthesis*). By this view of history, Paul's Law-free Gospel is the thesis, and Peter's Jewish-legal understanding of Christianity is the antithesis: from it emerges the universal synthesis of catholic Christianity, of which Acts is a chief document.[9]

It is possible that at the basis of Luke's story is an historical tradition of an encounter of Peter with a Roman officer who became a Christian. It is difficult, however, to square the story as it is told, including all the divine sanctions for the conversion, with Peter's refusal to have table fellowship with Gentiles as

---

[9] For a summary of the view of the Tübingen School, see A. Schweitzer on F. C. Baur, in *Paul and His Interpreters* (London: A. and C. Black, 1912), pp. 12-21. For a critique of the view, see J. Munck, *Paul and the Salvation of Mankind* (Richmond, Va.: John Knox Press, 1960), pp. 69-86.

reported in Gal. 2. Luke, however, lays heavy stress on the reluctance of Peter to go along with the Gentile mission and on the necessity of repeated divine intervention in order to convince Peter to visit Cornelius; thereby Luke demonstrates to his reader that the decision to open the common life of the Church to all without forcing submission to the Jewish Law was not Peter's idea, nor Paul's, but God's.[10]

In the chapter following Peter's report to the apostolic circle, Luke describes another period of persecution—this time by the civil authority, Herod Agrippa I —and after a brief term of imprisonment, from which he is miraculously delivered, Peter disappears from Jerusalem and from the narrative of Acts. A possible exception is the inclusion of "Symeon" (= Peter?) in the Apostolic Council detailed in Acts 15. But Peter's main mission is fulfilled for Luke when he has broken down barriers and become the first agent of Gentile evangelism.

Meanwhile, the apostolic circle had commissioned a man named Barnabas to exercise authority in Antioch, which was becoming a center for a newly founded Christian community (11:19-26). As his co-worker, he chose Saul of Tarsus, whose conversion had proved something of an embarrassment to the Jerusalem church (9:1-30). After effective evangelism in Antioch, Paul and Barnabas went on an evangelistic tour of Cyprus and southern and central Asia Minor (Chapters 13 and 14). Their procedure in each town was to preach first among the Jews, and then, when opposition was encountered, to turn to the Gentiles (14:27).

But not everyone at Antioch was pleased with the results of Paul's work, Luke tells us. Certain persons from Jerusalem (whether official inspectors or self-appointed busybodies is not stated) came to Antioch insisting that obedience to the precepts of Mosaic Law was necessary for participation in the life of the Christian community. Superficially, at least, this sounds like the situation of which Paul writes in Gal. 1 and 2. According to Acts 15 and Galatians, it was decided to have Paul and Barnabas go to Jerusalem to work out a settlement of a disagreement over the proper basis for admitting Gentiles to the church. Closer examination, however, shows that the consultation in Acts 15 and the one described by Paul in Galatians can scarcely be the same. In Acts, the meeting in Jerusalem is a kind of public hearing, at which the entire community (15:12) is present and listens to the verdicts handed down by the leaders of the apostolic circle. Paul makes a point in Gal. 2:2 that the conversation was a private one, with "those who were of repute." Titus is present in Paul's account; he is not mentioned in Acts. Even more striking is the difference between the agreement reached according to Acts and the one referred to by Paul in Gal. 2:10. According to Paul, it was agreed that he and his associates would carry on the evangelism of the Gentiles, while the Jerusalem group would restrict itself to work among Jews. The only further requirement was that Paul, and

---

[10] So Martin Dibelius, in *Studies in the Acts of the Apostles* (London: SCM Press, 1956), p. 122.

presumably the churches established by him, were to "remember the poor." This seems to be a reference to the practice attested to in the two preserved letters to the Corinthians by which the Gentile churches collected and submitted an offering to the Jerusalem church (see pp. 157, 189 for a discussion of the collection).

THE "APOSTOLIC DECREES." In Acts, however, Paul agrees to communicate to the Gentile churches the so-called "apostolic decrees." These were four: (1) abstinence from idolatry; (2) abstinence from blood—that is, from food containing blood and therefore unclean by Jewish dietary rules; (3) abstinence from eating animals that had been killed by strangling, again in accord with Jewish food laws; (4) abstinence from unchastity. In one group of New Testament manuscripts known as the Western text the words "and from things strangled" are omitted while others add a form of the Golden Rule. This allows for an interpretation of the three remaining requirements as strictly moral rather than cultic or dietary. "Blood" would be interpreted as a decree against committing murder. This would ease the problem somewhat by saving us from having to assume that Paul agreed to certain legalistic food laws as being prerequisite to acceptance into the family of faith. But even with the three rules, we are left with the sense that Paul must have compromised his teaching of justification by faith if he agreed to these laws for admission to Church membership. Although he would not have condoned such practices as were here forbidden in the churches under his care, it would have clouded the issue of faith to have held these particular rules up as prerequisite to accepting the Gospel of grace. Some scholars have conjectured that Paul agreed to these rules, but never sought to enforce them among the Gentile Christians; others have proposed that he made the simpler agreement reported in Galatians first and then accepted the more stringent rules later.

THE "NOAHIC" LAWS. It would appear that Acts 15 and Galatians are simply incompatible, so that Paul could not have accepted two such contradictory sets of regulations. Perhaps the clue to this difficulty is to be found in the correspondence between the fourfold requirement of Acts (in the non-Western text) and the way in which Judaism understood the force of the decrees connected with the Covenant of Noah in Gen. 9:1 ff. These Noahic laws were considered by first-century Judaism to be binding on all humanity, rather than as especially enjoined on Israel alone. The regulations of Acts 15 would be one version of the minimal requirements for Gentiles if they were to remain in God's good favor. Some scholars think they find a further trace of these "decrees" in Rev. 2:20-23. But it appears that Luke has included them here because he thought they were appropriate, not because he found them in a document reporting the decision reached at any Apostolic Council. The actual decision between Paul and the Jerusalem church was the one reported by Paul in Gal. 2; the decisions described in Acts 15 were written at a time when the tensions between Jewish and Gentile Christians had subsided—and, one might conjecture, after the full force of Paul's doctrine of justification by faith had been eclipsed by an end-of-the-first-century surge of moralistic Christianity, such as we see in James and other late New Testament books. For Luke, this council marks an important turning point in his story: the leadership of the Jerusalem church has passed from the apostles to the elders. Probably "Symeon" is Peter, but he is no longer the leader of the group; that role has been assumed by James, the brother of Jesus. Luke is showing that there was a common agreement and a unified set of ground rules by which the Church everywhere would from that time on operate. But already the center of attention for Luke has shifted from the historical and eschatological center in Jerusalem to the spread of the Gospel among the Gentile cities, culminating in Rome.[11]

THE CENTER OF ACTS.   The story of the conversion of Cornelius marks the center of the book, both in the aim of the author and in amount of material.[12] From that point on, Luke is interested in showing how the Gospel evoked faith among the Gentiles, first in the cities of Asia Minor, then on the mainland of Europe (Acts 16). Each step along the way is taken by divine hindrance (16:7) or divine call (16:9). None of the many civil authorities before whom Paul and his associates are brought can find anything worthy of punishment. The movement, Luke is telling his readers, is the work of God and is not in conflict with the laws of man. Whether it be in a jail (16:24 ff.), before the venerable Athenian court of manners and morals known as the Areopagus,[13] or at a public hearing before a Roman proconsul (18:12 ff.), Paul has an appropriate word from God. There are none, of whatever origin or station in life, who are to be denied an opportunity to hear the Gospel. And from every stratum there is a faithful response, whether from a jailer (16:34) or an Areopagite (17:34). Paul's preaching is varied in approach, ranging from capitalizing on the jailer's terror to quoting Greek poets before the members of the Areopagus. Paul's faithfulness in his mission provides him with opportunities to preach the Word before the rulers of the Greek cities, the territories of Palestine, the Jewish authorities, and finally in the city of Rome itself. In capsule form, the whole sweep of the world mission of the Church is discernible in the work of Paul and his aides. Its symbolic consummation is represented in his stay in Rome, where he is able to proclaim the Gospel of the kingdom, preaching about Jesus Christ without restraint (Acts 28:31). It is on this joyous note that the twofold work of Luke-Acts ends, even though Luke has given us full notice of the impending death of Paul (Acts 20:17-38).

---

[11] A full statement on the details of Acts 15, on the history of its interpretation and critical judgments concerning the historical elements in Luke's account, are to be found in E. Haenchen's *Die Apostelgeschichte* (Göttingen: Vandenhoeck & Ruprecht, 1959), pp. 396-414.

[12] Haenchen, *op. cit.*, pp. 305-308.

[13] Meaning "Hill of Mars." Originally the court met on this hill, overlooking the agora or market place. Later it met in its own building, though we cannot tell where Luke understood it to have met on the occasion he describes.

Before turning to consider the value of Acts for our knowledge of Paul, let us examine more fully the content of the early Christian preaching as we see it reproduced in Acts. Does it give us direct access to the way that the very first apostles preached?

EARLY CHRISTIAN PREACHING
ACCORDING TO ACTS

Even a casual reading of the brief sermon summaries that Luke has included in the Book of Acts will show the reader how different they are in theological perspective from Paul or even Mark. Although both Paul and Mark have their own distinctive features, they join in stressing the importance of the death of Jesus. For Paul, the death on the Cross is the central theme of his message, even though it is always closely linked with the Resurrection. The kerygmatic summary in I Cor. 15:3-6, or the hymn of Phil. 2, will show this clearly enough. But both the theological emphases and the terminology of the sermons in Acts are decidedly non-Pauline—even in the case of the sermons attributed to Paul (Acts 13:16-41; 14:15-18; 17:22-31). Furthermore, there is no real difference between the sermons of Peter and the sermons of Paul in Acts, in spite of Paul's acknowledgment in Gal. 1 and 2 of the great tensions and disagreements between them. Two questions confront us: What is the unity which links these sermons? And to what source should this unity be traced?

The following themes appear in the sermon summaries of Acts:

(1) Jesus is from the posterity of David.

(2) Jesus' ministry was approved by God, as may be inferred from the mighty acts which Jesus performed through the Holy Spirit.

(3) The Jews put Jesus to death, and, without realizing it, thus fulfilled the scriptures which point to his suffering.

(4) Gentiles ought to recognize God's concern for them in that his divine provisions for their needs are everywhere apparent.

(5) God has placed his stamp of approval on Jesus by raising him from the dead on the third day after his burial. Now God has exalted him and through him has sent the Holy Spirit. ·

(6) All men are called to repent and to receive salvation through the name of Jesus, who is destined to be the Judge of mankind.

The Acts Sermons and the Pauline Kerygma

While not all these themes appear in all the sermons, and other themes are to be found that have not been listed here, these are the recurrent motifs that Luke has reported in his accounts of the early Christian preaching. A most significant omission from this list is the interpretation of the death of Christ as somehow related to the forgiveness of sins. Nowhere does Peter or Paul say in Acts: Christ died *for our sins.* Yet this is paramount in Pauline theology. Attempts have been made by New Testament scholars to find a substratum of common affirmation behind the Acts sermons on the one hand and Paul on the other.[14] Except for the importance of the Resurrection as God's demonstration of his approval of the humiliated and crucified Jesus, there is no real identity. And even the Resurrection receives a different interpretation in Paul from the one given it in these sermons. For Paul it is the ground of man's justification as well as the basis of his hope of participation in the Age to Come (Rom. 4:25; I Cor. 15:20-22), whereas in Acts the Resurrection is the exaltation of the rejected Christ, by which he remains at God's right hand until the time has come for his work as Judge of all humanity.

The appearance in these sermons of certain unusual terms, such as the reference to Jesus in Acts 4:30 as "thy Holy Child," has led some interpreters to assume that we have here archaic theological language, antedating the more sophisticated terminology, for example, of Paul. Luke's use of rather awkward turns of expression in his otherwise smooth Greek narrative, especially in these early chapters of Acts, led others to the conclusion that Luke was utilizing an Aramaic source, which he had rendered into Greek.[15] But as we have already remarked (p. 303), the language of Luke-Acts is influenced by that of the Septuagint, which was of course the Bible of the Greek-speaking early Church for which Luke was writing and in which he was likely reared. As for the archaic theological terms, H. J. Cadbury has warned us:

> There is danger of arguing in a circle, since our ideas of early Christianity, with which the speeches in Acts are said to conform so exactly, are derived in large part from those very speeches.[16]

The sermons in Acts, it would appear, are not to be considered as evidence for the earliest Christian preaching, though one cannot exclude the possibility that there are some reflections of older kerygmatic tradition included in them. Rather, they are to be regarded as having been composed in the same manner used by historians roughly contemporary with Luke, who attributed speeches to various figures in their historical narrative. Whether the historian wrote

---

[14] The classic statement of the position that finds in Paul and the Acts sermons evidence for a pre-Pauline common *kerygma* is given by C. H. Dodd, in *The Apostolic Preaching and its Development in the New Testament* (New York: Harper & Row, 1951). A vigorous critique of this theory is given by C. F. Evans, in "The Kerygma," Journal of Theological Studies, N.S., VII, 1956, 25-41.

[15] This theory was propounded by C. C. Torrey in *The Composition and Date of Acts* (Cambridge: Harvard University Press, 1916). A more cautious assessment of the evidence is to be found in M. Black, *An Aramaic Approach to the Gospels and Acts* (Oxford: Clarendon Press, 1946).

[16] H. J. Cadbury, *The Beginnings of Christianity*, V, ed. F. J. Foakes-Jackson and K. Lake (London: Macmillan, 1933), 416.

about his own contemporaries or whether he wrote of a distant past to which he no longer had direct access, much less reliable documents, he saw his task as composing the speeches in such a way as to serve the over-all purpose of his book. There was an obligation to write the speeches so as to convey what the author deemed appropriate to the occasion he was describing.[17] What the author considered fitting was determined not by "what really happened," as a naive modern student of history might put it, but by what he thought the events meant. The fact that the speeches attributed to Paul do not correspond with the vocabulary and theological perspectives that we find in Paul's own letters would not in itself mean that Luke was not the companion of Paul and did not have access to Pauline material. It would signify only that Luke's purpose in setting forth his grand design of the divine plan of salvation, working out in history under the guidance of the Spirit, was better served by what Luke wrote for Paul than it would have been by direct quotations from Paul himself. The content and the unity of the speeches is to be derived from Luke's consistent point of view set forth in both volumes of his work, and not from his faithful reproduction of a particular way of proclaiming the kerygma that was shared by all the apostles. Even if there were such uniformity among the apostles, we should not be warranted in inferring it from the reports of the sermons in Acts. Luke's skillful literary method would have smoothed over the differences in serving his wider objective. The Acts sermons show us, therefore, not necessarily what the apostles preached, but what Luke thought they ought to have preached. The question remains, however: If Luke was so free in creating speeches for Paul and the other apostles, how much credence can we place in his account of Paul's travels and ministry?

ACTS AS A SOURCE FOR THE LIFE OF PAUL

We have already seen that both in regard to his speeches and to the Apostolic Council in Jerusalem, Luke has created material that serves his purpose rather than limiting himself to repeating whatever authentic information was available to him. Does this mean that Acts is worthless as an historical source? It does mean that for many of the historical questions to which we should like answers, Acts provides no information. But, in keeping with the conventions of the time, Luke does provide us in both Luke and Acts with references to contemporary incidents or persons by which we can ascertain the relative time of the events he is describing. This is most notably the case in the famous synchronism of Lk. 3:1, 2, where Luke ties in the beginning of the ministry of John the Baptist

---

[17] See the discussion of the style of speech writing among Hellenistic and Roman historians in H. J. Cadbury, *The Making of Luke-Acts* (London: S.P.C.K., 1961), pp. 184 ff. Also see the chapter on "The Speeches in Acts and Ancient Historiography" in M. Dibelius, *Studies in the Acts of the Apostles* (London: SCM Press, 1956), pp. 138-185.

with the reigns of various rulers in the eastern end of the empire. There are some historical difficulties involved in it,[18] but it does provide us a useful basis for establishing a relative chronology of the life of Jesus. That is, according to this chronology, Jesus would have begun his ministry in the year 26/27 or 27/28. Sinilarly, the references to pagan rulers in Acts have given us a fixed point: the accession to the governorship of Gallio, the Roman proconsul of Corinth in A.D. 52 (see pp. 158-159).

Paul's Itinerary and the Sources of Acts

It would appear further that Luke had access to a travel itinerary of Paul which he used as the basis for the Pauline section of Acts. It has been proposed that those sections of Acts in which Luke shifts from the customary third person plural to the first person plural of the narrative indicate the author's use of a travel diary. The account begins, "They went down to Troas" (Acts 16:8); but while referring to the same group, the writer without warning changes person to include himself: "We sought to go on to Macedonia" in 16:10. Some have thought that Luke joined Paul at this point, especially since the "we" passages are resumed when Paul returns to Troas on a later journey (20:5). There is no difference in literary style or in vocabulary between the "we" sections and the rest of Acts, so that we can be sure the author has reworked the whole carefully to suit his purposes. But the feeling that the events are being reported by an eyewitness is surely heightened by the "we" sections; further, there is no compelling reason to deny that a companion of Paul—perhaps Luke [19] —composed the whole, utilizing his own notes.

Although it has been proposed that Acts ends inconclusively because it was written before Paul's trial was over,[20] it is more likely that it ends as it does because the Gospel has by Acts 28 achieved the goal of being freely proclaimed in Rome, the capital of the Gentile world. The author of Acts does not leave us in any uncertainty as to the ultimate fate of Paul, however; the touching story of Paul's farewell to the elders from the church at Ephesus (20:17-38) makes it clear that Paul is to die for his testimony to the faith. The language of the valedictory speech of Paul uses terms and envisages situations in the Church which correspond to the post-Pauline era and which have their closest parallel in such deutero-Pauline writings as the Pastorals. This is especially noticeable in 20:28-30. Accordingly, we may infer that Luke has written the history of Paul and the beginnings of the Church at some time after the events which he is describing. The changed situation in which he finds himself is re-

---

[18] See the discussion in H. J. Cadbury, *The Making of Luke-Acts* (London: S.P.C.K., 1961), pp. 204-209. The difficulties are treated more fully by J. M. Creed in *The Gospel According to St. Luke* (London: Macmillan, 1930), pp. 48-50.

[19] So M. Dibelius, *Studies* (London: SCM Press, 1956), p. 104.

[20] According to A. Harnack, *Neue Untersuchungen zur Apostelgeschichte und zur Abfassungszeit der synoptischen Evangelien* (Leipzig: J. G. Hinrichs, 1911), pp. 63-114.

flected in the way he depicts the earlier state of affairs, but it also provides perspective on the meaning of what has occurred. If we assume, as it appears we must, that he is writing after the apostolic generation has passed, we can understand why the eschatological note, which is so dominant in Paul's letters, is muted here in Acts. What Luke has done, then, is not consciously to distort the history of Paul, but to place it in a wider setting of the overarching redemptive purpose of God, which is the main concern of his entire work.

THE ENDURING CONTRIBUTION OF LUKE

We are now in a position to evaluate what Luke has done. It is true that he has given us nearly all the information we have about the historical beginnings of the Church, even though we should like to have more details and to have them placed in a framework more suitable for modern historical inquiry. Specifically he has given us some additional information about Paul which we could not infer from Paul's letters and which we cannot evaluate historically: *e.g.*, his residence in Tarsus, his education under Gamaliel. But Luke's chief contribution is a theological one: he provided a perspective of meaning for the Church and its mission which enabled the Christian community to survive what might have been a fatal crisis in the nonfulfillment of the expectation of the *parousia*.

Paul has reckoned with a delay in the *parousia* (Phil. 1:23 ff.; II Thess. 2:3 ff.). Matthew's gospel had provided regulations for the Church's life (Mt. 5-7; 18), but there was no broad framework for comprehending the meaning of the Church in the long-range purpose of God. It was this need that Luke so brilliantly filled, by showing that the redemptive work promised in the holy scriptures and begun by the earthly Jesus was to be carried out under the power of the Holy Spirit through the Church. The *parousia* was still to come, and the judgment that would occur then was a solemn matter for all mankind. But its urgency was not so great, since the groundwork of redemption was already accomplished by the One who was seated at God's right hand. The carrying forth of the Gospel and the manifestation of redemptive power was the task of the Church, but God had already acted through the apostles to see that work to completion in principle, with the progress of the Gospel from Jerusalem to Rome. Even now his Spirit was at work in the Church to bring it to consummation throughout the world.

There are a number of questions which Acts hints at, but does not really formulate, much less answer. We feel as we read this book that there must have been a tension between the young Church and the Roman State, and that the author is trying to speak to that problem at least indirectly. He takes care to show that every time Jesus or his later followers were brought before civil authorities, there was no charge that could be made to stick against them. The tensions between Judaism and Christianity, of which we learn from Church historians and which are reflected in the oral traditions from this period later included in the rabbinic writings, are hinted at but not directly depicted. Luke is content to lay stress on the shift of focus of the Gospel from the Jew to the Gentile. One suspects, however, that the issue of the theological and institutional relationships between Judaism and Christianity was still a live one in the time that Acts was being written. Most clearly of all, the Church in Luke's day seems to have been struggling with the problem of changing from a free-moving evangelistic enterprise to a settled institution. Some scholars have seen in Acts a giant step in the direction of catholic or universal Christianity, as over against the local areas of the Church which continued to honor the apostle who had founded work there, and which followed the lead of his interests and emphases. Acts is surely concerned to stress the oneness of the Church and the common Gospel that is and ought everywhere to be proclaimed. In the later books of the New Testament, described in the following chapters, we see how these problems that lie just beneath the surface in Acts were dealt with more directly.

THE COMMUNITY
OF THE SPIRIT

John

CHAPTER FOURTEEN   It is a striking fact that the Gospel of John, one of the most profound and distinctive writings in the New Testament, poses more enigmatic problems than any other gospel writing. Earlier discussions of the origins and sources of the gospels have already pointed to problems; we must now focus our attention on some of the issues which have summarily been called "the Johannine Problem."

The question of authorship is sharply debated, although as early as the second century A.D. the writing was attributed to the apostle John, the son of Zebedee. An equally ancient tradition designates Ephesus, where John was supposed to have lived to an advanced age, to be its place of origin. This has also been challenged, and alternative cases have been made for Alexandria, and Antioch in Syria. While the weight of evidence inclines toward the Ephesian provenance, the identity of the author is uncertain.[1] It is possible that the author was indebted to traditions which indirectly derived from the apostle John, and a number of scholars maintain this position.

Even the text of the writing raises baffling questions. The gospel seems to reach a satisfactory conclusion at 20:31, but then another chapter follows. Chapter 21 serves principally to enhance the status of Peter and predict his death (21:15-19); it also intends to correct a mistaken notion on the part of some that the "disciple whom Jesus loved," an enigmatic figure who is mentioned but not named in the gospel, was not going to die until Christ's return (21:20-23). It appears that the last chapter also serves to identify this figure as the author of the gospel, which is one reason many believe that Chapter 21 is the addition of a later hand. Its presence has opened the door wider in the search for evidences of an editorial hand. The strange fact that certain sections of the gospel seem out of place—for example, Chapter 5 ends with Jesus in Jerusalem, while at the beginning of Chapter 6 he crosses the Sea of Galilee— has led to theories of editorial rearrangement. Numerous dislocations of the text and editorial touches [2] have been proposed, but the wide divergence in reconstructions testifies to their uncertainty.

JOHN AND THE SYNOPTIC GOSPELS: SIMILARITIES AND DIFFERENCES

One baffling problem concerns the relation of John to the three synoptic gospels: there are such obvious similarities and startling differences. In agreement with the Synoptics, John introduces the ministry of Jesus with an account of John the Baptist. The gospel contains familiar stories found in one or more of the Synoptics: these include the Cleansing of the Temple, the Feeding of the 5,000, the Stilling of the Storm, the Anointing of Jesus, the Last Supper, the Triumphal Entry into Jerusalem, the Hearings before the Jewish religious authorities and Pilate, the Crucifixion. In addition to these specific parallels there are numerous passages containing possible allusions to the Synoptics.

---

[1] For a discussion of authorship see C. K. Barrett, *The Gospel According to St. John* (London: S.P.C.K., 1955), pp. 83-119.

[2] One of the commonly acknowledged evidences of editorial work is found in the contradictory statement at 4:1-2.

But the differences between John and the Synoptics are more striking than the similarities. In the first place, even where John presents parallel material his version shows marked verbal variations. John sometimes has a different chronology of events. For example, the Cleansing of the Temple comes at the beginning of Jesus' ministry rather than toward the close, where the Synoptics place it. He has both the Last Supper and the death of Jesus take place a day earlier than in the Synoptics. In John the ministry of Jesus lasts about three years rather than the one year implied in the Synoptics. John also locates Jesus' ministry mainly in Jerusalem and Judea, as over against its Galilean orientation in the Synoptics.

There are notable differences in the form and content of Jesus' words. The parable, similes, and crisp sayings so characteristic of the Synoptics are missing; in their place are long discourses and dialogues on recurring themes. These are not the familiar themes of the Synoptics: righteousness, forgiveness, the coming of the kingdom, the apocalyptic Coming of the Son of Man, urgent calls to preparation and watchfulness. John pursues such themes as eternal life, light, darkness, blindness, sight, glory, truth. He prefers symbolical language, and often gives words and events a double meaning. In two series of sayings, one introduced by the words "I am," and the other by the words, "Verily, verily, I say unto you," Jesus makes striking pronouncements about himself and his mission. He explicitly affirms he is the Son of God in terms strange to the Synoptics. The greater part of John has no parallels in the Synoptics.

In explaining these similarities and differences, contemporary scholarship is in sharp disagreement. Some scholars account for the similarities on the basis of the author's knowledge of the Synoptics—at least, Mark and Luke—in written form. Others believe he was not acquainted with written gospels but did have access to certain oral traditions which later found their way into the written synoptic gospels. In recent years it has been argued that John differs so decidedly from the Synoptics that he could not have used them.[3] A strong argument has been made for the case that John was dependent on sources which developed quite independent from the Synoptic tradition.[4] Attention has been called to the Judean or southern Palestinian orientation of much in his gospel. This has been seen as persuasive evidence that John had access to sources which derived from southern Palestine.

Two serious problems confront the discussion of sources in John. In the first place, it is generally acknowledged that there is a common language, style, and theology which is present throughout the gospel. If the author has utilized sources, in varying degrees they now bear the marks of the author's interpreta-

---

[3] A thesis first developed by P. Gardner Smith, *Saint John and the Synoptic Gospels* (Cambridge: Cambridge University Press, 1938).

[4] See the thorough study of C. H. Dodd, *Historical Tradition in the Fourth Gospel* (Cambridge: Cambridge University Press, 1963).

tive language and thought. Because of this it is possible to speak of the unity of the gospel as a whole. But any effort to penetrate to supposed sources faces frustrating obstacles. Just how John utilized his sources is a question which has not been fully answered. This leads to the second and closely related problem, that of determining the extent to which the content of John is to be accounted for by his own creative theological imagination. Scholars vary in their estimates; to the extent that the scope is diminished, the greater the necessity to search for sources. The debate over John's relation to the Synoptics and his non-Synoptic sources is one of the most hotly contested of the problems posed by John.

THE RELIGIOUS BACKGROUND OF JOHN

The question of the background of John's religious thought has also prompted divergent opinions. In the late nineteenth and early twentieth centuries it was quite common to stress the strong influence of the Hellenistic mystery religions on John. His language of union with Christ, the centrality of eternal life and rebirth, and his sacramental teaching all were believed to have derived from this source. The emphasis later shifted to a Gnostic environment. One of the foremost proponents of this view proposed that portions of the Prologue and a large body of the sayings in the gospel derived from Gnostic circles, although the author of the gospel Christianized their meaning when he incorporated them.[5] Integral to this interpretation is the hypothesis that John was also influenced by a Gnostic myth of a divine redeemer who came from heaven to reveal to man the way of salvation. The major sources for the reconstruction of such a background are the writings of the Mandaeans [6] (see pp. 18, 19). While the earliest sections of the literature in its present form date from the seventh or eighth century, it is dependent on traditions which emerged as early as the first century. The major debate centers on the question of the nature of these earlier traditions, and particularly on whether or not there existed a pre-Christian redeemer myth of the alleged type. Other scholars have preferred to find the Gnostic-like background of John in the religious thought of the Hermetic literature.[7] This literature, dating from the third or fourth century A.D., derives from earlier traditions emerging in Egypt. While the question of influence is contested, one of the striking features of both the Mandaean and Hermetic literatures is the similarity to the style of portions of John. It seems necessary to

---

[5] The reference is to Rudolf Bultmann, *Das Evangelium des Johannes* (Göttingen: Vandenhoeck & Ruprecht, 1956). Unfortunately this major work has not been translated. For a discussion of Bultmann's source analysis see Robert M. Grant, *Historical Introduction to the New Testament* (New York: Harper & Row, 1963), pp. 160-162.

[6] For a discussion of this sect see C. H. Dodd, *The Interpretation of the Fourth Gospel* (Cambridge: Cambridge University Press, 1953), pp. 115-130.

[7] *Ibid.*, pp. 10-53, for a discussion of the Hermetic literature.

assume that John was influenced by a style common to his Hellenistic environment, whatever is said regarding the extent of his incorporation of sources.

Many scholars have laid a major emphasis upon the Jewish background in John. His obvious dependence on the Old Testament and on apocryphal literature, and his knowledge of rabbinical modes of interpretation [8] clearly point to the importance of the Jewish orientation of his thought. Interest in the Jewish background has received a new impetus with the discovery of the Qumran Scrolls.[9] Attention has been called to the dualistic language common to both, such as the contrast between light and darkness, truth and falsehood. It has been pointed out that John's dualistic view is much closer to the eschatological dualism of the Qumran sect (see pages 41-51) than the more metaphysical dualism of Hellenistic thought, especially Gnostic thought in some of its varieties. A further point of comparison are certain phrases common to John and the Scrolls: for example, "the spirit of truth," "sons of light," "do the truth."

THE DATE AND PURPOSE OF JOHN

The discussion of the background of John's religious thought has played a role not only in the interpretation of the writing, but also in the determination of its date and purpose. Scholars who have stressed the Hellenistic environment have tended to date the writing toward the end of the first century (A.D. 90-100); they have seen it as a missionary effort to communicate the Christian message in language and thought forms familiar to the Hellenistic world. Others have seen it as a defense against Gnostic distortions of the Christian faith. More recently, on the basis of similarities between John and the Qumran Scrolls, some have argued for a much earlier date of composition. Two of the problems confronting those who argue for an early date—for example, before the Gospel of Mark—have been, first, providing a convincing purpose for which the author wrote, and second, accounting for his use of the gospel form. The first problem has recently received a novel solution. It has been argued [10] that John wrote for a missionary purpose, but not the conversion of Gentiles. Rather, he wrote for the purpose of converting unbelieving Jews of the Diaspora synagogue. This position, which has not received sufficient critical consideration, seems to raise more problems than it solves.

---

[8] See Dodd, *The Interpretation of the Fourth Gospel*, pp. 74-96.

[9] There is now a large body of literature on the subject. For example, see Raymond E. Brown, S.S., "The Qumran Scrolls and the Johannine Gospel and Epistles," in *The Scrolls and the New Testament*, ed. Krister Stendahl (New York: Harper & Row, 1957), pp. 183-207.

[10] See John A. T. Robinson, *Twelve New Testament Studies* (Naperville, Ill.: Alec R. Allenson, Inc., 1962), pp. 107-125. Also, W. C. Van Unnik, "The Purpose of St. John's Gospel," in *Studia Evangelica*, LXXIII, ed. Kurt Aland, *et al.*, *Texte und Untersuchungen* (Berlin: Akademie Verlag, 1959), 282-411.

ASSUMPTIONS CONCERNING JOHN AND HIS GOSPEL

Whatever position is taken in answer to the questions of the nature of John's sources, the extent of his creative contribution, and the background, date, and purpose of his writing must be assumed in recognition of the diversity of opinions in contemporary studies. That John had some knowledge of the synoptic tradition, written or oral (the present authors assume knowledge of Mark and Luke), and also of non-synoptic tradition, seems a necessary assumption in the present state of study. While his thought is deeply rooted in Judaism and the Christian tradition, Hellenistic influences (even Gnostic influences) cannot be denied; they probably have been mediated through the author's Hellenistic Jewish environment. It seems certain that he was a Jew nurtured in the Judaism of the Diaspora synagogue. It is probable that the type of thought reflected in the Qumran Scrolls had influenced this environment. But there is no certain basis for claiming direct borrowing. There are more differences than likenesses between John and the Scrolls. Concerning the date of the writing, older arguments for a late date, such as the author's use of the Synoptics in written form, and the belief that his view of Christ (his concern and explicit language relating Jesus to God) reflects a later development, no longer carry the weight they once did.

There is one aspect of John's thought which may provide a clue to both his date and his purpose in writing. One of the principal features of the gospel is its stress on the presence of Christ and eternal life to and for the community of believers. In his obvious emphasis on these truths, the expectation of the Coming of Christ and the consummation of the kingdom appear subordinate. It may be that John, like Matthew and Luke, spoke to that problem which confronted the Christian community when the expected Coming of Christ failed to find fulfillment in the apocalyptic sense. At least, the burden of proof rests upon those who would find in the period before A.D. 70 a place for such a radical modification of the apocalyptic language and hopes of the Christian community. In stating his purpose John writes, ". . . but these are written that you may believe that Jesus is the Christ, the Son of God, and that believing you may have life in his name."—(20:31).

It has normally been argued that the words in the first part of the statement necessitate the assumption that John wrote mainly for nonbelievers. However, in one sense all the gospels were written to the Church to strengthen its belief in, and understanding of, Jesus as Christ and Son of God. Perhaps not enough attention has been given to the last phrase, "you may have life in his name." If equal stress is given to these words, then John would have written to the Christian community for the purpose of stressing that to believe in Jesus Christ means having life *now*. On the basis of an interpretation that differed from

Matthew and Luke, like them he sought to lead Christians to an understanding of their relation to Christ and the world at a time when the failure of Christ's expected return constituted a major problem for faith. Such a time would certainly have been after the fall of Jerusalem (A.D. 70), in the period A.D. 75-100.

This later date would also be supported by John's attitude toward the Jews. It has long been argued that his attitude reflects the hostility between Christianity and the synagogue after A.D. 70. The fact that the argument over the Law has been largely superseded by the conflict over the person of Jesus, especially his relation to God (or the divinity of Jesus), likewise suits the later period. Like Matthew and Luke, John may also be dealing with the problem of the relation of Christianity to Judaism. With them he acknowledges the Jewish roots of Jesus and the Church ("salvation is from the Jews"—4:22), but he goes much further in stressing the intensity of the Jewish rejection, and the contrast between the old and the new. Writing from the standpoint of one who had seen the Gentiles acknowledge the truth which the Jews had rejected, he interpreted the story of Jesus as the revelation of the "Savior of the world" (4:42) whose coming marked the end of the old and the beginning of the new.

However, John undoubtedly had more than one or two purposes in writing. Not least, he wanted to write a theological interpretation of the life, death, and resurrection of Jesus. Though he makes use of the gospel as a literary form, his main concern is not to repeat the story of the ministry of Jesus as found in the Synoptics or any other traditions he might have possessed. He aims to *reinterpret* the ministry in the light of his faith that Jesus was the eternal Son of God. And so it is that Jesus speaks and acts as the divine Son of God throughout the gospel. John assumes that his readers are familiar with the ministry of Jesus, and then proceeds to reinterpret the words and deeds of Jesus as remembered in the traditions, in order to discover their deeper meaning. This is an important point for the modern reader to keep in mind, for at first glance John's use of the gospel form suggests that he meant simply to record events, rather than to present an interpretation of those events.

THE PROLOGUE OF THE GOSPEL OF JOHN

John begins with a Prologue that sets forth the subject of his gospel (1:1-18)— namely, the Word of God (1:1-5). This is the Word that was with God from the beginning and through which all things were created and life was given to man. And this life, in turn, is the light that alone dispels the darkness of the world, the light to which John the Baptist had borne witness. But when the light of God came to "his own" (the Jews), many of them rejected him (1:10). Yet some of them received him and believed in him; to these Jews was given the power to become children of God (1:12). It was not, however, because they were earthly descendants of the Jewish people that they became children of God; rather, it was by an act of God's will. And God's will was accomplished when his Word became flesh and lived as a man among men (1:14), thereby revealing the "only Son" from the Father. Everyone who shared the "fullness" of Jesus' Sonship with those who believed in him also became children of God. Moses had given the Law, but it is only through the Son, Jesus Christ, that God's grace and truth are revealed. Since only the Son has seen the Father, only he can reveal the grace and truth through which men become children of God.

In short, then, John announces in his Prologue that he is going to tell his readers how God brought into being a new community through his only Son, Jesus Christ, through whom his life-giving Word was revealed. And he is also going to explain how the Jews' rejection of Christ was paralleled by the Gentiles' acceptance of Christ.

The terminology of the Prologue reveals how close John's religious thought was to that of the Hellenistic world in which he lived. For example, he describes the world as a place of darkness into which men are born and from which they can escape only by being born anew by one who brings light and truth from the divine world (Jn. 3). Immediately we are reminded of the Hellenistic practice of dividing reality into two realms of existence—the divine realm of light, truth, and life, and the lower world of darkness, falsehood, and death (see discussion, pp. 10 ff.). Apart from the language of rebirth, and the "only Son," it also bears resemblance to the dualistic language of the Qumran Scrolls, as we have already noted.

And yet John differs from Hellenistic religious thought in important respects. In the first place, he modifies the absolute distinction between the realm of light and the realm of darkness by affirming that God, through his Word, had actually created the lower world. Moreover, he asserts that the divine Son of God "became flesh"—that is, he dwelt as a man among men. Clearly, then, if the divine Son himself was clothed in a material body, there could be no absolute distinction between the realm of spirit and the realm of flesh. And John is emphatic on this point, for he affirms Christ's true manhood (2:3; 4:6-7; 11:35; 19:26-27), refers to Jesus' "flesh and blood" (6:53-55), and vividly describes his death as a human being by referring to the blood that poured forth on the cross (19:34). There is no doubt that in emphasizing Jesus' humanity John was combating a view of Jesus that tended to neglect or deny his humanity while stressing his divinity. This conception of Jesus, called *docetism* (from the Greek word "seem" or "appear"—he *seemed* to be a man), was fostered by Gnostic elements in the Church. This particular aspect of Gnostic thought is also opposed in I and II John, which clearly originated in the same milieu as the Gospel of John (see pp. 416 ff.). John was as eager as the docetists to acknowledge that Christ was a divine being, but he vigorously rejected any refusal to acknowledge that the divine Christ was also the man Jesus of Nazareth.

No term in John's Prologue is more pregnant with meaning or richer in religious association than the term *logos* (Word). This term had many shades of meaning in the Hellenistic world. The Stoics, for example, had popularized the *logos* as the rational principle that pervaded and constituted and ordered the universe. In the religious philosophy of the Hermetic literature, *logos* designates, among other things, a divine power enabling men to know God and themselves. And the term had come to have a particular religious significance to Greek-speaking Jews who read their scriptures in the Greek translation (Septuagint), for here *logos* was used to refer to the creative Word of God through which he had created the universe. The account in Genesis (1:3 ff.) records that the creation came into being when God *spoke,* and as time passed men decided that it was by God's *logos* that he had brought forth his creation.

Logos took on additional meaning in connection with the development of another concept in Judaism: wisdom. The Wisdom Literature of the Old Testament and the Apocrypha shows a growing interest in the place of wisdom in the creation of the world. There was even a tendency to personify wisdom, although the rigorous monotheism of the Jews kept them from suggesting that wisdom could exist independently. Later, however, under the influence of Greek speculation, *logos* was sometimes identified with wisdom as God's agent in creation. And, since the Law (Torah) was the embodiment of God's wisdom and his Word, there was also a tendency to ascribe to the Law all the attributes of Wisdom and Word.[11]

In the Old Testament, the Word of God appears not only as the means by which God created the world, but also as the vehicle by which God revealed his purposes for Israel and the world. The Old Testament prophets, for instance, often preface their prophecies with the phrase, "The Word of the Lord." Here the revelation consisted not merely of what the prophets had to say, but in the series of events that was set in motion by the prophets' words and actions. This use of *logos* as a vehicle of revelation was also common in popular Hellenistic philosophy and religion. Philo, for example, sees the *logos* as the divine instrument whereby is revealed the knowledge of God, and in Hellenistic religious thought it is through the *logos* that salvation is disclosed to man.

But what does all this have to do with John's use of *logos* in the Prologue to his gospel? Simply that he was using a term that had broad associations in the Hellenistic world among both Jews and non-Jews. Many efforts have been made to explain John's usage in terms of his dependence on either the Jewish or Hellenistic usage, but it would be more historically correct to recognize a common influence.

There is one sense, however, in which John's use of *logos* is unique, for when he says, "the Word became flesh," he *identifies* the *logos* with Jesus Christ. This means that John conceived of the *logos* primarily in personal and historical terms rather than in mythological or cosmological terms. His understanding of

---

[11] For a complete discussion, see J. Coert Rylaarsdam, *Revelation in Jewish Literature* (Chicago: University of Chicago Press, 1946).

the *logos* is determined by his understanding of the life and work of Jesus. True, John opens his gospel by naming the *logos* as the agent of creation, a reference that would be familiar to both Jews and non-Jews. But he quickly turns to the *logos* as the personal revealer of God, the One through whom salvation is revealed and given. And in the rest of the gospel, though the word rarely occurs, John retains this emphasis on its religious significance.

THE REVELATION IN THE WORLD

Like the Synoptists, John begins his story of the ministry of Jesus with an account of John the Baptist (1:19-34), though he completely subordinates the Baptist's role to that of Jesus. In several passages he depreciates John the Baptist's mission (1:6-8; 1:35-37; 3:25-30; 10:40-42), and from the very beginning ascribes words to him to indicate that the Baptist himself was aware of his subordination to Christ (1:15). John's account of Jesus' baptism completely omits the Baptist's message, and leaves him simply to proclaim Jesus as the "Lamb of God, who takes away the sin of the world" (1:29-34) and as the Son of God. In the Synoptics (except for Matthew) John does not recognize Jesus, but in the Gospel of John God reveals Jesus' identity to the Baptist through the Spirit. It is Jesus, upon whom the Spirit comes and permanently abides, who will baptize with the Spirit. In interpreting Jesus' relation to John the Baptist, John is utilizing a theological principle that he will develop more fully in the rest of the gospel—namely, that knowledge of Jesus' identity is revealed by God through the Spirit only to those who believe. Although John is deeply concerned with the historical foundation of Jesus' ministry ("the Word became flesh"), his primary interest is in reinterpreting that ministry in the light of the theological truth it has revealed.

It has previously been suggested (see pp. 303-304) that there is strong evidence of the existence in the first century of a sect which revered John the Baptist. In playing down the role of John the Baptist, John was undoubtedly hitting out at this rival sect in Asia Minor made up of the Baptist's followers. But quite apart from this motive, John's subordination of the Baptist was consistent with his tendency to treat everyone in his gospel as lesser actors in a drama that was played out for only one purpose: to reveal to the world the central figure, Jesus Christ. The Baptist speaks for every character in the gospel when he says: "He must increase, but I must decrease" (3:30). It is this emphasis that helps account for the artificiality of the dialogues between Jesus and the rest of the *dramatis personae* throughout the gospel; the others are important only in providing a setting for Jesus' words and deeds. This approach contrasts with that of the Synoptics, where hints of the historical tensions of the times often break through. John's purpose is not to reproduce the tradition represented in the Synoptics but to interpret it.

With the Baptist's proclamation that Jesus is the "Lamb of God," John introduces a subject that he later develops in interpreting the death of Jesus as the sacrificial lamb. Here at the very beginning, he alludes to the death as crucial to an understanding of the revelation and the mission of Jesus, the one who alone baptizes in the Spirit. While in the Prologue Jesus' divine Sonship was affirmed on the basis of his having been with God from the beginning and having seen God (1:1, 15-18), here his Sonship is affirmed on the basis of the fact that he will baptize through the Spirit. As John proceeds, he will disclose how the Sonship of Jesus was revealed in history and how the Spirit was imparted to men through Jesus Christ.

In John's version of the call of the disciples, he differs decidedly from the Synoptics (1:35-51), for here Jesus is recognized as the Messiah from the beginning. And Peter is named "the Rock" (Cephas) at his call rather than later in the ministry (Mt. 16:18). The climax is the story of Nathaniel's call. This is the first of a series of dialogues between Jesus and certain persons who take on symbolical significance. Nathaniel, the Jew "without guile," finds no basis in Jewish tradition for believing that Jesus is the Messiah ("Can anything good come out of Nazareth?"). But in spite of his doubt, he is willing to "come and see." For John, this is the essence of faith: the openness of mind that leads a man, in spite of doubt, to approach Christ to be shown. When Nathaniel approaches Christ, he is amazed by a knowledge that he cannot account for in human terms (1:47-48), and on the basis of this experience he believes. Christ responds by promising Nathaniel that a day will come when his belief will be founded on something far more profound than Christ's superhuman knowledge —the day when he will see "heaven opened, and the angels of God ascending and descending upon the Son of man." This is John's way of saying that a greater revelation will come to Nathaniel when he realizes that it is Jesus Christ through whom God has access to man on earth and through whom man has access to God in heaven. John is referring here to the death and resurrection of Christ, the moment in which this full revelation will be given. Nathaniel stands in vivid contrast to the unbelieving Jews who are later pictured as unwilling to open their eyes to the possibility that in the words and works of Jesus God is revealed (Jn. 7-9).

John divides his narrative of the ministry of Jesus into two phases. The first 12 chapters deal with Jesus' public ministry, which reaches its end when certain Greeks come to Christ. Beginning with Chapter 13, John portrays the final period, during which Jesus privately instructs the 12 disciples (13-17); this section is concluded with the Passion narrative (18-20) and reaches its climax with the coming of the Spirit. In general, this twofold division resembles the synoptic outline, in which the public ministry is followed by a withdrawal during the last days. But John's account of the conduct of the public ministry and the nature of the teaching is decidedly different from that in the Synoptics.

The New Life Given by Christ

In the first 12 chapters, John reconstructs the story of Jesus' public ministry around the framework of seven miracle stories and a series of discourses and dialogues, and several trips to Jerusalem at festival seasons. The first of the miracles sets the theme for the entire ministry of Christ (2:1-11). During a wedding feast attended by Jesus in Cana, a village in Galilee, the wine is depleted. At his mother's request, Jesus provides a superabundant supply. He takes six large vessels normally used for Jewish purificatory rites and has them filled with water, which he then miraculously changes into wine. This miracle, which is found only in John's gospel, may derive from an independent tradition. Indeed, some interpreters believe John had access to a collection of miracle stories—a "Book of Signs," as some label them.

But John's interest is not primarily in the physical miracles as such, and, in contrast to the synoptic gospels, he uses the term "signs" in referring to them. To John, Jesus' signs are manifestations of the power of God, which brings salvation to those who believe. In this sense, the miracle itself, met by faith, discloses the glory of God to the disciples (2:11). In John, the symbolic term "glory" refers not only to the transcendence and ineffable power of God, as in Hellenistic religious thought, but also to the power revealed in Jesus Christ (1:14, "We have beheld his glory")—the power that brings salvation. In the seven signs, Christ reveals God's power by doing God's works (5:36; 9:3). But the full manifestation of God's glory must include the death and resurrection of Jesus, and for John this is the greatest of all the signs, the one through which the meaning of all the others is revealed.

The word "sign" carries a second meaning in John's gospel, for each of the physical miracles serves as the vehicle for an unobservable truth. To put it another way: The signs are manifestations to the naked eye of God's power, but at the same time they are symbols of truth that cannot be observed directly. In the miracle at Cana, for example, the wine that Christ miraculously produces from the water is symbolic of the new life that he brings to mankind. It is the new life of the Christian community as contrasted to the old life of Judaism, symbolized by the water jars intended to be used for the ritual purifications required by Jewish Law. What the miracle really says is that Jesus is already engaged in the work through which man is purified and is thereby given access to salvation. Here, as in each of the succeeding six signs, we find a double meaning, for the observable deed carries with it a symbolic meaning.

In referring to the miracles as "signs," John differs from the synoptic gospels, in which the term "signs" generally refers to the apocalyptic events that were to mark the final coming of the kingdom. But since it is a basic theological belief for John that in Jesus Christ the true life of the kingdom was already revealed, he readily refers to the works of Jesus as manifestations of that life in history. This underlying belief also accounts for John's symbolical use of the term "hour." At Cana, for example, he tells his mother, "My hour has not yet come" (2:4). This is the hour of death and resurrection when God's revelation will be fully consummated (12:23-25), and when Christ will accomplish all that his signs foretell. But for John, who stands beyond that event in time, the term "hour" refers to that moment in history when the Eternal Word was made incarnate in Jesus Christ—that is, the time of Jesus' ministry. Since it was only with his death and resurrection that the meaning of all Jesus' words and deeds was finally revealed, John here refers to that last event as the "hour." But insofar as the coming of Christ into the world is the beginning of that hour, John can also say that the hour "now is" (4:23).

The miracle at Cana is followed by the Cleansing of the Temple (2:13-22). Here again John differs from the synoptic gospels, which place this event in the final days of Jesus' ministry. Some scholars believe that the passage originally came late in the gospel, but that at some point it was displaced. But it is generally agreed that John put the Cleansing of the Temple where he did because the change of order served his theological purpose. By placing it at the opening of the ministry, John emphasizes that the Spirit that was bringing into being a new community of worshipers was present in Jesus Christ from the very outset, but that the full coming of the community had to await the Resurrection and the consequent coming of the Spirit.

The climax of the story comes in Jesus' words: "Destroy this temple, and in three days I will raise it up" (2:19). John explains this saying symbolically: Jesus is really prophesying his resurrection, when the risen Christ will replace the Temple as the place where man finds God. Those who worship in his Spirit are the true worshipers (Jn. 4). As the changing of the water into wine symbolizes the new life that Christ gives, so the cleansing of the Temple symbolizes the spiritual worship of the new community of Christ that is brought into being through faith in the risen Lord.

This act, which heralds the day when the Temple worship will be superseded, fits into the over-all scheme of John's gospel. John builds the chronology of Jesus' ministry around a series of Jewish festivals, beginning with the Cleansing of the Temple at Passover (2:13), and closing with the Crucifixion at Passover (19:14). Between these events, Jesus makes significant pronouncements in or near Jerusalem at other festival seasons. It is probable that John has constructed this chronology in order to show that Jesus has supplanted all the old festivals of Judaism. He has revealed a new way to worship God, a way open to all men.

The New Birth

John 3, which purports to be a conversation between Jesus and a prominent Pharisee, Nicodemus, may be John's reinterpretation of Jesus' conversation with the Rich Young Man (Mk. 10:17-22). Here, however, the dialogue runs off into a discourse (3:16-21), which is obviously John's commentary on the conversation. The subject, entrance into the kingdom, is reminiscent of Jesus' teaching in the synoptic gospels. But when Jesus begins to discuss *how* one enters into the kingdom, he uses language peculiar to John's gospel. To enter into the kingdom one must be "born anew" (3:3, 7). The Greek phrase that is translated "born anew" can also be translated "born from above," and John undoubtedly intended that the phrase should convey this double meaning. To be born anew is to be born of the Spirit (3:6). All men are born of the flesh in their physical birth, but only those who are born anew by the Spirit enter the kingdom. Since the Spirit comes from "above," those who are born anew are also "born from above." This new birth has been made possible by the Son of Man, who has descended from heaven and ascended again (3:13). Those who believe in him "have eternal life" (3:15). This passage could readily be taken for a commentary on the statement in the Prologue: "But to all who received him, who believed in his name, he gave power to become children of God; who were born, not of blood nor of the will of the flesh nor of the will of man but of God" (1:12-13).

The entire dialogue with Nicodemus presupposes not only the earthly ministry but the death and resurrection of Jesus, and the faith of the Church. This is evident in the shift from the first person singular to the first person plural in the words, "we speak what we know, and bear witness to what we have seen; but you do not receive our testimony" (3:11). Here we have the Christian Church speaking through John; the birth through "water and the Spirit" (3:5) clearly refers to Christian baptism, which John considered the sacramental rite in which rebirth was consummated. Furthermore, the death and Resurrection are presupposed when John says that the Son of Man has descended and ascended again, making this rebirth possible (3:13). John contrasts the Old Testament story of Moses, in which a bronze serpent is set up so that Israelites who were bitten by snakes could be restored to physical health (Num. 21:4-9), with the lifting up of the Son of Man "that whoever believes in him may have eternal life" (3:14). The words "lifted up" in John are symbolical, for they refer both to the elevation of Christ on the Cross (death) and to the elevation of Christ to heaven (resurrection).

In the discourse that follows, John gives the purpose of Christ's mission to the world (3:16-17). It is because God "so loved" the world that he sent his only Son, and the ultimate purpose of that love is that the world might be saved through the gift of eternal life. But Christ's coming has brought judgment as well as salvation, for those who do not believe in him are already condemned. The judgment is this: the light (Christ) has come into the world and men have preferred darkness to the light because their deeds are evil (3:18-20). In their blindness they bring judgment on themselves.

For John, the great sin is unbelief, a logical outgrowth of his conviction that in Jesus Christ, God's truth ("I am the way, the truth, and the life") has been revealed. Unless a man knows the true way of life as revealed in Jesus Christ, he will inevitably walk the way of darkness or sin. In part, then, faith is belief in the proposition that Jesus is truly the Son of God. But John does not make faith simply an intellectual matter. He insists that the knowledge that Jesus is the Son of God cannot be verified by reason alone; it is revealed through the Spirit. This revelation is possible only when men open their minds and hearts (as Nathaniel did) to Jesus Christ. Involved here is an act of trust and commitment to the possibility that God was revealing himself through Christ. In short, faith means not just accepting certain propositional truths about Christ; it means entering into a personal relationship with Christ in which trust and obedience become the controlling factors in a man's life, thought, and action.

Moreover, belief in the truth that eternal life is given through Christ is possible only to those who enter into that life. Insofar as God alone is the truth, his truth can be known only as it is communicated directly by him to man. But the truth he communicates is not truth *about* himself, but rather *himself*. John believes that God communicated through Jesus Christ and that through him God's love and eternal life are communicated to man. To know the truth, then, is to know God, who reveals himself in Jesus Christ as the one who loves and who gives his Spirit to man. Such truth and knowledge can be comprehended only by entering into a union with God through his only Son, Jesus Christ.

In the discourse with Nicodemus, we have an example of how John transformed the eschatological teachings of Jesus and of the early Christian community. For John, life in the kingdom is presented primarily as a *present reality* rather than a *future expectation*, since eternal life has already entered into history with the coming of Jesus Christ. Baptism is not a baptism of repentance in expectation of the coming of the kingdom; it is being born anew as a child of the heavenly world of the Spirit. This approach recalls a phrase that was common in Hellenistic religious thought—"reborn into eternity."

Further, although John uses the title "Son of Man" to designate Jesus Christ, he no longer pictures an apocalyptic figure coming on the clouds of heaven to effect final judgment. The final judgment has already begun with the coming of the Son of Man; it is an event that is now occurring in history as a result of the coming of Jesus Christ. The Jewish and early Christian apocalyptic concept of the Son of Man has been appreciably modified in John by his concepts of the heavenly Son of God and the pre-existent *logos*. It is debated whether or not John's concept of the Son of Man was also influenced by Jewish speculation concerning Adam, or oriental speculation about a "primal man" (see pp. 103-104). Whatever influences might have been at work, John's central meaning has been shaped by his understanding of the work and words, death and resurrection of Jesus Christ.

The Savior of the World

In the dialogue with the Samaritan woman (Jn. 4), John develops the theme of the new life bestowed by Christ. When Jesus asks for a drink from Jacob's well, the woman is puzzled not only by the fact that a Jew would ask a Samaritan for a drink (John explains that the Samaritans and Jews were not on the best of terms), but also by Jesus' statement that he gives "living water" that becomes a "spring of water welling up to eternal life" (4:14). The water metaphor appears frequently in the Old Testament as a symbol of God's activity in giving life to men. In an eschatological passage in Zechariah, for example, it is prophesied that when the "day of the Lord" comes, "living waters" will flow out of Jerusalem and the Lord will become king over all the earth (Zech. 14:8-9). In rabbinic usage water was often used as a symbol for the Law. But John uses water as a metaphor for the Spirit, as he explicitly says (7:38-39). With the Coming of Jesus the Messiah, all the expectations of the final "day of the Lord" are being realized; not the least of them is the coming of the Spirit (7:38-39) and the life it brings.

When Jesus discloses intimate details of the Samaritan woman's past life, she calls him a prophet and asks him to answer the question that has divided the Jews and the Samaritans for centuries: Where is the proper place of worship—the Temple in Jerusalem, or Mt. Gerazim in Samaria, where the Samaritans worshiped (4:20)? Jesus answers that true worship occurs neither in Jerusalem nor on Mt. Gerizim, for the "hour is coming and now is" when worship "in Spirit and truth" shall prevail. The woman realizes that this answer is more than a prophecy, and replies that only the Messiah could possibly "show us all things" (4:25). Then, in response to her dawning faith, Jesus tells her, "I who speak to you am he" (4:26). This characterization of Jesus as the revealer of all things has associations both with Jewish speculation about the Messiah and with the Gnostic concept of a divine revealer who leads men into knowledge of truth. It is significant, however, that John never uses the noun *knowledge* (*gnosis*), though he frequently uses the verb *know*. Perhaps this reflects a conscious effort to avoid a term which might be misinterpreted.

In this dialogue between Jesus and the Samaritan woman, John explicitly links together the new life and the new worship that he has already alluded to in the sign at Cana and the Cleansing of the Temple. It is no accident that the setting for this dialogue is Samaria, for the coming of the Samaritans (4:39-42) demonstrates the universal nature of eternal life and true worship. The disciples would postpone the true and universal worship of God until the coming of the kingdom (four months until the harvest, 4:35); but Jesus declares that the hour has already come when the true God is being worshiped universally. While salvation is from the Messiah of the Jews (4:22), Jesus, who is that Messiah, has proved to be the universal savior of all men. So the

Samaritan friends of the woman confess "this is indeed the Savior of the world" (4:42). In calling Jesus "Savior," John is using a term that would have greater religious significance to Gentiles than the strictly Jewish term "Messiah" would have. Jesus has come to accomplish God's work (4:34), and that work is no less than the salvation of the world.

In the second of Jesus' signs, which follows immediately after the dialogue with the Samaritan woman, John illustrates the work that God has sent Christ to perform (4:46-54). Jesus heals a Roman official's son who is at the brink of death, and by so doing elicits the faith of the Roman official and his entire household. The fact that the man is a Roman emphasizes again the universal scope of the salvation Jesus brings. This sign points to the ultimate work of Christ—the healing of men at the brink of spiritual death through his life-giving word and through faith in its power. In the very hour that Jesus utters his healing word (4:53), the official's son recovers from his illness. But just as Christ's word restores physical life, so also is his word the source of eternal life to all who believe—Jew, Samaritan, or Roman.

The Work of the Father and the Son

The third of Jesus' signs, the healing of the man in Jerusalem at the sheep-gate pool (5:2-18), seems to be a reinterpretation of one of the Synoptic healings (Mk. 2:11; Mt. 9:6; Lk. 5:24). In the Synoptic account, however, it is Jesus' forgiveness of the man's sins that arouses a dispute with his Jewish opponents, whereas in John it is the fact that he makes himself "equal with God" by calling God "Father." Even the argument over his performing the miracle on the sabbath is subordinated to this central difficulty.

In the long discourse that follows the miracle (5:16-47), the true meaning of the sign is given. Jesus heals the man according to the Father's will, not his own; and the sign points to the final work of the Father, which is raising the dead and giving eternal life (5:20-21). Since the Father loves the Son and has sent him to accomplish his work, whoever hears the Son's word and believes God who sent him has eternal life, does not come into judgment, and has already passed from death to life (5:24).

In the fifth chapter, John develops several themes that he is to elaborate further in the rest of the gospel. Earlier, he had used mythological language in commending Christ's authority and power. Christ is the unique Son of God who has come from heaven (1:11; 3:13, 17, 31, etc.). Though John continues this theme, he speaks more and more of Christ's Sonship in terms of his doing the work of the Father. The Father has sent the Son to give eternal life to the world (3:16; 5:21, 26), but the Son's coming also involves judgment (3:17-21; 5:22-23). Those who believe the Son have eternal life; those who do not, stand under judgment. While John lays stress on the present reality of judgment and life, he frequently alludes to a future resurrection and judgment

(5:28-29; 6:39, 40, 44, 54; 11:24; 12:48). Some interpreters believe such references contradict the author's point of view, and have assigned them to a later editor. But there is no textual evidence for this. It is more likely that John retains the traditional resurrection hope, though his major emphasis is upon the reality of Christ's presence now as both judge and source of eternal life. The crucial point of later discussions is whether or not Jesus was "sent" from God.

The Greek word that John uses for "sent" is significant. In the Old Testament, it was used to refer to the office and work of a prophet or any other man who was believed to have been commissioned by God to speak or act in his name. One who was "sent" by God bore the authority and represented the power of the sender, and it is in this sense that the word is used elsewhere in the New Testament. The noun "apostle" comes from the same root, and means "one sent with a commission from God to speak and act on his behalf." This use of the term was also familiar to Hellenistic religious thought—in Gnosticism, for example, divine agents and their earthly disciples are "sent" as messengers of divine truth. But John claims that Jesus, being the Son, not merely represents the authority of God and speaks the word of God, but actually bears *in himself* that authority and power. The words he speaks *are* God's, and the works he does *are* the work of God. This is because he is himself God's Word.

This identity of Christ's work, authority, and will with God's leads to increasing conflict with the Jews. They continue (5:39) to seek for eternal life through their scriptures (Torah), while all the time the living Word is in their midst. John argues that if the Jews understood their scriptures, they would recognize Christ as the one prophesied by Moses (5:45-47). Their failure to understand their own scriptures, in which Moses himself wrote of Christ (5:46-47), is proof that they do not understand who Christ is.

The fourth (6:1-14) and fifth (6:16-21) signs, also reinterpretations of Synoptic miracles (Mk. 6:34-44, 45-52), further emphasize the divine power manifested in Christ's work. The fourth sign is John's version of the Feeding of the 5,000. When Jesus has finished feeding them, the people declare that he is "the prophet who is to come into the world" (6:14), and they wish "by force to make him king." The crowds do not understand the true meaning of the sign—they do not realize the nature of the one with whom they deal, and hence they fail to recognize that his kingship is "not of this world" (18:36).

The fifth sign is Jesus' walking on the water, and the climax comes in his words to the disciples, "It is I" (6:20). The English translation of these words does not convey the full significance of the Greek *ego eimi*, which literally means "I am." This was a technical phrase that had already been used as a name for God in the Greek translation of the prophet Isaiah. John uses it to signify the presence of God himself in the person of Jesus. Although the crowds saw in the miracle of the Feeding the power of an earthly king, here, in the words "I am," Jesus discloses to the disciples that God himself is with them. But even the disciples do not fully understand.

In the lengthy discourse that follows (6:25-65), John tries to explain the meaning of the Feeding of the 5,000. The crowds have seen it only as a miraculous work that reveals Christ's power to establish an earthly kingdom (6:26-27). But Jesus tells them that the Son of Man has not come to supply material needs but to give food that is the source of eternal life. The contrast between Moses and Jesus, already suggested earlier by John (1:17; 5:46), is further drawn when Jesus recalls that Moses miraculously gave the Israelites manna to sustain them in the wilderness, and yet they all died (6:49). Now Christ does what Moses could never do; he gives the "true bread from Heaven" which affords eternal life to the world.

In answer to the request that he produce some of this bread, Jesus says, "I am the bread of life; he who comes to me shall not hunger, and he who believes in me shall never thirst" (6:35). This is the first of a series of sayings that are prefaced with the words "I am," and are followed by a phrase with symbolic meaning, such as "bread of life," "the light" (8:12), "the door" (10:7), "the good shepherd" (10:11), "the resurrection and the life" (11:25), "the true vine" (15:1), "the way, the truth, and the life" (14:6). Although this form of pronouncement is not found in the synoptic gospels, it had been used from ancient times in the Orient as a mode of speech for a divine being. According to one Jewish view, when the Messiah came the heavenly manna would again descend from heaven as it had in Moses' day and would provide food for the faithful. According to another view, the manna was a symbol for the Law that was given through Moses.[12] But in John the heavenly food has a unique meaning, for here Jesus Christ is the "true bread." Just as he gives the living water (Jn. 4) that brings eternal life, so he offers the food that gives "life to the world." He accomplishes this by doing the will of the Father (6:38), by giving his flesh for the world. When John identifies the true bread with the "flesh" of Jesus, he emphasizes that it is through the words and deeds of the historical person Jesus Christ that God has given man eternal life.

This discourse on the true bread is followed by a dispute among the Jews, who ask how Jesus can give his flesh to be eaten (6:52). Jesus replies, "He who eats my flesh and drinks my blood has eternal life, and I will raise him at the last day. For my flesh is food indeed, and my blood is drink indeed." This answer seems to confirm the Jews' misunderstanding rather than to resolve it. But to his disciples Jesus explains that the flesh avails nothing; it is the "Spirit that gives life" (6:63). Only when they have seen the Son of Man "ascending where he was before" will they be given this food. In speaking of the ascent of the Son of Man, John refers once again to the resurrection of Jesus, which is necessary before the Spirit is sent; the Spirit alone reveals the truth of Christ's words and deeds and is the source of eternal life to those who believe.

John's account of the Feeding of the 5,000, and the discourse that follows, obviously reflect the eucharistic teaching of the early Church. As the community ate the bread and drank the wine, it was conscious of the fact that Jesus,

---

[12] See C. H. Dodd, *The Interpretation of the Fourth Gospel*, pp. 333-345.

the Son of God, the Messiah who had lived as a man among men, now shared his life through the gift of the Spirit. Although the Son truly revealed himself in the flesh, the full revelation came only when he sent the Spirit after the Resurrection. For John, the ultimate meaning of the sign of the Feeding of the 5,000 was the death and resurrection of Jesus Christ, through which eternal life was given to the world. And John interprets the feeding as the sign in Jesus' ministry of the eucharistic meal of the early Church. Through participation in the meal, the believers shared in the spiritual life bestowed by the risen Son of God.

John's language here is close to that of certain Hellenistic religious cults, which believed that through a sacred meal they entered into the life of the deity (see Chapter 1). Jesus says, "He who eats my flesh and drinks my blood abides in me, and I in him" (6:56), and the phrase "abide in" occurs with increasing frequency in the latter part of the gospel. John uses this term to express the mystical union between Christ and the believer, in a sense that is close to Paul's concept of being "in Christ." John explicitly interprets the Eucharist through this concept of mystical union. When John later deals more extensively with what he means by mystical union (Jn. 14-17), the difference between his understanding of the concept and the notions popular in his day become obvious. In John, the man is not absorbed by the deity, nor is there any deification of the man in which the distinction between man and God is broken down. And in his teaching about the Eucharist he avoids identifying the bread and wine as the body and blood in a way that would suggest they had some magical power when consumed ("The flesh is of no avail," 6:63). The words and the spirit are the source of life.

Since John's language was so closely associated with Hellenistic religious ideas, however, it was often subjected to superstitions and magical interpretations. Ignatius, for example, who was influenced by the type of theology we find in John, referred to the Eucharist with the easily misunderstood phrase "medicine of immortality."[13] But John's doctrine of the Spirit (as also Ignatius') stands clearly against such misinterpretations. Although John uses Hellenistic terminology and ideology in interpreting the Eucharist, he insists that it is the presence of the Spirit that determines the meaning and efficacy of the Eucharist.

The Children of God
and the Children of the Devil

John 7 and 8 are concerned largely with the controversy between Jesus and the Jews, especially the Pharisees. Actually, the controversy reflects the later antagonism between the synagogue and the Church, though ostensibly it

---

[13] *To the Ephesians*, 20:20.

is over the Law (7:24) in general and the sabbath observance in particular (and to this extent recalls the Synoptic reports of the actual conflict during Jesus' ministry). But the real issue is over Jesus' messiahship (7:40-52) and unique Sonship (Jn. 8). In his second "I am" saying, Jesus declares: "I am the light of the world; he who follows me will not walk in darkness, but will have the light of life" (8:12). The Pharisees charge Jesus with bearing witness to himself (8:13); and they insist that his testimony is invalid in the light of the Old Testament requirement that more than one witness is needed to establish a case (Num. 35:30; Deut. 17:6). But Jesus claims that the Father also bears witness to him. The very fact that the Jews do not recognize Jesus' claim is proof that they do not know the Father, since Jesus has come from the Father (8:14), and all he declares is what he has heard from the Father (8:26). Contrary to the Jews' claim, they are neither children of Abraham nor children of God, for they seek to kill Jesus (8:39-43); rather, their unbelief and hatred show that they are children of the Devil. They do not hear the words of God spoken by Jesus because they "are not of God" (8:47). Consequently, they are slaves of sin (8:34 ff.) and will die in their sins (8:24).

As John develops this conflict between Jesus and the Jews, he seems to build up a rigid determinism—for example, in such sayings as "no one can come to me unless it is granted him by the Father" (6:65; cf. 6:44). John seems to say that God has predetermined who can and will believe in Christ. John's determinism springs, not from any tendency to indulge in speculation about man, but rather from his firmly held concepts of faith and revelation. For John, faith is that trusting response to God's Word and action that is the only means of arriving at knowledge of and communion with God. John clearly understands that faith depends on both God's act *and* man's response. But throughout his gospel he emphasizes the divine side of the relationship: God's revelatory act in Christ. Unless God acts, man cannot know him. It is this emphasis that accounts for the many references to the fact that no one comes to God except he lead them, and except they be his children. Since John believed God's complete revelation was in Christ, God's true children are those who believe in Christ.

Conversely, John says that those who do not respond to Christ are not children of God but children of the Devil. Their actions reveal not the truth of God, but the lies of the Devil, who is the "father of lies" (8:44). John gives two reasons for the Jews' failure to believe in Christ, and thus for their subservience to the lies of the Devil. First, they judge by "appearances" rather than by right judgment (7:24); John means they place their traditional beliefs —that is, what *appears* believable to them—above God's revelation in Christ. Second, they seek "their own glory" (5:44; 7:18; 12:43)—that is, they take more delight in the pride that comes from being Abraham's children, the Chosen of God, than in the glory revealed in Christ, through whom Abraham's hope that all men become God's children by faith was fulfilled. Men become children of the Devil because their desires are his desires (8:44 ff.): they seek their own glory and close their eyes to the revelation of God's truth.

In spite of John's apparent determinism, it is evident that all men, without distinction, are potentially children of God. Though all are born in sin (Jn. 9) and must be born again (Jn. 3), God sent his Son to be the savior of the whole world. But only those who in faith are "taught by God" will recognize him as savior (6:45).

In the sixth sign (Jn. 9), John deals with the cardinal sin of unbelief. The occasion is the miraculous restoration of sight to a man who had been born blind. In the extended controversy with the Pharisees that ensues, two themes are dominant. On the one hand, there is the Pharisees' blindness to the possibility that Jesus' healing act can be in God's power, since Jesus is a sinner who has broken the sabbath laws. On the other hand, there is the blind man's confidence; his recovery is evidence enough that Jesus is from God and has acted according to God's will.

As with the other signs, however, it is only when we grasp the symbolism of this sign that we can understand its ultimate meaning. The clue is found in the man's confession that Jesus is the Son of Man whom he worships (9:38). The true miracle is not the man's recovery of his physical sight, but rather the opening of his "spiritual eyes" when Jesus reveals in faith that he is the Son of Man. John uses physical sight as a metaphor for the faith whereby man sees God in Christ (14:8-11). With the other signs, this sign anticipates the death and Resurrection; it was only the risen Lord who fully opened men's eyes and was worshiped by them.

In contrast to the healed man's faith and sight stands the blindness of the Pharisees. To them Jesus says: "For judgment I came into this world, that those who do not see may see, and that those who see may become blind" (9:39). What does John mean by this cryptic statement? He is saying that in reality all men are blind from birth, not physically but spiritually. The man who was born blind is a symbol of all men, for no man has the power within himself to penetrate the darkness in which he walks. He knows not where he goes, because he knows not where his true life is to be found (8:12). Only God's light can dispel the darkness and reveal the true life, for it is only in God that men have life. But only those who acknowledge their blindness can have their spiritual eyes opened; this acknowledgment is the beginning of faith and sight. On the other hand, those who claim that they see do not know they are blind. They walk in the light of their own knowledge, believing it to be the true light. This is the sin of the Pharisees: Christ cannot open their eyes to who he is because they already claim to know who he is—a demon-possessed man (8:48). Their judgment derives from their own preconceptions of what the Messiah will do and say. It is their claim to sight (their own understanding of how God will reveal himself) that brings judgment upon them. The Pharisees are symbolic of the children of the Devil who walk in darkness; the man born blind is symbolic of the children of God who walk in the light. For Christ is the "light of the world" (8:12 ff.), without which men do not know whence they go.

In contrast to the Pharisees, who are blind leaders of the blind (as evidenced by their maltreatment of the blind man), Jesus is portrayed in the tenth chapter of John as the "good shepherd" who cares for the sheep. This shepherd-sheep metaphor is commonly used in the Old Testament, where God frequently is called the shepherd of his people (Psalm 23; Is. 40:11; etc.).   King David, the ideal ruler, is also described as a shepherd (Ps. 78:70; Ezek. 37:24). And in Ezek. 34 the prophet utters God's promise that he will give his people a shepherd in the Davidic line who will lead them to salvation from the false rulers who are destroying them. Here the shepherd is a messianic figure. John was clearly influenced by the Old Testament in his use of the shepherd-sheep metaphor.

But the metaphor was also common in the non-Jewish world, for it had been used as a divine title in the religions of Egypt, Babylonia, and Persia. It also appears in the Hermetic literature, where one book is entitled *Poimandres,* a Greek word meaning "shepherd of mankind." The shepherd is *nous* (personification of mind), who reveals all truth to mankind. So the metaphor had associations for Jew and non-Jew alike.

Jesus, however, is the "good shepherd," the *true* shepherd of the sheep. All who came before him are robbers who would lead the sheep astray (10:8). He alone gives life to the sheep, through laying down his life (the Crucifixion) and taking it up again (the Resurrection). His sheep include not only the Jewish disciples who first believed, but others who are not of this fold (10:16). John refers here to the Gentiles who accepted Christ when the Jews rejected him, and who made up most of the early communities. These sheep know the Father and the shepherd, since the Father and the shepherd are one (10:29). It is ultimately God who calls the sheep through Jesus to the eternal life that no one can take from them, for he is the source of all life (10:25-30).

The Last Sign—Resurrection and Life

John brings Jesus' public ministry to its close with the seventh sign, the raising of Lazarus from the dead (Jn. 11). This is clearly intended to be a climactic finale, the greatest of the signs. Each of the preceding six signs points to this seventh, in which Jesus actually restores life to a dead man in the most dramatic demonstration of his divine power. As with the other signs, this miracle is seen as a manifestation of the glory of God (11:4) and the glorification of the Son.

This miracle is found only in John, and there are obvious problems over the historicity of the event. If this striking miracle was known to the other gospel writers, it is very difficult to explain why they omitted it; only two other accounts of raising the dead are reported, and the early Church would hardly have overlooked this one. As it stands, the story is typical of John's language and theology. Furthermore, it is not incidental to the public ministry but actually serves as the climax. The most that can be said is that John was working with traditional materials, on the basis of which he presented Jesus as the giver of eternal life. One explanation suggests that John is reinterpreting as a literal event the Parable of the Rich Man and Lazarus (Lk. 16:19-31), where the point is made that the Jews would not be persuaded even if someone returned from the dead to tell them the truth that Moses and the prophets had spoken. And indeed the raising of Lazarus does not convince the Jews that Jesus is the expected Messiah; rather it leads to the final conflict.[14] Whatever its background in tradition, it is the *symbolic* meaning of this miracle that is important to John.

Lazarus and his two sisters, who live in Bethany, are pictured as close friends of Jesus (11:3, 5). When Jesus receives word that Lazarus is ill, he says that it is not an "illness unto death" and delays two days before going to his friend. Only when it is certain that Lazarus is dead does Jesus go to Bethany with his disciples (11:14-15). As he approaches Bethany, Martha greets him with the pitiful words that Lazarus would not have died had Jesus been there sooner. When Jesus assures Martha that Lazarus will rise again, Martha shows her belief in the traditional Jewish view of a future resurrection, saying that she knows Lazarus will "rise again in the resurrection at the last day" (11:24). But Jesus corrects this misunderstanding with his reply: "I am the resurrection and the life; he who believes in me, though he die, yet shall he live, and whoever lives and believes in me shall never die" (11:26). This saying summarizes the view of eternal life that has been evident throughout the gospel. Jesus gives eternal life *now* to those who believe in him; those who believe, though they suffer physical death, will never lose the eternal life already bestowed by Christ. When Jesus asks Martha if she believes this, she replies, "Yes, Lord; I believe that you are the Christ, the Son of God, he who is coming into the world." To believe that Christ is the resurrection and the life is to believe that he is the Christ, the Son of God.

The "I am" saying of Jesus, followed by Martha's confession, forms the climax of the story and provides a clue to the symbolical meaning of the sign. For the glory of God that is revealed in the restoration of Lazarus to physical life is but a partial manifestation of the glory that is disclosed in God's gift of eternal life through Christ. The ultimate revelation of this life is to be given only in the death and resurrection, not of Lazarus, but of Jesus. Lazarus is the symbol of all men: Apart from Christ, they are already dead; through him, even in this world, they share in eternal life. John now has the High Priest unwittingly prophesy the gathering together of the true children of God

---

[14] For an excellent discussion, see Alan Richardson, *The Miracle-Stories of the Gospels* (London: SCM Press, 1941), pp. 120 ff.

through the death and resurrection of Christ: "You do not understand that it is expedient for you that one man should die for the people and that the whole nation should not perish" (11:50). Not only the Jews who believe, but also the Gentiles (the children of God scattered abroad), are to be gathered into one community (11:51-52) of life.

THE FULFILLMENT OF CHRIST'S HOUR

The events following the raising of Lazarus take place under the shadow of the imminent death of Christ. John concludes his account of the ministry of Jesus with a series of brief semi-public incidents. As in the synoptic gospels, the action occurs during the Passover season (12:1). In the home of Mary and Martha in Bethany, Jesus is anointed by Mary. But John, unlike Mark, has the anointing take place immediately before the Triumphal Entry (12:12 ff.; cf. Mk. 11:7-10). Whereas in Mark the anointing is interpreted as preparation for burial, in John the event symbolizes Jesus' anointment to kingship. After the anointing, Jesus enters Jerusalem and the people proclaim him "King of Israel" (12:13). Neither the crowd nor the disciples understand Jesus' kingship (12:16); it is only after his resurrection that they understand ("when Jesus was glorified"). He dies as the king of the Jews (19:12); but again the terminology is symbolic, for his kingship is "not of this world" (18:36).

In consternation, the Pharisees cry: "Look, the world has gone after him" (12:19). Again John places an unwitting prophecy on the lips of the Pharisees, for John writes from the vantage point of one who has seen men from all over the world, mostly Gentiles, enter into the Church. The coming of the Greeks to "see Jesus" (12:21) is John's dramatic way of announcing that Christ's death is near. With their coming, "the hour" in which the Son of Man will be fully glorified is near. The hour of Christ's death is the hour of judgment on this world whose ruler (the Devil) is cast out (12:31), and the death is the doorway to the Resurrection in which the victory over death and darkness (the realm over which the devil presides) is completely manifested. The world is judged for its unbelief; by their rejection of Christ, the Jews have shown themselves sons of the Devil (the ruler of this world, 8:44). At the same time, the "hour" of Christ's glorification is the moment when "all men" will be drawn unto him (12:32)—that is, when the whole world will acknowledge him as the *logos* who came to "his own" but was rejected (1:11). Christ is glorified by God because through him the whole world is given a share in the life of the Father.

The Meaning of Discipleship

After the Triumphal Entry, Jesus withdraws for a period of intimate association with his disciples (13:1 ff.). The evening meal is clearly John's version of the Last Supper recorded in the Synoptics, but John has it take place the day before the Passover eve. Whether or not John's dating is more correct than that of the synoptic gospels is not of great importance, for John was not primarily concerned with historical accuracy. By placing the meal the day before Passover eve, he has synchronized the crucifixion of Jesus with the traditional slaying of the lamb on the day of the Passover. John the Baptist had announced Christ to be the "Lamb of God who takes away the sin of the world" (1:29). Now as the Lamb of God Christ dies in fulfillment of John's proclamation. His bones are not broken on the Cross (19:36), just as scripture had enjoined that the paschal lamb's bones not be broken (Ex. 12:46; Num. 9:12). In contrast to the Passover, which celebrates God's leading of the Israelites safely out of their Egyptian bondage, John sees the death of Christ as the event through which God leads all men out of death and darkness into eternal life.

John, like the Synoptics, includes in his narrative of the last meal a reference to Judas' betrayal and the prediction of Peter's denial. But unlike them he omits any account of how the Lord's Supper was instituted.[15] In place of the account of the Last Supper, John substitutes the narrative of the Foot-Washing (13:2-20). The clue to the meaning of this act lies in the introductory words, "Having loved his own who were in the world, he loved them to the end" (13:1). The phrase "the end" may mean either "completely" or "to the point of death." John undoubtedly intends both meanings. The Foot-Washing must be understood against the background of Jesus' death, in which he completely revealed his love. In washing the disciples' feet, Jesus was performing a menial task that was usually the duty of the Jewish slave in the household. This act of humility surprised Peter, who wanted to stop Jesus from performing it. Peter's reaction is reminiscent of his rebuke to Jesus for announcing his coming death, as recorded in the Synoptics (Mk. 8:32 ff.). Peter is told that he does not know what Jesus is doing but that someday he will (13:7). Jesus' words to Peter, "If I do not wash you, you have no part in me" (13:8), are a symbolical reference to Christ's death, for it is through Jesus' death, resurrection, and the gift of the Spirit that Christians are washed and have a part in Christ.

John's account of the Foot-Washing recalls the image of Jesus as the Suffering Servant that is so vivid in the synoptic gospels. John's interest in presenting Christ as the divine Son has led him to a portrayal that conveys the heavenly glory of Christ, but only at the expense of the profound human emotions and sympathy with which Jesus entered into the sorrows and afflictions of a troubled people. And yet in this brief episode John makes it perfectly clear that the divine Son is none other than the Suffering Servant. In this one dramatic moment John recalls the lowly path trod by Jesus, a path that John has all but obliterated in his desire to show that Jesus has revealed the glory of God.

---

[15] For a discussion of this omission, see A. J. B. Higgins, *The Lord's Supper in the New Testament* (Chicago: Regnery, 1952), pp. 75-78.

It is significant that when John refers to the humble servant he turns his attention momentarily from Christ to the disciples. He speaks of discipleship in the terms of a lowly servant, and points out that there are implications for the disciples in the Foot-Washing. For to call Jesus teacher and Lord means that the disciples must follow the example of Jesus, since "he who is sent [the disciple] is not greater than he who sent him [Jesus]." The true disciple is recognized not only by his faith in the divine Son but also by his following the path of love and humble service trod by the historical Jesus; the disciples must love one another (13:35) even though this means death (15:13), as it did for Jesus. Again we see that although John often used the language of mythology, his divine redeemer is no mythological figure who inhabits the heavens. Rather, he is the historical person, Jesus, who saved men by entering into history. And eternal life is not a victorious journey through heavenly space; rather, it is a journey, here and now, along the path that Jesus has trod.

John sets up a vivid contrast between this description of the true disciple and his portrait of Judas, the false disciple. Judas is present through it all, already planning the betrayal. Paradoxically, he will help bring about Jesus' death, through which all men are washed clean, but he himself will not be made clean (13:11). That is why John remarks, "It was night," when Judas leaves (13:30). He is referring not to physical darkness but to the darkness of unbelief of one who fails to see that in Jesus is to be found light and life.

Judas' departure marks the first in the final sequence of events leading to Jesus' death, the moment of the glorification of the Son of Man and God himself. For by his death the Son of Man reveals the love of God for man. In anticipation of his death, Jesus leaves his disciples with one commandment: "That you love one another" (13:34). This is not a "new commandment," except in the sense that the love enjoined is for the first time revealed in Jesus Christ. The disciples are to love "as I loved you" (13:34), a love that is revealed in the life of humble service dramatized by the Foot-Washing and the death that it symbolically anticipated. Although there were tendencies in the early Church to interpret Jesus as a new lawgiver (see pp. 277-278), John presents Jesus as the giver of eternal life that may be shared by entering into union with him. Like Paul, John believes that the ethical life is the "fruit of the Spirit," not the product of rigid adherence to legal prescriptions.

The Farewell Discourses

The last meal provides the setting for a series of long discourses (Jn. 14-16) and a lengthy prayer (Jn. 17). There is some question about whether we have these chapters in their proper sequence, since the words at the close of Chapter 14 suggest a departure from the meeting ("Rise, let us go hence"). Yet it is clear that Chapters 14-17 stand in close relationship and must be read and interpreted as a unit. These discourses deal with Christ's departure from his disciples and his coming again. Although there is nothing comparable to them in the synoptic gospels, they undoubtedly represent John's interpretation of several synoptic passages. Chief among these is the apocalyptic discourse in Mk. 13, which speaks of the Coming of the Son of Man in the clouds of heaven. John's farewell discourses represent his interpretation of these expectations.

In John's gospel, the discourses are delivered to the original disciples on the last night of Jesus' life. There can be no doubt, however, that it is the risen Lord who is speaking and that the hearers are Christians living in John's own day. All that is said presupposes the death and resurrection of Jesus, the coming of the Spirit, and the Christian community's long history of experience. True, Jesus' words often seem to refer to the future, but this is because John continues to write within the dramatic framework of this historic ministry.

Several themes recur throughout the discourses. Chief among these is the relationship between Jesus and God, the Father. Jesus enjoys a mystical union with the Father, for he is "in the Father" and the Father is in him; the Father dwells in Jesus (14:11), and is with him in his hour of death (16:32). But this union of Jesus with the Father is not a mystical absorption in which the identity of either is lost. As he has throughout the gospel, John continues to recognize the distinction between Father and Son: the Father is greater than Christ (14:28). Rather, it is a union grounded in the love of the Father for Christ and Christ's love for the Father; the love of the Father is manifested in his faithfulness to the Son to the end (16:32); Christ's love is manifested in his perfect obedience to the Father's will (14:31; 15:10), finally sealed by his death. And so the words Christ speaks and the works he performs are not his alone but the Father's (14:10-11). John has continually emphasized that in Christ's words and works he was saying and doing his Father's will. But now it is the Father's last work, the death of Christ, that is on John's mind. The seven "signs" were mighty manifestations of power, but the death is to all outward appearances only a show of weakness. And yet, only those who see it as the perfect revelation of God's love can understand the true meaning of the signs and the words that Christ spoke.

This revelation is possible, however, only if Christ goes to the Father. And so Jesus repeatedly refers to his going to the Father (14:28; 16:7, 17, 28), in reference to both the death and the Resurrection. For John, Christ's going is important as the event by which Christ sends the Spirit. After his death there will be momentary sadness. But then there will be joy (16:16-24), for when the Spirit comes he will reveal the truth of life, death, and resurrection.

Jesus promises to come again. Though it is a point of controversy among interpreters, John seems to allude to a final Coming of Christ when he speaks of his going to prepare a place, and returning to take the believers with him (14:2-3). This aspect of the Coming should be related to the several references to the future resurrection already mentioned. But this Coming is overshadowed by another mode of Christ's Coming on the basis of which John seeks to understand any Coming in the future. Unlike those Christians who thought of the Coming largely in terms of some future event, John stresses Jesus' coming in the Spirit to the community. In several passages Jesus promises that he will send the Spirit. When the world is no longer able to see Jesus because he is not physically present, the Christian community will see him in the coming of the Spirit (14:18). The Spirit, being the Spirit of truth, will bear witness to the truth about Christ (15:26). He will reveal all the truths that the disciples could not "bear" (understand) during Jesus' ministry (16:12). Christ will speak to the community through the Spirit, because the Spirit will faithfully declare Christ's words; and, because these are also God's words, they will be true (16:14-15). Since it is only with the coming of the Spirit that all truth is revealed, it is only the Spirit who can reveal that Jesus is "the way, the truth, and the life" and that "no one comes to the Father" except through Christ (14:6). Only those who possess the Spirit will understand that to know and see Christ is to know and see God (14:7-9).

Clearly, it would be impossible to overemphasize the significance that the concept of the Holy Spirit had for John. Like Paul, John thought of the Spirit in terms of God's pervasive power through which God carried out his purposes in the world. It is as Spirit that God is present in the world. But since God fully revealed himself in Christ, it was in Christ that the meaning of Spirit was revealed. John speaks of the Spirit as *paraclete* (the anglicizing of the actual Greek word *parakletos*).[16] In Greek usage this term regularly means "advocate," one who pleads a cause in the legal sense. The term is not found elsewhere in the New Testament and John's usage has unique features in contrast to normal Greek usage. On one occasion he seems to use the term meaning advocate, but as one who convicts or convinces (16:8-11) the world; elsewhere the *paraclete* leads to truth (16:12-13; 14:26), witnesses to Christ (16:26), and even consoles (14:15-18). In the latter passages perhaps *counselor* is the best translation. Whatever influences were at work in John's use of the word (and the issue is unsettled), John by his own theological understanding gives it a new force in his gospel.

Apart from the Spirit, there could have been no community, for it is through the Spirit that the community knows that Christ lives and that the community itself lives by sharing in his life (14:19). And it is through the Spirit that the community knows that it shares in the union of Christ with the Father. But, as Christ's union with the Father is grounded in mutual love, so must the union of the community with Christ and the Father. It is by loving Christ and by keeping his commandment of love for the brethren that the community comes to know the love of the Father. Where such love is present, Jesus and

---

[16] A strong argument has been made that these "counselor" passages were the additions of a later editor. See W. F. Howard, *Christianity According to St. John* (Philadelphia: Westminster, 1946), pp. 74-80.

the Father come to make their home (14:21-24). This is eternal life as John sees it: life motivated and sustained by trust in the love of God revealed in Christ.

In the discourse on the vine, John allegorizes the union of Christ and the Church (15:1-17). Christ is the vine, and Christians are the branches that depend on the vine for life. This allegory is meant to help the Church understand the meaning of the union, for if the branches do not bear fruit they are cast forth. To "bear fruit" has a double meaning: in the first place, the Church must obey Christ's commandment of love in order that God may be glorified. In this the fruits of discipleship of the Church are demonstrated (15:8). But in the second place, it is through this love that the Church witnesses God's love to the world, with the result that other disciples are led to God (fruits). As the Great Prayer of Jesus (Jn. 17) reveals, the only reason for the Church's existence is to bear witness to the Father's love in word and deed. The Church realizes its union with the Father as it bears witness to that love through the Spirit given by Christ.

The Church can expect persecution in the world (15:18-22), because the world does not know the Spirit and does not receive it (14:17). The Spirit passes judgment on the world's sin (hatred) in the light of God's righteousness (love); insofar as the world does not desire forgiveness for its sins it turns away from God (16:7-11; 3:19-21). The sin (hatred) of the world, manifested in rejection of Christ's words and love and its persecution of him (16:18-24), has come under God's judgment. But as Christ loves to the end, so the Church, even though persecuted, must continue to manifest Christ's loving Spirit so that all the world may believe (17:20).

The Great Prayer

The farewell discourses conclude with a long prayer, purportedly by Jesus. But the language and thought are typically John's, and at one point John even has Jesus refer to himself in the third person (17:3). The prayer is a résumé of what John believes Jesus had actually done for the Church through his life, death, and resurrection and through the gift of the Spirit. John formulates all this as a great petitionary prayer to God on behalf of man. In the deepest sense, the prayer was not an invention of John, for it was inspired by what Christ had accomplished in obedience to the Father's will. Just what did John consider Christ's accomplishments to have been?

In his "hour" of death, Christ had glorified God by revealing God's love to man (17:1). By dying in obedience to God's will, Christ had finished his work; and when he was raised up into the presence of the Father, he had revealed through his Spirit that to know the only true God was to have eternal life (17:2-5). He had manifested God's name—that is, he had revealed the will, purposes, and love of God to the Church, and the Church had treasured and proclaimed this revelation (17:6). The Christian community knew that everything Christ said and did was a revelation of God, for it believed he had been sent with the commission and authority of God (17:7-8). Through the continuing presence of the Spirit, the community knew that it was under God's watchful care, and this knowledge was a source of joy (17:11-13). Because of its faithfulness to God's word revealed in Christ, the community had been separted from the world and had come to know its hatred (17:14). Yet, confident of God's victory over the world and its evil, the community had been kept from the grasp of evil power (17:15). Instead of being removed from the world, the community had actually been sent by Christ into the world to proclaim the truth that he himself had revealed (17:17-19). The community of disciples had, through their proclamation of the word, led many new believers into the community of Christ, and there they had come to know the love of God, which is eternal (17:20-24). They believed that Christ would continue to reveal this love throughout all the future (17:26).

This prayer has sometimes been called Christ's "High Priestly Prayer," a term that indicates what John seems to imply—namely, that in the prayer Christ consecrated the Church to its life and task in the world. But John clearly shows that it was not through any single word or prayer of the historical Jesus that this consecration took place, but rather through his *total life*. And the consecration did not cease with Jesus' death; rather, it continues to be consecrated through the Spirit throughout the life and history of the Church.

The Coming of the Spirit

This prayer is the climax of John's gospel. The speaker is Jesus, the Word of God, who is known not only through the words and deeds of his historical ministry, but also as the living Christ who is present in the community and who leads it to understand the meaning of his ministry for the world. It is through the inspiration and revelation of this Spirit that John has seen Christ's life as a prayer for his people, and it is this Christ whom John has been portraying throughout the Gospel. The ultimate truth about Christ and his works does not spring from a recounting of the literal words he spoke or of the literal works he performed; the truth is disclosed only by interpreting the historic ministry in the light of the meaning that the living Christ continued to reveal to the community in the days beyond the Resurrection right up to the time John wrote. We can now understand why John's portrait of Christ differs so decidedly from that of the Synoptics. Even the portrait in the Synoptics reflects the theological interpretation of the early community, but John has carried the interpretation much further. It is as though John had said: Let us re-tell the story of the life and work of Jesus on the basis of the meaning that has been revealed to the present day. Let him speak in language that will be meaningful to us. And let us reinterpret the events of his ministry from the standpoint of later happenings that have unfolded new meaning.

It has been said that John gave the Gospel to all the ages—that is, he freed the life and ministry of Jesus from its narrow Jewish setting and presented him as the savior of the world in language that would be familiar to non-Jews. But there is a more profound sense in which John gave Christ to the ages. By implication, John says that the historical Jesus is meaningful to men only when he is known as the Christ who lives in all ages, revealing himself and the Father to the Church.

This does not mean that John fails to affirm the significance of the Word become flesh, the historical ministry of Jesus. As we suggested earlier, he constantly presupposes the memory of the apostles as recorded in the synoptic tradition. Nowhere is this more clear than in John's Passion narrative (Jn. 18-20), which agrees with the Synoptic record on point after point. In fact, John may even include invaluable historical data that are not found in the Synoptics. But here again John's interpretative mind is at work. He uses Jesus' trial before Pilate as an occasion for the pronouncement, "My kingship is not of this world" (18:36). And on the Cross the last words are "It is finished" (19:30), words that have John's typical double meaning: it is not so much that Jesus' life is ended as that his work as Incarnate Word has been accomplished. And the accomplishment is not marked by the death on the Cross, though that is the conclusion of the earthly ministry. It is the gift of the Spirit that marks the accomplishment, as is indicated in John's final comment, "and he . . . gave up his spirit" (19:30). Here John refers not only to Christ's death but also to his giving of his spirit to the world. John's version of Pentecost is intimately related to Jesus' death and the Resurrection appearances of Jesus, the time at which the disciples receive the Spirit (20:19-23).

And the last word of John is consistent with his position throughout the Gospel: "Blessed are those who have not seen and yet believe." These words are intended for the readers of John's own day. It is not those Jewish disciples who saw Jesus in the days of his flesh who are blessed, nor even those who experienced the post-Resurrection appearances; blessed are those in all places and all ages who through their faith know Christ as present in the Spirit in the community of believers.

ETHICS FOR EXILES

I Peter and James

In its canon of New Testament letters, the Church has accepted not only letters attributed to the Apostle Paul, but also some attributed to other apostles. Foremost among the latter are those known as the "pillars" of the Jerusalem church (Gal. 2:9): Peter, James, and John. These were men whose importance to the early history of the Christian Church was keenly felt and whose very names seemed to guarantee the standards of canonicity.

Six letters attributed to them, together with one supposed to be written by the Apostle Jude, form the group we know as the "Catholic" or "General" Epistles: James; I and II Peter; I, II, III John; Jude.

While I Peter, I John, and perhaps James were known and used in certain areas at a relatively early date, there is not even indirect evidence concerning the others prior to the end of the second century. It is no wonder that their acceptance as "apostolic" writings into the canon was a rather slow process. At the beginning of the fourth century the Church Father, Eusebius, classified only I Peter and I John among the "undisputed" writings, while James, Jude, II Peter, and II and III John belonged to the class of books whose apostolicity and canonical standing were still under dispute. In the West, a clear decision to accept these smaller epistles as canonical was not forthcoming until the end of the fourth century, and even then II Peter is reported by Jerome to be "denied to be his [Peter's] by most." In the East, Didymus the Blind, an Egyptian theologian, denounced it as "forgery." As late as the fifth century, the official Bible of the Syrian Church, the *Peshitto*, numbered only I Peter, I John, and James among the accepted letters.

In fact, prior to being used for a whole group of writings, the designation "Catholic Epistle" seems to have been applied to I John because of its lack of specific address and therefore its designation as "general." Today, the designation is inappropriate because not all of the seven letters show a "universal" address. III John, together with Philemon, is a genuine private letter—the only such in our canon. The general designation, where it applies, however, is a clear hint of the decidedly literary character of the document; it is no longer a letter, but an "epistle."

It would of course be of greatest interest for us if these epistles had been written by those "apostles" under whose names they entered the canon, since our knowledge of those alleged authors is regrettably scanty. However, the chance of obtaining more data about these personalities from these letters is very slim. Scholars widely agree that the evidence against their authenticity is almost overwhelming. In some cases (James; Jude; II and III John), the letters themselves do not claim the authority of being written in the name of an apostle, and with the exception of I Peter and I John the history of their acceptance in the early Church clearly suggests a post-Apostolic date. Furthermore, in most of these epistles, including I and II Peter and James, there is no attempt to hide the marked dependence upon Paul's letters in form as well as in content.

I Peter addresses itself to churches in Pauline missionary territory, and mentions the name of Paul's companion Silvanus (= Silas). It follows exactly the general outline of the Pauline letters, including the Pauline form of the salutation ("May grace and peace be multiplied to you . . ."), an elaborate "thanksgiving" passage which is introduced by the same formula as in II Cor. 1:3 and Eph. 1:3, followed by a doctrinal and "ethical" section, and a personal conclusion reminiscent (for example) of I Corinthians and Galatians. The final salutation, "Peace to all of you that are in Christ," not only reflects Rom. 15:33 and I Cor. 16:23 f., but uses the Pauline formula "in Christ." This Pauline flavor is noticeable throughout. I Peter's insistence on the significance of Christ's death *for our sins* (2:24; 3:18) sounds Pauline, his notion of Christian freedom (2:16) seems to echo Gal. 5 and Rom. 6:18-22, and the admonition to use one's "gift" for one another, "as good stewards of God's varied grace" (4:10 ff.) reminds us of Pauline texts such as I Cor. 12 and Rom. 12.

The author of II Peter even quotes the body of Pauline letters along with other scripture (3:15 f.). The polemic of the author of James centering in the formula "no faith without works" can hardly be understood apart from the consequences which a later generation has drawn from the Pauline doctrine of justification. It is difficult to believe that men of so independent character as Peter and James would make themselves dependent upon Paul at all. And while we can account for Paul's Greek style, it is more than unlikely that "uneducated and common men" (Acts 4:13) like Peter and James had a command of the Greek language which, by literary and grammatical standards, is superior to that of most of the other New Testament authors.

Although under the circumstances it appears that these letters cannot contribute to the portrait of the apostles under whose names they have entered the canon, they are nevertheless most valuable sources for our knowledge of the post-Apostolic Church, its problems, and its ideas.[1]

"CATHOLIC EPISTLES"—LITERATURE OF CONFLICT

If in the history of the Church we can speak of "dark ages" about which we have little information, the period between A.D. 70 through 150 is one of them. Not that Christians did not write. But apart from those works that were received into the canon, only a random group of documents has survived. The bulk of them we know under the name *Apostolic Fathers* (see pp. 71-73).[2] What we catch from these sources are but sketchy glimpses of a wide landscape, the general shape of which we can only guess. We have a good many particulars, but we cannot tell exactly where they belong in the whole picture. We cannot even determine with certainty what the really pervading problems were, much less the details of developments of greatest importance, *e.g.*, regarding the ministry, Christian worship life, sacraments, etc. In order to reconstruct the situation in this "dark" period we often have no other choice than to infer what the

---

[1] For an introduction to the later books of the New Testament from this perspective see J. Christiaan Beker, *The Church Faces the World: Later New Testament Writings*, Westminster Guides to the Bible (Philadelphia: Westminster, 1960).

[2] A recent survey of the problems connected with this literature is found in R. M. Grant, *The Apostolic Fathers: A New Translation and Commentary; Vol. I: An Introduction* (New York: Nelson, 1964). This volume introduces a series which will comprise six volumes.

earlier phase probably was from the later development which is better attested. The danger of such a historical procedure is obvious. It may account for the surprisingly wide divergence among scholars even in the most elementary questions concerning the development in that age.

Combining canonical and noncanonical sources, we could try to establish a relative chronology for these books: James perhaps would come first, followed by I Clement; then Didache; I, II, III John; I Peter; Ignatius; Polycarp; Barnabas; Jude; II Peter. Last would come II Clement and the Shepherd of Hermas. But even if we had a precise chronological list, we would not have gained much, because another factor has to be taken into account. With the apostles, the Gospel had reached out far beyond the limited geographical scope of the earliest *kerygma*. The *kerygma* met with new situations at almost every outpost of the Christian mission. The historian of the post-Apostolic Church today must realize that he cannot assume that Christian developments in Rome are identical with or simply comparable to those in Asia Minor, Syria, Greece, or Egypt. He may be able to identify certain general trends, but he knows it would be wrong to suppose that the same stage of development was reached everywhere in the Church at the same time. Generalizations are of no help. There were great differences from province to province, from city to city. Even within the same congregation, the general outlook among Christians could be radically different. I Clement and I Peter seem to have been written at roughly the same time and from the same place, Rome. But their outlook is quite different. The very fact that Ephesians stresses the necessity of thinking of the Church in its *oneness* and of preserving what appeared to the author as the "unity" of a bygone golden age, may be an inadvertent indication that we have entered a period in which the local situation determined individual Christian development.

We have to be cautious concerning even the "general address" in some of our letters. The author may indeed intend his epistle to be a circular, to be read in various churches, perhaps even in the "Church at large." He tries to deal with problems in a wide frame; he appeals to the "general" truths of Christian faith. But he just cannot avoid speaking out of his local situation with its specific traditions and problems.

This is what makes any grouping of this literature under a common denominator somewhat arbitrary. Every book has its specific flavor, representing one of the innumerable local situations existing in the Church of those days. If we want to speak of "*the* Church" in the post-Apostolic Age, we must remember that we first have to think of the Church in Rome, in Corinth, in Ephesus, in the provinces of Asia or Macedonia, on the island of Crete, or in Spain.

This does not exclude the fact that to some extent all of these writings reflect certain common features. The great theme of the adaptation and transformation of the *kerygma* is the dominant factor, as we shall see. One theory of the history of the Church has been that *all* later development is an unfolding of seeds hidden in the history of the early days of the Church according to the will of God. There is certainly truth in this statement, inasmuch as it points to the undeniable historical continuity. But it is far too simple to describe this history *only* as an "unfolding." In the process we have not only "continuity" but also "discontinuity": not just modifications of former positions but denial, disavowal, rejection; not only "adaptation" but reform. Nor did the development follow an inner logic inherent in the Christian movement as such. If we take seriously the basic Christian message that God wants to meet man *in history* then we cannot fail to see that the development, especially in the formative period, was a response to the challenge of ongoing history, to pressures and dangers arising from outside the Church and from within. What was common to the churches of that period was perhaps not so much the *answers*, but rather the *problems* which they all were facing and the conflicts they all were involved in. All of the post-Pauline literature in the canon is literature of conflict. We must have an understanding of these conflicts in order to understand in what way the Christian *kerygma* has found its expression in those books.

THE CONFLICT WITH THE ROMAN GOVERNMENT

Perhaps the most influential writings among the Catholic Epistles are I Peter and James. They serve here as introduction to the basic lines of conflict along which the development in the post-Pauline Church seems to have moved.

The main conflict from outside that challenged and formed Christianity during this period was the conflict with the Roman authorities, which eventually led to the persecution of Christian minority groups by the civil authorities. This conflict was not deliberately sought by the Christians, neither was it precipitated by deliberate action of the state. It was an almost unavoidable consequence of the rapid growth of the Christian community and of the peculiar convictions of its members which distinguished them from other groups, even from Judaism. When the Pharisees and the Herodians questioned Jesus about paying taxes to Rome, Jesus is reported to have said: "Render to Caesar the things that are Caesar's and to God the things that are God's" (Mk. 12:17). Thus he had taken the moderate line of those Jews who refused to revolt against Rome and urged loyalty as long as it was made clear that there was no ultimate authority invested in the transitory institution of the state.

The same attitude prevailed in Paul. His appeal to the Roman Christians to accept the governing authorities as the gift of God (Rom. 13:1) has sometimes been interpreted as a demand that the Christian submit totally to every state "as authority over him." This is a misinterpretation. Paul put the will of God above the will of the state, which is an institution of "this passing age" destined to secure law and order in subjection to God's plan, though he had no quarrel with the claim of the Roman state to the loyalty of its citizens.

Nevertheless, both Jesus and Paul seem to have been executed by the Roman authorities on political grounds. The state quite obviously was not concerned with the content of their teaching, but with its effects. Groupings and movements which were likely to disturb the established order, the "peace" (*pax Romana*) which was based on wide tolerance in religious matters, created a situation which for the sake of law and order Rome was unwilling to tolerate. It was a matter of political expediency, not of religious intolerance, that there were early Christian martyrs.

The Persecution of Christians by the State

Actually, we have little precise knowledge of the various stages in this conflict. The first clear evidence of a serious encounter between Christians as a group and the Roman state comes from the time of the Emperor Nero (A.D. 54-68). In the summer of A.D. 64, a fierce fire raged through Rome for more than six days, devastating large areas of the city, especially west of the Tiber. According to the Roman historian Tacitus, there was a persistent rumor that Nero himself was responsible for the conflagration. In order to counter this suspicion, Nero laid the blame on "those who were hated on account of their

to Christ as to a god (*carmen dicere Christo*), bind themselves by an oath not to commit theft or robbery or adultery, not to break their word, and not to refuse to pay a debt. Beyond that, they had simply participated in eating a harmless meal of harmless food.

Trajan replied that Pliny had taken the right course, and that no general rule or fixed form of action could be laid down. Christians were not to be sought out actively, but if they were accused, they would have to be punished. If anyone denied that he was a Christian and agreed to worship the gods, he was to be pardoned, even if he had been under suspicion. And certainly no one was to be charged anonymously.

CHRISTIANITY AN ILLEGAL BUT NOT PERSECUTED RELIGION. According to Trajan's decision (which incidentally makes no reference to a precedent), it is clear that Christianity was to be regarded as an illegal religion. The "name as such" (*nomen ipsum*) was to be punished. To the average Roman citizen, including the governor, the Christian viewpoint seemed to be a "depraved and extravagant superstition." As a tolerant and enlightened polytheist, he could not see how the recognition of the state gods in any way threatened individual religious loyalty. However, even with this clarification, no general persecution was envisaged. In fact, we hear only of individual martyrdoms under Trajan and his successors, not of a general action against the Christians. Ignatius, bishop of Antioch, met his death on these terms; Symeon, son of Klopas and cousin of Jesus, was executed in Palestine. And one of the earliest reliable reports of a Christian martyrdom, that of Bishop Polycarp of Smyrna (155/156) illustrates most vividly the practice in Asia Minor based on the principles of that correspondence.[8]

I PETER: THE CONFLICT OUTSIDE THE COMMUNITY

It is astonishing how well the situation to which the author of First Peter addresses himself fits in with this frame. On the basis of the mention of "Babylon" (5:13), which as in Rev. 14:8 and 18:2 is a cryptic designation for Rome, and of the tradition which associates Mark with Peter in Rome, the letter is believed to have been written from Rome. No better alternative has been proposed. It is directed to Christians in Asia Minor. The list of five provinces (Pontus, Galatia, Cappadocia, Asia, Bithynia), which probably stands for Asia Minor as a whole, includes the areas of Pliny's actions. Allusions to the addressees' "former ways" make it quite clear that they are former Gentiles (1:14, 18, 21; 2:9 f.; 3:6; 4:2 ff.). The people in their environment react with surprise and open hostility to the Christians' withdrawal from the activities and

---

[8] See text and notes in *Early Christian Fathers*, Cyril C. Richardson, ed.; The Library of Christian Classics, I (Philadelphia: Westminster, 1953), 141-158.

pleasures of ordinary life, which the author paints in the colors of vices (4:3 f.). It is obvious that the new faith even splits families. Christian wives are urged to refrain from open attempts at converting their nonbelieving husbands, but rather to win them by their conduct as good wives (3:1 f.). Christians are being accused as "criminals" (2:12; 4:14 ff.), and there seems to be no way of appealing such an accusation. The Christian can show only by his correct behavior that he is innocent. For the rest, if he has a good conscience, he must be prepared to "suffer for righteousness' sake."

The word "suffer" dominates much of I Peter. Suffering here probably means more than just bearing the general hostility of one's surroundings [9]; if it is "suffering as a Christian," for the "name" (4:16), then it can hardly be doubtful that the threat of the "fiery ordeal" (4:12) is exactly the type of persecution Christians were facing under the rules laid down in the Pliny correspondence.[10] The Christian is advised not to act provocatively ("in your hearts reverence Christ as Lord"). However, when he is called to account, he should with a clear conscience affirm his allegiance and be prepared to take upon himself the consequences (3:13 ff.). The author's insistence on blameless conduct is aimed at keeping the issue clear. It seems that Christians were being accused of civil crimes such as murder, theft, "wrong-doing," "mischief-making" (4:18), and later Church Fathers refer to even more atrocious popular charges.[11] In the face of such accusations, it would have been difficult to make the issue clear as a religious question. In this situation of isolation the great danger for the new Christians was to yield to the pressure and become apostate: "Your adversary the Devil prowls around like a roaring lion, seeking someone to devour. Resist him, firm in your faith. . . ."—(5:8 f.).

At several points in the letter, the dangers of the present are placed in a wider context. The sufferings which the Christian has to undergo are a necessary episode, testing faith like the fire that purges dross and exposes true gold (1:6); they are signals that the great judgment which begins with the Church (4:17), and will not be restricted to one region only, is coming upon Christians throughout the world (5:10). In spite of this apocalyptic outlook, the author has not drawn the conclusion which we find in Revelation—namely, that his generation is witnessing the final battle, in which, under the cover of the Roman state, the powers of hell are fighting against God and his People. Rather, he shows considerable moderation. Although he warns that those who persecute will also be subject to judgment (4:17), he urges Christians to recognize the emperor and his governmental officials as the powers of order (2:13; 2:17). In the face

---

[9] The latter is the interpretation of W. C. Van Unnik, who consequently denies any reference to persecution in the epistle. See his articles "Christianity According to First Peter," in *Expository Times*, LXVIII (London, 1956), 79-83, and "Peter, First Letter of," in *The Interpreter's Dictionary of the Bible*, III (Nashville: Abingdon, 1962), 762.

[10] See the commentary by F. W. Beare, *The First Epistle of Peter*, 2nd ed. (Oxford: Blackwell, 1958).

[11] See especially Origen, *Against Celsus* VI. 27, 40; and Tertullian's *Apology*.

of the tests and troubles of the End of Time, the Christian entrusts himself humbly into the hands of the True Judge, waiting for the day when he will rejoice in glory. This attitude of loyalty and moderation toward Rome in fact characterizes the second-century Church, in which the prayer for the emperor was part of the liturgy,[12] and in which the attempt was made to work out a way of coexistence with the empire.

It is quite probable that the author of I Peter is drawing upon a traditional pattern when he is calling for "Joy in Suffering." [13] But what is more important is that, in making his point, he appeals to the Jesus tradition, and thus makes the *kerygma* the model for his teaching. The suffering Christ is invoked as the main example of the "suffering for doing right" which is demanded of the Christian (2:21 ff.; 3:17 f.). The test of persecution is a reason to rejoice, since the Christian thus shares the suffering of Christ (4:13) and will also share his glory. In his appeal to the Jesus tradition the author seems to reflect knowledge of the details of the Passion narrative (2:22 f.), just as he seems to be familiar with the tradition concerning the Sermon on the Mount (3:9, 14).

The Ethical Quest

The same appeal to the *kerygma* and its structure of humiliation and exaltation is at the basis of the author's teaching concerning the wider field of Christian morals. It is not by chance that in a writing which reflects the difficulties with the Roman state, we also find a serious attempt to deal with the question of Christian ethics. The basic message of the Church was concerned with a new life, bestowed by God through the Holy Spirit, a life which was to be radically different from the life of the world and its institutions. Nevertheless, since Christians were still living "in the world" they realized that they had to relate themselves to its customs and practices without perverting the new life. They were driven to formulate an ethical code which would help to make clear where the new life was endangered by the pressures of the day.

The need was heightened when the churches were flooded with Gentiles who had difficulty realizing that as members of the Church they had left "the world" and joined a group of "exiles." The immediate threat of persecution certainly did much to impress upon the Christian the awareness that he was not of this world. But in order to help him face this fact in his daily situation, there had to be some kind of a formal code.

The Church did not weave its norms of conduct out of thin air. Today we can distinguish the wide range of influences under which the Church, though often quite unconsciously and spontaneously, worked out the details. There

---

[12] Compare I Clem. 61; Polycarp, Phil. 12:3; Justin Martyr, *Apology* I. 17. 3; Tertullian, *Apology* 30.

[13] See W. Nauck, "Freude im Leiden," *Zeitschrift für die neutestamentliche Wissenschaft*, XLVI (Berlin: Töpelmann, 1955), 66-80.

are five main sources: first, there was the Old Testament, which Christians accepted as their sacred scripture. Second, there was the ethical tradition of various apocalyptic sects in Judaism which depended on the Biblical tradition, although in a peculiar form. The Dead Sea Scrolls have shed much light on this whole movement. Third, there were the teachings of Jesus, preserved by oral tradition and finally written into the Gospels. But since Jesus had not tried to give a systematic code of ethics, later Christians, especially in a Gentile environment, were confronted by many ethical decisions for which they had no ready answer from the tradition about his teachings. Evidences of reinterpretation reflecting the need to adapt this teaching to a new environment are already found in the gospels themselves. A fourth source of ethical standards was the instruction used in the Hellenistic synagogues for the training of proselytes. Hellenistic Judaism was indebted not only to Judaism, but also to the ethical teaching of Hellenistic philosophy, the influence of which is evident throughout the New Testament. A fifth source was the common store of Hellenistic ethical instruction, as it is represented by the preaching of the wandering stoic and cynic moralists, although in many cases it may be difficult to ascertain whether the borrowing was direct or mediated through the Hellenistic synagogue.

THE ETHICAL CODE AND BAPTISM. The parallel to the instruction of proselytes in the synagogue suggests that the teaching of the Christian "ethical code" was connected with baptism. There can be no doubt that the old rite of baptism as the initiation of the individual into the community of the God-given new life took on tremendous significance in the Gentile churches. The "rebirth" (I Pet. 1:3, 23; Jn. 3:3), or "illumination" (Heb. 6:4; Eph. 5:14), or "sealing" (Eph. 1:13 f.; 4:30; Hermas, Similitudes IX. 16.4), as it is variously described, mediates a new life affecting *all* phases of the new Christian's existence: forgiveness of past sins, strength and direction for right conduct in the present, and the gift of the Spirit which "seals" the Christian for eternal life in the New Age. We do not know much about the form in which baptism was administered, although the picture presented by Justin Martyr late in the second century may give us some idea.[14] Like Eph. 1:13 f., Acts stresses the general sequence of hearing the word, believing, and being baptized. It may be that when the head of the household took this step, other members (we do not hear about the children)[15] simply followed along (Acts 2:31, 41; 8:12; 9:18;

---

[14] Justin Martyr, *Apology* I. 61 ff. See the translation in *Early Christian Fathers*, Cyril C. Richardson, ed.; The Library of Christian Classics, I (Philadelphia: Westminster, 1953), 282 ff.

[15] For the recent debate concerning infant baptism see the (positive) study by J. Jeremias, *Infant Baptism in the First Four Centuries*, The Library of History and Doctrine (Philadelphia: Westminster, 1960), and the (critical) answer by K. Aland, *Did the Early Church Baptize Infants?*, translated with an introduction by G. R. Beasley-Murray, preface by J. F. Jansen (Philadelphia: Westminster, 1963).

10:47 f.; 16:33). Luke presupposes that, in the missionary situation of the early time, the rite originally was rather informal and spontaneous (Acts 2:41; 8:36-37). There is, however, reason to believe that in his records of baptisms he occasionally uses formulas of the baptismal liturgy of his time (Acts 16:30 f.; 8:37).

We have clear evidence of a concern about the proper form of the rite in the instruction contained in the Didache (Chapter 7):

> Concerning baptism, baptize thus: Having first rehearsed all these things, baptize in the name of the Father and of the Son, and of the Holy Spirit, in running water; but if thou hast no running water, baptize in other water, and if thou canst not in cold, then in warm. But if thou hast neither, pour water three times on the head in the name of the Father, Son, and Holy Spirit. And before the baptism let the baptizer and him who is to be baptized fast, and any others who are able. And thou shalt bid him who is to be baptized to fast one or two days before.

The most important feature here is that the solemn rite (which presupposes a trinitarian formula instead of the older form "in the name of Christ") is connected with a time of preparation marked by a fast on the part of both the baptizer and those to be baptized. "Preparation" for baptism here seems also to include some type of formal instruction. The phrase "having rehearsed all these things" refers to the first six chapters in which the conduct in the "way of life" is contrasted to the "way of death." A very similar pattern of ethical instruction is found in the Epistle of Barnabas (Chapters 18-20). It is quite probable that this "catechism of the two ways," which may have its roots in the proselyte instruction of the synagogue, was part of the baptismal instruction in the communities where the writings originated.[16]

Just how long it has been that the Church has given formal instruction in connection with baptism we cannot tell. But scholars today are inclined to trace a goodly amount of the didactic materials in the New Testament to the situation of "catechesis," *i.e.*, to baptismal instruction. In a similar way, baptismal liturgy is felt to have influenced the wording of many New Testament passages.

It has long been recognized that the books of the New Testament make use of local or regional liturgical traditions. It is relatively easy to recognize the use of hymns or hymnic fragments which by virtue of their rhythmic structure stand out from the context: the three hymns in Lk. 1-2, known as the *Magnificat* (Lk. 1:46-55), the *Benedictus* (Lk. 1:68-79) and the *Nunc dimittis* (Lk 2:29-32), the hymns in Revelation (4 f.; 11:17; 12:10 ff.; 15:3 f.; 19:1-8), the fragments in I Tim. 3:16 and Eph. 5:14. Suggestions for at least a hymnic background

---

[16] On the divergent views concerning the origin of this catechism see the introduction in J. P. Audet, *La Didaché: Instructions des apôtres* (Paris: Gabalda, 1958), pp. 122 ff.

have been made with respect to numerous New Testament passages (*e.g.*, Phil. 2:5-11; Jn.1:1 ff.).In their use of hymns, Christians were heavily indebted to the Jewish synagogue, but they certainly also created new hymns. The discovery of the *Odes of Solomon*, a second-century Christian Gnostic book of hymns to Christ and to the Christian virtues, is a welcome illustration.[17]

Beyond these materials there is the wide field of liturgical acclamations, doxologies, prayers, credal statements, and sacramental formulae which show the importance of Christian worship for the literature of the New Testament. With regard to baptism, Col. 1:15 ff. has been claimed as a baptismal confession; Ephesians (especially Chapter 1) is said to reflect part of baptismal liturgy. There can be no doubt that the main body of I Peter must in some way be connected with the rites of baptism.[18] The author addresses himself to new converts (1:12 ff.; 2:2; 4:3 ff.), and if we can take our clue from later baptismal liturgies or sermons it seems obvious that baptismal terminology abounds throughout the letter (*e.g.*, 1:23; 2:2, 3:21). Of special interest are the exodus typology in 1:2; 2:9 f., and the reference to Noah and the Flood in 3:20. Arguing from these facts, the suggestion has been made that I Peter preserves the liturgical formulary of a full baptismal service in the early Church,[19] consisting first of an initial prayer psalm (1:3-12) and a brief instruction (1:13-21) which immediately preceded the act of baptism (after 1:21). Then came a short exhortation (1:22-25), a hymn (2:1-10), a longer sermon (2:11-3:12), an apocalyptic address (3:13-4:7a), and finally the concluding prayer (here changed to an exhortation) ending with the doxology (4:7b-11c). According to this interpretation, 4:12-5:11, which is generally acknowledged as being in some way independent of the major section, would reflect a brief concluding service of the whole congregation.

Such an analysis may be too bold. But there is good reason to believe that in 1:3-4:11 we have preserved discourse materials which were meant to be delivered in connection with baptism. For converted Gentiles, the ethical implications of entering the new life were a serious matter. They had to renounce completely all the ways of their past (4:3). In the face of the conviction that

---

[17] R. Harris and A. Mingana, *The Odes and Psalms of Solomon*, 2 vols. (Manchester, England: University of Manchester Press, 1916-1920).

[18] Most scholars agree on this point. See for example F. W. Beare's commentary, *The First Epistle of Peter*, 2nd ed. (Oxford: Blackwell, 1958). For the suggestions concerning Colossians and Ephesians see E. Kaesemann in *Festschrift für Bultmann* (Stuttgart: Kohlhammer, 1949), pp. 133-148; and J. Coutts, in *New Testament Studies*, III (Cambridge, England: Cambridge University Press, 1956-1957), 115-127.

[19] The following analysis is that of H. Preisker in the appendix to the commentary by H. Windisch, *Die Katholischen Briefe*, 2nd ed., *Handbuch zum Neuen Testament*, XV (Tübingen: J. C. B. Mohr, 1951), 156-160. F. L. Cross, *I Peter: A Paschal Liturgy* (London: Mowbray, 1954), even suggests that I Peter constitutes the celebrant's part in the liturgy of a baptismal service on Easter Eve. See, however, the criticism by C. F. D. Moule, "The Nature and Purpose of I Peter," in *New Testament Studies*, III (Cambridge, England: Cambridge University Press, 1956-1957), 1-11; and T. C. G. Thornton, in *The Journal of Theological Studies*, new series, XII, 1961, 14-26.

baptism had freed them from sin, they needed advice as to how to keep their new status undefiled. Ethical instruction was a necessary part of the "Word," the "Good News" which preceded their baptism (1:12, 23; 2:8; 3:1). The details may have varied—but, being structured after the basic pattern of the *kerygma*, the emerging norm of conduct gave a concrete expression to the common faith and tended more and more to identify the Church as a cohesive social organism in the Roman world. I Peter is so valuable for our study of the Church's ethical teaching, because it provides us with an actual example of the content and the form of this teaching as it was delivered in connection with the baptism of converted Gentiles.

NEW FAITH AS THE FOUNDATION OF THE NEW ETHICAL LIFE.   The author of I Peter prefaces his instructions with a statement on the substance, source, and aim of the faith which lies at the heart of all ethical action (1:3-12). In baptism, Christians enter into a new life, they are "born anew." Our author, like the author of the Gospel of John, emphasizes the *radical* nature of this new life by speaking in terms of rebirth.

What is the source and substance of this new life? The source is God himself, who is the Father of Jesus Christ—the Lord to whom the Christian has committed himself. The substance of this life consists of a living hope—a word which the author uses almost interchangeably with faith (*e.g.*, 3:15). This hope is a gift from God that was made possible when God raised Jesus Christ from the dead and thereby revealed that men will obtain salvation. Since faith and hope are the source of the Christian's joy (1:6), Christians will not sidestep ethical decisions that bring them trials and hardships; their actions are not directed toward temporal ends, but toward proving their faithfulness to God who is the source of their joy (1:6-7). The new life is also characterized by love for Christ, through whom salvation has come, whom Christians have not seen, and whom even the prophets looked for. But Christians have come to know him through the proclamation of the Good News (Gospel) which the Holy Spirit revealed as true (1:8-12). It was the Church's faith as known through the *kerygma* that was the source of a new life.

This then is the foundation that the author lays for his ethical instruction— a sure knowledge that the new life is not to be measured primarily by what the Christian does, but by what he *hopes, believes, and loves*. This approach to ethical teaching is essentially the same as that of both Jesus and Paul.

A HOLY NATION, GOD'S OWN PEOPLE.   But the Christian's primary concern with faith does not free him from responsibility for his actions. He must be capable of making sober judgments in his daily life if he is not to betray the hope that is to be fulfilled when Christ is finally revealed (1:13). This means that Christians can no longer follow their desires as they did before they knew the God revealed through Jesus Christ (1:14). The central demand is that they conform in their conduct to the fact that he is holy (1:16); he is the judge of all men, and he judges them according to their deeds (1:17). Through Jesus Christ, God has released (ransomed) them from their bondage to pagan idolatries and from the futile dissipation of the way of life they had inherited from their fathers (1:18). But this means that they have really become exiles in the world (1:17). God's holiness has revealed the futility of any way of life except that lived in faith and hope in the God who raised Jesus Christ from the dead. Christians can no longer be at home with the world's ways.

What is the way of holiness? It is the way of love. Christians who have obediently responded to God's act of love proclaimed in the Gospel (the truth) have been purified and have been given a new birth in a new community of love. This community's life is born out of and sustained by one thing: the active power of God's saving Word disclosed in the Gospel. All other grounds of life are transient. The substance of the new life in the new community is the sincere love of the members for one another (1:22-25).

Notice how logically the author has proceeded through this opening discussion. First, he announced that the new life is grounded in faith (1:3-12). Then, he emphasized that faith inevitably demands holiness (1:13-21). And now he concludes that faith and the new life it brings are the foundations of a new community (1:22-25). This community is called "a chosen race, a royal priesthood, a holy nation, God's own people" (2:9). All of these are titles of honor which, in the Old Testament, explained Israel's role as the instrument of God's plan of salvation for all men. But the early Christians held that by rejecting Jesus, the People of Israel had forfeited this role. Through the death and resurrection of Jesus, God was finally calling his People together in a new way, fulfilling his promises to them through the coming of the Holy Spirit and using those who "were no people," the despised Gentiles, as his "New Israel," his People, his messengers for the execution of his plan. As a holy nation, then, the Church takes over the role of Israel. She is in exile in the world and Christians are aliens (2:11). And as long as the community lives in this world, its one authority for action is God's holy will, as revealed through Jesus Christ. This meant that the most the Church could do before the final salvation would mark the end of this world order, was to adjust herself to the world for the time being. Political, social, and economic institutions, and the temporal purposes for which they were set up, were all part of a life that would soon pass away. Consequently, the Church worked out no program of social or political reform. She accepted the social order as it was, although its acceptance did not imply absolute approval. The primary obligation of the Church was to live in and to bear witness to the world according to the will of God. Sometimes this meant separating herself completely from the practices of the world—as she did on matters involving pagan worship and the loose attitude toward sex relations. But on other points, the Church accommodated herself to the world—as in her relation to government and to social institutions like slavery.

The ethical instruction in I Peter reflects the teaching of the early Church on these matters. Beginning with 2:1, and continuing through 4:11, we have a series of exhortations. Study of the Greek text shows that each instruction begins with a technical phrase derived from a Hebrew formula.[20] This phrase is used in the same way elsewhere in the New Testament, especially in Paul's epistles to the Colossians and Romans, in I Thessalonians, in Ephesians, and throughout the Pastoral Epistles. In fact, all these passages, including those in I Peter, show similarity of content as well. For example, in Colossians (3:8-4:12) we find a series of exhortations to put off certain vices, worship God, submit to certain people, and be watchful. In Ephesians (4:22-6:8) there are similar exhortations regarding putting off sins, worshiping, submitting, and watching. And in I Peter are found instructions to put away insincerity (2:1), to worship (2:4-5), to abstain (2:11), to be subject (2:13), to submit (2:18; 3:1; 3:7), and to watch (keep sane and sober because the end of all things is at hand)—(4:7). Further, each of these epistles contains a brief statement about the new life of the Christian in terms of the New Creation (Col. 3:10 ff.; Eph. 4:24), and the same reference to the new life appears in I Peter in terms of regeneration (1:3). Apparently, there is imbedded in all these epistles a definite pattern of instruction defining the nature of the new life given in baptism and governing the conduct of Christians in the world.[21] Each teacher would use the basic pattern, but adapt the materials to the local situation.

According to I Peter, the one law that determines the life of the Christian community is the law of love. But this is not a vague or sentimental quality; basically, it is love for Christ as Lord (1:8). And to love Christ means to love what he loved—hence, Christians are to love one another. Now the author goes on to spell out in greater detail just what is meant by love. Since love is always concerned with the welfare of the brother, any words or deeds that harm him must be put aside (2:1). Like newborn babes, Christians should long for the holy life of love (spiritual milk) in order to be nurtured in preparation for their coming salvation. Obviously, since it was within this community that "the kindness of the Lord" (2:3) was known, it is here and not in any other community of the world that the life of love can be nurtured.

Christian Action in a Non-Christian World

Having dealt with faith and the new life as the basis of ethical action, and with the new community as the place in which the new life is nurtured, the author now turns to the relationship between Christians and the pagan world. The instruction takes the form of a catechism dealing with various

---

[20] D. Daube, *The New Testament and Rabbinic Judaism* (London: Athlone, 1956), pp. 90-105.

[21] See P. Carrington, *The Primitive Christian Catechism* (Cambridge, England: Cambridge University Press, 1940).

relationships: *government, slavery, marriage and the family.* These were relationships in which Christians, like all men in the Graeco-Roman world, were involved, and both Jews and thoughtful Gentiles had tried to formulate principles of action to govern them. The formula and content of the various duties prescribed in I Peter and in many other epistles of the New Testament (Col. 3:18 ff.; Eph. 5:22 ff.; I Tim. 2:8 ff.; 6:1 f.; Tit. 2:1 ff.) show a dependence on pre-Christian codes of ethical action.[22] These codes are commonly referred to as "household tables," because they describe the duties of the average person in his relationship at home and in the world. The foremost source from which these materials are borrowed is the Hellenistic synagogue which had already been influenced by the ethical teaching of Hellenistic philosophies.

GOVERNMENT.   The first specific instruction deals with the Christian's relation to the Roman government. We have already dealt with this aspect. The Christian's respect for the law and for the officials who enforce it did not stem from political convictions. They were simply accommodating themselves to the times, although their decision to do so was based on what they believed to be the will of God—that is, to do no moral evil. Ultimately, the Christian was a servant, not of the emperor, but of God. The instruction in I Peter says, "Honor the emperor"—only God is to be feared.

SLAVERY.   This same principle came into play when the Christian community tried to work out an ethical decision on the relationship between slaves and masters. This was an acute problem, for there were many slaves in the Christian community.[23] The fact that the instruction in I Peter, contrary to that found in Ephesians and Colossians, makes no mention of the masters' obligations to their slaves may mean that this instruction was intended mainly for slaves. Paul had already defined the relation of slaves and masters in the Church. There was no distinction among those who were in Christ (Gal. 3:28). But this freedom was a gift of God and not of the world. The Roman world had its own definite laws regarding free men and slaves; and Christians, who were subject to the Roman state, might even possess slaves. Paul even wrote a letter (Philemon) to a fellow Christian, urging him to permit a runaway slave to return without punishment.

So the instruction reads, "Servants, be submissive to your masters with all respect, not only to the kind and gentle, but also to the overbearing."—(2:18). Now, from the standpoint of the Christian faith, slavery was just as transient an institution as the Roman government itself. Consequently, the government's approach to the ethical relationship between slaves and masters was different

---

[22] See the discussion in E. G. Selwyn, *The First Epistle of St. Peter*, 2nd ed. (New York: St. Martin's Press, 1958), pp. 194 ff.
[23] See P. Allard, *Les esclaves chrétiens depuis les premiers temps de l'Eglise jusqu'à la fin de la domination romaine en occident*, 5th ed. (Paris: Lecoffre, 1914).

from the Christian approach. According to Roman law, the slave was a chattel in the hands of his master. He had no civil rights and his master could punish him as he pleased. The instruction here obviously implies that the slave should fulfill his obligations to his master in accordance with customary law and practice, and that he should be a good slave (cf. Col. 3:22 ff.; Eph. 6:5 ff.; I Tim. 6:1 f.; Tit. 2:9 f.; Didache 4:11). The slave must even go beyond what is expected of him and be kind and gentle to a master who may abuse him, for he is ultimately obligated to the will of God. The pattern for his conduct is none other than Christ himself: "When he was reviled, he did not revile in return; when he suffered, he did not threaten; but he trusted to him who judges justly."—(2:23).

Here we see clearly how the Christians conformed to convention while searching for an ethical code. For, while the slave fulfills his obligations to his master, his conduct is not governed only or primarily by law, but by the spirit of Christ. It is not surprising that in the early centuries many masters were led into the Church through the examples of their Christian slaves.

Unfortunately, this early Christian instruction was to be used centuries later as a justification for slavery. In America, during the early nineteenth century, many sermons were preached on this very text to justify slavery as a divine institution established by God's will as revealed in the New Testament. Nothing could have been further from the mind of the early Church. Slavery, like every human institution, existed by God's sufferance as long as this world order continued. Christians made no effort to justify slavery on the grounds of philosophical or social theory, for they did not expect the present order to last much longer. They did not try to defend it as a divine institution; they merely asked themselves the question: Given this relationship between Christians and the world, how can we act to bear witness to God's will?

MARRIAGE AND THE FAMILY.   The instruction in I Peter next deals with another common institution: marriage (3:1-7). The requirement that the Christian wife "be submissive" to her husband was in no sense peculiar to the Christian community (cf. Eph. 5:22 ff.; I Tim. 2:9-15; I Clement 1:3; Polycarp 4:2). Both Jewish and Gentile teachers pictured the ideal wife as faithful and obedient. But again, we find the ideal interpreted in a peculiarly Christian way. The instruction implies that the wives who are being addressed are married to non-Christian husbands. According to the Hellenistic philosopher Plutarch, the ideal wife should accept her husband's religion. But for a Christian wife to renounce her faith would be to act contrary to the will of God. And yet, she was not to withdraw from the relationship altogether. In all other respects she was to live up to the common ideal of the good wife in simplicity and with a "gentle and quiet spirit."

Here again we see how the Christian, though following a pattern of conduct not peculiarly Christian, in a relationship also not peculiarly Christian, is to act in such a way as to transform the whole relationship. When we recall the common hostility against the Christians, we can imagine how little peace there must have been in homes where Christian wives were regarded as insubordinate by their non-Christian husbands. But through the manifestation of the new life into which she had entered, she was to give new meaning to marriage so that her husband might be won to Christ, and the ultimate sanction for her fulfilling the role of wife was not in order to satisfy convention, but in order that she "do right" in the sight of God (3:6).

The instruction to husbands again brings up what was regarded as the proper conduct of husband toward wife (3:7). The Christian husband is to live "considerately with his wife." This translation does not quite do justice to the original Greek, which literally reads "live with her according to knowledge." The phrase undoubtedly refers to the "knowledge" that the husband has been granted through his new faith and which is spelled out in the reason given for his new way of life: "You are joint heirs of the grace of life." Although the husband is to maintain his traditional authority, through his faith he is to regard his wife as a joint partner in eternal hope and life. In the future world, there will be no difference (Mk. 12:25). He is no longer to think of her as simply the woman who bears his children or who acts as steward in the household. Their life together is to be transformed into a Christian relationship within the context of an institution that was in no sense peculiarly Christian.

THE AUTHOR'S APPEAL TO THE JESUS TRADITION.   The instruction concerning ethical action in relation to the world ends with a plea for "unity of spirit, sympathy, love of the brethren, a tender heart and a humble mind" (3:8). This instruction brings together two qualities of the new life that are most difficult to hold in balance: humility on the one hand, and acting in accordance with the will of God on the other (3:8-21). True humility means that Christians must return a blessing when they are reviled (3:9). It means defending their faith, not in arrogance, but in gentleness (3:13-15). Christians are to conduct themselves in such a way that their accusers will be shamed. And the pattern for humility is to be found in the example of Jesus Christ, who himself stood before the Roman procurator, Pilate, and then suffered on the Cross (3:17-4:1).

This is already the second instance in the course of the ethical exhortations in which the author makes an elaborate appeal to the Jesus tradition. In 2:21 ff. he had based the rule that the Christian slave should submit patiently even to punishment for doing right, on the example of the patient suffering of Jesus Christ. The same argument is used here when he stresses the suffering of the "righteous for the unrighteous" (3:18). However, the rest of the long kerygmatic digression does not seem to be to the point. In the next verse, mention is made of Christ's having "preached to the spirits in prison" who are identified as the unbelieving contemporaries of Noah who perished in the Flood (3:20). In the context of the exhortations, this reference may be intended as an encouragement for Christians not to shy away from bearing witness to unbelievers, just as Christ preached to the disobedient spirits.[24] But the quick transition from the "water" of the Flood to the "water" of baptism (3:21) and Christ's resurrection indicates that in this passage the author did not simply offer illustrations for his ethical teaching. He rather quotes (and adapts) preformed kerygmatic materials which only partly suit his aim. Most scholars think this represents a kind of credal statement.

The Structure of the Creed and Ethics

It is no surprise to find credal materials in a baptismal context. As we have seen, baptismal instruction included both the setting forth of the formal contents of faith and the ethical rules derived therefrom. We can infer from the later development that the act of baptism itself presented perhaps not the only, but certainly the most important, opportunity for a recital of the creed.[25] The Church Father Irenaeus (*Against Heresies* I. 9.4) speaks of the "rule of truth" being received in baptism. And the two major creeds still in use in our churches, namely the Apostles' Creed and the Nicene Creed, have a long history as baptismal confessions—a history which reaches back as far as we can trace their origins.

Some of the older credal formulae may have been rather brief. They could expressly or implicitly contain a reference to God the Father, but at least those connected with baptism always centered around the essence of the *kerygma, i.e.,* the person and work of Jesus Christ. Traces of such short formulae are still found in many New Testament books; Eph. 5:4 f.; Acts 8:37 (Western text), 16:3 among others, leave no doubt about a baptismal context. The earliest clear traces of a trinitarian affirmation (Didache 7:3; Mt. 28:19; cf. I Pet. 1:2!) also appear in the context of baptism.

The rich kerygmatic material in I Peter seems to imply a well-developed form of the Christological creed. It contains many elements which we know from pre-Pauline or Pauline tradition. Christ "was destined before the foundation of the world and manifested at the end of the time" (1:20; cf. Phil. 2:6; I Cor. 8:6; I Tim. 3:16). He died "for sins once for all" (3:18; cf. 1:18 f.; 2:24 f.). His "resurrection from the dead" (1:3) is described as the basis of our "dying to sin and living to righteousness" (2:23)—a term clearly connected with baptism (cf. Rom. 6:1-11). He is "sitting at the right hand of the Father,"* i.e.,* all "angels, authorities, and powers" are subject to him (3:22; cf. Phil. 2:11; I Cor. 15:24 ff.), and he will be "revealed" in glory (1:7). But there is evidence that we have moved to a more developed stage of Christological statements. To the traditional images for the death of Christ (his blood, his wounds, the lamb with-

---

[24] This is the interpretation given by Bo Reicke in his comprehensive book, *The Disobedient Spirits and Christian Baptism*, Acta Seminarii Neotestamentici Upsaliensis, XIII (Copenhagen: Munksgaard, 1946).

[25] About the various occasions which led to the formulation of a creed, see O. Cullmann, *The Earliest Christian Confessions*, tr. J. K. S. Reid (London: Lutterworth, 1949).

out blemish) is added the designation of the Cross as the "tree" (2:14) which has only a tentative forerunner in Paul (Gal. 3:3), but became very popular in the post-Apostolic period (Acts 5:30; 10:39; 13:29; Barnabas 5:13; Polycarp 8:1). As in the old formula of Rom. 1:4, the Resurrection is connected with the "Spirit" (3:19), but it seems to be distinguished from the Ascension (3:22). Among the gospel writers, only Luke seems to have knowledge of this latter tradition (Lk. 24:15 f.; Acts 1:2; 1:9-11). Furthermore, Christ's "ascent" is paralleled by the idea of his "descent" into hell or limbo (3:19 f.)[26] which probably is rooted in ancient mythical traditions, but is evident as part of the Christian *kerygma* only in later strata of the tradition (Eph. 4:9; Rev. 1:18; Gospel of Peter; Ignatius, Magnesians 9:2 f., etc.).

On the other hand, a more developed stage is indicated by the lack of interest in the notion of scriptural fulfillment which had been essential in the earliest formulations of the *kerygma* (cf. I Cor. 15:3). To be sure, most of the credal elements are linked to their Old Testament background. "Messianic" texts such as Is. 53 or Psalm 110 are presupposed in statements like I Pet. 2:24 f. and 3:22. The reference to Christ as the stone rejected by men but chosen and precious in the sight of God even contains a full scriptural "testimony" (2:4 ff.). But for the Gentile Christians, the scriptural proof was less important than the application of the *kerygma* to their new life. This does not mean that the Old Testament had become unimportant. Rather, the Old Testament was so completely absorbed by the Christian frame of mind that the average believer simply assumed it was a Christian book to begin with. The prophets have already fully announced what the Christian preacher says; furthermore, they knew that they were addressing the Christian generation (I Pet. 1:10-12). The Book of James and especially the letter of Barnabas demonstrate how even the Old Testament Law was Christianized by reducing it to its "moral essence" and eliminating the ceremonial law by "spiritual" exegesis.

Kerygma and ethical code are intimately connected in I Peter. But it is not so much the details of the Jesus tradition to which the author appeals in formulating his exhortations. It is the general structure of the *kerygma* in terms of Jesus' "suffering and his subsequent glory," of humiliation and exaltation, which he uses as his guiding principle in impressing the implications of the new life upon Gentile Christians. Here, the basic paradox of God's salvation has become manifest: God has chosen what is low and humble in the world, not what is high and exalted (5:5). In baptism, the young Christians have taken the first step toward conforming to this pattern. With Christ, they "died to sin and were raised to righteousness" (2:24). Now they have to be told how their whole lives should manifest this fact. They must be reminded that by joining this group of "exiles," rather than having entered into glory, they are thrown into an arena of

---

[26] See J. M. Robinson, "Descent into Hades," in *The Interpreter's Dictionary of the Bible*, I (Nashville: Abingdon, 1962), 826-828.

fierce fight, of temptation and suffering. The basic rule of conforming to the pattern under these circumstances which dominates the last part of I Peter (4:12-5:11) is summed up in 5:6: "Humble yourselves therefore under the mighty hand of God, that in due time he may exalt you."—(cf. 4:13; 5:1; 5:10).

This "due time" is not far off any more (4:7). The author again and again says that only a little while, a short span, separates this time of exile from the final glory (1:6; 1:17; 4:17; 5:10). In accordance with Jewish and Christian tradition, he thinks of this "end" as judgment. But for the Christian, this judgment is as little a frightening burden as are the trials of the present. The very fact of his suffering indicates that the judgment is already under way, and he knows that in the end it will be the occasion when his sharing in Christ's glory will become manifest.

Thus, it is the expectation of the final manifestation of God's righteousness that shapes the last contours of the ethical code. In formulating this code, Christians were not only looking back to the example of Jesus as they saw him through the medium of tradition. They were also looking forward to his Coming at the end of the Age. All actions of the Christian appear *sub specie aeternitatis,* "in the light of eternity."

Early Christian ethics have sometimes been called "interim ethics." This term would be inappropriate if it implied that ethical decisions were rather haphazard and casual because Christians were preoccupied with the shape of the world to come rather than with the shape of this world. To be sure, they knew that the shape of this world would pass away, that they were strangers and exiles. But they also knew that during this "interim" all their activity in the world was a witness to the message which they were commissioned to proclaim. It was their constant hope that through their conduct, other men might be led to glorify God. Thus, their ethical code, worked out only for a "temporary" situation, was nevertheless firmly and universally grounded in the structure of the message out of which it grew.

JAMES: THE CONFLICT WITHIN THE COMMUNITY

When we turn to the Epistle of James, it is evident how necessary it was to give concrete directions for the new life in the everyday situation of the average Christian and the average congregation. The whole epistle is concerned with one simple truth: It is not enough to "be" a Christian, if this fact does not show in one's conduct. The author sees the basic danger of the Christian message in its being misunderstood as merely intellectual doctrine. A life of complacency, inertia, and moral indifference is no possible mode of Christian existence. "James" vigorously denounces every attempt to restrict the new life to the realm of theory and mere talk instead of letting it have its effect on Christian action. Thus, his concern is not so much the formulation of the ethical code, but its application. The Church, which accepted the epistle into its canon, always saw the author as the representative of an activistic trend in early Christianity, as a warning voice that Christianity is an eminently practical religion.

James on Sin, Baptism, and Forgiveness

For us, the Book of James is important because it gives us some idea of how Christians faced the moral issue as it arose from within—that is, how they related themselves not just to the world around them, the challenge of persecution and of the pagan way of life, but to the worldliness in their own midst. For the Christian, as we have seen, sin was thought to have been basically dealt with in baptism. The new life meant forgiveness of past sins and included the expectation that, with the help of the Holy Spirit, the Christian henceforth would walk toward the goal of perfection, still involved in a daily fight with sin, but certainly without committing any major sin. Practice, however, revealed

THE OLDEST BAPTISTRY *ever found was in a tiny chapel at Dura Europos, on the Euphrates River in northeastern Syria. The walls of the chapel, which was destroyed in* A.D. 258, *were covered with paintings of Biblical scenes, traces of which are still visible. The person to be baptized stood in the shallow pool and had water poured over his head.*

that this principle did not square with reality. "Sin," even grave sin, remained a phenomenon within the communities, and had to be dealt with.

There seems to have been a common line which most writers of the post-Apostolic time followed. In the first place, they all stress the importance of the forgiveness of sins connected with the initial act of baptism, and the responsibility of the Christian to keep the "seal" of baptism undefiled. They also agree that sin after baptism is not *per se* a reason to regard a member as a "son of Satan" and to exclude him from the congregation. But they seem to recognize certain differences. Paul already had advised the expulsion of an open sinner (I Cor. 5:1 ff.), but he had stressed that the door must be kept open for him and for everyone who repents (II Cor. 2:5 ff.). Hebrews, presumably in a situation of persecution, mentions the denial of the Lord as a deliberate sin for which there is no forgiveness (10:26; cf. 12:25). I John tries to make a distinction between "mortal" sins and others that are "not mortal" (5:16 f.). The terminology of the Didache is particularly instructive. The respected members of the congregation are called "holy," and "holiness" is especially required in connection with the Eucharist. Only he who is "holy" can participate (10:6); he who has sinned must first "repent"—which includes giving a public confession of sins and performing such actions as fasting, praying, almsgiving (14:1; 4:6, 14, 17). Here we have one of the earliest traces of liturgical forms for the institution of penance. In the Book of Hermas, one of the major problems is that of a "second repentance" after baptism. What Hermas seems to be saying (Mandates IV. 3.1-6) is not that there is now for the first and only time a chance to repent and to obtain forgiveness of sins committed after baptism, but rather that the chance for such repentance, which always was available (even for the "saints") is now coming to an end and that therefore prompt repentance is needed in order to evade eternal wrath.

James does not seem to have a very sophisticated attitude toward the problem of sin. He simply assumes that "we all make many mistakes" (3:2). There are no special distinctions. Sin for him is basically action, wrong action, although he occasionally refers to the older idea of sin as a demonic power which stems from the root of concupiscence and causes death and sickness (1:15; 5:15 f.). In the case of "sickness," the mention of "sins" as being connected with it may be an echo of the healing stories of the Jesus tradition. However, it also could stem from popular beliefs, as they certainly are behind the procedure (which almost suggests an exorcistic ritual) of healing a sick person by the "prayer of faith," as it is described in 5:14:

> Is anyone among you sick? Let him call for the elders of the church and let them pray over him, anointing him with oil in the name of the Lord; and the prayer of faith will save the sick man, and the Lord will raise him up.

Sin has to be met by active repentance, by a return to the pattern of the new life, and by doing the "works" which in the judgment will outweigh the "multitude of sins." We shall see how important the idea of the judgment is for James' whole ethical orientation.

The Literary Character, Authorship, and Content of James

Again, we must realize that whatever insight we gain from James is but an isolated glimpse of a wide landscape. We do not really know where the epistle belongs in the over-all picture, and thus even the most elementary questions must still remain unanswered. For example, scholars are still divided over the question of its literary character. Is it really a letter as is suggested by the epistolary address? Even if the writing was meant for "general" circulation, the abrupt ending without any epistolary salutation would be puzzling. Or was it a sermon? The frequent use of "my brethren" as an address to the readers, and a strong sermonic flavor, including a rich rhetorical imagery, would speak for this possibility. But no formal plan is recognizable, no governing theme that structures the whole book. Pieces of sometimes more general, sometimes rather specific exhortation, seem to be strung together, often simply by means of catch-word connection. This does not mean, however, that in the treatment of the various themes we would find no coherence at all. In fact, some of the themes occur several times (trial and temptation: 1:2 f.; 1:12 ff.; steadfastness: 1:2 f.; 5:10 f.; rich and poor: 1:9-11; 2:5-7; 5:1-6), and others are alluded to or taken up again in a different context (prayer without doubt: 1:5 ff., cf. 4:3 and the "prayer of faith" in 5:16; quick to hear, slow to speak: 1:19, cf. the passages about the tongue and the necessity of bridling it: 1:26; 3:2-12, cf. 4:11 ff., evil talk against each other; doers and hearers of the word: 1:22 ff., cf. the discussion about faith and works in 2:14-26). In this sense, at least, a certain unity seems to emerge.

This loose structure, as well as the presentation with its display of skillful rhetoric, would suggest something like a treatise, written as a piece of literature but originally destined for public reading in congregations of a certain area. We remember that it was not unusual in Christian churches to read edifying letters in the worship service. This may account for the rudiments of the epistolary form as well as for the sermonic flavor.

What kind of person would have written such a treatise? The later tradition, which claims the apostle James as its author, has little to commend itself. Only the name James is mentioned in the address. The treatise itself does not identify this James with the apostle, and its outlook as well as the Greek style are anything but what we would expect, in the way of these things, of an Aramaic-speaking Palestinian Jew.

There is a passage in 3:1 that may give us some clue. The author warns the brethren not to let too many become "teachers." "You know," he continues, "that we who teach shall be judged with greater strictness." James obviously regards himself as belonging to that special group of teachers. Paul's list of charismatic offices in the Church mentions "teachers" along with "prophets and apostles" (I Cor. 12:28 f.); there can be little doubt that the origin of this function has to be linked with the Jewish "teacher," the rabbi.

The post-Pauline Church continued to count the teacher among the charismatic leaders and to honor him accordingly (cf. Eph. 4:11). Acts 13:1 represents the leading group in Antioch in terms of "prophets and teachers." The Didache furnishes most valuable evidence that in rural areas the charismatic offices of "prophet and teacher" were still held in high esteem. They had an active and privileged part in the worship life (15:1) and were to be supported by the local congregation if they stayed and settled down. In general, however, they seem to have migrated from place to place; very much like the migrating philosophers of Hellenism. This system had its weakness. For the congregations, it must have been difficult to separate the chaff from the wheat and to know the true charismatic from the false. The Didache gives some handy rules: if a prophet stays more than three days, if he asks for money or other things in his prophecy, then he is a false prophet. On account of his specific duties, a teacher may have been related to a local situation in a somewhat less casual way. That his "teaching" had to do with the catechetical (= baptismal) instruction seems to be presupposed by Hermas, in Mandates IV. 3.1. In this situation, the "teaching" seems not only to embrace the contents of faith, but also the ethical code. We may assume that, depending on the local situation and the background of the teacher, this latter aspect often dominated the instruction, sometimes even to the point of a flat moralism similar to the popular morals of the wandering philosophers of the Hellenistic world. The "teaching" referred to in Didache 11 must be the *Catechism of the Two Ways* with all its ethical rules. And another "teacher," the author of the Epistle of Barnabas, shows the same ethical preoccupation. He is the one who defines Christianity as "the new law of our Lord Jesus Christ which is not a yoke of compulsion" (Barnabas 2:6). His letter is addressed to a congregation where he had taught before (1:3-5). It is very likely that we have to think of the author of James in the same general terms. As the example of Barnabas shows, the literary form of a treatise slightly styled into the form of a letter which could be read publicly in worship, is nothing unusual for a teacher, and the heavy emphasis on ethical questions would be in line with what we would expect of him.

JAMES: BORROWER FROM TRADITION.   Even the obvious dependence of James on both Jewish and Greek moral teaching seems to be typical for a man of his profession. As a matter of fact, for almost every single exhortation, illustration, and particular doctrine, parallels may be found in either Jewish or Hellenistic literature, often in both.[27] It is especially the literature and tradition

---

[27] For this material see the excellent commentary of M. Dibelius, *Der Jakobusbrief* (Göttingen: Vandenhoeck, 1921; re-edited with a supplement by H. Greeven, 1956). An English translation will be forthcoming in the 20-odd volume commentary series *Hermeneia*, to be published by Prentice-Hall commencing in 1966.

of Hellenistic Judaism (Old Testament apocrypha, Philo of Alexandria) that seem to have served as a model for the form, and partly for the content, of his treatise. In order to give his exhortations the desired literary touch, he borrows freely from many sources: scripture, especially the Psalms; the poets; the philosophers; the rhetorical school tradition; and the store of popular wisdom. He likes the parabolic comparison (the rich man is like grass that withers; the tongue is like a little fire that sets ablaze a whole forest); he uses the commonplaces of popular philosophy (the image of the mirror, 1:23 f.; the wheel of existence, 3:6; the taming of all animals by humankind, 3:7); he takes over theological concepts (God as the unchanging Father of light, 1:17).

The thoroughly Jewish flavor in the general ethical tone even has led repeatedly to attempts to explain the whole epistle as an original Jewish document which has been reworked only slightly. The most interesting theory along this line took its clue from the enigmatic address: "James, a servant of God and of the Lord Jesus Christ to the twelve tribes in the dispersion." [28] It claimed that the original writing used the literary fiction of a "Testament" (= Epistle) of the patriarch Jacob (= James) to his 12 sons (= 12 tribes) as the frame of a grandiose allegory in which every son represented a specific ethical theme. Jewish tradition in fact knows such writings (cf. the apocryphal Testaments of the Twelve Patriarchs) as well as the motif of allegorizing the 12 tribes, and the title "Servant of the Lord" is frequently applied to Jacob in the Old Testament. However, there are too many difficulties connected with this theory, and scholars generally have abandoned it. According to the most likely interpretation, the term "twelve tribes in the dispersion" would mean *all* Christians (= all 12 tribes of Israel) living in the world as strangers and exiles (= in the Dispersion).

Apart from an occasional echo of baptismal language (1:18; 1:21) there is no direct reference to baptism in our treatise. As in the Epistle of Barnabas, the situation is not that of catechesis. But it would in any case be inappropriate to think of the "teacher" in his capacity as catechist only. As a charismatic leader, he would speak up, instructing the Church whenever he found it necessary. The author of Barnabas, for example, regards it as sufficient justification for his writing to say that he wants to "communicate something of that which I have received . . . in order that your knowledge may be perfected along with your faith."—(Barnabas 1:5). Unfortunately, we have no way of telling when or where James wrote. Those who do not retain the idea of James the Apostle as author usually date it in the time between A.D. 70 and 130. Even the situation to which the epistle speaks is far from being clear. Most of the warnings—to the rich, to the self-indulgent, the complaining, the deceitful, the talkative, the proud—seem to be very general and to have a purely literary ring. But there are some references which suddenly open up an alarming picture of the inner

---

[28] The reference is to Arnold Meyer, *Das Rätsel des Jakobusbriefs*, Beihefte zur Zeitschrift für die neutestamentliche Wissenschaft, X (Berlin: Töpelmann, 1930).

difficulties which a church of those days was facing and which actually are reflected in all the details of the epistle.

It is especially the little dissertation about the tongue, that "restless evil, full of poison" (3:1-12) which at closer scrutiny reveals a very real background. It leads directly up to a sharp attack against the evil of "jealousy and selfish ambition," against "boasting" of a wisdom which is "earthly, unspiritual, devilish" and results in "disorder and every vile practice" (3:13 ff.). Here the readers are directly addressed: These things happen in your midst! The problem seems to be quite similar to that which Paul had to fight in Corinth (I Cor. 3:3; 4:33; II Cor. 12:20 f.) and which Clement of Rome tried to set straight in his letter to the Corinthian church some 40 years after Paul (I Clement 1:1; 3:2 f., etc.). It is trouble stirred up by a group or by factions within the church and inevitably leading to rivalry, strife, and worse evils (cf. 1:5 ff.; 1:21). The "tongue" is involved not only by its sinful boasting, but also by the fact that Christians defame each other (4:11). True wisdom is characterized by peace (3:17). But instead of peace and a "meek" spirit, there are wars and fightings going on among Christians (4:1).

When the author asks why this is so, his answer first follows the pattern of popular philosophy: It is the "passions" of the human flesh that evoke fight and envy. *Apatheia,* the freedom from the passions of the material world, was the ideal of the Stoic wise men. But James goes beyond this preliminary answer. The Greek word used in the beginning of 4:4 is difficult to understand. It is derived from the word for fornication, which from the time of the prophets on had been an image for Israel's apostasy from God. Thus, for James the boastful mood among Christians and its atrocious consequences are outright apostasy. Friendship with the world means enmity with God. But all is not lost yet. God gives "more grace"—even after baptism—if the sinner submits to God, resists the Devil, and cleanses his hand and heart (4:7-8). This appeal is based on a quotation from Prov. 3:34 ("God opposes the proud but gives grace to the humble."). It is the same quote which appears in I Pet. 5:5, where it describes the basic paradox of God's salvation. Peter's summary of the ethical code is almost identical with James': "Humble yourselves before the Lord and he will exalt you."—(Jas. 4:10). Even if James knew I Peter, or is drawing upon the same preformed tradition, it is clear that in doing so he links his ethical appeal to the structure of the *kerygma.*

James on the Rich and the Poor

This can be shown at another important point of James' teaching: his dealing with the question of rich and poor. Verses 2-7 of Chapter 2 present a hypothetical scene which the author obviously regarded as virtually a true story. Two visitors—he thinks of non-Christian sympathizers—appear at the regular assembly of a Christian congregation, one of them well-to-do and well dressed, the other "a poor man in shabby clothing." The rich man is treated with great courtesy and attention while the poor man is not given any consideration at all. The point James wants to illustrate is the warning against "partiality" (Jas. 2:1). But he himself is far from being impartial. In his comment on the story, he does not hide a strong antipathy against "the rich." It is possible, though unlikely (cf. 5:4 ff.), that he tries to blame a group of rich people for an actual persecution of Christians when he says that they oppress Christians, drag them into court and deride the "name." Most important, however, is the reason he gives for his siding with the poor. It is again that paradox of God's salvation: "Has not God chosen those who are poor in the world to be rich in faith and heirs of the kingdom?"—(2:5).

A similar view of rich and poor is apparent in Luke. Here, too, the motif of the exaltation of the poor and the humiliation of the rich is an example for the paradox of God's salvation (Lk. 1:51-53; 6:20 ff.; 12:16 ff.; 16:19 ff.). In this predilection for the poor, an important religious heritage becomes visible. Jewish tradition had long known the equation "poor = pious" (Ps. 86:1 f.; 132:15 f.), and particularly the Wisdom Literature speaks of the great reversal of the relationship poor-rich which is to come. Apocalyptic circles and esoteric groups like the Qumran community seem to have characterized themselves as "the poor" (*anawim, ebionim*)—that is, as God's elect, the holy remnant of the End Time. This tradition seems to have found its continuation in the early Jerusalem church; Paul, in his references to "the poor of the saints" in Jerusalem (Rom. 15:26; cf. Gal. 2:20) seems rather to imply actual poverty, but the Jewish Christians who after their exodus from Jerusalem in A.D. 66-67 settled east of the Jordan and gradually became a sectarian group, retained this designation as their title of honor (Ebionites).

For James, although he must be seen in the light of this tradition, it is the practical relationship between rich and poor which informs his stand. The message that God accepts the lowly and rejects the proud only supports his conviction that, in social terms, "Christian" means "poor," and "rich" *per se* means "wicked" and doomed. In vivid colors he describes the miserable fate which awaits the rich (1:10-11; 5:1 ff.). In these texts, a strong apocalyptic flavor is noticeable. The change from exaltation to humiliation and *vice versa* (1:9) is not visible yet, but the Coming of the Lord is at hand (5:8). James no doubt has a very realistic imminent expectation; behind his pleas for patience we feel his own anxiousness to see the day when finally the rich will fall and the poor will be exalted in glory. He checks his own impatience by saying that what he is waiting for comes almost as a natural process. The day will come, as certain as the rain comes to the land in due season (cf. I Clem. 23:4 f.).

The Ethical Code in James

If in James the ethical code is related to the structure of the *kerygma*, it is this apocalyptic aspect, not the reference to the Jesus tradition, which is really important. Unlike the author of I Peter, James does not himself draw lines from the ethical code to the Jesus tradition. This lack has always puzzled the interpreters. At one point, he appears to allude to Gospel tradition (5:12), but only twice (1:1; 2:1) does he even mention the name of Jesus Christ; the references to the "Lord" can apply to God as well. And while a Christian (cf. I Peter) naturally quotes Christ as the example of steadfastness, James speaks of the prophets and of Job (5:10). The "end" of which the Christian message speaks is for him in the first place the judgment which will destroy the wicked and vindicate the righteous, not the revelation of Christ's victory (cf. 5:9).

In fact, the threat of judgment seems to be the orientation point for the author's whole understanding of Christianity. Whether a man's "religion" is right or wrong is a matter of how it will stand God's judgment in the light of the standards that are being applied there (1:26 f.). James' use of important theological concepts finds its framework here. Take, for example, the *law*: for James the law is not the dead-end street of salvation which is superseded by the Gospel. It is God's standard in the judgment, and therefore of utmost importance for the Christian. The judge, who can "save and destroy," has laid down his rules in the law so that they are known (4:12). Of course, this law does not include the ceremonial code of Judaism; its basic content is the rule of love (2:8), which is interpreted by such moral laws as "Do not commit adultery," "Do not kill" (2:11), "Do not speak evil against one another" (4:11). In this reduced form, however, it is as strict in its demand as was the old Jewish code: to break one of these rules means to break the whole law (2:10-11). This law is the "perfect," the "royal" law, the "law of liberty" (1:25; 2:8; 2:12) and as such really identical with the saving Gospel (the Word—1:21). "Doer of the word" (1:23) and "doer of the law" (4:12) are synonymous. With this equation of law and Gospel, James shares a tendency of the post-Apostolic Age, which not only characterizes Jewish-Christian thinking, but the general Christian approach as well (cf. Barnabas 2:6; Hermas, Similitudes V.6.3; Ignatius, Magnesians 2). Or take *righteousness*: righteousness is not a gift bestowed by God, but rather a claim which God acknowledges in his judgment; it is therefore righteousness man must "work" toward by taking notice of God's standards and heeding them (1:20 f.). Thus, to be justified is not the sinner's being declared righteous but one's classification as righteous in the Last Judgment by virtue of one's approved actions (2:21, 23, 24).

JAMES ON FAITH AND WORKS.   The verses last quoted form part of the famous passage on faith and works (2:14-26) which has caused theologians like Martin Luther, for whom Paul's formulation of the Christian faith was normative, to regret that the Epistle of James was ever included in the canon. The author, indeed, seems to reject flatly the idea of justification by faith. Faith alone is inadequate to render a man acceptable to God. In a passage that seems to be a direct criticism of Rom. 3:28, the author sternly opposes the claim that faith alone can save: "You see that a man is justified by works and not by faith alone." As we shall see, however, the real quarrel is not with Paul, but with a use of Pauline formulae which the author, in his concern for the ethical code, regarded as a danger.

The argument is presented in the form of a "diatribe," a dialogical style form very popular with the philosophical moralists who knew how to attract the attention of an audience in the street. James uses the same tricks here: the rhetorical question in the beginning (14), the grossly exaggerated example (15-17), the fictitious interjection (18) which starts a dialogue with argument and counter-argument, the surprise exegesis of the opponent's major proof texts (21-25), and finally, a catching slogan as conclusion (26). Again, the whole point cannot be understood apart from the dominating concept of judgment. The preceding passage (2:8-13) had closed with the clear statement that the standard of the judgment is nothing else but the "law of liberty," the Christian law of love—or, as verse 13 puts it, of "mercy": "Judgment is without mercy to one who has shown no mercy; yet mercy triumphs over judgment."

The following verses want to stress that there is simply no way around this requirement. Nobody will pass judgment (= be saved) just by *saying* "I have faith." Faith in the sense of mere words, as a recital of a formula—even if it were the most correct one (19)—does not substitute for the required acts of mercy (15-16). If the Christian message is not just theoretical doctrine, but also ethical code, guidance to the acts of love which alone count in the judgment, then no "faith" without "works" of mercy will do.

This all would be nothing new for Paul, who never thought of faith other than as a "faith active in love," and for whom, therefore, "works of love" were the immediate fruit of faith. But the author obviously has Christians in mind who would recite the Christian creed and yet would live as though this "faith" did not include the structure for a new life. We may recall the troublemakers of 3:13 ff. In James' eyes, what is lacking there is not just right doctrine, but commitment to the ethical code *which is part of it*. For him, this latter aspect is more important than all sophisticated talk about "faith." Let these people talk about the "law of freedom"; let them invoke Paul for their doctrine of faith alone; let them adduce scriptural examples of justification by faith alone (the case of the harlot Rahab must have been particularly impressive). Their *whole* talk about faith is out of gear. If it really came down to an alternative— faith *or* works—then the solution is completely clear: in God's judgment it was the acts of mercy and obedience that "justified" Abraham and Rahab, not the recital of a "faith."

We hear the serious warning behind all of the argumentation: Do not deceive yourselves (1:22)! In the Judgment, God does not accept "faith" in the form of mere words, correct as they may be. He demands active conformity to the rule of love. This emphasis seemed to be quite legitimate for a time when the trend was to identify "faith" more and more with a body of correct doctrinal beliefs. There may be reason to believe that the teacher James was not really up to the task of arguing with the "sophisticated" standpoint of his opponents on a doctrinal basis, and that he therefore led the discussion on a level where he was at home and could really make his point. At any rate, he made clear that the Christian's new life initiated in baptism can never remain in the lofty sphere of arguments. It must be lived. It has to develop, to grow; it must be nurtured and corrected, in order that the goal be attained which God himself has placed before the Christian. With this understanding of the ethical code, James is perhaps closer to Paul than we are sometimes willing to admit.

In the last verse of his book, James speaks of Christians who "wander away from the truth" and fall into "error." Perhaps here again we have a reference to the troublemakers who were mentioned earlier. At any rate, we may take this antithesis of truth and error as an indication that, in spite of his "practical" concern for right conduct, James is quite aware of the deeper conflict the Church of his time was facing when criticizing the behavior of these people on the basis of the ethical code: the conflict with false teaching. Never quite coming into the foreground, this conflict lurks behind all his arguments. It is the literature of this conflict to which we now turn our attention.

THE GROWING PROBLEM
OF FAITH AND ORDER
IN THE COMMUNITY

I, II Timothy; Titus; I, II, III John; II Peter; Jude

CHAPTER SIXTEEN

In its exposition of the Christian

ethical code, the Book of James showed no immediate con-

cern for the problems which arose out of the conflict with

Rome and which had so deeply influenced the ethical teach-

ing of I Peter. But behind its vigorous appeal for a true

commitment stands the other conflict which shaped think-

ing and acting of the Church during that period; the conflict

over false teaching. Not only here, but elsewhere in the later books of the New Testament as well, it has left far more noticeable traces than the parallel conflict with the Roman government. This fact does not mean that the conflict with the state was less important. It may suggest, however, that the conflict over false teaching, over heresy,[1] was much more dangerous in terms of the inner development of the Church. In the conflict with the Roman state, the lines were clearly drawn. The Christians made up a minority group, highly vulnerable to social ostracism and political disfavor, and therefore anyone who chose to join the Christian community was aware that he could find himself under suspicion at every moment and that he might have to suffer for the "name." Obviously, the death of Christ could not become an abstraction to Christians who were faced with the possibility of dying in his behalf. Thus, wherever the threat of persecution became apparent, it served, instead of curbing the movement, to deepen and strengthen the faith; it helped in bringing together the members of the community into a more closely knit group; and it taught Christians the patience to take upon themselves suffering and hardship, which was a major factor in the final victory of the ever expanding movement.

THE DANGER OF FALSE GNOSIS

The lines were not so clear in the conflict over false teaching. The trouble here lay in the fact that the Church did not enter this battle as a well-ordered organization with a well-defined doctrinal tradition and a well-prepared ethical code. Its self-consciousness, which originally assumed that only a very short span of time was left to it, slowly adapted to the new situation of its pilgrimage in the world. Thus it was still in search of ecclesiastical forms, and therefore open to all kinds of influences that promised assistance in working out the statement of faith, the norms of conduct, and the forms of organization which were needed. It now was no longer solely Judaism that played the role of a storehouse from which materials were drawn, but with the opening of the door toward the Gentiles, the whole religious world of the empire, with its manifold concepts and ideas, stood ready to be used. The Christian converts from the Gentiles brought with them factors from their specific religious backgrounds which influenced the development of doctrine, moral code, and Church order. A process of adaptation was under way, not planned and foreseen, but coming rapidly upon the Church.

In this situation the conflict over false teaching proved to be a tremendous catalyst in reformulating the *kerygma*. By working at this, the Church learned how to draw the lines between "right" and "false" teaching. The chances of this conflict may not have been seized upon in a really fruitful way by all the

---

[1] The word is derived from Greek *hairesis*, meaning a school, or party (cf. Acts 5:17; 15:5). The negative connotation of "sect" or "sectarian ($=$ false) doctrine" must have developed as early as in the post-Apostolic period (cf. II Pet. 2:1).

writers of the epoch, and we should not be surprised to find that occasionally, in the process of definition and adaptation, the *kerygma* itself appears to have exchanged its missionary bent for a rather defensive orthodoxy, or even that the center of the message itself has become obscured.

The problem of sources for this conflict proves to be an even greater handicap than in the case of the conflict with the state. This is not due to the scantiness of information. Actually, there is perhaps no area in the history of post-Apostolic times about which our sources contain so much detailed material. But the picture is so varied and bewildering that once more we are unable to piece the details together into a coherent whole.[2]

One thing is obvious. Gnosticism, which in many regions may first have appeared as a friend, helping with the formulation of Christian doctrine, soon was recognized as enemy number one. It would perhaps not be difficult to trace the development of this most comprehensive conflict, namely the struggle of the Church to free itself from Gnosticism, if we could use the approach of the early Christian heresiologists. One of them, the Church Father Irenaeus, demonstrates by the very title of his antiheretical work (*Detection and Overthrow of Gnosis Falsely So-Called*) that he regards Gnosticism as *the* heresy. In Book I, he gives a kind of genealogy of the whole Gnostic movement.[3] According to him, the "father of all heresies" is Simon Magus, the Samaritan "sorcerer" whose conversion and subsequent expulsion from the Christian community is told in Acts 8:9-24. The sect that gathered around him became, as Irenaeus thinks, the cradle for the whole plague of Gnostic religion. A certain Menander, he says, was Simon's successor, and in the next generation, with Satornilus of Antioch and Basilides of Alexandria, the "systems" of the Gnostic type spread all over the empire.

On the basis of the sources, there can be no doubt that Simon was indeed a more important figure than the account in Acts would suggest. He seems to have founded a sect which at the time of Justin Martyr had tremendous success in Syria [4] and which may have been the starting point for other Gnostic-syncretistic groups. But Irenaeus' fundamental statement that "from the sect of Simon all heresies [he means Gnosticism in its various forms] took their origin" oversimplifies the complex issue. It starts from the assumption that true Christianity in any event was earlier than the distortion which appears in Simon's doctrine. But if Simon, according to Acts 8:9 ff., had carried on his Gnostic preaching already before he was attracted to Christianity, the implication is that Gnosticism as such existed and developed in the pre- and non-Christian world. The picture modern research has been able to trace of Gnosticism reveals

---

[2] The classical attempt of a consistent interpretation is contained in the book by Walter Bauer, *Rechtgläubigkeit und Ketzerei im ältesten Christentum* (Tübingen: J. C. B. Mohr, 1934; new edition with an appendix by G. Strecker, 1963).

[3] *Against Heresies* I. 23.

[4] See Justin Martyr, *Apology* I. 26 and 56; II. 15; *Dialogue with Trypho* 120.

a wide range of "sources," influences, and motifs that have shaped this religious mood which was so readily adaptable to most any form of faith but was to unfold into clearly organized forms under the impact of the Christian movement as it became an increasingly complex institution.

Another point in Irenaeus' account needs modification: In his identification of Gnosticism as *the* heresy, he actually seems to subsume everything he regarded as heretical under the term "Gnostic." The Nicolaitans (Rev. 2:6), the Marcionites, even the Ebionites, all fall under this category. Again, this seems to be an oversimplification. To be sure, modern historical research has substantiated Irenaeus' statement to the extent that, in fact, groups like the Marcionites or Ebionites show trends in their teaching which are akin to the cosmological, anthropological, and soteriological speculations known to us from Gnostic sources. But this does not automatically make them "Gnostic schools," as Irenaeus wants it. The picture, indeed, is much more complicated, and the interrelationships between Christianity and Gnosticism much more delicate. For the literature we are treating here, this means that we cannot presuppose a clearly defined and organized "Gnosticism" as the enemy, although Gnostic trends may be present in the doctrine of the false teachers we encounter. In trying to describe the false teachers we have to take each case, each local situation in the various writings, by itself.

More important for the image of the post-Apostolic Church is the polemical method and the argumentation of the ecclesiastical writers themselves and their own definition of what is "Christian." Here, too, we cannot expect to find a unified pattern, but the attempt to understand how various writers dealt with the danger of false teaching will lead us deeply into some of the most controversial problems of the post-Apostolic period: the development of the notion of "tradition," of an organized ministry, of the forms of worship, of the Eucharist. We will only be able to draw some tentative lines, not more. They will show us once more in what decisive way the historical situation has shaped, modified, and transformed the witness to the *kerygma*.

THE PASTORAL EPISTLES

Apart from the Catholic Epistles, we have in our New Testament canon one group of writings in which the conflict with "false teaching" seems to dominate to such an extent that the fight against it appears to be their only immediate goal. This group is the Pastoral Epistles. Although they claim to be written by Paul to his fellow workers Timothy and Titus and contain numerous allusions to personal circumstances of the Apostle, most scholars today regard them as a product of the post-Apostolic period, for a number of reasons (see p. 166). The situations as they are presupposed can only be accounted for in the life of Paul if we assume a further period of freedom and a second imprisonment after Paul's first Roman imprisonment. But as the evidence for this second imprisonment rests almost exclusively on the Pastorals, we are moving in a circle. The necessity of dealing with them as one block is based on the one hand upon the fact that in the early manuscripts and canon lists they always are present or missing together, and on the other hand upon their obvious similarity in vocabulary style, conceptuality, and general content.[5] Everything seems to favor the assumption that in their present form they are the work of one person. We probably have to think of a Church leader of the third generation (if he is not Paul, he speaks as a member of that generation of Church leaders which Titus is thought to have appointed: Tit. 1:5) who communicates rules for the order of the Church and its ministry in an epistolary setting. I Timothy seems to have best preserved the form of Church order. II Timothy suggests a kind of last "will" or testament of the Apostle (cf. 4:6 ff.) which the Apostle wrote facing death. Titus centers around personal instruction. But all epistles deal with the same subject matter of rules for the churches and their leaders in a dangerous situation, and the specific epistolary frame can only underline the seriousness of the appeal.

The Danger of Heresy

The danger is described with the colors of an apocalyptic evil in II Tim. 4:3 f.:

> For the time is coming when people will not endure sound teaching,
> but having itching ears, they will accumulate for themselves teachers
> to suit their own likings and will turn away from listening to the truth
> and wander into myths.

The author clearly speaks of a danger from within, not of a threat from outside, as was the case with persecution. The "people" of whom he is talking are Christians; and "truth," *i.e.*, the "sound teaching" (I Tim. 6:3; 1:10; Tit. 1:9; 2:1; II Tim. 1:13), is the sum of Christianity as he sees it. "Sound teaching" is the reasonable norm for Christians against all morbid speculation. To follow it, in fact, is the only way to preserve the three ideal elements of earlier Christianity together: unity, purity, apostolicity.

Who are these "false teachers" and what are their arguments? The polemic of the Pastoral Epistles furnishes us with numerous details which at first glance seem to provide a rather full picture, including even names: Hymenaeus and Alexander (I Tim. 1:20; cf. II Tim. 4:14); Hymenaeus and Philetes (II Tim. 2:17); Phygelus and Hermogenes (II Tim. 1:15). But trying to combine all these indications into one coherent picture, we find ourselves at a loss.

---

[5] For a careful discussion see P. N. Harrison, *The Problem of the Pastoral Epistles* (Oxford: Oxford University Press, 1921).

I Tim. 6:20 has often been taken as the key in establishing the identity of the false teachers:

> O Timothy, guard what has been entrusted to you. Avoid the godless chatter and the contradictions of what is falsely called knowledge, for by professing it some have missed the mark as regards the faith.

A reading of the Greek text reveals better than the English translation the importance of this sentence. The word for "knowledge" is *gnosis*, and the combination (literally) "pseudonymous gnosis" is the very term which Irenaeus took over to characterize the whole Gnostic movement. Thus, it appears more than likely that the "false teaching" the Pastoral Epistles have in mind is in fact some form of Gnosticism. To some scholars it seems likely that the verse even yields evidence for a more exact identification of the specific group. The Greek word for "contradictions" here is *antitheses*, and we know, particularly from the detailed refutation by Tertullian,[6] that Marcion had written a work featuring this title. It was an exegetical treatise contrasting texts from the "Law" (Old Testament) with the "Gospel" (Marcion accepted only an expurgated version of Luke's gospel and 10 Pauline letters) and was written in support of Marcion's dualistic theology. If we could follow this theory, then the author of I Timothy would issue an official warning against this dangerous book, and the fact that he writes under the name of Paul would indicate the attempt to reclaim the authority of the Apostle for the teaching of his church against the false claim of the Marcionites.[7] The Pastoral Epistles would then have to be dated rather late—Marcion's *Antitheses* appeared around A.D. 140— and even the ingenious proposal to regard Polycarp of Smyrna as their author would not meet with unsurmountable difficulties.[8]

However, serious reasons speak against this tempting hypothesis. The main one is that, quite contrary to Marcion's attitude, the "false teachers" show definitely Jewish features. At least some of them are Jews (Tit. 1:10); they use "Jewish myths" (Tit. 1:14) which seems to imply a specific interpretation of the Old Testament. The allusion to "endless myths and genealogies" in I Tim. 1:4 (cf. Tit. 3:19) could be explained in this Jewish context. One would think of allegorizations and midrashic expansions of scriptural passages similar to those in the apocryphal Book of Jubilees, which actually is a paraphrase of the Genesis account.[9] In I Tim. 1:7 the opponents are rebuked as "desiring to be teachers of the law without understanding either what they are saying or the

---

[6] Tertullian, *Against Marcion*.

[7] This explanation has been cautiously adopted by F. D. Gealy in his excellent introduction to the Pastoral Epistles in *The Interpreter's Bible*, XI (Nashville: Abingdon, 1955), 358 ff.

[8] The reference is to Hans von Campenhausen, "Polykarp von Smyrna und die Pastoralbriefe," in *Sitzungsberichte der Heidelberger Akademie der Wissenschaften* (Heidelberg: Winter, 1951-52, Number 2).

[9] See "The Book of Jubilees," in *The Apocrypha and Pseudepigrapha of the Old Testament in English*, II, R. H. Charles, ed. (Oxford: Clarendon Press, 1913; reprint 1963), 1-82.

things about which they make assertions." Furthermore, they enjoin abstinence from certain foods (I Tim. 4:2; cf. Tit. 1:15); including wine (I Tim. 5:23), which would bring to mind Paul's difficulties with the advocates of Jewish dietary laws.

This last point, however, may not prove very much for a Jewish background. For Christians who enjoyed "freedom from the law," every abstinence or ascetic restriction could appear as a Judaizing tendency. To be sure, we know of strong ascetic tendencies within Jewish groups, especially the Essenes, but this ascetic trend was a general characteristic of the time. Philo of Alexandria describes the ascetic practices of the Essene sect of the Therapeutes as matching his own ideal, but justifies them on the basis of the Hellenistic anthropology which tended to overemphasize the "spirit" at the expense of the "material body." [10] That the abstinence enjoined by the false teachers is to be seen in this broader context of Hellenistic asceticism (which in part shaped Gnostic ethics and the ethics of Marcionism) can be inferred from the un-Jewish combination with abstinence from marriage (I Tim. 4:3). Answering a concrete question of his Corinthian correspondents, Paul had commended abstinence from marriage for the sake of the late world hour and of the unhindered service to the Lord (I Cor. 7:7 ff.); but he had done so in a context in which he also criticized the wrong notion, obviously abroad in Corinth, that to marry is "sin" (I Cor. 7:28, 36). Later Gnostic circles seem to have capitalized on the ascetic line in this statement, and to have claimed Paul as an important witness for their dualistic ascetic teaching about marriage. The *Acts of Paul*, for example, an apocryphal book showing marked Gnostic influence, summarizes Paul's message simply as "the word of God concerning resurrection and abstinence from marriage" (Chapter 5).

In spite of the negative attitude toward marriage, the false teachers of the Pastoral Epistles seem to concede to women an important role in the public life of the congregation. The strong injunction against the teaching of women in I Tim. 2:11 ff. is hardly understandable if it was not directed against emancipatory tendencies by which women were allowed, if not encouraged, to "teach" in the meetings. In the framework of the charismatic offices in the churches of Paul's time, a woman prophet seems not to have been unusual. Luke knows a Caesarean tradition of the four unmarried daughters of Philip who "prophesied" (Acts 21:9) and presents the Jewish couple Aquila and Priscilla as both engaged in missionary work (Acts 18:26). Paul, who regarded man and woman as one "in Christ" (Gal. 3:28; cf. I Cor. 11:12) seems to indicate himself that he could visualize women "praying and prophesying" in the Corinthian service (I Cor. 11:5). However, in the same passage, he also makes himself the advocate of a custom which stresses female subordination (11:3; 11:7-9). The

---

[10] See Philo, *About the Contemplative Life*, F. C. Conybeare, ed., 1895. The authenticity of this writing is not generally acknowledged, however.

same appeal to "good custom" is visible when in I Cor. 14:34 f. he orders that "as in all churches of the saints, the women should keep silence in the churches." This rule is no general axiom, however, but is meant to counter a specific development in Corinth. On the other hand, there can be no question that in many Gnostic groups the role of women was most important. Irenaeus says that Simon Magus always had with him a prostitute by the name of Helena, whom he called his first *ennoia* (mental conception). Women appear in many Gnostic writings as recipients of special revelation, and in the gnosticizing *Acts of Paul*, the Apostle is claimed as endorsing this tendency when his convert Thecla is pictured as teacher and preacher (Chapters 37, 39, 41, 43). This *Acts* also indicates that the public role of women in Gnosticism was matched by a general appeal of Gnostic teaching to women, and the warning in II Tim. 3:6-7 demonstrates that the author of the Pastoral Epistles also fears its destructive influence on weak women.

Both features, the encratitic attitude (*i.e.*, abstinence from sexual relations) and the prominence of women in the "false teaching," would fit very well the picture of Gnostics. There are more features that point in the same direction: the positive insistence that "everything created by God is good" (I Tim. 4:4), that "all men" are included in God's plan of salvation and should come to the knowledge of truth (I Tim. 2:4), and especially the negative reference to the doctrine that "the resurrection is past already" (II Tim. 2:18). Nevertheless, we are unable to link this false teaching with any of the great Gnostic systems. Even the names do not help us; they may be just of local importance. Although the author wants to give his fight against the heresy as universal a frame as possible, the impression cannot be avoided that he is speaking out of a specific local situation. We may at best find a certain resemblance to the false teaching in the Lycus Valley which Paul opposes in Colossians. In both cases, Jewish and Gnostic elements seem to have been combined into an undefinable local blend of magic-Gnostic religiosity.

Part of the difficulty in identifying the opponents stems from the polemical method applied. Paul, in his letters, usually gives at least fragmentary hints of his opponents' positions. To be sure, in the Pastorals, we still find, in the form of traditional parenesis, the ideal image of the leader who knows how to refute his opponents so that, God willing, they may be saved from their error. (II Tim. 2:24 f.; Tit. 1:9). Practically, however, the opponents are no longer being opposed by argument. On the contrary, the author gives the advice not to engage in controversy at all (II Tim. 2:23; cf. I Tim. 4:7; Tit. 3:9). The young leader must "avoid" the contact with this type of teaching and its representatives (I Tim. 6:20; II Tim. 2:16; 3:5). In spite of all the pathos and determination to "fight the good fight of faith," one senses behind these injunctions a certain insecurity: the danger obviously was serious. On the one hand, we hear of only "some" (I Tim. 4:1; 5:15; 6:10), of "certain individuals" (I Tim. 1:3, 19). However, these are not only "upsetting the faith of some"

(II Tim. 2:18) but of "whole families" (Tit. 1:11), and the author sees the doctrine spreading like gangrene (II Tim. 2:17). His anticipation is that the situation will become still worse (II Tim. 3:12 f.).

For his evaluation of heresy, the image of gangrene is revealing. False teaching appears as a creeping disease, an "unhealthy" matter which is in strict contrast to the "healthy" doctrine. Thus, his solution of cutting off the relationship to the "sick members" is the radical but necessary cure in order to protect the health of orthodoxy from deadly contact with the plague. Here we see that argument has been replaced by a formal pattern of antiheretical terminology. Developed as a means of defense, this pattern certainly cannot claim objectivity in its description of the enemy. Actually, we notice at all points that the false teaching is dealt with in a most summary fashion which leaves no room for individual differentiation: "If any one teaches otherwise and does not agree with the sound words of our Lord Jesus Christ and the teaching which accords with godliness, he is. . . ." There follows a spell of highly abusive terms, accusing the "heretics" of every vile and evil quality (I Tim. 6:3 ff.). A similar list appears in II Tim. 3:2 ff. It is placed in the framework of a general apocalyptic warning, but the context (verses 5b, 6) again shows that the author really has the false teachers in mind. A third list of vices in I Tim. 1:9 f. on first sight enumerates the categories of serious criminals for whose restriction the law is given. Neverthless, the summary in verse 10 makes it clear that the author even here thinks of the heretics he is fighting. Rather than describing his opponents, the author is using preformed "catalogues of vices," similar to those in Gal. 5:19-21, or Rom. 13:13. Recent research has shown that they have their origin in Hellenistic-Jewish parenthetical tradition; beyond this, they draw from a rich background of oriental forms.[11] This insight is fundamental. The pattern of antiheretical language is rarely formed *ad hoc*, but uses a standard stock of words and motifs. In the Pastoral Epistles we can watch this phenomenon in its formative stage.

Part of the pattern is the connection of "heresy" and "immorality." On the assumption that heresy is a disease, it was easy to think of this disease in moral terms. In all later antiheretical literature, the sequence is taken for granted: false doctrine/immoral life. The heretic is *per se* a morally irresponsible person. As a pattern, however, this "dogma" is not restricted to a Christian context. After all, Christians themselves experienced the hatred of those about them in the form of the accusation of "godlessness" as well as of moral turpitude.

Some features of this pattern may have a more real background; for example, the charge that the heretics used their preaching "as a means of gain" (I Tim. 6:5; Tit. 1:11). The account about Simon Magus in Acts 8 charges that love

---

[11] See B. S. Easton, "New Testament Ethical Lists," in *Journal of Biblical Literature*, II (Philadelphia, 1932, 1-12), and the recent book by S. Wibbing, *Die Tugend- und Lasterkataloge im Neuen Testament*, Beihefte zur Zeitschrift für die neutestamentliche Wissenschaft, XXV (Berlin: Töpelmann, 1959).

of money was the motive out of which he sought connection with the Christian community. There may be reason to believe that Gnostic teachers actually had considerable financial success, but this charge of mendicancy could hardly be avoided by any group of itinerant evangelists who had to make their living. Paul already had to defend himself against suspicion (I Thess. 2:5; cf. Acts 20:33 f.) and worked with his own hands. But for the Christian Church, he also had laid down the rule that the minister of the Gospel has a right to live on his ministry (I Cor. 9:6 ff.). This principle seems to have been generally recognized in the post-Apostolic Church. The Didache urges that a traveling prophet or teacher should if possible work in his trade if he wants to settle down. But in principle he has a right to his support by the local congregation (Didache 12 f.). Similarly, the Pastoral Epistles know of a regularly paid local ministry (I Tim. 5:17 f.). We may have to translate the Greek word *timē* (= honor) in the technical sense of "honorarium" so that the verse would recommend higher pay for good presbyters. There must have arisen occasional suspicion against the paid clergy—perhaps nourished by unfortunate experiences (Polycarp 11:1-2). Our texts often emphasize that a minister of the Gospel should not be a "lover of money" (I Tim. 3:3; I Pet. 5:2). The danger at this point was probably as great in the Church of the Pastorals as it was in the circle of the opponents. The problem is not resolved when the author contrasts the "good conscience" on his side (I Tim. 1:5, 19; 3:9; II Tim. 1:3) with the "bad conscience" on the other (I Tim. 4:2; Tit. 1:15). By this contrast, he is implying ill will and deliberate self-deceit on the part of the heretics. However, it seems likely that this reproach again is stock, and that the "false teachers" were as convinced as he was that they represented the true Church. This is the dilemma faced by an orthodoxy which was just starting to develop its own standards.

A New Concept of Tradition

Concerning these standards, the Pastoral Epistles are a most important witness of two positive ways in which the Church tried to find her own identity over against the false teaching: the appeal to a new concept of tradition, and the development of an established ecclesiastical ministry.

As we saw earlier, Paul made extensive use of Christian traditions, referring to kerygmatic materials which were "handed down" to him and which he, in turn, "handed on." To this process, he applies the technical term *paradosis* (see p. 56). In fact, inasmuch as the *kerygma* he proclaims is witness to God's act *in history*, it is itself "tradition," so that the terminology of *paradidonai* (hand on) and *paralambanein* (receive) can be applied to it (cf. I Cor. 11:1; 15:1; Gal. 1:9; I Thess. 2:13; II Thess. 3:6). Tradition includes both doctrinal and ethical materials (cf. I Cor. 11:23 ff.; I Cor. 7:10); it always issues from "the Lord" who authorizes it "in the Spirit." He, Paul, is one link in a chain of those who are "entrusted with the Gospel"—receiving as well as handing on.

In the situation of the Pastoral Epistles this rather free-wheeling concept of tradition was felt not to be safe enough from tampering. Thus, the term *paradosis* is replaced by *paratheke* (= deposit; I Tim. 6:20; II Tim. 1:12-14; the verb *paratithenai*—I Tim. 1:18; II Tim. 2:2). Paul's "dynamic" concept of tradition is replaced by a static one. The term belongs in the legal sphere, emphasizing the integrity of a given definition. Tradition in this understanding is a fixed deposit, something which has "once" been laid down and now can only be "guarded." With Paul, the author still calls it "Gospel" (II Tim. 1:8, 10; 2:8 f.; I Tim. 1:11), but other terms seem much more appropriate. In the first place, tradition now is "doctrine" (the word occurs 15 times in the Pastoral Epistles), and this doctrine is distinguished from false teaching by the adjective "sound" ("sound doctrine"—II Tim. 4:3; Tit. 1:9; 2:1; "sound words"—I Tim. 6:3; II Tim. 1:13; Tit. 2:8). Another important shift is noticeable when we consider the relationship of the Apostle, in whose name the author is writing, to this tradition. He is no longer seen as one link in the chain, but as the beginning of it; no longer as the mediator, but as the depositor of the Gospel which the later generations have to keep intact (I Tim. 1:11 f.; 6:14; II Tim. 1:13; 2:8; 3:14; Tit. 1:3). Tradition has become a body of fixed doctrine guaranteed by the authority of the Apostle. In this form, the Pastorals even equate it with "faith." In Paul faith was primarily trust in and commitment to God in response to the Gospel; it thus cannot really be measured and manipulated. To be sure, this nuance of trust is not lacking in the Pastorals. However, it seems that faith now *can* be measured and "handled" (II Tim. 2:15)—namely, by its congruence with the deposited body of correct doctrine. Faith still is the essence of the Christian's life (faith = Christianity: I Tim. 5:8; Tit. 1:13), but it is a faith of fixed and final content, identical with the "sound word," the healthy doctrine. This faith can be "kept" (II Tim. 4:7). It can be "disowned" (I Tim. 5:8), missed (I Tim. 6:21), departed from (I Tim. 4:1); it can be denied (I Tim. 5:8; 4:1)—all of these equivalents for "heresy." Faith has become the formal criterion for being a Christian.

The content of this faith is not presented systematically. The author simply presupposes it and occasionally quotes it in the form of traditional statements which have a flavor of venerable age. The introductory phrase is no longer: "the Lord says," but: "faithful is the saying" (I Tim. 1:15; 3:1; 4:9; II Tim. 2:11; Tit. 3:8). "Faith-ful," in accordance with the new understanding of faith, implies not so much trust as trust-*worthiness*. The quoted materials seem to come mostly from liturgical or credal tradition (I Tim. 1:15, 17; 3:16; 6:13-16; II Tim. 1:9 f.; 2:11 f.; Tit. 2:11 ff.). Concerning the apparent allusions to a formulated creed (cf. I Tim. 6:12) one notes that the polemic against false doctrine has already become an ingredient of the creed. Statements like I Tim. 2:4-5 are in all probability formulated in antithesis to false doctrine: God's will is that *all* men shall be saved—not just a selected group of Gnostics. There is *one* God and *one* mediator between God and man—not several gods and a multiplicity of intermediate powers; Jesus Christ, the *man*—not an incorporeal divine being. In the history of the early Christian Church, this development culminated in the formulation of the Nicene Creed, with its specific refutation of Arian doctrine.

On the other hand, it cannot be denied that the author has preserved a flavor of Pauline theology. Passages like II Tim. 1:8-10; 2:8 ff.; Tit. 3:5-8 are evidence of his "Paulinism." In the last of these passages, baptism is interpreted as the bath of rebirth to a new life which is bestowed by the gift of the Spirit, and justification is clearly grounded not in works of righteousness, but in Christ's deed of mercy—that is, in "grace."

In spite of all his heavy dependence upon traditional formulations, including Paul's, and his determined intention not to add anything, the author presents his "sound doctrine" in a language which often seems to be borrowed from popular Hellenistic-Jewish religiosity. He does not hesitate calling his faith "religion" (I Tim. 2:10; 4:7 f.) and using Hellenistic predications for his "Lord": Christ is God (Tit. 2:13), Savior (II Tim. 1:10; Tit. 1:4; 3:6), his appearance among men is an "Epiphany" (II Tim. 1:10; Tit. 2:11; 3:4) like the epiphany of a Hellenistic god or of the emperor-god. The image of "God-Father" (I Tim. 1:2) is in no way different from the transcendent God of Jewish-Hellenistic philosophy and piety (I Tim. 1:17; 6:15 f.; Tit. 3:4). Our epistles are impressive evidence of the extent to which this beginning orthodoxy felt free to assimilate concepts of its religious surroundings—not *in spite of*, but precisely *on the basis of*, the new understanding of tradition as a fixed deposit.[12]

According to the Pastorals, right faith implies right morals. To be an orthodox Christian means both to have faith and a "good conscience" (I Tim. 1:5, 19; 3:9). Much space in the epistles is taken by the discussion of the moral code, partly concerning ethical requirements for the ministry, partly the ethics for the whole Church. The antithesis to the "immorality" of the Gnostic heretics dominates, of course. But in trying to picture the situation which prompted these specific exhortations, we are at first struck by the seemingly low level of morality even within the Church. The rules for bishops and deacons (I Tim. 3) as well as for Timothy and Titus are so elementary that one should take them for granted. However, we must not forget that the author draws on preformed materials in the context of a Church order. Fragmentary "household tables" are discernible (I Tim. 2:8-15: men and women; 6:1-2: slaves; 6:17-19: the rich; Tit. 2:2-10: older men, older women, young women, young men, slaves). Use is made of a related form of "tables of duties" (I Tim.

---

[12] For this aspect see especially the important commentary by Hans Conzelmann, *Die Pastoralbriefe*, Handbuch zum Neuen Testament, XIII, 3rd ed. (Tübingen: J. C. B. Mohr, 1955).

3:1 ff.: bishop; 3:8 ff.: deacons [and deaconnesses?]; Tit. 1:5 ff.: elders and bishops).

Not only in these lists, however, is the influence of a Jewish-Hellenistic background visible. Even the theme of "suffering," which in I Peter and James was so closely connected with the structure of the Christian *kerygma*, is interpreted in terms of popular morals. For the Christian, to take upon himself "the share of suffering" means to lead a disciplined life, entirely devoted to the goal, like the soldier, the athlete, or the hard-working farmer (II Tim. 2:3 ff.; cf. 1:8). Thus it is not astonishing to see that the Christian ideal of right living comes very close to what any loyal citizen in the empire would strive for: "lead a quiet and peaceable life, godly and respectful in every way" (I Tim. 2:2). It is the intention of Christian life to live up to the highest expectations of the surrounding society. The good impression upon the outsiders for this church has become a most important concern (I Tim. 3:7; 6:1; Tit. 2:5, 8). In this connection it is almost self-understood that the authority of the state is fully acknowledged (Tit. 3:1), and that the prayer for the emperor is a loyal duty (I Tim. 2:2). Of course, the author knows about the Church's exile in the world (Tit. 2:11 ff.). He still places the commandment of love in the center of Christian morality (I Tim. 1:5). But the frequent combination "faith and love" (I Tim. 1:14; 2:15; 4:12; 6:11; II Tim. 1:13; 2:22; Tit. 2:2), which reproduces a Pauline formula, carries with it a different meaning: as faith is a body of fixed doctrine, so "love" seems to be the sum of a formal code of ethics. One thinks of Barnabas' definition of Christianity as "the new law of our Lord Jesus Christ." However, the author of the Pastorals would never call it "law." As a good Paulinist, he asserts that the law is good but that it is *abrogated* for the Christian. However, this understanding is made to serve his antiheretical argument: Christians are not to look for deep mysteries and senseless speculations in the law; they must realize that it is given not for good people but for bad people—for the heretics who must be told how God deals angrily with their wretchedness. Actually, the author's attitude to the whole Old Testament fits in with this understanding. The Old Testament is the inspired textbook for the teacher who has to reprove and to correct (II Tim. 3:16).

The Christian ethical code to which our author appeals has its strengths not in its relation to the structure of the *kerygma*, but in the fact that it accords with what is "normal" and "natural." The author is convinced that any person with a sound mind could accept his "sound teaching" in its doctrinal as well as its moral content. Against all excesses and extravagances of one's attitude toward the created world he recommends, in line with the Old Testament and with the philosophical moralists of his time, a middle way between asceticism and libertinism. The *whole* Creation is God's work and therefore good. There is no need to despise or abolish anything that is given: food, marriage, riches (I Tim. 6:7 ff.). Everything "natural" is good, if it is used according to God's will, *i.e.*, in moderation. "To the pure, all things are pure" (Tit. 1:15). There is a certain rationalistic trend in this argumentation. But by keeping what is "Christian" close to what is "natural," our author has shown the right insight into what the Church of his day needed against the invasion of world-contempt and spiritualism which accompanied the Gnostic movement.

The Christian Ministry

According to the Pastoral Epistles, the preservation and correct transmission of the true faith is a task of the ministry of the Church. These epistles are the only writings in the New Testament which deal specifically with the question of the ministry, and it is very significant that this is done in the context of the conflict with false teaching. If the Church was to be the "pillar and bulwark of truth" (I Tim. 3:15), it could fulfill this role only through an ordered and legitimized ecclesiastical office.

The historical development with regard to the Christian ministry during the post-Apostolic period is still a field of many open questions. In our sources, the constitutive ideas for its functions are presupposed rather than spelled out, and where ecclesiastical offices are mentioned the terminology is often confusing, indicating at least that the question was in great flux. Matters are further complicated by the fact that the sources, while speaking about the past, often use the situation of their own time as a model. The major handicap, however, is the scantiness of information about the general constitutional development in the early Church.[13] The Church was not planned as an institution with a projected long-range future. On the contrary, the process of adapting itself to the very possibility of an extended future was long and slow. What we can safely say about the general lines of the ministry in the post-Apostolic period is perhaps this:

1. There is a definite development from a rather loose organization to a more structured form of ecclesiastical order in which a hierarchy of offices emerged with a single "bishop" as head of the local congregation ("monarchical episcopacy").

2. The tendency toward more structured patterns of organization was at least enforced, if not initiated, by the needs of the conflict with heresy. The ministry in the Church became in the first place the guardian of tradition, legitimized by a special ordination, and thus was at the same time a guarantee of the effectiveness of all salutary activity in the Church.

3. The various stages of this development were not reached everywhere at the same time. Local differences, therefore, have to be taken into account.

---

[13] An excellent interpretation of all the pertinent materials is found in E. Schweizer, *Church Order in the New Testament*, tr. Frank Clarke, Studies in Biblical Theology, XXXII (London: SCM Press, 1959).

While in one church or one area the development toward a monarchical episcopacy seems to have made rapid advance, other churches still preserved for a long time more archaic forms of Church government.

The evidence from the Pastoral Epistles is rather disappointing, even though the frame in which the material is presented suggests a very comprehensive approach. Paul, the Apostle of the Gentiles, is writing to his missionary companions, instructing them how to establish an efficient ministry in the Church! Although the epistles do not develop a "doctrine" of the ministry, the author seems interested in laying down fundamental rules concerning the ministry in the light of his specific situation. The image of the Apostle Paul serves as the basic point of reference. Paul is not only claimed as the covering authority of the epistles, but, according to the author, offers himself as the true model for the ministry of the Church at all times.

Paul's life first illustrates the basis on which all Christian ministry is carried out: God's grace for sinners. He is the great example of the Christian experience of conversion: once an ardent foe of Christianity, a persecutor, the "foremost of sinners" (I Tim. 1:15), he now is the living witness to God's life-changing power. It is not his own merit, but God's mercy, that made possible his appointment to the "service of Christ" (I Tim. 1:12). What is this *diakonia*, this service? It is the ministry of the Gospel—a Gospel which leads into suffering (II Tim. 1:11-12; 2:10). Again, Paul's whole life is witness to this fact which every Christian minister must face: hardship and persecution are his share (II Tim. 3:10-12). But he is not fighting for his private cause. The Lord stands behind him and is watching over the precious deposit which he has left in the Apostle's hand so that it may accomplish its goal of being heard (II Tim. 4:17; cf. 1:12). The summary of Paul's life characterizes the goal set before every good minister: "I have fought the good fight, I have finished the race, I have kept the faith."—(II Tim. 4:7). One may find in this bold statement traces of the veneration of the great Apostle by a later generation which already sees him crowned with "the crown of righteousness" (II Tim. 4:8) and which tries to excuse his former life as "ignorance" (I Tim. 1:13).

At two points, Paul's ministry is defined by the terms preacher, apostle, teacher (I Tim. 2:7; II Tim. 1:11). It is striking that the title of apostle should be mentioned only in second place. For our author, Paul is first of all preacher, *keryx* (cf. I Clement 5:6). The Greek word naturally suggests the connection with the term *kerygma*. However, since our author interprets the *kerygma*, Paul's "Gospel," as implying a static concept of tradition, it would seem that for him, all three terms really point in the same direction. Paul's function is the proclamation *and* codification of the true, apostolic tradition, the right teaching. His deposition of the apostolic *kerygma* has set the standard for all Christian ministry after him.

If the image of Paul is the basic point of reference, Timothy and Titus are the more immediate models for the Church leader which our author has in mind. As recipients of the tradition from Paul, they stand with him in the post-Apostolic situation. Young, as our author presents them (I Tim. 4:12; 5:1; II Tim. 2:22; Tit. 2:6 f.), they are the prototypes of the "younger generation" which needs help and guidance and for which his Church order is intended.

The Church itself is like a small social organism, a family in which the minister has to recognize fathers and mothers, brothers and sisters beside him (I Tim. 5:1 f.). What distinguishes him is his public role. Here lies his great responsibility. His life must clearly show to everyone what it means to be a Christian, to have undergone a conversion from impurity to purity. He must renounce "youthful passions" and must set his mind on the true aims of righteousness, faith, love, and especially peace in order to be a "vessel for noble use" (II Tim. 2:20 ff.). He must set the example (I Tim. 4:12) of the integrity which Christians are to demonstrate in word and action so that no criticism can be leveled from outside (Tit. 2:7 ff.). Of course, he is not yet perfect, but he will make progress. For this, "soundness" and common sense are important qualities. There is no need for special ascetic exercise (4:7 f.). But hard work in the assigned duties is necessary—strict devotion, self-discipline, and willingness to suffer.

What are the minister's duties? What is the function of his ministry? Again, preaching is given the prominent place. II Tim. 4:1-2 defines this major task in strong, entreating language:

> I charge you in the presence of God and of Christ Jesus who is to judge the living and the dead, and by his appearing and his kingdom: *preach the Word*, be urgent in season and out of season, convince, rebuke, and exhort, be unfailing in patience and in teaching.

Thus, Timothy's ministry can be defined as that of an "evangelist" (II Tim. 4:5). But just as the *kerygma* has become doctrine, the evangelist actually is a teacher. His "preaching" has to do with the deposit of correct doctrine and the corresponding moral code. He is to instruct Christians in the face of threatening heresy. This is clearly the basic responsibility of "Timothy" (I Tim. 1:3) as well as of "Titus" (Tit. 1:5 ff.). But the conflict with false teaching in which he has to carry the main burden calls for a man who really has *all* the areas of Church life and Church order in which the application of right doctrine may be at stake, under his control.

Especially the image of Timothy contains evidence for administrative functions of the ministry. The long instruction concerning "widows" (I Tim. 5:3-16) presupposes that the Church engaged in organized charity.[14] Widows without family are supported by the Church, and it is the task of the ministry to

---

[14] For a full discussion of the charity of the early Church, see A. Harnack, *The Mission and Expansion of Christianity in the First Three Centuries*, I, tr. J. Moffatt (New York: Putnam's, 1908), 147-198. Republished by Harper in Torchbook paperback series, 1964.

watch over the correct "enrollment" (I Tim. 5:9) so that the Church is not unduly burdened. The minister also acts as a disciplinary authority in the Church, watching over the right procedure in disciplinary cases. He is not to show partiality and has to make sure that only well-founded complaints are brought against honorable elders (I Tim. 5:19 ff.). He has to rebuke the sinner (including the heretic), admonishing him once or twice; if this is without success, he has to draw the line and expel the "factious" person (Tit. 3:10; cf. I Tim. 1:20).

There is a third area which the ideal minister has to watch: the worship life of the congregation. According to I Tim. 4:13, he is not to neglect the public reading of scripture, or preaching and teaching; and some of the practical problems connected with worship—as, for example, the question of prayer—are dealt with in I Tim. 2.

What was Christian worship at this time, and what was the role of the minister in it? To answer this question we have to go somewhat out of our way.

CHRISTIAN WORSHIP

The prophet John informs his readers in the Book of Revelation that his first vision came to him on the "Lord's Day" (Rev. 1:10). In the time of Paul, Christians regularly assembled "on the first day of the week" (I Cor. 16:2). The Didache (14:1) and Ignatius (Magnesians 9:1) also refer to the "Lord's Day," and Barnabas (15:9) mentions a meeting "on the eighth day." The first day of the new week was the first day after the Jewish sabbath, the eighth day from the first day of the Jewish week. Justin Martyr, whose description of Christian worship for us is the most important source from the second century, refers to its with the pagan name as the "day of the sun." [15] According to tradition, Sunday was the day of Christ's resurrection, and from the earliest apostolic times had been a special occasion for the gathering together of all Christians wherever they might be. Long before there was an annual celebration of Christ's resurrection on Easter, the Church celebrated the Resurrection weekly on Sunday.

When the prophet John had his vision, he knew that Christians were gathering together throughout the churches of Asia Minor for worship on that very day. Sunday, the Lord's Day, dramatized not only to John, but to Christians everywhere, the unity that each professed. By providing a regular, consistent occasion for the worship of the risen Lord, and for instruction in the faith and in the Christian way of life, the Lord's Day was a vital factor in making the unity of the Church concrete and immediate to Christians.

The elements of the Sunday worship service were pretty much the same as

---

[15] See Justin Martyr, *Apology* I. 67. Compare F. A. Regan, *Dies Dominica and Dies Solis: The Beginnings of the Lord's Day in Christian Antiquity* (Washington, D.C.: Catholic University of America Press, 1961).

they had been in apostolic times: prayer, reading from the scriptures and other writings, preaching, instruction, and the singing of hymns and psalms. It is easy to show that all of these had their antecedents in the worship service of the Jewish synagogue.[16] The climax of each service was the fellowship meal in which the participants believed the risen Lord was present with them, and during which they renewed their hope for his coming again. It was the faith in the risen Lord that gave meaning to all Christian worship.[17]

The Old Testament, which formed the scriptures of the Church, was read as a regular part of the service. This reading aloud was for many the only way in which they could become familiar with the scriptures. No doubt the reading was often lengthy; Justin Martyr said that it went on "as long as there was time." We do not know whether or not there was any set order of reading from the Old Testament. In the service of the Jewish synagogue, from the third century A.D. on, the reading of the Law and the Prophets was planned in such a way that the entire Old Testament was completed in one year. Moreover, the readings were correlated with important religious festivals. Many scholars believe that this practice dates from a much earlier period; if so, it is possible that some such arrangement was practiced in the Christian Church as well, under the influence of the synagogue.[18]

In addition to the Old Testament, other writings were read in the church service. We remember that Paul wrote his letters to be read in the local churches. Later, Revelation was written to be read in the churches of Asia Minor; I Clement to be read in Corinth; the Shepherd of Hermas to be read in Rome, etc.

In recent years some scholars have theorized that the literary structure of some of the New Testament writings reveals that they were composed for liturgical reading—the Gospels of Matthew, Mark, and John in particular. Whether or not we accept this thesis, it is quite probable that the gospels *were* read in the churches. At first, some of the churches would have preferred one gospel over another. The first specific reference to the reading of several in one church comes from Justin Martyr, who says that the "memoirs of the Apostles" were read regularly along with the Old Testament. The reading of the scriptures was followed by preaching, teaching, and exhortation. This combination again seems to be a Jewish heritage. The so-called Second Letter of Clement, which in reality is a sermon, alludes to this connection in the course of its exposition (II Clem. 19:1 f.), and Justin Martyr tells us that

---

[16] See W. O. F. Oesterley, *The Jewish Background of the Christian Liturgy* (Oxford: Clarendon, 1925); C. W. Dugmore, *The Influence of the Synagogue Upon the Divine Office* (Oxford, England: Oxford University Press, 1944).

[17] For a more detailed discussion see O. Cullmann, *Early Christian Worship*, tr. A. S. Todd and J. B. Torrance (Chicago: Regnery, 1953); G. Delling, *Worship in the New Testament*, tr. Percy Scott (Philadelphia: Westminster, 1962).

[18] A. Guilding, *The Fourth Gospel and Jewish Worship: A Study of the Relation of St. John's Gospel to the Ancient Jewish Lectionary System*, 1960, tries to show that the structure of the fourth gospel follows the order of a synagogue lectionary.

after the lesson, the leader would give a sermon explaining and applying the passage read.

Prayer was also an important element in the worship service. As we have already seen, spontaneous and free prayers were common in the Pauline churches, especially among the Christian prophets. Under the influence of the synagogue and Jewish Christianity, however, the more traditional corporate or liturgical prayer took precedence over spontaneous prayer. In I Timothy it is urged that "supplications, prayers, intercessions, and thanksgivings be made for all men" (I Tim. 2:1), and men are urged to pray "lifting holy hands" (I Tim. 2:8). Fortunately, one of these liturgical prayers which was used in the church at Rome has survived and is found in I Clement 59-61. It is a good illustration of how prayers that were undoubtedly used in the Hellenistic synagogues of the Diaspora were adapted to Christian usage. The main elements are clearly visible: the invocation with an elaborate kerygmatic predication of God; the general prayer of intercession, including a prayer for peace and welfare and a prayer for the government; and the final doxology.

In addition to such prayers which, according to Justin, followed the sermon, the worship service included doxologies, or brief acclamations of praise to God, some of which are already found in the Pauline Epistles (Rom. 9:5; 11:36; 16:25-27; etc.). The later writings of the New Testament abound with both doxologies and benedictions, giving us glimpses into the worship of the Church, even though we are unable to establish their precise function.

Of particularly great importance in Christian worship was the Lord's Prayer,[19] which in the Gospel of Matthew is already presented as the one prayer that Jesus taught his disciples. Certainly it was in general use in the worship of the Church from an early period. The Didache, after instructing Christians to pray the Lord's Prayer, adds: "Pray thus three times a day" (8:3), an indication that it was used not only as a part of corporate prayer, but as a personal prayer as well.

Finally, part of the worship service was given over to psalms and hymns. In several places Paul had already mentioned the use of hymns among Christians (I Cor. 14:26; Gal. 3:16). Most of the psalms were taken from the Old Testament, but other psalms were probably used, too. We have dealt with the question of Christian hymns in another context (see p. 369 f.).

The Lord's Supper

All through the post-Apostolic Age, the Church continued to develop the liturgical mode of worship that had been present from the beginning. Since individual churches undoubtedly enjoyed considerable freedom in selecting the

---

[19] A classical study of the Lord's Prayer is E. Lohmeyer, *Das Vater-Unser*, 6th ed. (Göttingen: Vandenhoeck, 1962).

forms to be used, we find extensive variation from one church to another. This seems to be true even with regard to the Lord's Supper, which during this period gained special importance. The later New Testament writings do not provide us with any explicit records of the service itself, but other sources contain most valuable information. We still have a variety of designations for the meal that Christians were celebrating in every congregation. The Didache refers to the "breaking of bread," a term that had been used from the earliest times (Acts 2:42; 20:7). Ignatius and the Epistle of Jude (12) speak of *agape*—a Greek word meaning "love," and, in this connection, "love feast." Both terms suggest a rite related to the fellowship or social meals that early Christians had shared together. But a new term now gained increasing usage: *eucharist*, a Greek word meaning "thanksgiving." It is derived not only from the thanksgiving characteristic of the prayers used in the context of the rite, but also from the character of the rite itself as a "sacrifice of thanksgiving" to God for his gift of salvation in Jesus Christ. As in the earlier period, however, the primary meaning of the meal was Christ's presence in the midst of those who ate, and the hope it brought for his final Coming.

There is some difference of opinion among scholars as to whether the special rite of the Lord's Supper was ever observed apart from the fellowship meal in the first century A.D. It is perfectly clear from the Didache and from Ignatius that the fellowship meal had not completely disappeared, and we have further evidence to that effect in the letter of Pliny mentioned earlier (see p. 363). But the first certain evidence we have for the separation of the two is found in Justin Martyr,[20] who speaks of the Eucharist only and does not mention the fellowship meal. What probably happened was that the separation took place gradually in different churches during the late first and early second centuries A.D.

By the end of the first century A.D., certain liturgical forms for the Eucharist seem to have been developed. The Didache instructs Christians to come together on the Lord's Day, break bread, and hold the Eucharist "after confessing your transgressions" (Didache 14), an indication that a prayer of confession was already in use in the service. The writing also states (9:1-2) that concerning the cup, which here precedes the bread, the following words are to be repeated:

> We give thanks to thee, our Father, for the holy vine of David, thy child, which thou didst make known to us through Jesus, thy child. To thee be glory forever.

And concerning the bread (9:3-4):

> We give thee thanks, our Father, for the light and knowledge which thou didst make known to us through Jesus, thy child. To thee be

---

[20] Justin Martyr, *Apology* I. 65 and 67.

glory forever. As this broken bread was scattered upon the mountains, but was brought together and became one, so let thy Church be gathered together from the ends of the earth into thy kingdom, for thine is the glory and the power through Jesus Christ forever.

Concerning the rite itself, the rule is urged that only baptized members be allowed to eat and to drink of the elements (9:5; cf. Justin, *Apology* I. 66.1).

Then the author gives the final prayer for the Eucharist (10:25) which, as the other two, shows strong resemblance to the Jewish style of prayer. There is also a short responsive fragment which probably was arranged as follows (10:6):

> Liturgist: Let the grace come and let this world pass away!
> Congregation: Hosannah to the Son of David!
>
> Liturgist: If any man be holy, let him come! If any man be not, let him repent! Maranatha!
> Congregation: Amen.[21]

We cannot say how representative the prayers in the Didache were. Even the Didache, after giving the final liturgical prayer, says, "But suffer the prophets to give thanks as they will."—(Didache 10:7). Here we have an acknowledgment of the prophets' right to engage in free and spontaneous prayer. However, the difficulty was that prophets were not always available, and it seems that it is for this reason that the author offers a formulary which could be used as a regular substitute.

The tendency toward a more formal liturgical setting for the Eucharist certainly has been enforced by the Church's battle against false teaching. In his letters, Ignatius repeatedly insists that the Eucharist can be held only where bishop, presbyters, and deacons are present. Ignatius knew that in some churches members were partaking of the Eucharist isolated from the main body of Christians. Others were refusing to participate at all. He sensed a real danger here, for once the rite stopped being shared by all Christians, the unity of the community would be threatened. So Ignatius attacked misconceptions about the Eucharist and insisted that there was only one Eucharist—the one shared in by the whole Church and interpreted by its recognized leaders. His own interpretation gave the Eucharist special importance because here, in the immediate communion with "flesh and blood of the Lord," the Christian finds already the goal of his salvation: the "life that triumphs over death." Thus, the one bread, in its identity with Christ's body and blood, has almost magical powers. Ignatius calls it "medicine of immortality," or "antidote against death" (Eph. 20:2) in order to indicate the reality of the life which the Christian here already experiences.

---

[21] See H. Lietzmann, *Mass and Lord's Supper: A Study in the History of Liturgy*, translated with appendices by Dorothea Reeve; introduction and supplementary essay by R. D. Richardson (Leiden, Netherlands: E. J. Brill [Fasc. 4, 1955]), p. 193.

It is clear that for Ignatius the "bishop," who alone guarantees the effective distribution of this sacramental food, has a priestly function. The equation "with the bishop" = "in the realm of the altar" (Eph. 5:2; Trallians 7:2) is indicative of this fact. With the idea of the priestly bishop at the altar, the Christian ministry took on a new significance. Very soon this priestly mediation was to become the center of the Christian understanding of the ministry.

Ordination and Apostolic Succession

The Pastoral Epistles do not know of such priestly functions. A specific distinction of the ministry emerges not through the minister's role in worship, but through his all-important role as the guardian of the tradition which the Apostle had laid down. The Pastoral Epistles are a most important witness to the fact that, in order to insure the proper handing on of tradition, the Church took to a distinctive, public act of ordination at which the charge to "guard" the deposit and the spiritual authority for this office was conferred.

In Judaism, the tradition of the commissioning of Joshua by Moses (Num. 27:21-23) had served as the model for the ordination which the student of the Torah received from his teacher and which conferred the authority of exercising all the functions of a rabbi. The main rite was the laying on of hands. In Acts we hear of the installation of the Seven with prayer and laying on of hands (6:6), and of the sending out of Paul and Barnabas on their limited first mission (Acts 13:3) with the same rite. We notice that the laying on of hands is elsewhere in Acts connected with the gift of the Spirit, a fact which poses difficult problems because the relation to baptism is not completely clear (cf. Acts 8:17; 19:6). Behind these instances stands the more general idea of a transmission of charismatic power or of blessing by the laying on of hands (cf. Acts 9:12, 17; 28:8).

In the Pastorals the term "laying on of hands" refers to the ordination rite (I Tim. 4:14; II Tim. 1:6; cf. I Tim. 5:22), and the connection with the gift of the Spirit is indicated ("the gift which is within you"). Although it is the appointment to a regular office in the Church, the ministry is still regarded as a charisma, which is also stressed by the reference to the "prophetic voices" that designated Timothy before or when he was commissioned (I Tim. 1:18; 4:14). It is in the last instance the Spirit that guarantees the authority of the ministry, but the conflict with false teaching makes it necessary to bind this gift, once it is discovered in a man, to a regular ministry, an ecclesiastical office, in order to make sure that the right Spirit remains at work. The close interrelation of office and charisma, Spirit and tradition, is most characteristic of the situation. For our author, this is more important than the question of who ordains: in I Tim. 4:14 it is the presbytery; in II Tim. 1:6 the Apostle himself. This seeming contradiction is resolved once we remember that the author constantly re-projects the situation of his time into the apostolic frame of the epistle. But more: for him, the ordination by the elders is the legitimation by apostolic authority, the outward insurance of a correct "apostolic succession" in the preservation of the deposit.

The confounding of apostle and presbytery may also point to another dimension: in practice, the problem of the true "apostolic succession" through the ministry was that of local situations. The author has tried to give his comprehensive approach a vast geographical foil. Paul is seen as the central authority in the Church, Timothy and Titus as his assistants assigned to the task of establishing and supervising the ministry in churches of a large area. Many scholars have inferred from this scheme that Timothy and Titus represent something like archbishops or metropolitans as the later Church knew them. However, there is no clear evidence for either a centralized authority in the post-Apostolic Church, nor for the existence of such regional authorities. For all practical purposes both Timothy and Titus are conceived from the angle of a local situation which in the conflict with heresy always was the immediate battleground. They are the *ideal* of a more or less centralized local ministry which is at best just starting to be organized. This is the reason why it is also quite difficult to identify them simply as "bishops" of local congregations. For the projected ideal, the title of bishop in the sense of the monarchical episcopacy may be appropriate. But the glimpses of the actual situation as we catch them in the rules of the Church order, with their bewildering terminology of Church offices, show that with the Pastoral Epistles we are still in the middle of the transition, even though the later outcome is already in sight.

Bishop, Deacon, Presbyter

The tension which is felt to exist here between the ideal frame and the actual situation out of which the epistles arise makes it difficult to explain the various technical designations used here for the Christian ministry. To be sure, we no longer have the free variety of Pauline times, when every Christian, as a vessel of the Spirit, had a function to fulfill, and when Paul could mention apostles, prophets, teachers, healers, miracle-workers, believers, leaders, administrators, givers, etc., all in one breath. The Pastorals speak of specific "offices" with technical designations: bishop, deacon (perhaps deaconess), presbyter; even the "widows" seem to form a distinct group.

The word "bishop," which comes from the Greek *episcopos*, means primarily "overseer." It was used as the title of an administrative officer in civic and cultic societies in the Hellenistic world, but it also appears in the Septuagint as the description of various jobs of supervision (Judges 9:28; Num. 31:14; II Kings 12:11; Neh. 11:9; 14:23). The Qumran community knew the office of *Mebaqqer*, an elected member of the group who administered the property of the community and in Greek may well have been called *episcopos*. It is impossible to decide where Christianity found the precise antecedent for its own use of the title. The analysis suggests, in any event, that it was originally connected with the administration of local congregations and that the number of bishops was not restricted to one. Paul, who is the first to mention the title in a Christian context (Phil. 1:1), probably understood it in this sense.

The combination "bishops and deacons," which is used in Paul, points in the same direction. The word "deacon" comes from the Greek *diakonos* and means "servant." Paul uses it often in a general sense: every preacher "serving" through the Word, and also every Christian who "serves" his brother in accordance with the example of Christ, may be called a *diakonos*. In Phil. 1:1, however, it is clearly the title for a specific function in the Church. Acts 6, the appointment of the Seven, in which the word *diakonein* (to serve) is used, would indicate that the origin of the Christian function was in the ministry to outward needs in the Church. The combination "bishop and deacon" has never ceased to exist in the terminology of the Christian ministry. It is usually taken to imply a hierarchical subordination: the deacon "assists" the bishop in his functions. When Paul speaks of Epaphras, Tychicus, or Timothy as his "deacons" (Col. 1:7; 4:7; I Thess. 3:2), the idea of "assistants" certainly is in the foreground. To what extent such a subordination is implied in Phil. 1:1, we cannot tell.

"Elders" (Greek: *presbuteroi*, presbyters) can be simply the designation for a respected group of older members in a given community. In the Jewish communities and congregations such a body of "elders" was usually in charge of the administration. Luke speaks of a group of elders in the Jerusalem church (Acts 15; 21:18) and in other churches (Antioch, 11:30; Ephesus, 20:17). However, the distinction between general and technical use often is difficult to make. In many cases where the term occurs in the post-Apostolic literature [22] it cannot be decided with certainty which one is meant.

Whenever it is clear that "elders" is a title for Church leaders, however, the question arises how this office is related to that of bishop. After Paul, the role of "bishop" was probably quickly growing beyond pure administrative functions. In the Didache (15:1 f.), for example, the church in the province is admonished to elect local bishops and deacons to take the place of the migrant charismatics, especially with regard to worship life. The Didache does not mention presbyters. Conversely, other writings such as James, I Peter, and Revelation mention only presbyters, but not bishops. In many books, however, we find both terms (Luke-Acts, I Clement, Ignatius, Pastoral Epistles, Polycarp, Hermas). For Luke, the existence of the two titles is simply a terminological problem: "bishops" and "presbyters" are two designations for the same office (cf. Acts

---

[22] Compare I Clem. 44:5; 47:6; 54:2; 57:1; I Pet. 5:1, 5; Jas. 5:14; Polycarp, Philippians 6:1; 11:1; Hermas, Vision II. 4.2 f.; III. 1.8.

20:17, 28).[23] But when he maintains that Paul and Barnabas appointed "elders" in the churches of Asia Minor (Acts 14:23), yet Paul himself never mentions elders at all, it becomes clear that Luke's solution is too easy. For the historian it would seem that the patriarchal institution of elders as Church leaders first developed in independence of the administrative offices of bishops, and deacons, and that the two forms eventually merged—a process which is reflected in our sources in a variety of "types."[24]

The most advanced type in terms of the future development may be seen in the Epistles of Ignatius. Here, a clear hierarchical synthesis of the local ministry is presupposed, consisting of bishop, presbyters, deacons (the so-called "three-fold ministry": Magnesians 2; 6:1; Trallians 3:1; 7:2; Eph. 2:2; Philadelphians, Preface, etc.). *Deacons* are clearly subordinate to bishops and presbyters alike (Magnesians 2); they "serve" everybody (Trallians 2:3) and three of them accompany Ignatius as servants on his voyage to martyrdom. The role of the *presbyters* is not sharply defined. As the "synhedrium" of the bishop (Philadelphians 8:1), they belong immediately to the bishop; they surround him as the apostles surround Christ (Trallians 2:1 f.) and produce with him a harmony like the strings of a harp (Eph. 4:1). But it is quite clear that, beyond an honorary function, their share in active leadership is insignificant. The true leader of the congregation is the one *bishop*. As the guardian of true apostolic tradition and as the center of unity around which Christians gather at the altar of the Eucharist, he is the God-given bulwark in the fight against heresy. In his high vision of this office which he himself held in Antioch, Ignatius may be somewhat ahead of the reality, but he already can address other monarchical bishops by name in some of the churches of Asia Minor: Damas in Magnesia, Polybius in Tralles, Polycarp in Smyrna, and Onesimus in Ephesus. He implies that there is a bishop in Philadelphia, but he fails to mention the bishop in either Rome or Philippi. This omisson probably means that the monarchical episcopacy had not yet emerged in the two cities at this time. For Corinth, I Clement implies presbyterial leadership, even though he seems to indicate that the parallel leaders in his Roman surrounding are called bishops and deacons.

It is impossible to explain exactly how the monarchical episcopacy emerged. Bishop Polycarp, in writing a letter to the church in Philippi, introduces himself as a *member* of the presbytery (preface). This may suggest one explanation: out of a college of presbyters, one man rose to the position of president and was distinguished by the title "bishop." Another explanation would be that in a

---

[23] In modern times, the theory of an original office of presbyter-bishops has found a widespread following ever since J. B. Lightfoot's classical essay "The Christian Ministry," in *Saint Paul's Epistle to the Philippians*, rev. ed. (London: Macmillan, 1890), pp. 181-269. See also B. H. Streeter, *The Primitive Church* (New York: Macmillan, 1929).

[24] This is the thesis of Hans von Campenhausen, *Kirchliches Amt und geistliche Vollmacht in den ersten drei Jahrhunderten* (Tübingen: J. C. B. Mohr, 1953).

given situation, the number of bishops was gradually reduced until a one-man office resulted.

Compared with the relatively clear picture in Ignatius, the situation in the Pastoral Epistles remains ambiguous. Very little is said about the range of duties for bishops, deacons, presbyters, widows, and about their relationship to each other. The Church order only lists the prerequisites for the office. As we have seen, the moral standards are generally stock: a good reputation, married only once, temperate, managing his household well, not loving money. Special features include the warning not to appoint a recent convert as bishop (I Tim. 3:6), and the requirement that the bishop be well thought of by outsiders (I Tim. 3:7). According to the quote in I Tim. 3:1, the office of bishop is regarded as "old," and the sequence in the chapter probably implies superiority over the deacon. That the bishop's role, like that of Timothy and Titus, is primarily seen in the context of the fight against heresy, must be concluded from Tit. 1:9. But his relationship to the presbytery is not clear. Sometimes, bishops and presbyters seem to be identified (Tit. 1:5, 7). But the bishop always appears in the singular and is never mentioned together with the presbyters; furthermore, the presbyters are clearly treated as a special group of regular officers (I Tim. 5:17 f.) who among other things preach and teach. At any rate, in the projected ideal situation, presbyters would not have any leading function, but at best an assisting role. The actual situation may have been similar to that in Smyrna: the bishop (or the bishops) is (are) a member (members) of the presbytery, which, as a patriarchal body, was composed of an honored group of older Christians *and* of others who, regardless of age, were honored on account of their regular office.

Whatever the name of the regular leaders in the local congregations may have been, they carried an immense responsibility. We have no evidence that they were profound thinkers, but they were loyal to Christ and to what they believed to be the tradition of the apostles. They were the men who helped forge a strong community when the first enthusiasm of the primitive community was fading, and with it the effectiveness of the charismatic leadership. They sought to make the teachings of the Church and the Christian way of life relevant in a world that seemed less likely to come to an end than it had a few decades earlier.

We have seen that in the conflict with false teaching, the ministry had to become better organized in order to take effective action, and the tendency toward a more or less centralized authority in the congregation is unmistakable. But over against the "threefold" hierarchy and the monarchical bishop of Ignatius, the ministry in the Pastoral Epistles still is seen as the ministry of the *Word*. Even though the conflict with false teachings is forcing the definition of the Word in the direction of a fixed body of doctrine, this basic definition stands to be remembered.

THE JOHANNINE EPISTLES

Among the Catholic Epistles it is the group of the so-called Johannine Epistles that is dominated by the conflict with false teaching. With this group, however, we enter a completely different world of antiheretical argument. As to form, the category of "epistle" does not really apply to all three writings. III John is a genuine private letter, addressed to a private individual. In II John, the address "To the elect lady and her children whom I love in truth" could refer to an individual Christian woman and her family, but since no name is mentioned and the admonitions seem to be directed to a Christian congregation (cf. the change to the plural from verse 6 on), it may be a figurative expression for a particular church or for the Church at large. I John, though written with literary intentions ("I write to you"), is rather a tract or sermon without an epistolary frame, although it seems to be intended for an audience, well known to the author.

It has often been doubted that the three epistles originally belonged together. Scholars point to the fact that while I John is quoted early in the second century, the first traces of the other two appear almost a century later. However, linguistic evidence and content make a very strong case for I John and II John coming from the same hand; the epistolary frame of II John and III John renders it almost certain that these two have the same author, so that the unity of all three cannot easily be doubted. The lack of early references to the brief letters proves nothing. Possibly they originally appeared as an appendix to I John and were not counted separately. Irenaeus quotes II John as if it were part of I John,[25] and the Muratorian Canon has a curious reference to "two epistles" of John.

The question of authorship is closely bound up with the whole "Johannine question." Scholars now are generally agreed that I John and the fourth gospel must come at least from the same milieus, if not from the same hand. And although the thesis of apostolic authorship has been widely abandoned, the circle in which these writings originated has taken on a more definite profile, especially through comparison with the writings from Qumran.

Wrong Beliefs

To form an exact idea of the false teaching which the epistles are opposing is not easy. The Johannine style abounds in allusions and often veils what it has to say in somewhat mystical language. However, the main features appear with reasonable clarity.

---

[25] Irenaeus, *Against Heresies* III. 16.8.

Again the danger has arisen from within the Church. The false teachers were originally members of the Christian community where they lived unnoticed until, by their open separation—we may think of a separatist assembly, a conventicle—they revealed their true identity (2:19). They are "false prophets" (4:1), "antichrists" (2:18). The language pattern of this description has its roots in apocalypticism. The word "antichrist," to be sure, appears here for the first time in Christian literature. But Jewish apocalypticism, and especially the apocalyptic literature of Qumran, knew the figure of Belial as the personification of the hellish powers of the End of Time. The expectation of a powerful antimessianic figure had also become part of the Christian expectation from early times on (cf. II Cor. 6:14 f.; II Thess. 2:3-4; Mk. 13:14; the "beast" of Revelation). As the allusions in Revelation show (cf. Rev. 17), Christians were tempted to connect this figure with contemporary phenomena and, on this basis, to understand their hour as the time immediately preceding the End. In this context, the message of I John: "The antichrist is in the world already" (4:3) and therefore it is the "last hour" (2:18), may not have been surprising. New and surprising is the widening of the concept to a plural, "many antichrists" (2:18), and its identification with the heretics. The problem of heresy for our author obviously has dimensions which can only be accounted for as manifestations of the apocalyptic End.

It is the dangerous nature of the antichrist that he comes in disguise and is not easily recognized. Thus the aim of the epistles is to "unveil" his incognito by pointing to the marks which identify him. Recurring phrases like "if we say . . . ," or: "whoever says . . . ," introduce such distinctive statements which help the reader to draw the line between "true" and "false."

Except in III John, the author does not mention any names, and he never labels the heresy as "Gnosticism." But the evidence leaves no doubt that the apostates embraced some form of Gnosis. They are quoted as saying, "I know God" (2:4), and it is against this boastful claim of theirs that the author assures his Christians: "*you* know" (2:13; 2:14; 2:29); "it is not so that you do not know . . ." (2:21). The false teachers really are the ones who "do not know." This in particular applies to the knowledge of God with whom they claim to have close fellowship (1:6), whom they profess to "love" (4:20) and of whom they pretend to be "born" (4:7; 5:18). They cannot know the father because they "deny the son" (2:23).

Here, in the doctrinal field of Christology, is the first and most prominent mark of these heretics. They deny that "Jesus is the Christ" (2:22). This sounds at first like a Jewish denial of Jesus' messiahship, but another passage points in a different direction. What they deny is that "Jesus Christ has come in the flesh" (I Jn. 4:2; cf. II Jn. 7). It seems that Ignatius, especially in his letters to Ephesus, Tralles, and Magnesia, confronts a similar heresy. He denounces in strong terms people who do not confess Jesus Christ to have been a "flesh-bearer" (Smyrneans 5:2 f.). For them Jesus' whole life was only appearance.

He was not really born. He did not really grow. Ignatius' zeal for martyrdom makes him particularly alert against the implication that Jesus did not really suffer, but only *appeared* to. Against this "docetism" (from *dokein*, to appear) which robs his own martyrdom of its point, the most realistic, physical "imitation" of the Lord (Trallians 10; Smyrneans 4:2; cf. Irenaeus III. 18:5), Ignatius quotes the Christian *kerygma*, emphasizing the reality of all events of Jesus' life (Eph. 7:2; Trallians 9 f.; Smyrneans 4:1-2). In the antiheretical literature of the early Church we hear, indeed, of certain Gnostics who pretended that Jesus Christ had been a "bodiless phantom." [26] But for the Johannine Epistles, an even closer parallel may be found in the docetic doctrine of the arch-heretic Cerinthos of Ephesus, who taught that Jesus was the natural son of Joseph and Mary. At baptism, the heavenly "Christ" descended upon him, enabling him to proclaim the mysteries of the true God. But before the Crucifixion, "Christ" left him again, so that only Jesus suffered and was raised.[27] The allusions in I and II John still are too brief to allow the identification of the heretics with Cerinthian Gnosis. But the denial of Jesus being the Christ and the "Son of God" (4:15) would be in line with this particular form of docetism which furthermore is closely connected with Asia Minor, the probable home of the Johannine Circle.

Like Ignatius, the author of I John appeals to the kerygmatic tradition: against the heretical denial of Christ, the Christian "confesses" that Jesus *has* come in the flesh. The use of the word "confess" (I Jn. 1:9; 2:23; 4:2 f.; 4:15; II Jn. 7) suggests that this appeal is based on credal formulations, and it is precisely the center of the creed—Christ's death "for us," *i.e.*, the "expiation for our sins" (2:2; cf. 1:7)—that is endangered by a docetic Christology.

The false teachers boastfully claim to have the Spirit, to be pneumatics (4:1 ff.) and therefore to be "without sin" (1:8, 10). We cannot tell what concrete consequences this consciousness had in their case. But we know from other sources that the Gnostic feeling of superiority not only led to ascetic renunciation but was sometimes carried to the other extreme of antinomianism and moral libertinism, especially with regard to sex. "To a king, they say, there is no law prescribed." [28]

Wrong Behavior

Even in the New Testament we find the traces of both theoretical antinomianism and practical libertinism. Paul himself had to fight the notion that his "freedom from the law" meant freedom for sin (Rom. 6:1, 15; I Cor.

---

[26] Pseudo-Justin, *About the Resurrection* 2; Irenaeus, *Against Heresies* I. 24.2; Hippolytus of Rome, *Refutation* VII. 31.

[27] Irenaeus, *Against Heresies* I. 26.2; cf. III. 3.4.

[28] Clement of Alexandria, *Miscellanies* III. 30. Compare *Alexandrian Christianity*, H. Chadwick and J. E. L. Oulton, eds., The Library of Christian Classics, II (Philadelphia: Westminster, 1954), 30 ff. and 54.

6 f.; Gal. 5:13). The picture of the heretics fought in Jude and II Peter seems to indicate that they have drawn just these consequences: grace is here perverted into licentiousness (Jude 4; cf. II Pet. 2:2). The heretics promise freedom, but are slaves to their lusts (II Pet. 2:18), defiling the flesh (Jude 8: II Pet. 2:10) and following their instincts like irrational animals (Jude 10; II Pet. 2:12 ff.). It is in this context that the author of II Peter warns against certain things in the epistles of "our beloved brother Paul" which are "hard to understand, which the ignorant and unstable twist to their own destruction" (II Pet. 3:15 f.).

Heretics in the Johannine Epistles are not accused of sexual license. But one consequence of their spiritual self-assurance is obvious: they look down upon the nonspiritual Christians in the Church. Again and again our author lashes out against the lack of brotherly love on the part of these separatists. One cannot love God and at the same time hate the brother (4:20). For him, "love" is the essence of the Christian ethical code—love, however, not as a concept, but as the action of brotherly love. Here is one of the clearest criteria to find out where Gnostic error hides. "Knowing God" means keeping his commandment (2:4); and the sum of all the commandments is to love one's brother (2:9 ff.). Again, the main facts of the *kerygma* are invoked to make clear what this means. Jesus' life is the example which we are to follow (2:6); just as he laid down his life "for us," we ought to lay down our lives for the brethren (3:16). Or even simpler: "If anyone has the world's goods and sees his brother in need, yet closes his heart against him, how does God's love abide in him?"—(3:17). This is the tone of Jesus' own proclamation, and Christians must have felt that something very important was lacking in the Gnostic-heretical groups at this point. Ignatius expresses their criticism succinctly (Smyrneans 6:2):

> For love they have no care, none for the widow, none for the orphan, none for the distressed, none for the afflicted, none for the prisoner or for him released from prison, none for the hungry and thirsty.

In fact, the Church from earliest times on had interpreted Jesus' commandment of love as the corporate obligation to care for the less fortunate brethren, and Ignatius here gives us a glimpse of the range of charitable activity in post-Apostolic times: care for orphans and widows (Jas. 1:27; I Tim. 5:3 ff.; Hermas, Mandates VIII: 10), for those in prison (Heb. 13:3), for the sick (Jas. 5:14; Polycarp, Philippians 6:4), for strangers, especially traveling Christians (I Pet. 4:9; Heb. 13:2; I Clement 1:2, 11 ff.).

The lack of this spirit of brotherly love simply indicates the denial of Christianity. The Church was always very suspicious of Christians whose allegedly superior knowledge separated them from fellowship with other Christians. Love of self instead of love of brother is not what God commands. But we cannot overlook that the term "brother" often tended to remain within the narrow realm of the community and that the conflict with heresy saw the Church itself in danger of becoming "sectarian" in outlook. The Johannine Epistles, by keeping close to the *kerygma*, clearly strike the note of a universal Gospel (I Jn. 2:2, 29). But they also illustrate the peculiar dilemma of a Church which only had the Spirit as a criterion to ward off false teaching.

The Appeal to the Spirit

Unlike the writer of the Pastorals, the author does not appeal to the fixed norms of a deposited faith and to an authoritative ministry. If he exposes the distinctive marks of the antichrist, this is not a formal procedure in preparation for the excommunication of heretics, but it is a help in the much more comprehensive task of the Christian to distinguish the spirits, to orient himself in the fight between the "spirit of truth" and the "spirit of error." These marks themselves point to the real authority in the battle with heresy: the Holy Spirit, the Spirit of God. In the last instance it is the authority of this Spirit alone in which our author claims to speak, reminding his readers that they, too, have been "anointed" so that they are taught about everything (2:20, 27). Even the ambiguous witness with eye and hand to which he appeals in the famous opening of I John (1:1-3) and which may indicate his wish to put his writing under the authority of the Apostle John, ought probably to be understood in terms of the general Christian claim to having the "right" spirit. The "we" is not just a reference to the group of the Twelve, but actually includes all Christians who, through the gift of the Spirit, already *have* "eternal life." In their spiritual unity with their Lord they all witness to what they have "seen and heard" (1:3), what "was in the beginning" (1:1; cf. Jn. 1:1)—to the Word (*logos*) of life.

In the conflict about heresy, this spiritual claim had its weakness as well as its strength. The author of our epistles calls himself "the Elder." Scholars agree that this title probably points to some kind of spiritual authority rather than to a fixed jurisdictional one, and III John is generally taken as an illustration of the dilemma arising therefrom.[29]

The Elder seems to be in close contact with the church in which Gaius, the addressee, is to be located (III Jn. 1). Some brethren—probably itinerant evangelists (verse 7)—have been visiting there recently (verse 3), and Gaius is commended for hospitality extended (verse 5 f.). Actually the missionaries are now going back there, and the letter urges Gaius to help them again on their way "as befits God's service" (verse 6). But then, the author complains about a certain Diotrephes who does not "accept" the Elder and his circle (verse 9). Diotrephes refuses to receive the evangelists and even "excommunicates" those who are willing to receive them. It has often been suspected that, as in I and II John, some kind of heresy is involved here. But there is no indication that

---

[29] For the following see E. Kaesemann, "Ketzer und Zeuge," in *Zeitschrift für Theologie und Kirche*, XLVIII (Tübingen: J. C. B. Mohr, 1951), 292-311.

Diotrephes is a heretic. The charge against him is that he "likes to put himself first" (verse 9), and that he—successfully—breaks off communion with the circle of the Elder, who seems to be eager to see the situation corrected (verses 10, 13). This would much rather suggest the strong leader of a local congregation who wants to protect his flock from the influence of uncontrolled wandering "heretics."

With this evaluation, Diotrephes has no doubt overshot the mark. But it can hardly be denied that the Johannine spirituality could easily be misunderstood as "Gnosticism" in a situation where the local leader, determined to keep the ship of orthodoxy afloat, would throw out everything that smacked of "Gnosis." We saw earlier that the Gospel of John makes use of Gnostic terminology in its interpretation of the Jesus tradition. I John continues this line. Dualistic terminology abounds (light/darkness, truth/lie, God/the Evil One, love/hate, life/death). The "world" is not only regarded as "passing away" (2:15-17) but as being the domain of the Evil One (5:19), and the sinlessness of those who "know" is stressed emphatically (3:4 ff.). But especially at this last point, the evaluation of sin, the specific Johannine flavor becomes evident. The author says both: the Christian cannot sin, *and:* it is wrong to say we have no sin. The tension between the gift which has been bestowed and the responsibility to real-ize it (make it real) in action day by day, does not leave room for resignation before a paradox (2:1 f.). It is in the daily prayer for forgiveness that the Christian experiences what freedom from sin really means.

"John" is no Gnostic, even though he may have used Gnostic sources.[30] But the "Johannine question" strikingly reveals how difficult a task it was for the Church to draw the line between orthodox and heretical. On the one hand, the Church no doubt had to strive for a clearer, handier formulation of the *kerygma*; it had to develop a regular, authoritative ministry as we see it in Diotrephes. According to these standards, the weapons "John" was using in the antiheretical fight certainly are insufficient. But his call for "distinguishing the spirits" makes it clear that in the last instance the effectiveness of all the means used in the struggle rested in the one element which even the Church cannot "handle": the Spirit who alone makes alive.

JUDE AND II PETER

How serious, if not actually desperate, the problem of false teaching became for the Church, and how grave the danger was for it to lose its own identity in the battle against heresy, may be gleaned from the brief epistles called Jude and II Peter.

It is generally assumed today that both epistles are rather late and must

---

[30] The latter is the thesis of R. Bultmann, "Analyse des I. Johannesbriefs," in *Festgabe für A. Jülicher*, R. Bultmann, and H. von Soden, eds. (Tübingen: J. C. B. Mohr, 1927), pp. 138-158.

be dated around the middle of the second century. The author of II Peter, to be sure, presents a kind of "last will and testament" of the Apostle Peter (II Pet. 1:13-15), who is consistently presupposed as speaking. It is easy to show the artificial character of this literary frame: (1) He refers to a rather complete New Testament canon (Synoptic Gospels: 1:16 ff; 3:10; Pauline Epistles: 3:16; I Peter: 3:1). (2) He borrows extensively from Jude, who in turn depicts the Apostolic generation as being as remote from the present as are the Old Testament prophets (verse 17). Actually, out of the 25 verses of Jude, no less than 19 appear in one form or another in II Peter, often only slightly modified. (3) His letter implies a rather developed stage of the conflict with heresy.

The heresy against which both writings warn has certainly to do with Gnosis. II Peter emphasizes from the beginning the "knowledge" he has to offer (1:2, 3, 8; cf. 2:20), and his characterization of the false teachers reveals an anti-Gnostic bias: they are "worldly," "void of the spirit," "setting up divisions" (i.e., the Gnostic classifications of "spiritual" and "nonspiritual" people). We have already seen that the accusation of libertinism also points to a Gnostic background. A new aspect seems to be introduced by the attack on "authorities and excellencies," i.e., higher angels who must have played a role in "Jude's" cosmological system (Jude 8 ff.). Much of the material, however, repeats the general stock of antiheretical language (Jude 12-13, 16; II Pet. 2:12 ff.; the charge of immorality, Jude 7; II Pet. 2:14; of love of money, Jude 11; II Pet. 2:3, 14).

The author of II Peter characterizes the adversaries as apostates (2:15; 2:20 f.) who illustrate the truth of a rude proverb (2:22) and whose relapsing into the darkness out of which they had just emerged the Church can only deplore. The reality behind this stylized picture seems to be much more alarming, however. In the church to which "Jude" is writing, the heretics are not even separated from the Christian congregation. It is particularly painful to see them participate in the sacred meals, the love feasts (he speaks of their "carousing," Jude 12; cf. II Pet. 2:13). What one would expect in this situation is the advice to draw the lines and to throw out these men. But the letter contains no such proposal. It offers only the hope that the faithful may "convince some who doubt," and "save some by snatching them out of the fire" (Jude 23). A possible explanation is that the heretics are in the majority and Jude has only a small group of faithful Christians to write to. The church itself is in danger of being pushed into the ghetto of sectarianism.

The reaction to this situation on the part of "Jude" and "Peter" is deplorably weak. Of course, appeal is made to the Christian tradition. II Peter especially abounds in allusions to traditional kerygmatic language. But these appear in a general setting in which the tradition, the "faith," has definitely taken on the character of a deposit of fixed doctrine from the ancient time of the apostles, "once for all delivered to the saints" (Jude 3) of all generations. This "most holy faith" (Jude 20) which every Christian has "once for all" received in baptismal instruction (Jude 5) now must be defended. II Peter calls it the "commandment of the Lord and Savior through your apostles" (3:2), and clearly thinks of a fixed body of apostolic tradition, the transmission of which has been arranged for by the apostles themselves (1:15). It is in line with this that he only "reminds" (1:12, 15) his readers of the truth which is "at their disposal" (1:12).

The major traditional pattern on which both authors capitalize is apocalypticism. As in I John, we find the image of the heretics who, being predestined "long ago" for their condemnation, have entered the Christian community in disguise (Jude 3). Their appearance is the fulfillment of old prophecy—"Jude" refers to the apocryphal Book of Enoch (14 ff.) as well as to the predictions of "the apostles of our Lord Jesus Christ" (17). All the Christian can do is to preserve the faith, to pray and wait patiently, knowing that the punishment of the heretics is under way (20 f.). Obviously, this latter point was crucial in the dangerous situation. "Jude" goes to great pains, illustrating it by a catalogue of examples from the Old Testament which depict the destruction of the wicked: the unbelieving wilderness generation (5), the fallen angels of Gen. 6 (6), the "immoral" cities of Sodom and Gomorrah (7), Cain, Balaam, and Korah (11).

The author of II Peter repeats this apocalyptic argument. In his assumed role as the Apostle Peter, he first speaks of the false teachers in the form of eschatological prophecy: "There *will be* false teachers among you, who will secretly bring in destructive heresies . . ." (2:1 ff.). But he soon switches to the present tense (2:9 ff.) thus indicating that he sees the "prophecy" fulfilled. As in Jude, the major point of the apocalyptic picture is that the destruction of the heretics is near. They are "kept under punishment until the day of judgment" (2:9) or, using the venerable term of ancient Christian eschatology: until the "coming of the Lord" (1:16).

Again, this seems to be no longer self-evident. There are "scoffers" who raise doubts about this Coming and about the reality of such a judgment (3:3 ff.). Their argument is that even after the death of the previous generation ("the fathers") which, according to the predictions of Jesus and the apostles, had every reason to believe the End would come upon them, nothing has happened. Everything has remained as it was from the beginning of Creation—and probably will so continue (3:4). Obviously the author recognizes the seriousness of this argument, because for himself the delay of the expected *parousia* is a problem. In his answer, he first refutes the notion that the course of the world has remained unchanged ever since Creation. Once already, in the Great Flood, the created cosmos was destroyed, and "the heavens and the earth that now exist" will suffer similar destruction—this time by fire (3:5-7). However, the question of when the catastrophe will come must remain unresolved. God's chronology is different from ours (3:8). If the time seems to extend rather long—this is the author's own feeling—there is still no reason for criticizing

God's slowness, but rather for praising his forbearance, which gives the sinner a chance to repent (3:10). Obviously, several apologetic arguments have been combined here in an attempt to explain the delay of the *parousia*. They are not all equally convincing. It is their application that really counts: the catastrophe *is* coming; only the date is uncertain. Christians must doubly watch their actions in order to be prepared at every moment (3:11 ff.). The delay of the *parousia* should not lead to a decrease, but rather to an increase of their earnest expectation of the End (3:12).

We cannot determine whether or not the "scoffers" of II Pet. 3 are identical with the Gnostic foes. In I Clement 23:3 f. (cf. II Clement 11:2-4) a question similar to theirs is quoted as a "scripture," and although the source is unknown, it presupposes Jewish background. On the other hand, the context speaks for the identity with the Gnostics. That Gnostics would raise doubts about the traditional Christian eschatology is not surprising, given their interest in a vertical salvation from this "lower" world into "higher" worlds rather than for a horizontal one connected with a second Coming of the Lord in the future. It is an often recurring charge that Gnostics "deny the resurrection." Paul seems to argue against this position in I Cor. 15, and two heretics of the Pastoral Epistles, Hymenaeus and Philetus, are accused of maintaining "that the resurrection is past already" (II Tim. 2:18). The point probably was that they regarded the initiation into higher Gnosis as "resurrection." As Justin Martyr (*Apology* I. 26.4) says, Menander persuaded his followers that they would not die, and Irenaeus (*Against Heresies* I. 23.5) specifies that it was Menander's magical baptism which supposedly conferred immortality.

II Peter has been called an "apology of early Christian eschatology." [31] This certainly is true in a formal sense. But there is one important difference: the apostolic Church waited for the Coming of the Lord as the revelation of Christ's dominion over all the world. "Peter" is waiting for the judgment that will finally wipe out the ungodly and vindicate the righteous. When he is waiting for a "new heaven and a new earth in which righteousness dwells" (3:13), he is longing in the first instance for a world in which Christians finally will be at rest from their enemies. It is the whole misery of a hard-pressed Church that appears in this transformation. However, there can be no doubt: the more this Church allows the pressures and troubles of the present to take over and dominate its faith and hope, the more it has difficulty in preserving its own identity. The author of II Peter is certainly unaware how close he himself is to a "heretical" interpretation of Christianity. But when he describes it as the goal of faithful life that the Christian "may escape from the corruption that is in the world because of passion and become partaker of the divine nature"

---

[31] See E. Kaesemann, "An Apologia for Primitive Christian Eschatology," in *Essays on New Testament Themes*, tr. W. J. Montague, *Studies in Biblical Theology*, XLI (London: SCM Press, 1964), pp. 169-195.

(1:4), he has surely gone over the brink into pagan notions of apotheosis which are foreign to the *kerygma* he wants to preserve.

The Church in the post-Apostolic period shows the deep marks of the bitter conflict with forces that threatened to submerge the truth of the Gospel under a general Hellenistic syncretism. They are the result of painful experience. The Church saw the urgent need to reformulate the "faith" because it had come to it in a form insufficient to combat the ever new countenance of false teaching. But what emerged as "orthodox" faith proved by no means a guarantee against error. The danger of losing contact with the Gospel remained an ever present possibility, The Church also found itself under the necessity of developing an institutionalized ministry because the freedom of the Spirit, in which authority rested pretty much on the persuasiveness of each interpreter of the faith, proved ineffective in fighting the claims of the false teachers. But again, this ministry was not an automatic guarantee against error. The Church leaders often lacked the intellectual competence to draw the right lines. Nevertheless, in both cases the Church had to take the risk for the sake of the Gospel, which was to speak to a new generation. It had to sacrifice the innocence of its early days in order to grow to maturity.

THE COMMUNITY
AND THE CITY OF GOD

Hebrews and Revelation

CHAPTER SEVENTEEN From its very beginning, the

Christian community had looked forward eagerly to the

time when God would complete the work of transforming

his Creation. This mood of hopefulness and expectancy had

been strong in the Hebrew prophetic tradition, from which

Christianity had inherited so much. Jesus had appeared on

the scene of his public ministry announcing, "The kingdom

of God is at hand." His works were pointed to by him as

signs of the nearness of the kingdom. The apostles, together with the Aramaic-speaking Church of the first generation, prayed "Maranatha" (meaning "Our Lord, come!"). The prevailing atmosphere, therefore, was one of waiting for God to establish his new order.

The New Testament writers were agreed *that* God would establish the New Age; as to *when, where,* and *how,* there was not such unanimity. There is some evidence that single individuals—notably Paul—may have changed their views on this subject with the changing situations. Although we cannot be certain of the order of his letters, it appears that in I Thessalonians (which is usually thought to be among his earliest letters), he expected the coming of Christ to take place soon, and surely within his own lifetime (I Thess. 4:13-17). By the time he wrote Philippians, however, he thought he might not live to see the return of Christ (Phil. 1:19-25). His expectation of deliverance was not limited to his own future, but included the "eagerly awaited" redemption of the whole creation (Rom. 8:18-25).[1]

The writers of the gospels modified Jesus' own views of the coming of the kingdom of God in various ways. Although Jesus' message about the kingdom was basically apocalyptic, he did not engage in the bizarre speculations and doleful predictions about the events at the end of the Age, such as we read in Daniel or the Book of Enoch. The Synoptic Apocalypse, however, both in its older Markan form (Mk. 13:5-37) and in its greatly extended Matthean form (Mt. 24:4-25:46), has elaborated on the signs of the End and predictions of doom. We have already seen how Matthew has modified the eschatological message of Jesus by differentiating between the kingdom of the Son of Man (the present, mixed form of the Church, with good and evil within) and the kingdom of the Father (from which all evil will be purged).[2] Luke has eased the sense of urgency about the Coming of Christ by depicting him as already ruling at the right hand of God, while the Church extends the redemptive mission which he had launched.[3]

In the Gospel of John, the weight of attention has been shifted from the future fulfillment to the present availability of the life of the Age to Come. The effect of this shift is to lead Christians to look within the realm of their own experience for the realization of God's redemptive promise rather than to the future or to the Creation as a whole.[4]

In some of the later books of the New Testament, the hope of redemption has been modified in still other ways. In the Pastorals, for instance, it survives

---

[1] On the possibility that Paul's views of the future changed, see C. H. Dodd, *New Testament Studies* (New York: Scribner's, 1954), pp. 108-118.

[2] For a fuller discussion, see pp. 287-288.

[3] For the development of this view see pp. 302-303.

[4] This theme is treated throughout Chapter 14. The tendency to treat the inner life of the individual as the place where God is fulfilling his "historical" purpose is most evident in the work of R. Bultmann. See his *Theology of the New Testament,* II (New York: Scribner's, 1955) and *History and Eschatology* (Edinburgh: University of Edinburgh Press, 1957).

in largely formal expressions, such as "that Day" (II Tim. 4:8), by which the writer refers to the day of judgment. The author of II Peter tries to resolve the problem of the nonfulfillment of the Lord's Coming by suggesting that God's mode of calculating time is different from man's, so that the time which has elapsed since the promise of his Coming was uttered is not very great (II Pet. 3:8-10).

There are two New Testament writings, however, in which Christian hope continues to burn, though both were written toward the end of the first century: Hebrews and Revelation. Both are concerned with the establishment of the City of God, though they are not united in their views of the way in which God will establish it. The author of Hebrews, strongly influenced by Hellenistic thought, pictures the city as heavenly, the eternal archetype of a perfect Creation, revealed to men in God's own time. The author of Revelation, influenced by Jewish apocalyptic, portrays the City of God as coming down to earth out of heaven; that is, as the fulfillment on earth of the heavenly Father's purpose for his Creation. Yet both are alive with eager expectation that the God who has acted *decisively* through Jesus Christ for the world's redemption, will yet act *finally* in fulfillment of his goal.

JESUS CHRIST: GOD'S FINAL WORD TO MAN

Some time in the latter part of the first century a Christian leader wrote a "word of exhortation" (Heb. 13:22) to a group of Christians who were threatened by persecution. His writing later came to be called "To the Hebrews," and eventually it was accepted into the New Testament canon as an epistle of Paul. But Paul's authorship was questioned in the first few centuries, was later doubted by Calvin and Luther, and is generally denied today, for the language and theology differ markedly from that of Paul. Numerous other authors have been suggested (Luke, Barnabas, Silas, Apollos, Clement of Rome, and others), but the question of who wrote the epistle to the Hebrews remains one of the unsolved riddles of the New Testament.

The writing itself reveals a great deal about the unknown author, however. He was at home in the Greek language, and his vocabulary and style compare well with good literary prose of the period. The writing is not an epistle in the proper sense, for although it has an epistolary ending (13:24) it does not begin with the normal salutation. The ending may have been added later in an effort to enhance the claim for Paul's authorship. The epistle closely parallels a type of discourse common to Hellenistic rhetoric,[5] but the literary form has been modified under the influence of a type of Christian preaching. The author develops his argument within the framework of a series of quotations from the

---

[5] See A. H. McNeile, *An Introduction to the Study of the New Testament*, 2nd ed. (Oxford: Clarendon Press, 1953), pp. 225 ff.

Old Testament; he interprets the quotations in the light of the revelation of Christ; and then he exhorts his readers to specific action.

The language, style, and form of the writing indicate that the author had been educated in the Hellenistic tradition. For example, he uses terminology and concepts that show some familiarity with Platonic thought, as in his tendency to see earthly forms and phenomena in contrast to heavenly and eternal realities. Here he shows affinity to the writings of Philo, and some scholars have argued that the writing originated in Philo's home city, Alexandria. The author also resembles Philo in his method of interpreting scripture, in his dependence on the Jewish Wisdom Literature, and in his fondness for tracking down the derivations of words. On the other hand, he seems familiar with the rabbinical principles of interpreting scripture. In short, the author could have been either a Jewish Christian or a Gentile Christian; in either case, he had come to know Christianity as it was interpreted under the influence of Hellenistic Judaism.

Since the author tells us that he was a second- or third-generation Christian (2:3), the writing can be dated some time in the late first century A.D. And it is addressed to a community that is threatened by persecution (see pp. 359 ff.) and is in danger of apostasy. Only in the closing salutation, "Those who come from Italy send their greetings" (13:24), do we find any clue to the actual destination of the writing. This phrase has generally been interpreted to mean that the writing was first sent to Rome, and that there were Roman Christians with the author who sent greetings to their friends back home. The phrase may be a later addition to the text, but even so it would reflect a tradition that had already related the writing to Rome. Our surmise that the epistle was sent to Rome is strengthened by the fact that the first writing that shows acquaintance with Hebrews is I Clement, which is traditionally believed to have been written in Rome about A.D. 96. And it is true that toward the end of the reign of Domitian (A.D. 81-96) the Christians of Rome experienced some hostility from the government.

The writing has a very practical end in view: to strengthen the readers in their faith. The author strives earnestly to lead his readers to a fuller understanding of the truth for which they are being called upon to suffer. They have been called to share in eternal salvation in Jesus Christ, and he summons all the theological insights at his command to help them stand firm in their faith. It is this purpose that leads him to picture Christ as the great High Priest whose sacrificial death is the doorway to salvation. He embodies his appeal in a sermon to be read in the church to which the epistle was sent.

The Superiority of the Son of God

In his magnificent prologue, the author proclaims the finality of God's revelation in Jesus Christ (1:1-4). In ages past, God had revealed himself through the prophets, but now in the "last days" he has given his full revelation in his Son. The Son is the "heir of all things"; all God's promises to man are being realized through Christ (6:12, 17). Philo had referred to the *logos* as the "heir"—the divine, immanent principle that guides the world to its appointed ends. By heir, our author has primarily in mind God's Son, who brought salvation to the world. The author, like Paul and John, is clearly influenced by the wisdom and *logos* speculation of Hellenistic Judaism when he attributes to Christ pre-existence and a mediating role in Creation (1:3). But his major concern is not with cosmological speculation about Christ or the Creation, but with God's purposes in Creation as they are revealed in the salvation accomplished through the Son: *The end of Creation is redemption.*

He speaks of the finality of God's revelation in two senses: First, in the eschatological sense that with the coming of the Son the "last days" of this Age have been entered. And second, in the more philosophical sense that the Son has fully revealed the nature of God. To the Hellenistic mind, the very title "Son of God" would have suggested a unique relation of oneness with God. But our author is very explicit on this point. Christ reflects the glory of God, and bears the very stamp of God's divine nature. The Greek word translated as "reflects" is a Hellenistic term that was borrowed both by Philo and by the Jewish Wisdom Literature. A favorite analogy to explain how the transcendent God could manifest himself in the world was that of the sun and its rays. As the sun's rays (reflections) participated in the very essence of the sun's light, yet without diminishing that essence, so the divine life was mediated in the world without diminishing or disturbing the source from which it came. The author adopts this analogy to illustrate the unique relation between God and Christ.

The author comes to the crucial point of God's revelation in Christ when he refers to "purification for sins" and Christ's having "sat down at the right hand of the Majesty on high" (1:3). Here he turns to God's act of salvation in the historical death of the Son through which purification was accomplished, and to its consummation in the Son's exaltation to heaven. These are to be the subjects of the main section of his writing. The reference to the historical work of the Son, standing as it does in the midst of quasi-philosophical terminology, clearly relates God's final revelation to the historical person Jesus. In the death and exaltation of this historical person, God's salvation has been accomplished and Jesus' unique relation as Son has been revealed.

The author now elaborates on Christ's superiority to all other beings; he considers angels first (1:5-2:9), using Old Testament passages to support his thesis. Like other Christians of his day, our author regards the Old Testament writings as prophecies looking forward to Christ. Turning to a passage from the Psalms (Ps. 2:7) and to a passage from II Samuel, he points out that Christ has been called "Son" by God (1:5), whereas the angels have not. On the contrary, angels have been commanded by God to worship the Son (1:6), and according to Psalm 45 the Son has been anointed by God as the righteous ruler of God's kingdom (1:8-9). The author interprets Psalm 45, which was originally an enthronement psalm written to celebrate the anointing of a Jewish king, as a reference to God's appointment of Christ as the Messiah-King. This same theme of the victorious rule of the Messiah-King is also found in his next statement—namely, that God has promised that all the enemies of righteousness will be put in subjection to the Son (1:13); in contrast to Christ, angels are not to be served, but rather are to act as ministering servants to those who are to obtain salvation (1:14; 1:7).

But what practical point are the readers of the epistle to gather from this discussion of Christ's superiority to the angels? This is just what the author tries to make clear in the first of his series of exhortations to his readers (2:1-4). Since their salvation is given only through the Son himself, who is superior to all heavenly beings, he asks them how they can escape judgment if they neglect "such a great salvation." Clearly, they must pay close attention to this salvation, which was declared first by the Lord (Jesus), attested to by those who heard him (perhaps the apostles), and later by Christians. By making this reference, the author is firmly grounding his own message in the *kerygma* of the Church. Whatever his own interpretation of the *kerygma*, it is clear that he believes he is remaining true to its content and intent.

In developing this argument, the author is making use of a rabbinic principle of interpretation called *a minore ad majus* ("from the lesser to the greater"). If breaking the Torah that was given by lesser beings (according to Jewish tradition God had given the Torah through angels) brought judgment, a far worse judgment will result from disobeying the word of the Son of God, who is far superior. Later on in his writing, the author uses this same principle repeatedly.

Now the author quotes from another psalm, which he interprets as God's promise that in the Age to Come (the New Age) all things will be put in subjection to man, and not to angels (2:5-8). But anyone can see that all things are not yet subject to man; in particular, our author has in mind the power that death still seems to hold over man. The author calls upon his readers to fix their gaze on Jesus (2:9-18), who has suffered death but who has been exalted and crowned with honor and glory. It is to Christ that they must look for evidence of the New Age and of man's victory over death. Jesus has tasted death for every man. The author believes that the promises God gave to man have been fulfilled in the man Jesus, who through his suffering became the pioneer of salvation to many "sons" who share in his "sonship" and in the promises. This fulfillment was made possible because Jesus was a man ("partook of the same nature") and through his death destroyed the Devil, who holds man in the power of death. Here the author has preserved the apocalyptic mythology of the conflict between the Messiah and Satan that is found elsewhere in the New Testament.[6] But he concentrates on the victory over death—or the "fear of death," as he puts it—perhaps remembering that his readers are under threat of persecution.

The author does not say just how this victory has been won. But later on he speaks of Jesus' being "made perfect" through obedience (5:8-9), and we may assume that it was in Jesus' perfect obedience to God's will that he overcame the power of evil and the death that is the inevitable consequence of sin. But this mode of thinking about the meaning of Jesus' death is not central to the author's argument, for his major concern is not the destruction of the Devil but the expiation of sins by Christ acting as a faithful High Priest (2:17). Although the term "High Priest" is injected here, its meaning is not discussed until we come to the main theological argument of the writing (4:14-10:25).

Next, the author shows the superiority of Christ to Moses (3:1-4:13). Christians share in a "heavenly call" given by Jesus, who is the "apostle" and High Priest. This is the only place in the New Testament where Jesus is called "apostle." The term here has its usual technical meaning of one sent with the commission and authority of the sender (God).[7] But notice that it appears side by side with the term "High Priest," a fact that may give added meaning. According to rabbinic tradition, on the Day of Atonement the High Priest entered the Holy of Holies as the apostle of the people and represented them before God. Since the author later pictures Christ in these very terms (9:24), he may purposely be using the word "apostle" in an ambiguous way here.

In contrast to Christ's call, Moses had called the House of Israel into being. But Moses, as the representative of the House of Israel, was merely a servant; the author believes that what Moses said and did merely testified to, or foreshadowed, what Christ was to say and do (3:5). Since the true household that Christ built was merely foreshadowed by Moses and Israel, the author argues that Christ is far superior to Moses.

Again the author exhorts his readers to hold fast to their confidence in Christ, through whom the true household of God (the Church) has been built in order that they may remain members of that household (3:6-4:13). Quoting Psalm 95, he calls to his readers' mind the story of how Israel disobeyed Moses in the wilderness when they doubted God's promises that he would lead them to a new land (Num. 12:7 ff.). From the Psalm, he recalls how Moses warned them that unless they refrained from rebellion "today" they would not enter into God's "rest." Then he interprets the word "today" as actually foreshadowing the day in which Christ has called the true household into being. The author uses the term "today" in an eschatological sense to refer to "these last days" (1:2) when the Messiah, the Son of God, has come to lead God's people to God's "rest."

---

[6] See pp. 257 ff.
[7] For a discussion of the term see pp. 151 ff.

The "rest" that was promised to the Israelites was entrance into the Promised Land. But here again the author uses a term to foreshadow something that came later—the "rest" foreshadows the better promise that the author refers to variously as entrance into the heavenly sanctuary (10:19), into the city of the living God (12:22), or simply salvation (2:3). He is depending here on Jewish speculation about the statement in Genesis (2:2 ff.) that when God had finished the Creation he rested. But it was inconceivable to the Jews that God had ceased his divine activity after Creation. Philo, for example, insisted that the "rest" merely referred to God's continuing work; since it was of the very nature of God to create, this rest was a symbol of his effortless, unhindered, divine activity. One rabbinic interpretation was that the rest referred to God's completion of his work in judgment and salvation. All these interpretations were related to the meaning of the Sabbath, which commemorated the Creation. And the author of Hebrews says there remains "a sabbath rest for the people of God" (4:9). This is the true rest, the heavenly sanctuary, into which Jesus Christ, having been perfected through suffering, has already entered. It is the rest into which the People of God will enter if they are obedient and hold fast their confession of faith (4:11-14). To fall short of that "rest" is to come under the judgment of God, who discerns the inward thoughts of men (4:12-13).

Christ, the True High Priest—Hebrews 4:14-7:28

The author now turns to his central teaching about Christ, in which he compares and contrasts Christ's work with that of the Levitical priesthood. In his typical rhetorical style, he again introduces a subject that he will elaborate on later (Heb. 8-10). Throughout the early stages of the argument he emphasizes two points: First, because Christ was a man, and therefore was tempted as all men are, he can sympathize with men's weakness and give help in time of need (4:14-16). This point would be particularly meaningful to his readers, who were facing a threatening historical situation. In one of the few references to the historical ministry of Jesus found outside the gospels, the author recalls the Synoptic story of Jesus' agony in the Garden of Gethsemane (5:7-9): "In the days of his flesh, Jesus offered up prayers and supplications, with loud cries and tears, to him who was able to save him from death, and he was heard for his godly fear." The second point is that through Christ's obedience to God even unto death he fulfilled his own destiny as Son by becoming the source of eternal salvation to all who obey him (5:8).

Like the Levitical priests, Jesus is human, and so he can understand and sympathize with human weakness. This is a truth that must not be lost in face of the belief that he is a great High Priest who "has passed through the heavens, Jesus, the Son of God" (4:14). And just as the High Priest in the Levitical line is appointed by God to act on behalf of men in their relations to God, offering gifts and sacrifices for sins, so Christ is appointed by God and offers a sacrifice (5:1). But there is a difference: The Levitical High Priest is beset by human weakness and has sinned, and he must offer sacrifices for himself as well as for the people (5:2-3). But Christ, though a man, is without sin (4:15), and so does not need to offer sacrifices for himself.

There is also a difference in the way in which Christ was called to his ministry. Just as Aaron and his descendants in the Levitical line of priests were appointed by God and not self-appointed, so Christ was appointed by God (5:5-6). But Christ was called to his ministry as Son (5:5). The author again quotes Psalm 2, which he, along with other Christians, believed was a prophecy of Jesus' appointment as Messiah. This is an important point, for it shows that it is *as Messiah* that Jesus exercises his priestly role. But the author also quotes Ps. 110:4, "Thou art a priest forever after the order of Melchisedek," which he also interprets as a reference to Christ. Now the first verse of this Psalm, "The Lord says to my Lord: sit at my right hand, till I make your enemies your footstool," was commonly interpreted by Christians as referring to Christ's exaltation to heaven as Messiah (Mt. 22:44; Mk. 12:36; Acts 2:34; I Cor. 15:25; Eph. 1:20; etc.). But our author is the only New Testament writer to use the reference to the order of Melchisedek. What he intends to do is to show the superiority of Christ's order of priesthood (Heb. 7) to the Levitical order; but before he does that he again exhorts his readers (5:11-6:12).

He reprimands them for their dullness of hearing (5:11) and for their sluggishness in faith and conduct (6:11-12). Although they ought to be teachers, they themselves are in need of being taught again the first principles of God's word. But he proposes to leave elementary doctrines and go on to mature teaching (6:1-3), despite their need to be fed milk rather than solid food (5:12). Exactly what the author means by "milk" and "solid food" is not clear. Usually the solid food is taken as the author's interpretation of Christ as a priest after the order of Melchisedek (5:10). It has even been suggested that the author, under the influence of Gnosticism, thinks of solid food as esoteric knowledge about Christ that only the mature (5:14) are able to receive.

When the author uses the terms "dullness" or "sluggishness," he is not referring simply to his readers' understanding of doctrine. The meaning of "dullness" depends upon the meaning of the word "mature," which is a translation of the Greek word meaning "perfect." As used in the mystery cults, this term referred to the state of those who had been initiated. In Gnostic circles, it referred to those who were in possession of the secret knowledge whereby the Gnostic was guaranteed salvation from the material world. Paul uses the term to refer to Christians who through the Spirit have come to know the wisdom of God revealed in Christ (I Cor. 2:6-10).

But in Hebrews, "perfection" has a somewhat different connotation. Essentially, it refers to the status of one whose sins have been forgiven through the sacrificial death of Christ (9:26). "For by a single offering he has *perfected* for all time those who are sanctified" (10:14). The author stresses that as a consequence of this forgiveness the believer has had his conscience purified (9:14; 10:22). Once he has been purified he must sin no more, for a Christian who sins after baptism can expect no further forgiveness for sins (10:8, 26). The perfecting that is accomplished by Christ through the forgiveness of sin and the cleansing of the conscience demands a moral purity of life. What is "hard to explain" because they are "dull of hearing" is the truth that having been forgiven they must maintain moral purity of life or they will forfeit their salvation. This is implied by the author's statement that those who live on milk are "unskilled in the word of righteousness" (5:13), whereas solid food is for those who have been trained "by practice to distinguish good from evil" (5:14). In this latter passage, the author is using a philosophical term for the capacity of a person to distinguish between right and wrong.

What is "hard to explain" is also implied in his warning that it is impossible to "restore again to repentance those who have once been enlightened, who have tasted the heavenly gift, and have become partakers of the Holy Spirit, and have tasted the goodness of the word of God and the powers of the age to come, if they then commit apostasy . . ." (6:4-6). Here the author refers to the forgiveness of sins received in baptism and the power to live according to the new life bestowed upon them. According to the author, this includes the power to refrain from apostasy. Apostasy may include the actual denial of Christ under persecution but it also has the figurative meaning found in the Old Testament of denying God through immoral action. Bearing "thorns and thistles" (6:8) may refer to moral corruption as well as to an outright renunciation of faith in Christ. In short, the author is insisting that there is no further repentance for those who deny Christ in word *or* deed.

The author now turns to his interpretation of Christ's work in terms of priesthood. Although Hebrews is the only New Testament writing to speak of Christ's work in these terms, the author may not have been the first to do so. Jewish speculation had already proposed that the Messiah would come from a priestly line. We find evidence of this in the Jewish apocalyptic writing, *The Testament of the Twelve Patriarchs*, and in the Dead Sea Scrolls a Messiah from the line of Aaron is expected. [8]

The thesis of Christ's priesthood is developed in relation to the mysterious Old Testament personage, Melchisedek (Heb. 7), who is mentioned in two Old Testament passages, Gen. 14:17-20 and Ps. 110:4 ff. According to the account in Genesis, Melchisedek, king of Salem and priest of the Most High God, had

---

[8] The stress on the superior priesthood of Christ parallels the claim at Qumran that theirs was the true priesthood, in contrast to the "wicked" priests in Jerusalem. But the theory of Y. Yadin which attributes Hebrews to the Dead Sea community has not found wide acceptance. See Y. Yadin, "The Dead Sea Scrolls and the Epistle to the Hebrews," in *Aspects of the Dead Sea Scrolls, Scripta Hierosolymitana*, IV (Jerusalem, Israel: Hebrew University Press, 1957), 36-55.

met Abraham returning from his battle to release Lot from captivity. Melchisedek blessed Abraham and took from him a tenth of all he had.

By a method of interpretation common in the author's day, though it seems far-fetched today, he seeks to establish the superiority of Melchisedek over both Abraham and the Levitical priesthood descended from Abraham. This superiority clearly shows, he argues, that perfection was not attainable through the Levitical line; otherwise the other order of priesthood through Melchisedek would not have been necessary (7:11). The point of the author's involved interpretation is to show that it is in the priesthood of Melchisedek alone that the priesthood of Christ is foreshadowed. Melchisedek was not from the tribe of Levi, nor was Christ (7:13). Melchisedek was made a High Priest forever, and so was Christ (7:3; 7:24). Christ's priesthood was not validated by his being in the line of Levi but by his "indestructible life" (7:16). The Lord, as the scripture testifies, swore that Christ was a High Priest forever (7:21).[9]

There is one other important line in the author's argument. If Jesus, in the order of Melchisedek, represents a priesthood that supersedes the Levitical priesthood, then the Law that established that priesthood is superseded (7:12), and a former commandment is set aside (7:18). The author, like Paul, believes that with the coming of Christ the Law has been set aside. But there is a difference in the two views. Paul thought of the Law in terms of its unrealizable ethical demands, and so the Law held him in bondage to sin and death. With the coming of Christ, the power of the Law was broken, for man is justified by faith and not by works of the Law. The author of Hebrews thinks of the Law in terms of the cultus, with its priesthood, sacrifices, and sanctuary, none of which he believes can provide forgiveness of sins. But with the coming of Christ, the true priesthood, sacrifice, and sanctuary are revealed, and through them true forgiveness is made possible. With Christ a new covenant is given that is superior to the old one that established the cultus (7:22). And a better hope grounded in better promises is given whereby man is able to draw near to God (7:18, 25). It is to establish the superiority of the new priesthood, sacrifice, sanctuary, covenant, promises, and hope that the author now compares Christ and the Levitical priesthood.

The Heavenly Sanctuary—Hebrews 8:1-10:18

Having established Christ as a priest after the order of Melchisedek (Heb. 7), the author mentions Melchisedek no more. His purpose has been served, for he has shown that in Christ a priesthood that supersedes the Levitical priesthood has found its fulfillment. The author now turns to the climax of his theological argument, in which he explains how Christ's priesthood is superior to the Levitical priesthood.

---

[9] For a discussion of the complicated problems raised by the author's reference to Melchisedek and of previous speculation about this figure, see Alexander C. Purdy and J. Harry Cotton, "The Epistle to the Hebrews," *The Interpreter's Bible*, XI (New York: Abingdon, 1955), 660.

The author draws his comparison in terms of a High Priest in a heavenly sanctuary built by God (8:1-2), and in terms of the setting up of an earthly priesthood and the building of an earthly sanctuary according to the Law revealed to Moses on Mt. Sinai (8:5). Here the author alludes to the instructions regarding the tent (tabernacle) in the Book of Exodus (24-27). According to this account, Moses was to "make everything according to the pattern which was shown you in the mountain" (Ex. 25:40). Throughout his discussion, the author has in mind this tent that was set up in the wilderness, rather than the Temple at Jerusalem, which he had probably never seen. His description of the sanctuary is clearly drawn from the Biblical account.

There had been a good bit of speculation among the Jews about this statement to Moses. The word "pattern" had led them to the conclusion that the earthly Temple was a copy of an invisible heavenly sanctuary in which angels continually interceded for the sins of men. The author of Hebrews was undoubtedly influenced by such speculation. But he was also influenced by Hellenistic dualism, which tended to think of earthly phenomena as copies or shadows of heavenly realities. He uses the words "copy" (8:5; 9:23, 24) and "shadow" (8:5; 10:1) in contrast to the "true" (8:2; 9:24; 10:1), the "perfect" (9:11), "the real" (10:1). Philo spoke of the Temple as a symbol of the true temple, the invisible world of ideal forms whose Holy of Holies is the heaven, and whose High Priest is the *logos* who leads men to understand that the material world is patterned after the immaterial world.[10]

And yet the author of Hebrews is not primarily interested in the cosmos or a replica of the tent in the heavens, but rather in the revelation of the true priest Jesus Christ and the heavenly sanctuary that God has made through him. Not only has Christ obtained a priesthood that is more excellent than the old; he has also mediated a covenant that is better. The author finds his authority for this New Covenant in a prophecy of Jeremiah (8:8-12). From the beginning, Christians had believed that this promise of a New Covenant prophesied by Jeremiah had been fulfilled in Christ (Mt. 2:18; 26:28; Mk. 14:24; Lk. 22:20). The author of Hebrews is peculiarly interested in the promise of the "forgiveness of sins" (8:12) that will bring about a new relationship between God and man through the true sacrifice of Jesus Christ.

He describes the earthly sanctuary with its ineffectual priesthood and sacrifices (9:1-14). Here he is dependent on the Exodus account (Ex. 25 ff.). Obviously he was not aware that this description (9:1-5) derives from an idealized account by priestly scribes who wrote long after Moses' time. Nor was he apparently aware of certain discrepancies between his own description and that in the Exodus account.[11] But, as he himself says, he is not concerned with details (9:5). The major features that are important for his interpretation are the

---

[10] See E. R. Goodenough, *By Light, Light* (New Haven: Yale University Press, 1935), pp. 108 ff., 116 ff.

[11] For these discrepancies, see Purdy and Cotton, "The Epistle to the Hebrews," *Interpreter's Bible*, XI (New York: Abingdon, 1955), pp. 685-687.

two inner tents. The outer of the two, known as the Holy Place, was open to all classes of priests, though not to the people; in this area the daily sacrifices were offered. The inner tent, the Holy of Holies, only the High Priest was allowed to enter, once a year on the Day of Atonement (9:7). This great occasion, described in Lev. 16, preoccupies our author and he deals with it as representative of the whole Levitical system of sacrifices. On that occasion the High Priest entered through the curtain to sprinkle sacrificial blood upon the mercy seat. The sacrificial blood of a bull was sprinkled for the sins of the High Priest himself and of the other priests, for, being human, they too were liable to sin. And the sacrificial blood of a goat was sprinkled for the sins of the people. The author argues that these animal sacrifices could only guarantee ritual cleansing after some infractions of the laws dealing with ritual purity (9:10), such as those found in Lev. 11. But he contends that none of these sacrifices could perfect the conscience (9:9).

Now the author explains that the outer tent is actually a symbol of the present age, and that as long as it stands it is impossible to enter into the inner sanctuary—the heavenly sanctuary (9:8-9). He seems to mean that until the "New Age" came, no matter how often the High Priest entered the Holy of Holies, he never actually entered into the presence of God. But with the exaltation of Christ to the right hand of God (8:1), the New Age has come (9:26) and the true High Priest has entered the heavenly sanctuary, into the presence of God himself (10:24). And in entering that sanctuary he offered himself and not the blood of goats and bulls (9:11-12).

The superiority of Christ's offering of his life is that it purifies the conscience from dead works through forgiveness of sin. His offering of a life without blemish (sin), through the Spirit, was able to purify men from all sins (9:14; 2:9-18) and so perfect those who were consecrated by that offering (10:14; 10:29). The superiority of Christ's sacrifice is also substantiated by the fact that it was a single sacrifice that could never be repeated (7:27; 9:25-26; 10:10, 12, 14), whereas in the tent sacrifices had to be continually offered, showing that the conscience was never purified from sin. By implication, this single offering was sufficient for all time, since it need not, indeed it could not, be repeated. It marked the end of the Old Age of sin and the beginning of the New Age in which sin and death were overcome by Christ, who was now seated at the right hand of God (10:12-13; 2:9-15). Interpreting words from Psalm 40 as words of Christ, the author can say that Christ himself came to do away with all other kinds of sacrifice (10:5-7) by doing the "will of God," and in his death he consecrated once and for all those who believe.

Christ's sacrifice was superior in yet another sense, for through his sacrificial death he had become the mediator of the New Covenant. Alluding to his earlier statement that through Christ the believers are led into God's "rest" (3:7-4:10), the author now declares that the promises of the New Covenant are better than those of the Old, for those whose sins are forgiven will receive the promised eternal inheritance; they will enter into the heavenly sanctuary with Jesus Christ (9:15, 19). As the former covenants were ratified by the sprinkling of blood (9:15-22), so Christ, through his death, has ratified the New Covenant; those who are consecrated by Christ's offering of himself in perfect obedience to God's will are heirs of the better promises.

The author concludes this section with an exhortation (10:19-39) in which he shows the implications of Christ's priesthood for the reader. Although in the Jewish cultus only the High Priest was allowed to enter the Holy of Holies (which was believed to be the peculiar place of God's presence), Christ's "brethren" have confidence that they may enter into the heavenly sanctuary (10:19)—that is, into the heavenly presence of God himself. This is the climax of the author's argument, and he urges his readers to hold fast their confession of Christ and to remain faithful. For, having had their conscience cleansed in baptism (10:22), if they now sin deliberately there is no longer any sacrifice for sins; only judgment awaits them (10:26-31). They must continue steadfast in good works and in confidence lest they lose their reward (10:23-25; 35-56).

No matter how elegant this rhetorical argument may have seemed to the first century, to the modern reader it inevitably sounds rather strange. But the patient reader cannot fail to discover the main point of the discourse. The author's basic conviction is remarkably clear: Because man is sinful, his relationship to God is broken, and man himself cannot restore the relationship. Jesus Christ, through his sacrificial death, accomplished what no man could do for himself: he made forgiveness of sins possible and opened the doorway to a new relationship with God through the promise of salvation.

Our author never explicitly explains why a sacrificial death was necessary. In this he resembles the earliest Christians, who, though they proclaimed a relationship between Christ's death and the forgiveness of sins, never explained that relationship. There is certainly nothing in the writing that suggests the concept of an angry God who must be appeased before man can be forgiven. Nor is there any explicit suggestion, as in John and Paul, that it is through Christ's death that God's love is revealed and the believer is made a new creature or is born again.

Two questions stand unanswered: (1) Why was the sacrifice necessary? (2) How did it benefit man? In answer to the first question, the most we can say with certainty is this: The author of Hebrews seems to accept the Old Testament principle that in the relationship God had established with his People (through covenants) and in the Peoples' continuing effort to maintain that relationship (through worship) sacrifice was of primary importance. What was true of the Old Covenant foreshadowed the situation under the New Covenant established through Jesus Christ.

It is equally difficult to decide just how man is to benefit from Christ's sacrifice. The author seems to presuppose that his readers will accept the crucial significance of sacrifice for establishing relations with God. On the basis of this presupposition, he is content to argue the finality of Christ's sacrifice and to summon them to faith that through his sacrificial death their sins are forgiven. The primary benefit seems to be found in the assurance that the believers experience through this acceptance of the effectiveness of Christ's death and the power this faith gives them to endure temptations and to maintain a pure conscience.

The distinctiveness of our author's teaching about sacrifice perhaps can be seen best in relation to Paul. Paul also agrees that Christ's sacrificial death was necessary for man's salvation. But he explicitly sees that death as a revelation of the love of God. Furthermore, man appropriates the benefits of that sacrifice as through faith he enters into Christ's sufferings through the Spirit of Christ who dwells in him.[12] It is the absence of the Pauline concept of faith and of the indwelling Spirit that, among other things, distinguishes our author's teaching on sacrifice, as well as on many other points, from that of Paul.

The Way of Faith—Hebrews 11:1-13:21

Chapter 11 is one of the best-known passages in Hebrews. It is a roll call of the heroes of the Old Testament who followed the way of faith. The author hopes to strengthen his readers by reminding them that they are not alone in their struggles, and to inspire them to faithfulness by recalling the example of their forebears in the faith.

In his opening lines he gives the only explicit definition of faith that appears in the New Testament (11:1-4). When he says that faith is the "conviction of things not seen," and that through faith we know the world is made out of things that do not appear, he is speaking in language that was common in Hellenistic philosophical thought. This is the way of thinking that conceived of the material world as the shadowy and passing image of the heavenly world of reality. This heavenly world is what is in the author's mind when he says it was through faith that Abraham looked forward to "the city which has foundations, whose builder and maker is God" (11:10). Into this scheme of thought the author inserts Jewish apocalyptic language when he refers to the "city of the living God, the heavenly Jerusalem" (12:22). And earlier he has spoken of the heavenly world of reality in terms of a heavenly sanctuary, the true tent, the Holy of Holies. All this metaphorical language points to unseen realities. So he pictures the great Old Testament heroes of faith as "strangers and exiles on the earth" (the material world) looking for a "homeland," "a better country, that is, a heavenly one" (11:13-16). It is into this heavenly world that Christ had gone when he "passed through the heavens" (4:14).

Our author says that it is through faith that we understand the existence of such a world. A philosopher like Philo would have said it was through the

---

mind (*nous*) or *logos* (reason) that man knew of its existence. But our author, deeply influenced by the Christian understanding that all truth is a revelation of God, uses the term *faith*. Nevertheless, in so far as the author speculates about an invisible world he clearly reflects the concern of Hellenistic philosophy for a rationally acceptable interpretation of reality understood in terms of a transcendent order beyond this world of time and space.

But when our author calls the Old Testament roll of those who have been approved by God for their faith, he stresses another aspect of the meaning of faith: the more familiar Biblical concept of faith as that immediate, trusting response to the word of God and to the promises substantiated by that word. Abel, Enoch, Noah, Sarah, and especially Abraham are examples of this faith. Abraham responded obediently to God's call and journeyed into a strange country, trusting only in God's promise that he would lead him to a new land. The author comments that all these heroes were really seeking for something far more than the partial fulfillment of the promise, such as Abraham's arrival in Canaan. It was really the City of God toward which they journeyed, though they did not know the way. Here the author uses faith very nearly in the sense of hope, since in his mind the entrance into the city of God had to await the fulfillment of the promise in Christ.

In the last list of persons (11:23-38), faith has the meaning of patient endurance, a meaning that we have frequently met earlier in the epistle. In this list, which covers the period from Gideon to the Maccabeans, he recalls men and women who risked their lives, suffered, or died a martyr's death in obedient response to God's word. All these, though faithful, did not receive what was promised (11:39-40). This was because God intended for them the promise that was revealed and fulfilled only through Jesus Christ.

The author summons up this host of witnesses before his readers in order to encourage them (12:1). Having given them grounds for faith, he now gives them living examples of faith. And in the center once more he places Jesus Christ, the pioneer and perfecter of faith. Like the faithful in all ages, Jesus suffered; but by his suffering and elevation to the right hand of God he has revealed the true substance and meaning of faith.

Now the author calls his readers to recognize that, in view of the suffering of the faithful people of the old covenant and of Christ himself, they must expect to undergo the discipline of suffering in resisting sin and abuse (12:5-11). The Greek word for discipline literally means "education" (*paideia*). The author develops the thesis, found frequently in Jewish Wisdom Literature, that it is through the discipline of suffering that God educates his people in righteousness. The Stoics had also emphasized that a man must endure suffering as part of his education into true manhood. This was in contrast to the classical Greek concept of *paideia*, which was concerned more with the full-rounded education of the mind, body, and soul according to the ideal of the true, the good, and the beautiful. Quoting from Proverbs (3:11-12), the author says it is through endurance that Christians realize their sonship to God even as Christ did (5:8). If Christians endure present pain, they will share in God's holiness when they reach the heavenly city. So they must stand firm (12:12) under affliction lest they fall into sin, for which there is no more repentance (12:17). For they do not have to do with the Covenant of Moses delivered on Sinai (12:18-21), awesome as that event was; they have to do with the covenant mediated by Jesus Christ (12:22-24), and with those of all ages who have been faithful to the promises, and with God who is the judge of all men. If those did not escape who failed to obey Moses, who was merely a man, what chance of escape do they have who reject God, who speaks from heaven through his own Son, Jesus Christ (12:25-29)? For what they confront is not the lightning and thunder on Mt. Sinai, but rather the shaking of the foundations of the heavens and the earth in judgment; in this finale only those who have received God's unshakable kingdom will not be consumed. In thankfulness for such a kingdom, Christians are to offer acceptable worship to God with awe and reverence (12:28-29). The author refers not only to worship in the formal sense, but to worship of God through good deeds (13:15).

In this last exhortation and warning, the author reveals his own belief in a final apocalyptic cataclysm and a judgment on mankind. In this he retains the two-age view of the primitive Christian community, a view that stands in strange juxtaposition with the Hellenistic dualism that we have found in the writing. But it reveals his Christian understanding that the divine world and the human world (history) are not ultimately two separate realms. The one God who has created all things has revealed himself in history through Jesus Christ. He is not only the One through whom all things had their beginning, but through whom all things have their end. The whole created world moves to a single appointed end, which Jesus Christ has already inaugurated in bringing in the New Age.

The author concludes his writing with a series of specific admonitions on the treatment of fellow Christians, and on marriage, money, and respect for leaders, together with statements of doctrine (13:1-17). If this chapter was actually a part of the original writing, he undoubtedly was directing his remarks to specific problems confronting the church to which he wrote. And they were problems that were being faced by all the churches in the first century. The book ends with one of the most beautiful of New Testament benedictions (13:20-21), in which he reminds his oppressed readers that they are in the care of "our Lord Jesus," the great "shepherd of the sheep" who will provide them with the strength to do what is pleasing in his sight.

We can imagine how encouraging this message must have been to its first afflicted readers. And its message, in a time of social confusion, must have brought hope to Christians in other communities as well. But it would have had a particular appeal for the Hellenistic world, for men were wandering in a strange land (the world) of sin and imperfection, and were looking for a savior who could lead them to a heavenly home (see Chapter 1). The forgiveness of sins, the universality of Christ's salvation, the familiar dualistic teaching, even the persuasive style of the author's argument, would have made a strong appeal. In an age when men sought desperately for a sense of community, our author's presentation of a great company of people gathered together in a fellowship of suffering, journeying toward the heavenly city, must have been peculiarly stirring. And the portrayal of the great pioneer and perfecter of faith as an historical person, not a mythological figure, provided a clearer image of the God whom they had worshiped from afar.

THE REVELATION OF THE NEW JERUSALEM

There was one circle in which were seen clearly the implications of the growing struggle between the City of Earth (Rome) and the coming City of God. This was the Christian group in Asia Minor that produced the prophet, John, the author of the Book of Revelation. Tradition has identified this prophet with John the Apostle, and has ascribed to him the authorship of the Gospel of John, the Letters of John, and the Book of Revelation. If this tradition were reliable, it would mean that we have an extended body of literature that comes to us from the hand of one of Jesus' most intimate followers and that might be presumed therefore to represent a point of view very close to Jesus' own.

In fact, however, there are serious difficulties connected with the theory that John the Apostle wrote the books with which he has been credited. Since he was a Galilean fisherman, uneducated and perhaps even illiterate (Acts 4:13), it is most unlikely that he could have written—in Greek—a work of the theological subtlety of the Gospel of John. Efforts to demonstrate that the Gospel of John was originally written in Aramaic have not been particularly convincing to most scholars. The skill of the apologetic that the Gospel of John contains suggests that it was written by a man who had had protracted contact with and intimate knowledge of the Greek world. It has been argued that the Gospel and the Letters of John, which both language and theological content show came from the same circles, were written by John when he was very old and had had a lifetime in which to theologize. Even if this proposal were to be considered plausible, there is some evidence in the New Testament that the disciple John was martyred at the same time as his brother James—i.e., A.D. 44. If this evidence is valid, then none of the books bearing the name of John could have been written by John, the son of Zebedee, the disciple of Jesus. It would have been a simple matter for the early traditions of the Church to confuse a notable leader named John from the church in Ephesus, or from some other city of Asia Minor, with the disciple of the same name.

The Book of Revelation, which is the only book in the New Testament that claims to have been written by John, differs radically in style and perspective from the Gospel and Letters of John. In the gospel, the emphasis falls on the spiritual life of the Church as an ongoing fact, free from time-bound considera-

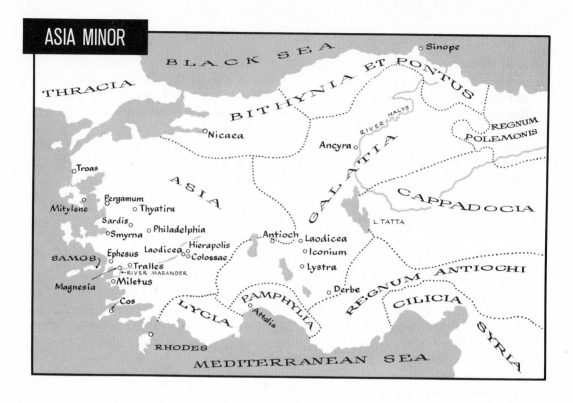

tions. In Revelation, the author is gravely concerned to stress the crisis that is now impending. For him there is no indefinite or unlimited period of time stretching out into the future, but rather a conviction that very soon the conflict of the powers of evil against God and his people will reach its climax. We might conclude from this that Revelation was written by a disciple, since this understanding of God's purpose would be likely to exist among the followers of Jesus. But John the Prophet also looks backward with veneration to the times of "the twelve apostles of the Lamb" (Rev. 21:14)—a phrase more appropriate to one who, with awe and reverence, has heard about the apostolic leaders than to one who was himself a member of the Twelve.

Purpose of the Book of Revelation

The book was written at a time when efforts were being made to cripple the Church. The community was ill prepared to meet the crisis precipitated by the Christians' refusal to participate in emperor worship, for it had become half-hearted in matters of Christian faith and life. "Because you are lukewarm, and neither cold nor hot, I will spew you out of my mouth," John reports Christ as saying to one of the Asian churches (Rev. 3:16). The genius of John the Prophet, as the author of Revelation may fittingly be called, was not primarily foresight, but insight into the real nature of the problems confronting the Christian community. He saw with clarity the issues on which the Christians must make decisions, and the far-reaching consequences of those issues. John's ultimate concern, therefore, was not for a solution to the immediate problem of the empire's demand that Christians worship the emperor. Rather, he viewed the immediate crisis as a crucial stage in the final conflict between God and the evil powers. Steadfastness in this crisis would lead the community on to complete victory, in which God's purpose for his creation would be achieved. We must examine the Book of Revelation again, therefore, not from the viewpoint of the community in conflict, as in Chapter 11, but with the aim of understanding how through this conflict the community saw the fulfillment of its hope.

Promises and Predictions

After a brief but impressive introduction (Rev. 1:1-8), John addresses in turn seven of the churches of Asia Minor, pointing up in each case each church's weaknesses, strengths, and prospects. Some had been lulled to sleep and needed to be aroused; some had flirted with paganism and needed to be warned in the strongest terms of the consequences of such behavior. John himself had been exiled to the tiny, barren isle of Patmos as a result of his courageous testimony to the faith, and the faithful Christians in the churches addressed could expect the same fate or worse.

THE LETTERS TO THE CHURCHES.   The words addressed to the individual churches are not merely general comments; in each case, the remarks are peculiarly appropriate. For example, Pergamum is warned about Satan's throne,

THE GREAT ALTAR OF ZEUS *at Pergamum: a reconstruction. With its grand proportions and its magnificent sculpture, this was one of the wonders of the ancient world. The allusion to Satan's throne in the letter to the church at Pergamum (Rev. 2:13) may have been a reference to this colossal structure of early architectural artistry.*

an apparent reference to the fact that the emperor was worshiped as divine in Pergamum long before the emperor cult was begun in Rome. Pergamum had been from the beginning the setting for "Satan's throne"—i.e., the seat of imperial worship in the East. To Sardis, John wrote a warning of the coming of the Lord "like a thief," an unmistakable reference to a famous incident in which the seemingly impregnable city of Sardis had been captured by the Persians, who entered the acropolis through a tiny crevice while the fabulous King Croesus sat in complete confidence in his splendid palace. The spiritual blindness of Laodicea is stressed because, ironically, it took pride in its great hospital dedicated to Aesclepius, the god of healing, and in its famed eye salve, which was supposed to cure blindness. It is fitting for John to heap scorn on this city for its pride of riches, since at a time of earthquake when other cities had had to ask for financial assistance from the empire, Laodicea had, in proud self-sufficiency, announced that she had ample resources to meet the emergency.[13] In spite of these words of warning to the churches of Asia Minor, and in spite of the troubles that were soon to fall upon these churches, the Christians were to remain confident in God's love for them, and in the fulfillment of his purpose through these difficulties. The New Age could not come without these birthpangs, and the people of God must meet them informed and confident.

THE VISIONS.   The ingenuity of the writer is nowhere more apparent than in the series of apocalyptic visions that occupy the rest of the book (Rev. 4:1-22:19). The recurrence of the number seven is one of the most striking features of this section: there are seven seals (6:1-8:1), seven trumpets (8:2-11:15), seven visions of the kingdom of the dragon (11:16-13:18), seven visions of the coming of the Son of Man (14:1-20), seven bowls (15:1-16:21), seven visions of the fall of Babylon (17:1-19:10), and seven visions of the End (19:11-21:4).[14] Perhaps the greatest difficulty in interpreting this book has resulted from the effort to discover a chronological sequence in this series of visions. This method of interpretation has appeared in two forms: the futuristic, which sees in these visions pictures of the successive situations that will arise in the last days; and the historical, which relates the visions to the ongoing history of the Church, and identifies the symbolic figures of the book with historical personages. The futuristic method ignores the clear historical allusions of the writing. And the historical method must constantly be revised with the passage of time, since as historical crises pass it becomes clear that there was no basis for seeing in them the fulfillment of John's prophecies. There is scarcely a demagogue of international fame who has not been identified by interpreters

---

[13] Tacitus, *Annals*, 14:27.
[14] Based on Ernst Lohmeyer's outline.

of prophecy as the beast of Rev. 13. Napoleon and Hitler were awarded this label, to name only two. In the 1930's Biblical literalists opposed to President Roosevelt's New Deal even claimed that the Blue Eagle which all merchants were required under the terms of the National Recovery Act to display was "the mark of the beast" (Rev. 13:17)!

The most plausible approach to the apocalyptic section, and hence to the entire book, requires (1) an awareness of the historical crisis—actual or impending—that was the immediate provocation for the book, and (2) a recognition of the cyclical structure of the writing. The historical situation that gave rise to the book was the empire's opposition to Christianity. The Christians of Asia Minor had come under suspicion of subversion because of their refusal to join in the worship of the emperor. On the eastern edge of Asia Minor were located the Parthians, a warlike people who remained a constant threat to the peace of Rome, and whose border was the one perennially unsettled boundary of the entire empire. There can be no doubt that any show of disloyalty to the emperor in the region of Asia Minor would be viewed with special suspicion, since it might indicate collusion with those perennial trouble-makers, the Parthians. The involved and highly figurative language of a book like Revelation would serve to communicate a message of resistance to those who understood the imagery, but would at the same time conceal the message from eyes for which it was not intended. Since this kind of writing had become common in late Judaism, neither the form nor even some of the specific images had to be invented. The author simply had to rework these well-known materials in terms of the new crisis of faith that he saw looming on the horizon.

It is misleading to suppose that the series of visions of the end is intended to describe a sequence of events in strict chronological fashion. Rather, the images and prophecies are presented in cyclical form in order to bring out the full implications of the end in a manner in which a single set of visions could not. It is as though the author were saying to the reader: "I have described the end under the figure of the trumpets; now, lest you have missed something of the fullness of meaning, I shall go back over the same territory, but this time I shall use the figure of the kingdom of the dragon."

The apocalyptic section begins with a magnificent vision of the throne of God (Rev. 4). With typical Jewish reluctance to picture God, only the throne and its surroundings are described (4:2). But this description conveys a sense of the awesome majesty of God, surrounded by the symbols of his universal authority. Clearly, however, God's authority is not limited to heaven, since John outlines the things which, it has been revealed to him, "must take place after this" (4:1). There can be no mistaking that the author shares the apocalyptic viewpoint which is characteristically deterministic: these things *must* take place. But the author is not a fatalist. He regards the history of the world as moving by divine will and in fulfillment of a wise and gracious purpose, and not as proceeding by chance. The ultimate outcome of this determined course of history will be the achievement of God's program of redemption for his Creation. Unlike Paul, however, John does not expect the redemption of all things; he looks forward to the unending punishment of the wicked spirits and of the dragon, their leader.

For his imagery in the description of the divine throne, John draws heavily on Old Testament resources. The living creatures resemble the cherubim, which are designated as the guardians of God's throne both in the historical shrines of ancient Israel (Ex. 25:18 ff.; I Kings 6:23) and in the prophetic visions (Ezek. 1:5 ff.). The 24 elders seem to represent the People of God of every generation, who fall in adoration before him. The prose descriptions break over periodically into poetry, as in the ascription of praise with which Revelation 4 closes:

> Worthy art thou, our Lord and God,
> To receive glory and honor and power,
>> for thou didst create all things,
>> and by thy will they existed and were created.

THE VICTOR. At the opening of Rev. 5 there appears a figure, both majestic and humble, both conquering and submissive, who dominates the Apocalypse, and, according to John's conviction, dominates the unfolding of God's purpose. Although this figure is not named, the opening words of the book make it clear that it is Jesus Christ, who is both Lion (5:5) and Lamb (5:6). He comes in humility, yet he is the one through whom victory over the powers opposed to God will be won. He is the only one worthy to unroll the seven-sealed scroll, which is a symbol for the unfolding purpose of God (5:2). What follows in the rest of the book is an elaboration through complicated symbolism of what will be achieved according to God's plan. Fearful conditions will arise on earth: war (6:2, the white horse), civil strife (6:3-4, the red horse), famine (6:5-6, the black horse), and plagues (6:8, the pale horse). There will be astronomical disturbances (6:12-17)—reminders that, as the New Testament writers understand it, the fate of the whole universe is involved in the fulfillment of man's destiny.

In the midst of this destruction and misery, however, God is at work bringing together his faithful witnesses. They look forward with eagerness to the final deliverance of the Creation from its subjection to the control of the evil powers (6:9-11), even though they know that their fidelity to God will bring about their martyrdom. The word "martyr" is simply a transliteration of a Greek word meaning "witness"; the implication is that the Christian who is faithful in his witness to what he believes to be the truth will meet a martyr's death. These witnesses are considered by John to be the special objects of God's loving care; they are granted the privilege of everlasting shelter in the presence of God. It is at moments like this that the prophet shifts over to poetry:

> Therefore are they before the throne of God,
> and serve him day and night within his temple;
> and he who sits upon the throne will shelter them with his
> presence.
> . . . The Lamb in the midst of the throne will be their shepherd,
> and he will guide them to springs of living water;
> and God will wipe away every tear from their eyes.
> —REVELATION 7:15, 17

Terrifying as some of John's visions are, there can be no doubt that the primary intent of his book was not to frighten but to comfort the Christians living under the shadow of persecution. No matter how oppressive the situation might become, they were to have confidence that beyond tribulation lay peace and God's victory.

THE VANQUISHED.   New pictures of the struggles with the evil powers are presented under the figure of the seven angels with the trumpets (Rev. 8:1-2). The angels announce the scourges that are to come upon the earth, and release fearful, fantastic creatures that spread death and destruction on the idolaters of the world. As numerous as locusts, and more horrible than dragons, these creatures torture with their scorpion-like stings, and kill with sulphurous fumes and fire (Rev. 8 and 9). Even though a third of mankind is slaughtered, the suffering is still not at an end (9:18). The Holy City itself is to be visited with judgment, and the prophets of God bring drought upon the surrounding land (Rev. 11). The wicked try in vain to destroy the witnesses, just as the dragon (Satan) tries to destroy the child who is destined to rule over the earth (Rev. 12). In cunning fashion, the dragon gives supernatural powers to "the beast" (Rev. 13), who is a symbol of the emperor, with his demands for divine honors. The special powers are designed to lure the unwary into worshiping him, on the supposition that he is divine.

The prophet reveals the beast's identity by a cryptic number, 666. This figure must have had meaning for John's original readers, but now we can only guess at what it meant. Probably the number was arrived at by adding the numerical values of the letters in the emperor's name. This would be an obvious kind of cryptogram, since in Greek and Hebrew the letters of the alphabet also served as numbers (alpha was 1; beta was 2; iota was 9; and so on). Since the number of combinations to give the sum of 666 is almost infinite, it is impossible to determine with certainty which emperor the author had in mind. One likely conjecture is Nero: the letters of Nero Caesar add up to 666, if spelled in Hebrew. The fact that Domitian was probably emperor at the time of John's writing raises no serious problem, since it was customary for apocalypticists to re-use materials from earlier times without recasting them and bringing them up to date. Although the identity of the figure hidden behind the number cannot be known, certainly the intent of the symbol is unmistakable: it

THE EMPEROR DOMITIAN *was the first of the Roman rulers to command that he be acclaimed as "Lord and God." It was probably during the lattter part of his reign (A.D. 81-96) that the Book of Revelation was written as an encouragement to Christians to defy his demand for divine honors.*

is a veiled allusion to an emperor claiming divine honors—in all probability, Domitian.

In contrast to all these demonic figures, John now turns to a sevenfold picture of Christ, through whom the promise of victory is fulfilled. He is portrayed as the Lamb in its purity (14:1-5), as the herald of the Gospel throughout the earth (14:6-7), as the herald of doom for the emperor-worshipers (14:8-11), as the Son of Man who both announces the judgment (14:14-16) and executes it. In vivid imagery based on Isa. 63, he is pictured as trampling out the grapes of God's wrath just as the ancients pressed out the wine from the grapes with their feet in the winepresses. His feet and garments are spattered with the blood of the fallen as a man in a winepress would be stained with the juice from the grapes (14:17-20; cf. Isa. 63; 3, 4).

Following a magnificent hymn of praise to God for his might and majesty ("Great and wonderful are thy deeds, O Lord God the Almighty!"—15:3), John introduces two new series of seven woes each: one series is to fall on all the earth, in a vain effort to bring it to repentance (Rev. 15-16); the other is to fall on Babylon—that is, Rome—the scourge of God's People in John's day as Babylon was in the days of the ancient prophets (Rev. 17). The proud splendor and moral corruption of Rome are described under the unforgettable figure of a harlot, gorgeously clad in scarlet, trying to entice all the world to engage in emperor worship. John, like the Hebrew prophets, looks upon idolatry as closely related to adultery. The harlot was seated on seven hills (Rev. 17:9), which are the seven hills of Rome.

The seven heads of the beasts are almost certainly seven emperors, but which seven are meant is difficult to determine. Since three emperors sat on the throne in a single year (Otho, Vitellius, and Galba, in 68-69), it is impossible to tell whether or not the writer included all three in his computation. Estimates are further affected by the weight we attach to the theory that the king who "was and is not" (17:11) is the same as the one who was earlier pictured as mortally wounded and healed (13:3). Perhaps both these references are allusions to the belief prevalent in the first century that Nero would come back from the

THE COLOSSEUM *from the air. Built by Vespasian and Titus as an arena for great public spectacles, it seated more than 50,000 people. In the later years of the empire, many Christians were slain here by Roman gladiators and wild animals.*

dead to lead Rome's traditional enemies on the eastern border, the Parthians, against Rome. Since Nero died under mysterious circumstances, reportedly by suicide, there was much speculation about his death. The rumor spread that perhaps he was not really dead, but would return. Finally, the theory arose and became widespread that he would be raised from the dead to lead the attack on Rome. If Nero is the man behind John's symbol here, we have additional evidence of the prophetic insight that saw in the purely local persecution of Christians under Nero the first rumblings of a tremendous conflict that was later to develop between the Church and the empire. The completeness of the destruction of the city of seven hills (Rev. 17:9) is celebrated in an awesome dirge (Rev. 18):

> Fallen, fallen is Babylon the great!
> It has become a dwelling place of demons,
>> a haunt of every foul spirit,
>> a haunt of every foul and hateful bird;
>> for all nations have drunk the wine of her impure passion. . . .
> Alas, alas, for the great city
>> that was clothed in fine linen, in purple and scarlet,
>> bedecked with gold, with jewels, and with pearls!
> In one hour all this wealth has been laid waste.
> —REVELATION 18:2, 3, 16, 17

THE FINAL VICTORY. The final chapters of the Revelation portray in majestic fashion the finale of the present Age and opening of the new. Conflict and judgment are at an end; the adversary and his demonic aides are banished and enchained forever; the hostile nations are destroyed in the great battle of Armageddon, after which the birds of prey swarm over the field of the fallen warriors to gorge themselves on their flesh (Rev. 19). Then begins the period of 1,000 years (Rev. 20), which is an initial stage of the reign of God over his Creation. But even under these ideal conditions, man continues to disobey God. The period ends in a final judgment of man, the destruction of death itself, and the renewal of the entire Creation (Rev. 21). The book closes with a description of the serenity and plenty that come upon God's Creation when, at last, it is subject to his will:

> Then I saw a new heaven and a new earth; for the
> first heaven and the first earth had passed away.
> . . . And I heard a great voice from the throne
> saying, "Behold, the dwelling of God is with men.
> He will dwell with them and they shall be his people."
>
> Then he showed me the river of the water of life,
> bright as crystal, flowing from the throne of God
> and of the Lamb . . . ; also, . . . the tree of life with

its twelve kinds of fruit, yielding its fruit each
month, and the leaves of the tree were for the healing
of the nations.

And night shall be no more; they need no light of
lamp or sun, for the Lord God will be their light, and
they shall reign for ever and ever.

—REVELATION 21:1, 3; 22:1, 2, 5

SUGGESTIONS

FOR

ADDITIONAL

READING

For a general survey of the history of critical study of the New Testament, and for discussions of the origins of the individual books of the New Testament, the best available is *An Introduction to the Study of the New Testament*, by A. H. McNeile, which was revised by C. S. C. Williams and published in a second edition in 1953 (London: Oxford University Press). Part III of M. S. Enslin's *Christian Beginnings* (New York: Harper & Row, 1938), written in Professor Enslin's own brand of colorful prose, includes concise statements on the date and authorship of the New Testament books. Perhaps the finest brief survey of the history of the first-century Church is *The Beginnings of the Christian Church*, by H. Lietzmann (London: Lutterworth, 1953). An excellent Roman Catholic study is Alfred Wikenhauser, *New Testament Introduction* (New York: Herder & Herder, 1963). An imaginative introduction which approaches the New Testament from the standpoint of worship is Charles F. D. Moule, *The Birth of the New Testament* (New York: Harper & Row, 1962). *The Interpreter's Dictionary of the Bible*, 4 vols. (New York: Abingdon, 1962) is the most complete modern dictionary in the English language. A good history of modern study of the New Testament is Stephen Neill, *The*

Interpretation of the New Testament, 1861-1961 (New York: Oxford University Press, 1964). Two books which discuss the central issues of debate over contemporary problems of New Testament study are Reginald H. Fuller, *The New Testament in Current Study* (New York: Scribner's, 1962) and Rudolf Schnackenburg, *New Testament Theology Today* (London: Geoffrey Chapman, 1963). An introduction particularly valuable for discussion of the rise of the New Testament Canon and the major problems of New Testament interpretation today is Robert M. Grant, *A Historical Introduction to the New Testament* (New York: Harper & Row, 1963). A learned, conservative, but somewhat eccentric "introduction" is: D. Guthrie, *New Testament Introduction, The Pauline Epistles* (Chicago: Intervarsity Press, 1961), and *New Testament Introduction, The General Epistles and Revelation* (Chicago: Intervarsity Press, 1962).

CHAPTER ONE

THE SEARCH FOR COMMUNITY IN THE GRAECO-ROMAN WORLD

For an introduction to Graeco-Roman background, see F. C. Grant, *Roman Hellenism and the New Testament* (New York: Scribner's, 1962), pp. 1-112. For selected texts from Graeco-Roman and Jewish sources, see C. K. Barrett, *The New Testament Background: Selected Documents* (New York: Macmillan, 1957). A detailed description of the religions of the Graeco-Roman world may be found in H. R. Willoughby, *Pagan Regeneration* (Chicago: University of Chicago Press, 1929). A very instructive presentation is found in A. N. Sherwin-White, *Roman Society and Roman Law in the New Testament* (Oxford: Oxford University Press, 1962). On Gnosticism, see R. M. Grant, *Gnosticism and Early Christianity* (New York: Columbia University Press, 1959), and Hans Jonas, *The Gnostic Religion* (Boston: Beacon Press, 1958).

CHAPTER TWO

THE SEARCH FOR COMMUNITY IN ISRAEL

A thorough study of the period may be found in Werner Foerster, *From the Exile to Christ: A Historical Introduction to Palestinian Judaism*, translated from the German by Gordon E. Harris (Philadelphia: Fortress Press, 1964). For a popular study of the intertestamental literature, see Lawrence E. Toombs, *The Threshold of Christianity* (Philadelphia: Westminster Press, 1960). For a comprehensive survey of the Dead Sea Scrolls and their significance, see F. M. Cross, *The Ancient Library of Qumran* (New York: Doubleday, 1961). A complete translation of the documents, with somewhat eccentric interpretation, in A. Dupont-Sommer, *The Essene Writings from Qumran* (New York and Cleveland: Meridian, 1961). For excellent material on the Qumran sect and documents, see Helmer Ringgren, *The Faith of Qumran* (Philadelphia: Fortress Press, 1961).

CHAPTER THREE

THE NEW COMMUNITY AND ITS CONVICTIONS

On the apostolic *kerygma*, see C. H. Dodd, *The Apostolic Preaching and its Developments* (New York: Harper & Row, 1951). For a view of the different forms of the *kerygma* in the rise of Christianity, see R. Bultmann, *Theology of the New Testament*, Vol. I (New York: Scribner's, 1951). For a study of the theme of humiliation/exaltation as providing the underlying unity of the New Testament message, see Eduard Schweizer, *Lordship and Discipleship* (Naperville, Ill.: Alec R. Allenson, Inc., 1960). On oral tradition, see listings under Chapter 4. For a brief introduction to problems concerning the text of the New Testament, see Vincent Taylor, *The Text of the New Testament* (New York: St. Martin's Press, 1961). On the canon of the New Testament, see the comprehensive article by F. W. Beare in *The Interpreter's Dictionary of the Bible* (New York: Abingdon, 1962). On the question of the gospels as historical records, see H. E W. Turner, *Historicity and the Gospels* (London: A. R. Mowbray & Co., 1963).

CHAPTER FOUR

JESUS IN THE GOSPELS

Two general introductions to the gospels are Vincent Taylor, *The Gospels: A Short Introduction*, 7th ed. (London: Epworth Press, 1952), and Frederick C. Grant, *The Gospels: Their Origin and Their Growth* (New York: Harper & Row, 1957). An excellent, brief, non-technical commentary on the synoptic gospels, employing methods from history and source criticism, is Francis W. Beare, *The Earliest Records of Jesus* (New York: Abingdon, 1962). Two classic studies of form criticism of the gospels are Rudolf Bultmann, *History of the Synoptic Tradition* (New York: Harper & Row, 1963) and Martin Dibelius, *From Tradition to Gospel* (New York: Scribner's, 1935). The best general introduction to form criticism is Vincent Taylor, *The Formation of the Gospel Tradition* (New York: St. Martin's Press, 1953). R. Bultmann and K. Kundsin: *Form-Criticism* (New York: Harper & Row, 1962) is a re-issue in paperback of classic essays on form-critical method.

CHAPTER FIVE

THE CLAIMS OF JESUS

A helpful, brief introduction to the life and ministry of Jesus may be found in "The Life and Ministry of Jesus," by Vincent Taylor, in *Interpreter's Bible*, VII, 114-144. The author has expanded this article into a book, *The Life and Ministry of Jesus* (New York: Abingdon, 1955). The introductory chapters of two other books set the ministry of Jesus in the context of the contemporary Jewish world: T. H. Manson, *The Servant-Messiah*, Chapters 1-4 (Cambridge: Cambridge University Press, 1953); Martin Dibelius, *Jesus*, tr. C. B. Hedrick and

F. C. Grant, Chapters 1-4 (Philadelphia: Westminster, 1949). Helpful studies of the miracles in the gospels are: Alan Richardson, *The Miracle-Stories of the Gospels* (London: SCM Press, 1941); Reginald H. Fuller, *Interpreting the Miracles* (Philadelphia; Westminster, 1963); and S. Vernon McCasland, *By the Finger of God* (New York: Macmillan, 1951). The latter, though concerned with demon possession and exorcism in the light of modern views of mental illness, also tries to see these phenomena in relation to Jesus' own mission and message. A classic discussion of the form and method of Jesus' teaching is that of M. Goguel, *The Life of Jesus*, tr. Olive Wyon (New York: Macmillan, 1944). A valuable little book on the same subject is E. C. Colwell, *An Approach to the Teaching of Jesus* (New York: Abingdon, 1947). Three articles in Volume VII of *Interpreter's Bible* are helpful introductions to Jesus' teaching: C. T. Craig, "The Proclamation of the Kingdom," pp. 145-154; A. Wilder, "The Sermon on the Mount," pp. 155-164; W. R. Bowie, "The Parables," pp. 165-175. An excellent extensive treatment of the Sermon on the Mount is H. Windisch, *The Meaning of the Sermon on the Mount*, tr. S. M. Gilmour (Philadelphia: Westminster, 1951). Joachim Jeremias, *The Sermon on the Mount*, Facet Books, Biblical Series No. 2 (Philadelphia: Fortress Press, 1963), is an excellent short pamphlet on the Sermon on the Mount. Also see Harvey K. McArthur, *Understanding the Sermon on the Mount* (New York: Harper & Row, 1960). Of the many excellent books on the parables, none is better than J. Jeremias, *The Parables of Jesus*, rev. ed., tr. S. H. Hooke (New York: Scribner's, 1963). An indispensable tool for the serious study of Jesus' teaching is T. W. Manson, *The Teaching of Jesus* (Cambridge: Cambridge University Press, 1948). Brief but lucid interpretations of Jesus' proclamation of the kingdom of God are found in A. Wilder, *New Testament Faith For Today*, Chapter 3, "The Proclamation of Jesus" (New York: Harper & Row, 1955); and M. Dibelius, *Jesus*, Chapter 5 (Philadelphia: Westminster, 1949). The most complete study of the interpretation of Jesus' proclamation of the kingdom, his ethical teaching, and his mission in relation to their eschatological context is A. Wilder, *Eschatology and Ethics in the Teaching of Jesus*, rev. ed. (New York: Harper & Row, 1950). For a more systematic treatment of the ethics of Jesus, see L. H. Marshall, *The Challenge of New Testament Ethics*, Chapters 1-6 (London: Macmillan, 1950).

CHAPTER SIX

THE CROSS OF JESUS

For a helpful interpretation of the problem of the "messianic consciousness" of Jesus, based on a study of his message, mission, and death, see Chapters 3-5 in T. W. Manson, *The Servant-Messiah* (Cambridge: Cambridge University Press, 1953). Three varying but suggestive interpretations of the meaning of Son of Man are found in R. Otto, *The Kingdom of God and the Son of Man*, rev. ed., tr. F. V. Filson and B. Lee-Woolf (London: Lutterworth, 1943); G. S. Duncan, *Jesus, Son of Man* (New York: Macmillan, 1949); and R. Fuller, *The Mission and Achievement of Jesus* (Naperville, Ill.: Alec R.

Allenson, Inc., 1954). There is brief, lucid interpretation of the meaning of Son of Man in M. Dibelius, *Jesus,* Chapter 7 (Philadelphia: Westminster, 1949). The same book (Chapter 9) provides a concise summary of the nature of the opposition leading to Jesus' death. A view which represents Jesus' death in relation to his total mission and message is found in W. Manson, *Jesus the Messiah,* Chapter 7, "The Passion and Death of the Messiah" (Philadelphia: Westminster, 1946). A detailed study of the trial of Jesus is given by Paul Winter, *On the Trial of Jesus* (Berlin: Walter deGruyter, 1961).

CHAPTERS SEVEN, EIGHT, NINE
[ON PAUL AND HIS MESSAGE]

For an excellent brief reconstruction of the life and thought of Paul, see *Paul,* by M. Dibelius and W. G. Kuemmel (Philadelphia: Westminster, 1953). A fuller statement of Paul's thought, based on his religious experience, is a reverent work by James S. Stewart, *A Man in Christ* (New York: Harper & Row, n.d.). A fresh and illuminating, though highly technical, analysis of Paul's thought is given in Volume I of Rudolf Bultmann's *Theology of the New Testament,* tr. Kendrick Grobel (New York: Scribner's, 1951), pp. 187-352. For a technical study of Paul's thought against the background of first-century rabbinic teaching, see *Paul and Rabbinic Judaism,* by W. D. Davies (London: S.P.C.K., 1948). A detailed reconstruction of the issues and developments in Paul's relationships with the Jerusalem Christians is given in *St. Paul and the Church of Jerusalem,* by W. L. Knox (Cambridge: Cambridge University Press, 1925). Paul's break with Jewish Christianity is the recurrent theme in *The Birth of Christianity,* by M. Goguel (New York: Macmillan, 1954), which also includes descriptions of the historical situations out of which the books of the New Testament emerged. On Paul's apostolic vocation, see W. A. Beardslee, *Human Achievement and Divine Vocation in the Message of Paul* (Naperville, Ill.: Alec R. Allenson, Inc., 1961). On demonology in Paul see G. B. Caird, *Principalities and Powers* (Oxford, England: Clarendon Press, 1956). C. K. Barrett, *From First Adam to Last* (New York: Scribner's, 1962), deals with Paul's Christology. See also C. K. Barrett, *The Epistle to the Romans* (New York: Harper & Row, 1957). In addition to the relevant sections of the commentaries on Acts, the reader will find more detailed analysis of life in the Gentile churches in such commentaries on the Corinthian Letters as *The First Epistle to the Corinthians,* by James Moffatt (New York: Harper & Row, 1938), and the exegesis of I and II Corinthians by C. T. Craig and F. V. Filson, respectively, in Volume X of *Interpreter's Bible* (New York: Abingdon, 1953).

CHAPTER TEN
THE DEATH OF PAUL AND THE END OF THE APOSTOLIC AGE

For a careful reconstruction of the fall of Jerusalem and the end of the apostolic age, see M. Goguel, *The Birth of Christianity* (New York: Macmillan, 1954), Part II, Chapters 2 and 3. Macgregor, in *Inter-*

preter's Bible, IX, 349-352, gives a concise statement of the various theories about the fate of Paul in Rome. The best commentary on the English text of James is by James Moffatt, in *The General Epistles* (New York: Harper & Row, n.d.). An excellent brief introduction to the book of James is given by Goguel in *The Birth of Christianity* (New York: Macmillan, 1954), Part IV, Chapter 6. See the discussion of Ephesians by F. W. Beare in *Interpreter's Bible*, Volume X (New York and Nashville: Abingdon, 1953). For a theological discussion of the unity of the Church, see E. Best, *One Body in Christ* (London: S.P.C.K., 1955).

CHAPTER ELEVEN
THE COMMUNITY CONFRONTS MAJOR CRISES [MARK]

For a popular introduction to Mark, see Curtis Beach, *The Gospel of Mark: Its Making and Meaning* (New York: Harper & Row, 1959). See also D. E. Nineham: *Saint Mark*, Pelican Gospel Commentaries (Baltimore: Pelican, 1963); and J. M. Robinson: *The Problem of History in Mark* (Naperville, Ill.: Alec R. Allenson, Inc., 1957).

CHAPTER TWELVE
THE NEW WAY OF RIGHTEOUSNESS [MATTHEW]

See Edward P. Blair, *Jesus in the Gospel of St. Matthew* (New York: Abingdon, 1960); G. Bornkamm, *et al.*, *Tradition and Interpretation in Matthew's Gospel* (Philadelphia: Westminster, 1963); and K. Stendahl, Exposition of Matthew in *Peake's Commentary on the Bible*, ed. M. Black and H. H. Rowley (London and New York: Nelson, 1962).

CHAPTER THIRTEEN
THE EPOCH OF THE CHURCH IN THE REDEMPTIVE PLAN OF GOD [LUKE–ACTS]

A perceptive work on the literary and historical background is H. J. Cadbury, *The Making of Luke-Acts* (London: S.P.C.K., 1961). More detailed essays along form-critical lines are found in M. Dibelius, *Studies in the Book of Acts* (Philadelphia: Westminster, 1956). An imaginative and suggestive theological study of Luke-Acts is H. Conzelmann's *Theology of St. Luke* (New York: Harper & Row, 1960). A brief survey of research on Luke-Acts appears in C. K. Barrett, *Luke the Historian in Recent Study* (London: Epworth, 1961).

CHAPTER FOURTEEN
THE COMMUNITY OF THE SPIRIT [JOHN]

For a concise discussion of the problems confronting the interpreter of the Gospel of John, see the article by W. F. Howard, "The Gospel According to St. John," in *Interpreter's Bible*, VIII (New York: Abingdon, 1952), 437-462. Two short books dealing topically with the Gospel of John are E. C. Colwell and E. L. Titus, *The Gospel of the*

Spirit (New York: Harper & Row, 1953), and W. F. Howard, *Christianity According to St. John* (Philadelphia: Westminster, 1946). Among the many excellent longer commentaries in English on John, none is more important than E. C. Hoskyns, *The Fourth Gospel*, ed. F. N. Davey (London: Faber & Faber, 1947). Important for a study of sources is C. H. Dodd, *Historical Tradition and the Fourth Gospel* (Cambridge: Cambridge University Press, 1963). For a popular introduction and interpretation, see Alan Richardson, *The Gospel According to Saint John* (New York: Collier Books, 1962). An excellent nontechnical commentary is R. H. Lightfoot, *St. John's Gospel* (New York: Oxford, 1960). One of the most successful efforts to provide guidance on the theological perspective and literary method of the author of John is found in A. Wilder, *New Testament Faith For Today* (New York: Harper & Row, 1955), pp. 142-164.

CHAPTER FIFTEEN

ETHICS FOR EXILES [I PETER AND JAMES]

For a discussion of the historical problems connected with I Peter, see F. W. Beare, *The First Epistle of Peter* (Oxford: Blackwell, 1947), pp. 1-41. An important article dealing with the ethical teaching of I Peter is W. C. van Unnik, "The Teaching of Good Works in I Peter," *New Testament Studies*, I, No. 2 (Nov., 1954), 92-110. For a theological interpretation of the development of ethical teaching, see R. Bultmann, *Theology of the New Testament*, II, tr. K. Grobel (London: SCM Press, 1955), 203-231, and W. Beach and H. R. Niebuhr, *Christian Ethics* (New York: Ronald, 1955), pp. 46-57. The best popular commentary is Bo Reicke, *The Epistles of James, Peter and Jude*, The Anchor Bible, Vol. XXXVII (Garden City, New York: Doubleday, 1964). On baptism, see G. R. Beasley-Murray, *Baptism in the New Testament* (New York: St. Martin's Press, 1962).

CHAPTER SIXTEEN

FAITH AND ORDER IN THE COMMUNITY [LATER EPISTLES]

A good popular introduction to the Epistles is J. C. Beker, *The Church Faces the World: Late New Testament Writings* (Philadelphia: Westminster, 1960). On the development in theology and Church organization see Maurice Goguel, *The Primitive Church* (New York: Macmillan, 1964). Two excellent commentaries on the Pastoral Epistles in English are C. K. Barrett, *The Pastoral Epistles in the New English Bible* (Oxford: Clarendon Press, 1963, and J. N. D. Kelly, *The Pastoral Epistles* (New York: Harper & Row, 1963). On worship, see C. F. D. Moule, *Worship in the New Testament* (Richmond: John Knox Press, 1961). An interesting discussion of the "false teaching" confronting the early Church may be found in M. Goguel, *The Birth of Christianity*, tr. H. C. Snape (New York: Macmillan, 1954), pp. 393-435. A discussion of false teaching, especially as it relates to the Pastoral Epistles, appears in the introduction to the commentary on I and II Timothy and Titus by F. D. Gealy, *Interpreter's Bible*, II (New York: Abingdon, 1955), 350-360. An illuminating book on the development of organization in the early Church is J. Knox, *The Early Church and the Coming Great Church* (New York: Abingdon, 1955). An older important work on the origins of the Christian ministry is B. H. Streeter, *The Primitive Church* (New York: Macmillan, 1929). A balanced nontechnical chapter dealing with worship in the New Testament may be found in D. H. Hislop, *Our Heritage in Public Worship* (Edinburgh: Clark, 1935), pp. 59-92. An important work on the subject of the Eucharist is A. J. B. Higgins, *The Lord's Supper in the New Testament* (Studies in Biblical Theology, No. 6) (Naperville, Ill.: Alec R. Allenson, Inc., 1952). For a general survey of the historical development of the New Testament Church, see H. Lietzmann, *The Beginnings of the Christian Church*, tr. B. L. Woolf (New York: Scribner's, 1952), especially pp. 191-221; 236-248. The most thorough study of the development of the Church in relation to its environment is A. Harnack, *The Mission and Expansion of Christianity in the First Three Centuries*, tr. J. Moffatt (New York: Harper & Row, 1961). For a theological interpretation of the development of organization, see R. Bultmann, *Theology of the New Testament*, tr. K. Grobel (New York: Scribner's, 1955), I, 133-152; II, 95-126; 231-236.

CHAPTER SEVENTEEN

THE COMMUNITY AND THE CITY OF GOD [HEBREWS AND REVELATION]

A concise discussion of the historical, literary, and theological problems posed by Hebrews is the introduction to Hebrews by A. C. Purdy, *Interpreter's Bible*, II (New York: Abingdon, 1955), pp. 577-594. In a recent study of Hebrews, *The Epistle to the Hebrews* (London: Hodder & Stoughton, 1951), W. Manson propounds some unusual theories about the purpose of the book. A short nontechnical commentary influenced by Manson's book is W. Neil, *The Epistle to the Hebrews* (London: SCM Press, 1955). The most complete survey of the historical setting of the Book of Revelation is that of W. Ramsay, in *The Letters to the Seven Churches* (New York: Armstrong, 1905). An excellent commentary on Revelation is *The Revelation of St. John*, by M. Kiddle (New York: Harper & Row, 1940). The fullest technical analysis of Revelation is *The Revelation of St. John*, by R. H. Charles (New York: Scribner's, 1920). For an illuminating survey of the changing interpretations of New Testament eschatology in the present century, see Chapters 1-3 of A. N. Wilder, *Eschatology and Ethics in the Teaching of Jesus*, rev. ed. (New York: Harper & Row, 1950). Three popular interpretations of Revelation are John W. Bowman, *The Drama of the Book of Revelation* (Philadelphia: Westminster, 1955); Hans Lilje, *The Last Book of the Bible* (Philadelphia; Muhlenberg Press, 1957); and Thomas Kepler, *The Book of Revelation* (New York: Oxford University Press, 1957). An excellent treatment of the relation of the Church and the Roman government is O. Cullmann, *The State in the New Testament* (New York: Scribner's, 1956). A similar study, though dealing more extensively with non-Christian sources and covering a period up to the beginning of the fourth century, is R. Grant, *The Sword and the Cross* (New York: Macmillan, 1955). A series of historical essays dealing largely with various Roman emperors up to the fourth century is Ethelbert Stauffer, *Christ and the Caesars*, tr. K. and R. Smith (Philadelphia: Westminster, 1955). For a brief analysis of the development of eschatology in the New Testament, see H. A. Guy, *The New Testament Doctrine of the Last Things* (London and New York: Oxford University Press, 1948). An existentialist interpretation of eschatology is offered by R. Bultmann, in *The Presence of Eternity* (New York: Harper & Row, 1957).

APPENDIXES

I. ABBREVIATIONS

The following abbreviations are widely used to identify books of the Bible. In this book, these abbreviations are used only when followed by a chapter (or chapter-and-verse) number; where no chapter or verse is cited, and with extracted material, the names of the books are spelled out.

OLD TESTAMENT ABBREVIATIONS

Gen.	Genesis	I Kings	I Kings	Eccles.	Ecclesiastes
Ex.	Exodus	II Kings	II Kings	Song	Song of Solomon
Lev.	Leviticus	I Chron.	I Chronicles	Is.	Isaiah
Num.	Numbers	II Chron.	II Chronicles	Jer.	Jeremiah
Deut.	Deuteronomy	Ezra	Ezra	Lam.	Lamentations
Josh.	Joshua	Neh.	Nehemiah	Ezek.	Ezekiel
Judg.	Judges	Esther	Esther	Dan.	Daniel
Ruth	Ruth	Job	Job	Hos.	Hosea
I Sam.	I Samuel	Ps.	Psalms	Joel	Joel
II Sam.	II Samuel	Prov.	Proverbs	Amos	Amos

Abbreviations (cont'd)

Obad.	Obadiah	Nahum	Nahum	Hag.	Haggai
Jon.	Jonah	Hab.	Habakkuk	Zech.	Zechariah
Mic.	Micah	Zeph.	Zephaniah	Mal.	Malachi

NEW TESTAMENT ABBREVIATIONS

Mt.	Matthew	Eph.	Ephesians	Heb.	Hebrews
Mk.	Mark	Phil.	Philippians	Jas.	James
Lk.	Luke	Col.	Colossians	I Pet.	I Peter
Jn.	John	I Thess.	I Thessalonians	II Pet.	II Peter
Acts	Acts	II Thess.	II Thessalonians	I Jn.	I John
Rom.	Romans	I Tim.	I Timothy	II Jn.	II John
I Cor.	I Corinthians	II Tim.	II Timothy	III Jn.	III John
II Cor.	II Corinthians	Tit.	Titus	Jude	Jude
Gal.	Galatians	Phm.	Philemon	Rev.	Revelation

II. A RECONSTRUCTION OF Q

The following reconstruction of the hypothetical Q document was prepared by Frederick C. Grant for *Harper's Annotated Bible* (New York: Harper & Row, 1955), and is used by permission. Scarcely two scholars agree in every detail on what to include as Q material, but here one may see the major themes of Q and gain an impression as to how extensively Matthew and Luke have relied on this source.

The Contents of Q

The ministry and message of John the Baptizer
    Luke 3: [2b], 3a, 7b-9 John's preaching of repentance (cf. Mt. 3:1-10)
    3:16, 17 John's prediction of the coming Judge (cf. Mt. 3:11, 12)
The ordeal of the Messiah
    4:1b-12 The Temptation (cf. Mt. 4:1-11)
Jesus' public teaching
    6:20-49 The Sermon on the Plain (or Mountain; cf. Mt. 5:3-12, 39-48; 7:12, 1-5, 16-27; 10:24, 25; 12:33-35; 15:14)
The response to Jesus' preaching
    7:2, 6b-10 The centurion's faith (cf. Mt. 8:5-13)
    7:18b, 19, 22-28, 31-35 John's emissaries; Jesus' words about John (cf. Mt. 11:2-6, 7-19)
    9:57b-60, 61, 62 Various followers (cf. Mt. 8:19-22)
The mission of the Twelve
    10:2-16 The mission of the disciples (cf. Mt. 9:37, 38; 10:7-16, 40; 11:21-23)
    [10:17b-20 The return of the Twelve]
    10:21b-24 The rejoicing of Jesus (cf. Mt. 11:25-27; 13:16, 17)

Jesus' teaching about prayer
    11:2-4 The Lord's Prayer (cf. Mt. 6:9-13)
    [11:5-8 The parable of the friend at midnight]
    11:9-13 Constancy in prayer (cf. Mt. 7:7-11)
The controversy with the scribes and Pharisees
    11:14-22 The charge of collusion with Beelzebul (cf. Mt. 12:22-30)
    11:23-26 The story of the unclean spirit (cf. Mt. 12:43-45)
    11:29b-32 The warning contained in the "sign of Jonah" (cf. Mt. 12:38-42)
    11:33-36 Jesus' sayings about light (cf. Mt. 5:15; 6:22, 23)
    11:39b, 42, 43, 46-52 The controversy with the scribes and Pharisees (cf. Mt. 23:4-36)
Jesus' teaching about discipleship: the duties of disciples when persecuted
    12:2-12 The testimony of disciples amid adversaries (cf. Mt. 10:26-33; 12:32; 10:19, 20)
    12:22-31 On freedom from care (cf. Mt. 6:25-33)
    12:33b-34 On treasure (cf. Mt. 6:19-21)
    12:39, 40, 42-46 Three parables on watchfulness (cf. Mt. 24:43-51a)
    12:49-53 Messianic divisions (cf. Mt. 10:34-36)
    [12:54-56 Signs of the times (cf. Mt. 16:2, 3)]
    12:57-59 The duty of speedy reconciliation (cf. Mt. 5:25, 26)
    13:18-21 The parables of the mustard seed and the leaven: the steady growth of the kingdom despite opposition (cf. Mt. 13:31-33)
    13:24-29 The narrow way (cf. Mt. 7:13, 14; 7:22, 23; 8:11, 12)
    13:34, 35 The fate of Jerusalem (cf. Mt. 23:37-39)
    14:11=18:14 On self-exaltation (cf. Mt. 18:4; 23:12)
    14:16-23 The parable of the great supper (cf. Mt. 22:1-10)
    14:26, 27 On hating one's next of kin, and on bearing the cross (cf. Mt. 10:37, 38)
    14:34, 35 The saying on salt (cf. Mt. 5:13)
    [15:4-7 The parable of the lost sheep (cf. Mt. 18:12-14)]
    16:13 On serving two masters (cf. Mt. 6:24)
Sayings about the Law
    16:16-18 The Law and the Prophets until John; on divorce (cf. Mt. 11:12, 13; 5:18, 32)
    17:1, 2 On offenses (cf. Mt. 18:6, 7)
    17:3, 4 On forgiveness (cf. Mt. 18:15, 21, 22)
    17:6 On faith (cf. Mt. 17:20b)
The coming *parousia*
    17:23, 24, 26, 27, 34, 35, 37b The *parousia* (cf. Mt. 24:26-28, 37-39; 10:39; 24:40, 28)
    19:12, 13, 15b-26 The parable of the entrusted talents (cf. Mt. 25:14-30)
    [22:28-30 The apostles' thrones (cf. Mt. 19:28)]

III. PASSAGES OF MATTHEW ASSIGNED TO M AND OF LUKE ASSIGNED TO L

The following lists of passages assigned to M and L were prepared by C. S. C. Williams for the Revised Edition of *Peake's Commentary on the Bible*, eds. Matthew Black and H. H. Rowley (New York and Edinburgh: Nelson, 1962), and are used by permission. As in the case of Q, scholars are not agreed as to what should be included, but here we have a representative listing of the passages drawn from the written—or, in the case of M, possibly oral—sources from which Matthew and Luke drew respectively.

Passages Assigned to M

1:1-2:23	Infancy stories
3:14f.	Reason for the Baptism
4:13-6	Fulfillment of Isa. 9:1f.
5:1, 5, 7-10, 14, 16f., 19-24, 27f., 31, 33-7, 38-9a, 41, 43 6:1-4, 5-8 10b, 13b, 16-18, 34 7:6, 12b, 15, 19f., 22	Passages in Mt.'s Sermon on the Mount, some of it editorial but much of it from reliable sources, if not from Q from which Lk. has omitted it
8:17	Fulfillment of Isa. 53:4
9:13a	Fulfillment of Hos. 6:6
9:27-31	The healing of two blind men (cf. Mt. 10:46ff.)
9:32-6	The healing of the dumb demoniac, and preface to the Mission of the Twelve
10:5b	Command to go to the House of Israel
10:8b, 16b, 23, 25, 36, 41	Sayings chiefly of a missionary character
11:1	? editorial
11:14f.	(cf. Mk. 9:13)
11:20	? editorial
11:28-30	The invitation to the heavy-laden (cf. Sir. 51:23-7)
12:5-7	Probably three sayings of Jesus spoken at different times, here expanding the story of the plucking of corn
12:17-21	Fulfillment of Isa. 42:1-4
12:36f.	Judgment on idle words
12:40	(cf. Lk. 11:30)
13:24ff., 44, 45f., 47ff., 51f.	Parables of the tares, hidden treasure, pearl of great price, draw-net, with an ending (to a parabolic source?)
14:28-31	Peter on the water
14:33	(cf. Mk. 6:51b)
15:12-14a	The Pharisees and the blind
15:23f.	Pro-Jewish-Christian expansion of the story of the Syro-Phoenician woman
16:12	Explanatory note about the "leaven"
16:17-19	Probably three separate sayings attributed to Jesus, bearing on Peter and inserted here to expand the commission to him (cf. on 12:5-7)
17:6f.	Expansion of Mk.'s story of the Transfiguration
17:13	Explanatory note about "Elijah"
17:24-7, 18:4	The coin in the fish's mouth, which reads like Jewish-Christian Midrash (but cf. Lk. 14:11, 18:14)

18:10	Introduction to the story of the lost sheep (cf. 18:14, a conclusion to it)
18:16-20	Expansion of the duties to fellow-Christians
18:23-35	Parable of the unforgiving servant, no doubt authentic
20:1-16	Parable of the laborers in the vineyard, also authentic
21:10bf.	Introduction to the story of Christ in the Temple
21:14-16	Healings in the Temple and the fulfillment of Ps. 8:3
21:28-32	Parable of the two sons, no doubt authentic
21:43	Explanatory note
22:6f.	A late addition to the parable of the wedding-feast, and 22:11-14, the parable of the wedding-garment, probably a different parable, the beginning of which is lost, that Mt. has conflated awkwardly

23:2f., 5
23:7b-10
23:15-22 } An expansion of the woes against scribes and Pharisees
23:27b-28
23:32f. } (but for 33 cf. Lk. 3:7)

24:10-12	Three sayings, probably originally separate, serving here to expand the beginnings of the messianic woes
24:14b	A conclusion to a section or lection
24:20b	'Flight . . . on the sabbath,' a Jewish-Christian addition
24:30a	An expansion based on Dan. 7:13
25:1-13	Parable of the ten virgins, probably authentic
25:31-46	The picture of the last assize, no doubt authentic also
26:1	Introductory to the Passion narrative
26:25	A secondary addition to show that Jesus knew the betrayer (cf. Lk. 22:23, which seems more primitive)
26:50	(cf. Lk. 22:48)
26:52b-54	(cf. Rev. 13:10
27:3-10	Death of Judas and fulfillment of Zech. 11:12 (cf. Ac. 1:15ff.)

27:19, 24f., 62-6 and } A cycle of Christian Midrashic stories about Pilate, much of which
28:11-15 } may be secondary

27:43	A fulfillment of Ps. 22:9
27:51b-53	Portents at Jesus' death, also Midrashic in character
28:2-4	The earthquake and the angel at the tomb, possibly three originally separate phrases, the second of which may have at one time referred to Christ, brought together here by Mt. to expand the story of the Resurrection (cf. on 12:5-7, 16:17-19 above)
28:11-15	The bribing of the soldiers, which may be secondary material
28:16-20	The command to baptize

Passages Assigned to L

1:5-2:52	Infancy narratives
3:10-14	Teaching of John the Baptist
3:23-38	The genealogy of Christ
4:16-30	Christ's rejection at Nazareth
5:1-11	Draught of fishes and Simon's call
5:39	Old and new wine (but cf. the variant reading of Mk. 2:22)
7:11-17	Raising of the widow's son at Nain

7:36-50	The woman who was a sinner
8:1-3	The ministering women
9:51-6	Rejection in the Samarian villages
10:1	Mission of the seventy(-two)
10:17-20	Their return
10:25-8	The lawyer's question (but cf. Mk. 12:28-31)
10:29-37	The good Samaritan
10:38-42	Martha and Mary
11:1-8	Teaching on prayer (but cf. Mt. 6:9-13)
11:27f.	Blessedness of the Mother of Christ
11:37-41, 53-4, 12:1	Inward as against outward purity
12:13-21	Parable of the rich fool
12:35-8	On watchfulness (but cf. Mt. 25:1ff.)
13:1-9	Call to repentance
13:10-17	The woman with a spirit of infirmity healed
13:31-3	Departure from Herod and Galilee
14:1-6	The man with dropsy healed
14:7-14	Teaching on humility
14:28-33	On counting the cost
15:1-32	Parables of the lost sheep, the lost coin and the lost (prodigal) son
16:1-13	The shrewd steward
16:14f., 19-31	Misuse of wealth and Dives and Lazarus
17:7-10	The servant's wages
17:11-19	Healing of ten lepers
17:20f.	Kingdom of God (but cf. Mk. 13:21)
18:1-8	The importunate widow and unjust judge
18:9-14	The Pharisee and the publican
19:1-10	Zacchaeus
19:11-27	Parable of the pounds (but cf. Mt. 25:14-30, the parable of the talents)
19:37-40	Entry into Jerusalem (cf. Mk. 11:9f.)
19:41-4	Lamentation over the city
20:18	The strength of the stone
21:5-36	The Apocalyptic discourse (cf. C. H. Dodd, *Journal of Roman Studies* 37 [1947], 47-54); cf. Mk. 13

CHRONOLOGICAL CHART

ROMAN EMPERORS	PROCURATORS OF JUDEA	CHRISTIAN WRITINGS	

Augustus, 30 B.C.

B.C. 1
A.D. 1

10 ——

	Coponius, A.D. 6-9	
	Ambibulus, A.D. 9-12	
	Annius Rufinus, A.D. 12-15	
Tiberius, A.D. 14	Valerius Gratus, A.D. 15-26	

20 ——
| | Pontius Pilate, A.D. 26-36 | |
30 —— Gaius Caligula, | Marcellus, A.D. 36-37 | |
     A.D. 37 | Marullus, A.D. 37-41 | |
40 —— Claudius, A.D. 41 | Cuspius Fadus, |
| A.D. 44-46 |
| Tiberius Alexander, |
| A.D. 46-48 |
| Ventidius Cumanus, |
| A.D. 48-52 |

50 —— | M. Antonius Felix, | I, II Thessalonians,
| A.D. 52-60? | A.D. 50-52
Nero, A.D. 54 | | Galatians, A.D. 53-54
| | I Corinthians, A.D. 54-55
| | II Corinthians, A.D. 55-56
| | Romans, A.D. 56-57
| | Captivity Epistles,
| | A.D. 58-60

60 —— | Porcius Festus,
Galba, A.D. 68 | A.D. 60-62?
Otho, A.D. 69 | Albinus, A.D. 62-64?
Vitellius, A.D. 69 | Gessius Florus,
Vespasian, A.D. 69 | A.D. 64-66

70 —— | | Gospel of Mark, A.D. 70
| | James, A.D. 75-100
| | Ephesians, A.D. 75-100
80 —— Titus, A.D. 79 | | Gospel of Matthew,
Domitian, A.D. 81 | | A.D. 85-100
| | Gospel of Luke-
| | Acts, A.D. 85-100
90 —— | | I Peter, A.D. 90-95   Gospel of John,
| | Hebrews, A.D. 90-95   A.D. 90-110
Nerva, A.D. 96 | | Revelation, A.D. 90-95   Epistles of John,
Trajan, A.D. 98 | | I Clement, A.D. 95   A.D. 90-110
| | Didache, A.D. 100-130
100 —— | | Pastoral Epistles,
| | A.D. 100-130
| | Shepherd of Hermas,
| | A.D. 100-140
| | Epistles of Ignatius,
110 —— | | A.D. 110-117
Hadrian, | | Jude, A.D. 110-130
   A.D. 117-135

120 ——
130 —— | | II Peter, A.D. 130-150

IMPORTANT EVENTS IN EARLY CHURCH	IMPORTANT EVENTS IN JEWISH HISTORY	

	Maccabean Revolt, 167 B.C.
	Dead Sea Sect at Qumran,
	   105 B.C.(?)-A.D. 66
	Pompey takes Jerusalem, 63 B.C.
	Herod the Great (King of Judea),
	   37 B.C.-4 B.C.	

Birth of Jesus, 6-4 B.C.?	Herod Antipas (Tetrarch of Galilee), 4 B.C.-A.D. 39	1 B.C.
	Archelaus (Ethnarch of Judea), 4 B.C.-A.D. 6	1 A.D.
	Philip (Tetrarch of Iturea), 4 B.C.-A.D. 34	———— 10
	High Priest Caiaphas, A.D. 18-36	———— 20
Preaching of John the Baptist, A.D. 27-29?		———— 30
Ministry of Jesus, A.D. 29-33?		
Crucifixion, A.D. 30-33?		———— 40
Conversion of Paul, A.D. 33-35?		

Peter imprisoned by Herod Agrippa,
   A.D. 41-44?
	Theudas' revolt, A.D. 40?
	Herod Agrippa I (King of Judea),
	   A.D. 41-44	

Execution of James, son of Zebedee,
   A.D. 44
	Jews banished from Rome by Claudius,
	   A.D. 41-49?	

Paul in southern Galatia, A.D. 47-49?		———— 50
Paul in Corinth, A.D. 50-51		
Paul in Ephesus, A.D. 52-54		
Paul arrested in Jerusalem, A.D. 56		
Paul in Rome, A.D. 60—		———— 60
Death of James, brother of Jesus, A.D. 62		
Flight of Christians to Pella, A.D. 66-67	War with Rome, A.D. 66-73	
	Jerusalem and Temple destroyed, A.D. 70	———— 70
		———— 80
	Council of Jamnia, A.D. 90?	———— 90
		———— 100
		———— 110
Martyrdom of Ignatius, A.D. 117?		———— 120
		———— 130

INDEX

Abel, 292n
About the Contemplative Life, Philo, 396n
About the Resurrection, Pseudo-Justin, 418n
Achaia, 182, 182n
Acrocorinth, 181
Acropolis, 177
Acts of the Apostles: authenticity of sermons in, 143n, 317-319; center of, 316; Church as redemptive instrument, 66-67; as historical source, 154-163, 319-321; program for disciples, 310 ff.; sermon themes in, 317-319; sources of, 320-321; theological content compared with that of *Paul* and *Mark*, 317 ff.
Adam, 193, 196, 205, 232, 304, 337
Adultery, 284
Against Celsus, Origen, 366n
Against Heresies, Irenaeus, 15, 15n, 16, 69, 416n, 418n
Against Marcion, Tertullian, 395n
Agape meal, 409
'Ain Feshka, 46
Aland, K.: *Did the Early Church Baptize Infants?*, 368n; "The Problem of Anonymity and Pseudonymity in Christian Literature of the First Two Centuries," 232n
Albinus, 30, 241

Aleppo, 274
Alexander the Great, 5, 6 ff., 233
Alexander Jannaeus, 26, 43
Alexandria: Jewish colony in, 8, 23; library, 8; locale of writing of *Gospel of Matthew*, 274
Alexandrian Christianity, H. Chadwick and J. E. L. Oulton, 418n
Allard, P., *Les esclaves chrétiens depuis les premiers temps de l'Eglise jusqu'à la fin de la domination romaine en occident*, 374n
Ammonites, 25
Amos, 32
The Ancient Library at Qumran and Modern Biblical Studies, Frank M. Cross, 42n
Anderson, Hugh, *Jesus and Christian Origins*, 94n
Annals, Tacitus, 361n
Annas, 241, 243
The Ante-Nicene Fathers, 15n, 230n
Anthropos Son of Man, C. H. Kraeling, 104n
Antinomianism, 418
Antioch, 310, 314
Antiquities, Josephus, 54, 98n, 158n
Antiochus IV (Epiphanes), 23-25, 129, 254
Antiochus the Great, 10

The Church at the Close of the First Century A.D

BASED ON MAPS IN *THE WESTMINSTER HISTORICAL ATLAS*, PLATES XV AND XVI B

LEGEND

ROMAN PROVINCES

THE LATER JOURNEYS OF PAUL ―――

CITIES AND TOWNS •

(A CHURCH EXISTED IN EACH CITY SHOWN;
QUESTION MARK INDICATES CHURCH EXISTENCE IN DOUBT